Tenants Rights

San Francisco Tenants Union
Tenants Rights Handbook

Twenty-First Edition

The First Eviction

San Francisco Tenants Union
Tenants Rights Handbook
Twenty-First Edition

Production Coordinator: Eihway Su

Editors/Authors: Jessica Alexandra, Lehua Asher, Richard Backer, Renee Curran, Jennifer Fieber, Kendra Froshman, Terrrie Frye, Becca Gourevitch, Ted Gullicksen, Keeeth!, Harry Kershner, Tim Lee (San Francisco Rent Board), Roger Levin, Alex Merchant, Ryan Murphy, Kristen Nygaard, Trina Roderick, Kim Rohrbach, Heidi Smith, Eihway Su, Rebecca Sutton, J. Scott Weaver, Susan Weisberg, Dave Wilbur, Jason Wolford, Miguel Wooding

Editorial Review: Eihway Su, Ted Gullicksen, Roger Levin, Ora Prochovnick, Miguel Wooding

Copy-Editing: Eihway Su, Loretta Stec, Greg Shaw, Kathy Harr, Mara Math, Lindsay Kimpel

Index: Eihway Su, Karen Gifford, Jan Wright *Design:* Joshua Pfeffer

Graphics: Eihway Su, Brett Bellas, Kathy Harr (cover), Thuy Ngo, Occuprint, Occupy Democracy Resources, Occupy Design, Linda Pettibone, Jan Pence, Susan Prentice, *radicalgraphics.org*

Additional Contributions: Dave Anderson, Anti-Displacement Coalition, Pat Arnsfield, Rudy Balderama, Bay Area Legal Aid, Paul Behrend, Daniel Berko, Carol Bettencourt, Causa Justa, Karl Cohen, Allen Cohn, Harold Darling, Tom Drohan, Janis Eggleston, Tom Elke, Eviction Defense Collaborative, Lisa Giampaoli, Carolyn Gold, Becca Gourevitch, Luke Hickman, Holly Holman, Mark Hooshmand, Carlos Jato, Marissa Jimenez, Brian Klein, Don Medearis, Philip Morgan, Cathy Mosbrucker, Richard Nagle, People With Disabilities Foundation, Ora Prochovnick, Dean Preston, Jennifer Rakowski, San Francisco Rent Board, Jamie Sanbonmatsu, Jules Sarkar, Sara Shortt, Joey Smith, Robert Smith, Steve Shubert, Jared Solovay, Ruby Steele, Joseph Tobener, Tenants Together, Liz Thornton, Cindy Vaias, Deepa Varma, Volunteer Legal Services Program of the Bar Association of San Francisco, Daniel Wayne, Robert Wilson, Stephanie Yee, Jim Youll, David Zlutnick

The Tenants Rights Handbook is not available for sale but is provided to all members of the San Francisco Tenants Union.

GCC/IBT 869-M

Library of Congress Card No. 96-92517

ISBN 978-0-9911006-7-5

Acknowledgments

The *Tenants Rights Handbook* is the result of years of effort by countless individuals and groups dedicated to furthering our rights to live in decent and affordable housing. The acknowledgments here are undoubtedly incomplete; credits are given to those we can name, and many thanks and apologies to those we left out.

Tenant Survival, was edited by Terry R. McCune and published in 1972, by the Tenants Action Group, a predecessor to the San Francisco Tenants Union. A couple of versions of *Tenant Survival* were produced. In 1976, another edition of *Tenant Survival* by the Tenants Action Group was published.

An update of the *Tenant Handbook* was published by the San Francisco Tenants Union in June 1977.

An update of the *Tenant Handbook* was published in November 1978 by Rick Ames, Dave Brigode, Michael Canright, Anne Dewesbury, and Steve Shapiro of the Tenants Union. That edition was based on the California Tenants Handbook by Myron Moskovitz. Other contributors to that edition included Jamie Fogle of the Goodman Building Tenants Union with cover art; Black Sheep Press printed the cover; 409 House and John Hansen did mimeographing; the Rehabilitation Unit of the Langley Porter Institute collated the book, and Ann McAndrew typed the text. An "Interim Update" was published by the San Francisco Tenants Union in July 1980, by Steve Shapiro and Steve Norris. It also cites the California Tenants Rights Handbook by Moskovitz, Warner, and Sherman.

Understanding Landlording which derives from work written by Mike Jacob in collaboration with Linda Lillow, with help from Jake Buckwalter and Sally Van Meter, was published by the Santa Barbara Rent Control Alliance (later known as the Santa Barbara Tenants Union) in October 1977. *Understanding Landlording* was later revised and expanded by Linda Lillow, Jake Buckwalter, Sally Van Meter, and others. Members of the California Housing Action & Information Network (CHAIN) provided support, feedback, and criticisms. It was printed and circulated by the California Housing Research Foundation in cooperation with CHAIN in an undated edition. *Understanding Landlording* was first included in the July 1981 edition of the San Francisco Tenants Union *Tenants' Rights Handbook* which was an update of the *Tenant Handbook* by Margy Ortiz, Lisi Lord, Michael Canright, and Steve Shapiro.

A new edition of the *Tenants Rights Handbook* was compiled by Jim Faye, Roger Levin, and Connie Brandon in July 1986. The graphic design and layout was by Jim Faye; the cover art by David Prowler; word processing by Connie Brandon, Cliff Ghames, Jim Faye, Roger Levin, Eve Lynch, and Cara Valentino. The West Bay Law Collective provided equipment and office space.

The 1986 edition was republished with updates inserted at the beginning of the book four times: in November 1987 with a two page update; August 1988, three pages; April 1989, five pages; and June 1990, six pages. Michael Harney and Lenore Gerard prepared the inserts.

The first perfect-bound edition of the *Tenants Rights Handbook* was published by the San Francisco Tenants Union in July 1991. That edition was revised and updated by Jim Faye, Ted Gullicksen, Roger Levin, and Ellen Lyons. Others who assisted included Larry Becker, Connie Brandon, Ira Dorter, Lenore Gerard, Cary Gold, Richard Hack, Michael Harney, Steven Herold, Bill Sparks, and Jean Turk. Mary Jane Foran and Cathy Mosbrucker helped with *Evictions*; Jane Wilson with *Landlord Research*, and Marianne Truitt with *Capital Improvements*. Graphics credits went to Carlos Ferreira, Christina George, Ron Richardson, Peter Tripodi, Joe Sloan, and Bruce Bortin. M.E. Klimek contributed photographs. It was printed by Graffik Natwiks.

A separate mini-update was published in 1993 with contributions by Jim Faye, Ted Gullicksen, Michael Harney, Roger Levin, and Ellen Lyons.

What the Tenants Union called the Fifth Edition of the *Tenants Rights Handbook* was published in 1994. The Editorial Committee consisted of Connie Brandon, Ted Gullicksen, Roger Levin, and Miguel Wooding. Research and writing credits went to Larry Becker, Ira Dorter, Jim Faye, Steven Herold, Ellen Lyons and Wolf Schweiger.

The Sixth Edition was published in August 1996 with Jim Faye, Ted Gullicksen, Roger Levin, Ellen Lyons, and Miguel Wooding on the Editorial Committee. Research and writing credit went to Larry Beach Becker, Connie Brandon, Robert Collins, Janis Eggleston, Cary Gold, Elley Lyons, and Wolf Schweiger. Noelle Hanrahan, Mavel Hussein, and Chester Zemany helped with production.

The Seventh Edition was published in October 2000. Miguel Wooding, David Wilbur, Roger Levin, Ted Gullicksen, and Jim Faye were on the Editorial Committee. Samantha Zutler, Wolf Schweiger, David Noor, Ellen Lyons, Laura Hicks, Steven Herold, Robert Haaland, Jim Faye, Ira Dorter, Connie Brandon, and Larry Beach Becker helped with research and writing. Additional graphics were contributed by David Noor and Charles Denefeld, along with photography by the California Department of Corrections. Mara Math and Maureen Burke copy-edited.

The Eighth Edition of the *Tenants Rights Handbook* was published in June 2004. Joshua Pfeffer, Greg Shaw, Kathy Harr, and Miguel Wooding coordinated the work. Chapter editors/authors were Lehua Asher, Ted Gullicksen, Keeeth!, Harry Kershner, Roger Levin, Kristen Nygaard, Trina Roderick, Heidi Smith, Rebecca Sutton, Dave Wilbur, and Miguel Wooding. Ora Prochovnick reviewed much of the work and gave valuable suggestions. Loretta Stec, Greg Shaw, Kathy Harr, Mara Math, and Eihway Su, among others, copy-edited. The index was prepared by Karen Gifford.

Acknowledgments

Joshua Pfeffer designed and laid out the book. Our graphics team included Thuy Ngo, Joshua Pfeffer, Linda Pettibone, Brett Bellas, and Susan Prentice. Other contributors include Pat Arnsfield, Steve Shubert, Liz Thornton, Joey Smith, Cindy Vaias, and Janis Eggleston.

The Ninth Edition was published in December 2005. Eihway Su, Ted Gullicksen, Terrie Frye, Roger Levin, Miguel Wooding, and Kathy Harr coordinated the work. Chapter editors/authors were Lehua Asher, Richard Backer, Terrie Frye, Ted Gullicksen, Keeeth!, Harry Kershner, Roger Levin, Kristen Nygaard, Trina Roderick, Heidi Smith, Eihway Su, Rebecca Sutton, Dave Wilbur, and Miguel Wooding. Editorial review was provided by Ora Prochovnick. Loretta Stec, Greg Shaw, Kathy Harr, Mara Math, and Eihway Su copy-edited. The index was modified by Eihway Su who made the index electronic. Eihway Su also made minor changes to the layout. Josh Pfeffer updated the cover.

The Tenth Edition was published in May 2007 with changes by Eihway Su including contributions by Terrrie Frye to *Tenant Resources*. Josh Pfeffer updated the cover. Ted Gullicksen reviewed the changes and coordinated the printing.

The Eleventh Edition was published in June 2008 with changes by Eihway Su as well as updated OMI/Ellis Comparison and Protected Classes charts by Brendan Conley with Miguel Wooding, and additional text by Miguel Wooding. Roger Levin reviewed the changes and recommended listing the changes. David Zlutnick suggested *radicalgraphics.org*. Josh Pfeffer updated the cover. Ted Gullicksen reviewed the changes and coordinated the printing.

The Twelfth Edition was published in September 2009 with changes by Eihway Su and contributions by: Kendra Froshman wrote the buyout section. Index changes were made by Jan Wright. Terrrie Frye researched the updates for *Tenant Resources* and Ted Gullicksen updated *The Story So Far*. Additional updates in law were obtained from *Tenants Together*. The cover was provided by Josh Pfeffer. Miguel Wooding and Kim Rohrbach reviewed the edits. Ted Gullicksen also coordinated the printing.

The Thirteenth Edition was published in March 2011 with changes by Eihway Su and contributions from Roger Levin, Kim Rohrbach, *Tenants Together*, Joseph Tobener, and Miguel Wooding. The updates included Terrrie Frye's research for *Tenant Resources*, and changes to *The Story So Far* by Ted Gullicksen. Ted Gullicksen also coordinated the printing as well as reviewed the changes along with Ryan Murphy. Josh Pfeffer updated the cover.

The Fourteenth Edition was published in November 2012 with changes by Eihway Su and contributions by: Jessica Alexandra suggested numerous corrections and citations. Roger Levin rewrote Costa-Hawkins/6.14 with Tim Lee of the San Francisco Rent Board, fixed an error in the Ellis section, added citations, clarified use of security deposits and relocation payments, and reviewed changes. Ryan Murphy edited the changes as well as simplified wording for *Renting Basics*, and revised the OMI/Ellis Comparison chart with Miguel Wooding. Foreclosure strategies were obtained from Tenants Together and the Eviction Defense Collaborative. Becca Gourevitch added changes to foreclosures. Renee Curran edited *Renting Basics,* and added a resource. Updates and corrections for disabilities were provided by the People With Disabilities Foundation and Kim Rohrbach. Ora Prochovnick improved wording and a citation for *Discrimination* and reviewed changes. Joseph Tobener illuminated real world rent increases under Costa-Hawkins, and offered a citation. Susan Weisberg pointed out a correction for 6.14. Terrrie Frye double-checked *Resources* by email and phone. Stephanie Yee assisted with law updates. Lindsay Kimpel proofread the Table of Contents and *The Story So Far*. Noelle Hanrahan sent Miguel Wooding's photo taken by Jan Pence, and Susan Prentice wrote the dedication. Hugo Kobayashi updated the cover with Ted Gullicksen who also reviewed and handled the publication.

The Fifteenth Edition was published in November 2013 with changes by Eihway Su and contributions from: Susan Weisberg rewrote *Renting Basics* and *Repairs and Services* for readability and *Rent Increases* and *Security Deposits* with Ryan Murphy. *Resources* were updated with Terrrie Frye's assistance. Ted Gullicksen updated the condo and Exemption for Capital Improvement Passthroughs sections, reviewed the changes, and coordinated the printing. Jason Wolford added the Airbnb and home exchanges section. Roger Levin suggested updates for Airbnb, open houses, and online payments. Joseph Tobener gave permission to cite from his Web site. The Volunteer Legal Services Program's *A Practical Guide to Representing Tenants in San Francisco 2011* provided information on defending evictions. Tenants Together passed on court rulings and with Eviction Defense Collaborative presented foreclosure strategies. The Regional Human Rights/ Fair Housing Commission's *A Practical Reference Guide to the Laws Affecting Rental Housing in California* supplied information.

The Sixteenth Edition was published in October 2014 with changes by Eihway Su and contributions from: Susan Weisberg collaborated on rewriting *Changes In Use*, *Eviction Defenses*, *Rent Increases*, and *Roommates* for readability; Roger Levin provided information on certificates of occupancy and foreclosures; Alex Merchant updated the results of demolition appeals, Richard Nagle recommended adding information for cosigners and electronic fund transfers; Joseph Tobener suggested clarifying credit reports; and Ted Gullicksen reviewed the work and coordinated the printing.

The Seventeenth Edition was published in September 2015 with changes by Eihway Su and contributions from: Jennifer Fieber summarized the changes to short-term rentals; Roger Levin, Kim Rohrbach, Renee Curran, Ora Prochovnick; Jason Wolford, Paul Behrend, Tom Elke, Adam Lazar, Allen Cohn, and Dean Preston of Tenants Together provided information and updates on tenant rights. Susan Weisberg suggested edits. The photograph of Ted was offered by Iris Biblowitz.

The Eighteenth Edition was published in December 2016 with

changes by Eihway Su and contributions from: Susan Weisberg edited *Roommates* and *Eviction Defenses* and the adding non-family roommates section written by Alex Merchant who also stated an opinion on notices. Jared Solovay clarified that no-fault evictions were not allowed during lease terms, base rent includes new parking, and overcharging subtenants may be illegal use. Kim Rohrbach recommended procedures for Rent Board petitions. Tom Elke illuminated tenancies at will and provided a nonmaterial breach case with added commentary by Roger Levin. Roger Levin also added a discrimination case and explained subtenant Costa-Hawkins rent increases along with Joe Tobener, Robert Smith and Rudy Balderama. Roger Levin also requested a release clause in letters responding to estoppel requests. Daniel Berko cited a case for release of liability for partially vacated tenancies and J. Scott Weaver suggested revoking guarantees. J. Scott Weaver, Ora Prochovnik, Robert Smith, Deepa Varma, Lisa Giampaoli, Roger Levin and Joseph Tobener weighed in on the effect of a ruling on an amendment to owner move-in evictions of children. Joseph Tobener and Carlos Jato presented a case for preventing rent increases after an illegal demolition. Joseph Tobener also suggested information on disability rights as did Rudy Balderama and Lisa Giampaoli. In addition, Lisa Giampaoli related exemptions for seniors from school tax. Robert Wilson's case on compounded interest for security deposits was included. Carol Bettencourt of the Eviction Defense Collaborative offered an opinion on San Francisco State properties exemption from the Rent Ordinance. Roger Levin, Renee Curran, Jessica Alexandra, Robert Smith, and Deepa Varma assisted with updating resources.

The Nineteenth Edition was published in May 2018 with changes by Eihway Su and contributions from: Jared Solovay elaborated on and corrected CC 1946.7, security deposits, condo conversion lifetime leases, marijuana cultivation, and typos. Jules Sarkar also informed us about security deposits, Small Claims telephone appearances, and 1946.7. Roger Levin noted the updated masking of unlawful detainers, Section 8 voucher discrimination case, "tenant" definition, Rent Board does not have deposit increases hearings, and revoking guaranties statute. In addition, Roger Levin with Brian Klein pointed out the debt service passthrough for new owners. Deepa Varma also commented on the updated masking law. Jennifer Rakowski, Roger Levin, and Marissa Jimenez of the San Francisco Rent Board clarified Rent Board procedures. The Anti-Displacement Coalition with Tom Drohan and Causa Justa explained habitability strategies. Jamie Sanbonmatsu, Jim Youll, Lisa Giampaoli, and Robert Smith amended procedures for working with the Department of Building Inspection. Scott Weaver wrote the buyouts section, quoted case law for eviction notice periods and the housing preference program fire displacement. Joseph Tobener gave case law for no nonpayment eviction from an illegal unit and suggested a letter describing disability instead of completing the 37.9(i) request. Mark Hooshmand caught the error in the annual rent increase. Alex Merchant and Tom Elke offered opinions that severing a co-tenancy under the Rent Ordinance would not apply under *Schmitt v. Felix*. Dave Anderson called attention to the limited application of marijuana's federal law. Daniel Wayne reminded us of advantages of taking a case to court instead of the Rent Board. Holly Holman researched telecommunication services requirements.

The Twentieth Edition was published in February 2020 with changes by Eihway Su and contributions from: Scott Weaver summarized various of the following updates and offered a sample notice for revoking a guarantee and buyout letters. Elke & Merchant LLP notified us of the change in counting days for notices. Also, Alex Merchant and Catalina Muñoz explained permit application notice requirements and TICs, and that Block Book Notice Requests are reported to the owner. Jennifer Rakowski and Marissa Jimenez presented San Francisco Rent Board procedures and tenant rights. The Eviction Defense Collaborative's Cary Gold detailed Prop F. Joe Tobener cited a case for late charges in an eviction, elaborated on family trusts in OMIs, and provided a code and case citation for smoking through Holly Holman. Holly Holman with Roger Levin gave us the status of Presidio and Treasure Island housing and a remedy for illegal rent increases for subsequent tenants. Holly Holman also corrected the days for temporary displacement. Paul Behrend, Piper Wheeler, Roger Levin, and Jared Solovay suggested a caution for vacating original tenants. Jared Solovay also clarified original tenant v. original occupant. Jason Wolford reminded us eviction without just cause only applies to master tenants residing with their subtenants. Daniel Wayne informed us on the difference between giving up a tenancy and temporarily vacating, Julian Sarkar corrected the description of statutory damages. Noe Neighborhood Council demonstrated how to set up alerts for permit applications. Deepa Varma found a reference for interpretation of ambiguous contracts and forwarded info on AB 1482 from Housing Is A Human Right. Info on AB 1482 also obtained from Richard Nagle, Tenants Together and Joe Tobener. Ora Prochovnick noted the Alternative Dispute Resolution timeline.

The Twenty-First Edition of the handbook was published with changes by Eihway Su and contributions from: Roger Levin gave a new source for law online, Jennifer Rakowski of the SF Rent Board provided info on the termination of tenancy from the death of a tenant.

ONLY ALAN WAS PREPARED TO ACKNOWLEDGE THE ELEPHANT IN THE ROOM.

Table of Contents

Items and page numbers in *italics* refer to the text in boxes on the corresponding page.

Table of Contents

Chapter 8: *Harassment* — 83

Chapter 9: *Discrimination* — 93

Chapter 10: *Roommates* — 100

Chapter 11: *Changes in Use* — 114

Chapter 12: *Eviction Defenses*   128

Table of Contents

Chapter 13: Eviction Process in Court — 160

Chapter 14: Taking Action — 171

Appendix A: Resources — 186

Appendix B: List of Changes — 199

Appendix C: San Francisco Law and Regulations Excerpts

Appendix D: California Law Excerpts — 270

Appendix E: Table of Statutes, Regulations, and Cases — 311

Index — 322

HOMES:

EVERYBODY GETS ONE BEFORE ANYBODY GETS TWO

While we know what it's like to struggle with landlords for decent and affordable housing, it's important to put these day to day struggles in context and to realize that we can never stop fighting for our collective rights. While we have the relatively recent right to habitable housing, tenants have yet to win the right to affordable housing or housing free from the fear of eviction. In San Francisco, we at least have a modest version of rent control (which only restricts the rent increase, but doesn't ensure it's affordable when we move in) and just cause eviction protections (which prevent only arbitrary evictions), but getting those modest protections took decades of fighting and remains constantly under attack. Before we were even able to win some housing rights, tenants had to struggle to get basic human rights, such as the right to vote. Even that right has come under attack as "Tea Party" conservatives have called for limiting voting to property owners only.

The struggle for our rights in this country dates back to when the first Europeans colonized the "New World" over 400 years ago. Many of these white settlers, who fled the entrenched feudal system of their various homelands for the new promised land, probably were surprised to find a similar property-based class system already established in the Americas. American feudalism is rarely mentioned in American history classes for schoolchildren.

In later years, tenant farmers who had fought in the American Revolution were outraged to find that only white, male, property owners were given the right to vote. Shay's Rebellion, in 1787, was one of the first tenant-organized protests against the emerging government and its property class supporters and financiers, who had passed laws to tax poor tenant farmers. The laws were passed to pay off the wealthy who had "loaned" the money to finance the war against Britain. Shay and his followers were quickly squelched by a privately funded militia operating with the blessing of the new government.

The struggle by tenants for economic and political justice predates the American Revolution. The landlord-tenant relationship is deeply rooted in feudal times, in which tenant-farmers (serfs) paid their lords and masters to live on and use a plot of land. In the original landlord-tenant relationship, the tenant would pay "rent" in the form of crops and other services. The rent was both for the use of the land and for the lord's "protection," which often was protection from the landowner's own gang of marauding thieves, murderers, and rapists. In the original feudal arrangement between landlord and tenant, the landlord was not legally responsible for the conditions of the tenant's housing and charged tenants the highest amount of rent that one was able to pay. When all available land is owned and controlled by landlords, tenants are forced to pay monopoly rents to the landlord class.

Tenants Begin to Organize

Only after organizing were landless people given the rights of citizenship and voting. After acquiring voting rights, tenants continued organizing to obtain other basic economic and social rights. Technological changes and the inaccessibility of capital forced many farmers from their small homestead to the cities. Most of these farmers joined the growing tenant class. Here, often allied with labor unions and churches, tenants began pressuring the government to recognize society's interest in housing its people and in establishing laws to protect tenants.

Until relatively recently, if a house burned down, the tenant was required to continue paying rent since the condition of the housing itself was not considered relevant to the rental agreement. In 1974, the California courts finally recognized that a tenant had an obligation to pay rent only if the landlord fulfilled her obligation to provide housing "services," such as plumbing, heating, and electricity.

As the polarization between rich and poor has intensified, some cities and states have gone beyond requiring minimal habitability standards and have passed laws regulating how, and for what reasons, tenants could be evicted and how much landlords can charge for rent.

The City Finally Responds to the Crisis

In 1979, in response to the housing crisis, the San Francisco Board of Supervisors, passed the city's Rent Control law to address rising rents and increasing evictions. The law's introduction:

"...Tenants displaced as a result of their inability to pay increased rents must relocate but as a result of such housing shortage are unable to find decent, safe and sanitary housing at affordable rent levels. Aware of the difficulty of finding decent housing, some tenants attempt to pay requested rent increases, but as a consequence must expend less on other necessities of life."

The housing crisis has not improved and has even been followed by worse crises, such as the "dot-com" boom at the turn of the century and the "housing bubble" during much of the first decade of the 21st century. Rent control, did alleviate some of the pressure by placing a cap on rents for occupied rental units and providing some protection against arbitrary evictions by landlords. However, this law was passed by a landlord-controlled Board of Supervisors which realized that voters were about to approve a much stronger rent control law if the Board did not act. The 1979 rent control law, had a gaping loophole that created a whole new set of problems which led to the ensuing and ongoing housing crises: *vacancy decontrol.*

The weak rent control law passed in 1979 regulated rents on occupied apartments, but allowed landlords to charge whatever the "market" would bear for vacant apartments. This form of rent control limits rent increases, but does little to preserve the affordability vacant housing stock. Rents on empty units soar when real estate speculation, a severe supply and demand imbalance, and easy credit during good economic times all cause property values to skyrocket. This creates an economic motivation for landlords to try to evict long-term tenants. Not surprisingly, as rents in vacant units have risen, so have evictions and harassment of tenants.

Condo Conversions Soared Along With Rent Increases

In addition to the skyrocketing rents in the late 1970s, there was also an epidemic of condominium conversions which resulted in San Francisco adopting a condominium conversion law which limited conversions. This law did not have loopholes, but landlords found a way around it: Tenancies In Common (TICs).

These so-called TICs are almost identical to a condominium, but rather than owning title to the individual unit, the buyers of the units have a percentage ownership in the entire building and an "exclusive right of occupancy" to one of the units in the building. TICs were covered by the condo conversion law, but in the 1980s, a California Supreme Court case ruled that condo conversion laws did not cover TICs unless that "exclusive right of occupancy" was recorded on the deed of the property. Real estate speculators then began selling the units without recording that agreement on the deed and TIC—or condo conversions—again became epidemic.

Today, the number one housing problem in San Francisco is the conversion of rent controlled apartments into condominium and condominium-like units. Most evictions in San Francisco are for the purpose of condo conversion and the steadily declining rental housing stock has made it more difficult and more expensive to find an apartment in San Francisco.

The High Tech and Housing Bubbles Hit

In the late 1990s, the high tech economy in Silicon Valley began to boom which brought thousands of well-paid workers to the Bay Area (at the time, a Silicon Valley industry group reported that 40% of all Silicon Valley workers were living in San Francisco) who were able to buy expensive condominiums or pay top dollar for rents. San Francisco's vacancy rate dropped to less than 1% and rents on vacant units increased at a rate of over 30% a year. The dual loopholes of vacancy decontrol and unlimited TIC-type condo conversions caused evictions in the city to soar as landlords sought to either convert to condos or raise rents on vacant units.

Between 1997 and 1998, evictions nearly doubled, increasing 86%. The city's housing struggles took on a new face as gentrification drastically changed the city. With 2-bedroom condominiums selling for $500,000 (and $1,200,000 these days), the demographics of the city began changing. As middle and working-class renters were evicted from their apartments, they were replaced with people who were far wealthier. Those evicted certainly could not afford to buy a luxury condominium and they also found they could not afford the high rents on vacant apartments. A San Francisco Tenants Union study at the time found that 83% of tenant evicted for Landlord Move-In (then the most common way to evict for condos or to increase rents) moved out of San Francisco.

While evictions and conversions proved to be the most effective means of gentrification, since it forces low and moderate income people from the city and replaces them directly with wealthier people, construction of new expensive condominiums, and phony "live/work" units soared, bringing even more rich people to the city. With all of this, San Francisco began losing some of its flavor and progressiveness. As artists were forced from real live/work units in the South of Market area, they were replaced by people who then began complaining about the nightclubs in the neighborhood, forcing many to close. Neighborhoods which previously voted progressively suddenly started voting conservatively. Politicians got elected who sounded and talked an awful lot like conservative Republicans (though they were too savvy to actually call themselves Republicans).

Following the burst of the dot-com bubble in 2002, rents, evictions, and conversions slowed, but soon enough the housing bubble was in full swing and property values began going through the roof. Speculators began buying up properties all over the city, converting them to TICs and condominiums and selling them for huge profits, sometimes in a matter of weeks. By 2004, evictions for conversions soared again to levels even higher than what was experienced in the dot-com bubble. By 2008, the number of evictions and rents on vacant apartments were at levels which few thought would be possible.

In 2008, the housing bubble began to burst around the country, but San Francisco remained immune as property values here continued to dramatically increase. Rents (up 30% from 2007!), evictions, and conversions continued to increase as well. In addition, since 2007, when the city adopted a law prohibiting the conversion of any building into condominiums if multiple evictions occurred or if any senior or disabled tenant was evicted, most evictions have happened through coerced buyouts. Not until the end of 2008, when the world's banking and financial systems collapsed, did San Francisco begin to show any signs of the bubble bursting.

The Great Recession

In 2009, the country's financial and banking system caused the "great recession," the worst economic turmoil since the Great Depression of the 1930s. It was the housing boom and real estate speculation which caused the collapse, and during the housing bubble, tenants paid dearly via evictions and soaring rents. Tenants lost again as the working class lost jobs and had wages cut. The U.S. government bailed out the landlords and banking industry by paying off their paper debts and mortgages that had been used to bid up the price of those assets in the first place. Incredibly, the government called upon both the working class and the tenant class to pay higher taxes to pay off the debts of landlords, bank shareholders and property speculators even though tenants and the working class were victims or benefited very little from the financial go-go years.

Adding insult to injury, as tenants were being forced from their homes in record numbers during the housing bubble, our state and national governments cared very little. California state legislators, in fact, even rolled back renters rights considerably since 1995, making it easier to evict tenants or raise our rents. When homeowners faced the loss of their homes, the federal government made saving their homes a number one priority. Of course, the government should try to keep people housed, but it should value saving the homes of renters and homeowners equally rather than treating tenants as second class citizens.

The legal system treats tenants differently too, since the laws generally are written and enforced by white, male property owners, just as our founders envisioned 230 years ago. Landlords have successfully used the courts numerous times to get laws limiting evictions or rents tossed out by landlord-friendly judges. These judges, for example, are almost always property owners and many are, in fact, landlords or real estate investors. Even in San Francisco, where 56% of the residents are tenants as of the 2020 census, the city's Rent Board Commission—which enforces rent control—has just two tenants among the five members.

Compare, for example, the startlingly different laws involved in evicting a tenant from his home versus evicting a homeowner. A tenant's eviction process is a "summary" one, which means that the procedure moves fast. If a tenant is one day late with the rent, he can be evicted in a few short weeks. On the other hand, failure to make a mortgage payment will lead to warnings, and then a series of notices over a period of many months. When the case finally reaches court, the homeowner is entitled to the benefits of the slow, creaky legal process with full due process protections.

After the Recession

In 2010, San Francisco was one of only four cities in the country which saw property values increase from 2009 and was again the country's second-most-expensive market. In the first quarter of 2012, San Francisco had a vacancy rate of 3.2%, the lowest in the country, and the largest increase in rent on a yearly basis (5.9%) nationwide, as wealthy, young workers for businesses like Twitter and Facebook moved in. As the tech boom continues the housing crisis is much worse than during the 1990s. Although developers push for more construction, very little of the new housing is affordable. Here are some key numbers:

- Median rents for a vacant one bedroom in San Francisco for May 2022 was $2,895. At minimum wage of $16.32/hour, full-time employment would mean rent is 100% of gross pay. Severe rent burden is defined as spending more than half of one's income on rent. Low-paid workers, who need to stay where their employment and support systems are, cram together into small spaces, have long commutes, or are homeless.

- In 2019 (there was no full count due to the coronavirus for 2021), 8,011 people were counted in San Francisco as homeless, including 5,180 not in shelters. (*https://hsh.sfgov.org/about/research-and-reports/pit-hic*) Despite much wealth, 12% of the population was below the poverty level in the 2010 census.

- The chief economist for the City of San Francisco estimates that 100,000 new rental units are needed to noticeably lower the price of market-rate units. (*archives.sfexaminer.com/sanfrancisco/leveling-sf-housing-field-could-take-100000-new-units/Content?oid=2703869*) To have an idea of how much housing this is, this is the number of housing units that were added to San Francisco between the 1920s and 2014. Rent-controlled housing does not

PROFIT OVER PEOPLE?

require new construction, and is a fast, cheap, and environmentally-friendly way to increase affordable housing.

COVID-19 Pandemic

The COVID-19 pandemic forced many tenants out of San Francisco housing as they lost their jobs, causing a high vacancy rate. Rents dropped as much as 30% in San Francisco. Some politicians understood that a massive increase in the homeless could have a devastating impact not only on the homeless but the wider population, creating a ripple effect of destruction. Legislation was passed that helped mitigate the disaster, but in 2021 rents shot back up.

San Francisco Renters Fight Back

As much as the system is stacked against us and San Francisco gentrified, tenants would be in a far worse position if we weren't organized and fighting back. Led by the San Francisco Tenants Union, the city has a strong tenants movement which at City Hall and at the ballot has passed many laws helping tenants and defeated others that hurt tenants. Strengthening rent control which covers 75% of the tenants as of 2018 (62% Rent Ordinance, 14% deed restricted affordable housing, *www.sfchronicle.com/bayarea/article/If-Prop-10-passes-SF-supervisors-ready-to-alter-13359811.php*) has been a priority as the cheapest, fastest, environmentally-friendly, and non-disruptive method to achieve affordable housing. Legislative highlights include:

- Rent Increases Reduced or Restricted, 1992 (Prop H cut increases in half), 2000 (Prop H) restricted the landlord's ability to passthrough capital improvement costs).

- Rent Control Expanded or Retained for Owner-Occupied Buildings with 2-4 Units, 1994 (Prop I expanded rent control), 1998 (Prop E retained rent control).

- Housing Code Enforcement Improved, 1994 (Prop G).

- Owner Move-In Evictions Limited to One Per Building, 1998 (Prop G).

- Repeal of Rent Control Defeated, 2002 (Prop R), 2008 (Prop 98).

- Condo Conversions Limited, 2002 (Prop R defeated expansion of conversions), 2006 (restricted conversions), 2013 (limited conversions to 2-4 unit owner-occupied buildings and 10 year moratorium on conversion lottery).

- Relocation Payment Provided or Increased for Evicted

Tenants, 2005 (relocation payments for Ellis Act), 2006 (Prop H increased relocation payments).

- Severance of Garages and Other Services Made Illegal, 2006.

- Eviction Disclosure Required for Sellers, 2006 (Prop B).

- Buyout Agreements Regulated, 2014.

- Low-fault eviction protections, restrictions on rent after no-fault evictions, and the right to add roommates within the Housing Code limits sponsored by Supervisor Jane Kim, 2015.

- Advocated for legislation that passed the San Francisco Board of Supervisors unanimously to enforce penalties to reduce the illegal postings of Airbnb which have removed much affordable housing from the market. Influenced incumbent politicians to advocate for tenants including pressuring Airbnb to follow the law to register hosts. Airbnb finally agreed to enforce registration of hosts. 2016.

- Led on legislation for reducing fraudulent owner move-in evictions which passed unanimously at the San Francisco Board of Supervisors, 2017.

- The Tenants Union forces oversight of renovations that evict tenants "temporarily," 2017.

- After failed litigation by Airbnb and other short-term rental agencies, registration of short-term rentals is enforced, adding potentially five thousand units back to the housing market in 2018.

- After a successful appeal by the City of San Francisco, the restriction on owner move-in eviction of school workers is reinstated pending a petition to the state Supreme Court in 2018.

- Major advocates for Prop F, which provides tenants with an attorney during an eviction attempt, 2018.

- Campaigned for winning pro-tenant Supervisors Gordon Mar, Matt Haney, Rafael Mandelman, and Shamann Walton, giving progressives a majority on the San Francisco Board of Supervisors, 2018.

- Passthroughs of mortgage costs from a change in ownership to tenants are restricted, 2018.

- One of only two counties to vote yes on Prop 10 to Repeal Costa Hawkins which limits rent-control state-wide, 2018.

- Buyouts law updated to require disclosure of tenant displacement, 2019.

- Continued fight against "renovictions," 2019.

- Leading role in ensuring real estate donation money becomes toxic for progressive candidates statewide, 2019.

- Prevented Mayor Breed's attempt to replace a Rent Board tenant commissioner with over 30 years of experience with an inexperienced tenant commissioner, forcing her to appoint a trusted tenant attorney, 2019.

- Ensured that services for tenant counselors would not be cut to fund attorneys for eviction defense, 2019.

- Under pressure from tenant activists, state-wide rent control with just cause evictions passed, 2019.

- Campaigned for San Francisco District 5 Supervisor Dean Preston, a tenant rights advocate, who won over a known evictor, given us a progressive majority to override Mayor Breed, 2019.

- Extended just cause eviction to post-1979 constructed rental units, 2019.

- Defeated Senate Bill 50 which may have demolished affordable rental units since there were no enforcement provisions for preventing demolition, 2020.

- Campaigned for Supervisor Preston's Eviction Protection Ordinance which was passed by 10-1 so it could override Mayor Breed's veto. The ordinance stopped evictions of tenants who can't pay because of COVID-19 related income loss but doesn't stop landlords from collecting the debt. 2020.

- As part of the San Francisco Anti-Displacement Coalition, requested and received extensions of the Mayor's eviction moratorium. 2020.

- Endorsed and campaigned for progressive San Francisco Supervisors Connie Chan, Aaron Peskin, Dean Preston, and Hillary Ronen who won, retaining a progressive majority that supports tenants. Myrna Melgar was our second choice. 2020.

- San Francisco Supervisor Dean Preston (endorsed and campaigned for by the SF Tenants Union), continues to lead on legislation to protect tenants during the pandemic. 2021.

- Under pressure from the San Francisco Board of Supervisors (Chan, Haney, Mandelman, Mar, Melgar, Peskin, Preston, Ronen, and Walton endorsed by the SF Tenants Union), Mayor Breed finally agrees to Prop I (supported by the SF Tenants Union) funding for rent relief. 2021

- San Francisco Supervisor Dean Preston (endorsed and campaigned for by the SF Tenants Union), continues to lead on legislation to protect tenants during the pandemic. 2022.

Through fighting back, tenants have gained substantial rights over the years, but the reality is that changes in the laws have not ended the historical adversity between landlords and tenants. The landlord-tenant struggle is more than an issue of good versus evil. The struggle is based on two very competing interests that have nothing to do with the personalities of the landlord or the tenant. A landlord sees the rental unit as a commodity. A tenant sees his home as part of a community. This commodity versus community conflict is basically at the root of every landlord-tenant dispute. In San Francisco, this conflict is greater than in almost any city in the United States as San Francisco has one of the highest property values in the country, meaning that there's a lot of profit which can be made off our homes.

The issue that likely caused you to join the Tenants Union, is *not* an isolated incident in the city. It is the direct result of a housing crisis gone haywire. It is important to remember that we are all in the same boat and that by working together we will begin to resolve this crisis. **Renters do have rights.** After all, a home is not just a place to sleep, but is also a place for living and enjoyment. A home and shelter seems as American and uncontroversial as apple pie, but fighting for this right conflicts with landlords' ideas of "private property" and "making a profit."

Too often people are concerned with their rights only when they or someone they know is being personally threatened. It is precisely this attitude which allows abuses to continue. Perhaps the biggest problem with San Francisco tenants is that **we do not recognize ourselves as a class and a majority.** Tenants in the city sometimes are a self-disempowered majority. By remaining isolated from one another, we make a serious personal and political mistake. Until tenants assert their rights for affordable, safe, and decent housing, abuse will continue. If you have ever found yourself wondering what you can do about your housing situation or about preserving affordable housing, we hope this book is a starting point. Getting involved with your local Tenants Union and staying committed to the fight for basic economic rights for everyone, including tenants, will go a long way to solving this housing crisis. Don't just be a member of the San Francisco Tenants Union: become an active member and together we can keep San Francisco affordable, livable, and diverse.

Chapter 2: *Understanding Landlording*

Next to slavery, the landlord-tenant relationship is the most destructive and unjust institution ever developed by humans. Except in rare instances where it is based among families, friends or members of a particular community, the landlord-tenant relationship is an economic relationship. Landlord-tenant disputes arise from this economic relationship, which pits a landlord who wants to profit from her investment against a tenant who seeks to live peacefully in her home.

The government encourages and empowers this unjust economic relationship by giving landlords billions of dollars in annual tax breaks and cash subsidies. These government subsidies generally are paid for by imposing high taxes on the wages and salaries of the working and tenant classes.

Unfortunately, the American housing institution that has developed and been refined over the years is based on a single principle: profit to landlords and real estate speculators. No consideration is made for the well-being of the families who make the property their home or for the community in which they live. Even some nonprofit housing developers are realizing they can make up shortfalls in their own budgets by managing and investing in the property they control in a manner similar to a profit-making real estate venture.

The system of providing housing and shelter in this country is in need of radical reform. While recognizing the current reality, this handbook is written to deal with practical realities. Nevertheless, a basic appreciation of the legal and economic parameters of the landlord-tenant relationship is useful to tenants to better confront and deal with their landlords and, hopefully, to encourage activism to abolish this terribly unjust and inhumane institution.

It is a good idea for tenants to understand subtle differences between different types of landlords and how landlords profit from people's homes. Landlording is a big money business, one that often provides an outsized profit in exchange for little actual work. An examination of the wealthy and powerful in this country reveals that the fortunes of many are based on land holdings and real estate speculation. Even progressive-minded people often fall into landlording as an investment deal they "simply can't resist."

There may be some "good" landlords, but we certainly know there are horrendous ones. No matter how nice a person you think your landlord may be, the issues inherent in a landlord-tenant relationship are systemic, and problems are virtually certain to arise. Control of land has been the battleground (both literally and figuratively) in this country from the time it was settled by Europeans, who promptly evicted the Natives. In this chapter we examine the different characteristics of landlord types and how the current economic structure and tax laws benefit the property owners at the expense of the unpropertied class.

Landlord Types

All people, including tenants and landlords, are unique individuals with character strengths and flaws. Most tenants are willing to give their landlords some slack and the benefit of the doubt until they get screwed. Some tenants may live contentedly in their home for years until one day a continuing little annoyance simply becomes just too much. Others are primed from the get-go and refuse to let the landlord get away with anything.

As a tenant who has decided to assert your rights, it is essential that you know as much as possible about your landlord's personal style and financial resources before charging into battle. There are some landlords who take personal pride in maintaining a quality building, even some who value long-term tenants. These landlords will respond to your request immediately and might even sincerely thank you for bringing the problem to their attention. There are other landlords, however, who may consider your request a personal attack and want to retaliate. Appreciating these differences in attitudes will help you prepare appropriate strategies to solve your problem(s).

If possible, try to develop a personal relationship with the landlord or manager. This may make it easier for you to get repairs done. Bear in mind, though, that such a relationship may turn against you if serious differences arise. Try to remember that landlording is a business and self-interest in business often overshadows friendships.

When you first move in, talk with your neighbors. They may have information that can be helpful when dealing with the landlord, such as: Where does your landlord live? Where does he work? How much other property does he own? Does the landlord seem to be willing to spend the money to make needed repairs? Does your landlord hire workers to care for the property or do it himself? Does he communicate with tenants in writing or through informal verbal conversations?

Landlords are different and warrant different tactics. What follows are brief descriptions of these landlord types as we have experienced them as tenants and as tenant counselors.

Big vs. Small

The more apartment buildings owned or managed by your landlord, the more likely you will be considered a faceless name. Tenants' needs usually are not important to a large landlord. A significant problem is that large property owners often have buffers between themselves and their tenants. Resident managers, property managers and repair people will handle some problems and cause you others. If the manager has been authorized to act as the landlord's agent, the landlord is legally responsible for the manager's actions as well as the manager. **It is very important that you document your communications in writing with the people with whom you interact in connection with your tenancy (mail your letters with a certificate of mailing, different from certified).** Find out and record the names of the people with whom you are communicating and determine what authority they have in making decisions. Most of these "buffers" usually are agents of the landlord and have some authority. Although you should not rely on the promises of the person who fixes the toilet that the owner will not try to pass on the cost of repairing it, if the landlord's property manager tells you the same thing, you should document it as a possible defense against a potential rent increase.

Large landlords also have financial and legal advisers helping them to maximize profit. You may find yourself being nickeled and dimed to death as they use every opportunity for rent hikes, or you may find your teeth chattering as they wait until winter is almost over before turning on the heat in the building.

Smaller landlords who only own a few rental units generally will not have such bureaucratic shields. More than likely you will be dealing with the owner directly, and there should be fewer excuses when you need her attention to some problem with the property. On the other hand, small landlords may be excessively defensive if you suggest that they are not quick enough with repairs or otherwise criticize their business practices. Smaller landlords may be less likely to navigate the local rent laws for capital improvement increases, etc., but they may ignore basic laws protecting tenants, since they firmly believe that no government can tell them what to do with *their* investment property. You definitely should not take the word of any landlord as the law regarding any landlord-tenant issue. Instead, seek advice from the Tenants Union or other housing rights advocates as to the truthfulness of their statements and legality of their actions.

Professional vs. Amateur

To professional landlords, investing in housing is simply another business endeavor. Professional landlords often have extensive property holdings and renters are merely a source of income who provide them with a rate of return on their investment. They often do not consider the fact that their investment is someone's home. These professionals usually will have property managers running their day-to-day affairs. Professional landlords make investment decisions and do not often bother with the petty details of running their business. Cost efficiency is usually their paramount concern. Thus, they are more likely to make capital improvements to the building in order to upgrade the property and increase their rent profits. Evictions and rent increases are routine and systematic; these landlords know the rules and break them carefully. Treat such professionals in a businesslike fashion; be smart and stay alert.

Not all professionals own huge buildings on lower Nob Hill. In the 1980s a new type of professional evolved. These are usually younger owners of a limited number of buildings. These landlords usually do not know all the ins and outs of milking their buildings for maximum profits, but they often are involved with property speculation and other get-richer-quicker schemes, like trying to evict long-term tenants through "owner-move-ins" in order to remove the building from rent control.

Amateur landlords, in contrast, often are part-timers and usually own only one or a few buildings. They may rent their apartments out themselves and may make deals with prospective tenants or tenants. They are more likely to be emotional, take complaints as personal attacks, and take impulsive, illegal actions such as lockouts and harassment. They sometimes make mistakes, both legal and financial, and often cut corners to save money. For example, many will try doing repairs themselves. Sometimes the problem is not getting the repairs done; it's getting them done right. Many amateur landlords are prone to some of the problems described in the "Absentee vs. Landlord-Occupant" following section.

Absentee vs. Landlord-Occupant

The absentee landlord is the type you rarely see, if ever. If your building is in excellent condition, and the landlord never bothers your household, you may feel lucky to have only a post office box to which to send the monthly rent check. Hold back the rent, however, and you may quickly get the landlord on your doorstep, demanding the rent. If your home is in decent shape, it probably is just as well that you have an absentee landlord, as you can probably get away with minor violations of the lease. But you may find it a problem to get immediate attention to repair problems and may have to send registered letters or call in your own repair people.

Owner-occupants are often the toughest landlords to deal with if the landlord-tenant relationship turns sour. The landlord is easily available if something needs to be repaired. Also, since most owner-occupants take pride in the building in which they live, the work often gets done quickly. Some owner-occupant landlords are always around, however, prying into your business, entering unannounced to "visit" you, and "inspecting" your living space. Things can deteriorate very quickly if you get on the owner-occupant's bad side. We have seen outrageous conduct by owner-occupant landlords and urge you to use common sense in dealing with them.

Old/Long-Term Investor vs. New/Short-Term Speculator Ownership

The longer a landlord has owned the building, the less likely he may feel the need to evict tenants in order to raise the rent. Long-term landlords are more likely to have a positive cash flow (income exceeding cash expenses). The building's mortgage is usually paid off or the monthly mortgage payment is far less than the current monthly rental income. Thus, the monthly rental income stream is often pure profit. A stable, hassle-free tenant population is usually an important consideration for these landlords. They also may be less likely to put money back into the property, which ultimately will cause serious repair and maintenance issues. Many tenants will accept the trade-off between this "deferred maintenance" and continued low rents, however.

Whenever a building is sold to a new landlord there almost certainly will be problems for the tenants. For example, eviction attempts of long-term tenants who pay less than "market" rents often are inevitable. The new landlords also may try to raise rents to help pay off their increased mortgage payments. Services may be reduced to save money or they may try to change the terms of the tenancy in order to assert their power or their personal wishes. Tenants should prepare themselves for these and other hassles when their building is put on the real estate speculation merry-go-round, but should be aware that the San Francisco Rent Ordinance provides significant protections for tenants, even when property changes hands. (See the section "Sale of Building" in "Chapter 4: Renting Basics" for more information.")

Now, with a basic understanding of the types of people who shape the landlord class, let's take a look at the financial side of being a landlord. This is the heart of what motivates a landlord's behavior and ensures large campaign contributions to those politicians who will continue the unjust landlord-tenant institution.

How Landlords Make Money

Most of the problems you will face as a tenant will come down to money. The repairs that are not being made, the eviction the landlord is threatening, or the exorbitant rent increase all have one thing in common: the landlord says he does not have the money or wants more money. Never mind that the increased monthly rent means that tenants have less money for their children, food, medical care, or other necessities. The current market economy is a zero-sum game in which the landlord's goal is to increase his

personal wealth which, by definition, will come at the expense of the tenant's financial well-being.

Your landlord may plead poverty and moan about his property tax bill (that the tenant actually pays when he pays rent each month), but you can be sure that you will not meet the landlord when picking up your food stamps. The economic dynamic between landlords and tenants is not much different from that between bosses and workers; landlords often will make it appear that they are not making much profit from "their" building, when in fact they are making handsome profits. The landlord class makes a killing from owning real estate.

Although this section of the handbook is not designed to be a thorough analysis of the economics of landlording (the subject is more complex than is possible to cover in this handbook), the following paragraphs offer a basic explanation of how landlords profit from their real estate investments. As you will see, landlording generates large sums of money and wealth in many more ways besides your monthly rent check.

There are four basic sources of wealth and income that a landlord receives from his rental property: (1) equity in the building; (2) appreciation in the value of the property and speculation on its anticipated increase; (3) income from rents; and (4) tax loopholes (write-offs) and tax shelters. One reason why property ownership is such a favored investment is that these four sources of income and wealth, in combination, provide the landlord with a steady cash flow (rental income), a sound and safe investment asset (equity and potential appreciation), and tax shelters for reducing or eliminating otherwise taxable income (tax loopholes).

We will begin our discussion with equity, since an understanding of this concept is crucial to understanding how wealth flows to a landlord.

Equity

Equity is defined as the net value that the landlord has in the building. For example, if the property is worth $500,000 and the bank has an outstanding mortgage of $200,000 on the building, the landlord has an equity value of $300,000. In many ways his investment in the building is similar to other investments, such as stocks or bonds. Landlords, like all investors, expect their investments to increase in value. This is not an unrealistic expectation considering the U.S. government plans for an inflation increase of 3% to 5% a year by managing increases in the nation's money supply.

Studies often show that real estate investments perform better than other investments, even in geographic areas where housing is not skyrocketing in value. In a city like San Francisco (where the cost of land is among the highest in the world) it is an especially lucrative investment. In other words, simply buying and holding on to property (whether it is a vacant lot or a 40-unit apartment building) is an investment which is far more stable than the stock market and often brings the investor much greater returns. When the real estate market is appreciating (see the "Appreciation and Speculation" following section), returns are magnified tremendously, even without considering the significant benefits from rental income and tax shelter advantages.

Even if the real estate market is temporarily flat or falling, equity makes real estate a good investment option because the investor only needs a relatively small amount of money for a down payment. A bank puts up the vast majority of the investment, sometimes as much as 100% of the purchase price. The increase in the landlord's equity is created by the monthly rent checks paid by tenants.

When a landlord buys property, he will typically make a down payment of 20% of its value (this is called the initial equity); the remainder of the money comes from a bank or other financial institution. (This loan is called the mortgage.) The landlord pays installments on the mortgage until the loan is paid off; the rental income protects the bank and secures the original investment. After the landlord (or tenant) pays off the mortgage, the rental income becomes an additional source of profit. At any point in time, the initial equity (down payment), plus the part of the mortgage which has been paid off by the tenants, plus any appreciation in the value of the property is the landlord's total equity in the property.

Before the landlord pays off the mortgage and owns the property outright, he can use its equity in many ways. Because equity is considered part of net worth, the landlord can use the property as collateral for other loans. Real estate equity is almost always used by speculating landlords to build a vast portfolio of real estate holdings while using very little of their own money. After acquiring one building they can use the equity buildup in that building as collateral for additional loans to purchase more property, which can then be used as collateral for still more buildings, and so on. Meanwhile, tenants pay the monthly rents, which in turn are used to pay the landlord's mortgage, property taxes, insurance and building maintenance and to keep the landlord's credit rating secure.

Even if the landlord is not an aggressive property speculator and he does not use the equity in one property to leverage other purchases of property, a landlord can make a small down payment on a building and watch the equity grow as the mortgage is paid off by the tenants and the building appreciates in value over time.

Appreciation and Speculation

Ownership of a building enables speculation. From 1990 to 2005, the median sales price for a residential building in San Francisco increased approximately 300% from just under $300,000 to over $800,000. This increase is known as "appreciation" and it builds the equity value in the investment. (Remember equity equals down payment + mortgage paid + appreciation.) It is the equity buildup that enables landlords to make a killing by buying and selling buildings. The way the real estate market is today, even

when a landlord does nothing to maintain or improve a building, it increases in value over time.

The following is an example of how profit is made from appreciation:

Assume that a landlord bought a 4-unit building priced at $1,000,000 five years ago. Assume the landlord made a $100,000 down payment, took out a $900,000 mortgage and resold the building five years later for $1,500,000. This is a fairly realistic example of the appreciation in the San Francisco housing market. The landlord's profit is calculated as follows:

	Resale Price	$1,500,000
minus	Unpaid Mortgage	$700,000
	Proceeds from Sale	$800,000
minus	Initial Investment	$ 100,000
	Landlord Profit	$700,000

Let's look at this profit calculation in a slightly different way. The purchase price of the building was $1,000,000 and the resale price was $1,500,000. Is the landlord's profit a 50% increase? **No. Remember—the landlord's initial investment was only $100,000.** The landlord's profit is a whopping 700% on his initial investment.

This profit is further sweetened by another government subsidy that taxes the landlord's profit at favorable capital gain rates. Capital gains are subject to a 15% tax rate, while working people pay taxes in excess of 60%, when income taxes, payroll taxes, property taxes, sales taxes and other taxes are added together. Furthermore, the profit is taxed only when the building is sold, even though the landlord has access to the equity before then, as banks will lend money on the increased value. By refinancing (borrowing money on the appreciation of the building), speculators can increase the buying power of their original small investment. This process is called pyramiding. Real estate empires have been built by borrowing money several times on the same property. Each time the property is refinanced the tenants have to shoulder the cost of a higher mortgage and increased interest costs through passthrough of the costs to the tenant.

The foregoing example is a perfect illustration of the lucrative field of speculation. Speculation occurs when a landlord or real estate company buys up property, holds it for a short time, and then resells it for a much higher price. In the process, the owner might do some minor repairs or slap a new coat of paint on the building to help raise the resale value, but generally he will not invest much money in the upkeep of the building.

What speculators are counting on is that property and housing prices will continue to increase and that they can make huge profits without doing much work. Every time the building is refinanced, the mortgage payments increase and the tenants are expected to bear the burden of the increases, even though the owner ultimately will make huge profits.

Chapter 2 – Understanding Landlording

The cost of housing, and rents, continues to increase far beyond the original cost of the property, and we, the tenants (and even homeowners), pay for it. This principle is nicely described in the book *How to Get Rich While You Sleep*:

> …[I]t's nice to drive by [the income property] and know that these tenants are actually in there worrying about how to pay you the rent so that you might make all your expenses, reduce your indebtedness and build your estate. It's nice to be able to show your friends this property and say, 'Even while I was asleep last night, that building over there was making me money and helping me build my estate.'

The reason that the practice of landlording and speculation continues to be a very profitable business is that everyone needs a home. Most people cannot stop renting just because they think it is too expensive.

Rental Income

Rental income is the magic ingredient that builds equity by providing the cash flow. What you pay in rent becomes the landlord's gross income; what is left over after expenses is the landlord's net rental income. While it is a small part of the overall profit picture, rental income is important because the cash flow it provides makes everything else work. While a patient landlord can wait and reap the substantial benefits of equity, appreciation, tax advantages and maybe speculation, rental income is one component of the picture that the landlord can manipulate directly and need not wait for time and market forces to provide the financial benefits. Thus, most landlords will watch their rental income closely. For example, poor cash flow often results from a landlord's higher mortgage expenses because he just bought a building. Time will make the cash flow positive, but until it does, landlords will try to raise rents. In addition, tenants will face difficulties in getting repairs done and long-term tenants are likely to face eviction attempts.

As in any business, the landlord begins with a set of fixed and variable expenses. Fixed expenses will include the mortgage and property taxes, and the varying expenses will be the building's operating costs such as maintenance. The fixed expenses account for 65–95% of the building's total expenses. Only a small amount is subject to inflation, which varies from year to year. For the variable costs, the landlord gets an additional break from San Francisco rent control laws, which enable him to increase rents up to 7% per year based on inflation. He may request additional increases to pay for "capital improvements." ("See Chapter 7: Rent Increases.") These capital improvements, which tenants pay for, allow the landlord to increase the monthly rent, even though they significantly increase the equity of the building as well! As many landlords have discovered this new profit strategy, the number of capital improvement cases has increased dramatically.

The total rent collected by the landlord is defined as gross income. The landlord deducts mortgage payments, property taxes, and money spent on maintenance and repair from the gross income. The money remaining is the landlord's "cash flow." (On top of this are the billions of dollars in tax subsidies given to landlords each year by the federal and state government in the form of phony "depreciation" deductions that landlords use to reduce their taxes on other income. See the discussion under the "Tax Advantages" following section.)

It is important to understand that this rental income is not the source of the landlord's profit or return on his investment; rather it is the money the landlord uses to pay off his investment. When a landlord pays bills, the first priority will be the mortgage payments, the second priority property taxes, and third priority, typically, insurance and utility costs. These are the basic expenses that will keep the landlord's investment safe from foreclosure or disaster and will enable him to build equity and reap tax benefits. The *last* priority for many landlords is maintenance and repairs. A landlord who is interested in making the highest profit and having maximum cash flow possible will make cuts in this area.

Tax Advantages

Another important financial consideration for landlords is the lucrative tax advantages that come with real estate ownership. Some of these tax benefits occur every year when landlords prepare their tax returns. Another one kicks in when a landlord sells a building. The former category includes a phony deduction called "depreciation" and other tax write-offs for expenses; the latter is the favorable "capital gains" tax rate, which is a reduced tax rate that applies to property sales.

The concept of depreciation treats your home, in the eyes of the tax laws, as it treats other commercial business expenses. It assumes, without any economic justification, that the real estate is "wearing out" over time, similar to the same process that occurs with new industrial and business equipment. Even though the building actually is increasing tremendously in market value each year (as San Francisco real estate virtually is guaranteed to do), the tax laws allow a landlord to pretend that his real estate investment is decreasing in value. This theoretical decrease in value is treated as if it were an actual cash expense paid by the landlord. Thus, a landlord can deduct the depreciation value from his taxable income the same as if he made a charitable donation or paid the property tax bill.

Even though depreciation only operates on a theoretical bookkeeping level that may warrant a discussion in a college accounting textbook, the government allows the landlord to treat it as an actual annual cash expense. Although the original builder of the housing deducted its full cost when it was built, nevertheless, the government allows every rental building to be "depreciated" year after year. Each new owner is allowed to treat the building as if it were brand new housing, and as the real estate continues to increase in value, the tax subsidies to landlords grow larger and larger. Think about that the next time you prepare your own tax return and ask yourself how many deductions the government lets you take to reduce your taxable income.

There are two formulas for calculating depreciation: "straight-line" and "accelerated." Using straight-line depreciation, the landlord can spread the depreciation benefits equally over the building's "useful life." For example, if a building is claimed to have a useful life of 25 years and its initial value is $1,000,000, a landlord can deduct $1/25$ (or $40,000) from his income tax each year as if he were losing that money. Current tax rules allow the building write-offs over about 30 years. In the 1980s, the full cost of rental property could be deducted in as little as 19 years, even though many San Francisco buildings were over 100 years old and probably would still be standing another 100 years later.

This theoretical depreciation loss is used to "shelter" other income. Sheltered income can be from rent, from sales of other buildings, from other investment income (interest and dividends) or even from "earned" income from wages. This incredible government tax subsidy of depreciation is a primary reason why many buildings are owned by doctors, attorneys and other persons in high-income occupations; depreciation will shelter the person's regular taxable income as well as provide a sound investment that builds equity.

Most wealthy individuals will have at least a portion of their investments in real estate because of these tax shelters. An indirect consequence for tenants, besides having to pay higher taxes to subsidize these tax loopholes, is that many federal and state legislators also have financial interests in real estate. Accordingly, it is difficult to get legislation passed that eliminates these tax subsidies. If these subsidies were eliminated, the cost of housing would decrease dramatically, as speculators no longer would be competing with one another to bid up the price of our housing. If the price of housing were reduced, rents also would be reduced substantially.

More common, and more outrageous, than straight-line depreciation is accelerated depreciation. This works similar to the straight-line method described previously, but rather than equal depreciation deductions each year, the landlord receives larger depreciation deductions in the first years of ownership. This results in significantly greater deductions on the landlord's income tax return. In later years the amount will be less, but by then the building often is sold. Obviously, this is a great tool for speculators and actually creates a financial incentive to buy and sell buildings quickly. After having milked the building for the bulk of its depreciation value even though the building actually is increasing in value, the building can be sold at a profit. In addition, these phony depreciation deductions continue indefinitely. When an owner has depreciated a building and then sells it, the new owner can begin this depreciation game all over again at the higher purchase price. In this manner, the total depreciation on any building can add up to many, many times its original construction cost.

Besides depreciation, landlords get other ongoing tax breaks from the federal and state governments, which are especially annoying because the San Francisco rent control law allows rent increases for the very same items! If you get a capital improvement rent increase because your landlord finally painted the building, for example, your landlord not only gets the money from your increased rent checks to fix up the building, he also can write off the costs of doing the work on his federal and state tax returns and receive a fat check from the government. This process is commonly known as "double-dipping." Landlords also can write off all of their operating expenses, such as mortgage interest, property taxes, insurance and all sorts of other items like travel costs, office and computer costs, telephone costs, etc.

In other words, landlords are heavily subsidized by taxpayers in yet another form of welfare for the rich. Keep in mind that this landlord subsidy increases each year even as the renter's tax credit has been restricted to those of very low income, and remains at the measly sum of $60. Government funding of affordable housing has virtually disappeared as well. If the amount of money the government spends on subsidizing landlords were spent to create housing, society would have fewer problems with homelessness, and tenants would pay far less of their income in rent.

Building sales and speculation are important sources of landlord profit by themselves, but they are further sweetened because the profit is taxed at a special "capital gains" tax rate. As ludicrous as it sounds, once a landlord has taken advantage of the myriad tax loopholes and tax shelters that apply to real estate, the government continues the subsidies by giving them a special tax rate. When a landlord sells a building, the profit is called "capital gain." In a truly generous manner, the government tax rate on capital gains is generally less than one-half the tax rate paid by working people on their wage and salary income.

San Francisco landlords receive an additional benefit from the government because many major cities typically impose a "transfer tax" on property sales. The transfer tax rate in San Francisco is about one-half of those typically found in other Bay Area cities. In a nutshell, many tax advantages are available to landlords. This discussion shows how easy it is for those millionaires you often read about in the newspaper to actually make a million dollars in cash, but to claim zero taxable income and to receive a tax refund courtesy of the government!

This section has provided a very brief explanation of how landlords make money. However, we would like to add that we have serious questions about the ethics of landlording as a career at all. Most people work every day and get paid only for the amount of time they are working. This is not the case with landlording; landlords make money because people need housing. Our economic and political systems make it very easy for landlords to capitalize on that need by treating landlording as a business similar to selling widgets; tenants have been reduced to mere components of a landlord's profit statement, and are not treated as people in need of housing.

Chapter 3: Researching Landlords, Buildings, and Laws

Whether you are facing an eviction, thinking about moving to a new apartment, or trying to get repairs made, you may find it useful to know more about your building, its owners and tenant law. All of this information is available, but it is spread out among several different agencies. Don't let this scare you; each of these agencies has offices and clerks who can help you find what you need. The following pages can help direct you to the appropriate agency for your specific needs.

Landlord and Building Information

Department of Building Inspection

The San Francisco Department of Building Inspection (DBI) is the repository of permits, complaints, inspection reports, and citations for all buildings in San Francisco. This is where tenants obtain copies of records that may be offered as evidence in court or at a Rent Board hearing to prove that a landlord has failed to correct a defective condition or that work was done without the necessary permits or review by the city inspectors.

For more information on using DBI for repairs and services, see the section "Department of Building Inspection" in "Chapter 6: Repairs and Services." For more information about what DBI does and contact details, see "Department of Building Inspection" under "Government Agencies" in "Appendix A: Resources." For info on the permit process see "Permit Process" in "Chapter 11: Changes in Use."

Department of Planning

Many permits for substantial work must be approved by the San Francisco Department of Planning as well as the Department of Building Inspection, and it is here that you get a chance to raise issues like the loss of affordable housing that might result from the landlord's plans. For more information on the permit process, see the "Permit Process" section in "Chapter 11: Changes in Use."

See "Department of Planning" under "Government Agencies" in "Appendix A: Resources" for more details and contact information.

Department of Public Health

For information about what the Department of Public Health (DPH) does and contact information, see "Department of Public Health" under "Government Agencies" in "Appendix A: Resources. "Also the sections "Lead, Mold, Filth, and Pests," "Removing Mold Problems," and "Lead Paint and Lead Hazards" in "Chapter 6: Repairs and Services" provide more information on what DPH does.

Assessor and Recorder

The San Francisco Assessor and Recorder Office is where you can find and obtain copies of documents recorded for every property in San Francisco, going back to decades. The type of records available include deeds, purchase price, mortgages (called deeds of trust), private and government liens (including those for unpaid taxes, water and garbage bills), partnership agreements, whether the owner is behind on mortgage payments (Notices of Default), lawsuits involving the property (Notices of Action or *Lis Pendens*) and judgments against the owners, and dozens of other esoteric documents which may reveal something about your landlord's financial situation or real estate modus operandi.

Information you can find online going back to 1990 include the name of the owner, building construction date, sale date, property value, number of legal units, restrictions on the use of the property, block and lot number, condominium approvals or other subdivision documents, defaults on payments, liens, notices of substandard building or foreclosure, etc., can be found on *https://sfassessor.org*. Click on the "Property Search" button and follow the instructions. Click on the link in the middle of the search result page for "Assessor Recorded Documents" The documents shown seem to be two weeks behind, but one can find out the name of the grantor, "R" (former owner). "Trustee Deed" indicates the bank has full ownership. Information on fictitious businesses can be found here, as well. If your Internet is too slow for the Assessor database, you may access the Recorder data at *https://recorder.sfgov.org*. Notices of Constraints on Property (limit on rent after owner move-in or Ellis Act evictions) are "NTC CNST" if you search by address. It is listed as #233 if you are searching for any notices of constraint in the entire database.

"So, we agree. A marzipan extension to a Gingerbread Cottage does meet local building code?"

"We'll convert it to condos and revitalize the area!"

BILL PROUD

There are two methods of finding the building and ownership information in the office— microfiche and computer. The property information is somewhat harder to search on microfiche, but more thorough. The General Index is an alphabetical listing, dating back to 1973. It is updated weekly and kept on microfiche next to the readers. Insert the microfiche card in the reader and look up your building.

The index is organized in several ways —alphabetical by owner's name, street address, and number. The alphabetical index provides a list of all properties in San Francisco owned by individuals using their own name and not a fictitious business name. (Many properties are listed only by the majority owner so it may be necessary to find out who this is.) The street address index shows all property addresses in the city. Look up any address, and you'll find the principal owner's name and mailing address. The number index arranges the same information by assessor's block and lot number. (All properties are given block and lot numbers; you can find yours by looking at the maps in the corner across from the computer print-out table.) You can also get your block and lot number, and sometimes the name of the primary owner, by looking up your address in a book on the counter. Microfiche with general information about each property is kept in file boxes behind the counter—ask the clerk for the record you need once you have found it in the index.

Two sets of computer terminals on the tables can be used by the public. (The information is organized in the same manner as described in the previous paragraphs.) One set will give you general information about your building, including the number of legal units it has, the owner, and the property tax assessment. You can find where your landlord lives by checking for "owner occupancy" tax exemptions on property a landlord owns. Or you often can find out by getting a copy of the tax bill for your building. The tax bill will have an address on it which often is the landlord's home address. The other set of computers can be used as an index (like the General Index on microfiche described previously) to the more detailed records available through the microfilm. The menu prompts are relatively easy to follow.

Whether you use the computers or the microfiche, each entry lists the type of document on file (many are abbreviated—use the index in the front of the microfiche binders to find out what the abbreviations mean), a date, a cross-reference name, the recorder's file number and bookmark. This bookmark refers you to a "book and page" (or reel and image) where the actual document is found on microfilm, for example, E785/932. Once you have located a document you want to view, pull the appropriate reel from the file cabinets (organized numerically by reel number). Insert the reel in the microfilm viewers and locate the page you want. Page numbers are found on the upper right corner of the document. Using the viewers is a bit tricky at first — assistance is available if you cannot figure them out. It is a good idea to review the documents immediately before and after the document you found in the index as there may be related papers. Copies of documents can be made—copy order forms are available at the front counter.

Finally, make sure to consult the computer printouts found on a large table. This report is organized by block and lot number and is updated weekly. It is the most current index of transactions available and is essential if you are researching a recent sale. The printouts include a filing date for each record, and you will notice that there is some lag time between filing and indexing. (It may take two to three weeks before a filed record shows up on the printouts.) If you are looking for more recent records, you can ask the clerk. You may be able to view records that have not been indexed yet. See "Assessor/Recorder's Office" under "Government Agencies" in "Appendix A: Resources" for contact information.

Rent Board

The San Francisco Rent Board has records of petitions filed by tenants and landlords, eviction notices, buyout agreements, and wrongful eviction reports. You can go there or call and ask a counselor to tell you what records they have on your landlord. If a case was appealed to the Rent Board Commissioners, info might be found by searching for key words (including names) on the Rent Board's website, *https://sfrb.org*.

All Rent Board decisions bear, on the front page, a section labeled "Law Construed," with corresponding "Index Codes" (for example A5, B6, etc.), that relate to issues considered in the decision. If you go to the computers in the work stations in front of the help counter at the Rent Board, you can hit a button reading "Index Codes," and the entire Index Code list will appear, i.e., the Code and its corresponding "translation." For example, the letter "A" relates to the category Rent Increases; "A49—Rent Increase—1.21—Tenant Not in Occupancy" is how one entry reads, but the list goes from A1 to A80; the broad "A" issue of Rent Increase has been minutely subdivided, and some decisions are very subtle. If you are interested in reading a decision involving that issue, you just hit the "carrot" [">"] to the left side of the screen, and it will open a list of all Rent Board cases in which that Index Code appears. On the right-hand side, there's another button for every case reading "Decision" that you can hit, and it will open the text of the decision itself, which can also be printed out at cost. This sounds more complicated than it actually is, and anyone there will show you how to do it. It's only available at the office however, not online.

If you are searching for a specific case, it is advisable to search under the name instead of addresses due to clerical error. You can also search under phone numbers. The database goes back to 1987. However, if you are looking for buyout agreements, the tenant's name is removed for privacy and the agent for the landlord may be named instead of the landlord. Most Decrease in Housing Services petitions are settled in mediation, which is not searchable in the database. See "Rent Board" under the "San Francisco" section of "Government Agencies" in "Appendix A: Resources" for more information about the Rent Board.

Additional Online Information

The type of dwelling unit (apartment or condo), property value, and previous tenants can be found at *https://www.propertyshark.com* and *https://www.spokeo.com*. Information on LLCs (limited liability companies) can also be found on *https://www.corporationwiki.com* which is free. The "registered agent" can be the attorney who accepts the mail instead of the owner, however. Searching online using search engines such as Google with the landlord's name and adding a middle initial, family member's name, phone number, or email address can yield additional information about an owner. *https://www.linkedin.com* is a good source of information about a person, but you will need an account which will show you have visited the person's site. Information on subdivision status of a property is available by going to *http://bsm.sfdpw.org/subdivision/tracking*.

Names of the landlord or tenant in court cases can be found by using the online resources in the sections that follow.

Court Records

It can be useful to look up information about your landlord in the court records to find out whether or not she has ever sued or been sued before. Surprising information may be gleaned through court documents. You can find court cases by party names or case number at *https://sfsuperiorcourt.org* (click on "Online Services"), although eviction records are restricted starting 2017, or follow the instructions in the following sections for in person research.

More information about the courts can be found under the "California" section of "Government Agencies" in "Appendix A: Resources."

Superior Court — Limited Jurisdiction

The California Superior Court— Limited Jurisdiction is where most of the eviction (Unlawful Detainer) cases take place. It is also where actions for damages of less than $25,000 are filed. You can find information at the Public Viewing Room. The indices of court cases filed in the current calendar year are located in binders

"We've decided it would be better for his later development if we speak to him only in legalese."

of computer printouts, divided alphabetically by plaintiff's name and defendant's name. One index contains Unlawful Detainer (eviction) cases broken down by plaintiff and defendant. Be sure to page through these binders because, although the cases filed earlier in the year are blended with the composite index, those cases filed in recent weeks and days are not yet shuffled into the main deck, so to speak.

Current cases and cases going back about ten years can also be found using the computer terminal available for public use. Printed instructions are provided, or you can follow the computer screen prompts. You can locate cases by the plaintiff's name, defendant's name, or the attorney's name. Older cases are indexed on microfiche. Check with the Clerk's office for the microfiche reader and the card file of microfiche sheets.

After you have found the number of the case you are interested in, complete a request card and the clerk will pull the file for your review. You will need to leave your driver's license with the clerk for this. Inactive cases may have to be ordered from the warehouse, which could take a few days. The clerk will copy portions of the file you wish for $0.50 per page (9/21).

Superior Court — Unlimited Jurisdiction

The Unlimited Jurisdiction division of the California Superior Court is where cases seeking damages in excess of $25,000 are filed. (Most wrongful eviction suits filed against landlords are heard here.) This is also where probate cases (estate divisions) and divorces are filed.

As in the Limited Jurisdiction division, you must know the case number before you can review the case file to find out what the action is about. Both divisions are in the same room, but you use different indices and computers and go to different "windows" for assistance. The indices for cases filed since January 1987 are stored on computer. If it is an earlier case, it may be on computer if the case isn't finalized. Otherwise, pre-1987 case indices are stored on microfiche. These microfiche sheets are available from the person at the information desk. Readers are found along the wall — use them as described previously.

The clerks at the counter may help you access the computer indices

(1987 to present) if they aren't too busy. There are instruction sheets near the computers, and often someone in the room can help you figure them out if the sheets aren't enough.

To view the case file, fill out a request card and the clerk will pull the file. If you want to copy a specific document, tag it with a paper clip, count the number of pages, and fill out a copy request form. The more pages you are copying, the more likely it is you will have to pick them up the next day. There is no self-service copying in Court clerk's offices.

Small Claims Court

The California Small Claims Court is where landlords and tenants fight over security deposits as well as other lawsuits for $10,000 or less. Some landlords are so familiar in this court that the court clerk maintains a rubber stamp with their names. To research in person prior small claims court cases involving your landlord (cases available online, as well), ask the clerk to let you look up your landlord's name in the indices. Technically, the small claims court is also a division of the Superior Court, but, aside from being in the same building, there is very little integration with the other two divisions.

Laws (See also Appendices C and D: Law Excerpts and Regulations)

Law Libraries

The public San Francisco law library is an invaluable resource when a tenant is doing her own eviction defense or legal research. The staff is very helpful and will often assist in your search or answer your inquiry. You can read and copy the City and State codes including Housing, Building, Planning, and Health. (The main library also has code books.) Many books relating to tenant-landlord law are available for reading, including many used by lawyers in their daily practices.

If you want to look up any of the cases cited in this handbook, we reference them in the *Table of Cases* using the *California Appellate*

"The judicial rulings are over there. This section is all lawyer jokes."

Reports (Cal. App., also abbreviated CA) and the *California Reports* (Cal., or C). For instance, the landmark California case of *Green v. Superior Court* is cited as 10 Cal.3d 616. This cites volume 10 of the "official" case publication for California Supreme Court decisions, *California Reports*, 3rd series, starting at page 616.

Law Books

An excellent resource for legal research for non-lawyers is the Nolo Press book, *Legal Research: How to Find and Understand the Law,* by Stephen Elias (available at the library, many bookstores or through Nolo Press in Berkeley). Also an excellent, if somewhat technical, reference for landlord-tenant law is the *California Practice Guide: Landlord-Tenant Law* by Friedman, Garcia, and Hagarty, published by the Rutter Group.

Laws on the Web

San Francisco Rent Board's Web site, *https://sfrb.org,* includes the entire text of the San Francisco Rent Ordinance and Rent Board Rules and Regulations, as well as brief overviews of topics of interest to tenants. Summaries and updates can also be found on the San Francisco Tenants Union Web site, *https://ww.sftu. org.* San Francisco's municipal codes (Administrative, Building, Electrical, Environment, Fire, Health, Housing, Mechanical, Planning, Plumbing, Police, and Subdivision Codes) can be found on *https://www.amlegal.com* and *elaws.us.*

Translations of California tenant law for laypersons can be found at *https://www.nolo.com* (under the "Legal Articles" menu, then click on "Tenants"). *https://www.courts.ca.gov* has information about handling your own court case. (See also "Chapter 14: Taking Action" for more information.)

State law can be found at *https://leginfo.legislature.ca.gov,* the California Code of Regulations at *https://www.dir.ca.gov/dlse/ ccr.htm,* and California Building Standards Code (also known as California Code of Regulations, Title 24) at *https://www.dgs. ca.gov/BSC/Codes.* For the full text of federal laws, which include laws against housing discrimination and laws affecting subsidized housing (public housing, Section 8, and housing projects) you can search on *https://uscode.house.gov,* which also can be searched by keyword.

Case law can be found by searching under the names of the plaintiff v. the defendant. A search engine with which you can choose to limit your search to a specific court or jurisdiction is at *https://lp.findlaw.com.* LexisNexis (*https://www.lexisnexis. com/clients/CACourts*) and Google Scholar (*https://scholar. google.com*) allow searches by word in case law. Civil Jury Instructions (interpretation of law and other information) is at *www.courts.ca.gov/partners/juryinstructions.htm.* A database for legal professionals that a layperson can also use is *https://www. martindale.com.*

Chapter 4: **Renting Basics**

Protections for the Tenant Under the San Francisco Rent Ordinance and State Law

The San Francisco Rent Stabilization and Arbitration Ordinance, (San Francisco Administrative Code Chapter 37) passed in 1979, provides protection for tenants in most of the residential rental units in San Francisco. We will refer to the ordinance in this book as the Rent Ordinance.

Starting April 1, 2020, every online listing for a rental unit covered under the Rent Ordinance, excluding listings by landlords or master tenants who will reside in the same rental unit as their tenants or subtenants, must contain a disclosure in at least 12-point font that includes the following: "This unit is a rental unit subject to the San Francisco Rent Ordinance, which limits evictions without just cause, and which states that any waiver by a tenant of their rights under the Rent Ordinance is void as contrary to public policy." This text should also be included in print advertisements, if practicable. (SF Administrative Code § 37.9F)

If a unit is not covered by the Rent Ordinance, state law applies. An owner of residential property covered under the Tenant Protection Act of 2019 (CA Civil Code § 1946.2) must disclose to the tenant as follows in no less than 12-point type:

"California law limits the amount your rent can be increased. See Section 1947.12 of the Civil Code for more information. California law also provides that after all of the tenants have continuously and lawfully occupied the property for 12 months or more or at least one of the tenants has continuously and lawfully occupied the property for 24 months or more, a landlord must provide a statement of cause in any notice to

SF v. CA Exemptions to Rent Control/Just Cause Eviction (Part 1)

	SF Administrative Code § 37.2(r). See "What Does the Rent Ordinance Cover?" for more info.	California Civil Code § 1946.2 and § 1947.12
Disclosure	None	Required if covered, or if exempt as a single-family home.
Length of Tenancy	Rooms in transient housing where the tenant has occupied the room fewer than 32 consecutive days. SF Administrative Code § 37.2(r)(1)	Less than 12 months tenancy. CC § 1946.2(a), § 1947.12(a)(2)
Certificate of Occupancy Date	Rental units with an initial certificate of occupancy issued after 6/13/79 are only exempt from rent increase limitations of the Rent Ordinance except for (SF Administrative Code § 37.3(g)): 1. Costa-Hawkins Rental Housing Act limitations (SF Administrative Code § 37.3(d), § 37.3(f)). 2. Replacement units under SF Administrative Code § 37.9A(b). 3. Development agreement with the City under SF Administrative Code Chapter 56. 4. Accessory Dwelling Units under SF Administrative Code § 37.2(r)(4)(D).	Housing that has been issued a certificate of occupancy within the previous 15 years unless a mobilehome. CC § 1946.2(e)(7), § 1947.12(d)(4)
Government-Assisted Housing/ Affordable Housing	Units in project-based government-assisted or government-regulated housing except units with tenant-based assistance are protected by parts of the Rent Ordinance. SF Administrative Code § 37.2(r)(4)	Some affordable or other rent-controlled housing. CC § 1946.2(e)(9), § 1947.12(d)(1) and (3)
Transient Housing	Rooms in hotels, motels, inns, tourist houses, rooming and boarding houses where the tenant has occupied the room fewer than 32 consecutive days. SF Administrative Code § 37.2(r)(1)	Transient and tourist hotel occupancy are exempt from just cause eviction. CC § 1946.2(e)(1)

terminate a tenancy. See Section 1946.2 of the Civil Code for more information."

(1) For any tenancy commenced or renewed on or after July 1, 2020, as an addendum to the rental agreement, or as a written notice signed by the tenant, with a copy provided to the tenant.

(2) For a tenancy existing prior to July 1, 2020, by written notice or addendum to the rental agreement no later than August 1, 2020.

More info about which residential units are covered is in the rest of this section. The Rent Ordinance and state law restrict the amount rent can be increased for a residential unit unless the unit is exempt. (See "Chapter 7: Rent Increases" for details of the rent increase limitations.) In addition, evictions under the Rent Ordinance and state law requiring "just cause" can only be for the specified reasons. (See the chart "SF v. CA Just Cause for Eviction" in "Chapter 12: Eviction Defenses.")

The Rent Ordinance is a weaker version of rent control than has been enacted in other cities. Rent control works like regulatory price controls imposed on utility companies. In other words, its purpose is to make sure that an essential service remains affordable. Despite state law that allows rental agreements to be changed with proper notice, in *Birkenfeld v. City of Berkeley* ((1976) 17 Cal. 3d 129, and numerous other cases, the courts have ruled that rent control ordinances and just cause evictions are allowed because they do not materially interfere with other law.

Unfortunately, there is a major loophole in the Rent Ordinance: Though it limits the amount that rent can be increased on *occupied* units, landlords can usually raise rents on vacant units to market level (as high as the landlord can get away with). When the vacant unit is re-rented, it is once again covered by the Rent Ordinance, but at the new rent. This "vacancy decontrol" loophole provides the incentive to evict long-term tenants and has allowed San

SF v. CA Exemptions to Rent Control/Just Cause Eviction (Part 2)

	SF Administrative Code § 37.2(r). See "What Does the Rent Ordinance Cover?" for more info.	California Civil Code § 1946.2 and § 1947.12
Substantially Rehabilitated Housing	Same as "Certificate of Occupancy Date" above.	Not applicable.
Unusual Residences	**Some nonprofit cooperatives**, units in a **hospital, convent, monastery, extended care facility, asylum, residential care facility for elders, or school dormitory**. SF Administrative Code § 37.2(r)(2) and (3)	**Dormitory, nonprofit hospital, religious facility, extended care facility, licensed residential care facility for the elderly, adult residential facility.** CC § 1946.2(e)(2) and (3), § 1947.12(d)(2)
Sharing Property with Landlord	A tenant residing in the same rental unit as the landlord can be evicted without "just cause." SF Administrative Code § 37.9(b)	1. If the tenant shares bathroom/ kitchen with the owner's principal residence, the unit is exempt from just cause eviction. CC § 1946.2(e)(4) 2. Owner-occupied residence where the owner-occupant rents no more than two units or bedrooms, including, but not limited to an accessory dwelling unit or a mobilehome are exempt from just cause eviction. CC § 1946.2(e)(5) 3. A 2 dwelling units structure where the owner occupied 1 of the units as his/her principal place of residence at the beginning of the tenancy and neither unit is an accessory dwelling unit, if the owner continues in occupancy. CC § 1946.2(e)(6), § 1947.12(d)(6)
Single Residential Unit	Some dwelling units which are separate from title to any other dwelling unit do not have rent increase protections. SF Administrative Code § 37.2(r)(7). See also the section "Definition of a Single Residential Unit" in "Chapter 4: Renting Basics."	Dwelling units separate from title to any other dwelling unit are exempt from rent control/just cause eviction unless: • The owner is a real estate investment trust, a corporation, or limited liability company with corporation member or management of a mobilehome park **OR** • Required disclosure was not given. • See also the section "Definition of a Single Residential Unit" in "Chapter 4: Renting Basics." CC § 1946.2(e)(8), § 1947.12(d)(5)

Francisco rents to soar despite rent control. (See the box "Vacancy Control" in "Chapter 7: Rent Increases" for exceptions.)

The Rent Ordinance establishes a Rent Board to enforce the Rent Ordinance and to arbitrate disputes between tenants and landlords arising out of the law. The Rent Board commissioners (five persons appointed by the mayor — two landlords, two tenants, and one "neutral" property owner but not a landlord— plus five alternates from the same groups) enact rules and regulations, hold bi-weekly public meetings and hear appeals. The Rent Board office staff performs the day-to-day administration of the Rent Board: providing information to tenants and landlords, facilitating mediation, and holding hearings.

This book is only a summary of the Rent Ordinance and the Rent Board's procedures for enforcing it, the San Francisco Rent Board Rules and Regulations (SF Administrative Code § 37.6) and state law. "Appendix C" and "Appendix D" contain important law and rules. There is no substitute for reading the text of the law itself and the accompanying rules and regulations. For an inexpensive amount you can purchase copies of the Rent Ordinance and Rules and Regulations from the Rent Board or find them on *https://sfrb. org*.

What Does the Rent Ordinance Cover?

The San Francisco Rent Ordinance and what it covers or excludes applies to:

> *All residential dwelling units in the City and County of San Francisco together with the land and appurtenant buildings thereto, and all the housing services, privileges, furnishings and facilities supplied in connection with the use or occupancy thereof, including garage and parking facilities.* (SF Administrative Code § 37.2(r))

The term "rental unit" is defined as "a residential dwelling unit, regardless of zoning or legal status, in the City and County of San Francisco." (SF Rent Board Rules and Regulations § 1.17) "Illegal" rental units, such as most "in-laws," rented commercial space used for residential use with the implied or express consent of the landlord, or parking supplied in connection with the use of a rental unit, are included in the definition of "rental unit" in the Rent Ordinance.

Despite the previous statement, the protections of the Rent Ordinance do not apply to all residential units in San Francisco. The Rent Ordinance defines coverage backwards by listing the types of property "exempt" from coverage—that is, not covered by the ordinance. In other words, if a tenant lives in a residential dwelling unit in San Francisco that does not

fall within one of the exempted categories listed in the Rent Ordinance, then the unit is covered and the tenant enjoys the protections of the Rent Ordinance, starting at the inception of the tenancy. If there is a disagreement with the landlord over whether the rental unit is or is not covered under the Rent Ordinance, the tenant may submit a request for determination of jurisdiction in the Tenant Petition form from the Rent Board.

The types of residential units exempt from coverage in the Rent Ordinance are in the following subsections.

Certificate of Occupancy Date

Effective January 2020, rental units with a certificate of occupancy after June 13, 1979 or which the Rent Board has certified has undergone a substantial rehabilitation are no longer exempt from the Rent Ordinance. However, these newer units are allowed to set the initial and subsequent rent with the following exceptions (SF Administrative Code § 37.3(g)):

- Costa-Hawkins Rental Housing Act limitations (SF Administrative Code § 37.3(d), § 37.3(f)).

- Replacement units under San Francisco Administrative Code § 37.9A(b). Search the "Assessor Recorded Documents" on the San Francisco Assessor and Recorder's Office website for the restriction.

- Accessory Dwelling Units with rent limitations under San Francisco Administrative Code § 37.2(r){4}{D}. Look for "ADU" under "Planning Applications."

- Unauthorized units that existed before June 13, 1979 and were brought up to code after that date are still covered under the Rent Ordinance. (*Da Vinci Group v. San Francisco Residential Rent Stabilization Board* (1992) 5 Cal. App.4th 24; *Burien, LLC v. Wiley* (2014) 230 Cal. App. 4th 1039)

- Development agreement with the City under San Francisco Administrative Code Chapter 56. Within 10 days after the execution of the development agreement, the agreement shall be recorded with the County Recorder.

See the section "Unauthorized Units" in "Chapter 11: Changes in Use" for info on how to look up the initial certificate of occupancy. For the interpretation of multiple certificates of occupancy in the Costa-Hawkins Rental Housing Act, see the later section "Single Residential Unit" in this chapter.

If the rent is increased substantially above market rate, a tenant may be able to successfully sue or prosecute the landlord for wrongful eviction or harassment since the excessive rent increase could amount to an eviction without just cause. (SF

Subsidized Housing

Tenants in public housing projects (San Francisco Housing Authority Developments), Section 8 projects, and United States Department of Housing and Urban Development (HUD) subsidized buildings where the subsidy is connected to the building, not to the tenant, are not covered by San Francisco's Rent Ordinance. Instead, they have their own protections governed by HUD or by the San Francisco Housing Authority. These units *are* covered by state and local laws, except the Rent Ordinance, covering housing conditions, discrimination, etc.

HUD-insured buildings without subsidized rents (such as Golden Gate and Vista Del Monte) have always been covered by the Rent Ordinance.

Tenants receiving *tenant-based* rental assistance like Section 8 vouchers, Housing Opportunities for Persons With AIDS (HOPWA), or HUD-Veterans Affairs Supportive Housing *are* covered by the eviction protections of the Rent Ordinance (SF Administrative Code § 37.9(g) and (h)), and in some cases, the rent increase sections as well.

If the rent is *not* a fixed percentage, commonly 30% of the tenant's income, for example Section 8 vouchers, then whenever the rent goes above the "Payment Standard," a standard rent amount set by the Housing Authority, rent increases are subject to the annual and banked rent increase controls of the Rent Ordinance. (SF Administrative Code § 37.3(a)(10)) No capital improvement passthroughs, operating and maintenance increases, "comparable" rent increases, or other rent increases are allowed. (SF Administrative Code § 37.2(r)(4))

SF Police Code Article 33 prohibits housing discrimination against tenants based on their source of income. This law prohibits landlords from refusing to accept a tenant solely because his rent comes from a housing subsidy program. It also prohibits landlords from refusing to participate in the housing subsidy program with an existing tenant who subsequently becomes eligible for a housing subsidy. But most importantly, landlords can no longer arbitrarily "opt out" of housing subsidy programs to clear out the unit in order to raise the rent. Tenants trying to use this law to fight discrimination should also raise state discrimination statutes addressing arbitrary discrimination since the local law may be preempted by state law. See *Chapter 9: Discrimination* for more information.

You can contact the Housing Rights Committee of San Francisco or Bay Area Legal Aid (see *Appendix A: Resources*) if you have questions specific to subsidized housing.

Residential Hotels

A residential hotel is any building containing six or more guest rooms or efficiency units, as defined by California Health and Safety Code § 17958.1, not including a building which is primarily used by transient guests. (CA Health and Safety Code § 50519) Under state law, residential hotel tenants have the same rights as any other tenant once they have occupied their rooms for 30 consecutive days. (Short-term occupants, on the other hand, can be locked out of their rooms once the time they've paid for runs out and are generally at great risk of eviction for arbitrary reasons.) The hotel operator cannot require an occupant of a hotel room to move or to check out and reregister before the expiration of the 30-day occupancy period if a purpose of the move is to deny the occupant tenant status, "musical rooming." The occupant can sue for actual damages, $500 statutory penalty, and reasonable attorney fees for the prevailing party. (CA Civil Code § 1940.1)

The occupant in a hotel (SF Housing Code § 401 similarly defines a hotel as a building containing six or more guest rooms) receives the benefits of the San Francisco Rent Ordinance after 32 consecutive days in the same room. Hotel residents also have visitor rights. (See "Uniform Hotel Visitor Policy" under "San Francisco Administrative Code" in *Appendix C: Law Excerpts and Regulations*.) A federal appeals court upheld that the U. S. Postal Service may deliver mail to the front desk or a central collection box rather than individual mailboxes, overriding San Francisco and California law for mailboxes. (*City and County of San Francisco v. USPS*, No. 12-15473 (9th Cir. 2013), SF Administrative Code Chapter 41E.3, CA Civil Code § 1941.1) For loss of housing services including violations of the Residential Hotel Visitor Policy, petition the Rent Board for a rent reduction if the room is covered by the Rent Ordinance.

For rooms covered by the Rent Ordinance, kitchen facilities or lobbies supplied in connection with the use of the room require "just cause" to be taken away. (See the section "Just Causes for Eviction Under the SF Rent Ordinance" in *Chapter 12: Eviction Defenses* for more information.) Any severance that is allowed should have a rent decrease. (SF Administrative Code § 37.2(r))

Administrative Code § 37.10A(i), (j); § 37.10B(a)(5))

Government-Assisted Housing

Units in project-based government-assisted or government-regulated housing are exempt from the Rent Ordinance except Midtown Park Apartments receive benefits of the Rent Ordinance. (SF Administrative Code § 37.2(r)(4), § 37B) However, tenants living in townhouses owned by San Francisco State, for example, should be covered under the Rent Ordinance unless maybe the unit was rented by a student as part of being enrolled at SF State. (*City and County of San Francisco v. The Regents of the*

Chapter 4– Renting Basics

University of California et al. (2019) S242835. Although ostensibly a tax case, this case demolishes the argument made that a state entity is completely exempt from local regulation, including the Rent Ordinance.) Tenants with tenant-based assistance are protected by parts of the Rent Ordinance. (See the box "Subsidized Housing" for more information.) Treasure Island housing is exempt from the Rent Ordinance as it is government-regulated housing, *https://sftreasureisland.org/living-treasure-island*. Presidio housing is also exempt from the Rent Ordinance as well as state law as it is federal land and since there is almost no federal landlord-tenant law, federal contract law principles have to be applied.

Transient Housing

Rooms in hotels, motels, inns, tourist houses, rooming and boarding houses where the tenant has occupied the room fewer than 32 consecutive days are exempt from the Rent Ordinance. (SF Administrative Code § 37.2(r)(1)) See the box "Residential Hotels" for more information.)

Substantially Rehabilitated Housing

Units that have undergone "substantial rehabilitation" as certified by the Rent Board are no longer exempt from the Rent Ordinance. However, these units are allowed to set the initial and subsequent rent with the same exceptions as the post-1979 certificate of occupancy units. (See the previous section "Certificate of Occupancy Date.") Substantial rehabilitation is renovation work on a building that is at least fifty years old and essentially uninhabitable.

Unusual Residences

Employees who dwell in their units as part of their employment with no separate claim as tenants are exempt from the Rent Ordinance. (See the section "Resident Managers Under the San Francisco Rent Ordinance and California Law Requiring Just Cause Eviction" near the end of this chapter for more information.)

Nonprofit cooperatives owned and controlled by a majority of the residents, or dwelling units solely owned by a nonprofit public benefit corporation, the majority of whose directors are residents of the dwelling units, where the corporate bylaws require that rent increases be approved by a majority of the residents are exempt from the Rent Ordinance. (SF Administrative Code § 37.2(r)(2))

Units in a **hospital**, **convent**, **monastery**, **extended care facility**, **asylum**, **residential care facility for elders**, or **school dormitory** are also exempt from the Rent Ordinance. (SF Administrative Code § 37.2(r)(3))

Sharing Rental Unit with Landlord

See the section "Roommates(s) Living with Owner" in "Chapter 10: Roommates" for information.

Single Residential Unit

Under the Costa-Hawkins Rental Housing Act (CA Civil Code § 1954.50 et. seq.), a state law effective in 1996, tenants who rent a dwelling unit which is separate from title to any other dwelling unit (commonly called a single-family home) lost rent increase protections from the Rent Ordinance starting January 1, 1999 with exceptions listed in the following sections. However, other sections of state law, Civil Codes § 1946.2 and § 1947.12, provide limitations on rent increases and evictions for those units without Rent Ordinance protection.

Additional Definitions of a Single Residential Unit

- Buildings that have been converted legally or illegally to a rooming house are considered multiunit, not a single residential unit. (*Chun v. Del Cid* (2019) B295140)

- An illegal dwelling unit in addition to a legal unit would not be a single residential unit unless the units were rented together. However, two legal units rented together may not be considered a single residential unit under the Rent Ordinance since it is zoned as two units. (*https://sfrb.org/topic-no-019-partial-exemption-certain-single-family-homes-and-condominiums-under-costa-Hawkins*)

- Illegal removal of a dwelling unit did not allow the rent to be increased for the remaining unit under the Costa-Hawkins Act, although not a binding decision by the Rent Board. (Case #T151421)

- A single apartment above a commercial unit would be considered a single residential unit.

- If the subdivider (the person or group of people who have divided the property into condominiums with separate titles) has not sold all the units separately to bona fide purchasers or has only one unit but has not lived in that unit for one year after subdivision, then the unit does not qualify as an exception to rent control under the Costa-Hawkins Act. (CA Civil Code § 1954.52(a)(3)(B)(ii))

Rent Ordinance Rent Increase Limitations Still Apply to Single Residential Units in the Following Circumstances:

- If the tenancy started before 1996 and was covered under the Rent Ordinance, the unit continues to be rent-controlled under the Rent Ordinance until the current tenant moves out. For single residential units, if the original tenancy began before 1996 and a newer tenant moved in after that date but paid rent directly to the

landlord, this newer tenancy would be considered to be a continuing tenancy. Therefore when the original tenants vacate, an unlimited rent increase would not be permitted under the Costa-Hawkins Act.

- Termination of the preceding tenancy by the owner for no fault of the tenant (see the section "Fighting "Fault" Evictions" in "Chapter 12: Eviction Defenses" for tenant "faults"), or by changes in terms of the rental agreement under California Civil Code §827, excluding a legal increase in rent or fees, causes the new tenant's rent to be regulated by the Rent Ordinance. (CA Civil Code § 1954.52(a)(3)(B)(i))

- Code violations that were serious, not caused by a disaster, and unabated for at least sixty days for remaining tenants or six months for replacement tenants after being cited by a city agency before a tenant vacated the unit, would cause the remaining or replacement tenants' rent to be regulated by the Rent Ordinance. (CA Civil Code § 1954.52(d), § 1954.53) The sixty-day period may be extended by the agency issuing the citation.

- Even if a landlord can raise the rent under the Costa-Hawkins Act, if the rent is increased substantially above market rate, a tenant may be able to successfully sue or prosecute the landlord for wrongful eviction or harassment since the excessive rent increase could amount to an eviction without just cause. (SF Administrative Code § 37.10A(i), (j); § 37.10B(a)(5)) You can check for the current market rental rates for a comparable unit by neighborhood on *https://www.padmapper.com.*

When landlords are not confident that they can increase the rent under the Costa-Hawkins Act, they sometimes try to claim in a lawsuit that the original tenant no longer lives in the unit and so any remaining roommates can have their rent increased. (See the section "Rent Increase When Original Occupant Vacates" in "Chapter 10: Roommates.")

Just Cause Eviction Requirement for Single Residential Units

Tenants in single residential units that are not otherwise exempt from the Rent Ordinance, still have the "just cause" eviction protections of the Rent Ordinance. (See "Chapter 12: Eviction Defenses" for more information on just cause eviction.) If the unit is not covered under the Rent Ordinance, state law for just cause eviction applies. See the later section for more info.

California Law Disclosure and Ownership Requirement for Single Residential Unit Exception

For a tenancy in a single residential unit that began or renewed on or after July 1, 2020 or if the lease is for a mobilehome July 1, 2022, in order to be exempt from state rent control or just cause eviction, the rental agreement must be written and include the following statement: "This property is not subject to the rent limits imposed by Section 1947.12 of the Civil Code and is not subject to the just cause requirements of Section 1946.2 of the Civil Code. This property meets the requirements of Sections 1947.12 (d)(5) and 1946.2 (e)(8) of the Civil Code and the owner is not any of the following: (1) a real estate investment trust, as defined by Section 856 of the Internal Revenue Code; (2) a corporation; or (3) a limited liability company in which at least one member is a corporation." For tenancies that existed before July 1, 2020, the statement does not have to be in the rental agreement. (CA Civil Code § 1946.2(e)(8), (f); CA Civil Code § 1947.12(d)(5))

If the owner is one of the following, these properties do not qualify for the single residential unit exception from state rent control (CA Civil Code § 1947.12(d)(5)(A):

- A real estate investment trust, as defined in Section 856 of the Internal Revenue Code.

- A corporation.

- A limited liability company in which at least one member is a corporation.

Landlord's Duty of Habitability

See "Chapter 6: Repairs and Services" for information on habitability.

Tenant's Duty of Habitability

The tenant must:

- Properly operate all electrical, gas and plumbing fixtures, and keep them clean and sanitary.

- Not damage the structure or dwelling unit or the facilities, equipment or accessories or permit any other person to do this on purpose or by unrestrained carelessness.

- Only use parts of the dwelling for living, sleeping, cooking or dining as intended to be used.

- Dispose of waste, in a sanitary way (unless otherwise agreed to in writing).

- Keep the premises which she occupies clean, as the condition of the premises permits.

(CA Civil Code § 1941.2)

- Inform the landlord about repairs that are needed unless the landlord already knows about the problem. (See "Chapter 6: Repairs and Services" for more information.)

Although nearly everyone lives up to these standards, you should be aware that the law allows landlords to use the tenant's failure to comply with these requirements as a defense to not meeting their own obligations, and even as a reason to evict. Be careful about making repairs or improvements yourself since most rental agreements require the tenant to have permission from the landlord before making alterations.

Leases and Rental Agreements

A *lease* or *rental agreement* is a contract between the landlord and the tenant specifying the rights and obligations of each party for the temporary possession of the property in exchange for "reward" which is usually rent. (CA Civil Code § 1925) The Rent Ordinance uses the term "consideration" to include payments other than monetary for rent. (SF Administrative Code § 37.2(p)) If, for example, a landlord has a romantic relationship with the tenant, a "tenancy at will" or "estate at will" has been created when the landlord allows the tenant to be in possession but does not charge the tenant any rent.

The rental agreement may be written or oral. (CA Civil Code § 1622) If the oral agreement is followed by a written agreement, then the written agreement replaces the oral agreement. (CA Civil Code § 1625, § 1697) If there is a cosigner in a shared rental unit, it is recommended that the contract states that the cosigner's obligations terminate when the tenant the cosigner is aiding leaves.

The agreement must be legal, possible, and definite. (CA Civil Code § 1596, *Ladas v. California State Automobile Assn.* (1993) 19 Cal.App.4th 761, 770) In the absence of other law in the sections preceding California Civil Code 1654, the courts would interpret ambiguous terms against the writer of the agreement.

A tenant has legal rights and duties when entering into a rental agreement, such as the right to habitable premises and the duty to notify the landlord of repairs that need to be made if the landlord doesn't know about the problem. These legal rights and duties are "implied" in every rental agreement; they are part of the contract whether or not they are expressly stated in the agreement.

There are three basic types of rental agreements:

- The written lease for a term of longer than 30 days (usually 6 months to a year).

- The written rental agreement, usually month-to-month, which is not a lease.

- The oral rental agreement which is just a "handshake," usually from month-to-month. (For more info see the

section "Proving That a Rental Agreement Directly with the Landlord Exists" in "Chapter 10: Roommates.")

The distinguishing characteristics of each type are discussed in the following sections. But no matter what kind of agreement you have, as soon as your landlord accepts rent from you, a binding rental contract is created. At this point, both you and your landlord have certain legal rights and responsibilities towards one another. Since you have paid rent to the landlord, you have acquired the right to occupy the premises: the so-called "right to possession." Your landlord cannot kick you out or otherwise regain possession of your place without taking you to court and having the sheriff evict you, with few exceptions. (See the section "Bypassing the Courts: Lodgers and Hotels" in "Chapter 13: Eviction Process in Court.") No matter what kind of rental agreement you have, if the building is sold all the provisions of the original agreement remain in effect. (See the section "Sale of Building" later in this chapter.)

See the section "Proving That a Rental Agreement Directly with the Landlord Exists" in "Chapter 10: Roommates" for more information about proving the existence of a rental agreement.

Leases vs. Month-to-Month Rental Agreements

What's the difference between a lease and a month-to-month rental agreement? A month-to-month agreement continues indefinitely until it is terminated by either the landlord or the tenant. If you have a month-to-month rental agreement, you can terminate it at any time with a thirty-day written notice to the landlord. (See the section "Notices and Other Communications Between Landlord and Tenant" later in this chapter.)

A lease is an agreement to rent for a specified period of time. In order to be a lease, the contract must specify a date upon which the tenancy begins and the date that the tenancy ends—for example, from May 1, 2021 to April 30, 2022. A lease for a period of more than a year must be in writing. (CA Civil Code § 1624) Thus, an oral agreement to rent a place from December 1, 2021 to December 31, 2022 is not a lease. It is an oral month-to-month rental agreement even if it is titled "Lease." For a lease to be extended automatically if the tenant is still in possession or did not give a notice of termination, the extension clause must follow the requirements of California Civil Code § 1945.5.

After the expiration of the time period for a lease, the agreement continues month-to-month if the rent is paid monthly. At the end of each month the agreement expires at midnight and renews itself in the same instant. It is a rental agreement with no termination date specified. (CA Civil Code § 1945 and § 1944)

Can the landlord refuse to renew the rental agreement and evict the tenant? In San Francisco the answer depends on whether the rental unit is covered by the San Francisco Rent Ordinance or California law requiring just cause eviction. (See the section earlier in this chapter "Protections for the Tenant Under the San Francisco Rent Ordinance and State Law.") If, like most units in San Francisco, the unit is protected by the Rent Ordinance or state law requiring just cause eviction, then the landlord cannot evict just because of the expiration of the rental agreement. *Expiration of the rental agreement is not a "just cause" for eviction.* If the unit is not covered by the Rent Ordinance or state law for just cause eviction, then the landlord can refuse to renew the rental agreement and evict at the end of the rental agreement if the tenant has not vacated. In this case, a Notice to Quit is not required. (See "Chapter 12: Eviction Defenses" for more information on evictions.)

Each type of rental agreement has pros and cons. A lease can have definite advantages under some circumstances. If, for example, you have a stable source of income and lifestyle and you truly love the home you've found, a lease assures you that you will be able to live in your place for the period of the lease term as long as you keep up with your lease obligations. However, if circumstances change and you have to—or want to—move, you may be liable for all money due during the remaining lease period. (See the section "Breaking a Lease" later in this chapter for more information.)

If you have a lease for a stated period of time, then the landlord cannot change any term of the agreement during that time without your permission. Even without a lease, if the unit is covered under the Rent Ordinance, the landlord may not make material, unilateral changes in a month-to-month rental agreement unless authorized under the Rent Ordinance. (SF Rent Board Rules and Regulations § 12.20)

Oral vs. Written Rental Agreements

If everyone seems to be on good terms, signing a contract may seem overly formal. But remember, if there are problems, it will be up to you to prove both that you are a tenant and the terms of your tenancy. If your agreement is in writing, you will not need to depend on your memory—which invariably will be different from your landlord's. In addition, during the term of a lease which must be in writing if the lease period is over a year, the landlord can't evict you unless you have broken a term of the lease or the law. (See "Chapter 12: Eviction Defenses" for more information.)

For rent-controlled units with month-to-month rental agreements, however, tenants are often better off with an oral agreement than a standard form rental agreement. The San Francisco Rent Ordinance and state law provide limits on rent increases and restrictions on evictions without a just cause, so these will apply whether you have a written agreement or not. Most standard rental forms have clauses that are unfavorable to the tenant, so written month-to-month rental agreements only place extra limitations on the tenant. (See the "Other Undesirable Rental Agreement Clauses" section later in this chapter for more information.) If you have an oral agreement for a rent-controlled apartment, you do not have to sign a new written agreement if the terms differ in any substantial way from your oral agreement. (SF Administrative Code § 37.9(a)(5), SF Rent Board Rules and Regulations § 12.20, CA Civil Code § 1946.2)

Requirements and Protections in Rental Agreements

You should get a copy of the rental agreement at the time of signing. If you didn't, the owner is required to provide you with a copy within fifteen days after you sign it, and provide an additional copy once each calendar year upon request if you made an agreement with the owner or owner's representative. (CA Civil Code § 1962) If any changes are agreed upon and made later, get a copy of the changes signed and dated by the owner or owner's representative.

The owner or agent is required to provide, and keep current, information disclosing (1) the name, telephone number, and "usual" street address of all persons who are authorized to manage the premises, and upon whom notices and demands can be made; (2) the name, telephone number, and address of the person to whom rent payments shall be made, the form(s) in which rent payments are to be made, and the days and hours that person shall be available to receive rent payments if payments may be made in person; or (3) the financial institution and account number into which rent payments may be made, if that financial institution is within five miles of the rental property, or the information necessary to establish rent payment by electronic transfer. If the owner fails to provide an address for notices, the tenant may give notice of litigation by registered or certified mail to the address the rent is paid. (CA Civil Code § 1962.7)

If the owner or agent no longer has a copy of the rental agreement or if the rental agreement is oral, the owner or agent must still provide the tenant in writing with the information described previously in (1)–(3) once a year, within fifteen days of the tenant's request, except the requirements of (1) can be made by posting in at least two conspicuous places in the tenant's building instead of providing the information in writing. The owner must still, however, provide in writing to the tenant the rest of the information required in (2) and (3). (CA Civil Code § 1962, § 1962.5)

An owner who takes over the property from the previous owner is prohibited from seeking to evict a tenant for nonpayment of rent during the period the new owner did not provide updated contact information. However, the tenant still owes the rent if the owner decides to collect it through a deduction from the security deposit or a lawsuit (CA Civil Code § 1962).

If the rental agreement is negotiated in Spanish, Chinese, Tagalog, Vietnamese, or Korean, the landlord is required to provide a copy

Chapter 4– Renting Basics

in that language along with the English version. (CA Civil Code § 1632)

Additional required disclosures before renting include informing the prospective tenant of the presence of mold/asbestos/lead/or other chemicals specified in the law as causing cancer or other reproductive toxicity, shared utilities or submetered water rights, information about and how to report bed bugs, demolition application, prohibited smoking areas, the manner of a death of a previous occupant in the unit within the last three years except death from AIDS-related complications do not require disclosure (CA Civil Code § 1710.2), and for some rental units how to access the registered sex offenders registry (CA Civil Code § 2079.10a).

Beginning April 1, 2020, every online listing for a rental unit covered under the Rent Ordinance, excluding listings by landlords or master tenants who will reside in the same rental unit as their tenants or subtenants, must contain a legible disclosure in at least 12-point font that includes the following text: "This unit is a rental unit subject to the San Francisco Rent Ordinance, which limits evictions without just cause, and which states that any waiver by a tenant of their rights under the Rent Ordinance is void as contrary to public policy." This text should also be included in print advertisements, if practical. (SF Administrative Code § 37.9F) Check this book's index under "disclosure requirement" for more information.

Disclosure Under California Law Requiring Just Cause Eviction or Rent Control

An owner of residential property covered under California Civil Code § 1946.2 (just cause eviction) must disclose to the tenant as follows in no less than 12-point type: "California law limits the amount your rent can be increased. See Section 1947.12 of the Civil Code for more information. California law also provides that after all of the tenants have continuously and lawfully occupied the property for 12 months or more or at least one of the tenants has continuously and lawfully occupied the property for 24 months or more, a landlord must provide a statement of cause in any notice to terminate a tenancy. See Section 1946.2 of the Civil Code for more information."

(1) For any tenancy commenced or renewed on or after July 1, 2020, as an addendum to the rental agreement, or as a written notice signed by the tenant, with a copy provided to the tenant.

(2) For a tenancy existing prior to July 1, 2020, by written notice to the tenant no later than August 1, 2020, or as an addendum to the rental agreement.

See the previous section "California Law Disclosure and Ownership Requirement for Single Residential Unit Exceptions" for more info.

Rights That CANNOT Be Signed Away

You cannot sign away any of the following rights:

- Implied warranty of habitability. (CA Civil Code § 1942.1, § 1953)

- If you began renting your place on or after January 1, 1976:

  - Deposits (including so-called "nonrefundable" deposits) to be refunded to you.

  - Entry requirements for the landlord. (*Jordan v. Talbot* ((1961) 55 Cal. 2d 597)

  - Notices or hearings required by law.

  - Prevention of personal injury or property damage ("duty of care").

  - Suing your landlord (*Jaramillo v. JH Real Estate* (2003) 111 Cal. App. 4th 394), and making the landlord appear at a hearing or trial.

  (CA Civil Code § 1953)

- Eviction with just cause under California Civil Code §. 1946.2.

- Rent increase limitation under California Civil Code §. 1947.12.

- Attorney' fees provided to the landlord if the landlord prevails in a lawsuit are also awarded to the tenant if the tenant prevails. (CA Civil Code § 1717)

- Cash or an electronic funds transfer payment of rent or security deposit may not be required unless the tenant has bounced or put a stop payment on a previous check to the landlord. (CA Civil Code § 1947.3)

- Renewal of a lease that is automatic is voidable by tenant unless renewal clause was presented as required by law. (CA Civil Code § 1945.5)

- Retaliation by the landlord provides defenses for the tenant. (CA Civil Code § 1942.5)

- Submetering of water rights. (CA Civil Code § 1954.215)

Additional rights you cannot give up under San Francisco law:

- Security deposit interest. (SF Administrative Code § 49.4)

- San Francisco Rent Ordinance rights including maintenance and repair cannot be signed away (SF Administrative Code § 37.9(e)) **except** as specified in the following section.

Rights That CAN Be Signed Away

Your rights under the San Francisco Rent Ordinance can be signed away in two cases:

- The landlord informed the tenant, in writing, that the tenant did not need to accept a proposed change in the rental agreement and the tenant still accepted the change, in writing. Even without this disclosure, the tenant should not agree to the change so the proposed change was unilateral and not allowed. (SF Rent Board Rules and Regulations § 12.20)

- Buyout agreements. (*Larson v. City and County of San Francisco* (2011) 192 Cal. App. 4th 1263)

Often, San Francisco landlords try to avoid the restrictions of the Rent Ordinance by pressuring tenants into signing "buyout agreements" (sometimes called "cash for keys"). The tenant agrees to move out—and give up any potential rights related to his home, such as relocation payments—in exchange for a sum of money. Tenants are not obligated to sign any agreements that entail giving up their rights. If a landlord or prospective landlord asks you to sign any such agreement you can go ahead, but you should ask yourself just what his motives might be. A landlord who asks you to give up your rights or bargaining power will probably prove to be bad news a few months down the road. Make sure you get what you pay for! Not only because it is the right thing but because you're entitled to it by law.

Other Undesirable Rental Agreement Clauses

Often the landlord proposes a rental agreement which contains restrictions that are uncomfortable for the tenant. This often happens with "standard form" agreements. These clauses may be legal but you should try to have them removed:

Late Charge

Except for late rent payments due to COVID-19 with a declaration by the tenant (CA Civil Code § 1942.9, check for amendment), charges for late rent may be valid. However, under certain circumstances, a tenant can challenge them if the amount seems "unreasonable." The landlord probably has the right to collect the legal rate of interest plus legitimate processing and administrative charges, since these are the landlord's "costs," provided there is a late fee clause in the rental agreement. The tenant can dispute in court charges beyond what are actual damages as penalties to which the landlord is not entitled by law. The only situation where the payment of a fixed amount should be enforced is when it would be extremely difficult to determine the actual cost. (CA Civil Code § 1671, *Orozco v. Casimiro* (2004) 121 Cal. App. 4th Supp. 7, *Del Monte Properties v. Dolan* (2018) 26 Cal.App.5th Supp. 20) However, the safer route is to pay the disputed amount under protest and sue for the amount. (Accompany the check with a signed and dated letter stating the reason for the protest, and write on the check "paid under protest.")

There is no such thing as an automatic grace period for late rent. Unless your agreement specifically provides for a grace period, the late charges stated in a rental agreement will start to accrue immediately after the due date. If there is a grace period before the late charges are assessed, that does not change the fact that your rent is still late, and habitual late payment of rent is a just cause for eviction. Also, a warning about postdating checks: a postdated check can still be immediately cashed by a financial institution unless the customer alerts the bank to delay processing the check.

Overnight Guest and Pet Restrictions

A landlord cannot refuse permission for a reasonable number of days for overnight guests if there is a clause requiring permission for guests. If the unit is covered under the Rent Ordinance (see the earlier section "What Does the Rent Ordinance Cover?"), the landlord cannot refuse keys in addition to those required for the adult occupants, within reason and at cost upon request. (SF Administrative Code § 37.13) However, the prohibition of visiting pets is enforceable, but assistance animals are not considered pets. (See the section "Reasonable Accommodations and Modifications" in "Chapter 9: Discrimination" for more information.) A pet agreement may help convince the landlord to accept a pet: *https://www.sfspca.org/sites/default/files/documents/pet_agreement.pdf*. For animals that are allowed, there cannot be a requirement that an animal be declawed or devocalized. (CA Civil Code § 1942.7)

"Merger" Clause

These clauses state, usually at the end of the rental agreement, that the written agreement is the entire agreement between the tenant and landlord. This means that any verbal promises made to you by the landlord after the agreement was signed and not also included in writing may be completely void. If your proposed agreement contains any such provisions, try to have them scratched out. Then you and your landlord should initial and date two copies of the document, one for each of you. The better alternative is to make sure all promises are put in writing and made part of the rental agreement, signed and dated by both you and the landlord, with each of you keeping a copy.

Chapter 4– Renting Basics

House Rules

Many rental agreements include specific house rules. When you sign the agreement, you are agreeing to follow those rules. House rules that are referred to in the rental agreement although not actually in the agreement are enforceable if they are reasonable and not arbitrarily applied.

Utilities Paid by Tenant

Some rental agreements specify that the tenant must pay utility costs except for those specified in the agreement. The tenant should receive copies of the bills before paying.

Shared

If utilities paid for by the tenant, such as gas, electricity, water, sewer, garbage and telephone service, are shared with areas outside of the tenant's unit, the sharing of utilities must be disclosed in writing prior to the tenancy or upon discovery by the landlord along with the portion the tenant will pay. (CA Civil Code § 1940.9, *The Rutter Group California Practice Guide: Landlord-Tenant*) Caution: a dwelling without its own PG&E meter is often an unauthorized unit. See the section "Unauthorized Units" in "Chapter 11: Changes in Use."

Submetered Water

For buildings with two or more residential units under a single master meter, a landlord who intends to charge separately from rent for water service in a submetered property shall clearly disclose the separate billing procedure and estimated costs, in writing in at least 10-point type, before executing the rental agreement. This law does not apply to a submetering system that measures only a portion of a dwelling unit's water usage.

Required disclosures by the landlord:

1. A statement that the tenant shall notify the landlord of any leaks, the landlord is required to investigate and repair the problem within 21 days, otherwise, the water bill will be adjusted. (See CA Civil Code § 1954.210 for the calculation.) The landlord must provide a mailing or email address and a local or toll-free number for the tenant to contact the landlord about the leak.

2. A statement that the landlord shall provide any of the following information if asked by the tenant:

   a. The location of the submeter.

   b. The calculations used to determine a monthly bill.

   c. The date the submeter was last certified for use, and the next scheduled certification, if known.

3. A statement that if the tenant believes that the submeter reading is inaccurate, the tenant shall first notify the landlord in writing and request an investigation. A tenant shall be provided with notice that if an alleged submeter malfunction is not resolved by the landlord, a tenant may contact the local county sealer and request that the submeter be tested. Contact information for the county sealer shall be included.

4. A statement that this disclosure is only a general overview of the laws regarding submeters and that the laws can be found at Chapter 2.5 (commencing with Section 1954.201) of Title 5 of Part 4 of Division 3 of the Civil Code, available online or at most libraries.

(CA Civil Code § 1954.204)

Posting and Distributing of Information by Tenant

Tenants have the right to post political signs. (CA Civil Code § 1940.4) Political signs may be posted or displayed in the window or on the door of the premises leased by the tenant in a multifamily dwelling, or from the yard, window, door, balcony, or outside wall of the premises leased by a tenant of a single-family dwelling.

You can also post or deliver flyers unless your landlord forbids posting and delivery of flyers from all solicitors in the common hallways, the landlord restricted access by visitors to the hallways by locked doors, and the rental agreement clearly states the prohibition. (*Golden Gateway Center v. Gateway Tenants' Association* (2001) 26 Cal. 4th 1013)

For buildings with 5 or more units, an occupant or guest may hang or place literature on the door of tenant units, or where that is not practical on the floor in front of the units which plainly include the name and telephone number and address of a distributor that the affected tenant may contact to opt out of future literature. (SF Administrative Code §49A.3)

Desirable Clause in Rental Agreement

Attorney's Fees for Landlord

Some rental agreements specify that the tenant must pay the attorney fees if she loses a lawsuit. However, the clause is required by law to apply to the prevailing party regardless of the contract, so the landlord is required to pay attorneys' fees if the landlord loses the lawsuit, also. (CA Civil Code § 1717)

Paying Rent

There is **NOT** an automatic grace period for when rent is due. Any grace period for late fees only means that the late fee is not

charged until after the grace period; the rent is still late. If the rent due date falls on a Sunday or holiday as specified in California Civil Code § 11 and § 7, the due date for paying the rent on time is extended to the next business day (as defined in California Government Code §§ 6700-6730). Mail your rent checks early since habitual late payment of rent (which may be as few times as three times a year) is cause for an eviction. (See the section "Refused Rent" in "Chapter 12: Eviction Defenses" for more information on showing proof of offering rent.)

The landlord is not allowed to require payment in cash or electronic funds transfer unless the tenant has bounced or put a stop payment on a previous check to the landlord. In that case, the landlord may serve a thirty-day notice requiring payment in cash for a period of no more than three months. A copy of the bounced check should be attached to the notice. The landlord is required to accept third-party payment of rent where there is an acknowledgment in writing that the third party does not claim tenancy rights. (CA Civil Code § 1947.3) You cannot give up your rights for this law. A service fee for a bounced check may be charged. (CA Civil Code § 1719(a)(1))

When you pay the rent, it's a good idea to specify what it is you are paying for, especially if the landlord might apply the rent to other charges. If you are paying rent late every month and are charged a late fee as a result, it can be a good idea to pay the next month due before you pay the last month's. (Warning: banks may pay a postdated check immediately, unless the customer has alerted the bank that he wants to delay processing of the check.) If the rent continues to be due from more than a year ago, it is no longer a reason for eviction. (CA Code of Civil Procedure § 1161(2)) This strategy can also prevent eviction for habitual late payment. If you dispute a charge, you can specify that you are only paying the amount you actually owe. If the tenant doesn't specify what the payment is for, then the landlord can decide at the time the payment is made. If neither tenant nor landlord specifies what the payment is for, then generally it goes to the oldest debt first. (CA Civil Code § 1479) Put a note on the check saying, for example, "May 2022 Rent." You could also write instead "Rent through [month, date, and year]" to be more clear about being paid up in rent. If you are paying rent by electronic fund transfer, write a note to the landlord (keeping a copy for yourself and mailing with proof of mailing) that the transfers are for rent only unless directed otherwise by yourself in writing.

You have a right to a signed receipt when you pay the rent. (CA Code of Civil Procedure § 2075, Civil Code § 1499) If the landlord refuses to give you a receipt, make sure you document in some other way that you paid the rent.

If you are covered under the Rent Ordinance (see the earlier section "What Does the Rent Ordinance Cover?"), and the landlord refuses in bad faith to accept, acknowledge, or cash the rent check within thirty days (such as refusing to cash the check to try to evict the tenant for nonpayment of rent even though there is no legitimate reason to not cash the check), it is harassment.

The tenant can sue for three times the actual damages or $1,000, whichever is greater, and other relief if the bad faith can be proven. (SF Administrative Code § 37.10B (a)(10), (11)) Some courts have taken issue with the "bad faith" language in the ordinance.

Waiver of Breach of Rental Agreement by Landlord

If you move in and subsequently breach (violate) your rental agreement, and the landlord with full knowledge of the breach continues to accept your rent, the landlord may be judged to have given up the right to object to this breach at a later time. For example, if your agreement prohibits pets and the landlord continues to take your rent even though she knows that you have a dog, you can argue that the landlord cannot legitimately object later that you have broken your agreement. This situation is legally termed a "waiver" of that part of the agreement by the landlord. The key for tenants is proving the landlord actually knew of the breach and continued to accept the rent.

Some rental contracts contain clauses to the effect that any past waiver of an agreement by the landlord may be revoked, and the agreement returned to its previous condition, with a thirty-day written notice by the landlord. If this should happen and the landlord may be using the breach to attempt an eviction, it is time to seek legal advice. (For more information see the section "Breach of Rental Agreement" in "Chapter 12: Eviction Defenses.")

Breaking a Lease

Although some types of contracts allow for cancellation rights, rental agreements are not one of them. Until a new tenant is found, the old tenant is liable for the rent, even if she has moved out. So what can you do if you want to get out of a lease?

First, carefully read your contract to be certain that you even have a lease. It must include a date that the tenancy begins and a date that the tenancy ends.

Second, your landlord may be willing to let you break the lease either because he is understanding or, more likely, because he thinks that a new tenant would be willing to pay more rent or sign a new lease more advantageous to the landlord (a "novation").

Third, if there is no provision against subletting in the lease, the tenant may sublet to a replacement tenant without getting permission from the landlord. However, almost all rental agreements prohibit subletting without the permission of the landlord, though the landlord cannot unreasonably refuse permission. (CA Civil Code § 1951.4) See the section "Changing Roommates" in "Chapter 10: Roommates" for more information.

Fourth, even if the rental agreement prohibits subletting or

Examples of Letters for Moving Out

These letters are examples of notifications to landlords about moving out. The letter on the top-right is for a month-to-month agreement. In the letter on the bottom-right, the tenant goes a step further by providing the landlord with a list of people able and willing to rent the apartment since the tenant is breaking a lease. The letter on the bottom-left is for tenants needing to break a lease without offering replacement tenants.

October 8, 2022

Dear Sir or Madam:

As you know, I occupy unit #3 of your building at 558 Capp St. under a lease that runs from January 1, 2022 until December 31, 2022.

Due to circumstances beyond my control it is necessary for me to move on November 30, 2022. As I paid my last month's rent when I moved in, I will make no rent payment on November 1, 2022. Please apply my last month's rent to the month of November.

I apologize for any trouble I may put you to by moving out before the end of my lease term and will cooperate with you in every way to see that a new tenant is found promptly. Of course, I will rely on you to mitigate any damages as much as possible.

Sincerely,
Terri Tenant

January 10, 2023

Dear Landlord:

This is to notify you that as of February 12, 2023, I will be vacating the premises at 558 Capp St. #2, San Francisco, CA. As required by state law, I would appreciate it if either you or one of your agents would drop by two weeks before the day I vacate to inspect for damages and cleanliness. Please contact me to make an appointment for this inspection.

Sincerely,
Terri Tenant

October 16, 2022

Dear Landlord:

As I previously told you verbally on October 15, 2022, I am moving out of this apartment on November 30, 2022. Because I wish to keep damages to a minimum, I am including the names, addresses, and phone numbers of four people who have expressed an interest in renting this apartment on or about December 1, 2022 at the same rent that I pay. I assume that you will find one of these potential tenants to be suitable, unless of course you have already arranged to rent the apartment.

Sincerely,
Terri Tenant

---

assignment, the landlord has the legal duty to "mitigate the damages." This means that he cannot simply sit back, let the place remain vacant, and make no effort to find a new tenant while still expecting to collect the rent from you. Furthermore, the old tenant is responsible only for the amount of rent while the place is vacant, plus certain "reasonable" costs that the landlord incurs in re-renting. (CA Civil Code § 1951.2) The landlord cannot "double dip" or "double let" by collecting rent from both you and a new tenant. (CA Civil Code § 1950) The tenant has the burden of proof to show that the landlord did not act in good faith to find a new tenant to rent the unit. (*Polster, Inc. v. Swing* (1985) 164 Cal. App. 3d 427, 433) Presumably, a tenant meets this burden if the tenant found prospective tenants to rent the unit. You might accomplish this by talking to friends, or placing ads on *https://www.craigslist.org*. You should look for someone who meets the regular reasonable application standards of the landlord.

Fifth, if the place is in such terrible shape that no reasonable person could live there, then the landlord has breached the lease, and you can move out because the landlord has "constructively evicted" you by making the place uninhabitable. (See the section "Constructive Eviction" in "Chapter 6: Repairs and Services.")

Sixth, for victims and household or immediate family members of domestic violence, sexual assault, stalking, elder or dependent adult abuse, or human trafficking, or a crime that caused bodily injury or death or included the exhibition of a deadly weapon or threat of or use of force, a tenant may break a lease with fourteen-day notice and documentation. (CA Civil Code § 1946.7 in "Appendix D: California Law Excerpts") If the tenant is terminating the tenancy because an immediate family member is a victim and the tenant did not live in the same household as the immediate family member at the time of the act, and no part of the act occurred within the dwelling unit or within 1,000 feet of the dwelling unit of the tenant, the tenant shall attach a statement including that the tenant intends to relocate as a result of the immediate family member being a victim of an eligible act. Domestic violence is defined for this purpose as "abuse" so does not require physical violence. Tenants invoking Section 1946.7 do not need to be a spouse or romantic partner. A roommate or housemate would qualify as well, as the Family Code defines domestic violence as "abuse perpetrated against . . . cohabitants" (with a cohabitant defined as "a person who regularly resides in the household"). (CA Family Code §§ 6211, 6209) Stalking includes a pattern of conduct intended to follow, alarm, place under surveillance, or harass the victim resulting in fear for her or an immediate family member's safety, or would cause a reasonable person to suffer substantial emotional distress. The landlord is restricted from disclosing the information provided.

Seventh, a military servicemember may terminate a lease at any time after entry into military service or the date of the military orders. (50 U.S.C. § 3955(a)(1)) A service member's dependent also has rights for terminating lease obligations. (CA Military and Veterans Code § 409)

See the section "Changing Roommates" in "Chapter 10: Roommates" for information on breaking a lease which includes housemates.

Notices and Other Communications Between Landlord and Tenant

For a month-to-month tenant in California (regardless of whether or not under the Rent Ordinance), any change in the rental agreement by the landlord requires at least a thirty-day written notice. (CA Civil Code § 827) Different requirements apply to a lodger where the landlord retains access to all areas of the rental unit. (See the section "Roommates(s) Living with Owner" in "Chapter 10: Roommates" for information.)

For your landlord to raise a tenant's rent, she must give at least a thirty-day written notice of her intention to do so. A ninety-day notice is required if the landlord wants to raise the rent more than 10% in any calendar year. (See "Rent Increases under California Law" and "Rent Increases under San Francisco Rent Control" in "Chapter 7: Rent Increases" for more information.)

If the landlord wants to change the terms of a rental agreement for a tenant covered by the Rent Ordinance, the landlord must provide written notice of the changes and the tenant that he does not need to accept the changes unless the changes are required by law. Even without this disclosure, the tenant should not agree to the change so the proposed change was unilateral and not allowed. (SF Rent Board Rules and Regulations § 12.20; *Foster v. Britton*, No. CGC-11-514035, Cal. Super. Ct. May 24, 2012) If the tenant does not agree to the changes, he should write to the landlord clearly stating that he does not agree. This will document the fact that he has rejected the change in case the landlord tries to evict for breach of the rental agreement.

If you are the one giving notice to move out, and are on a month-to-month rental agreement, you must give at least a thirty-day written notice of your intentions. A requirement in the rental agreement that the termination notice by the tenant be increased to sixty days is probably unenforceable since California Civil Code § 1946 limits the required termination notice by the tenant to thirty days or fewer, and California Civil Code § 1953 prohibits giving up that right. If you give less than the required notice, the landlord has a duty to reduce her losses by trying to re-rent to someone else. Notices terminating a tenancy can be given at any time during the month; they do not have to be given the same day rent is due.

If you are moving out but a co-tenant is remaining, see the section "Breaking Up" in "Chapter 10: Roommates." In the case of the tenant's death or incapacity to contract, the estate of the deceased is not liable for the rent due to lack of notice to the landlord. (CA Civil Code § 1934, *Miller & Desatnik Management Co. v. Bullock* (1990) 221 Cal.App.3d Supp. 13)

For notice by mail, the notice should be sent by certified or registered mail. For delivery in person, make sure you have proof of the delivery, for example, by delivering the notice with a witness. (CA Civil Code § 1946, § 789)

The tenant does not have to give notice before the termination date of a lease; he can just move out by the specified date. The landlord doesn't have to give a termination notice at the end of a lease either except if the unit is covered under the Rent Ordinance or state law for just cause eviction, the landlord can only evict with just cause and must give notice. (See the section earlier in this chapter "Protections for the Tenant Under the San Francisco Rent Ordinance and State Law" in "Chapter 4: Renting Basics" and "Chapter 12: Eviction Defenses.")

Communications other than termination notices do not always have to be in writing. However, written communication can prove to the court or the Rent Board that you have fulfilled obligations under the law, such as giving the landlord notification of needed repairs. It is good practice to send notices to the landlord by regular mail as well as either certified or registered mail, always keeping a copy for yourself.

Negotiations are often handled best through written rather than oral communication since emotional outbursts are less likely to occur. See "letter, example" in this book's index for suggestions and the section "Write Letters" in "Chapter 14: Taking Action." Emails or texts can be used for casual communications, but letters are still better if they may be used in court since the courts aren't up-to-date on technology.

Sale of Building

Tenants often panic when they see a "For Sale" sign on their building. Though the sale of your building is a cause for concern, there's no need to panic. If the unit is covered under the Rent Ordinance or state law (see the section earlier in this chapter "Protections for the Tenant Under the San Francisco Rent Ordinance and State Law"), the new landlord does not have extra rights because he's just bought the building—you

cannot be evicted, have your rent raised, or have your rental agreement changed. (*Kirk Corp. v. First American Title Co.* (1990) 220 Cal. App. 3d 785, 809) The owner is required to inform tenants of these rights that remain under the new owner before the sale of the building if the building is covered under the Rent Ordinance. Also, tenants covered under the Rent Ordinance must be informed that the owner's right to show the unit is restricted (CA Civil Code § 1954) and that tenants do not have to sign an estoppel agreement (see the following section) unless required under the rental agreement. (SF Administrative Code § 37.9(k)) A new right due to a sale of the building is the owner (or agent) does have a right to enter to replace a regular toilet with a low-flow toilet. (SF Housing Code, Chapter 12A, § 12A09)

This does not mean there's nothing to worry about. When a building is sold, typically one of three things happens: (a) The building continues on as investment rental property (the owner lives elsewhere and profits off the rents), (b) the building is converted into condos or a form of joint ownership called "tenancy in common (TIC)" for sale as homes for buyers or (c) the owner seeks to live in one or more of the units and may want family members to live in other units. Most tenants hope for option (a) as it is the least likely route to evictions. Conversion of the building into owner-occupied will often mean evictions for the entire building. Generally speaking, it's the smaller rental property which investors buy to convert to owner occupancy since only property with six or fewer units can be converted to condominiums. (See the "Condominium Conversions" section in "Chapter 11: Changes in Use" for more information.)

If your building is for sale, keep in mind that your rights do not change, but try to find out how the realtor is marketing the building and what potential buyers are planning. If it looks like evictions may be part of the plan, see "Chapter 12: Eviction Defenses" for information on how to deal with them. If you are on good terms with your current owner, ask her if she is willing to give you a long-term lease, maybe even a lifetime lease. A lease will prevent the new owner from evicting you for a no-fault eviction cause. A lease can be recorded at the San Francisco's Assessor/Recorder as a memorandum attached to the property's deed to solidify evidence of the lease. If the building will be marketed as tenancies in common (TICs), see the section "Fighting the Sale of Your Home" in "Chapter 11: Changes in Use" for strategies.

Estoppel Agreement or Rental Questionnaire: Should I Sign It?

A realtor often gives tenants a "Request for Information Under San Francisco Administrative Code Sections 37.9(i) and (j), "estoppel agreement," "rental questionnaire," "tenancy statement,"

or something similar to sign. The realtor is trying to tie you down to what you agree your rental agreement is for use in marketing the property for sale.

You do not have to fill out or sign these forms unless your rental agreement requires that you do so or you fall into a protected tenant status (senior, disabled, a household with children or a school worker or have a familial relationship with a child or a school worker). Any statements you make, either written down or omitted, are "presumed to be true." (CA Evidence Code § 622) For example, if you had an oral agreement with the owner that you could use the backyard and you fail to include this in your estoppel, you may lose that right. Furthermore, you may lose the right to correct any factual errors you have made in the estoppel.

Estoppel agreements generally have standard questions and categories that do not always include everything you want to communicate to the buyer. It is important to be sure that the buyer has information to your benefit that is not included in the rental agreement, such as: an oral agreement that you may have pets despite the written rental agreement's prohibition; the right to parking, storage, backyard use or laundry facilities; that you have permission to have four people living there even though the rental agreement says three; what you paid for the security deposit and so on.

The best way to get estoppel information to the realtor/owner is often to ignore the form and send back basic information in your own informal letter. If your rental agreement requires that you sign an estoppel, attach an addendum when you send it in. For instance, you might say "I moved in in 2002 and paid a security deposit of $1,750. My security deposit interest has never been paid. I have received all the annual rent increases and since 2006 I have had a dog and a cat with the consent of the owner." Add "To the best of my knowledge, the above information is correct as of the date of this writing. However, I reserve the right to supplement, correct, amend, and/or modify this response in the future. I hope this information has been helpful. If you have any questions, please feel free to write to me at the above address." You might also let them know about problems with the place: "As we have discussed on several occasions, there are a number of repairs that need to be made, including but not limited to the following..."

If you are senior, disabled, or a household with children or a school worker or have a familial relationship with a child or a school worker, it is crucial to answer the question. The restriction on owner move-in evictions of qualified tenants provides that an owner who wants to move herself and/or her close relative(s) into your unit may request information about whether you are in one of these "protected" categories. If the tenant falls in a protected category, and fails to respond to the owner's request within thirty days, then the tenant will not be covered by the owner move-in eviction prohibition for such tenants. Therefore, if the estoppel agreement or rental questionnaire asks if you are protected under the eviction prohibition and you are, you must answer this. If you are not sure if you qualify, you can write your own statement with a description of your disability, putting the burden of the determination of disability on the owner. Make sure you have proof of your response by the deadline such as mailing with proof of mailing and supporting evidence of the disability.

You are not required to answer a question about whether you anticipate becoming a member of a protected class in the future. Answering "yes" for becoming a member of the protected class in the future might make you a target for eviction before obtaining the protection.

Rental Agreement for New Owner

Many new owners try to force tenants to sign a new rental agreement. **If the unit is covered under San Francisco's Rent Ordinance, you do not have to sign a new agreement which is materially different from your current agreement!** (Rent increases allowed by the Rent Board are not material changes. It would be safer to sign a lease with otherwise the same terms as the month-to-month agreement if the tenant does not anticipate needing to move out before the lease ends.) Only if your new owner offers you substantially the same agreement that you now have could you be required to sign it. (SF Rent Board Rules and Regulations § 12.20) **Under state law requiring just cause eviction, you only have to sign a renewal of a lease with materially the same terms.** In fact, refusing to sign an agreement that is substantially the same as one that has expired is a just cause for eviction. If necessary, the tenant has the right to break the lease. (See the section earlier in this chapter "Breaking a Lease.")

All agreements, written or oral with the old owner are now the new owner's agreement with you except there are some differences in foreclosures. (See the section "Foreclosure by a Bank" later in this chapter.) Similarly, the new owner is bound to any legal orders or judgments that the old owner was bound to. For instance, if the San Francisco Department of Building Inspection ordered the old owner to make repairs, the new owner is bound by this order, or if the Rent Board has ordered a rent reduction, the new owner must adhere to this requirement. In addition, the new owner must inform the tenant to whom and where to pay the rent. (CA Civil Code § 1962)

Special Rental Situations

Foreclosure by a Bank

Not surprisingly, things do not always go smoothly during a foreclosure and it is recommended that tenants in foreclosures speak to a Tenants Union counselor or consult the organization Tenants Together to get help regarding a specific situation. (See "Appendix A: Resources" for the contact information for Tenants Together.) See also the box "Foreclosure Process" for more information.

Notice of Foreclosure or Ownership Change

Within fifteen days of obtaining ownership of the unit, the new owner must provide notice to the tenant of the new owner's identity (it may be a bank) and where to pay rent. (CA Civil Code § 1962(c)) The new owner must also provide tenants notice of additional rights under San Francisco law— i.e. "just cause" eviction protections. An owner is not allowed to evict a tenant until this notice has been given. (SF Administrative Code § 37.9D) Before the new ownership takes effect, the tenant may want to try

Foreclosure Process

The California home-buying process usually involves the use of the deed of trust, which involves three parties; the trustor (borrower or the "owner" on the Assessor's record), the beneficiary (lender, often a bank), and the trustee (neutral third party named in the deed of trust receiving the right to foreclose). The deed of trust usually includes a "power of sale" clause that gives the trustee the legal right to enforce collection of the debt.

Defaulting on one's loan causes the start of foreclosure, the process by which the lender takes over the home in order to recover their principal investment. Once the home is either sold at auction or "repossessed" by the lender, it is no longer owned by the former owner (trustor). When there is a power of sale clause in the deed of trust, the non-judicial process of foreclosure is used.

The non-judicial foreclosure begins when the trustee files a Notice of Default. This is a letter to the owner notifying him of his default of the loan. This notifies the owner of the intent of the lender to follow through on their right to collect on the debt. The

copy of the notice, which is recorded at the County Recorder's Office, is mailed to the address of notice for the deed of trust.

The next step is the filing of the Notice of Trustee's Sale. The filing must wait until at least three months after the Notice of Default. (CA Civil Code § 2924) The notice will list the date of the sale. The notice must also contain the telephone number of the trustee. (CA Civil Code § 2924f)

No sooner than twenty days after the Notice of Trustee's Sale is posted and published, the home may be sold at a public auction. If no one bids at the auction, the lender assumes ownership of the property and may dispose of the property. To find out if there is a continuance of the auction, which could postpone the auction for up to a year, call the trustee.

If the property is sold, the new owner will have a Trustee's Deed Upon Sale as proof of ownership The new ownership is supposed to be recorded at the Assessor's Office within fifteen days of the sale, but this doesn't always happen and can be retroactively recorded.

See the section "Foreclosure by a Bank" for more information.

to obtain a long-term lease from the old owner, with a clause that allows breaking the lease if necessary.

Often, banks fail to notify tenants of foreclosure for several months. In many circumstances, tenants become aware of the looming foreclosure only after receiving numerous letters addressed to the defaulting owner. To find out information about possible foreclosure or if the property has already been foreclosed, look for a Notice of Default, Notice of Trustee's Sale, or Trustee's Deed (the bank has full ownership) at the Assessor's Office or Web site. (See the section "Assessor and Recorder" in "Chapter 3: Researching Landlords, Buildings, and Laws" for more info.) A lien may be a sign of a future foreclosure, as well.

If the building has been foreclosed and the address of the new owner provided, it is important to be proactive and notify the new owner in writing of your status as a tenant since usually the new owner knows nothing about the tenant. In some circumstances, if the tenant doesn't want to deal with ongoing harassment, it may be a good idea to send the owner a copy of part of the rental agreement to prove tenancy. (Usually, it is preferable to not disclose to the new owner the restrictive clauses in the rental agreement.) Among other reasons, it is important to notify the new owner of your status as a tenant as soon as possible so that the new owner cannot treat you as the former owner of the unit. A former owner's rights are different from that of a renter; for instance, a former owner can be evicted from a property much faster than a tenant.

Eviction Protections for Tenants During Foreclosures

San Francisco laws offer greater protections to tenants than state law. A tenant living in a home that is covered by the Rent Ordinance cannot be evicted by the foreclosure owner—typically a bank—unless the owner has a "just cause" for eviction. A change of ownership is not one of the sixteen "just causes" for eviction under the Rent Ordinance. (SF Administrative Code § 37.9(a)) "I'm the bank and I want you out" is not a just cause. (*Gross v. Superior Court* (1985) 171 Cal. App. 3d 265) So long as the tenant living in the foreclosed property continues to pay the rent and abide by the terms of the rental agreement, the bank can only evict in a few circumstances. (See the section "San Francisco Rent Ordinance Evictions" in "Chapter 12: Eviction Defenses" for more info on "just cause" for eviction.)

A tenant living in a home that is not ordinarily covered by the Rent Ordinance (for example, a rental unit constructed after 1979) also cannot be evicted by the bank until the end of the tenant's fixed term lease or unless the bank has a "just cause," whichever occurs later. (SF Administrative Code § 37.9D)

In addition, for tenants not covered under the Rent Ordinance, federal law gives most of these tenants the right to remain in their home for either the duration of their fixed term lease or ninety days, whichever is longer. The federal law does not override additional protections of local or state law. There are some exceptions to the tenant protections. A purchaser may elect to not honor the tenant's lease and evict with ninety days notice if the purchaser will occupy the unit as a primary residence. The law does not apply to a tenant who is a child, spouse, or parent of the former owner nor to a renter who is not a "bona fide" tenant. (Protecting Tenants at Foreclosure Act of 2009, restored 2018. 12 U.S.C § 5220 note)

Rent Payments During Foreclosure

More often than not, the tenant does not receive a written notice informing him of the new owner's identity and is left unsure as to whom and where to pay the rent. When a bank is the new owner, the bank sometimes refuses to accept a tenant's rent checks. The law prohibits a successor owner from seeking to evict a tenant for nonpayment of rent during the period the successor owner did not provide updated contact information. (CA Civil Code § 1962) However, the tenant still owes the rent if the landlord decides to collect the rent through a deduction from the security deposit or a lawsuit. Also, if the judge is not convinced that the contact information provided by the new owner was insufficient, or that the bank refused payment, the tenant may still need to pay back rent. Consequently, it is very important to save rent during the period you don't know where to send it or the bank won't accept it, so that if the owner later demands multiple months of rent the tenant cannot be evicted for nonpayment. Some tenants have found it useful to set up an escrow account for any unpaid rent to prove that the money is accounted for when needed. Don't expect that because a bank is not collecting rent checks they will not ask for that money later on. It may be useful to write letters to both the old and new owner to inquire whom the rent should be paid to. Send the letters with certificate of mailing (different from certified) and keep copies for yourself. The letters could be used as proof that attempts were made to pay the rent and insufficient contact information was provided.

Also see the previous section "Notice of Foreclosure or Ownership Change" for rent that is not due because of the lack of disclosure to a prospective tenant of a mortgage default.

Repairs and Utility Shut Offs During Foreclosures

Owners losing properties to foreclosure often fail to pay utility bills. As a result, many tenants have their utilities shut off during or after a foreclosure. Tenants have the right to transfer utility bills formerly paid by the owner to their name. (See the section "Utility Shutoffs" in "Chapter 8: Harassment.")

Banks have been claiming they are not responsible for repairs because they are merely trustees, not owners. Finding the person who is responsible for making repairs can be challenging since banks hide their responsibility under layers of bureaucracy. Persistence will be necessary. See "Chapter 6: Repairs and Services" for more info.

Security Deposits During Foreclosures

Tenants have the right to have their security deposit returned

after they vacate, although banks may argue that they are not a "successor in interest" and therefore not required to return the security deposit to the tenant. (CA Civil Code § 1950.5(h)(1))

If the new owner does not notify the tenant regarding the status of the security deposit, the tenant should upon finding out about a new owner demand, in writing, repayment of the deposit from both the old and new owners. The letter should state that since there has been no notification regarding the transfer of the deposit, § 1950.5(j) treats both the old and new owner jointly and severally liable for the return of the deposit. Though the tenant should send this letter immediately, she is not entitled to the return of the deposit until after vacating the unit and therefore cannot sue successfully for the return of the deposit until that time. Demanding the deposit when the ownership changes documents that the tenant did not receive the deposit at that time and the tenant may get the deposit back at this time. If the deposit has not been returned after vacating, the tenant may sue both the old and new owner for repayment. See the box "Sale of Building and Security Deposits" in "Chapter 5: Security Deposits" for more info.

Buyout Offers or "Cash for Keys" During Foreclosures

In a foreclosure situation, it is common for a tenant to be offered payment from the bank in exchange for moving out and relinquishing all rights related to the rental unit. Often times, these "cash for keys" or "buyout" offers are made by unscrupulous agents of the bank seeking to avoid tenant protections and increase profits. It is not surprising to hear stories about a bank lying to a tenant about his rights. Especially for San Francisco tenants since they have some protections from eviction, it is important to recognize that a tenant is not obligated by the law to sign a "cash for keys" agreement. Constant contact regarding a "cash for keys" settlement may even constitute harassment. (See the section "Buyouts, Almost Always a Bad Idea" in "Chapter 8: Harassment" for more info.)

Resident Managers

A resident manager is both a resident and a manager. The *resident* part of the term means that the resident manager lives in the building, along with her fellow tenants. The *manager* part of the term means that she is the agent for the landlord, assuming various responsibilities for the landlord. Often acting as the buffer between the landlord and the tenants, the resident manager may have to explain why repairs (that may affect her as well as the other tenants) cannot be made, while the landlord is inaccessible.

The duties of resident managers vary from doing nothing more than reporting problems to the landlord—i.e., keeping the landlord insulated from the tenants—to doing virtually everything there is to do including showing apartments, deciding

who to rent to, making repairs, cleaning the property, writing and issuing notices to tenants (notices of entry, eviction notices, etc.), testifying in court in eviction proceedings, collecting the rent, and keeping the books.

Many resident managers begin as regular tenants, and are later asked by the landlord to become resident managers. As a result, the types of people that become resident managers vary from the tenant down the hall, who has a regular full-time job and merely acts as a buffer and information conduit for the landlord, to the professional full-time resident manager, who has years of professional experience and does nothing else for a living.

California and San Francisco law requires that buildings of sixteen or more units have a resident manager. These laws do not, however, state what the duties of the resident manager consist of. Although logic would suggest that one of the most important purposes of requiring a *resident* manager is to provide help in case of emergencies, the law is silent on how often the manager should actually be *resident* (e.g., nothing says that when the resident manager goes on vacation for thirty days, the landlord must find a replacement). For any apartment house of more than four but less than sixteen apartments, if the owner does not reside on the premises, a notice stating the owner's name and address, or the name and address of the owner's agent in charge of the apartment house, shall be posted in a conspicuous place on the premises. (CA Code of Regulations, Title 25, Article 5, § 42; SF Housing Code § 1311)

Resident Managers Under the San Francisco Rent Ordinance and California Law Requiring Just Cause Eviction

The courts have held that some resident managers may be mere "licensees," and not tenants, and therefore not entitled to the protections of the Rent Ordinance. A key test is whether the person is on the premises solely due to her employment, or if she has a separate, independent claim of tenancy. Where the resident manager signs a contract declaring that she is a "licensee," and that her occupancy of the apartment is merely incidental to employment, the courts have held that the resident manager is not a tenant under the Rent Ordinance. (*Chan v. Antepenko* (1988) 203 Cal.App.3d Supp. 21) California law would also allow eviction for this just cause. (CA Civil Code § 1946.2(b)(1)(J))

Factors that favor the interpretation that the manager is a tenant include: the manager was a tenant prior to being hired as a manager, has given the landlord rent (although paying rent is not a requirement to prove tenancy as services may be provided instead of rent, CA Civil Code § 1925), has given the landlord a security deposit, or has a contract designating her as a tenant or allowing her to continue to reside on the premises after the employment is terminated, providing that she pays rent.

Resident Managers as Workers

Many resident managers are among the most exploited workers.

Working for Your Landlord

All workers in California are covered by the minimum wage law, including those, like resident managers, live-in aides, and many hotel workers, whose boss is also their landlord. The Industrial Welfare Commission has published orders that detail the rules regarding pay and working conditions for various job classifications. They require that employers pay at least minimum wage for all hours worked. **Minimum wage in San Francisco is $16.32 per hour as of July 1, 2021 and $16.99 per hour as of July 1, 2022.**

Hours worked "includes all the time the employee is suffered or permitted to work, whether or not required to do so." For tenant-managers required to live on the premises, all hours spent performing "assigned duties" count as hours worked, and the tenant should be paid for all of them.

If, like *resident* managers, you must live in the place in order to keep your job ("as a condition of employment"), these laws put an absolute cap on the amount of rent the landlord may charge, whether it is charged in money or deductions from wages. If you are not required to live there but you do, then the limit applies to the amount that can be counted toward your wage. If your pay plus the maximum allowed rent (and food in some cases) credit adds up to less than minimum wage for all hours worked, then your boss has violated the minimum wage law. A worker cannot legally contract with an employer to violate the minimum wage laws. Also, the agreement must be voluntary and it must be written. No credit toward minimum wage is allowed for lodging that is not used.

For 2022, the rent limits on an apartment are: two-thirds of the ordinary rental value for a single employee, but cannot exceed $790.67/month with 25 or fewer employees or $847.12/month with 26 or more employees. For a couple, two-thirds of the ordinary rental value, but cannot exceed $1169.59/month with 25 or fewer employees or $1253.10/month with 26 or more employees. For a room, the rental value cannot exceed $65.83/week for 25 or fewer employees, $70.53/week for 26 or more employees.

Contact the Labor Standards Enforcement Division of the California Department of Industrial Relations or search online for California Industrial Welfare Commission Orders for wage order #5, Public Housekeeping Industry, for more info.

They are usually on call 24 hours a day, and must be available to perform various and sundry tasks, many of them very unpleasant, such as cleaning up garbage, serving eviction notices, and dealing with irate tenants, not to mention collecting rents in an uncertain economy. Resident managers often receive a reduction in rent equaling less than the minimum wage. Many resident managers do not realize that their work is in violation of the law. See the box "Working for Your Landlord" for more information.

Live/Work Rental Units

All units with the express or implied consent of the landlord occupied as a residence—whether or not they are legal or zoned for commercial use—are residential rental units, so they are covered under the Rent Ordinance as long as the unit is not otherwise exempt. (See the section "What Does the Rent Ordinance Cover?" at the beginning of this chapter for the exemptions.) The big issue in determining whether a live/work unit is protected by the Rent Ordinance is whether the landlord permitted residential use.

The San Francisco Planning and Building Codes allow for "citywide live/work zoning controls" to facilitate the preservation and creation of affordable live/work housing for artists. The Building Code and Health and Safety Code are somewhat relaxed compared to regular residential housing, to allow for the special needs and realities of live/work housing. For more specifics contact the Planning Commission or the Department of Building Inspection. Unfortunately, speculators have used these laws to create high-priced bogus "live/work" condos that are not required to meet the usual safety and planning criteria.

Squatting

"Squatting" means finding empty housing and moving yourself in without an agreement with the landlord. Squats can be short-term housing or long-term housing. Squatting has always been an option people all over the world have chosen to meet their housing needs. Sometimes this choice is made for political reasons by people who have a strong conviction that the idea of paying money for housing (and others making money off housing) is simply immoral. More often though, squatting has become an economic necessity. San Francisco's homeless demonstrates how many people can't afford to rent in San Francisco.

Many people independently choose to squat and set out to identify suitable houses and move themselves in, or it's more structured: Homes Not Jails developed an organized squatting movement which identified and set up squats for people who are homeless.

Police Interactions

When squatting, people should anticipate that there will be an encounter with the police and should immediately begin preparing for this. Probably the most important step, and the first step to take, is to **create the appearance of tenants' rights**. This is pretty easy and can forestall actions to evict or arrest you as a trespasser, giving you time to establish more solid rights.

Creating the appearance of a tenancy is based first on the fact that police are not supposed to arrest you as a trespasser unless

they are acting on the complaint of the property owner. More importantly, police training in a trespassing situation instructs them to first determine if the person may be a tenant. Police are instructed to ask for rent receipts, utility bills or mail at the address. S.F. Police Training Bulletin 84-05 says "if any material showing a right to possession is produced, however arguable it may be, the burden shifts to the property owner or agent to prove the elements required for a trespass violation…members should not presume a person to be a trespasser." (See the "San Francisco Police Department Training Bulletin" near the end of "Appendix C: San Francisco Law and Regulations Excerpts.") If the burden is shifted back to the owner, that means the police should tell him it's a "civil matter" and must be addressed in court.

To create the appearance of tenants' rights, first make the place look like a home. Get furniture and possessions inside. If the police come by and see that you're cooking dinner, reading or watching television they're much more likely to buy an argument that you have permission to be there. If it obviously looks like you're just crashing in for the night, they're likely to ignore their training and procedures and haul you off to the station "and let God and a judge sort it out later" (as one officer told squatters).

The second step is to get some utilities in your name and mail sent to your squat. At first, squatters often do whatever is necessary to get the electricity and water working, but once you have an idea the squat might be a solid one, it's a good idea to get them turned on in your name. This is relatively easy, since most utility companies won't ask for any proof of tenancy. You should also arrange for services like telephones and cable if you can afford them. Doing all this will give you a fistful of paper to show the police and raise serious doubts in their mind about whether you're actually a trespasser.

If you have a place looking like your home and have some mail and utility bills, you're likely to be successful in a face-off with the police, even if the owner is there as well. It's also a good idea to have all your arguments down: "Mr. Smith has been letting us live here to keep an eye on the place and fix it up, but seems to have changed his mind because he found someone else who'll pay him money to be his caretakers."

In most cases, though, the first complaint will likely come from a neighbor who's suspicious. In such a case, having documentation is doubly valuable, but also gently remind the police that they need some type of complaint from the owner to evict you as a trespasser. You might even call their bluff and provide the police the name of the owner and ask them to call him.

Tenants' Rights for Squatters

In San Francisco, there are no "squatters' rights," such as a right to occupancy after thirty days of squatting. The first step to acquiring rights is to obtain tenants' rights. Until some level of tenants' rights are acquired, the squatter is a trespasser.

Getting tenants' rights as a squatter is difficult but not impossible. The two basic problems squatters have in gaining tenants' rights are: (1) They are not paying any rent. (2) They are living there without the landlord's permission. As daunting as it seems to get past these hurdles, it can be done!

First, rent does not necessarily have to be cash. Rent is frequently paid through labor, for example, resident managers, caretakers, etc. What makes a rental contract is "consideration": that is, you are getting housing in exchange for something. In the case of squatting, squatters are getting housing in exchange for watching over it, making repairs, cleaning it up, etc.

Second, the landlord's permission does not necessarily have to be explicitly stated or written down. A rental agreement can be implied by the conduct of the landlord. Many squatters have found themselves in a situation where the landlord has known about the squat and has given up trying to get rid of them. Squatters can make an argument that, when discovered by the landlord, they made an agreement with him to live there in exchange for maintenance and security of the property. (One Homes Not Jails squat was successful in establishing such tenants' rights and even successfully fought the landlord's attempt to demolish the housing to build condos.)

Sometimes squatting can actually lead to the total legal possession of the housing, through what's called "adverse possession." The squatters may get lucky and find a squat which seems to have abandoned. If police and neighbors have been dealt with successfully and after many months the landlord still hasn't complained or been seen, the squatters might start laying plans for gaining adverse possession.

Generally, the law says that a claim to adverse possession can be made after five years of possession and after the adverse possessors have paid the taxes on the property. The property also needs to be "cultivated or improved," which can be repairs, painting, etc. (CA Code of Civil Procedure §§ 321, 325) Adverse possession has been interpreted to mean "open and notorious" possession, in the sense that the squatting has been done on a level where the squatters' presence is not hidden and the landlord could have reasonably known of the possession. In other words, squatters who arrive at midnight and clear out by 5 a.m. every day for five years might not meet the requirements of "open and notorious."

When a squatter gets into the position where adverse possession becomes a possibility, the greatest hurdle is often the payment of taxes. The landlord can pay the taxes on the 364th day of the 5th year and defeat the squatter's claim to adverse possession (which is exactly what happened at a San Francisco squat in the 1970s). If squatters begin getting a substantial length of possession under their belt, it is imperative that they begin saving up to pay the taxes in order to finalize their claim.

Chapter 5: **Security Deposits**

Before a tenant moves in, the landlord will nearly always ask for extra money in addition to the first month's rent. "Security deposits," "cleaning deposits," "last month's rent," "key deposit," even "pet charges" are all deposits, even if they are termed "fees" or "costs." Any money that a tenant gives to the landlord on or before initial occupancy, except for first month's rent, an application screening fee or a holding deposit, is a "security deposit" under the law, and is refundable (CA Civil Code § 1950.5) unless the rental unit is totally destroyed (see the section "Destruction of Rental Unit" later in this chapter). The information in this chapter applies to both rent-controlled and non-rent-controlled tenancies unless specified otherwise.

A landlord may not require a security deposit more than two months' rent for unfurnished property or more than three months' rent for furnished property, in addition to any rent for the first month paid on or before initial occupancy. Servicemembers have further limitations on their deposit charge. (CA Civil Code § 1950.5(c)) Also, the landlord cannot require a security deposit in cash unless the tenant has bounced or put a stop payment on a previous check to the landlord. (CA Civil Code § 1947.3)

Application Screening Fee

The "application screening fee" is a fee that a landlord is allowed to charge to cover their "actual out-of-pocket costs" of tenant screening. This fee cannot be more than the landlord actually spends, and a receipt for the expenses and time spent by the landlord to obtain and process the report shall be given to the applicant. As of December 2021 the fee could not be more than $55.58 per tenant. (*https://caanet.org/kb/max-screening-fee*) When passing on the fee for a credit report, the landlord must provide a copy of the report to the tenant if requested. (CA Civil Code § 1950.6) The landlord must keep the credit report in a secure location (15 U.S.C. § 1681m(c) of the Fair Credit Reporting Act) and destroy it when it is no longer needed (15 U.S.C. § 1681w).

"Holding" Deposits

"Holding" deposits are when the prospective tenant pays the landlord to not rent the unit to anyone else for a specific period of time. Legally, "holding" deposits are option contracts, and are wholly separate transactions from your rental agreement. They are often not refundable, depending upon the agreement made at the time of the transaction. However, the tenant can dispute charges beyond what are actual damages as penalties to which the landlord is not entitled to by law even if the contract states an amount beyond the actual damages. (CA Civil Code § 1671)

The particular terms of "holding" deposits vary widely, depending on the needs of the particular people involved. Like any other agreement, they should always be in writing, in case there is a problem later. At a minimum, you should include at least these

"Surely, it's no longer legal to require a deposit of your first-born child?"

basics: the amount of the deposit, paid by who to whom, the date paid, whether (and/or by when) it is refundable (wholly or partly), for how long the place will be reserved, and for whom (for example, for you or for a friend).

Destruction of Rental Unit

If the rental unit is totally destroyed for reasons beyond the tenant's control, the landlord does not have to return advance payments of rent since the rental agreement is cancelled, unless there is an agreement otherwise, for example, on the rental agreement. (*Pedro v. Potter* (1926) 197 Cal. 751)

Use of Security Deposits

Under California Civil Code § 1950.5, a security deposit may only be used to secure the landlord against future tenant defaults. § 1950.5(e) states that the landlord may only deduct amounts from the security deposit that are "reasonably necessary" for this purpose, and § 1950.5(b) gives the following examples:

(1) Default in the payment of rent.

(2) The repair of damages to the premises, exclusive of ordinary wear and tear. (CA Civil Code § 1929) Ordinary wear and tear may include ordinary soiling that is not removable by ordinary cleaning.

(3) The cleaning of the premises upon termination of the tenancy *necessary to return the unit to the same level of cleanliness it was in at the inception of tenancy*. The part in italics applies only to tenancies beginning after Jan. 2003.

(4) Future defaults by the tenant to restore, replace or return personal property or accessories, exclusive of ordinary wear and tear, if the rental agreement allows for this use of the security deposit.)

[For more information see *Kraus v. Trinity Management Services, Inc.*, 23 Cal. 4th 116, 141 (2000)]

One common method of calculating the deduction for replacement of an item prorates the total cost of replacement so that the tenant pays only for the remaining useful life of the item that the tenant has damaged or destroyed. For example, suppose a tenant has damaged beyond repair an eight-year-old carpet that had a life expectancy of 10 years, and that a replacement carpet of similar quality would cost $1,000. The landlord could properly charge only $200 for the two years' worth of use that would have remained if the tenant had not damaged the carpet. One approach for determining the amount that the landlord can deduct from the tenant's security deposit for repainting, when repainting is necessary, is based on the length of the tenant's stay in the rental unit. This approach assumes that interior paint has a two-year life. (Some landlords assume that interior paint has a life of three years or more.) Using this approach, if the tenant lived in the rental unit for two years or more, the tenant could not be charged for any repainting costs, no matter how dirty the walls were. (CA Dept. of Consumer Affairs)

Landlords can deduct from your deposit if you change the carpet or paint without asking, even if the changes are improvements, if the rental agreement requires permission from the landlord. However, the landlord could not deduct for a reasonable number of small nail holes in the wall or burned out lightbulbs (*https://realestate.findlaw.com/landlord-tenant-law/what-can-a-landlord-deduct-from-a-security-deposit-for-cleaning.html*).

Sale of Building and Security Deposits

If your landlord sells your building (or the building is foreclosed on), within a "reasonable time" the landlord must do one of the following:

- return the balance of your security deposit directly to you along with an itemized list of any deductions he made from it. (In this case, you would have to pay a new deposit to the new landlord.)

- or transfer the balance to the new landlord and notify you of this either personally or by first class mail, informing you of the name, address and telephone number of the new landlord. (In this case, you would have to restore the amount of the original deposit after the new landlord sends you either your whole deposit or an itemized list of deductions.)

(CA Civil Code § 1950.5(h-j))

If your building was sold and you didn't get your deposit back from your old landlord at that time, your present and old landlord will be liable for it when you move out. If your landlord is putting your building up for sale, ask him in writing which of these two alternatives he has chosen.

Preventive Medicine

The first step in getting your full security deposit back begins when you move into your unit. At this time, it is necessary that you carefully inspect the place. Any damage that exists at the time that you move in may be (and usually is) held against your deposit, unless you take steps in advance to prevent this from happening. Go through the entire place with either the landlord or reliable witnesses and make notes of each and every defect that exists prior to your moving in. Check windows for cracks, look under sinks and in all closets, etc. Note the state of cleanliness. Have the landlord or your witnesses sign the list of defects. The law requires that you leave the place in the same state of cleanliness that you found it in when you moved in if you moved in after January 2003. You can use the checklist in this chapter for when you move in and out of the unit.

The second step in getting your deposit back takes place when you give your 30-day notice of your intent to move. (See the section "Notices and Other Communications Between Landlord and Tenant" in "Chapter 4: Renting Basics." If you have roommates who will remain, see the section "Breaking Up" in "Chapter 10: Roommates.") At this time, you should set up an appointment with the landlord to make an initial inspection of your unit (a "walkthrough"). Unless your tenancy is terminated by a 3-day notice, your landlord is required to inform you of your right to request an inspection before moving out. This notice of a right to request an initial inspection could be on the rental agreement, but the inspection would occur sometime during the two weeks before you move out so that you have a chance to fix anything that your landlord says she will deduct from your deposit. The landlord is supposed to try to find a time that is acceptable for you and give 48 hours written notice of the time of inspection. This written notice can be skipped if you and your landlord both sign a waiver. Unless you withdraw your request, your landlord can proceed with the inspection even if you are not there. After the inspection, the landlord must give you an itemized statement of deductions she would make from your deposit if you were leaving the unit in its current condition. Try to have your landlord sign the statement. In case she refuses, be sure to have witnesses present. The statement shall be given to you, if you are present for the inspection, or shall be left inside the premises if you are not present. (CA Civil Code § 1950.5(f))

Carefully document repairs made in response to the list of deductions from the inspection with photos, receipts, etc. If you make the repairs before you move, the landlord can't legally deduct them. However, she can still deduct for damage that occurs between the initial inspection and your vacancy date or couldn't see because of your belongings.

Moving Out

We recommend that tenants try to exchange the key for the full deposit when moving out. Make another inspection appointment (a walkthrough) for the day you move out and give notice to the landlord, enough in advance of the appointment, that you expect the full deposit amount at this time. Communicate your expectation either in writing or with a phone call, followed up with a letter, always keeping copies in either case. That way, the

Move-In/Move-Out Checklist	Condition on Arrival	Condition on Departure
Bedroom(s)		
Floor & Floor Covering		
Walls & Ceiling		
Windows & Coverings & Doors		
Light Fixtures		
Other		
Bathroom(s)		
Floor & Floor Covering		
Walls & Ceiling		
Windows & Coverings & Doors		
Toilet		
Sink(s) & Counter(s)		
Shower/Bathtub		
Light Fixtures		
Ventilation System		
Other		
Kitchen		
Floor & Floor Covering		
Walls & Ceiling		
Windows & Coverings & Doors		
Sink & Counter(s)		
Stove & Oven		
Refrigerator		
Light Fixtures		
Cupboards		
Other		
Living Room		
Floor & Floor Covering		
Walls & Ceiling		
Windows & Coverings & Doors		
Light Fixtures		
Other		
Other		
Furnace/Heater		
Smoke Detector		
Dining Room		
Garage/Parking Space		
Storage Space		
BackyardDeck		
Other		

Address of premises checked: _____

Checklist completed at the beginning of the tenancy on (date)_____ approved by

_____(landlord) and _____ (tenant).

Checklist completed at the end of the tenancy on (date)_____ approved by

_____(landlord) and _____ (tenant).

landlord cannot claim to be taken by surprise and unprepared to pay at the time of the appointment. If there actually are problems, this is also the best time to work them out, since you still have the move-in checklist, the deduction list from the previous inspection and the key, thus the psychological threat of keeping possession if the landlord refuses to cooperate. (If the tenant actually keeps the key, implying the tenant is still in possession of the unit, the tenant may still be liable for rent. Even if the tenant is moving out, the landlord doesn't legally have to pay the deposit at the time of move.) If the landlord can't or won't make an appointment, you should document in a letter to the landlord, (keeping a copy and mailing with a certificate of mailing), that you tried to meet with the landlord, but the landlord did not agree to the appointment, and describe the condition in which you left the unit.

When you turn over the key, try to get the landlord to sign a statement that she received it but have a witness with you in case she refuses. If you mail the key, send it certified mail with a return receipt requested on or before the last day for which you paid rent. That way, the landlord can't claim you were still living there after you moved out.

Documenting the condition in which you left the unit can best be accomplished by both witnesses and photographs. When taking photographs try to include the headline of a newspaper in at least the first photo, and keep the newspaper. Also, take both detailed photos and location photos that show that the detailed photos are of your home, not your friend's home that you are trying to pass off as your own. Digital photos are fine evidence, but keep in mind that you will need to provide the equipment to clearly view the photos in a courtroom in case of a trial. Documentation serves two purposes: first, it may prevent you from having to sue the landlord because she may decide to just give you back your deposit once it is clear that you will win in court. Second,

Sample Letter for Return of Security Deposit

This is an example of a letter to a landlord for when you are having trouble getting your security deposit back. In this letter, the facts of the case are concisely spelled out and documentation of your case is enclosed. This demonstrates to the landlord that you are prepared for court, if necessary. Also, the security deposit law is cited, as this law specifies when a landlord must return a deposit, what can be deducted from it, and what the penalties are for noncompliance.

December 1, 2022
558 Capp St.
San Francisco, CA 94110

Dear Landlord:

I am writing to you to request that you return my security deposit, in its entirety, pursuant to the terms of both our rental agreement and California Civil Code § 1950.5. Civil Code § 1950.5 requires that you return my deposit in full within 21 days of the day that I vacate the unit or furnish me with an itemized list of damage supposedly caused by me, along with copies of receipts for the expenses of repairing such damage.

As of today, I have received neither my full deposit nor an accounting of why I haven't received it. As you know, I requested that you meet me at the apartment on the day that I vacated it for the purpose of inspecting it and working out a resolution to any possible problems regarding my deposit. You chose not to be present on that occasion. Because of your absence, I felt it necessary to document the excellent condition in which I left the apartment. Please find enclosed copies of the photographs that I took on that day as well as copies of photographs that I took on the day that I moved in. (I have also included the checklist that I made on the day that I moved in.) The apartment was in better condition when I moved out than when I moved in. The law only requires that I leave the apartment in the condition that I found it less "ordinary wear and tear." Given the fact that I lived in the apartment for four years, I would be allowed considerable "ordinary wear and tear." I and my guests were very gentle on the apartment. Also enclosed are copies of the statements of the persons who witnessed the condition in which I left the apartment.

Civil Code § 1950.5 also provides for penalties of up to twice the amount of the deposit for "bad faith retention" of a security deposit. Because of your unwillingness to return my deposit within the period provided by law, I will have made a prima facie case of "bad faith" and therefore expect to be awarded these statutory damages.

Very sincerely,

Joe Hill

documentation will allow you to prove your case in court if necessary.

If unwanted possessions are left behind, be sure to tell the landlord in writing that what remains is trash, document the items in a list and take photos for your own records. You may be charged for the removal of the items if they are large, but you won't be charged extra rent.

It is important to let the landlord know how and where to send your deposit after you have moved out. Since the landlord is legally required to send you a written, itemized statement accounting for any deposit money not returned to you, the failure of the landlord to send such a statement may later be used as evidence of the landlord's "bad faith," leaving the landlord potentially liable for twice the amount of the deposit in punitive damages, in addition to your deposit and litigation costs. (CA Civil Code § 1950.5(l))

No later than 21 calendar days after the tenant has vacated (departed from) the premises, the landlord shall give the tenant, by personal delivery or by first-class mail, an itemized statement indicating the reason for and the amount of any security deposit received, any use of the deposit, and return any remaining portion to the tenant. (CA Civil Code § 1950.5(g)) The landlord may not make a claim against the tenant for defective conditions from before the tenancy began.

For deductions of at least $125, the itemized statement must also include documentation of the labor and money spent on repairs and cleaning. The landlord must provide bills, invoices, or receipts for any materials purchased or for labor costs, unless the landlord or the landlord's employee did the work, in which case the landlord must submit a statement describing the work done and the time it took to perform.

If the landlord cannot obtain documentation, then an estimate of the costs may be substituted. If the landlord cannot provide written documentation because the person or company who performed the work has not yet submitted such documentation, the estimate must contain the name, address, and telephone number of the person or company who did the work. An estimate could also be substituted if the work could not be "reasonably completed" within 21 days. If the landlord submits an estimate, then the actual documentation must be subsequently provided to the tenant within 14 days of the work actually being completed. Tenants can give up this right to get documentation of the actual costs of deductions, but may still obtain it by requesting the documentation within 14 days of receiving an itemized statement. If the security deposit deduction is less than $125, tenants may also obtain the documentation by requesting it within 14 days of receiving the itemized statement.

Your landlord may try to deduct money from your deposit for rent for days after you moved out. Unless you are moving out before the end of a lease without a replacement (see the "Breaking a Lease" section in "Chapter 4: Renting Basics"), or did not give sufficient

---

Suing for Refund

If three weeks have passed and you still haven't received your deposit or if the landlord has deducted what seems to be an unreasonable amount, you should make a *written* demand for it (see the sample letter), keeping a copy of this for yourself. If the landlord's response is unsatisfactory, you can sue him in Small Claims Court for the actual deposit money remaining *plus* twice the amount of the deposit in punitive damages if the total amount is $10,000 or less. The court may award the tenant the additional amount for bad faith retention by the landlord even if the tenant has not requested the additional amount. For amounts over $10,000 you will need to sue in Superior Court and will probably require an attorney.

You can sue even if you don't have a receipt for your deposit. The existence of a deposit is rarely challenged and casual evidence is accepted in Small Claims Court. (CA Civil Code § 1950.5(o)) The landlord has the burden of proof for the reasonableness of the amounts used from the security deposit. (CA Civil Code § 1950.5(l)) See the "Sue Your Landlord" section in "Chapter 14: Taking Action" and "Appendix A: Resources" for more information on the courts and legal assistance.

---

notice in writing (see the "Notices and Other Communications Between Landlord and Tenant" section in "Chapter 4: Renting Basics)" she isn't allowed to do this.

If possessions that are still wanted are left behind, write the landlord within eighteen days of moving out. The letter must ask for and describe the possessions, include your mailing address, your signature and the date (keep a copy and mail with a certificate of mailing, different from certified, or even better, send the letter with delivery confirmation). You will owe the landlord reasonable costs for removing and storing your possessions. The landlord and you must agree to a time to claim pick up your possessions that is no more than 72 hours after you have paid for your landlord's costs or within a reasonable time (three days is considered reasonable) after you landlord has received your letter if there are no costs. If you do not notify your landlord, she should notify you about your belongings or risk being liable for your loss. (CA Civil Code §§ 1965, 1980-1991; Code of Civil Procedure § 1174)

Interest on Deposits

Since 1983, landlords have been required to pay simple interest annually on deposits held for one year or more including deposits collected before 1983. Interest is required for *all* residential tenancies (*not* just the units covered by the Rent Ordinance), except where the rent is assisted by a government agency. The landlord must give the tenant interest in the form of either a direct payment or a credit against the tenant's rent. (SF Administrative Code § 49.2)

Although many landlords pay the interest on schedule, there are those who require a reminder note. If the landlord still fails to pay, the tenant may either sue in Small Claims Court or try deducting the amount from the next rent check. Be warned, however, that this latter option poses the risk of the landlord attempting to evict for not paying the full rent due. SF Administrative Code § 49.2 should provide a good defense, but, whenever a tenant chooses this option, the tenant should be prepared for all the hassle and expense of defending an eviction.

When you move out, your landlord must pay the interest he owes you (pro-rated for a partial year if you have lived in your unit for at least one year) within three weeks, but he is allowed to keep the interest if your deposit is not enough to cover unpaid rent and/or damage to the unit.

Be careful about asking your landlord for the interest on your deposit if he hasn't billed you for your portion of the Rent Board fee (see the box "Rent Board Fee"). Your request for interest may remind the landlord about the fee, which would cause you to lose money if the fee is higher than your interest payment.

Each January, the Rent Board will announce a new interest rate—calculated by averaging the "Discount Window" rates posted by the Federal Reserve Bank in each of the previous 12 months—that will be in effect from March to February of the following year. Starting June 15, 2003, the rate in effect when the payment is due should be used to calculate your interest. If you have an anniversary date that falls between August 4, 2002 and June 14, 2003, you will have to pro-rate different rates for that year—3.4% for the months between August 4, 2002 and February 28, 2003, and 1.2% for the months between March 1, 2003 and June 14, 2003.

The following are the interest rates for security deposits:

September 1, 1983–August 3, 2002....................5%
August 4, 2002–February 2003.......................3.4%
March 2003–February 2004............................1.2%
March 2004–February 2005............................1.2%
March 2005–February 2006............................1.7%
March 2006–February 2007............................3.7%
March 2007–February 2008............................5.2%
March 2008–February 2009............................5.2%
March 2009–February 2010............................3.1%
March 2010–February 2011............................0.9%
March 2011–February 2012............................0.4%
March 2012–February 2013............................0.4%
March 2013–February 2014............................0.4%
March 2014–February 2015............................0.3%
March 2015–February 2016............................0.1%
March 2016–February 2017............................0.2%
March 2017–February 2018............................0.6%

March 2018– February 2019............................1.2%
March 2019– February 2020............................2.2%
March 2020– February 2021............................2.2%
March 2021– February 2022............................0.6%
March 2022– February 2023............................0.1%

What are the consequences if the landlord doesn't pay every year? Must the landlord pay interest on top of the unpaid interest owed on the tenant's security deposit? There are a couple of arguments that tenants can make. First, we can look at general California law about what happens when someone has a right to collect money for damages, where the amount "can be made certain by calculation." Since security deposit interest is a simple calculation and it becomes due on a fixed date (the anniversary of the date the deposit was paid), state law says that the security deposit interest becomes a lump sum that's due on the anniversary date, and if it's not paid the landlord should pay interest on that lump sum. (CA Civil Code § 3287)

What rate of interest should the landlord pay? According to state law, assuming the rental agreement doesn't provide for a particular interest rate, the rate would be 10% per year. (CA Civil Code § 3289) The tenant could then sue the landlord both for the interest on the deposit and for interest on the unpaid interest that became due. (See case #CSM-15-849481, which does not set a precedent, for more information.)

In addition, one can argue that since § 49.2(b) gives the landlord only two choices about how to pay the interest—send payment to the tenant or allow the tenant to take it off the rent—by failing

Rent Board Fee

The San Francisco Rent Board is funded by a fee. (SF Administrative Code § 37A.1) The owner is assessed an amount each November for units covered under the Rent Ordinance (see the section "What Does the Rent Ordinance Cover?" in *Chapter 4: Renting Basics*) and also post-1979 units with a development agreement stating inclusion, and is allowed to pass on half of the costs to tenants. For tenants in occupancy as of November 1, 2021 (2021-2022 tax year), the owner can charge tenants $29.50, except residential hotel rooms can only be charged $14.75. Rent Board fees from November 1999 on are "bankable"; that is, an owner may save them up and charge them later. If the tenant does not pay the fee when requested, the owner may deduct the amount from the security deposit interest. The owner could also sue for the money, but tenants cannot be evicted for refusing to pay as it is not rent. (SF Administrative Code § 37A.6) If your owner hasn't been paying you your deposit interest and sends a request for the fee, it might be a good time to ask her to deduct the fee from the interest and send the balance to you.

to pay the interest, the landlord has chosen to take it off the rent. As a result, the next time the landlord accepts rent, the landlord has unlawfully accepted more than the rent due. This could serve as the basis for an unlawful rent increase petition at the Rent Board or for a defense to a notice to pay rent or quit. (As always, it's safer to pay the rent rather than have to fight an eviction lawsuit, but if the landlord does sue, the tenant should raise the issue.)

Increases in Deposits After the Tenancy Begins

Some landlords have been attempting to raise the amount of the original security deposit as well as the rent. It is the position of the San Francisco Tenants Union that tenants in units covered under the Rent Ordinance (see the section "What Does the Rent Ordinance Cover?" in "Chapter 4: Renting Basics") are under no obligation to pay any security deposit increase demanded after the tenancy has begun. This seems clear that continually increasing deposits, would defeat the express intent of the Rent Ordinance to halt uncontrolled rent increases, which have forced so many tenants to move. It would also be a "unilateral change in terms of the tenancy" to which the tenant does not need to agree. (SF Rent Board Rules and Regulations § 12.20 prohibits evictions for violating a clause that was unilaterally imposed by the landlord, unless the change in the rental agreement is authorized by law.)

While the issue has not yet been resolved by the courts, but it is clear that nonpayment of requested increased security deposits is *not* one of the "just causes" for eviction under the Rent Ordinance and no tenant has yet been evicted for this reason. If you are faced with a proposed increase in your deposit you may wish to notify the landlord that this is illegal and that you refuse to pay it. If threatened with an eviction notice though, you may take the safer course and pay the increase under protest. (Accompany the check with a signed and dated letter stating the reason for the protest, and write on the check "paid under protest.") You may sue the landlord in Small Claims Court after first making a request for its return. These last options would not involve a risk of eviction.

Last Month's Rent Deducted from Security Deposit

Under the pressure of finding a home, many tenants have signed agreements containing clauses which state, "security may not be used as last month's rent," or words to that effect. That clause is enforceable against you. Even so, however, a tenant may wish (or need) to use the "security deposit" as last month's rent to save up money for the move. In addition, some tenants are afraid with good reason that their landlord will either be unable or unwilling to return their security deposit after they move out.

If tenants go ahead and use the security for last month's rent anyway, the landlord's legal remedy is to give the tenants a three-day notice to pay rent or leave and, after this three-day period runs out, start eviction proceedings in court. Since the tenants are leaving anyway, this remedy is not often used, because the tenants will be out long before a court judgment could be obtained against them.

In addition, the security can only be applied against defaults in the tenant's rent or to repair damages to the place caused by the tenant. If the security equals the rent and the place is left in good shape, then the landlord has not been damaged in any way. Some tenants' rental agreements do call a portion of the deposit "last month's rent"; in such cases the landlord is contractually bound to allow the tenants to apply that amount to the last month's rent. If a portion is labeled "last month's rent" (and not "applicable toward last month's rent") then the last month's rent, as set by contract, is the amount set forth in the agreement, not the amount to which the landlord may have increased the rent.

Finally, if back rent is owed and/or the tenants have caused repairs to be needed, remember that the landlord can still sue the now ex-tenants in an ordinary (not an eviction) lawsuit. After all, the only reason rental agreements contain this clause in the first place is so the landlord will not be "stuck" by "bad" tenants. Such clauses force all tenants to pay up front and lose use of their deposit during the tenancy merely to save the landlord the inconvenience of having to sue later if problems develop. The presumption seems to be that all tenants might (or will) cause the landlord harm.

Partial Refund as "Payment in Full"

Let's say you moved out of a place owing no rent and leaving it in good condition, and you're eagerly awaiting a full refund of your deposit so you can finally afford to pay the next month's rent on your new place. A letter arrives three weeks later containing a check for only a fraction of the money you're owed along with a letter from your landlord claiming serious damages to the unit by you. You really need the money, but the question is this: if you go ahead and cash the check, does this mean you're agreeing that landlord's claims are true and that actually you're accepting only part of the original deposit as "payment in full"?

California Civil Code § 1526 says that you can go ahead and cash the check as long as you write "accepted as partial payment only," or words to that effect, by your endorsement. California Commercial Code § 3311, on the other hand, says that if the landlord sent you the money in good faith as full satisfaction of the claim, then you give up your rights to the remainder of the money if you cash the check. (You can regain your right to sue for the full amount under this law if you send the money back to the landlord within 90 days after you cash the check.) The federal court ruled that the two statutes conflict and that, since the Commercial Code is more recent, it is the one that is in effect. (*Directors Guild of America v. Harmony Pictures* (1998) 32 F. Supp. 2d 1184) Under the Commercial Code, you can argue that the landlord had not made a good faith offer, but you would have a difficult time if it went to court.

Chapter 6: **Repairs and Services**

Obligations of the Landlord

When you buy a bicycle, you have every right to expect that there will be pedals so you can make the bike go. You also assume that it will come with wheels, decent brakes, a seat, and handlebars. And of course your new bike would have a warranty so that if something goes wrong you could get it fixed. In California, and most other states, a similar idea applies to the place you rent. As the California Supreme Court unanimously stated:

The modern urban tenant is in the same position as any other normal consumer of goods. Through a residential lease, a tenant seeks to purchase 'housing' from his landlord for a specified period of time… A tenant may reasonably expect that the product he [or she] is purchasing is fit for the purpose for which it is obtained, that is, a living unit…The tenant may legitimately expect that the premises will be fit for such habitation for the duration of the term of the lease. (Green v. Superior Court (1974) 10 Cal. 3d 616 20)

This is a simplified definition of an important tenant right, the legal term for which is the "implied warranty of habitability." (See the section "Rent Strikes" for more information on habitability.) As a renter, you are a consumer from your landlord who is making a profit. You have the right to expect that the home you rent will be safe, decent, and sanitary.

You have the right to expect your home to possess at least the following:

- Effective weatherproofing and weather protection… including unbroken windows and doors.

- Plumbing or gas facilities…in good working order.

- A water supply…capable of producing…hot and cold running water…furnished to appropriate fixtures, and connected to a sewage disposal system.

- Heating facilities…maintained in good working order.

- Electrical lighting, wiring, and equipment…maintained in good working order.

- Buildings, grounds, appurtenances, and all areas under control of the landlord at the time of the rental agreement, in every part clean, sanitary, and free from all accumulations of debris, filth, rubbish, garbage, rodents, or vermin.

- An adequate number of appropriate receptacles for garbage and rubbish, in clean condition and good repair… with the landlord providing serviceable receptacles thereafter, and being responsible for the clean condition and good repair of such receptacles under his or her control.

- Floors, stairways, and railings maintained in good repair.

(CA Civil Code § 1941.1)

- The temperature of the hot water of not less than 110 degrees (CA Code of Regulations, Title 25, Division 1, Chapter 1, Subchapter 1, Article 5, § 32)

- Some balconies, decks, entrances, stairways, and walkways must be inspected periodically. (CA Health and Safety Code § 17973)

This is an update of a law passed in 1872 as a Statement of Public Policy by the California State Legislature; it reads in part:

The lessor of a building intended for the occupation of human beings must…put it into a condition fit for such occupation, and repair all subsequent dilapidations thereof, which render it untenantable. (CA Civil Code § 1941) However, what is law and what actually happens are often different things. What can you do when the home you are paying for isn't up to standard?

Landlord responsibilities usually cover what is considered reasonable to the average person. See *Chapter 8: Harassment* for information on landlord behavior that would be considered harassment. See *Chapter 9: Discrimination* for information on illegal discriminatory actions.) California Health & Safety Code § 17920.3 lists substandard conditions. (See "Appendix D: California Law Excerpts" for this law, and the sections "Heating Requirements," "Lead Paint and Lead Hazards," "Asbestos and Other Chemicals Causing Cancer or Reproductive Toxicity," and "Mold" later in this chapter.) The San Francisco Housing Code, Fire Code, and Health Code provide basic habitability standards for your rental unit and are much more specific than state law. (See *https://www.amlegal.com* and the sample Department of Building Inspection Notice of Violation later in this chapter for more information.)

Some services become the responsibility of the landlord if they were provided as part of your rental unit when you moved in. Stoves, refrigerators, dishwashers, air conditioners, etc. are not covered in California Civil Code § 1941.1 However, if you rent a home with appliances already furnished by the landlord, then he is responsible for maintaining them. It helps if there is a specific agreement stating that the landlord is furnishing the appliances, but it is not required. In addition, if your rental unit is covered under the Rent Ordinance (see the section "What Does the Rent Ordinance Cover?" in *Chapter 4: Renting Basics*), furnishings are specifically included in the housing services provided by your

"It's our landlord!"

landlord. Your landlord might make the claim that the appliances were left by the previous tenants and that he is not responsible for them. But if he does make this claim, you have the right to take them when you move out.

If the rental unit is covered by the Rent Ordinance, parking, storage, laundry rooms, decks, patios, gardens, or kitchen facilities or lobbies in single room occupancy hotels, supplied in connection with the use of a unit, may only be taken away from the tenant with "just cause." See the section later in this chapter "Parking, Storage, or Laundry Room Severance."

Construction Requirements

Windows and Doors

Window specifications including ventilation requirements are in San Francisco Housing Code § 504, and California Civil Code § 1941.1. California law requires that windows and doors are not broken and provide effective protection from the weather. For security requirements, see the "Security" section later in this chapter. The law also includes requirements for exits, including two exits except for some second floors of an individual unit, or second floors with an occupant load of ten or less. (San Francisco Housing Code § 801)

Earthquake Retrofit

Types of Buildings that Require Retrofit

Chapter 34B of the San Francisco Building Code requires certain buildings to undergo mandatory seismic retrofit. To check the status of your building go to *https://sfdbi.org/soft-story-properties-list*. The buildings that are initially included have all of the following:

1. The building's permit for construction was applied for before January 1, 1978.

2. The building has three or more stories, or two stories over a basement or underfloor area that extends above grade. An "underfloor area" can be a crawl space or cripple story, finished or not.

3. The building contains five or more dwelling units.

4. The building is of Type V wood-frame walls construction

and has a Target Story or "soft story." Generally, a basement story, an underfloor area, or any story whose walls are substantially different from those of the next story up will be a Target Story. The intent of this retrofit program is to limit the structural retrofit work to the ground story or to a basement or underfloor area.

Some buildings that have all of the previous characteristics may be exempt from the retrofit if the building has satisfied the optional evaluation of the Department of Building Inspection. See *https://sfdbi.org/softstory* for more information.

Notice for Retrofit

For loss of parking, driveways, storage, laundry rooms, decks, patios, or gardens on the same lot, or kitchen facilities or lobbies in single room occupancy hotels, supplied in connection with the use or occupancy of a unit, the tenant must be given a 30 day written notice for the temporary loss of the housing service. The notice must include the length of time of the severance and the landlord must have permits by the date the notice is given. Permits by address may be found at *https://dbiweb02.sfgov.org/dbipts*.

Compensation for Retrofit

The required compensation for units covered under the SF Rent Ordinance does not exceed 15% of the monthly base rent, pro-rated, and a comparable service may be provided instead. Otherwise, if the written agreement states a rate for the service, that is the rate for calculating the compensation. If there is no written rate and the service was provided at the beginning of the tenancy, the current replacement value is used as the rate, but other factors may be considered. Half of the compensation shall be made by the service of the notice, the other half is due when the severance begins. (SF Administrative Code § 65A) If the tenant must move out of their home due to uninhabitable conditions during the retrofit, see the section "Capital Improvement Evictions" in "Chapter 12: Eviction Defenses."

The tenant may file a Tenant Petition for section "E. Other" (SF Administrative Code Chapter 65A.5) to determine the appropriate amount of compensation owed to the tenant or to challenge the sufficiency of any substitute housing service provided by the landlord. The tenant may also file a Report of Wrongful Severance of a Housing Service if the landlord failed to give the tenant proper written notice before removing the service. (See the section "Petition the Rent Board" in "Chapter 14: Taking Action" for more information.)

Contractor

Construction work that costs $500 or more including labor and materials, must be done by a licensed contractor. (CA Business and Professions Code § 7028 and § 7048) You can check to see whether a contractor is licensed at *www.cslb.ca.gov*.

Health Requirements in Addition to Construction Requirements

Lead, Mold, Filth, and Pest Nuisances

Health nuisances such as lead, mold, filth and pests are prohibited under San Francisco law. (SF Health Code Article 11, § 581) California law also requires the landlord to keep areas under her control free of filth and vermin and provide adequate trash receptacles. (CA Civil Code § 1941.1) The San Francisco Department of Public Health is authorized to adopt rules and regulations to implement these laws. Enforcement of the San Francisco law include relocation payments, fines of up to $1,000 per violation for each day the violation is permitted to continue and/or imprisonment. (SF Health Code § 596, § 600) For more information on lead and mold, see the sections "Lead Paint and Lead Hazards" and "Mold" later in this chapter.

For multifamily properties, the owner must provide containers for the amount reasonably anticipated to be generated of recyclables and compostables, in addition to trash. (SF Environment Code § 1904)

Tenants must be notified in writing about planned pest control, including identification of the pest, the pesticide that is proposed to be used, warnings about the effects of the pesticide, the frequency of the treatment, and contact information for the pest control company if any. If the pest poses an immediate threat to health in a common area, making compliance with notification prior to the pesticide application unreasonable, the landlord shall post the notification as soon as practicable, but not later than one hour after the pesticide is applied. (CA Business and Professions § 8538, Civil Code § 1940.8, § 1940.8.5)

Bed Bugs

Bed bugs have become a particularly nasty problem in San Francisco and other cities. To confirm you have bed bugs when you suspect you have them, use a bedbug-sniffing dog or you can make your own trap, *https://njaes.rutgers.edu/fs1117/*.

Landlords are prohibited from showing or renting a dwelling unit that the landlord knows has a bed bug infestation. (CA Civil Code § 1954.602) The landlord must give written information to tenants about recognizing signs of bed bugs and their habits, and how to report infestations. (CA Civil Code § 1954.603)

Landlords often try to make bed bugs the tenant's responsibility— "you brought them in!"—but as for all pests, the landlord is obligated to keep the premises free of them. For bed bugs, the rules and regulations and additional information, including the procedure for making a complaint to the Department of Public Health, can be found at *https://www.sfdph.org/dph/EH/Housing/BedBugs.asp*. The rules and regulations require training and at the beginning of the employment and annually thereafter for managers, maintenance and housekeeping staff to identify and control bed bugs. Also, management must respond to tenants' complaints of bed bugs within 48 hours with a plan of action and execute the action within 72 hours.

The landlord must inform tenants of units inspected by a pest control operator of the pest control operator's findings in writing within two business days of receipt of the findings. For confirmed infestations in common areas, all tenants shall be provided information of the pest control operator's findings. (CA Civil Code§ 1954.605)

Air Quality (Besides Lead, Mold, Filth) and Fire Hazards

Secondhand smoke and other odors may be considered a nuisance and an interference with a tenant's right to quiet enjoyment of her home. Smoking is prohibited in "enclosed" common areas in residential buildings and smoking by tenants is restricted outside the entrances and windows. The "enclosed" area does not have to be completely enclosed to qualify as enclosed. However, violations by tenants would not be considered a decrease in services for the neighbors under the Rent Ordinance if the owner has complied with required communications about not smoking and removed ashtrays, but the tenant potentially has a successful lawsuit against the landlord. (*Birke v. Oakwood Worldwide* (2009) 169 Cal. App. 4th 1540) In addition, the Department of Public Health can collect damages of up to $500 a day and attorneys' fees and penalties against the smoker. The law also applies to smoking of plants besides tobacco. (SF Health Code § 1009.21, 1009.22, 1009.25, 1099.26) Also, a tenant may sue the smoker for nuisance. (CA Civil Code § 3479)

California Fire Code (CA Code of Regulations, Title 24, Part 9, § 308.1.4) prohibits the use of charcoal burners and other open-flame cooking devices within 10 feet of combustible construction except for:

(1) One- and two-family dwellings.

(2) Where buildings, balconies and decks are protected by an automatic sprinkler system.

(3) LP-gas cooking devices having LP-gas container with a water capacity not greater than 2 and 1/2 pounds.

The California Health and Safety Code and Bay Area Air Quality Management District prohibit emissions of air contaminants that present a nuisance or annoyance to a considerable number of people, or that threaten public health or property. During regular business hours, complaints are dispatched to an inspector, with very few exceptions, no later than thirty minutes

after receipt of the complaint. Inspectors proceed directly to the area of the suspected source to determine the cause of the complaint. Inspectors contact complainants in person unless the complainant has asked not to be contacted. (It is also possible to file a complaint anonymously.) Inspectors prepare a written report for each complaint investigation, and you may request a copy. The Bay Area Air Quality Management District may issue a Notice of Violation to facilities or individuals that it determines are violating air quality regulations, and may prosecute these violations through administrative, civil, or criminal processes. (See "Bay Area Air Quality Management District" in the "California" section of "Government Agencies" of "Appendix A: Resources," and the section "Asbestos and Other Chemicals Causing Cancer or Reproductive Toxicity" later in this chapter for more information.)

Smoke Detectors

Smoke detectors in rental units are required. (California Health and Safety Code § 13113.7, § 13113.8; Code of Regulations, Title 24, § 907.2.10.2) Smoke alarm(s) must be installed in each sleeping room and on the ceiling or wall outside of each separate sleeping area in the immediate vicinity of the bedrooms. In addition, when a dwelling unit has more than one story, a smoke alarm shall be installed on each story and in the basement. The owner is responsible for maintaining smoke detectors, but only if the tenant notifies the owner that a smoke detector is inoperable. The tenant is responsible for replacing the battery, however, similar to replacing lightbulbs.

The owner has the right to enter the tenant's unit to test the smoke detector with proper written notice. (See the section "Privacy and Landlord Entry" in "Chapter 8: Harassment" for more information.)

Fire Extinguishers

Generally, the owner must provide a fire extinguisher on each floor which has common hallways. (*https://sf-fire.org/fire-safety-requirements-building-owners*) Call the Fire Department for the fire extinguisher regulations for your building layout.

Fire Alarm Systems

Buildings that are required to have a fire alarm system must comply with the sound level requirement for sleeping areas in § 18.4.5.1 of the National Fire Protection Association (NFPA) 72's National Fire Alarm and Signaling Code (2013 edition), as amended, upon either (a) completion of work under a building permit with a cost of construction of $50,000 or more (exception for mandatory seismic strengthening under Chapter 4D of the

Building Code), or (b) July 1, 2021, or (c) for buildings sold or transferred after September 1, 2017, twelve months after the sale of the property, whichever occurs first. (SF Building Code § 401.8)

Carbon Monoxide Detectors

Carbon monoxide detectors are required for all dwellings having a fossil fuel burning heater or appliance, fireplace, or an attached garage. (California Health and Safety Code § 17926, §17926.1) The owner shall install a carbon monoxide device approved and listed by the State Fire Marshal. (CA Health and Safety Code § 13263)

Disclosure Requirements for Smoke, Carbon Monoxide and Fire Safety

Owners of residential units in San Francisco are required to designate units as smoke free or smoking optional for tobacco. The information should be updated and the tenant notified that the tenant may obtain the information upon request. The owner is required to inform potential tenants which units in the building are smoke free or smoking optional unless all the residential units are smoke free. For rental agreements starting on or after January 1, 2012, the owner must specify the areas on the property where smoking is prohibited. (SF Health Code § 19M, CA Civil Code § 1947.5)

Buildings with at least three dwelling units are required to disclose to tenants (San Francisco Fire Code § 409.2, § 409.3):

(1) The location of fire extinguishers, fire escapes, and fire alarm system, the date last serviced (San Francisco Fire Code § 907.8.5 for the fire alarm), and confirmation that the building fire alarm system is certificated under § 907.7.4, if applicable.

(2) The location of emergency exits, and a statement that they must remain unobstructed.

(3) How to confirm the smoke alarms and carbon monoxide detectors are in working condition, and when they were last replaced.

(4) The phone number for the San Francisco Fire Department for reporting suspected violations of § 409.

(5) The owner shall provide an oral and written explanation and post the Disclosure Information for new residents before occupancy, and update the written and posted information by January 31 of each year.

(6) The owner shall post at the entry to the building, or other location that the Fire Marshal approved, the phone number of the person who can give the Fire Department or other building inspector prompt access to the building to conduct safety inspections.

The owner must provide information on emergency procedures to most buildings with three or more dwelling units. (CA Health and Safety Code § 13220)

Ventilation for Urban Infill Sensitive Developments

Enhanced ventilation is required for urban infill sensitive use development within the Air Pollutant Exposure Zone. The map is available by searching on *https://www.sfdph.org* and the details in SF Health Code Article 38.

Security

Specifications for doors including locks are required by San Francisco law. (SF Housing Code § 706) California specifies a regulation deadbolt for the main entry and security devices for windows (except for louvered windows, casement windows, and all windows more than 12 feet vertically or six feet horizontally from the ground, a roof, or any other platform. (CA Civil Code § 1941.3) Metal gates also have security requirements. (SF Building Code § 1003A.5)

Some court cases have indicated that security is part of the landlord's responsibility as well. If your doors and windows do not have strong locking devices (such as deadbolts), and there is a history of break-ins in the building, you would most likely be able to include these security measures in any action you took to get repairs made. A court decision held that the landlord may be liable to the tenant if the landlord had reason to anticipate danger to tenants and failed to take reasonable precautions. (*Kwaitkowski v. Superior Trading Co.* ((1981) 123 Cal. App. 3d 324) In another case, the court ruled that a tenant could withhold rent if the landlord failed to provide adequate security. (*Secretary of Housing and Urban Development v. Layfield* (1978) 88 Cal. App. 3d Supp. 28) In another decision, a tenant was injured by a neighbor after repeatedly complaining to the landlord with no action by the landlord, the court ruled the landlord had to pay the tenant's costs. (*Madhani v. Cooper* (2003) 106 Cal. App. 4th 412)

To establish that security-related repairs are the landlord's obligation, you must be sure that the landlord is verifiably made aware of the dangerous condition(s), and of any security breaches that have occurred on the property previously. If these factors are present, you have a right to demand that the landlord correct them by making repairs.

Landlords are required to rekey at least one of the locks on doors that are exclusive to the unit when the unit is permanently vacated. (SF Administrative Code § 49B.2) Tenants covered under the Rent Ordinance (see the section "What Does the Rent Ordinance Cover?" in "Chapter 4: Renting Basics") have a right to keys for each adult occupant without charge, and additional sets of keys, within reason, at cost, upon request. (SF Administrative Code § 37.13)

For a protected tenant with a restraining court order or a police report, the landlord is required to change locks to exclude the person named in the restraining order or the police report. If the landlord does not change locks within 24 hours of a written request by the tenant with a copy of the court order or police report, the protected tenant may change the locks without the landlord's permission if the lease was executed on or after January 1, 2011. (CA Civil Code § 1941.5, § 1941.6)

Additional Rights

Besides the basic habitability standards required under state and local law, landlords may also be responsible for providing or maintaining "services" which are provided as part of the rent, such as those described in the following sections. Tenants do not have the same options as with habitability to force landlords to provide or restore them, however. For example, the Department of Building Inspection will not cite a landlord for not providing such services; nor are options such as repair and deduct available. However, tenants covered under the Rent Ordinance's rent control can petition the Rent Board for a decrease in rent. (See the "Decrease in Housing Services Petitions" section later in this chapter.) If the unit is not rent-controlled, the tenant can sue.

Quiet Possession

A tenant has the right to "quiet possession," use of the premises reasonably free from interference by the landlord. (CA Civil Code § 1927) See "Chapter 8: Harassment" for more information.

Roommates

If you are covered under the Rent Ordinance you have the right to move in immediate family members and replace departing roommates, even if your rental agreement says otherwise. See "Chapter 10: Roommates" for more information.

Communication Devices

Tenants in buildings with at least four dwelling units have the right to install communication services for video or telecommunications from a provider of the tenant's choice. (SF Police Code Article 52) Installation of a satellite dish or antenna, one meter in diameter or less for video or wireless signals, is permitted in areas of exclusive use by the tenant. (Federal Communications Commission's Over-the-Air Reception Devices Rule) Installation of communication cable is allowed also. (1984 Cable Act, 47 U.S.C. § 541)

Telephone

A minimum of one usable telephone jack and wiring that connects

the equipment on the premises to the telephone network are required. (CA Civil Code § 1941.4)

Circuit Breaker Access

The legal occupant of the dwelling shall have access to all circuit breakers of their dwelling. (California Electrical Code § 240.24(B))

Water Conserving Fixtures

As of 2019, all homes must have low-flow toilets, showerheads and interior faucets. (CA Civil Code § 1101.4, § 1101.5)

Charging Station for an Electric Vehicle

A tenant has the right to install an electric vehicle charging station with limitations. (CA Civil Code § 1947.6)

Write the Landlord a Letter First

If you are on speaking terms (better yet, on good terms) with your landlord, you are at an advantage. This does not mean you have to become buddies, but if you have established a relationship and are able to communicate, a lot of time and energy may be saved if there is a problem later; in fact, the problem may be averted altogether. If you have discussed repair problems with your landlord and nothing is done, however, you will need to take further action. Some advance preparation will make this much more successful.

We suggest that from the beginning of your tenancy you keep copies of all written (including email) communications with the landlord, and a log of verbal and text communications, noting dates, times, and who is talking to whom about what. These, plus a folder with all the rent receipts, bills and any other communications connected with your tenancy, will be a good record of events in case you need it later. When you can produce any promises, agreements or relevant conversations it will be difficult for the landlord to deny at a hearing or trial that the events you have documented took place, especially if your records are very specific. The positive psychological value for you is also enormous.

If your home is not up to standard, gathering evidence that a third party can easily understand is critical. A report from a city inspector becomes public record, citing the owner if violations are found. (See the following section for information on using the city inspectors.) Such reports carry great weight toward getting repairs made and as evidence. In addition, photographs, other physical evidence of problems and witnesses are all very useful. Take photos through the time period to show the development of the problem.

Since landlord-tenant law is almost entirely civil (as opposed to criminal) law, the standard by which disputes will be decided is the "preponderance (weight) of the evidence" that a judge or jury will hear (as opposed to the criminal standard of "beyond a reasonable doubt"). Consequently, if you can accurately and persuasively present your side, your chances of winning your case will be tremendously increased should relations with your landlord go sour.

The law says that landlords are not responsible for problems that they have no way of knowing about. For this reason, you should make sure to **write the landlord about problems with the unit and keep a copy of the letter.** Verbal notice (and even constructive notice—the idea that the landlord *should have known* about the problems since they would have been evident upon reasonable inspection) may be good enough, but your evidence is many times stronger if you have written letters. Receiving a letter can make a landlord wake up and recognize that the problem you have been nagging her about is something she really should deal with now. And a paper trail documenting the history of the repair issues is a key first step in the success of many remedies, including a Rent Board Decrease in Housing Services petition, repairing and deducting, or a rent strike, discussed in the following sections. The San Francisco Tenants Union and even the San Francisco Apartment Association can help you with a letter to your landlord.

It is good practice to mail your letter by certified mail with a return receipt requested, or with delivery confirmation, or a "certificate of mailing." With either delivery confirmation or certificate of mailing, the landlord cannot claim she didn't receive the notice

---

Example of Letter Requesting Repairs

August 25, 2022

Dear Sirs:

I reside at 558 Capp St. and regularly pay my rent to your office.

On August 22, 2022, the water heater in my unit failed to function. On that date, I notified your manager Mr. Repair of the problem. He called PG&E on that date and they sent a man out who put a tag on the machine saying that it was no longer serviceable or safe and that it should be replaced. I gave Mr. Repair a copy of the PG&E slip on August 23, 2022 and he said that he would see about having the heater replaced immediately.

So far the heater has not been replaced and no one has told me when it will be. I assure you that it is a real hardship to be without hot water. I would appreciate hearing from you as soon as possible. My telephone number at work is 282-6622.

Sincerely,

Terri Tenant

by not picking it up from the post office. A certificate of mailing, which is cheaper than certified mail or delivery confirmation, is a form on which you write your name and address and the landlord's name and address. The postal clerk will then hand cancel both the certificate and the envelope. This will serve as evidence that you gave your landlord notice.

Department of Building Inspection

If your landlord does not respond to your written requests for repairs, it may be time to bring in the Department of Building Inspection (DBI). DBI is the lead city agency responsible for enforcing laws requiring landlords to provide tenants with safe and habitable housing. DBI inspectors are responsible for citing violations of San Francisco laws such as the Housing, Building, Fire, Plumbing, Electrical, and Health Codes which are often more stringent than state law, as well as violations of state law. For contact information see "Department of Building Inspection" under "Government Agencies" in "Appendix A: Resources." For more info on the permit process see "Permit Process" in "Chapter 11: Changes in Use."

In theory, DBI is supposed cite the landlord for any violations, tell the landlord what repairs must be made and give a time limit, promptly schedule a hearing if the landlord fails to make the repairs and, if the landlord still hasn't corrected the problems, refer the matter to the City Attorney's Office for prosecution. It doesn't usually work that way. Tenants often need to be vigilant in following up that DBI does its job.

The main reason to get an inspection of your rental unit and building, despite the lack of enthusiasm that DBI often displays, is to get evidence of the problems that concern you. A written inspection (by DBI, Fire or Health Departments), especially when bolstered with witnesses, photographs, and copies of letters to your landlord about the problems, provides nearly conclusive legal documentation of the condition of your unit, to which the Rent Board or court judge will give great weight. It proves that the problems existed and that your landlord knew about them. The tenant has the legal burden of proof in habitability cases, and the single greatest problem with tenant complaints is the lack of clear and compelling evidence backing up claims.

Call the Department of Building Inspection's Housing Inspection Department for problems with the Housing Code (repairs and services as opposed to unpermitted construction but not including plumbing or electrical problems). Call the Plumbing or Electrical Inspection Divisions for plumbing and electrical problems. There is a major difference between housing inspectors and building inspectors; if you email or use the web form, you may get the wrong one. A housing inspector will respond within 2 business days to schedule an appointment. Be sure to leave your phone number so he or she can access your building. Your complaint description will appear online instantaneously but your personal information won't appear. Call the Department of Building Inspection's Building Inspectors for stop work orders for unpermitted work.

Don't Call DBI If You Live in an Unauthorized Unit

If you live in an "illegal" unit that needs repairs and the landlord is not responding, you probably should not request a DBI inspection. The inspector may not even care about the defects you called about but simply cite the landlord for having an unauthorized unit. If the landlord is cited for an unauthorized unit, he will be ordered to shut it down or legalize it, which may be impossible, which can result in the tenant's eviction. Common characteristics of unauthorized units are they are off the garage or in the basement and have shared PG&E meters and mailboxes. To find out if your unit is unauthorized, see the section "Unauthorized Units" in *Chapter 11: Changes in Use.*

If your unit is unauthorized, document the problems through other means, such as photographs, letters, and inspections by people other than DBI inspectors such as private inspectors or contact the Code Enforcement Outreach Program (CEOP). The Department of Public Health (DPH) says that they are required to report housing code violations to DBI, but tenants may be able to prevent the code violations being reported to DBI by telling DPH that they cannot pass on the information. DBI cannot cite the unit unless they come in the unit because of a complaint or warrant.

Even if your unit is unauthorized by DBI standards, if the building is covered under the Rent Ordinance the Rent Board will treat it like any other residential unit.

Be flexible about making yourself available on the date and time the inspector can get to your home. Do not cancel an appointment unless absolutely necessary. (The inspector may also note if the place is dirty because of the tenant, so make the place look responsibly clean!) You may wish to get together with your neighbors to request inspections at several units on the same day, which will save everyone time and may reveal similar and/or connected problems.

Before the inspection, make a list of the problems in your unit so you won't forget any of them when the inspector arrives. Go through each room and list all defects, large or small. Refer to the "Move-In" checklist in "Chapter 5: Security Deposits." Be sure to check out hallways and all other common areas as well. (The inspector will not be able to cite for a leaky roof, only for a leaky ceiling, so mediation is recommended to fix a leaky roof.) Provide a copy of your list to the inspector and keep one for yourself. Then, let the inspector conduct the inspection as she sees fit, without interruption. If the inspector does not notice something, point it out, and if there is a major problem ask that it be cited, but don't get into arguments.

Ask when the inspection report with the reinspection date will be

DEPARTMENT OF BUILDING INSPECTION

City & County of San Francisco
1660 Mission Street, San Francisco, California 94103-2414
Housing Inspection Services   R1_____ R3_____

NOTICE OF VIOLATION

Date:_____
Rating: [ ] Good   [ ] Fair   [ ] Poor

Address:_____   [ ] Apt   [ ] Hotel

Block:_____Lot:_____   Complaint [ ]   **Annual Routine** [ ]   Other [ ]

1.   [] Repair Damaged: [] **walls** _____
     [] **Ceilings**_____HC 1001, 1301
2.   [] **Painting** required at: [] walls_____
     [] Ceilings_____HC 1001, 1301
3.   [] Removed or cover damaged paint in approved manner to prevent a **lead hazard**_____
     [] See attached Lead Hazard Warning_____HC 1301
4.   [] Repair [] replace [] **window glass** [] sash cords [] window frame_____HC1010
5.   [] Eliminate [] **mold/mildew** [] walls_____HC 1301, 1303
     [] Ceilings_____HC 1010
6.   [] Repair [] Replace floor coverings\carpets_____
     [] Clean_____HC 1001
7.   [] **Repair plumbing:** [] toilet_____[] sink_____
     [] Plumbing Permit Needed_____HC 1001
8.   [] **Repair electrical** [] switch/light_____[] receptacle_____
     [] Electrical Permit Needed_____HC 504
9.   [] Provide adequate **lighting** at:_____
     [] Electrical Permit Needed_____HC 504
10: [] Repair [] Replace [] Provide **smoke-detectors**_____
     [] Central Alarm_____HC 909
11. [] Repair [] Replace [] Provide battery operated **smoke detectors** [] in lobby [] top of **each public**
     stairway [] every third floor below top of stairway/unit_____HC 911
12. [] Provide [] Recharge [] Date-tag fire **extinguisher** (Type 2A-10bc)_____HC 905
13. [] Eliminate egress obstruction_____HC 801
14. [] Repair [] Replace []**Handrails**_____HC1001
     [] Building Permit Needed [] stairs_____HC 801
15. [] Repair [] Replace [] Provide [] **doors**_____[] locks_____HC 706
     [] Door closers_____[] **viewers**_____HC 912
16. [] Remove [] Clean [] **rubbish/trash**_____HC1307 & 807
     [] Storage_____HC 904
17. [] Eliminate rodent/cockroach infestation_____HC 1306
18. [] Provide heat between 5:00 & 11:00 AM and 3:00 & 10:00 PM. [] Set time to correct hours.
     [] Maintain a minimum room temperature of 68 degrees fahrenheit. [] See attached list_____HC 701
19. [] Provide Ventilation at:_____HC504 & 707
20. [] Provide Utility Shutoff Tool_____[]Post Enclosed Diagram in Public Area_____HC 712
     [] Other_____

_____
_____
_____
_____
_____
_____
_____
_____
_____
_____
_____

All items checked MUST be completed within 7 / 15 / 30 days. **Reinspection Date**_____

Contact Housing Inspector_____ at 558-_____
For every inspection, after the initial re-inspection, a $71.92 fee will be charged until the violations **are abated.**
SFBC 305(g).

Arrival Time:_____   Abated Date:_____   (P:\CHKLIST)

available, and be aware that you must request a certified copy from DBI if you are using the report in court by visiting their offices and paying a small fee. Tenants do not automatically receive a copy, even if there are serious problems in their building.

To make this authority work, tenants need to encourage the inspectors to actually use it. This means making sure you get the inspector back for a re-inspection after her initial order to correct has expired, and then urging the inspector (politely! you want her on your side) to cite the owner.

If the landlord has not fixed ("abated") the problem within the required time, the DBI inspector is supposed to issue a "Notice of a Director's Hearing. The landlord has thirty days to apply for a permit that is required, sixty days to obtain one, and ninety days to complete the work including inspections.

At the hearing, the landlord gets a chance to say why the code violations are still not fixed. Often the landlord calls the inspector to try to talk him out of scheduling the hearing, so you should make sure the hearing is scheduled. The inspector is supposed to post a public notice on the building with details about the hearing, but the landlord often removes it, although that is illegal. Find out when the hearing is scheduled, and notify any other tenants in your building who may be able to attend and support you. Tenants are permitted to speak, so if the landlord makes false statements, the tenant can speak up. Bring printouts of photos as evidence. Usually at the hearing the landlord is given more time to finish the work.

DBI inspectors technically have the power to arrest—without a warrant— a landlord who is violating the Housing Code, but this authority is rarely, if ever, used. San Francisco Housing Code § 204 (see "Appendix C: San Francisco Law and Regulations Excerpts") provides for civil and criminal penalties, including fines and jail time for certain grievous code violations. However, the law specifies that an arrest cannot take place until after the inspector's initial order to correct the problem ("Notice of Violation") has expired, which could be ninety days if the landlord is required to get a permit. The process for the "arrest" is the issuance of a "Notice to Appear" in court, much like what would be issued in a traffic case, so don't expect to see your landlord dragged off in chains. If the tenant can prove bad faith on the part of the landlord and is covered under the Rent Ordinance, he can sue for three times the actual damages or $1,000, whichever is greater, and other relief, under San Francisco Administrative Code § 37.10B, but some courts have taken issue with the "bad faith" language in the ordinance. Outstanding violations can, however, result in tax liens on the property with costly fees, especially when you request a Director's Hearing. This lien sometimes becomes part of the landlord's tax and the bank's title company is informed about the lien.

Petitions for Lack of Services

Tenants in units rent-controlled under the Rent Ordinance (see the section "What Does the Rent Ordinance Cover?" in "Chapter 4:

Renting Basics") may file a petition with the Rent Board for a denial of future rent increases, a reduction in rent until problems are fixed, and a retroactive reduction in rent for the time when the landlord knew about the problems but didn't fix them. For many tenants, this can be a way to get some compensation for lack of repairs and it hits the landlord right in the pocketbook, which may spur the landlord to fix the problem. The process can take months, however, as after the petition is filed, there is a mediation which if unsuccessful is followed by a hearing. (Also see "Chapter 14: Taking Action" for more info on petitioning the Rent Board.)

Decrease in Housing Services Petitions

The logic of the "Decrease in Housing Services" petition (SF Rent Board Rules and Regulations § 10.10) is as follows: The rent a landlord charges for an apartment is based on all the amenities provided, both the basic ones like ceilings that protect you from the rain and the special ones like storage areas or laundry facilities. These are called "housing services." If a housing service that was either provided at the beginning of the tenancy or was reasonably expected under the circumstances is withdrawn or reduced, then the value of that service should be taken off the rent. The landlord refusing to repair a leaky ceiling is taking away a housing service, and if she does it without a corresponding rent decrease it is considered to be an unlawful rent increase.

Housing services, according to San Francisco Rent Ordinance § 37.2(g) are: "Services provided by the landlord connected with the use or occupancy of a rental unit including, but not limited to:
    elevator service,
    furnishings,
    heat,
    janitor service,
    laundry facilities and privileges,
    light,
    maintenance,
    painting,
    parking,
    quiet enjoyment of the premises, without harassment by the landlord as provided in § 37.10B,
    repairs,
    refuse removal,
    replacement,
    telephone,
    water,

Details for the Petition for Decrease in Housing Services

To successfully petition for a decrease in housing services, you need to have evidence of all six of the following for each housing service you have listed on your petition. Otherwise, the Rent Board judge may deny your petition.

1. The landlord was required to provide the service. You can show this in any of four ways:

   a. The service was reasonably expected under the circumstances. If the law requires the landlord to provide the service, then it is certainly reasonable to expect the service. This is why lack of adequate heat, for example, is a "decrease" in housing services even if the heater never worked. In addition, although the landlord is not required to provide a refrigerator, if there was a refrigerator when you first viewed the apartment, then a broken refrigerator that never worked, even at the start of the tenancy, could still constitute a decrease in housing services since it is reasonable to expect that any refrigerator that is present works.

   b. The service was promised at the start of the tenancy.

   c. The service was provided at the start of the tenancy.

   d. The service was provided starting after the tenancy began and you paid additional rent for the additional service.

2. The landlord has not provided the service for a period of time and there was a demonstrable actual decrease in services to the tenant.

3. The dates the service was not provided. When did the problem begin? Has it been fixed since then? If so, when? Approximate month and year if not sure.

4. The date the landlord first knew or should have known of the decrease in services. If the landlord had no reasonable way of knowing that there was a problem, then the landlord is not responsible for it. Except for limited circumstances, rent decreases can be retroactive for only one year prior to the filing of the decrease in services petition. (See the "Petition for Lack of Services" section.)

   There are three ways you can show notice to the landlord:

   a. Show written notice to the landlord of the problem. Judges love this kind of evidence, and that's why we always recommend that, whenever you have a problem, you write to the landlord saying what the problem is, date it, keep a copy, and mail it with a certificate of mailing (different from certified mail). Attach a copy of the letter, email or text to the petition.

   b. Show oral notice to the landlord of the problem. This can be a harder to prove, since the landlord might just deny your testimony, but it still constitutes notice. If a friend was with you when you talked to the landlord about the problem, then your friend's testimony could help you show oral notice to the landlord. You can also bolster your evidence of oral notice by writing a letter to the landlord and referring back to earlier conversations you have had with him (or his employee). For instance, you could say, "As you know, the heater in my apartment has not been working for three months. Back in January (or this past winter or as specifically as you can remember) I asked the manager to fix the heater. She came by to look at it a week later but didn't fix it."

   c. Show constructive notice, in other words, show that the landlord should have known about the problem. (SF Rent Board Rules and Regulations § 10.10(d)(2)) For example, the landlord should probably know about a problem in the common areas of a building. Also, if a window was broken when you moved in, then the landlord should have seen that upon reasonable inspection of the place when the unit was vacant even if you didn't say anything. We recommend that you mention it in a letter to the landlord and keep a copy to strengthen your evidence.

5. The reduction is substantial. This is a point where tenants often lose decrease in services petitions outright. It is very important that you describe in detail how it negatively affected your tenancy, your health, your normal routines, etc., and is not a mere inconvenience or cosmetic problem. For example, the landlord demolished a deck that you and your neighbor had been permitted to use. When you first saw the place, the deck was a big part of the reason you took the place, and you later passed up a good deal on another place because you wouldn't have had a deck. You spend hours on the deck tending your plants and frequently bring your guests out there. Your neighbor has never even stepped onto the deck. The reduction in services to your neighbor might not be substantial, while for you it is.

6. The value of the service. When you file the petition you have to state a value—a monthly dollar figure. The same kinds of evidence apply for showing the value as for showing the problem is substantial. If there are statutory penalties for the lack of service, that can be used for the value. The judge is never going to give you more than the value you determine, so estimate on the high side (but don't be unreasonable). If the judge agrees that a service has been decreased but disagrees with the amount, the petition will not be thrown out. Rather, you will be awarded less.

rights permitted the tenant by agreement or the Rent Ordinance, including the right to have a specific number of occupants whether express or implied, and whether or not the agreement prohibits subletting and/or assignment [see "Chapter 10: Roommates"], and any other benefits, privileges, or facilities."

Under SF Administrative Code § 49A.5:
    right to organize and meet with the landlord.

These would also include, we believe:
    air conditioning,
    alarms and security systems,
    backyard,
    intercoms,
    refrigerators,
    stoves.

In addition, parking, storage, laundry rooms, decks, patios, gardens, or kitchen facilities or lobbies in single room occupancy hotels, supplied in connection with the use of a unit, may only be taken away from the tenant with "just cause," except for temporary seismic work required by Building Code Chapter 34B. Any reduction that is allowed by just cause should have a corresponding decrease in rent. For loss of these services due to Building Code Chapter 34B, see the earlier section "Earthquake Retrofit." (SF Administrative Code § 37.2(r)) The tenant may report illegal severance by filing a Report of Alleged Wrongful Severance of a Housing Service Pursuant to Ordinance § 37.2(r) with the Rent Board. See "Chapter 12: Eviction Defenses" for more information about "just cause." See also the following section "Parking, Storage, or Laundry Room Severance" for more information.)

No guidelines are offered as to what any given service is worth. You can research past rulings at the Rent Board. (See "Chapter 3: Researching Landlords, Buildings, and Laws.") Also use your own research, experience and intelligence. Here's an example of a decrease in housing services, and how to estimate its value: Let's say the landlord shuts off the radiator used to provide heat to the apartment. A decrease in services has occurred for which the tenant may receive a rent reduction. You cannot determine what heat rents for in your neighborhood. The reduction in services can be figured out by calculating the cost of buying and running a replacement electric heater per month. Also, you can determine value — for example, you would only be willing to pay 70% of the rent if there is no heat. If you have poor circulation, or work from your home, you might determine that heat is worth 50% of your rent. You would seek a rent reduction of a dollar amount based on these percentages.

The Rent Board Rules and Regulations provide for a decrease in rent going forward until the repairs are made or the service is restored. Rent reductions will also be awarded retroactively for *up to one year before the tenant filed the petition, and longer than one year when there is evidence of continued notice to the landlord*

every month before the last year. Written notice is the best, but oral notice, adequately demonstrated, will support a petition going back more than one year. (SF Rent Board Rules and Regulations § 10.10(c))

Be aware that you must be able to prove that the landlord failed to do anything about the problem within a reasonable time. (See the box "Petition for a Decrease in Housing Services.") A reasonable time would usually be thirty days, but less than thirty days could be reasonable in some cases (if your only toilet won't flush, for example). The lack of a Notice of Violation from the Department of Building Inspection (DBI) and/or the Department of Public Health (DPH) or Fire Department, although not required, is important evidence, so try to get DBI/DPH/Fire to come out and cite the landlord unless the unit is illegal. (See the box "Don't Call DBI If You Live in an Unauthorized Unit!") See the sections "Preparation for 'Decrease in Housing Services' and 'Failure to Repair and Maintain' Hearings" later in this chapter for more information.

Sometimes the very activity of building maintenance can adversely affect the comfortable, quiet use of your home. If the outside of the building is being painted, for example, the scaffolding may block your window; a new roof means noise and fumes; and so on. Living around repairs in progress may well be inconvenient, but don't expect damages from the Rent Board. An Appeals Court decision held that "reasonably necessary" repair and maintenance which temporarily interferes with the tenant's full use of housing services, but does not substantially interfere with the right to occupancy as a residence, does not constitute a decrease in services. (*Golden Gateway Center v. San Francisco Residential Rent Stabilization & Arbitration Board* (1999) 73 Cal. App. 4th 1204, 1212) The tenant would probably need to show that the repair was not reasonably necessary or the performance was not reasonable to have a successful petition for decrease in services. (SF Rent Board Case #AL 130111) In one such case, the court ruled against the landlord for tearing out existing facilities and leaving them in a dilapidated, unsafe, and unusable condition for years at a time while no construction whatsoever took place. (*Ocean Park Associates v. Santa Monica Rent Control Bd.* ((2004) 114 Cal. App. 4th 1050)

Parking, Storage, or Laundry Room Severance

The San Francisco Rent Ordinance states that parking, storage spaces, or laundry rooms provided in connection with a residential rental unit cannot be severed from a tenancy without "just cause," except for temporary seismic work required by Building Code Chapter 34B. (SF Administrative Code § 37.2(r). See the section "San Francisco Rent Ordinance Evictions" in "Chapter 12: Eviction Defenses" for more information on "just

"Let's not panic until we know if it's going in or coming out."

cause.") In other words, a landlord may not remove parking, storage, or a laundry room without "just cause" just as she could not remove the bedroom, even if the severance is accompanied by a rent reduction. Some landlords try to convert these spaces to accessory dwelling unit without a just cause. For conversion of these spaces to an accessory dwelling unit, the landlord is supposed to notify affected tenants of the intention to convert by posting for 15-days in a common area of the building; and by mail.

The best way to stop the illegal removal of these spaces is to request a Discretionary Review before the permit has been issued. (See the section "Building Permits" in "Chapter 11: Changes in Use" for more information.) The tenant may also file a Report of Alleged Wrongful Severance of a Housing Service Pursuant to Ordinance § 37.2(r) with the Rent Board which sometimes works to stop the project or sue for wrongful eviction. (See the section "Accessory Dwelling Units" in "Chapter 11: Changes in Use" for more information.) The tenant may also sue for an injunction which has been successful in the past, making it clear the tenant had a right to the parking without needing to go to trial.

Any reduction that is allowed by just cause should have a corresponding decrease in rent. For loss of these services due to Building Code Chapter 34B, tenants will not be entitled to a rent reduction, but are entitled to compensation or substitute housing service. If a garage was furnished with the unit when the tenant moved in for no specific amount separate from the rent and the garage is demolished because it is unsafe, the Rent Board will order a reduction in the tenant's rent in the amount of the value at time the tenant first rented the garage with the allowable annual increases. If the tenant acquired the garage *after* the beginning of the tenancy and no money or consideration was paid to the owner—in other words, the service was provided for free—then no rent reduction will be granted if the service is removed.

A parking or storage space in the same building as the residential unit but on a separate rental agreement becomes part of the rent for purposes of calculating the annual rent increase allowed under the Rent Ordinance. (See "Chapter 7: Rent Increases.") Even when the parking or storage space is rented after the inception of the tenancy, the additional amount paid for the service is added to the base rent. The anniversary date for the annual rent increase stays the same as before the parking or storage space was added, even if the tenant has not had the parking or storage space for an entire year. The rental of a garage by a tenant who does not live on the same lot and is not rented in connection with the use of the tenant's rental unit is not covered by the Rent Ordinance and restrictions may apply. (SF Planning Code § 204.5)

Failure to Repair and Maintain Petitions

"Failure to Repair and Maintain" petitions apply only when you receive notice of a rent increase. If your landlord has neglected *requested* normal repair, replacement or maintenance *required by law*, you may file a "Failure to Repair and Maintain" petition for a denial of any proposed rent increase except for certified capital improvements, rehabilitation and energy conservation.

In order to block the increase in whole or in part, you must file this petition within sixty days of receipt of the rent increase notice and you must be able to prove that the problems were *substantial* violations of the law. Lack of heat would be grounds to stop a rent increase, but a broken (but not unsafe) oven would probably not qualify.

You should write letters to the landlord requesting the repairs (keep copies and mail with a certificate of mailing, which is different from certified mail, or, even better, send the letter with delivery confirmation). If the repairs are not made, request an inspection from the Department of Building Inspection (DBI) and get a copy of the DBI report or Notice of Violation (NOV). An NOV is usually required.

In the petition, provide copies of your letters to the landlord and the NOV. The Rent Board will typically dismiss tenant's oral notices to the landlord as inadequate and—no matter how serious the repair obviously is—dismiss the tenant's unsubstantiated claim that the repair is required by law. In addition, the petition must be accompanied by a copy of the notice of rent increase, a statement of the nature and extent of the necessary repairs and/or maintenance, together with the supporting documentation. (SF Administrative Code § 37.8(b)(2), SF Rent Board Rules and Regulations § 10.11)

While this petition is pending, you should pay the demanded rent increase to protect yourself from eviction for nonpayment of rent. If the petition is granted, the Administrative Law Judge will order repayment of the rent increase and issue a list of needed repairs. If the landlord makes the repairs, then she can give the rent increase. The tenant's anniversary date is not affected by the postponement of the increase; it remains the effective date of the notice of the rent increase.

At the hearing the tenant must prove that the work was required by law, that the landlord was notified of the problem(s), and failed to perform the necessary work. The Rent Board can defer the rent

increase until repairs are satisfactorily made. If the tenant petition is granted, any excess rent paid by the tenant between the effective date of the rent increase and the decision by the Rent Board judge must be refunded to the tenant.

A tenant can file both a "Decrease in Housing Services" petition and a "Failure to Repair and Maintain" petition, but only if *the failure to repair and maintain results in a substantial decrease in housing services.* (SF Rent Board Rules and Regulations § 10.10) Since a tenant petition for "Failure to Repair and Maintain" must be filed within sixty days after receipt of a rent increase notice, tenants who file such a petition should also simultaneously file a "Decrease in Housing Services" petition, since tenants may qualify for a rent reduction through the "Decrease in Housing Services" petition in addition to stopping a rent increase. The reverse is not necessarily true since a tenant may qualify for rent reduction with a petition for "Decrease in Housing Services" but not qualify for a petition for "Failure to Repair and Maintain" for stopping a rent increase if there is no proposed rent increase. See the following sections "Preparation for 'Decrease in Housing Services' and 'Failure to Repair and Maintain' Hearings" for more information.

Preparation for "Decrease in Housing Services" and "Failure to Repair and Maintain" Hearings

In hearings for these petitions, the burden of proof is on the tenant. This means you should prepare for the hearing as if you expect the landlord to dispute everything you claim. See the box on "Petition for a Decrease in Housing Services" for what you need to prove. Bring as much of the following documentation as possible to the hearing:

- Photos of maintenance or repair problems. Label and date each photo.

- Copies of all complaint letters to the landlord and responses.

- Information through the city agency:

  - Property ownership.

  - Department of Building Inspections and Health Department inspections and notices of violations.

  - Previous Rent Board cases involving your landlord.

See "Chapter 3: Researching Landlords, Buildings, and Laws" for how to obtain public information on the property. See the "Petition the Rent Board" section in "Chapter 14: Taking Action" for more on presenting your case.

If parallel problems involve multiple tenants in the building, ask the other tenant(s) if they will come to a meeting to discuss filing

many petitions at the same time for a joint hearing. A stack of Decrease in Housing Services Petitions would serve the same purpose as a petition for multiple units. The petition for multiple units is called "Tenant Petition Based on Decreased Housing Services for Multiple Units in the Same Building." Because this petition is often misused it is only available upon request from the Rent Board with instructions from a counselor. It requires a representative for the entire building and must have parallel issues listed in the same order which is consistent in narrative with some individualizing of value. Each tenant must personally appear at the arbitration hearing even if the tenant has an authorized representative or the petition may be denied, but the case may be settled by a representative at the mediation (Form 523).

Suing Your Landlord

If the landlord is not providing habitable premises, the tenant can sue for money as well as for injunctive relief (an order that the landlord do some specified act). If the tenant can prove bad faith on the part of the landlord and is covered under the Rent Ordinance (see the section "What Does the Rent Ordinance Cover?" in "Chapter 4: Renting Basics"), he can sue for three times the actual damages or $1,000, whichever is greater, and other relief, by law. (SF Administrative Code § 37.10B. Some courts have taken issue with the "bad faith" language in the ordinance.) A lawsuit may award more damages to the tenant than a petition to the Rent Board since the Rent Board will only award for loss of housing services and not for statutory, emotional distress or punitive damages. (See the section "Sue Your Landlord" in "Chapter 14: Taking Action" for more information.)

Whether or not a tenant is covered under the Rent Ordinance the tenant may sue for breach of the implied warranty of habitability (see the section "Rent Strikes" later in this chapter) and/or under a claim of unfair business practices in addition to actual, statutory, emotional distress or punitive damages. (CA Business and Professions Code § 17200, *Stoiber v. Honeychuck* (1980) 101 Cal. App. 3d 903, 928) The damage award for unfair business practices is cumulative, so an award does not reduce an award under other causes of action such as breach of the warranty of habitability. (CA Business and Professions Code § 17205) A tenant must be in possession of the rental unit to proceed with a claim for unfair business practices. See the "Sue Your Landlord" section in "Chapter 14: Taking Action" for more information.

There is a state law that lets tenants sue to have their rental unit taken away from their owner. State and local code enforcement agencies, any tenant or any tenant organization may seek a court order prohibiting an owner from maintaining a property in substandard condition. If the owner does not correct the defects, the law permits a court to order that the property be taken out of the owner's control and placed in "receivership," at which point the landlord is forbidden to collect rent, interfere with the operation of or sell the property. The "receiver" may collect rent and borrow money to make necessary repairs. In addition, if the property "substantially endangers the health and safety of the residents," the court shall order the owner to:

(a)Pay relocation and storage benefits to each tenant, including moving costs, insurance, replacement value of lost, stolen or damaged property, and utility connection charges.

(b)Offer the displaced tenants the first right to re-occupy the property once the property is habitable.

(c)Pay the code enforcement agency all costs for inspection, investigation, enforcement and attorney's fees.

(CA Health and Safety Code § 17980.7)

In a similar situation under Los Angeles' Rent Escrow Account Program (REAP), the City can place properties into REAP when a landlord fails to repair habitability violations. Once the property is placed in REAP, tenants pay a reduced rent into a city escrow account instead of the landlord until repairs are made. Four landlords filed a lawsuit saying their constitutional rights had been violated when their buildings were placed into REAP. The United States Court of Appeals for the Ninth Circuit rejected the landlords' challenge to the REAP program. The court wrote: "landlords are not a protected class, and they have no fundamental right to rent uninhabitable housing."

Repair and Deduct

One method of getting repairs made is to have the repairs made yourself and deduct the cost from your rent. Under certain circumstances, the law backs you up if you do this. California Civil Code § 1942 allows you to withhold up to one month's rent twice every twelve months to make necessary repairs on your rental unit for problems falling under California Civil Code § 1941.1 (included in "Appendix D: California Law Excerpts"), and other uninhabitable conditions. See the following section "Rent Strikes" for more information on uninhabitable conditions. Apply this law by the following steps:

1. **You must notify the landlord as to what repairs are necessary.** While verbal notice is legally sufficient, written notice is a much better idea since it provides a record of the communication. If you do give verbal notice, you should have someone witness it. If you give written notice, send it by certificate of mailing (different from certified mail) or, even better, send the notice with delivery confirmation. Always make sure you **keep a copy**. You should also have a copy of the Notice of Violation from the Department of Building Inspection or Health Department.

2. **You must give your landlord a "reasonable" time in**

Example of Letters for Repair and Deduct

To _____, Landlord of the premises located at _____

NOTICE IS HEREBY GIVEN that unless certain dilapidations on said premises are repaired within a reasonable time, the undersigned tenant shall exercise any or all rights accruing to him pursuant to law, including those granted by California Civil Code § 1942.

Said dilapidations are the following:

_____

_____

_____

(Signature of Tenant) (Date)
558 Capp St.
San Francisco, CA 94110

---

558 Capp St.
San Francisco, CA 94110
October 21, 2022

Dear Landlord:

I have repeatedly requested repairs which have had no response from you. (Please see my letters dated September 15, 2022 and October 14, 2022.) Since you are not taking care of the repairs, I have elected to do so myself and deduct the cost from this month's rent pursuant to Civil Code § 1942.

Enclosed is a copy of the receipt from Andy's Heaters for repairs made on October 20, 2022 in the sum of $200. Also enclosed is my check for the difference in rent in November for the sum of $2,000.

A reminder that it is illegal for a landlord to retaliate in any manner against a tenant who has used this "repair and deduct" remedy.

If you have any questions, please call me.

Sincerely,

Terri Tenant

which to make the repairs. Thirty days is considered reasonable by law. If you give less than thirty days notice, you should be ready to prove that the time you gave was reasonable. For example, you would give less than thirty days notice if your only toilet wasn't working. In that situation, 24 hours or less might be reasonable notice.

3. **If your landlord doesn't make the repairs** after you have given reasonable notice, then you can independently arrange for the repairs to be done or make them yourself, and **deduct the costs of labor and materials from your rent**.

It is very important that you send a copy of the paid bill and copies of any applicable receipts along with whatever rent remains due (if any) to your landlord. Send these copies along with a letter of explanation of the deduction for the repairs from the rent. It is critical that you keep the receipts and a copy of the letter for yourself.

There are some limitations to § 1942. You are limited to using one month's rent to make repairs. Repair costs often exceed one month's rent. However, you can apply this right twice in any 12 month period (i.e., in two different months, not two months' worth of rent deducted over the course of several months) and the two months can be consecutive.

The most effective way to use this law (as with most tactics) is to apply it as a group with other tenants, especially if the repairs that need to be made are ones that affect the building. (For more about organizing, see the following sections and "Chapter 14: Taking Action.")

Your landlord may try to collect the rent you have deducted by issuing you a "Three-Day Notice to Pay Rent or Quit." If he does, you have two options. First, you may decide to pay the demanded amount in full within the three days and then sue the landlord to get it back. Since by paying the rent you complied with the notice, this should prevent the landlord from filing an eviction lawsuit and thus prevent your tenant record from being tarnished. You can then try to recover your costs by suing in Small Claims Court for up to $10,000.

Second, if you have a strong case with good evidence that you followed the procedure outlined in Civil Code § 1942, you may decide to stand firm and fight the retaliatory eviction attempt in court if it comes to that. Many landlords will send a three-day notice just to see if they can intimidate the tenant into paying the deducted money, and will back down once the tenant calls their bluff. You should be aware, however, that if the landlord actually gets to the point of filing an eviction lawsuit in court, tenant screening agencies will report that the eviction lawsuit was filed even if the lawsuit was meritless. Future landlords may prefer a tenant without records of such actions, even if you can show you won the case. And of course, if you haven't followed the law correctly, the landlord may win the eviction. If you are thinking of this option, talk to a Tenants Union counselor or a tenant attorney to help you evaluate your case before you make a final decision. (See the box "Retaliation Is Illegal" and "Chapter 12: Eviction Defenses" for more info on defending yourself.)

Illegal Rent

California law makes it *illegal* for a landlord to demand or collect rent where there are serious repair problems in a unit and a complaint has been filed against the landlord by the Department of Building Inspection or other public agency.

This law applies to rental agreements entered into after January 1, 1986. (CA Civil Code § 1942.4) In order to use this law, the following conditions must be met:

(1) The unit is in substantial disrepair.

(2) The public agent has inspected the unit and filed a complaint against the landlord requiring that she make the necessary repairs.

(3) 35 days have passed after the service of the complaint by the public agent without the landlord correcting the problem(s).

(4) The tenant did not cause the problem(s).

At this point, it is illegal for the landlord to demand or collect rent from the tenant. In addition, the landlord may be liable to the tenant for "actual damages" caused by the defects as well as for punitive damages from $100–$5,000. "Actual damages" includes emotional distress. (*McNairy v. C.K. Realty*, 150 Cal. App. 4th 1500 (2007)) The prevailing party is awarded attorney fees.

This law empowers the courts to order the landlord to fix the problems. If the landlord disobeys this order, she can be held in contempt of court. Some judges have ruled, however, that after the habitability defects have been fixed, the tenant owes back rent reduced for the lack of services.

See the "Sue Your Landlord" section in *Chapter 14: Taking Action* and *Appendix D: California Law Excerpts* for the law.

Rent Strikes

When a tenant rents a dwelling from a landlord, she has entered into a legal contract with the landlord. As in any legal agreement, each person in the agreement has certain obligations and responsibilities. The responsibilities of the tenant include paying rent, using the premises only as agreed upon, etc. As the phrase "implied warranty of habitability" suggests, it is the responsibility of the landlord to provide a safe and sanitary place to live.

The California Supreme Court has expressly held that the "implied warranty of habitability" exists in all residential rental agreements. (*Green v. Superior Court* (1974) 10 Cal. 3d 616) This means that it is the landlord's duty to provide tenants with safe and sanitary housing—as defined in Civil Code § 1941.1 and local building and health codes—in exchange for collecting rent. The Court declared in the Green decision that "public policy requires

that landlords generally not be permitted to use their superior bargaining power to negate the warranty of habitability rule."

If either party in a legal agreement fails to carry out their obligations under the agreement, the other party may have a basis for not carrying out their side of the contract. If a tenant fails to pay rent, the landlord has a legal basis to evict the tenant. Similarly, if the landlord substantially fails in the legal obligation to provide a decent place to live, the tenant has a legal ground for withholding rent. This is the basis for a rent strike. The fact that tenant has continued to occupy the property does not necessarily mean that the property is habitable. (California Civil Jury Instructions/CACI No. 4320)

The "implied warranty of habitability" is a legal theory which has been developed and defined through various court cases throughout the country. In California, a case was based on this concept. (*Hinson v. Delis* ((1972) 26 Cal. App. 3d 62) In most cases where a tenant exercises his rights under California Civil Code § 1942 (see the "Repair and Deduct" previous section), there is no question that the one or two months' rent withheld was withheld legally. As a result, few instances of this particular action by the tenant are ever challenged in court. However, rent withholding in the form of a rent strike is not so clearly defined, and therefore

---

NOTICE OF RENT WITHHOLDING

To_____, landlord of the premises located at
_____.

   NOTICE IS HEREBY GIVEN that because of your failure to comply with the implied warranty of habitability by refusing to repair certain defects on the premises, as previously demanded of you, within a reasonable time after such demand, the undersigned tenant has elected to withhold this month's rent in accordance with California law. Rent payments will be resumed in the future as they become due only after said defects have been properly repaired.

   Dated:_____

   Signature of Tenant:_____.

Authority: *Green v. Superior Court* (1974) 10 Cal.3d 616, 111 Cal.Rptr. 704

---

tenants on rent strike are much more likely to be taken to court.

If the landlord violates the "implied warranty of habitability" by failing to maintain or repair the dwelling, the Court ruled that tenants should not be evicted for withholding rent if all of the following apply:

- **The defects are "material,"** that is, **serious and significant** to a "reasonable person" (not minor, technical, or only cosmetic).

- The problem was not caused by the tenant or his visitors.

- The tenant has notified the landlord of the problem(s) and has allowed him a "reasonable" amount of time to repair the defect(s).

- **The tenant actually has the rent.** You may be required at some point to deposit the contested amount of rent with the court until your case is concluded. If you do not have it, you will almost certainly lose no matter if you can prove the place was bad, because the court will never reach that issue. Remember that many judges are skeptical of even the most legitimate rent withholding, believing that tenants are merely trying to get out of paying rent. **So never spend your withheld rent!!** Any withheld rent should be kept in a bank account separate from any other accounts you may have.

A California Supreme Court decision strengthens the rights of tenants in rent withholding situations. This decision held that:

- Tenants have a right to withhold rent until repairs are made, even if the tenants knew of the defects when they moved into the rental unit. (Id. at 54)

- Once the tenant has notified the landlord of the defects, the tenant doesn't necessarily have to wait a "reasonable time" but can withhold rent immediately. (Id. at 55)

- Tenants may exercise these rights against the current owner of the premises, even if the defects existed before the current owner purchased the property. (Id. at 57)

(*Knight v. Hallsthammer* (1981) 29 Cal. 3d 46)

If the tenant withholds more rent than the judge decides is the proper amount, the tenant is not penalized for having been unable to guess the right amount to withhold. (CA Code of Civil Procedure § 1174.2, *Strickland v. Becks* (1979) Cal. App. 3d Supp. 18)

In addition, state law makes it illegal for a landlord to demand rent where there are serious repair problems that were not fixed for 35 days after a complaint was filed against the landlord by a public agency. See the box "Illegal Rent."

A rent strike is most effective when a group of tenants is involved rather than just an individual. The energy, organization, and mutual support of tenants working together are critical factors in the success of a rent strike. For example, you might have moved into a building with a sagging front porch and stairs, which have continued to deteriorate. Each entry to and departure from the building may be dangerous and the landlord has done nothing to correct the problem, even though you have written to her several times. All of the tenants in your building might join a rent strike to pressure the landlord to replace the porch and stairs. If you live in a building that you think has the potential for being organized, see "Chapter 14: Taking Action" and contact the Tenants Union.

The following steps provide a basic outline of what is involved in a rent strike:

(a) A list of problems should be sent to the landlord with proof of mailing such as delivery confirmation or at least a certificate of mailing which is different from certified mail and does not require a signature. Keep a copy of the list.

(b) Estimates for the repairs should be obtained and copies should be sent to the landlord.

(c) The appropriate city inspectors should be called out to inspect the building so that there is an official report on record of all the code violations. A written complaint should also be filed with the Department of Building Inspection if appropriate for that department. You should also have a copy of the Notice of Violation from the Department of Building Inspection or Health Department.

(d) If rent is going to be withheld, a letter explaining this (and the reasons for it) should be sent to the landlord and/or to his attorney with an additional explanation about the special bank account in which the rent is being held.

If the landlord still won't make repairs, tenants have two legal paths to choose from to begin their rent strike. One is to file a lawsuit against the landlord seeking a judicial declaration that the tenants are obligated to make rental payments only after the landlord complies with his duty to substantially obey the housing codes and make the premises habitable. (*Hinson v. Delis* ((1972) 26 Cal.App.3d 62) Or they can begin withholding rent, wait for the landlord to file an eviction action against them, and base their defense to the eviction on the landlord's breach of "implied warranty of habitability." This second approach is as effective legally as the first, but is far more risky.

Caution with Rent Withholding!

We should emphasize that although rent withholding is powerful leverage against your landlord especially if done with other tenants, it can be a risky option because it brings with it the potential for an eviction attempt for nonpayment of rent. It is treated very seriously by courts and not looked at kindly by landlords. It should be used

Retaliation Is Illegal

Your landlord is prohibited by law from taking retaliatory action against you for 180 days or longer after you exercise your rights as a tenant. These rights include complaints to the landlord or a government agency, "repair and deduct," consulting a tenants rights organization or an attorney, or organizing your building. If the tenant is in default for rent, however, the law would not apply. There are limits to how often the retaliation may be asserted under California Civil Code § 1942.5.

The landlord cannot evict you, raise your rent or decrease any services if his motive is to get back at you for some action you've taken to assert your tenant rights. The courts have consistently ruled that after 180 days have passed, the landlord still cannot legally evict a tenant if the reason for the eviction is the tenant's exercise of any rights under the law, except retaliatory Ellis Act evictions are allowed. (See the section "Ellis Act" in *Chapter 12: Eviction Defenses*.) While tenants always have the burden of proving the landlord's eviction attempt was retaliatory, judges will examine a landlord's motive for the eviction. Therefore, any time the tenant can provide convincing evidence that the landlord's motive was retaliation for the tenant's exercise of a legal right, the eviction attempt should fail.

This doesn't mean that your landlord won't try to retaliate against you. It does mean that if you resist the landlord's attempts to intimidate you and the issue goes to court, the law provides you with a strong defense for your actions. Furthermore, if you think your landlord is trying to retaliate against you, you may take her to court for violating the law. If you win, you may collect between $100 and $2,000 in penalties from your landlord for each act of retaliation you can prove, as well as your attorney's fees.

The Rent Ordinance also prohibits retaliation. (SF Administrative Code § 37.9(d)) See also the section on retaliation under "Affirmative Defenses" in *Chapter 13: Eviction Process in Court.*

with discretion, only when other methods are useless under the circumstances. But it can also be the most effective method for forcing a landlord to make repairs.

If you decide you want to withhold rent, do not do so until you have talked to a Tenants Union counselor or a tenant attorney. A tenant who withholds rent should be ready to use the previously mentioned court cases and to construct a legal defense, because the likely response by a landlord to tenants withholding rent is to

begin an eviction proceeding. This will begin with a "Three-Day Notice To Pay Rent Or Quit (Vacate)," followed by a summons and complaint for "Unlawful Detainer" if you continue withholding rent after the three-day notice period. (If you receive an Unlawful Detainer Summons, contact the Eviction Defense Collaborative or a tenant attorney immediately because **you have only five calendar days to "answer" an Unlawful Detainer Summons or you will lose.**) Therefore, you must be confident of your grounds for withholding rent because the forum where you will argue your right to do so is the courtroom, and if you lose, you not only lose your argument, you also lose your home.

When you and your landlord go to court, the judge, or jury if the case goes that far, will decide what the reasonable rental value of your place is after you and the landlord have presented your evidence. Therefore, *evidence of the defects* in the place that another person can relate to and understand *is essential*; this includes photographs, videos, witnesses, certified Building Inspectors' reports and copies of your notices to the landlord of the problem(s). Remember, you must also be able to prove in court that the defects are "material," that is, that the defects would be serious and substantial to the average "reasonable" person. Also, it is *absolutely critical* for you to be able to show that *you actually have the withheld rent*. This may be the first thing you will have to show in court.

If you present your case successfully, at the conclusion you will be obligated to pay the landlord only the "reasonable" rent for the time the defect(s) went uncorrected, since you were getting housing of significantly reduced value than the rent the landlord was demanding. The court may decide, for example, that you should pay only 75% or even no rent at all until the necessary repairs are made. And the personal satisfaction of successfully employing the rent strike, a tenant's most powerful weapon to deal with unethical landlords who break the law, is incalculable.

Prosecute Your Landlord

For tenants covered under the Rent Ordinance (see the section "What Does the Rent Ordinance Cover?" in *Chapter 4: Renting Basics*), your landlord can be convicted of a misdemeanor and be punished by a fine of up to $1,000 or by imprisonment for up to six months, or both, if she has, in bad faith which can be proven:

(1) failed to provide housing services required by law;

(2) failed to perform maintenance required by law;

(3) failed to exercise due diligence in completing maintenance once undertaken or failed to follow appropriate protocols to

minimize exposure to potentially harmful noise, dust, mold, or building materials.

(SF Administrative Code § 37.10B)

You can report these crimes by contacting the City Attorney.

"Constructive Eviction"

Another alternative to staying put and fighting it out is to make use of the theory of "constructive eviction." "An eviction is constructive if the landlord engages in acts that render the premises unfit for occupancy for the purpose for which it was leased, or deprive the tenant of the beneficial enjoyment of the premises." (*Cunningham v. Universal Well Services, Inc.* (2002) 98 Cal. App. 4th 1141) This option may be most useful for tenants who want to break a lease because they find their home unlivable. If your home is in such terrible shape that it is truly impossible for you to live there, you can move out and not owe rent, even if you have a lease. You do not have to give the normally required thirty-day notice. (*Kulawitz v. Pacific Paper Company* (1944) 25 Cal.2d 664) Instead, send the landlord a letter explaining why you are moving. You have, in effect, been evicted from your home because of the impossible living conditions. You are then relieved of responsibility to pay rent from the date you move out, and can sue for back rent for the time that you lived there and overpaid rent for an uninhabitable place, as well as damages from the landlord's negligence. (CA Civil Code § 1714)

It should be emphasized that a constructive eviction requires *serious* problems with your home, which make it "untenantable." This means more than simple inconveniences or minor problems; the problems must be so bad that no reasonable person could be expected to live there. You must also be able to prove that the landlord knew of the problems and had a reasonable time to correct them. You should have a file complete with letters, photos, and, ideally, Department of Building Inspection and/or Department of Public Health Inspection reports. Lastly, you must be able to show the problems were not your fault.

We do not ordinarily recommend that you take this action because (1) it adds one more home-seeker (you) to the competitive housing market, (2) relieves pressure on the landlord to make the needed repairs, and (3) actually gives the landlord an opportunity to increase the rent on the new tenants who move in. However, if you feel the living conditions are absolutely unbearable and do not have the time or energy to fight for repairs, this is an option to consider. The landlord may try to sue for thirty days' rent (though it is rare), and you would then have the responsibility of proving that a "constructive eviction" had occurred. (You would use the same arguments and evidence that you would for rent withholding, as discussed in the previous section.) More commonly, the landlord will try to keep your security deposit, in which case you would take her to court and most likely win it back.

If you are covered under the San Francisco Rent Ordinance and forced to vacate your unit due to disaster, the landlord must offer the renovated unit to the displaced tenant within thirty days of completing the repairs. (See the section "Fire or Other Disaster" at the end of this chapter.)

Heating Requirements

San Francisco can get cold. If your landlord is neglecting your heating system it's not only inconsiderate, it's also against the law. If you are suffering from no or inadequate heat, then your landlord is violating the San Francisco Housing Code as well as the warranty of habitability.

Landlords, except for hotels, must provide heat capable of maintaining a room temperature of 70 degrees at a point three feet above the floor. The requirement for hotels is 68 degrees between the hours of 5:00 a.m. and 11:00 a.m. and 3:00 p.m. and 10:00 p.m. All individual heaters installed in the dwelling unit must be permanently attached. (SF Housing Code § 701) The complete law may be found in "Appendix C: San Francisco Law and Regulations Excerpts."

If you are not getting adequate heat, here's what you should do:

1. **Notify Your Landlord.** With something as necessary as heat, you probably want to tell your landlord right away over the phone or in person. **Follow up with a letter, keep a copy, and mail it with a certificate of mailing** (different from certified), or even better, send the letter with delivery confirmation. Tell the landlord what the law is. If the problem isn't fixed, tell the landlord you will call the Department of Building Inspection and have him cited for breaking the law. Remind him that failure to provide heat is a criminal violation of the San Francisco Housing Code and you are prepared to assert your rights.

2. **Contact the Department of Building Inspection,** except if you live in an unauthorized unit, and request an inspection. (See the section "Department of Building Inspection" earlier in this chapter.)

3. If you are covered under rent control by the Rent Ordinance, **petition the Rent Board to decrease your rent.** You can use the statutory penalties in #5 and #6 for the money value. (See the section "Petitions for Lack of Services" earlier in this chapter.)

4. You also have the right to "repair and deduct" or to withhold rent, but it is rarely a useful remedy for a lack of heat because the repairs are too expensive or because they require permits. You also risk an eviction attempt for withholding rent. Talk to a Tenants Union counselor or an attorney before you try this tactic.

5. Talk to an attorney about suing your landlord or sue in Small Claims Court. San Francisco Housing Code § 204 provides for civil penalties. If the tenant can prove bad faith on the part of the landlord and is covered under the Rent Ordinance (see the section "What Does the Rent Ordinance Cover?" in *Chapter 4: Renting Basics*), he can sue for three times the actual damages or $1,000, whichever is greater, and other relief, under San Francisco Administrative Code § 37.10B but some courts have taken issue with the "bad faith" language in the ordinance. Outstanding violations can result in tax liens on the property with costly fees, especially when you request a Director's Hearing.

6. Prosecute your landlord if bad faith on the part of the landlord can be proven by contacting the City Attorney for criminal penalties. (SF Administrative Code § 37.10B, Housing Code § 204(c)) Landlords can be fined between $500-$1,000 and/or be imprisoned for up to six months for not providing heat. Under California law, the landlord could be guilty of a felony. (See the section "Utility Shutoffs" in *Chapter 8: Harassment* for more information.) Let your landlord know what the penalty is, but be prepared to take other actions as the City is reluctant to prosecute landlords.

Mold

Mold was called "the asbestos of the nineties." Homes have been evacuated due to mold; courtrooms have been filled with mold cases; an entire industry has sprung into life around the issue of indoor air quality. What does all this have to do with the fuzz growing on your shower curtain?

Basic Facts About Mold

Mold is a common type of fungus found everywhere, indoors and outdoors, and even in some of the world's most beloved cheeses. It grows in damp conditions and uses organic materials such as wood, paper, cloth and leather as a food source. Some molds produce spores that travel through the air, forming new colonies when they land in places with enough moisture and food. As the mold grows, the food source is "eaten" and decomposes. If left unchecked, mold can cause serious structural damage to buildings and can destroy porous substances such as books, fabric and furniture.

Mold is a housing problem whenever there is excess indoor moisture, which is likely to develop from:

• Roof, ceiling, window or plumbing leaks.

• Floods, wet basements or crawl spaces.

- Inadequate ventilation of steam from showers, cooking or dishwashing; or clothes dryers not vented to the outside.

- Improper repair or cleanup of prior water damage that leave mold colonies that will reactivate.

- Big spills of liquid onto carpet or upholstered furniture.

Mold grows in new buildings as easily as in old ones. In fact, some modern luxury buildings have had the worst problems with mold because they are so tightly sealed that moisture cannot escape. Chronic water incursions will get mold started, and usually result from chronic lack of maintenance.

Mold colonies take 24 to 48 hours to begin growing. If moisture can be dried out within that time, the mold growth will be prevented or contained. There aren't many landlords who take only a day or two to fix a leaky roof, however. And the worst mold usually grows where it can't be seen—that roof may be leaking behind the sheetrock, for example, or into the carpet padding—and it can be hard to convince landlords who don't take care of their property to fix an "invisible" problem. The landlord's idea of a fix is often to just wipe down the walls with bleach, when in fact the wallboard might need to be ripped out entirely. Remediation of a home that is badly mold-damaged should only be done by qualified people and can be an expensive proposition.

It is very important to do what you can yourself to control excess moisture in your home. You know best where problems may be arising. Make sure to open windows or use exhaust fans if moisture builds up while you shower, cook or use a dishwasher or dryer. If you have a drip pan in your refrigerator, keep it clean and dry. If there is a little mold on your window or your bathroom tiles, clean it promptly. However, gather evidence of the mold before cleaning for proof if needed.in the future. If it can't be controlled, notify your landlord. Like most repairs, it is best to address the problem early.

Medical Impact of Mold

A breath of "fresh air" in San Francisco is likely to contain many mold spores. Low levels of mold will not often have a great impact on health. But high levels of certain types of mold have been linked to medical problems, particularly to respiratory problems like asthma. Many factors influence the odds that mold will cause medical problems, including the species of mold, the age and health of the person breathing the spores, the amount of exposure to the mold, and the environment for mold growth.

Certain common molds feed on decaying plants and are unlikely to indicate a problem with your home. Other species are rarely found in the outside air, but thrive on water-damaged building materials. The second group is of greater concern, particularly toxic molds that disperse harmful substances called "mycotoxins."

Certain groups of people are more susceptible to mold-related health problems than others. The very young and old are more vulnerable than healthy college students. People with compromised immune systems may have fatal reactions to mold levels that would have minimal impact on healthy immune systems. Similar individuals within the same home suffer different impacts depending on the extent of their exposure to the mold. A person returning home only for sleep may have a fraction of the exposure of an infant sleeping most of the day near the mold.

There is broad agreement in the medical community that many people are allergic to certain molds and will suffer from typical allergic symptoms such as watery eyes and nasal irritation. The good news about typical allergies is that the problems often clear up soon after departure from a moldy environment. Doctors also agree that problems can arise when molds or fungi grow on or inside the body. These diseases can range from well know minor ailments such as the fungus known as athlete's foot to serious problems like a mold growth in the lungs called aspergillosis. Conditions like aspergillosis require treatment even if you move away from the initial source of the mold exposure.

The widest range of problems has been associated with "toxic molds" that disperse mycotoxins. Scientists have identified the species that emit mycotoxins, but they have only recently developed tests that can measure mycotoxins in the environment. Although doctors agree that molds can cause allergic reactions, there are many views about the impact of toxic molds. Symptoms that have been reported include loss of respiratory function, cognitive problems, skin rashes, digestive problems and debilitating loss of energy. Some victims have compared these problems to chronic fatigue syndrome.

Medical evaluation of severe reactions to mold can be expensive. If you have reason to believe that mold is causing your health problems, be persistent in pressing doctors to conduct tests. Most medical school curriculums spend little time on mold, and you can't assume that your doctor has read the current research. An allergist/immunologist will be familiar with basic allergy tests even if he isn't an expert on toxics. Allergists can use blood tests or scratch tests to check for standard (IGE) allergic reactions to mold. If you find a doctor specializing in mold, she may be able to suggest other tests and is more likely to be familiar with current research on toxic molds. However, if you get into litigation, be aware that a defense lawyer may convince a judge to rule that allergy test results will not be allowed into evidence.

Testing for Mold

The Toxic Mold Protection Act of 2001 was the first law in the country to regulate toxic mold exposure in the home and

workplace. It requires landlords who know or should know of the presence of mold to disclose that fact to prospective or current renters (CA Health and Safety Code § 26147) and provide prospective tenants with the booklet *Information on Dampness and Mold for Renters in California* from the California Department of Public Health. It also charges the California Department of Health Services, with the assistance of a volunteer task force (including tenant representatives), to develop and adopt permissible exposure limits for indoor molds, and to develop standards or guidelines to: assess the health threat posed by indoor molds, determine valid methods for mold sampling and identification, provide practical guidance for mold removal and abatement of water intrusion, develop standards for mold assessment and remediation professionals, and develop public education materials about mold health effects, cleanup/ removal methods and prevention techniques. The state is taking contributions from the public to cover the budget to implement this law. Let's hope tenant advocates fill their penny jar faster than the insurance industry or the realtors!

You can run a variety of tests to identify the mold and the extent of the problem in your home. Tape tests or bulk tests can identify the species of the mold growing on a particular spot, but provide limited information on the magnitude of the problem. Dust tests can give you an idea of the quantity of mold spores that collect over time. Air tests pump air over a growth medium to measure the concentration of mold you take into your lungs every day.

State standards have not established a certain level of mold as dangerously high, so ask your environmental tester to interpret test results. In air testing, mold levels in indoor air are compared to mold levels in outdoor air. If the mold levels of dangerous molds in your home air are five times the level of air outside your door, then you have a problem with mold growth in your building.

A full battery of environmental tests requires that you pay an expert to collect samples, pay a lab to analyze the samples and an expert to interpret the results. Is it worth it? If you and other tenants in your home enjoy excellent health and there is minimal visible mold, you probably shouldn't spend $2,500 to gather comprehensive data. But if you suspect that mold is the reason that your child has been to the emergency room twice in the last year and persistent repair requests to the landlord have fallen on deaf ears, then you may have to take legal action to get a solution.

If you want to prove the full extent of a personal physical injury from mold, you'll have to collect sufficient scientific and medical evidence. Environmental and medical tests have to be included in evidence of personal physical injury, or else a judge may prevent the jury from hearing all your medical claims. Attorneys often file *in limine* motions requesting the judge to rule that certain evidence cannot be heard by the jury. In addition, you must have a doctor willing to testify that the symptoms you have been experiencing are a result of the mold growing in your home.

You can provide an attorney with medical records and photos of your problem and request that your attorney advance the costs of the tests. If the attorney is reluctant, you could volunteer to pay a few hundred dollars for initial tests in hopes of convincing the attorney to advance more extensive test costs. Positive results from an initial round of tests may also persuade your doctor, HMO or medical insurer that you need additional medical tests. An initial round of tests may also persuade a city inspector that the mold problems need to be cited and abated, although typically, the mold must be visible before inspectors will cite the landlord. Try to have enough people available to observe the mold inspector or tester when she comes as she may quickly go to different rooms.

If mold forces you to leave your residence, you are much better off with tests that show the extent of the problem during the tenancy. You could get a court order to run tests after your departure, but then the landlord may argue that the problem developed after you left.

Since mold problems are usually related to water intrusion, many attorneys currently prefer to emphasize water intrusion as a habitability issue or as a source of property damage. Less testing and less expert testimony may suffice in these cases if mold is photographed to merely demonstrate the effects of a leakage nuisance instead of analyzed to prove the mold's medical impact.

Removing Mold Problems

Whatever course of action you take to get your landlord to fix the mold problems in your home, by all means do what you can yourself to control the water sources and the mold after gathering evidence of the mold for proof in the future if needed. As we've stressed, time is mold's friend, and you don't want to be breathing mold spores while prodding a landlord to get to work.

The first step is to identify and eliminate the sources of moisture. Then, if your home has only a small amount of mold, your landlord should be able to clean it up safely if the proper precautions are taken. For larger amounts of contamination, only a qualified person should perform the cleanup as mold remediation is specialized work. Like lead paint, mold becomes airborne when disturbed, and must be contained as it is cleaned.

Mold is a "health nuisance" by law. (SF Health Code, Article 11, § 581) The Nuisance Code is enforced by the San Francisco Department of Public Health (DPH). (The "Lead Paint and Lead Hazards" section later in this chapter describes how to work with DPH.) The code states that mold must be "visible or otherwise demonstrable." If you make a complaint against your landlord and have a DPH inspector come to your home, she will not cut a hole in your wall to see if there is mold growing behind it. But if she can smell mold, even if she can't see it, she will cite your unit. (The inspector may also note if the place is dirty because of the tenant, so make the place look responsibly clean!)

The Department of Building Inspection (DBI) will also cite the landlord if the mold is visible and is sometimes more responsive than the Department of Public Health. In one case, a DBI inspector required a landlord to hire a certified industrial hygienist to clean up a mold situation. Insist that your landlord and his workers follow safe procedures and call DBI if your landlord doesn't!

Leaks and building structural problems that are creating the conditions for the mold are habitability issues well-referenced in state and local codes. Tenants should use all the remedies described previously in this chapter to get these problems taken care of, such as complaining to the Department of Building Inspection and the remedies for constructive eviction.

Compensation for Mold Problems

Besides a personal injury lawsuit, mold problems can form the basis for a number of legal actions, including claims of violation of the warranty of habitability, property damage, nuisance claims or reduction in rent from the San Francisco Rent Board.

If your health or property has been significantly damaged by mold, you should come to the Tenants Union to get a referral to tenant attorneys who are experienced in mold claims. If a tenant has been forced to move out of her home due to mold, she could bring a lawsuit on the grounds of bad faith and violation of the implied warranty of habitability. If the tenant moves out temporarily under the SF Rent Ordinance, the requirements of a temporary capital improvement eviction applies. (See the section Capital Improvement Temporary Evictions" in *Chapter 12: Eviction Defenses.*") Tenants can also file a personal-injury suit tied to health effects of exposure to mold. Although there is not yet scientific consensus on the whys and hows of mold-related illness, in civil cases legal proof is simply a preponderance of the evidence. The jury must believe the cause and effect are more likely than not to be related. So it would be important to have substantial documentation of the condition of your home and of your health to prove tangible damages. Expert testimony from all of the following might be required: microbiologists, toxicologists, ventilation experts, mold remediation experts, dermatologists, pulmonary specialists, allergists, and psychologists. Tenants are more likely to recover damages for mold-related allergies than to prove permanent illness caused by mold. Extreme cases of mold have caused victims to became quite ill and lose most or all of their personal belongings. There have been some very large settlements won from homebuilders and insurers, which in turn has caused many insurance carriers to drop mold coverage from homeowners' and renters' insurance policies.

Lead Paint and Lead Hazards

Lead paint is common in most San Francisco homes—most

housing built before 1978 has it and the vast majority of San Francisco's housing was built before then. Cities on the East Coast have been dealing with this issue since the late 1960s, and now lead paint provisions are routinely built into city and state housing codes there. Steps are finally being taken in that direction here and tenants are developing some solid remedies.

Childhood Lead Poisoning

Lead paint is the major source of lead poisoning. Lead is dangerous for anyone, but its effects are most profound on children under the age of six because their central nervous systems are still developing. Elevated lead levels will cause slowed mental and physical growth, learning disabilities, hyperactivity and mental retardation. The amount of lead necessary to harm a child is very small and childhood behaviors make it pretty easy for children to get lead into their bodies. Deteriorating lead paint can create lead dust that children will get on their hands and then into their bodies when they put their fingers (or some object) in their mouths. Or children might eat a chip of lead paint when they mouth a windowsill with chipped lead paint. A chip of paint the size of a postage stamp will harm a child, but an adult is not in danger unless the amounts are far higher. Usually adults get poisoned through sanding lead paint or working in an industry that uses lead.

Lead-contaminated soil is another hazard. High levels of lead have been found in soil in San Francisco, mainly due to the use of leaded gasoline over many years, and also from the lead-based paint shed from the exterior of buildings. Other possible home lead hazards include ceramic ware, painted toys, imported canned goods and candies, and some home remedies.

Because lead poisoning mimics many common childhood sicknesses, parents are advised to have children tested regularly for lead poisoning. (Sometimes doctors must be told to do this since medical education on lead poisoning has been lax on the West Coast.) Children should be tested starting at age six months to one year up until the age of six.

There is no real medical treatment to reverse the effects of lead poisoning unless the child is near death, and the only accepted means of dealing with it is prevention.

Does My Home Have Lead Hazards?

Lead poisoning becomes most acute in poorly maintained housing. Lead paint can lie benign under other paint in housing that is well cared for. But the lead eventually will work its way to the surface and into the environment when normal maintenance and repairs are not made. Not surprisingly, lead poisoning is most

common in children living in rental housing.

A landlord must give every tenant the Environmental Protection Agency (EPA) pamphlet "Protect Your Family From Lead in Your Home," or a state-approved version of the pamphlet for most rental property built before 1978. Zero-bedroom dwellings, such as studios and single-room occupancy housing, are exempt on the theory that children will not be occupying the unit. Both the landlord and tenant must sign an EPA-approved disclosure form to prove that the landlord told the tenants about any known lead-based paint or hazards on the premises. Property owners must keep this disclosure form as part of their records for three years from the date the tenancy began. A landlord who fails to comply faces penalties of up to $10,000 for each violation and three times what the tenant suffered in damages. (42 U.S.C. § 4852d, Residential Lead-Based Paint Hazard Reduction Act of 1992, commonly known as Title X) However, not all landlords know the law, and not all know their property has lead hazards anyway.

The San Francisco Department of Public Health (DPH) estimates that 260,000 housing units in San Francisco were painted with leaded paint prior to 1978, one of the highest number of housing units in any U.S. city. But if the paint is intact—not chipping or wearing off—it is not a risk.

You can purchase lead test kits at most hardware stores, and certified professionals also do lead-based paint testing. A lead-based paint test is legal and legitimate, but is not very useful for determining lead-based paint hazards. The lead-based paint test merely gives a surface-by-surface result of whether or not the paint is positive for lead; these results do not usually indicate whether or not there is a hazard. It is not worth the bother unless the paint is deteriorated or the landlord is planning on doing work on the surfaces. You can consult a list of private inspectors who will test your home for lead, DPH, or find other resources at the California Department of Public Health's Lead Poisoning Prevention Branch, *www.cdph.ca.gov/programs/CLPPB/Pages/default.aspx.* DPH may also inspect your home if you make a complaint against your landlord (the complaint is not anonymous); this procedure is described in the following section.

Removing Lead Paint Hazards

Lead hazards are included as a "health nuisance" in the Health Code. (SF Health Code, Article 11, § 581)The code's definition of lead hazards is quite extensive: "…any condition that exposes children to lead from any source, including but not limited to lead-contaminated water, lead-contaminated dust, lead-contaminated soil, lead-based paint on impact surfaces, friction surfaces, or accessible surfaces, or deteriorated lead-based paint." This language gives the DPH broad authority to order the control or elimination of lead hazards.

DPH enforces the nuisance laws (SF Health Code, Article 11, § 596) using procedures similar to those of the Department of Building Inspection (DBI). If you have a child under age six in

your home, and you believe your home has lead hazards, you can contact DPH and issue a complaint against your landlord. We recommend a call followed up with a letter. If young children are frequent visitors to your home, or if you are pregnant, call DPH and tell them your situation. At its discretion, DPH will investigate complaints in homes without young children. DBI will also cite peeling paint.

DPH will send an inspector to your home to investigate. He may take paint, soil, or dust samples. If the inspector finds lead hazards, he will send the landlord a "Notice to Abate," which will specifically cite the locations of lead hazards and the probable cause (e.g. flaking paint around bedroom window caused by a leaking window frame). If the landlord does not abate the hazards within a maximum of thirty days, DPH will either get the problems fixed itself or post a Notice of a Director's Hearing, which will be held a few weeks later or a few days later if the paint constitutes a severe and immediate hazard to life, health or safety. After the hearing, the landlord has some more time to comply with a Director's Order to Abate, and to pay for a re-inspection by DPH. If the problems still do not get fixed, DPH will contract to have the problems fixed and bill the landlord for all expenses, putting a lien on the property if they don't get paid. Generally by this point, the case will have been referred to the City Attorney's office for action.

Article 26 of the San Francisco Health Code, the Comprehensive Environmental Lead Poisoning Investigation, Management and Enforcement Program, provides tenants with rights to have lead problems corrected if their children have tested positive for lead. Doctors and clinics are required to report elevated blood lead levels to DPH. (SF Health Code § 1621) In children, blood lead levels of 20 micrograms/deciliter (or consecutive tests of 15-19 micrograms/deciliter 3–4 months apart) are considered poisoned. For such poisoned children, a Public Health Nurse shall make a home visit to provide extensive teaching. In addition, a certified lead inspector/assessor shall perform an

---

WARNING! Don't Try to Abate Lead Yourself!

Do not try to remove lead paint yourself until you have learned the proper procedures to follow! Sanding, sawing, scraping, burning, etc. will cause the lead to become airborne in high concentrations which can easily be ingested or breathed in so that anyone living there will become severely poisoned—including adults and pets. Most paint remover solutions will also cause the lead to be airborne. Workers should be equipped with proper respirators and protective clothing (which should not be worn except while doing the lead abatement work).

environmental investigation and issue a report of lead hazard findings. The building owner and DBI shall also receive notice of lead hazard findings which are under the owner's control. (SF Health Code § 1617)

Tenants can use the same measures to compel their landlords to fix lead hazards as they do with any other serious code violations. See the previous sections in this chapter. For tenants covered under the Rent Ordinance's rent control, the tenant can petition the Rent Board. The Rent Board has ordered a rent reduction for at least one tenant whose child was poisoned. The Rent Ordinance specifies that lead remediation is assumed to be caused by deferred maintenance unless the landlord shows evidence otherwise. If the landlord does not show evidence otherwise, the cost of the lead remediation cannot be required to be paid by the tenant as a capital improvement passthrough. (SF Administrative Code § 37.3(e))

For lead poisoning, the Tenants Union has referrals to attorneys who specialize in lead litigation. In California, there is little case law so far on lead poisoning, because there are no state laws which expressly prohibit lead paint. However, lead hazards are defined. (CA Health and Safety Code § 17920.10) Also, in other states, landlords have been pressured to clean up lead paint largely because civil lawsuits for large damages have made it more economical for them to act responsibly than to be sued. Any such lawsuit would be based on the landlord's violation of laws rather than just the presence of lead paint. For instance, a tenant may be able to show that lead poisoning damages occurred because of the landlord's negligence in repairing code violations which caused lead to be released into the environment and poison a child. The suit would have to prove the landlord knew there was a danger and refused to correct it.

Proper Procedures for Lead Removal

Improper lead removal is one of the more serious causes of lead poisoning. The federal Environmental Protection Agency's "Lead Renovation, Repair and Painting Rule" (RRP Rule) became effective in 2010. The RRP Rule requires all renovation, repair, and painting firms, including sole proprietorships, working in housing where children are routinely present, and built before 1978, to be EPA certified for the work. Certified firms are provided a certificate and an identification number; ask to see it and check it at *https://cfpub.epa.gov/flpp/pub/index.cfm?do=main.firmSearch*.

The EPA rules also require the landlord to be a certified firm and use or be a certified renovator in two circumstances. (1) If the landlord does the renovation herself, then she must have firm and renovator certification. (2) If an employee of the landlord does the renovation work, then the landlord must have firm certification and the employee must be a certified renovator. A property management company acting as an agent for the landlord has the same responsibilities as the landlord under the RRP Rule. Therefore, if the property management company uses its own employees to do the work, the property management company must be a certified firm and one of the employees must be a certified renovator.

You can get information from DPH on how to work safely with lead-coated surfaces. If your landlord is doing renovation work, you should warn her (in writing, keeping a copy) of the dangers of disturbing lead paint. The warning can state that improper work practices will result in lead hazards, a violation of Health Code § 581. Ask her to contact the DPH to get information on how to do the work safely.

Activities that disturb painted surfaces on the interior and exterior of buildings built before December 31, 1978 are regulated. The owner must:

• Notify occupants three business days before work begins of the start date for the disturbance of lead-based paint.

• Provide occupants with a copy of the U.S. Environmental Protection Agency pamphlet titled "Renovate Right."

• Restrict access by third parties to the regulated area, except to areas required for access or egress during the course of the work, such as common areas, and where no alternative exists for access or egress, in which case dust generation shall be controlled through the use of HEPA-attached tools or other suitable containment.

• Contain the work debris within the regulated area.

• Remove all visible work debris at the completion of the work or when access to the regulated areas is required by law.

• For interior work, except for owner-occupied units, protect with the use of 6 millimeter plastic any horizontal surfaces, curtains, blinds, shades and furniture in the areas from work debris when it is impracticable to remove such items from the areas during the course of the work.

• Penalties for violations of up to $500 per violation per day and additional fees for the cost of enforcement.

(S.F. Building Code § 3423, §327)

• Contact the owner, DPH, DBI, or the EPA's hotline at 1-800-424-LEAD for violations.

Lead abatement is a just cause for temporary eviction of no more than thirty days. If safe to do so, it is best to stay in the unit while lead abatement work is being done so that this eviction is not abused. See the section "Lead Abatement Evictions" in *Chapter 12: Eviction Defenses* for more information.

Unauthorized Units and Lead Removal

A call to the Department of Building Inspection (DBI) to get an unauthorized unit inspected for lead hazards may result in the unit being ordered to be demolished and the tenant evicted. To encourage tenants in unauthorized units to report lead hazards, San Francisco law provides special relocation assistance to anyone whose unauthorized unit is shut down pursuant to a lead inspection. Tenants who are forced to move under these circumstances are required to receive from the landlord a payment of five months' fair market rent for a comparable home, in addition to the return of their security deposit. (SF Administrative Code § 72.3(b)(1)(C)) If the landlord does not provide the payment, the tenant's remedy is to sue.

The Department of Public Health is the agency responsible for lead inspection, unless the inspection is for lead-based paint disturbance or removal, which DBI deals with. DPH does not enforce code pertaining to unauthorized units, so call them if possible instead of DBI. DPH says that they are required to report housing code violations to DBI, but tenants may be able to prevent the code violations being reported to DBI by telling DPH that they cannot pass on the information. DBI cannot cite the unit unless they come in the unit because of a complaint or warrant.

Asbestos and Other Chemicals Causing Cancer or Reproductive Toxicity

Asbestos used to be a common building material. It was most commonly used in acoustical ceilings, textured wall paints and plaster, vinyl or linoleum floor backings, and boiler and heat duct insulation. Dwellings built prior to 1981 are assumed to contain asbestos. Under state Proposition 65 (passed in 1986), owners of rental property built before 1981 are required to disclose to residents that the building does or may contain asbestos or other chemicals specified in the law as causing cancer or other reproductive toxicity. (CA Health and Safety Code § 25249.6) For information on lead, see the previous section "Lead Paint and Lead Hazards." For information on pesticide applications, see the earlier section "Lead, Mold, Filth, and Pest Nuisances." For information on secondhand smoke, see the earlier section "Air Quality (Besides Lead, Mold, Filth) and Fire Hazards."

Asbestos is most dangerous when airborne or easily crumbled (friable); it breaks down into microscopic fibers which can lodge themselves in the lungs, causing severe illness. Asbestos is most apt to become airborne when renovation work is being performed, where there's water damage, crumbling ceilings or walls, or when there's a deteriorating heating system.

Currently, the law in this area only defines "safe" levels of airborne asbestos in schools and in the workplace. Dangerous levels of asbestos—even when airborne—have not yet been specifically defined by state or local law. However, the law requires that any person filing an application for a building permit to perform work in an apartment house or a residential hotel which includes asbestos-related work shall, before beginning any asbestos-related work, to notify tenants who will occupy areas of the location and quantity of asbestos-containing material. (Cal/OSHA-Title 8 Regulations, Subchapter 4, Article 4, § 1529(k)(2)(B)) Warning signs that mark the regulated areas must be displayed a distance so that an employee may be warned. (Cal/OSHA-Title 8 Regulations, Subchapter 4, Article 4, § 1529(k)(7)) In addition, state legislation mandates contractors and other employers who perform asbestos-related work to register with the Asbestos Contractors' Registration Unit. The registration requirement applies when work involves 100 square feet or more of asbestos-containing construction materials that have an asbestos content of more than 0.1%. More information on disclosure of asbestos can be found at *www.dir.ca.gov/dosh/ACRU/ACRUinfo.htm*.

A tenant is limited in the options he can pursue to eliminate any hazard; options such as rent withholding are not advisable unless the tenant is willing to risk eviction in hopes of winning a rare court ruling. Tenants covered under the Rent Ordinance's rent control can pursue the safer strategy of filing a petition with the San Francisco Rent Board for a "Decrease in Housing Services." (See the earlier section "Petitions for Lack of Services.") In the case favoring tenants, the Rent Board awarded a rent deduction for a potentially dangerous level of contamination from asbestos. However, the tenant had to hire a private company to test for the asbestos in the air and much of the argument revolved around the shoddiness of the asbestos removal techniques used. In the other Rent Board case, the Board ruled in favor of a landlord who sought to pass on costs of asbestos removal to the tenants as a capital improvement.

For possible dangerous asbestos in your home, you should:

- Arrange for testing to document that the asbestos has become airborne. You should attempt to get the Department of Building Inspection to do this testing, but you may have to find a private company. You may also make a complaint with the California Air Resources Board. (See "Government Agencies" in "Appendix A: Resources" for contact info.)

- Give written notice to the landlord, including a copy of the test results, and demand that he safely abate the asbestos. (Mail with a certificate of mailing or, even better, with delivery confirmation.)

- Contact the construction workers and inform them of their rights under the California Occupational Safety and Health Act of 1973 (Cal OSHA).

- File a Petition for Decrease in Housing Services with the Rent Board if you are covered under the Rent Ordinance's rent control; you will have to show how the asbestos has significantly affected you.

- Sue your landlord including, if you are covered under the Rent Ordinance, under San Francisco Administrative Code § 37.10B for three times the actual damages or $1,000, whichever is greater, and other relief if bad faith on the part of the landlord can be proven. Some courts have taken issue with the "bad faith" language in the ordinance.

- Call your legislators and demand that laws be passed defining asbestos in the home as a hazard and a Housing Code violation.

If faced with a capital improvement rent increase for a unit covered under the Rent Ordinance for asbestos removal, tenants should try to fight it. Asbestos removal, it can be argued, is normal maintenance and repair of the landlord's investment and the costs should not be borne by tenants.

"Cosmetic" Repairs

There may be occasions when you want changes made to your home which do not qualify as violations of law. For example, you would like new paint on the walls or the old carpets replaced. Your landlord may not legally be required to repaint or remodel "cosmetic" features where the condition does not pose a hazard. (See the previous section "Lead Paint and Lead Hazards" for more information on lead hazards.) A carpet that can be tripped on is an example of a hazardous condition that the landlord should repair, but there is no requirement that she recarpet, or repaint, etc., simply after a certain period of time.

Nevertheless, tenants have obtained significant rent reductions from the Rent Board for such conditions as a water-damaged carpet, cracked plaster revealing the wood underneath on a

"The paintballs were the only way my landlord was going to paint the building."

kitchen ceiling, and a stained countertop that has lost its finish. A Notice of Violation from the Department of Building Inspection would substantially improve the success of these petitions. What else can you do if the landlord refuses to make such changes?

(1) Get estimates as to how much the job will cost and ask the landlord if she would be willing to share the cost with you. Many landlords will agree to this since it improves the value of their property and, if the tenant is willing to provide the labor or make the arrangements, this saves the landlord the time and hassle.

(2) If the landlord refuses to pay for any of the improvements, you might offer to absorb the entire expense.

(3) Even if you are willing to pay for changes yourself, many rental agreements require that the tenant get approval from the landlord for any alterations to the rental unit. *If the tenant performs the work—even if it improves the unit— without permission, the landlord could evict the tenant for violation of the agreement.* So if your rental agreement has such a clause, be sure to get permission for any alteration in writing, signed by the landlord. If the rental agreement specifies that a tenant cannot commit "waste," a landlord can argue that any "change" is "waste," which is also, grounds for eviction. Written permission, with the landlord's signature, before you begin any alterations is critical to protect yourself from possible eviction.

Does a tenant have the right to be reimbursed for the costs of improvements if the landlord had not agreed to make them? Not likely. But if you can remove the improvement without damaging the property, you may take it with you when you move out as long as you restore the property to its previous condition. An exception is a "fixture," an item of personal property attached in such a permanent manner that it is deemed to have become part of the realty (shelving standards screwed into walls, for instance). Fixtures belong to the owner of the realty, even if they were installed by the tenant. (CA Civil Code § 660) The landlord may claim an improvement is a "fixture" and belongs to him, but courts tend to favor the tenant, usually concluding that the tenant intended the item for her own use rather than to attach it permanently to the realty. (See also the section on "Disability" in *Chapter 9: Discrimination* for information about improvements made for a disability.)

Fire or Other Disaster

If displaced by fire or other disaster, tenants who are not covered by the Rent Ordinance do not have a right to return unless it is provided for in the rental agreement. (CA Civil Code § 1933) Probably the best thing you can do is attempt to negotiate a right to return while you still have belongings in the unit.

However, under the San Francisco Rent Ordinance (see the section "What Does the Rent Ordinance Cover?" in *Chapter 4:*

Renting Basics), if a tenant is forced to vacate her unit due to fire or other disaster, the landlord must offer the renovated unit to the displaced tenant within 30 days of completing the repairs. The tenant has up to 30 days after the landlord offers the unit to inform the landlord whether she wants to accept or reject the offer, and she must re-occupy the unit within 45 days of receipt of the offer. The rental conditions remain the same as before the displacement. However, the landlord may petition the Rent Board for a capital improvement passthrough, to have the tenant pay for costs not reimbursed by insurance coverage. (SF Rent Board Rules and Regulations § 12.19. See the section "Capital Improvements" in *Chapter 7: Rent Increases* for more information.) If the landlord refuses to allow the tenant to return to the unit, this is a wrongful eviction and the landlord is liable to the displaced tenant for actual and punitive damages.

Tenants often ask: "Do I still have to pay rent to the landlord after a fire or other disaster forces me out? Am I entitled to a return of my deposit and the rent I already paid through the end of the month?" The answer depends on whether or not you can still live in your home. If you have been constructively evicted by the fire—in other words, your home has become uninhabitable— your rental obligation ends. If you are still living in the unit, you may still owe rent, although the reasonable rental value may be diminished due to damage caused by the fire. Talk with the landlord about working out a fair rent pending repairs. If he won't reduce the rent, consider filing a Decrease in Housing Services Petition at the Rent Board if you are covered under the Rent Ordinance's rent control. If the unit has been damaged to such a degree that an important reason for renting the unit no longer exists, (for example, there is now only one bedroom that is inhabitable and you have a roommate who needs a separate bedroom,) you can terminate the rental agreement as long as you were not the cause of the damage. (CA Civil Code § 1932)

If a tenant is forced to move out due to a fire or other disaster but the premises are not totally destroyed, the law is silent as to when the landlord must refund any unused portion of rent already paid or the deposit,. Most landlords would probably agree to pay immediately but, at worst, the money should be refunded three weeks after the tenant vacates. (CA Civil Code § 1950.5; also see *Chapter 5: Security Deposits*.) However, you may want your landlord to hold your deposit as evidence that you plan to return to the unit once the repairs are made. If the premises are totally destroyed, the landlord does not have to return advance payments of rent, since the rental agreement is effectively cancelled, unless there is an agreement otherwise, for example, on the rental agreement. (*Pedro v. Potter* (1926) 197 Cal. 751)

It is a good idea to submit a written claim to the landlord's insurance company soon after the damage is assessed. Make a list of all items damaged or destroyed. If you get personal belongings cleaned, or if you must eat at restaurants, keep the receipts. When you estimate the actual monetary loss, you should claim the replacement value, although insurance companies are notorious for avoiding paying for the true value of loss.

Consider carrying renter's insurance. Renter's insurance will protect your personal property in the case of fire or other disaster when the landlord is not negligent, as well as from theft. Another protection of renter's insurance can be that if you cause damage to the building, or to another tenant's property, or if a guest is injured in your home, damages may be covered by your policy. Policies start around $15 a month (2021). It is legal, under California law, for a landlord to include a clause in the rental agreement requiring a tenant to pay for renter's insurance. However, in a court case, the landlord was not able to evict a tenant for breach of the rental agreement because the tenant did not have renter's insurance as required by the rental agreement. (*Nivo 1 LLC v. Antunez* (2013) 217 Cal. App. 4th Supp. 1)

If you lose your possessions or you are forced to move because of a disaster, must your landlord give you relocation expenses and reimburse you for your losses? Unhappily, there is no required relocation payment and the landlord has no obligation to cover a tenant's losses from a fire or other disaster unless it can be proved that the landlord (or agent) was negligent in causing the disaster which resulted in the losses. (CA Civil Code § 1714) If the fire was accidental or caused by a third person's negligence or criminal conduct, the landlord is not responsible for the tenant's losses.

A couple of examples where a landlord could be found negligent:

Example One: The landlord (or property manager) knew the electrical system in the building was dangerous (short circuits, frayed wiring, overloaded circuits) and did nothing to repair it, and the fire was caused by the malfunctioning electrical system.

Example Two: The landlord knew that flammable materials were stored in an area of the building without sprinklers and ignored the risk by not removing the danger, and the fire was accidentally caused by a careless smoker or other person.

Landlords can temporarily rent at a reduced rate to a tenant who has been displaced by a disaster. See the section "Expiration of Good Samaritan Occupancy Status" in *Chapter 7: Rent Increases* for more information.

San Francisco tenants who experienced a fire in a rent-controlled apartment may qualify for a Displaced Tenant Housing Preference Certificate which provides a lottery preference for affordable housing. The tenant must not be able to return to the unit within a period of six months. (SF Administrative Code §§ 47.2, 47.3) See "Appendix A: Resources" for info about the Displaced Tenant Housing Preference Program. Contact info is listed under "Government Agencies" > "Mayor's Office" > "Housing and Community Development."

Chapter 7: **Rent Increases**

State law is usually the only law that applies to rent increases, but the San Francisco Bay Area cities of Alameda, Berkeley, Campbell, Concord, East Palo Alto, Emeryville, Fremont, Hayward, Los Gatos, Mountain View, Oakland, Richmond, San Francisco, San Jose, and Union City have rent increase laws, as well. San Mateo, San Rafael, and properties with 3 or more units in the unincorporated areas of Marin County (including Marin City) have just cause for eviction protection.

Rent Increases Under California Law

Until 2030, California state law limits how much rent may be increased unless your rental unit is exempt. See the section "Protections for the Tenant Under the San Francisco Rent Ordinance and State Law" in "Chapter 4: Renting Basics" for more info. The San Francisco Rent Ordinance would apply instead of state rent control if the unit qualifies for the Rent Ordinance.

For units covered only under California rent control, annual rent increases are capped at 5 percent plus the cost of living increase or 10 percent, whichever is lower, for tenants who have occupied the unit for 12 months or more. Search online for "sf cpi" to find the cost of living increase between April 1 of the current year and the previous year. For April 2022, the cost of living is 5% over the previous year for the San Francisco Area, so the **total annual increase is up to 10% until April 2023**. (The California Apartment Association recommends using the March number for the prior calendar year if the April number is not available, *https://caanet.org/where-are-the-new-cpi-figures-for-rent-increases-under-ab-1482.*) The base rent used to calculate the rent increase as of January 1, 2020 is the rent that was in effect on March 15, 2019. (CA Civil Code § 1947.12) Rent increases which are discriminatory (see "Chapter 9: Discrimination"), retaliatory (see the box "Retaliation Is Illegal" in "Chapter 6: Repairs and Services"), or rent increases over 10% of costs following a state of emergency declaration (CA Penal Code § 396, *https://caloes.ca.gov/cal-oes-divisions/legal-affairs/price-gouging*) are prohibited. Tenants with rent debt due to COVID-19 and who have submitted a declaration may not have fees increased or charged for services previously provided without charge. (CA Civil Code § 1942.9, check for amendment)

For rent increases of ten percent or less, a thirty-day written notice must be given. For rent increases over ten percent, including any rent increases in a twelve month period which cumulatively exceed ten percent, a ninety-day written notice is required. So, if a landlord gave a five percent increase on May 1, 2022 and then a seven percent increase on July 1, 2022, the second increase would require a ninety-day notice. (CA Civil Code § 827)

Service of the notice is by delivering the notice to the tenant personally or by mail. If served by regular mail, service is complete at the time of the mail deposit in a post office or mailbox, but at least five days are added to the notice time. Out of state mail requires additional days. (See California Code of Civil Procedure § 1013 in "Appendix D: California Law Excerpts.") The rent increase notice starts counting on the day after the service is complete. (CA Code of Civil Procedure § 12) For example, if you receive a rent increase notice in person on April 30, May 1 is the first day of the notice period until you must pay the new rent. If the last day of the notice falls on a weekend or holiday (as defined in California Code of Civil Procedure § 12a), the notice period is extended to the next day that is not a holiday.

The number of times in a year in which a owner can raise the rent is limited to two unless your unit is exempt from rent control. However, if you have a lease, your rent cannot be raised during the period of the lease even with a written notice, unless the terms of the lease allow this. Excluding the exceptions in this section, tenants who do not have rent control can have their rent increased by any amount, at any time, so long as the landlord provides the proper written notice.

You may request the SF Rent Board contact your landlord (use the request form called Report of Excessive Rent Increase Under the Tenant Protection Act) if you believe your landlord has increased your rent in noncompliance with California rent control. The Rent Board will not enforce the law, but having a government agency contacting your landlord may encourage compliance.

Single Residential Units

Single residential units (alienable separate from the title to any other dwelling unit) and exempt from rent control (CA Civil Code § 1947.12(d)(5)) where the tenancy began or renewed on or after July 1, 2020 must include the following statement in the written rental agreement: "This property is not subject to the rent limits imposed by Section 1947.12 of the Civil Code and is not subject to the just cause requirements of Section 1946.2 of the Civil Code. This property meets the requirements of Sections 1947.12 (c)(5) [sic] and 1946.2 (e)(7) of the Civil Code and the owner is not any of the following: (1) a real estate investment trust, as defined by Section 856 of the Internal Revenue Code; (2) a corporation; or (3) a limited liability company in which at least one member is a corporation." (Check for amendments to this law at *https://leginfo.legislature.ca.gov.*) For tenancies that existed before July 1, 2020, the statement does not have to be in the rental agreement.

Rent Increases Under San Francisco Rent Control

The San Francisco Rent Ordinance (see the section "What Does the Rent Ordinance Cover?" in "Chapter 4: Renting Basics") would apply instead of state rent control if the unit qualifies for the Rent Ordinance. (CA Civil Code § 1947.12(k)(3)) The Rent Ordinance limits how much the rent can be increased, how often,

Vacancy Control

The San Francisco Rent Ordinance limits the initial rent in the following cases.

1. After the following just causes for evictions, the subsequent tenant's initial rent is limited:
   a. Capital Improvement
   b. Condo Conversion Sale
   c. Demolition Without a Development Agreement with the City of San Francisco
   d. Ellis Act
   e. Owner Move-In
   f. Lead Abatement

   The tenant may file an Unlawful Rent Increase Petition for illegal rent for these causes.

2. Single residential units (title is separate from other dwelling units) may have rent limitations.

3. Subtenancies may have rent limitations after the original tenant vacates.

4. Change in terms under California Civil Code § 827, except for a legal change in rent, resulting in termination of the preceding tenancy.

5. Nonrenewal of an agreement with the government that provided for rent limitation to the preceding tenancy.

See the specific section in "Chapter 12: Eviction Defenses" for more info on #1, "Single Residential Unit" in "Chapter 4: Renting Basics" for #2, "Chapter 10: Roommates" in "Rent Increase When Original Tenant Vacates" for #3, and San Francisco Administrative Code § 37.3(f) in "Appendix C: Law Excerpts" for #4 and #5.

and for what reason. Some increases can be given to tenants without prior Rent Board approval while others require prior approval. In addition, the rent control law provides a mechanism for tenants to contest rent increases, as discussed in the later section "Contesting Rent Increases Which Do Not Require Rent Board Approval."

Rent Increases Not Requiring Approval of the Rent Board

Annual Rent Increases

The San Francisco Rent Ordinance allows a landlord to increase your rent once a year without going to the Rent Board for permission, although the proper notice must be given, as discussed in the previous section "Rent Increases under California Law." Starting July 1, 2022, a landlord is required to report information about their rental unit to the Rent Board to obtain a license to impose the rent increase. The annual rent increase is computed as 60% of the increase of the San Francisco-Oakland Consumer Price Index from the previous year (the residential rent component of the Bay Area Cost of Living Index) but capped at 7%. (SF Administrative Code § 37.3(a)(1)) The federal Department of Labor Statistics furnishes this info to the Rent Board around December 20 each year. The allowable percentage increase is published by the Rent Board each January for the period from March through the following February. The annual increase can be given only once every 12 months, on or after your "anniversary date" (SF Rent Board Rules and Regulations § 1.11), which is 1 year after your current rent became effective.

Example: Sam moved into his rent-controlled flat on November 1, 2013. His monthly rent at the time he moved in was $2,000.00 and the unit is covered by the Rent Ordinance. The landlord cannot raise Sam's rent until November 1, 2014 — 1 year after he moved in. Then his landlord may impose a 1% increase of $20. With proper notice, Sam's rent may be increased to $2,020.

The anniversary date may change according to when the landlord imposes the annual rent increase. For example, if Sam's landlord did not impose the rent increase until December 1, 2014, December 1 would become Sam's anniversary date.

The "annual rent increase" (SF Rent Board Rules and Regulations § 1.12) is calculated based on the tenant's base rent. Base rent is defined as that rent charged a tenant upon initial occupancy, plus any allowable annual rent increases later added by the landlord. (SF Administrative Code § 37.2(a)) In the previous example, Sam's base rent when he moves in is $2,000. His base rent after the 2014 rent increase is $2,020. Base rent does not include passthroughs of the landlord's costs for capital improvements, water penalties, or PG&E costs, but it does include annual and banked increases as well as those based on operating and maintenance costs and comparable units. (The following sections discuss these types of allowable rent increases.)

"Banking" Past Annual Rent Increases

A landlord may "bank," or save up, the annual rent increases that were not imposed in prior years, and then increase the rent for the accumulated amount in a later year. Banked rent increases may be given in addition to the current annual rent increase without obtaining Rent Board approval. However, the banked increase may only be added on or after the tenant's anniversary date, with the proper notice. (See the previous section "Rent Increases under California Law" for the notice requirement.)

In general, a landlord can bank rent increases going back as far as April 1982. Banking is a little different for landlord-occupied 2-4 unit buildings, which were not brought under rent control until December 22, 1994 after the passage of 1994's Proposition I. The

Chapter 7– Rent Increases

Rent Board passed a "good landlord" regulation for landlords of Proposition I units who had not raised rents in the years prior to 1994, allowing additional rent increases. (SF Rent Board Rules and Regulations § 6.11(b)) If the landlord of Proposition I units gave a rent increase between May 1, 1994 and December 22, 1994, then the rent should have been rolled back to the May 1, 1994 level since May 1, 1994 is the starting date for rent control of Proposition I units.

The allowed annual increase limitations from April 1982 to date:

April 1982–February 1984	7.0%
March 1984–February 1992	4.0%
March 1992–December 7, 1992	4.0%*
December 8, 1992–February 1993	1.6%*
March 1993–February 1994	1.9%
March 1994–February 1995	1.3%
March 1995–February 1996	1.1%
March 1996–February 1997	1.0%
March 1997–February 1998	1.8%
March 1998–February 1999	2.2%
March 1999–February 2000	1.7%
March 2000–February 2001	2.9%
March 2001–February 2002	2.8%
March 2002–February 2003	2.7%
March 2003–February 2004	0.8%
March 2004–February 2005	0.6%
March 2005–February 2006	1.2%
March 2006–February 2007	1.7%
March 2007–February 2008	1.5%
March 2008–February 2009	2.0%
March 2009–February 2010	2.2%
March 2010–February 2011	0.1%
March 2011–February 2012	0.5%
March 2012–February 2013	1.9%
March 2013–February 2014	1.9%
March 2014–February 2015	1.0%
March 2015–February 2016	1.9%
March 2016–February 2017	1.6%
March 2017–February 2018	2.2%
March 2018–February 2019	1.6%
March 2019–February 2020	2.6%
March 2020–February 2021	1.8%
March 2021–February 2022	0.7%
March 2022–February 2023	2.3%

* Note that there are two different percentages for the year 3/92–2/93. The banking allowed would be either 1.6% or

4%, depending on when in this period the anniversary date falls; the landlord cannot bank both rent increases for the same year. For annual rent increases after the years listed, check the Rent Board's Web Site.

Example: Tom has resided in a residential rental unit covered by the San Francisco Rent Ordinance since May 1, 1981. His landlord has not increased Tom's rent since he moved in. He pays $500 per month (his base rent). On March 1, 2003, Tom receives a notice that his rent will be increased 70.2% effective May 1, 2003 to $851.00. This increase includes the May 2003 annual increase of 0.8%, plus 69.4% in banked increases (5/82-7%, 5/83-7%, 5/84-4%, 5/85-4%, 5/86-4%, 5/87-4%, 5/88-4%, 5/89-4%, 5/90-4%, 5/91-4%, 5/92-4%, 5/93-1.9%, 5/94-1.3%, 5/95-1.1%, 5/96-1.0%, 5/97-1.8%, 5/98-2.2%, 5/99-1.7%, 5/00-2.9%, 5/01-2.8%, and 5/02-2.7%). The landlord cannot raise the rent again until May 1, 2004 and has no more banked rent increases.

The banked amount is not compounded; in other words, the landlord cannot impose the increase on each year's banked rent after adding in the annual increase. The last base rent is used to compute the banked amounts. (SF Rent Board Rules and Regulations § 4.12 (a))

The landlord is supposed to provide a breakdown of the banked rent increase percentages, but even if she doesn't, if the total amount is correct the increase is permitted. (SF Rent Board Rules and Regulations § 4.12 (b)) A landlord does not have to take all banked increases to which she is entitled at once. If she does not take the entire banked increase, the remainder stays banked and may be imposed on or after the next anniversary date. You may be able to negotiate a smaller banked increase by informing your landlord that she will not lose the ability to take it later.

Reinstating Original Rent If Rent Was Lowered

It's pretty rare, but suppose that your landlord lowers your rent. Can she later raise the rent back to the old rent without regard to the usual Rent Ordinance limits, or is she permitted to raise the rent only the usual allowable amount? The Rent Board's policy depends on whether the reduction was a favor to a tenant who is facing financial difficulties or was in response to a falling rental housing market. If the landlord made it clear that the rent reduction was related to the tenant's hard times, then she would be able to increase the rent in the future based on the old (pre-reduction) base rent. (*https://sfrb.org/topic-no-264-temporary-rent-reduction-agreements*) If the new rent amount was not due to the tenant's financial difficulties, the new rent becomes the base rent, the effective date of the new rent becomes the anniversary date, and no banking prior to the reduction in rent is allowed.

If you are trying to negotiate a reduction in rent, make it clear that the reduction is not a favor from the landlord, and is due to a falling housing market. Avoid explaining the possibility of reserving the right to raise the rent in the future unless it's the only way to get a temporary reduction. See also the following section "Expiration of Good Samaritan Occupancy Status."

Expiration of Good Samaritan Occupancy Status

Good Samaritan occupancy status is when a landlord agrees in writing for the tenant to start a temporary occupancy following an emergency such as a fire or earthquake that required the tenant to vacate his unit unexpectedly. The "Good Samaritan" landlord agrees to rent the tenant a replacement unit at a reduced rent for a specified period of up to twelve months. The reduced rent can be up to 10% above the base rent the tenant was paying for his previous unit at the time of the emergency. For example, if a displaced tenant moves from a $1500/month apartment into one that would ordinarily rent for $2000, the landlord can charge no more than $1650/month. An exception is if the owner of the replacement unit is the same as the owner of the original unit. In this case the reduced rent is the same rent the tenant was paying for the previous unit at the time of the emergency—$1500 in our example. The agreement must be in writing and must include a statement that the agreement is temporary, refer to San Francisco Administrative Code Section 37.2(a)(1)(D), and state that the tenant has been displaced from his previous unit as certified by an official authorized by law. The landlord and tenant may agree, in writing, to extend the reduced rent up to a total of 24 months.

The Good Samaritan Status Period rental agreement may state what the new base rent for the unit can be after the Good Samaritan rental period expires. In this case, within sixty days after the expiration of the Good Samaritan Status Period the landlord may give notice of a rent increase from the temporary reduced rent to the new rent.

If sixty days elapse after expiration of the Good Samaritan Status Period without the landlord serving a notice to increase the rent (to no more than the previously agreed upon rent for the unit) or serving an eviction notice under San Francisco Administrative Code § 37.9(a)(16), the tenant's occupancy is no longer temporary and the landlord cannot evict the tenant from the rental unit unless there is a just cause other than the expiration of the Good Samaritan Occupancy Status. The tenant's current reduced rent rate will become the tenant's initial base rent and the landlord may not increase it by more than the amounts allowed by the Rent Board.

General Obligation Bond Passthroughs

Landlords may pass through 50% of the cost of most general obligation bonds to tenants. To impose the passthrough, the landlord must provide a copy of the completed Bond Measure

Passthrough Worksheet to the tenant on *https://sfrb.org*. (The current assessed value of the property, which is required on the form, may be found at *https://sfassessor.org*.) The passthrough must be imposed on the tenant's rent increase anniversary date, and the proper notice must be given. (See the earlier section "Rent Increases under California Law" for additional notice requirements.)

The passthrough shall not become part of the tenant's base rent (and thus not included in calculating future annual rent increases). If imposed in 2020 or before, it must be discontinued after twelve months. Starting 2021, the passthrough applies for the same number of months as the property tax bills for the calculation. (See SF Administrative Code § 37.3(a)(6) in "Appendix C: San Francisco Law and Regulations Excerpts" for the details.) Bond measure passthroughs may be banked and imposed in future years. However, starting 2021, passthroughs are limited to going back three years. The tenant may file a challenge petition to the general obligation bond passthrough within one year of its effective date.

General obligation bonds include school bonds. Seniors (65 or older) may apply for exemption from some school bonds, *https://www.sfusd.edu/senior-citizen-exemption-office*.

Water Passthroughs

Water Revenue Bond Passthrough

A landlord may pass through 50% of the charges for the Water System Improvement Revenue Bonds authorized in the November 2002 election to any unit in compliance with any applicable law for water conservation devices. (SF Administrative Code § 37.3(5), Rent Board Rules and Regulations § 4.14) To impose the passthrough, the landlord must provide a copy of the completed Water Revenue Bond Passthrough Worksheet on *https://sfrb.org*. The landlord must also provide copies of the water bill(s) if the tenant requests them. The tenant may file a hardship appeal with the Rent Board. (See the section "Hardship Appeal at Tenant's Request" in "Chapter 14: Taking Action.")

Water Penalty Passthroughs

Landlords may pass through 50% of penalties for excess water use to the tenants in buildings with a common meter (see "Submetered Water" in "Chapter 6: Repairs and Services" for excess water charges for submetered water) if the landlord provides tenants with written certification that:

- Permanently-installed retrofit devices designed to reduce the amount of water used per flush or low-flow toilets (1.6 gallons per flush) have been installed in all units.
- Low-flow showerheads which allow a flow of no more than 2.5 gallons per minute have been installed in all units.
- Faucet aerators (where installation on current faucets is physically feasible) have been installed in all units.
- No known plumbing leaks currently exist in the building and that any leaks reported by tenants in the future will be promptly repaired.

Additionally, the landlord must provide the tenants with a copy of the water bill. If the increase causing a penalty is over 25%, and where that increase does not appear to result from any known use, then the landlord may not impose any increase unless inspection by a licensed plumber or Water Department inspector fails to reveal a leak.

If requested, the landlord must make a good faith effort to represent tenants' interests at an appeal hearing (based on increased occupancy) before the Water Department.

The passthrough is calculated on a per room basis. If the tenant objects to the calculations or procedure, she can file a Summary Petition (there is no hearing; see the section "Summary Petition for Unlawful Rent Increases" later in this chapter) with the Rent Board. The Rent Board will decide if the passthrough is justified and may require an inspection by the Water Department. The tenant must object within sixty days following receipt of the notice of excess water use charges. This passthrough will not become part of the tenant's base rent and will not continue unless the penalties continue. (SF Administrative Code § 37.3(5)) The tenant's failure to pay the demanded amount is not a just cause for eviction, as the passthrough is not defined as a rent increase. (SF Administrative Code § 37.2(q)) The owner must seek relief for nonpayment in court or through an arbitration/mediation service. (SF Rent Board Rules and Regulations § 4.13)

Gas, Electricity or Steam Heat Passthroughs

SOME UTILITY PASSTHROUGHS REQUIRE RENT BOARD APPROVAL, AS EXPLAINED BELOW.

A landlord may have the tenant pay for increased costs for utilities. (SF Administrative Code § 37.3(a)(4)) From November 1, 2004–December 31, 2008, the landlord was required to file a Rent Board petition for approval of utility passthroughs. (The Rent Ordinance defines utilities as only including gas and electricity, but the Rent Board petition for utility passthroughs

also includes steam heat.) Beginning January 1, 2009, the landlord is required to file a petition only where the landlord is comparing utility costs for the 2 most recent calendar years. (SF Rent Board Rules and Regulations § 6.16) A Rent Board Administrative Law Judge (ALJ) must approve the petition for the passthrough to take effect. For all other base years, the landlord is required to file only a Utility Passthrough Calculation Worksheet form, available at *https://sfrb.org*, which does not need approval by the ALJ. The method for calculating the passthrough is in the Rent Board's utility passthrough petition and worksheet forms.

Every petition and worksheet must be filed with the Rent Board before giving the tenant a notice of rent increase for the passthrough. Where a petition is required, the tenant does not have to pay the passthrough until an ALJ orders the payment. However, any passthrough that is granted will be retroactive to the effective date of a valid notice of increase. Where a worksheet is required, the passthrough is due on the effective date in the notice of rent increase. (See the previous section "Rent Increases under California Law" for notice requirements.) If the landlord has filed a petition for approval of the utility passthrough, the Rent Board will mail a copy of the petition to the tenant shortly after it is filed.

The tenant can object to the passthrough by filing a petition. (SF Rent Board Rules and Regulations § 10.13. See the section later in this chapter "Contesting Rent Increases Which Do Not Require Rent Board Approval.") The tenant's petition must be filed within one year of the effective date of the passthrough. The petition will be reviewed by an ALJ and decided without a hearing unless the ALJ determines that a hearing is required. If the petition is decided without a hearing, the tenant will receive a written decision in the mail. If a hearing is required, the parties will receive written notice of the hearing.

If the landlord has filed a Utility Passthrough Calculation Worksheet instead of a petition, the landlord must serve the tenant with a copy of the worksheet, date-stamped by the Rent Board, with the notice of increase for the passthrough. The Rent Board reviews 10% of all worksheets filed with the Board to determine if the passthrough is correctly calculated. If the Board determines that a hearing is required, the parties will receive written notice of the hearing. If the landlord fails to serve the tenant with a copy of the worksheet or if the tenant believes that the landlord did not properly calculate the passthrough, the tenant may file a petition at the Rent Board to challenge the imposition of the passthrough within one year of the effective date of the passthrough. A hearing will be scheduled and the landlord will have the burden of proving that the passthrough was correct.

The utility passthrough does not become part of the tenant's base rent, and thus is not included in the calculation for the annual rent increase. The passthrough can only be imposed at the same time as the annual increase and applies only for the twelve-month period after it is imposed. In order to bank a utility passthrough, the landlord must have filed a timely Petition for Approval of

Utility Passthrough or Utility Passthrough Calculation Worksheet with the Rent Board. In such case, the landlord may "bank" all or a portion of the utility passthrough and impose it at a later date, so long as it is imposed at the time of an annual rent increase. (SF Rent Board Rules and Regulations § 5.13(b) and § 6.16(m)) By this method, more than one utility passthrough may be imposed at the same time. The notice of rent increase must specify the dollar amount of each utility passthrough. Each utility passthrough must be discontinued twelve months after it is imposed. If the passthrough is not discontinued after twelve months, the tenant can file a petition at the Rent Board for a refund. There is no time limit for filing such a petition.

If payment of a utility passthrough causes a financial hardship for the tenant, the tenant may seek relief by filing a Hardship Application form with the Board within one year of the effective date of the passthrough. Payment of the passthrough is suspended from the date of filing until a decision is made on the Tenant Financial Hardship Application. For a passthrough based on a petition from the landlord, the hardship application cannot be filed until the tenant receives the notice of rent increase or decision of the Administrative Law Judge, whichever is earlier. ("See the section "Hardship Appeal at Tenant's Request" in "Chapter 14: Taking Action" for more info.)

Original Tenant Moves Out

The landlord may be able to raise the rent when all of the "original" tenants have left but other tenants remain. What defines an "original" tenant, however, is a complicated question. A tenant does not have to be named on the agreement, nor does the tenant have to have lived there from the beginning in order to be protected from rent increases. See the section "Rent Increases When Original Tenant Vacates" in *Chapter 10: Roommates* for discussion of this situation.

Rent Board Fee

See the box "Rent Board Fee" in *Chapter 5: Security Deposits*.

Contesting Rent Increases Which Do Not Require Rent Board Approval

Even though some types of rent increases do not need the approval of the Rent Board, as described in the previous section, tenants may challenge them for certain reasons. A tenant can object because of improper procedure or calculation for a rent increase or passthrough, or because the increase is not justified due to the landlord's lack of maintenance and repair. Rent increases which clearly fall outside the guidelines because the landlord believes the unit is exempt from rent control can also be challenged.

Before filing a petition with the Rent Board it is usually a good idea to write the landlord a letter, explaining specifically why you believe the rent increase is incorrect. There are two reasons for doing this: first, the landlord may agree and simply cancel the rent increase; and second, a letter shows a good faith effort by you to give the landlord notice, and will be great evidence if you do end up going to the Rent Board. See the following sections and *Chapter 14: Taking Action* for more info, including appeals based on financial hardship.

A landlord must give you a thirty or ninety-day (ninety days for rent increases over 10%) written notice of the rent increase and inform the tenant on or before the date the notice is given which portion reflects the annual increase, the banked amount (if any), the costs of any capital improvements, rehabilitation or energy conservation work which has been certified by the Rent Board, or any passthroughs. (SF Rent Board Rules and Regulations § 4.10) If the landlord fails to give the required notice in the proper form, or if the rent increase is in excess of the allowable amount, the entire rent increase may be "null and void." However, if the landlord has not provided a breakdown of the banked rent increase percentages but has imposed an allowable banked rent increase, that increase will be permitted to stand. (SF Rent Board Rules and Regulations § 4.12 (b))

If your landlord has not been paying the interest on your deposit (see the section "Interest on Deposits" in *Chapter 5: Security Deposits*) this may be a possible defense to a rent increase.

If a tenant receives a rent increase notice that he believes is defective, it is best to check with the Rent Board (if the rental unit may be covered under the Rent Ordinance) before the increase goes into effect. If the Rent Board determines that the rent increase notice appears to be defective, they will ask the tenant to file a Summary Petition or a petition for a hearing. (See the following sections.) In order to prevent the landlord from attempting to evict for nonpayment of rent, it may be best for the tenant to pay the disputed increase under protest until the determination by the Rent Board. (To pay under protest, accompany the check with a signed and dated letter stating the reason for the protest, and write on the check "paid under protest.") If the tenant is right, the landlord will have to refund any excess rent paid by the tenant and is subject to prosecution for a criminal misdemeanor. (SF Administrative Code § 37.10A)

In some instances, where landlords are not confident that they can increase the rent legally, they may file a lawsuit claiming, for instance, that no original tenant lives in the rental unit and so the remaining roommates can have their rent increased, or some similar argument. These lawsuits are called "declaratory relief actions." Tenants can defend themselves from such rent increases by filing a response in court called a "demurrer." The reasoning is that the landlord is trying to exhaust the resources of low-income tenants by forcing them to defend themselves in court, ultimately driving them out of the unit and raising the rent for a new tenant, and the matter is better resolved at the Rent Board. The Tenants

Chapter 7 – Rent Increases

Union has a list of attorneys who can file the demurrer.

Summary Petition for Unlawful Rent Increases

The Summary Petition provides a way to challenge a defective rent increase notice if you believe that the proposed rent increase notice clearly does not comply with the Rent Ordinance. With a Summary Petition there is no hearing. You must file the petition at least seven to ten days before the increase is to take effect to give the Rent Board sufficient time to review your petition and notify the landlord before the rent increase takes effect. You should include a copy of the landlord's rent increase notice, your rent increase history, notification from the Rent Board about capital improvements (if any), and a statement of why you believe the rent increase should not be allowed, together with any supporting documentation. (SF Rent Board Rules and Regulations § 9.10)

If the increase is incorrect, the Rent Board staff will send you and the landlord a letter stating that the *entire* rent increase is "null and void," not just the overcharge. The landlord will then have to start the process over with a new notice.

The Summary Petition process can only be used for rent increase notices which are clearly and on their face defective—for example, a 25% annual rent increase on the tenant's first anniversary date. In other cases, tenants will have to file a petition alleging unlawful rent increases. (See the following section "Unlawful Rent Increase Petition.")

Unlawful Rent Increase Petition

A tenant may file an Unlawful Rent Increase Petition at the Rent Board alleging that a proposed rent increase exceeds the allowable increase. (Passthroughs that are incorrect are challenged with a different petition. See the following section, "Passthrough Challenges by Petition." A rent increase notices that is clearly defective on its face and will not take effect for at least 10 day may be challenged with a Summary Petition. See the previous section "Summary Petition for Unlawful Rent Increases.") The Rent Board counselors will sometimes do the calculation of the proper rent increase.

The tenant may also file the Unlawful Rent Increase Petition if she believes that at some time in the past (after April 1, 1982 for most units; after May 1, 1994 for Proposition I units) the landlord has unlawfully increased the rent over the allowable limits. (See the section "Rent Increases Not Requiring Rent Board Approval.") If the landlord has unlawfully increased the rent, the past rent increase(s) may be determined to be "null and void" under the Rent Ordinance. This will result in the rent being recalculated

by the Rent Board from that time forward. Even though a rent increase may be determined to be null and void as far back as April 1982 (May 1, 1994 for Proposition I units), the Rent Board judge can only allow a refund of rent overpayments back to three years prior to the filing of the petition. (SF Administrative Code § 37.8(e)(7)) Furthermore, a landlord can try to keep the tenant from being allowed a refund of rent overpayments by arguing that the tenant "sat on her rights" and waited too long to file to the detriment of the landlord (a legal theory called "laches").

An alternative to petitioning the Rent Board for back rent would be to sue the landlord for the amount owed, which could also include attorney's fees, court costs, and interest. (SF Administrative Code § 37.11A) Keep in mind, though, that the Rent Board knows the rent law far better than the courts do, and a tenant's chances may be much better before the Rent Board than in court.

If you receive notice of a rent increase because your landlord does not think you are covered by rent control and you believe that your unit is covered, you should file a petition with the Rent Board alleging an unlawful rent increase.

Failure to Repair and Maintain Petition

To stop rent increases except for certified capital improvements, rehabilitation and energy conservation when the landlord has failed to provide required repairs and maintenance, see the section "Failure to Repair and Maintain Petitions" in "Chapter 6: Repairs and Services" for info.

Passthrough Challenges by Petition

A tenant may file a petition at the Rent Board alleging that a passthrough of the landlord's costs has been incorrectly imposed or not discontinued when it should have been. The Challenges to Passthroughs Petition may be used for gas and electric passthroughs, water revenue bond passthroughs, general obligation bond measure passthroughs (see the previous sections on passthroughs) or capital improvement passthroughs that have not been discontinued when they should have been (see the section on "Capital Improvements" later in this chapter).

Rent Increases Requiring Rent Board Approval

If your landlord wants an increase in excess of the annual rent increase or in addition to the "automatic" increases or passthroughs described in the previous sections, he must obtain prior approval from the Rent Board. To do so, the landlord must file a petition with the Rent Board for a hearing on the proposed rent increase (except for some utility passthroughs that do not require a hearing; see the section "Gas, Electricity or Steam Heat Passthroughs"). At the hearing, the landlord must prove actual cost increases. An exception is when the landlord contests the unit as the tenant's principal place of occupancy; see the section "Tenant Not in Occupancy" later in this chapter. The landlord must provide supporting documentation with the petition. This is to give tenants a chance to review the reason for the increase in order to prepare a defense.

The Rent Board will notify the tenant of the landlord's application for a rent increase and the hearing date. See the sections "Hearing for Capital Improvement Passthroughs" and "Hearing for Operating and Maintenance Expense Rent Increase" later in this chapter, and the "Petition the Rent Board" and "Preparing for a Hearing" sections in *Chapter 14: Taking Action* for more info.

Only after filing the petition may the landlord give the tenant written notice of the proposed rent increase. The tenant is not obligated to pay the petitioned portion of the increase until approved by the Rent Board. However, if the increase is approved, it will be retroactive to the effective date of the rent increase notice. (SF Rent Board Rules and Regulations § 5.13) Tenants who choose to wait for the Rent Board to approve the increase before paying should set aside the money to avoid being evicted for nonpayment.

The following types of rent increase require a petition from the landlord to the Rent Board and the Rent Board's approval:

1. Passthrough to the tenant of the landlord's costs for capital improvement (usually includes energy conservation measures) and rehabilitation.
2. Rent increase for increased operating and maintenance costs.
3. Removal of a tenant from rent increase protection because the unit is not the tenant's principal place of occupancy.
4. Increase of rent to that charged for comparable units.
5. Banked rent increases that were not given for at least three years prior to 1994's Proposition I (owner-occupied 2-4 unit buildings).

In addition to protesting the increase at the Rent Board, rent increases in excess of what is allowed by the Rent Board is subject to criminal prosecution. (SF Administrative Code § 37.10A)

Capital Improvements

The San Francisco Rent Ordinance and Rent Board Rules and Regulations state that, with Rent Board approval, landlords can pass through the costs of certain capital improvements made to properties covered under the Rent Ordinance. This is an area where landlords can try to get major rent increases.

The Rent Board defines "capital improvement" as work that substantially adds to the useful life or value of a property, or adapts it to new uses, and which may be amortized (paid off) over the useful life of the improvement. (SF Administrative Code § 37.2(c), SF Rent Board Rules and Regulations § 1.13) The amortization schedules for specific items are in SF Administrative Code §§ 37.7(c).

The Rent Board allows the landlord to pass through the costs of capital improvement work, plus interest, to tenants in most cases, as long as the landlord complies with the Rent Board requirements. The interest rate charged to the tenant is either the actual interest that the landlord is paying on a loan for the work, or an "imputed" interest rate set each year by the Rent Board. Interest can be no more than 10% in either case. (SF Rent Board Rules and Regulations § 7.14)

A new roof, seismic upgrades, and a remodeled kitchen are a few examples of capital improvements. Generally, routine maintenance does not qualify as capital improvements. For instance, if your landlord patches the roof, this would be considered an ordinary repair, not a capital improvement, but if she replaces the entire roof, it may be a capital improvement, subject to tenant objection.

The main defenses to capital improvement increases are because of hardship exemption and as summarized in the box "Defenses to Capital Improvement Passthroughs." You would protest the increase at a Rent Board hearing or file for hardship exemption. (See the section "Hearing for Capital Improvement Passthroughs" later in this chapter and the section "Hardship Appeal at Tenant's Request" in "Chapter 14: Taking Action" for more info.) If permits are required, you can protest them before they are approved. If you think that your landlord is planning to apply for a permit, you can request alerts for both the Department of Building Inspection and the Department of Planning. (See "Permit Process" in "Chapter 11: Changes in Use.") Landlords sometimes evict tenants in order to perform capital improvements. For defenses and the tenant's rights in these evictions, see "Chapter 12: Eviction Defenses. "

Passthrough Amounts for Capital Improvement

Five or Fewer Units (SF Administrative Code § 37.7(c)(4)): For petitions filed on or after November 14, 2002 for properties with five or fewer units, landlords can pass through to tenants 100% of the costs of capital improvements, but a tenant's rent can be raised no more than 5% per year, with exceptions for work required by law and energy conservation are described in the following sections.

Hardship Exemption for Capital Improvement Passthroughs

Tenants may qualify for exemption from capital improvement rent increases including any already imposed increases as well as future increases. See the section "Hardship Appeal at Tenant's Request" in *Chapter 14: Taking Action* for more info.

Defenses to Capital Improvement Passthroughs

The following costs cannot be passed through to the tenant:

(1) SF Administrative Code § 37.7(b)(6) prohibits passthroughs for code violations by the current or previous landlord which were unabated by the current landlord for 90 or more days which resulted in the work unless there was a good faith effort to complete the work within the 90 days. Also costs due to compliance with a Fire Life Safety Notice and Order as shall not be allowed.

(2) Legalizing an existing dwelling under Planning Code § 207.3. (SF Administrative Code § 37.7(a))

(3) Lead remediation that was deferred maintenance. (SF Administrative Code § 37.3(e))

(4) The work within the tenant's unit is not required for health or safety or to reduce excessive maintenance costs.

(5) Some tenants benefit but not all the tenants charged with the rent increase.

(6) Unnecessarily expensive items for the building and the socioeconomic status of its current tenants (sometimes called "gold-plating"). Where the Board finds that an item's cost is substantially excessive, but that the item itself is a reasonable improvement, then the Board shall approve a reduced cost that it finds to be reasonable.

The following objections are more technical defenses:

(7) The work the landlord claims to have done was not done, was done without the appropriate permits, was completed more than five years ago, or does not comply with the codes.

(8) The landlord did not pay as much for the work as claimed or received insurance money for the cost.

(9) The landlord miscalculated the amortization.

(10) The landlord served the rent increase notice to the tenant before filing a petition with the Rent Board.

(11) The tenant moved into the building within six months after the beginning of capital improvement work and the building wasn't sold between the start of the work and the start of the tenancy.

(SF Rent Board Rules and Regulations § 7.10(e), § 7.12, § 7.15, Topic 312 on *https://sfrb.org* under the menu heading "Landlord & Tenant Info." See also "Hardship Appeal at Tenant's Request" in *Chapter 14: Taking Action*.)

Six or More Units (SF Administrative Code § 37.7(c)(5)): For petitions on or after November 14, 2002, tenants in properties with six or more units have a choice of either splitting the cost of the capital improvement with the landlord or getting a permanent cap on how much their rent can be increased due to capital improvements, with exceptions for work required by law and energy conservation are described in the following sections. The choices are: (1) the landlord can pass through only 50% of the capital improvement costs, or (2) **at** the tenant's option, 100% of the costs can be passed through on the condition that a tenant's rent will never increase more than 15% due to capital improvements, for the duration of the tenancy. Choice (2) means that once a tenant's rent has been increased 15% of his base rent (rent charged a tenant upon initial occupancy plus allowable annual rent increases that was added), no further capital improvement rent increases are allowed for that petition or any future petitions during his tenancy except since the base rent at the time of the filing will be used for any future petitions, there may be more rent increases.

The tenant's choice between the 50% passthrough or the 15% rent increase cap is made individually; for example, in a ten unit property, two tenants might choose the 50% passthrough and eight tenants the 15% cap. Tenants have fifteen days after the judge's decision on the petition to notify the Rent Board of their choice on a Rent Board form. If a tenant were to take no action, then the 50% passthrough would be given.

For the 50% passthrough option, the rent can be increased by 10% per year until the capital improvement is paid off. For the 15% rent increase cap, the rent increases 5% in year one, 5% more in year two (using the same base rent for calculation as in year one), and 5% more in year three. The tenant will then receive no further rent increases and will pay the 15% higher amount until the capital improvement is paid off.

Which of the two choices is better for individual tenants will depend on a number of factors. Generally, tenants who get large capital improvements will look to the 15% cap while tenants with moderate or small capital improvements will benefit by the 50% passthrough. One basic guideline is whether or not a 50% passthrough would result in an increase greater than 15%. For example, if the capital improvement will result in 10% rent increases three years in a row, then the 15% cap is likely the best choice. Other factors include how long the tenant intends to reside in the unit and what the base rent is.

Required Seismic and Code Work Capital Improvement Passthroughs

Petitions filed after November 14, 2002 for seismic or capital improvement work required by law after November 14, 2002, can be passed through at 100% subject to a 10% annual rent increase limit or $30 whichever is greater. If the total monthly proposed capital improvement passthrough exceeds the greater of $30.00 or 10% of the tenant's base rent at the time the petition is filed, the landlord must limit the initial passthrough to $30.00 or 10% of the tenant's petition base rent, whichever is greater. The landlord may accumulate or "bank" the remaining portion of the passthrough and impose it in subsequent years at the rate of $30.00 or 10% of the tenant's petition base rent per year, until the full passthrough amount is completely imposed. (SF Rent Board Form 528) The 10% annual rent increase limit is in addition to passthroughs for other types of capital improvement. These passthroughs will be amortized over a twenty year period. (SF Administrative Code § 37.7(c)(3))

Energy Conservation Measures Capital Improvement Passthroughs

In general, energy conservation measures are capital improvements and would be subject to the provisions previously described. However, certain energy conservation measures which are filed after November 14, 2002 and which directly benefit the tenant (if, for example, the tenant is paying for utilities separate from rent) can be passed through at 100% in addition to passthroughs for other types of capital improvement. Allowable increases include for the replacement of a refrigerator which are at least 5 years old with new EPA Energy Star compliant refrigerator. Such refrigerator costs would be amortized over ten years. (SF Administrative Code § 37.7(c)(2)(B))

Calculating the Passthroughs for Capital Improvement

Calculations of the appropriate passthrough include allocation based on equal division among all units or based on the square footage of each unit. Where an improvement does not benefit all units, only those units benefited may be charged the capital improvement passthrough. For example, the cost of a new roof would be allocated to all units in the property, but the cost of new carpeting in one unit would be allocated to that unit only. (Topic 304 on *https://sfrb.org* under the menu heading "Landlord & Tenant Info.") Costs for units where the rent cannot be raised (because of a lease restriction, owner occupancy or other reason) may not be allocated to the other units.

For capital improvement petitions filed after November 14, 2002, 100% of the certified capital improvement costs may be passed through to the tenants. All residential units on the same property must be counted. Commercial units do not count toward the number of units on the property, although a portion of the cost must be allocated to commercial units that benefit from the capital improvement. A reasonable portion of capital improvement cost for a common area must also be allocated to areas exclusively controlled by the landlord, such as a management office.

A new tenant cannot be charged for a capital improvement completed before the tenancy began since the owner was free to set a new market rent at the time the unit was vacant. In addition, capital improvement costs cannot be passed through to units that are first rented during the construction period or rented within

six months after the work began, unless ownership changed during that period and the new owner took over after the new tenancy commenced.

Example:

1. The Rent Board approves a capital improvement passthrough dollar amount for an entire property.

   $200,000 = Total Capital Improvement Passthrough

2. The total amount gets divided by the number of units in the property (including commercial units, assuming all equally benefit) at 100% passthroughs.

   For a 10 Unit Property $200,000/10 = $20,000, each unit's share

3. Each unit's share is divided by the applicable amortization period, for example, ten years.

   $20,000 amortized over 10 years = $2,000, each unit's amortized share per year

4. The unit's amortized share per year is then divided by 12 months to calculate the monthly rent increase.

   $2,000/12 = $166.67 rent increase per month

Filed before November 14, 2002: Here's an example for passthroughs filed before November 14, 2002. If the tenant pays $1500 in rent, the 10% annual increase cap means the rent can increase up to $150 per month in any year. Since the $166.67 is greater than the cap, the rent will be increased by the 10% cap amount each year until the total increase has reached $166.67.

Year One: Rent increase of $150.00 (10% of the tenant's rent)

Year Two: Rent increase of $16.67 (On top of $150 increase in Year One; Tenant now pays $166.67 more rent than before the capital improvement passthrough each month.)

Years Three–Ten: No further increases; tenant continues to pay $166.67 more rent per month until capital improvement passthrough is paid off in year Ten.

Filed after November 14, 2002: For passthroughs filed after November 14, 2002, a tenant's rent cannot be increased more than 5% annually for properties with five or fewer units or 10% annually for properties with six or more units except see previous sections for exceptions for work required by law and energy conservation, and the following sections for variables related to 50% passthroughs and lifetime 15% cap. If the increase is less than the 5% or 10% caps, respectively, then the tenant's rent goes up one time and the tenant pays that increase for the amortization period. But if that increase is greater than 5% or 10% of the rent, respectively, then the tenant will receive sequential annual capital

improvement passthrough rent increases (of 5% or 10%) until his rent increase has reached the total allowed passthrough amount (in the example, $166.67 per month).

50% Passthrough: If the tenant chooses the 50% passthrough, then the landlord can pass through only $10,000 instead of $20,000. The $10,000 divided by the amortization of ten years for this example comes to $1,000 a year. Divided by 12, the monthly increase to the tenant is $83.33. For a $1,500 rent, for example, this is less than the 10% cap, so the rent goes up $83.33 in year One and the tenant pays that increased rent for the 10 year amortization period.

> Year 1: Rent Increase of $83.33
> Years 2–10: No further increases; tenant continues to pay the $83.33 each month for the remainder of the amortization period.

15% Lifetime CIP Cap: Under this option the amortization periods are ignored. The tenant gets three 5% rent increases and pays that increased amount until the $20,000 capital improvement is paid off. This option will typically be taken for very large capital improvements or by tenants with lower rents. For this example, assume the tenant's rent is $500 per month.

> Year 1: Rent increase of $25 (5% of $500)
> Year 2: Rent increase of $25 (5% of $500; Total Capital Improvement Passthrough is now $50)
> Year 3: Rent increase $25 (5% of $500; Total Capital Improvement Passthrough is now $75 which is 15% of $500)
> Years 3–20: No further increases; tenant continues to pay the $75 increase until she has paid the entire $20,000 capital improvement passthrough, which would happen in approximately 21 years.

For this example, the 15% cap would result in a lower monthly rent increase, but the tenant would continue paying the higher rent for a far longer period than if she had chosen the 50% option.

General Procedures for Capital Improvement Passthroughs

Capital improvement rent increases can be imposed anytime—not just on a tenant's rent anniversary date—but they do *not* become part of the base rent for the purposes of future annual rent increases, nor do they change the anniversary date. (SF Rent Board Rules and Regulations § 7.16, SF Administrative Code § 37.9(a)(1)(A)(ii)) For example, assume your rent was originally $1500 and your anniversary date is June 1. You begin paying the

$120 on December 1, and you can receive an allowable annual increase effective the following June 1.

If a landlord fails to discontinue a capital improvement passthrough at the appropriate time, the tenant may file a Challenges to Passthrough petition at the Rent Board (see the "Passthrough Challenges by Petition" section earlier in this chapter) to request a refund of the overpayments. There is no time limit for filing such a petition.

Before rent increases can be passed through to tenants, capital improvement work must be approved and certified by the Rent Board. The landlord begins the process by filing a petition for certification of capital improvement expenses at the Rent Board. The landlord must file the petition after completion of the work, but no longer than five years later. The landlord has to provide accurate data concerning the property's rent history for each unit, such as names, phone numbers and move-in dates of each tenant involved; prior annual rent increases, capital improvement increases and PG&E increases for all the units involved; and a schedule amortizing the current capital improvement costs allocated to each unit.

The landlord's petition must also include: support documentation, including a schedule showing who did the work, exactly what work was done, when the work was finished, how much it cost, how and when it was paid for, copies of permits, and before and after photos if available. Petitions for $25,000 or more must include either copies of competitive bids for work and materials or receipts for time and materials billing for all contractors and subcontractors. If the landlord cannot provide these, she must pay for the Rent Board's cost of hiring an independent estimator. An estimator may also be necessary if the work is extensive, the documentation is unclear, and/or there are numerous tenant objections.

Upon receipt of the petition, the Rent Board briefly reviews the landlord's petition. The Rent Board may administratively dismiss a landlord's petition for capital improvements without a hearing if it is defective; however, this is rarely done. (SF Rent Board Rules and Regulations § 7.17) If the landlord's petition is complete, the case will be scheduled for a hearing. All parties are notified by mail at least ten days before the hearing date. (SF Rent Board Rules and Regulations § 11.10) The whole petition process, from filing to decision, takes several months and can be slowed down a bit more if an estimator's report is required. **Landlords cannot legally serve tenants with notices of proposed capital improvement rent increases until after they have filed their petition with the Rent Board or the proposed increase will be null and void.** (SF Rent Board Rules and Regulations § 7.10 (c)) This does not mean the landlord will ultimately be denied the passthrough; she can give the tenant a new notice once the petition is filed. It does delay the increase for the tenant, however.

The petition only has to be filed—not approved—before the notice of proposed increase is given. A tenant who has been properly

served with a written notice of a capital improvement increase has two choices: He can pay the proposed increase amount on the effective date, or he can wait until the Rent Board approves the increase — which can take anywhere from several months to a year. If the tenant chooses to wait and the Board certifies the work, he will have to pay the landlord retroactively for the rent increase amount that has accrued since the effective date on the notice. On the other hand, if a tenant pays the proposed rent increase before the Rent Board certifies the work and the Board decides not to certify all or part of the work, the landlord will owe the tenant a refund. Tenants who choose to wait should put aside money to cover the proposed increased amount in case the Board does approve the increase.

Hearing for Capital Improvement Passthroughs

The burden of proof is on the landlord in these hearings.

1. If your landlord gives you a notice of rent increase for capital improvements, check to see that it is technically correct. (See the section at the beginning of this chapter "Rent Increases under California Law" for more info on proper rent increase notices.)

2. Call or visit the Rent Board to inquire whether or not your landlord has filed a capital improvement petition.

3. If your landlord has filed a petition, ask to see the case file. Plan to spend enough time at the Rent Board to thoroughly review the file and make notes.

    a. Jot down the case number for future reference.

    b. Read the file cover to cover. You can't take it with you but you can get copies of pages for a small fee.

    c. Make notes on all items you disagree with.

    d. If you disagree with the work, you must be able to prove to the Rent Board that the work does not meet the requirements set forth in the Rent Ordinance or Rent Board Rules and Regulations. You may want to read § 37.7 of the Rent Ordinance and Part 7 of the Rules and Regulations yourself to get a first-hand idea of what is and isn't legitimate. The Rent Board counselors can also be helpful.

    e. Assemble a defense based on factual evidence:

    f. Write a statement challenging each point that you disagree with in the petition and/or supporting documents. Be specific, detailed, but as brief as possible. The judge isn't going to want to read your statement if it's illegible, too long or disorganized.

    g. If you question your landlord's calculations, ask a Rent Board counselor to verify them.

4. Provide your own "before" and "after" photos. If you want to present video evidence, you will need to provide equipment to view the video.

5. Bring witnesses who can support your claim: friends, family, neighbors, roommates, and workers.

5. Attend the hearing!

Operating and Maintenance Expense Rent Increase

A landlord may, in some cases, increase the rent for operating the property. (SF Rent Board Rules and Regulations § 6.10) The landlord must prove that there has been an increase in total expenses over the 12 month period immediately prior to filing the petition (the "adjustment year") compared to the prior 12 month period (the "comparison year," calendar years may also be used), and that the increase exceeds the annual allowable increase for the unit. *This rent increase can only be granted by the Rent Board judge after a hearing.*

Operating and maintenance costs can include but are not limited to: water and sewer charges, janitorial service, refuse removal, elevator service, security system, insurance, debt service (includes mortgage payments), real estate tax, management, repairs, and pest control. These costs shall not include installation or upgrade of systems for compliance with a Fire Life Safety Notice and Order under this section: SF Administrative Code § 37.8(e)(4):

- *For petitions filed before December 11. 2017*: If the property has been purchased within two years of the date of the previous purchase, consideration shall not be given to that portion of increased debt service which has resulted from a selling price which exceeds the seller's purchase price by more than the percentage increase in the Consumer Price Index for All Urban Consumers for the San Francisco-Oakland Metropolitan Area by the U.S. Department of Labor between the date of previous purchase and the date of the current sale, plus the cost of capital improvements or rehabilitation work made or performed by the seller.

- *For petitions filed on or after December 11, 2017*: the Rent Board shall not consider increased debt service or increased property taxes from a change in ownership except the Rent Board may consider increased property taxes that has resulted from the completion of needed repairs or capital improvements with respect to any petition filed on or after December 11. 2017; and except that the Rent Board may consider increased debt service and increased property taxes pursuant to Section 37.8(e)(4)(A)(i), if the landlord demonstrates that the property was purchased on or before April 3, 2018 and had

---

Hardship Exemption for Operating and Maintenance Expense Increase Passthroughs

Tenants may qualify for exemption from operating and maintenance expense rent increases. See the section "Hardship Appeal at Tenant's Request" in *Chapter 14: Taking Action* for more info.

reasonably relied on its ability to pass through those costs at the time of the purchase.

• *For petitions filed on or after July 16, 2018*: the Rent Board may consider management expenses only to the extent those expenses are reasonable and necessary.

If the landlord can document these costs, the net cost increase, divided by 12 months and the number of units in the property including commercial units (Topic 322 on *https://sfrb.org* under the menu heading "Landlord & Tenant Info") may be given to the tenant(s) in the form of a monthly rent increase. If the per unit increase does not exceed the annual allowable rent increase, no increase in the rent will be granted. Prospective/future costs not actually incurred and paid by the landlord cannot be part of the rent increase, except for property taxes, which are always allocated to the year in which they are payable regardless of when or whether they are paid.

The increase may be charged to the tenant only at the time of the annual rent increase. The maximum allowable increase from the base rent for an Operation and Maintenance petition is 7% and it becomes part of the tenant's base rent. In properties with 6 or more units, landlords may not impose more than a 7% increase within any 5 year period. (SF Administrative Code § 37.8(b)(1)(A))

See "Petition the Rent Board" in "Chapter 14: Taking Action" for more info.

Hearing for Operating and Maintenance Expense Rent Increase

The burden of proof is on the landlord in these hearings, but be sure to follow these guidelines:

1. Is all the documentation in the petition file? If bills, calculations, or letters are not included, you can access them at the Rent Board by making a document request (which can include copying for a small fee).

2. Are all the bills labeled clearly? Are they for the time period specified in the petition? Do they support the landlord's calculations?

3. Are there duplicate bills? Were repairs actually made? Did they affect your apartment?

4. Are the landlord's calculations correct? (Bring a calculator!)

5. Take extensive notes on the file. Write down any inaccuracies or things that aren't true.

6. If the case is very big, ask a friend or another tenant to go through the file with you.

Gas, Electricity or Steam Heat Passthroughs That Do Not Require Rent Board Approval

Some utility passthroughs do not require Rent Board approval. See the earlier section in this chapter "Gas, Electricity or Steam Heat Passthroughs."

Tenant Not in Occupancy (Rental Unit Is Not the Principal Residence)

If a tenant is not using her rental unit or with the consent of the landlord reasonably proximate rental units in the same building as her "principal place of occupancy," the landlord can petition to remove the rent increase limitation under the Rent Ordinance. (SF Administrative Code § 37.3, Rent Board Rules and Regulations § 1.21) The burden of proof is on the landlord. The Rent Board will consider factors including:

1. The premises are listed as the tenant's address for a motor vehicle registration, driver's license, voter registration or with any public agency.

2. Utilities are billed to and paid by the tenant at the premises.

3. All of the tenant's personal possessions are at the premises.

4. The tenant does not have a homeowner's tax exemption.

5. The premises are the place the tenant normally returns to as her residence, excluding hospitalization, vacation, family emergency, travel necessary for a job or education, or other reasonable temporary absence.

6. Other persons testify that the tenant uses the premises as her principal place of residence.

An absence of several years could be reasonable for going to college, for example. Long absences where the tenant is not subletting would be a stronger argument that the absence is temporary since a tenant would be unlikely to pay rent for years without planning to return. Another example, if the tenant lived half of the time somewhere else for work, other factors could prevent a rent increase. However, a homeowner's exemption for taxes on another property is likely to make a claim that the rental unit is the principal place of occupancy unsuccessful.

The landlord's petition would be based on the circumstances that existed before the petition was filed, so the tenant does not have a chance to cure the problem after the petition is filed.

Miscellaneous Landlord Petitions

A landlord may try to raise the rent for a reason other than those specified in the Rent Ordinance. Examples include: disputes over additional costs or a dispute over whether a rental unit is exempt from the Rent Ordinance. In addition, a landlord may petition to raise the rent for a "comparable unit," where the length of occupancy is a factor in determining the rent. (SF Administrative Code § 37.8(e)(4)(B), SF Rent Board Rules and Regulations § 6.11) The Rent Board will schedule a hearing but these petitions are rarely granted.

Chapter 8: **Harassment**

In California it is illegal for the landlord (or anyone else, for that matter) to take the law into their own hands. A landlord or their representative cannot lock you out, take away your personal property, violate your right to privacy, cut off utilities, or harass or terrorize you in any way. If a landlord wishes to evict you, she must follow legal procedures. In California, only the sheriff can evict a tenant, unless the tenant is the sole lodger, and any efforts by a landlord to take possession of the tenants' unit either directly or indirectly without using the proper legal channels, may constitute harassment and give the tenants a legal case against the landlord.

Due to tenant activists, 2008's Proposition M added language in the San Francisco Rent Ordinance that defines tenant harassment, and allows a tenant to remedy the violation if bad faith on the part of the landlord can be proven by suing under for three times the actual damages or $1,000, whichever is greater, and other relief including criminal prosecution. (SF Administrative Code § 37.10B. See "Appendix C: San Francisco Law and Regulations Excerpts" for the text of this law.) However, in recent years the Rent Board was unable to act on harassment complaints from tenants because of *Larson v. City and County of San Francisco* (2011) even while landlord harassment to get long-term tenants to more out increased. Thanks to more work by tenant activists in 2013, Administrative Code §37.9(l) allowed for hearings on Alleged Wrongful Endeavor to Recover Possession Through Tenant Harassment with possible referral to the city for prosecution. Though this legislation does not guarantee action on the part of the Rent Board, it is worth trying in cases with a repeated pattern and practice of egregious landlord misbehavior. This chapter explains other strategies for stopping harassment. See also "Chapter 9: Discrimination" for more information about harassment that is discrimination.

Privacy and Landlord Entry

This section discusses protecting your privacy against intrusion by your landlord and his agent. For your rights against intrusion by others, see "Security" in "Chapter 6: Repairs and Services."

Your landlord may not enter your home without your permission except in limited situations. These circumstances are spelled out in the law. Except in cases of a legitimate emergency, if your landlord wishes to enter your home for one of these following reasons, she must give reasonable written notice stating the date, approximate time, and purpose of the entry. (See later paragraphs in this section for a limited exception for oral notices.) The notice may be personally delivered to the tenant, left with someone of a suitable age and discretion at the premises, or left on, near, or under the usual entry door of the premises in a manner in which a reasonable person would discover the notice. Twenty-four hours (minimum) is presumed to be reasonable notice unless there is evidence otherwise. If mailed, the law presumes reasonable notice if the landlord or agent sends it to the tenant at least six days prior to the date of entry. The landlord must also come during regular business hours (presumably Monday through Friday, 9 am–5 pm, except for open houses, see "Fighting the Sale of Your Home" in "Chapter 11: Changes in Use") unless you arrange another convenient time.

In the case of oral notices of landlord entry, the tenant and landlord may agree orally to an entry to make repairs or supply agreed services, if the agreement includes the date and approximate time of entry *and* if the entry is within one week of the oral agreement, except entry for reading water submeters must be in writing. An oral notice can also be given if it was preceded within 120 days by a written notice of entry to exhibit the dwelling to prospective or actual purchasers.

A landlord or landlord's agent is limited to the following reasons to enter a tenant's unit:

- Civil Code § 1954

  · In case of emergency.

  · To make necessary or agreed repairs, decorations, or alterations; supply necessary or agreed services; or exhibit the dwelling unit to prospective or actual purchasers, mortgagees, tenants, workers, or contractors or to make an inspection before a tenant moves out when requested by the tenant. (CA Civil Code § 1950.5(f)) See also the section "Other Forms of Harassment by the Landlord" later in this chapter for more information on when the repairs becomes harassment.)

  · The tenant has abandoned or surrendered the premises.

  · Pursuant to court order.

  · For the purpose of installing or repairing a water submeter, and reading a submeter if installed before 2018.

  · For the purpose of inspecting balconies, decks, entrances, stairways, and walkways as required under California Health and Safety Code § 17973.

- To test a smoke detector as well as install the smoke detector or a carbon monoxide detector. See the section "Air Quality (Besides Lead, Mold, Filth) and Fire Hazards" in "Chapter 6: Repairs and Services" for more info."

If a landlord (or his agent) doesn't follow these rules violating your right to privacy, here are some different ways you can respond:

(1) Start with a polite phone call, telling him that an unauthorized entry is illegal and that you want it stopped immediately. **Follow up the call with a letter** (keep a copy, and mail with a certificate of mailing which is not the same as certified mail) reiterating the points made in your earlier phone conversation. For more info on your rights for showing the unit to prospective buyers/renters, see the section "Fighting the Sale of Your Home" in *Chapter 11: Changes in Use.*

(2) In more serious situations, the police may need to be called to help resolve the dispute. Don't tell the dispatcher that it is about a "tenant" or "landlord." If the landlord is still on the premises, the police may arrest the landlord. You have a right to make a citizen's arrest if the police are unwilling to arrest your landlord for trespass. (CA Penal Code § 837) At least, get the badge numbers and names of the police, make an incident report, and get the case number so you can easily obtain a copy later.

(3) Work with your neighbors, who are probably also being harassed.

(4) If you fear for your safety or are worried about continued invasions of your privacy, consider changing the locks and denying the landlord a copy of the key. No law requires you to provide a key to the landlord (although your rental agreement may). However, most rental agreements contain a provision prohibiting building alterations without landlord consent. Changing the locks will be a violation of the prohibition and may be used as grounds for eviction. If you decide to change locks, a well-documented history of complaints and incidents of abuse will be important for legitimizing your action. Also, the landlord may change the locks, again, to allow entry as permitted by law.

A cheaper alternative to changing the locks is to get a keyed chain door guard, available at hardware stores. The keyed chain guard can be locked from the outside but is mounted on the inside with screws. In case of an eviction attempt for altering the premises without the landlord's consent, the lock can easily be removed if the one-way screws that come with the locks were replaced with regular, short screws. By using short screws, entrance into the unit by the landlord for an emergency would not cause serious damage to the door.

(5) If your landlord continues to interfere with your privacy and you document this interference through letters (sent with a certificate of mailing which is different from certified mail), witnesses, photos, and/or video, you may sue your landlord under the Rent Ordinance for three times the actual damages or $1,000 whichever is greater if bad faith on the part of the landlord can be proven, and other relief including criminal prosecution. (SF Administrative Code § 37.10B(a)(12)) Interference with privacy under the Rent Ordinance includes requests for Social Security numbers credit information, or citizenship status after the tenant (including subtenant) has been approved if the requests are made under bad faith on the part of the landlord, but would probably not include security cameras in public areas if the purpose is to increase security. (SF Administrative Code § 37.10B(a)(13))

(6) Finally, you may consider suing your landlord for breach of privacy and seek injunctive relief; a court order prohibiting the landlord from entering the dwelling. (See the section "Restraining Orders and Injunctions" at the end of this chapter.) You will probably need an attorney to represent you. You might want to read *Guntert v. City of Stockton* ((1976) 55 Cal. App. 3d 131) for more information.

Prohibition on Illegal Landlord Acts to Influence a Tenant Move-Out

Under California Civil Code § 1940.2, tenants have a statutory right to monetary damages for specified illegal acts caused by their landlord. § 1940.2 states "it is unlawful for a landlord to do any of the following for the purpose of influencing a tenant to vacate a dwelling":

Obtain property from a tenant by wrongful use of force or fear, or under the pretense of authority as specified in California Penal Code § 518. (Also CA Civil Code § 789.3)

Use, or threaten to use, force, willful threats, or menacing conduct constituting a pattern that interferes with the tenant's quiet enjoyment of the premises as specified in California Civil Code § 1927, that would create an apprehension of harm in a reasonable person. (The phrase "course of conduct" is used in § 1940.2. CA Penal Code § 646.9(f) and 18 U.S.C. §2266(2) define "course of conduct" as two or more acts evidencing a continuity of purpose.)

Commit a significant and intentional violation of illegal entry into a tenant's unit as specified in California Civil Code § 1954.

Threaten to disclose information relating to the immigration or citizenship status of an occupant, or other person known to the landlord to be associated with an occupant.

A tenant who prevails in a civil action against their landlord, including an action in small claims court to enforce his rights under this section is entitled to a penalty of up to $2,000 for each violation. See the section "Stopping These Types of Harassment" later in this chapter for more remedies.

Buyouts, Almost Always a Bad Idea

Has Your Landlord Offered to Pay You Money for You to Give Up Your Rent-Controlled Apartment?

Know Your Rights Before You Make Any Drastic Decisions!!

Buyouts have become a common method for landlords to get around the eviction protections of the Rent Ordinance in order to jack up the rent for your apartment. Landlords almost always use a "carrot and stick" approach. They dangle money in front of you (carrot) and they suggest that you might have to move out (stick). These discussions often (but not always) happen either shortly before or shortly after the sale of a building. There are often veiled threats from the landlord at around this time, like "I am thinking of moving in," or "I may Ellis Act the building," (These are referred to as "bluff evictions.") The best way to fight this manipulation is to remain calm and learn your rights. The San Francisco Tenants Union is here to help you learn your rights. We also have a list of tenant-friendly attorneys.

Always Do the Math

The possibility of having $10,000, $20,000, or even $60,000 in your pocket just to give up your rent controlled apartment might sound tempting. But if you do the math, you will probably find that the money goes away pretty quickly. Let's say your rent is $1,500 per month, but a comparable unit would cost you $3,500. A good Web site to check out rental prices is *https://www.padmapper.com*.) That's a difference of $2,000 per month. In this situation, a $20,000 buyout will last you only 10 months, a $60,000 buyout will last you less than three years. After that, you will be losing money. In addition, if you have any roommates, you will have to think about what their split of the buyout will be.

There are only a couple of situations where the numbers make any sense: 1) If you plan on moving out of the Bay Area in the very near future. 2) If, after learning about your rights, you find that the landlord would have a clear right to evict you anyways. Emptying a multimillion dollar building of tenants increases the value of the building by 25%-35%, so tenants need to keep that in mind when money is offered

Insist that the Landlord Follow the Law

The Rent Ordinance requires landlords to give you a copy of "buyout disclosure form" and that if there is ultimately an agreement, to file a copy of the agreement with the Rent Board (with the tenant's identity removed). (SF Administrative Code 37.9E) If the landlord has been saying that he "may decide"

Examples of Letters You Can Write to Your Landlord

Letter No. 1 - If you don't want to have any discussions regarding buyout.

Dear Landlord,

I have received your phone call/letter/email requesting that we discuss giving up my Rent Controlled tenancy in exchange for money. I do not see any good reason to give up my tenancy and therefore must decline your offer to have such discussions. If you believe there is reason for further discussions, please provide, in writing, what those reasons are.

Sincerely,
Tenant

Letter No. 2 - If you are willing to have discussions, but want to set ground rules.

Dear Landlord,

I have received your phone call/letter/email requesting that we discuss giving up my rent-controlled tenancy in exchange for money. I will agree to discuss this, but only under the following ground rules:

1) You agree to file with the Rent Board the required disclosure form.

2) (Optional) If you believe you could have grounds to evict me, then please provide me with the required notice and file it with the Rent Board. We can begin negotiations at that point.

3) If we ultimately reach an agreement, you agree, in advance, that you will not ask me to waive any legal rights that I might have if you do not perform the action on the notice.

4) If we ultimately reach an agreement, you agree to file the buyout agreement with the Rent Board.

Sincerely,
Tenant

---

to move in to your unit, then you should insist that he take the steps necessary to do this legally. That means serving you with usually a 60 day notice and filing a copy of it with the Rent Board. That is the only way you will really know whether or not it was a "bluff eviction." If the landlord begins discussions without filing the disclosure, the tenant can file a Report of Alleged Wrongful Eviction with the Rent Board.

Chapter 8– Harassment

Never Waive Your Rights If the Landlord Does Not Move In or Remove the Unit (and the Entire Building) Under the Ellis Act from the Rental Market

It is too often the case that a landlord and tenant will reach an agreement, and then, the landlord, at the last minute insists on a "waiver" provision that would force you to give up any rights you may have against the landlord. Even if you received an Owner Move In notice, you would not be able to sue if the landlord does not move in. This is the biggest landlord abuse with respect to buyouts. If, after receiving a notice, you engage in negotiations with the landlord, make it clear early on that you have no intention of waiving your rights if the landlord doesn't move in. If he balks at this, that's a pretty good sign that he does not intend to follow through with moving in.

You Have the Right to Rescind Any Agreement within 45 Days of the Agreement

If you reach an agreement, the buyout provision of the Rent Ordinance allows a tenant to "rescind" (cancel) the any agreement within 45 days after it is signed. That means that you will not have to move. If you do rescind, then you will have to pay back any money that the landlord has paid you.

Condo Conversion Prohibition

The prohibitions for condo conversions are similar to no-fault evictions when a tenant has vacated under a buyout agreement after October 31, 2014. Since conversion to condos is usually the ultimate goal when tenants are evicted for no fault, stopping the conversion can be a powerful defense. (See the section "Condo Conversion Law" and the "Condo Conversion Prohibited" chart in Chapter 11: Changes in Use for more information.)

Lockouts

If a landlord locks you out or removes personal property with the intention of ending your tenancy, she is violating California Civil Code § 789.3(b) and the same rights and remedies are available to tenants as discussed under the section "Utility Shutoffs" that follows.

Lockouts are crimes for which a landlord can be arrested and jailed. The most commonly used California Penal Codes in such cases are § 418 (Forcible Entry), § 594 (Malicious Mischief), and § 602.5 (Unauthorized Entry). Breaking any of these laws is a misdemeanor under California law. Also these acts, in bad faith, are misdemeanors under the Rent Ordinance. (SF Administrative Code § 37.10B) If the landlord strikes you or seriously threatens or intimidates you this may be an assault or battery which may be charged as felonies and carry even stiffer landlord penalties.

If you think you might be locked out, it is a good idea to carry a recent rent receipt, utility bill, or your driver's license with your current address on it with you any time you leave your home. This can be shown to the police as proof that you are a legal tenant and have a right to be let back in. The burden of proof is supposed to be on the landlord to prove that she hasn't locked you out or that you are a trespasser, but in practice it doesn't always work that way.

If you are locked out you have the right to:

> Call the police and have them assist you in convincing the landlord to let you back in. Don't tell the dispatcher that it is about a "tenant" or "landlord." Remind the police that Penal Code § 418 gives them jurisdiction in the matter. They have been good at getting the tenant back in within 24 hours. Filing an Alleged Report of Wrongful Eviction with the Rent Board improves your ability to have a police escort to get back in.

> Break back in. (It is not illegal to break into your home.)

> Sue for your loss of housing services and other costs. (CA Civil Code § 789.3(b), SF Administrative Code § 37.10B) Or sue for injunctive relief, a court-ordered act. (CA Code of Civil Procedure § 527.6, SF Administrative Code § 37.10B) This can involve obtaining what is called a Temporary Restraining Order (TRO) against your landlord. (See the section "Restraining Orders and Injunctions" at the end of this chapter.)

A good case to read concerning lockouts is *Jordan v. Talbot* ((1961) 55 Cal. 2d 597). In that case, tenants were awarded $9,500 damages. The California Supreme Court also held that:

> Rental agreement terms that allow the landlord to enter or evict at will or on short notice are illegal.

> A tenant's possession cannot be disturbed except by the proper legal process.

> Forcible entry is committed even when a landlord enters with a passkey.

> A person who obtains possession of property by forcible entry does not have the right to keep possession.

Your rights to privacy, to be protected against utility cutoffs, lockouts, and harassment in general are touchy matters for all concerned, so be careful. Try to learn whether the landlord knows that what she did is illegal. If the landlord honestly didn't know, you might only have to inform her of the rules. If the landlord knew the conduct was illegal and still carried it through (or tried to carry it through), you will have to decide how much of a confrontation you're willing and able to handle.

If an assault or battery has been committed and the police refuse to arrest your landlord (as they usually do) claiming that it is a civil matter and they don't have jurisdiction, you might try a citizen's arrest under Penal Code § 837. You always have the right to self-defense. Your best choice of action may depend on information you learn about past behavior of your landlord.

towards his tenants. Your neighbors may be very helpful when you try to gather this information.

The laws in this section are the ones most commonly used to defend tenants' rights in these matters, but they aren't the only means of action you have. Be creative and try to get back possession of your home as soon as possible. Possession is both your right and your strongest bargaining position. Remember that old saying, "Possession is nine-tenths of the law." It is especially true in cases of this kind.

Utility Shutoffs

Shutting off a tenant's utilities with the intent to terminate the occupancy is another form of harassment and is strictly illegal. Any landlord who willfully causes the interruption or termination of any utility "including but not limited to water, heat, light, electricity, gas, telephone, elevator, or refrigeration, whether or not the utility service is under the control of the landlord" with the intent to terminate the occupancy, is acting wrongfully and is liable for damages. It does not matter if you are behind on your rent or facing an eviction action. The tenant can sue for:

A court order to turn the service back on.

Actual damages, i.e. whatever expenses the tenant actually suffered from the illegal act.

Punitive damages of up to $100 per day or any part of the day that utilities were unavailable to the tenant (with a minimum of at least $250).

Reasonable attorney's fees.

California Civil Code § 789.3

The tenant can also sue if covered under the Rent Ordinance for three times the actual damages or $1,000, whichever is greater if bad faith on the part of the landlord can be proven, and other relief including criminal prosecution. (SF Administrative Code § 37.10B) For cutting off the utilities, the landlord is subject to penalties, including imprisonment under the San Francisco law as well as under California law:

A landlord risks possible imprisonment under California Penal Codes § 591 and § 593 for unlawfully and maliciously removing, injuring, or obstructing any line used to conduct electricity, or any part or connected apparatus. The penalty is imprisonment up to three years and a fine up to $10,000 dollars.

Penal Code § 593c makes a landlord guilty of a felony for willfully and maliciously obstructing, removing

or injuring any pipe maintained for the purpose of transporting gas, or any part thereof, or equipment connected with any such pipeline.

A landlord is guilty of a misdemeanor under Penal Code § 624 for willfully obstructing, or injuring any pipe for conducting water, or any connected equipment.

You might want to show your landlord these laws (in *Appendices C and D: Law Excerpts and Regulations*).

There are times when utilities for a building are cut off by the company because the landlord has not paid the bill. Usually the occupants will receive notice from the company before this happens. (CA Public Utilities Code § 777, § 777.1) The San Francisco Public Utilities Commission (SFPUC) has a policy of collection through the lien process (a charge on the property) rather than terminating water and waste services. You should contact the landlord immediately when your utilities are cut off, and follow-up, including your neighbors if possible, with a letter.

State law requires that PG&E and the SFPUC continue to provide service to master metered, multi-unit, residential buildings when a public health or building officer certifies that the termination would result in a significant threat to the health of the occupants or the public. (CA Public Utilities Code §§ 777.1(e)(5), 10009.1(e)(5)) Tenants will need to work their way up from the desk staff to the supervisors and contact the legal department for PG&E if necessary. Also, contact the City Attorney who has successfully invoked this law. The Department of Building Inspection (DBI) also has the authority under San Francisco Building Code § 102A.20 to issue an emergency order to continue gas and electrical service in a building when the service is about to be discontinued due to the owner's failure to pay. DBI can enforce the provision of utilities since failure to provide utilities to a housing unit could render a building unsafe. (SF Building Code § 102A, SF Housing Code § 1001)

The tenants may need to have the utility account transferred to their names to assure continuation of the service. (In these cases, PG&E can require you to meet their usual credit requirements.) State law allows a tenant who becomes a customer under these circumstances to withhold rent for the cost of the utility service. (CA Civil Code § 1942.2, Public Utilities Code § 10009.1(d)) A safer route than withholding rent is to file an unlawful rent increase petition with the Rent Board if the tenant is covered under the Rent Ordinance's rent control. (See "What Does the Rent Ordinance Cover?" in "Chapter 4: Renting Basics" and "Unlawful Rent Increase Petition" in "Chapter 7: Rent Increases.") The utility companies might attempt to have tenants pay the money the landlord owes, but the law says that tenants can't be forced to pay any past due balance owed by the landlord. (CA Public Utilities Code §§ 777(b), 777.1(a), 10009(b), 10009.1(a)) You should call the Public Utilities Commission and assert your rights vigorously. (See the box "Bureaucracies" in "Chapter 14: Taking Action" for tips.) You should also consider legal action against the landlord for reimbursement of any costs incurred. § 777.1 includes a clause for awarding of reasonable attorney fees to the tenant.

Debt Collection

If your landlord is harassing you in connection with collecting a debt, you have additional protections under either the Federal or California Fair Debt Collection Practices Acts. (FDCPA, CA Civil Code §§ 1788–1788.33) The FDCPA protects consumers from nasty debt collectors of all types. It applies to anyone who regularly engages in debt collection in the ordinary course of business on behalf of themselves or others. This description applies to landlords and property managers, so if any of the harassment you experience is connected to collecting rent, utility bills, late fees, etc., you can use the protections provided in this law.

Threats prohibited by the FDCPA include: the use of force, violence or criminal means to harm a person, reputation, or property; false criminal accusation (for example, if the landlord says that you'll go to jail for not paying your rent); or defaming the debtor. (CA Civil Code § 1788.10)

Harassment prohibited includes: swearing at you for not paying your rent on time, anonymous phone calls, misrepresenting who has to pay for long distance phone calls, repeated phone ringing "to annoy the person called," and "unreasonable" frequent communication with the debtor. (CA Civil Code § 1788.11)

Communication with other people restricted regarding your debt: debt collectors can't contact your employer except to verify your employment, locate you (which shouldn't be necessary for a landlord), or to garnish your wages after they get a judgment against you. The latter two communications must be written. Debt collectors are also prohibited from contacting your family besides your spouse, except for the purpose of locating you. Postcards to embarrass the debtor, advertisements naming the debtor, and "deadbeat lists" disclosing the debtor's name and the nature of the consumer debt are also prohibited. (CA Civil Code § 1788.12)

Misrepresentation prohibited: Generally debt collectors aren't supposed to lie to you or mislead you about your debt. For example, debt collectors can't give you a false name, claim to be attorneys if they're not, write you letters on a lawyer's stationery if that lawyer isn't actually representing them, or indicate that they are working for a government agency unless they are and are acting on behalf of that agency. Your landlord shouldn't tell you that you will have to pay attorney's fees, late fees, etc. unless these fees are actually allowed (and they generally are not allowed unless explicitly provided for in your rental agreement). They can't even threaten to sue you, hire a collection agency, or report you to a credit agency unless they really are planning to do so. (CA Civil Code § 1788.13)

Abuse of the judicial process or of the attorney-client relationship is prohibited. (CA Civil Code §§ 1788.14-16)

Nonwaivable rights for the Fair Debt Collection Practices. (CA Civil Code § 1788.33)

To enforce this law, the debtor can sue the debt collector for actual damages, a statutory penalty for "willfully and knowingly" violating the FDCPA of up to $1,000, and attorneys' fees and costs. (CA Civil Code § 1788.30) There is a one year statute of limitation for bringing a suit under this act, and suing under the FDCPA does not prevent other lawsuits (such as under federal law or as a tort). You should start by communicating the issues with your landlord in writing and keeping a copy for yourself.

If the landlord hires someone else to collect a debt rather than doing it themselves, federal law provides additional protections. The federal Fair Debt Collection Practices Act requires debt collectors to inform debtors the first time they write them that they have 30 days in which to dispute the debt. (15 U.S.C. Section 1692g) If the debtor (i.e., tenant) writes back saying they don't agree with any or all of the debt amount, the debt collector is supposed to stop all collection activity until they have verified the debt. (This step is often easily satisfied by the debt collector calling the landlord to ask whether the figures are correct.)

Federal law applies to attorneys, while California law is limited to non-attorneys. If you get a letter from an attorney about a debt the landlord claims you owe (including a 3-day notice to pay rent or quit) they're also supposed to tell you that you have 30 days in which to dispute the debt. See "Nonpayment of Rent" in "Chapter 12: Eviction Defenses" for more info.

Sexual Harassment

What Are the Laws?

Sexual harassment is discrimination on the basis of sex, and it is illegal under the California Fair Employment and Housing Act (FEHA), the Unruh Civil Rights Act, and the federal Fair Housing Act (FHA). (See "Chapter 9: Discrimination" for more info about these laws.) The Unruh Civil Rights Act defines sexual harassment as "sexual advances, solicitations, sexual requests, or demands for sexual compliance…that were unwelcome and persistent or severe, continuing after a request by the plaintiff to stop." To make a claim you need to show that your right to enjoy your home is substantially reduced—you do not need to show that you have suffered any other direct economic loss as a result of the harassment. If the harasser works for the landlord in any capacity, such as resident managers, maintenance workers, repair contractors, or real estate agents, the landlord may also be held liable along with the actual harasser. Neighbors who engage in sexual harassment could be individually liable under an anti-intimidation provision of the law, but the landlord probably wouldn't be liable in these situations unless there is something the landlord could do, but doesn't, to prevent the harassment. Under the Unruh Act, you also need to show that you can't "easily terminate the relationship without tangible hardship." This can be often be met in San Francisco by showing that your rent

(because of rent control) is significantly lower than market rent for comparable vacant units.

What Can You Do?

Write a letter. Be as specific as possible. Describe exactly what happened or what comments the harasser made to you, how it made you feel, and what you would like to happen. (See "Chapter 14: Taking Action" for suggestions.) If the harassment continues, document each incident, including any witnesses who 'might be present. Always document any communications with your landlord in writing, keeping a copy for yourself and mail with a certificate of mailing, different from certified mail. To enforce your rights under the Unruh Civil Rights Act documenting communication is even more important than ever since Unruh requires that you make a specific request that the harassment stop.

Get allies. Try talking to other tenants in the building or in another building owned by the same landlord. Chances are good that if the landlord is harassing you, he may also be harassing someone else. Corroborating testimony and evidence of other incidences of similar behavior can be very powerful for any legal case against the harasser.

Make a complaint to the U.S. Department of Housing and Urban Development (HUD), the Human Rights Commission, or the California Department of Fair Employment and Housing (DFEH). Any complaint should be filed within one year of the incidents. Consider suing or using the HUD or DFEH administrative process. If you decide to sue, you have two years from the date of the harassment to file your suit under FEHA or the federal FHA and one year under the Unruh Act.

Relief available includes monetary damages, injunctive relief (a court order telling the defendant to stop the action), and attorneys' fees. Monetary damages might include any actual costs incurred, like moving expenses or expenses incurred due to an eviction, the additional costs of higher rent, physical, and emotional damages due to being harassed, and, if you sue in court and the violation is found to be intentional, punitive damages. Injunctions that could be issued include: stopping the harassment, changes in the operation or management of the housing, training programs for employees, and other preventive steps.

The administrative processes are probably cheaper and quicker than suing in court, and you can get all of the damages you would get in court except punitive damages. After you file a complaint, HUD gets 100 days to decide if your case has merit. If HUD decides that your case does have merit, they will issue a "charge"—if HUD does not issue a charge, you can still sue.

If HUD decides to issue a charge, you have two choices if you want to continue. You can sue in court, represented by the Department of Justice, and you will get all the damages you would have gotten if you had gone to court at first. (The two-year statute of limitations on filing a lawsuit still applies, but the clock stops from the date you file your complaint until HUD decides whether or not to file a charge.) The second option is to get a hearing in front of a Rent Board judge. The hearing will be held within 120 days after the charge is issued, and within 60 days after the end of the hearing, the Rent Board judge must render a decision. The decision is final unless modified within 30 days by the Secretary of HUD. You can appeal (on limited grounds), first within HUD and then to a federal appeals court. See "Chapter 14: Taking Action" for additional suggestions.

Noise and Nuisance from a Neighbor

It is against the law to make excessive noise. California Penal Code § 415 punishes by imprisonment in jail for a period of not more than 90 days, a fine of not more than $400, or both for any person who maliciously and willfully disturbs another person by loud and unreasonable noise.

In San Francisco, Article 29 (see the following section "Other Forms of Harassment by the Landlord") and Article 1, § 49 of the Police Code also set noise guidelines. Generally, a device that amplifies sound more than 5 decibels in excess of the background noise is a violation, when measured in one dwelling unit three feet from any wall, floor, or ceiling when the windows and doors of the dwelling unit are closed with the noise coming from outside the unit. Also, "no fixed noise source may cause the noise level measured inside any sleeping or living room in any dwelling unit located on residential property to exceed 45 dBA between the hours of 10 pm to 7 am or 55 dBA between the hours of 7 am to 10 pm with windows open except where building ventilation is achieved through mechanical systems that allow windows to remain closed." The dBA is measured by a sound meter fitted with a decibel A filter. However, activities with a permit from the City and County of San Francisco for different noise limitations are exempt. (SF Police Code § 2909)

Living in a city as densely populated as San Francisco, people expect a certain level of noise. However, if you are harassed by loud, inconsiderate, or hostile neighbors within your building, the following steps may be taken:

(1) Work with other neighbors, who are probably also bothered, in keeping a log of what the noise was, what day and time it occurred, how long it lasted, and any other person present who could confirm the noise. Decibel meters are inexpensive, easy to purchase, and useful for measuring the noise level.

(2) Speak with the offenders, explaining that the noise is a problem.

(3) Request a free Alternative Dispute Resolution Session from the San Francisco Rent Board. (See "Alternative Dispute Resolution" in "Chapter 14: Taking Action.") Or try other mediation services such as Conflict Intervention Service. (See "Appendix A: Resources.")

(4) Write a letter to the offenders and send a copy to the landlord with a certificate of mailing (different from certified mail) and keep a copy for yourself).

(5) Call in the police to make a report and request the police report number.

(6) Notify the landlord that the neighbors are causing a substantial interference with the habitability of the premises ("implied warranty of habitability") and ask her to notify the neighbors to stop under threat of eviction. Be very careful, however, about siding with the landlord against other tenants—it is not the preferred method.

(7) File a petition for Decrease in Housing Services with the Rent Board if you are covered under the Rent Ordinance's rent control. The Rent Board has awarded rent reductions for noise from a neighboring unit (SF Rent Board Case #AL 190090) or for the landlord's failure to provide quiet enjoyment (see definition of quiet enjoyment and case #AL180101) as long as the breach is not caused by the landlord.

(8) If the problem continues, you may sue the landlord.

(9) Consider withholding rent. Always contact the Tenants Union before using this tactic since it is risky.

Other Forms of Harassment by the Landlord

A tenant has the right to the "quiet possession" of the rental unit. (CA Civil Code § 1927) "Quiet possession" includes two requirements. First, the landlord may not take an action that substantially interferes with the tenant's lawful use of her home. Second, the landlord must take action to provide a tenant with the "quiet enjoyment" or "quiet possession" of the tenant's home if the landlord is aware that the tenant's lawful use of the property is jeopardized. For example, a landlord may be obligated to take action to stop an overly aggressive real estate agent if he becomes aware that the agent is substantially interfering with the "quiet enjoyment" of a tenant's home.

Besides the types already discussed, some landlords may wage a more subtle campaign of harassment, ranging from nasty phone calls, notes, numerous visits to the rental property to "check on his things," to extreme cases where violence breaks out. Some landlords have even resorted to poisoning pets and torching

buildings. Although such extreme acts are rare, common sense says you should move out if your relationship with the landlord has deteriorated to the level where this is a real possibility. Document as much as possible, move out, and then sue the landlord. The police should definitely be called and criminal charges should be filed. See also the box "Retaliation Is Illegal" in "Chapter 6: Repairs and Services" for dealing with retaliation.

Harassment may take many lesser forms, such as:

Construction or repair work which seriously disrupts your life. SF Police Code, Article 29, § 2908 prohibits loud construction between the hours of 8 pm and 7 am without a special permit. In addition, see also the previous section "Noise and Nuisance from a Neighbor" in this chapter, "Using the Department of Building Inspection" in *Chapter 6: Repairs and Services*, and "Permit Process" in *Chapter 11: Changes in Use*. Failure to exercise reasonable care in completing maintenance or to follow appropriate protocols to minimize exposure to noise, dust, mold, or building materials with potentially harmful health effects, in bad faith, is a form of harassment under the Rent Ordinance. (SF Administrative Code § 37.10B(a)(3))

Repeated calls or visits to your home or workplace.

Mail tampering.

Refusal to accept or acknowledge receipt of rent, or to cash a rent check for over thirty days, in bad faith, if covered under the Rent Ordinance. (See the section "Paying Rent" in *Chapter 4: Renting Basics*).

Stopping These Types of Harassment

- Work with your neighbors, who are probably also being harassed, in gathering evidence of the harassment such as written communication from the landlord, witnesses, photos, videos, etc. The recording of conversations is allowed where there is a reasonable expectation the conversation can be overheard. (CA Penal Code § 632) The recording of communications is also allowed for the purpose of obtaining evidence reasonably believed to relate to the committing by the other party of extortion, kidnapping, bribery, felony involving violence against the person, threat to inflict injury to the person or property or any member of his or her family, communication with intent to annoy by telephone or electronic communication device using obscene language about the other person or threatening injury to the other person or property, or repeated communication with telephone calls or electronic communication devices to annoy another person. (CA Penal Code § 633.5, § 653m) Also, as a general rule, if you can observe something from a public place, you are allowed to photograph it legally. (Mickey Osterreicher, General Counsel for the National Press Photographers Association, *National Geographic Traveler*,

Example of a Letter About Harassment

The letter on the right addresses the landlord's responsibility to assure that your apartment is not unreasonably noisy, as well as landlord entry violations.

August/September 2013) Maintain a log, detailing each incident including the date, time, who was present, and what occurred.

- Speak with the landlord, explaining the problem.

- Request a free Alternative Dispute Resolution Session from the San Francisco Rent Board. (See "Alternative Dispute Resolution" in "Chapter 14: Taking Action.") Or try other mediation services such as Conflict Intervention Service. (See "Appendix A: Resources.")

- For failure to exercise reasonable care in completing maintenance or to follow appropriate protocols to minimize exposure to noise, dust, mold, or building materials with potentially harmful health effects, in bad faith, file a petition for Decrease in Housing Services with the Rent Board if you are covered under the Rent Ordinance's rent control. (SF Administrative Code § 37.10B(a)(3))

- Notify the landlord in writing to cease further harassment or face legal action. (Mail the letter with a certificate of mailing which does not require a signature unlike certified mail, and keep a copy.)

- File a lawsuit in small claims. You can seek a penalty of up to $2,000 for each violation under California Civil Code § 1940.2, and not less than three times actual damages or $1,000, whichever is greater, and whatever the court rules is appropriate if bad faith on the part of the landlord can be proven under the Rent Ordinance including possible punitive damages (SF Administrative Code § 37.10B(c)(5)).

- Consult an attorney for filing a case in Superior Court and/or file for a temporary restraining order, injunction, or criminal penalties including jail for up to six months if bad faith on the part of the landlord can be proven under the Rent Ordinance. (See the following section "Restraining Orders and Injunctions" and SF Administrative Code § 37.10B(c) for more information.)

- Contact the Postal Inspector regarding mail tampering or you can prosecute. (18 U.S.C. § 1701, § 1708)

Restraining Orders and Injunctions

If you are victimized by harassment in one of the forms

June 8, 2022

Dear Landlord:

The apartment in which I am living is verging on being uninhabitable due to the conduct of the apartment manager and neighboring tenants.

Noise is beyond the level agreed upon in the lease and the law. Tenants leave stereos and TVs on at high volume well beyond the 10 pm limit set by Article 29 of the San Francisco Police Code, and loud guests are easily heard through the walls well beyond 10 pm. Furthermore, unreasonably loud noise, including stereos and loud conversations by tenants and the manager, continue at all hours of the day and night. I have attached a log of what the noise was, when, and for how long the noise continued, as well as the decibel level according to my decibel meter, recordings of the noise, and police reports.

This incessant noise from other tenants is bothersome and in violation of the lease. Since this makes it impossible for me to peacefully enjoy my home, a legal nuisance exists which is under your control as the landlord and which is your responsibility to abate. Allowing these constant disturbances to continue violates my rights under the lease.

The manager is also in violation of Civil Code Section 1954 governing entry by the landlord. On numerous occasions he has claimed the emergency inspection privilege of Section 1954 to enter the premises without there being an emergency. He stands at the door demanding to be let into the apartment, disrupting my quiet enjoyment when I have expressly stated that I desire to be left alone. My apartment is kept clean and safe and there is no reason for frequent inspections or entry by the manager. His behavior is clearly unreasonable. Further, I suspect the manager of entering my locked apartment when I am not home, since no one else should have a key. I have discovered food missing and my possessions have been tampered with. This is also in violation of my right to quiet enjoyment of my premises and clearly a violation of my rights to privacy. I have, also, attached a log of when and what were the violations of my privacy.

This is a formal demand for you and the manager to act within the bounds of the law. If the violations mentioned above continue, I will be forced to sue for compensatory and punitive damages.

Sincerely,

Marisa Mayday

Example of a Temporary Restraining Order Complaint

On May 18 and June 4, 2022, the Defendant (landlord) entered the Plaintiff's (tenant) rental unit without permission at approximately 6 am each morning and verbally assaulted tenant telling her that she and her two children "must vacate the premises immediately or else," even though the Defendant had not served the Plaintiff any prior written eviction notice.

The Plaintiff returned home on the evening of June 7, 2022 to find the Defendant waiting outside the Plaintiff's home with two large unidentified males. The Defendant told the Plaintiff she "couldn't enter her home and that the Plaintiff would box up the Defendant's belongings and leave then in the back yard for her to pick up in four days." Police were notified and upon investigation, allowed the Plaintiff to enter her home. The Defendant was informed by the police that preventing the Plaintiff from entering the Plaintiff's home was illegal.

---

discussed previously, you might consider obtaining a court order restraining the other person from future actions that violate your rights. If you do not allege violence, threats of violence, or stalking, there is usually a fee of $435 (listed under "protective orders," effective 4/21) for the petition and response, but you may qualify for a fee waiver. Tenants may file the order on their own, although it is advisable to seek legal help so that your petition is not dismissed on a technicality.

To obtain a restraining order and more information, go to the Access Center (see "Access Center" under "Governmental Agencies" in "Appendix A: Resources") or *https://www.courts.ca.gov/selfhelp-abuse.htm*. Ask the court clerk for forms that are needed in addition to the forms listed on the Web site. IMPORTANT: Your restraining order paperwork will go to the restrained person in your case and he will get a chance to see everything you write. If you are staying somewhere you do not want the restrained person to know about, do NOT write it on these papers. You can use a program called "Safe at Home" (*https://www.sos.ca.gov/registries/safe-home*) that gives you a secure address to use for your court papers (or for banking, etc.).

You must provide enough information in your petition to convince the judge that you need protection from your landlord or his agent because all of these facts apply:

- The landlord's conduct is intentional.

- The landlord has done a series of acts (more than one)

which seriously alarms, annoys, or harasses the tenant.

- The tenant has suffered a lot of emotional distress.

- The landlord's conduct has no legitimate reason and is not protected by law.

The law defines "harassment" for temporary restraining orders (TRO) as "unlawful violence, a credible threat of violence, or a knowing and willful course of conduct directed at a specific person that seriously alarms, annoys, or harasses the person, and that serves no legitimate purpose. The course of conduct must be such as would cause a reasonable person to suffer substantial emotional distress, and actually cause substantial emotional distress to the plaintiff." (CA Code of Civil Procedure § 527.6(b)(3))

When filing the TRO, do not recount all details of prior incidents but provide specific and accurate facts. Give dates, times and the form of harassment (verbal, physical or written). The more recent these incidents, the better or the court may say you've waited too long. Ask the Access Center to review the paperwork. Make at least five copies (some courts want copies after filing so ask the court clerk first). File the forms at Superior Court. Keep copies of the papers in different safe places.

You will need someone other than yourself and at least eighteen years of age and not to be protected by the order to serve the papers and also serve blank forms of Response to Request for Civil Harassment Restraining Orders (Form CH-120), Proof of Firearms Turned In or Sold (Form CH-800), and How Can I Respond to a Request for Civil Harassment Restraining Orders? (Form CH-120-INFO) on the person you want a restraint on. Have your server fill out a Proof of Personal Service (Form CH-200) and give it to you so you can file it with the court.

Go to the hearing! The judge will review the pleadings and will either grant or deny the application. The only information the judge uses in making a decision is the allegations you write in your TRO, so make sure these show "great or irreparable harm." A hearing on whether to issue a permanent injunction will be within fifteen days, at which time both the tenant and the landlord may appear in court to give verbal testimony and to offer other documentary evidence. The judge may either issue a permanent injunction or deny the request. If the order is granted and the landlord violates it, she will be subject to arrest for contempt of court. The party who wins the case may be awarded court costs and attorney's fees.

See the "Breaking a Lease" section in *Chapter 4: Renting Basics* and the "Nuisance" section in *Chapter 12: Eviction Defenses* for more information for victims and household family members of domestic violence, sexual assault, stalking, elder or dependent adult abuse, or human trafficking. See the section "Security" in *Chapter 6: Repairs and Services* for changing locks for a protected tenant with a restraining court order or a police report.

Chapter 9: **Discrimination**

What Is Discrimination?

Discrimination is treating a person or group of people less favorably because of some perceived characteristic. Discrimination is illegal if that characteristic is protected by laws. Housing discrimination most often occurs when a person is a prospective tenant. Most landlords know that discrimination is illegal, so they are careful not to say, "We don't rent to your kind." Instead, they will try something more subtle, such as telling you that the apartment has already been rented, or that the ad had an error and the rent is actually higher, or pretend to consider your application. In an extremely tight housing market, landlords can be very selective about the tenant and practice discrimination. Laws are only as good as the tenants' ability to enforce them.

Federal, State, and Local Anti-Discrimination Laws

Any state or local anti-discrimination laws may be preempted, that is voided, by State or Federal laws that "occupy the field" of housing discrimination law (CA Government Code § 12993(c)). If a conflict exists between federal, state and local laws, laws made by the superior legislature preempt laws made by the lower legislative body. Federal laws will preempt state and local laws, while state laws will preempt local laws. However, federal law for the Fair Housing Amendments Act does not invalidate state or local law, unless the state or local law would be discriminatory housing under the federal law. (42 U.S.C. § 3615)

If a discrimination lawsuit went to trial based solely on a local anti-discrimination law, the court would rule that the law was invalid if the law is in a field occupied by state law. Why bother enacting a law that is preempted by a superior legislative body? Because preemption is applied by the courts, there is no fixed rule that the law is void unless the law has already been challenged in court.

San Francisco's anti-discrimination laws are still on the books, and the Human Rights Commission has said that it will continue to enforce them. A number of local laws that are similar to anti-discrimination laws have been ruled valid, such as the law that prohibits discrimination against people with AIDS is valid because it promotes public health (but not because it prevents discrimination). (*Citizens for Uniform Laws v. County of Contra Costa* (1991) 223 Cal. App. 3d 1468) Similarly, the section of the San Francisco Housing Code prohibiting landlords from denying housing to families might be allowed because its purpose is to promote "housing access to families," not to prevent discrimination.

A fair amount of overlap exists between federal, state and local laws. Federal law include the Fair Housing Act and Fair Housing Amendments Act (42 U.S.C. § 3601 *et seq.*). State antidiscrimination laws include the Fair Employment and Housing Act (CA Government Code § § 12900–12996), the Unruh Civil Rights Act (CA Civil Code § 51 *et seq.*), and Civil Code § 54.1. Locally, the San Francisco Rent Ordinance (SF Administrative Code § 37.10B) includes anti-discrimination laws. (See *Appendices C and D: Law Excerpts and Regulations.*) Most discrimination claims can be brought under any or all of these laws.

Discrimination includes any of the following:

Refusal to rent housing accommodations.

Refusal to negotiate for the rental of housing accommodations.

Representation that a housing accommodation is not available for inspection or rental when that housing accommodation is available.

Provision of inferior terms, conditions, privileges, facilities, or services in connection with those housing accommodations.

Harassment in connection with those housing accommodations.

The cancellation or termination of a rental agreement.

The provision of segregated or separated housing accommodations.

Who Is Protected?

Under federal, state, and local laws, the opportunity to seek, obtain, and hold housing without discrimination is a civil right. Landlords violate one or all of these laws if they discriminate on the basis of:

- age (exemption for senior and homeless youth housing)
- ancestry
- color
- disability
- familial status
- gender identity
- genetic information
- height
- income source
- marital status
- medical condition
- military or veteran status

- national origin
- race
- religion
- sex
- sexual orientation (homosexuality, bisexuality, or heterosexuality)
- weight
- other arbitrary discrimination except for a valid business reason that is applied to all of that trait. (*Harris v. Capital Growth Investors XIV* (1991) 52 Cal.3d 1142. For example, the Rent Board would probably allow passthroughs limited to units with low rent only. See "Chapter 7: Rent Increases" for more info on passthroughs.)

The California Fair Employment and Housing Act (FEHA) protection also protects against discrimination based on the perception that a person has a protected characteristic or the association with a person who has, or is perceived to have, any protected characteristic. Exemptions include:

Refusal to rent a portion of an owner-occupied single-family house to a roomer or boarder living within the household, provided that no more than one roomer or boarder is to live within the household, and the owner complies with California Government Code § 12955(c), which prohibits discriminatory notices, statements, and advertisements. However, advertising for a particular sex when living areas are shared is also not discrimination. (CA Government Code § 12927(c)(2))

Senior housing, which may discriminate against children and is allowed to qualify applicants based on their age.

The Fair Housing Act includes discrimination for criminal history if the policy or practice has a discriminatory effect because of race or national origin. See *www.hud.gov/sites/documents/HUD_OGCGUIDAPPFHASTANDCR.PDF* for more information.

It is not prohibited to discriminate against people with low income, so long as the landlord uses uniform standards based on the prospective tenant's ability to pay rent. An income-to-rent ratio (for example, rent is no more than 30% of income) is allowable. However, a policy automatically excluding any prospective tenant receiving public assistance would be arbitrary discrimination and not allowed. Refusal to rent based on monetary considerations must bear some reasonable relation to the tenant's ability to pay rent.

More Information on Specific Characteristics Protected by Anti-Discrimination Statutes

Disability

Defining Disability

The Americans with Disabilities Act only applies to housing made available by a public entity, and private entities that own, lease (to and from), and operate places of public accommodation. The Fair Housing Amendments Act of 1988 (FHAA) protects persons with handicaps from discrimination and requires landlords to make reasonable accommodations to rules, policies, and regulations in order to permit a handicapped person to enjoy full and equal use of a housing unit. The Act uses the term "handicap" to have the same legal meaning as "disability." (*Bragdon v. Abbot* (1998) 524 U.S. 624, 631) The FHAA defines "handicap" as any of the following:

A physical or mental impairment which substantially limits one or more major life activities.

A history of such impairment.

Being regarded as having such impairment.

The California Fair Employment and Housing Act (FEHA) and the Unruh Civil Rights Act, also prohibit discrimination against a tenant or prospective tenant based on a disability. The FEHA and the Unruh Civil Rights Act, however, define disability far more broadly than the FHAA to include mental or physical impairments that merely "limit" a major life activity, and looks at the disability *without regard to the mitigating, i.e. corrective measures used to treat or correct the disability.*

"Mental Disability" includes any mental or psychological disorder or condition (including anyone identified by the Diagnostic and Statistical Manual of Mental Disorders—Fourth Edition, DSM IV) that limits a major life activity, including:

Mental retardation, organic brain syndrome, emotional or mental illness (for example, chronic depression or obsessive-compulsive disorder) or specific learning disabilities.

"Physical Disability" is defined as having a physiological disease, disorder, condition, cosmetic disfigurement, or anatomical loss that:

Affects neurological, immunological, musculoskeletal, special sense organs, respiratory, including speech organs, cardiovascular, reproductive, digestive, genitourinary, hemic and lymphatic, skin, and endocrine systems.

Limits a major life activity (without regard to corrective measures and broadly construed to include physical, mental, and social activities in addition to work).

In addition, physical and mental disabilities include, but are not limited to, chronic or episodic conditions such as HIV/AIDS, hepatitis, epilepsy, seizure disorder, diabetes, clinical depression, bipolar disorder, multiple sclerosis, and heart disease.

There may be other mental or physical conditions that would qualify as a disability. See the following sections and the section "What Can You Do?" at the end of this chapter for strategies for asserting rights for disabilities.

Reasonable Accommodations and Modifications

Reasonable accommodations require the landlord to change her policies, rules, practices, or services to enable a disabled tenant an equal opportunity to use and enjoy the housing, for example, rules about animals, change of the rent due date, extra time to cure or quit, etc. The Code of Federal Regulations requires owners of apartment complexes with accessible units to adopt suitable means to assure that information regarding the availability of accessible units reaches eligible individuals, and to take reasonable steps to maximize the use of such units by eligible individuals. (24 CFR 8.27)

A landlord will be required to cease eviction proceedings at whatever stage they are in, even if made aware of the tenant's disability and need for an accommodation only after notice of the eviction was provided to the tenant, or after the eviction complaint was filed. (*Radecki v. Joura*, 114 F.3d 115 (8th Cir. 1997)).

The landlord has a right to require supporting documentation of a disability where the disability is not obvious, but usually the type or severity of the disability does not need to be disclosed unless it is required to make a decision related to the disability such as an accessible unit. Such information must not be shared with other persons unless needed to make a decision to grant or deny a reasonable modification request or unless required by law (e.g., a subpoena). Information verifying that the person meets the definition of disability can usually be provided by the individual herself (e.g., proof that an individual under 65 years of age receives Supplemental Security Income or Social Security Disability Insurance benefits or a credible statement by the individual). A doctor or other medical professional, a peer support group, a non-medical service agency, or a reliable third party who is in a position to know about the individual's disability may also provide verification of a disability.

Reasonable modifications require a landlord to allow a disabled tenant to alter the unit at the tenant's expense, so the tenant can have "full enjoyment of the premises." However, the tenant's right to modify the unit may be conditioned on the tenant's agreement to restore the unit to its preexisting condition when reasonable. (CA Civil Code § 54.1)

Where reasonable, for example, the tenant has a poor credit history, the landlord may require the tenant to place into an interest bearing account the amount to restore the unit to its condition before the modification. (CA Civil Code § 54.1) Charging a higher fee to a person in a wheelchair because of the wear and tear that is predictable because a person in a wheelchair is living in the unit is unlawful. The interest in the account would belong to the tenant. See the Joint Statement of the Department of HUD and Justice on Reasonable Modifications Under the Fair Housing Act, 3/5/08, for more info: *https://www.mvfairhousing.com/modification.php.*

Additionally, the 9th Circuit Court has held that under United States Code, Title 42, § 3604(f)(3)(B), landlords may be required to assume reasonable financial burdens in accommodating handicapped residents. The case concerned a landlord's refusal to waive guest parking fees for a disabled resident's home healthcare aid. The Court further held:

"The reasonable accommodation inquiry is highly fact-specific, requiring case-by-case determination. In a case such as this one, a reviewing court should examine, among other things, the amount of fees imposed, the relationship between the amount of fees and the overall housing cost, the proportion of other tenants paying such fees, the importance of the fees to the landlord's overall revenues, and the importance of the fee waiver to the handicapped tenant." (*United States v. California Mobile Home Park Management Co.* (1994) 29 F. 3d 1413, 1417))

The Fair Housing Amendments Act (FHAA, 42 U.S.C. § 3604) requires that in public and common-use areas for buildings with four or more units constructed for first occupancy after March 13, 1991:

All common areas are readily accessible and usable by handicapped persons.

All doors are wide enough to allow passage by wheelchair.

The FHAA, also, requires that dwellings have:

All light switches, electrical outlets, thermostats, and other environmental controls within the dwelling units are placed in accessible locations.

S. GROSS

Bathroom walls are reinforced to allow the placement of grab bars.

All rooms within the dwelling are maneuverable by wheelchair.

For actions that remain illegal under federal law, such as growing marijuana, the landlord would not have to make reasonable accommodations. (*Ross v. Ragingwire Telecommunications* ((2008) 42 Cal.4th 920) The reasoning used in deciding the case could be extended to a case where a resident seeks an accommodation for medical marijuana use in rental housing.

Disability and Animal Support

The Fair Housing Amendments Act of 1988 applies to service animals, assistance animals, or companion animals for reasonable accommodation. "Service animal" is not expressly defined in the Fair Housing Act, so emotional support animals, including species other than dogs, are potentially allowed with no specific training required. The courts have ruled that landlords may not require proof of special training or certification of the animal. (*Green v. Housing Authority of Clackamas County* (1993) 994 F.Supp. 1253, 1256 (U.S. District Court))

The animal must be necessary to afford the individual an equal opportunity to use and enjoy a dwelling or to participate in the housing service or program. The animal must provide a disability-related benefit to the individual. The animal can be excluded if it would cause a financial or administrative burden, fundamentally alter the nature of the housing program, pose a direct threat to health or safety, or cause substantial physical damage to the property of others that cannot be reduced by a reasonable accommodation. (2/17/11 HUD memo, *https:// www.equalhousing.org/wp-content/uploads/2014/09/2011-ADA-Regulations-Section-504.pdf*)

Local ordinances prohibiting housing discrimination combine with state and federal laws and case law (*Auburn Woods I Homeowners Association v. Fair Employment and Housing Commission* (2004) 121 Cal.App.4th 1578), to require landlords to reasonably accommodate a tenant (or a tenant's visitor) with a disability who wishes to be exempt from any landlord's animal rules. While the federal FHAA has exemptions to prohibitions on discrimination, these do not apply under the California Fair Employment and Housing Act unless one of the situations mentioned previously in the "Who Is Protected?" section applies.

The Unruh Act (in *Osborne v. Yasmeh* (2016) Cal.App.4th 2016 WL 4039863) and the Fair Housing Act do not allow a deposit to be charged for the animal (*https://www.hud.gov/sites/dfiles/ PA/documents/HUDAsstAnimalNC1-28-2020.pdf*) but the animal owner is responsible for damage outside of normal wear and tear. In California, fines are imposed for interfering with a disabled person's ability to exercise their rights for a trained guide dog, signal dog or service dog, or for interfering with those dogs. "Service dog" means any dog individually trained to do work or

perform tasks for the benefit of an individual with a disability, including, but not limited to, minimal protection work, rescue work, pulling a wheelchair, or fetching dropped items. (CA Penal Code § 365.5 et seq.) Dogs in training are also usually protected. (CA Civil Code § 54.1) and cannot be charged an extra fee or deposit (CA Civil Code § 54.2) In addition, there cannot be a requirement that the animal be declawed or devocalized. (CA Civil Code § 1942.7)

Service animals might help with: mobility, guidance, hearing, seizure alerts, miscellaneous daily needs, coping with conditions such as arthritis, cancer, carpal tunnel syndrome, chronic pain, developmental and hearing impairments, eating disorders, obesity, diabetes, heart disease, high blood pressure, HIV, lupus, mood disorders, post-traumatic stress disorder, psychiatric conditions, seizure disorders, and many other conditions.

Neither service animals nor assistance animals require you to be totally or catastrophically disabled. Nor do you have to be eligible for or receiving disability benefits to qualify for the assistance of a service animal or assistance animal. Your landlord may therefore be required to make an exception for you from any restrictions against having animals if all of the following apply:

- You have a medical condition (physical or mental) that meets the legal definition of a disability.

- You need to live with an animal (cat, dog, bird, tarantula, etc.) to cope with your condition.

- Your doctor or other medical professional, a peer support group, a non-medical service agency, or a reliable third party who is in a position to know about the individual's disability will sign a simple statement verifying that you have such a condition and confirming that living with an animal would be beneficial for your health. Your landlord has a right to request such proof of a need for reasonable accommodation where the need is not obvious, but usually the type or severity of the disability does not need to be disclosed.

- You can maintain and care for your animal without causing damage to your landlord's property, without causing serious problems, and without interfering with your neighbors.

(May 17, 2004 Joint Statement of HUD and DOJ Reasonable Accommodations Under the Fair Housing Act, *https://www.hud.gov/sites/documents/huddojstatement.pdf*)

Pets Are Wonderful Support (PAWS) recommends that the letter states that the animal is an essential part of the treatment, not to use the word "pet" but "assistance animal," specify how the animal helps with the disability, and that the letter must be on the doctor's letterhead.

You can call the police to enforce your rights and tell them what law you are asserting when you call, but sometimes the officers are not fully aware of the law, and it is possible that they may take the other side. Your best bet is to try to educate the person attempting to exclude your assistance animal. ID tags for service dogs are available through county animal control, but there is no government assessment of an animal's training. (CA Food & Agriculture Code § 30850)

Personal Care Attendants

A tenant with a disability may require the services of a live-in personal care attendant to assist with day-to-day activities. Although the attendant lives on the property, he is an employee of the tenant with the disability and does not have a landlord-tenant relationship with the landlord. A tenant with a disability cannot be charged more rent or additional security deposit for the attendant. (*www.pdffiller.com/40772958-2014_Fair_Housing-_Handbookpdf-2014-13-Edition-FAIR-HOUSING-HANDBOOK--Human-RightsFair--Various-Fillable-Forms*)

People with AIDS/HIV

The FEHA prohibition against discrimination on the basis of disability includes discrimination against people with AIDS or people who are HIV positive. San Francisco's ordinance makes it illegal to refuse to rent to a person because that person has AIDS or HIV, or to evict a person because they suffer from AIDS or HIV. (SF Police Code § 3801, § 3804)

Familial Status

Discrimination based on the size of familial or non-familial households is prohibited in San Francisco. Landlords may not refuse to rent or otherwise deny (for example, by eviction) a dwelling unit to a family, where a family is one or more persons related or unrelated, living together as a single integrated household, as long as the minimum floor area is provided. See

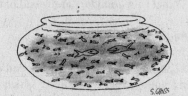

S. GROSS

"I guess we're family. We live together, love each other, and we haven't eaten the children yet."

"Adding Family Members" in "Chapter 10: Roommates."

In addition, discrimination prohibited by San Francisco Police Code § 102 includes:

Unreasonable rules or rental agreements that exclude or discriminate against persons with children.

Segregating families with children to a particular part of the building.

Evictions based on the number of occupants.

Additional rent or deposits based on the actual or potential number or age of persons living in the housing accommodations.

Rent charges based on additional occupants.

The Fair Housing Amendments Act and FEHA also prohibit discrimination against a tenant or prospective tenant based on familial status. See the section "What Can You Do?" at the end of this chapter for more strategies.

Height and Weight

San Francisco Police Code § 3304 prohibits discrimination for height or weight.

Income Source

The FEHA and California Government Code §§ 12955 and 12927 prohibits housing discrimination on the basis of one's source of income which is "lawful verifiable income" that is paid either directly to the tenant, tenant's representative, or landlord. Landlords must evaluate prospective tenants based on the aggregate income of the applicants seeking to share a residence. A landlord's inquiry about the amount or source of income does not alone constitute discrimination.

Where the tenant is receiving a government rent subsidy as a Section 8 Housing Voucher, FEHA does not consider it a source of income. However, discrimination against persons receiving Section 8 is expressly prohibited and was upheld in court with a review by the California Supreme Court denied. (*City and County of San Francisco v. Post* (2018) 22 Cal.App.5th 121)

Age

The Unruh Civil Rights Act expressly forbids discrimination on the basis of age. (CA Civil Code § 51.2) The Federal Fair Housing Amendments Act protections may be available to the tenant when the age discrimination is related to family status. Age discrimination can occur when a landlord refuses to consider renting to a family with small children. It can also arise when a landlord does not want an older tenant who may

Chapter 9– Discrimination

be looking to settle down, or a tenant who may not reflect the youthful image the landlord is trying to project in the building. See the section "What Can You Do?" at the end of this chapter for possible strategies against this discrimination.

In the case of "senior citizen housing," discrimination is allowed against those under 62 years of age, if the senior citizen housing follows the strict federal and state laws allowing such discrimination. (CA Civil Code § 51.3) Housing for homeless youths is not considered age discrimination. (CA Government Code § 12957)

Sexual Orientation

In addition to the FEHA express prohibition against discrimination on the basis of sexual orientation in housing, several California cases have held that sexual orientation is a protected class for any business transaction under the Unruh Act. See the section "What Can You Do?" at the end of this chapter for possible strategies against this discrimination.

Marital Status

Discrimination against unmarried cohabiting couples is prohibited by the FEHA and the Unruh Civil Rights Act. The California Supreme Court ruled in *Smith v. Fair Employment and Housing Commission* ((1996) 12 Cal. 4th 1143) that the FEHA provision prohibiting discrimination in housing on the basis of marital status did not burden a landlord's free exercise of religion even if their strongly-held religious beliefs forbid them to rent to unmarried mixed gender couples. The Court held that religious beliefs did not require landlords to rent apartments, and therefore they can avoid any burden on the landlord's religious exercise without violating the religious beliefs. The religious exemption that the landlord sought could only be granted by completely sacrificing the rights of prospective tenants not to be discriminated against by the landlord in housing accommodations on account of marital status. Thus, the Court held FEHA does not violate the State or Federal Constitution. (See the section "What Can You Do?" at the end of this chapter.)

Race

Occasionally tenants experience harassment because they are associating with people of another race. This is clearly illegal.

The Federal Fair Housing Amendments Act, FEHA, and the Unruh Civil Rights Act prohibit race discrimination. A letter to the landlord (or landlord's agent) demanding he cease the discriminatory action may be enough to cause the landlord to back down. However, if the harassment continues, a lawsuit or administrative action may be brought against the landlord. (See the section "What Can You Do?" at the end of this chapter.)

Retaliation—Protected Acts of the Tenant

FEHA (CA Government Code § 12955(f)) and California Civil Code § 1942.5 prohibit any owner of housing accommodations from harassing, evicting (except retaliatory Ellis Act evictions are allowed, see "Fighting an Ellis Eviction" in "Chapter 12: Eviction Defenses"), or otherwise discriminating against any person in the rental of housing accommodations when the owner's dominant purpose is retaliation against a person who has engaged in any of the following conduct prior to, or close to the owner's retaliatory or discriminatory conduct:

Opposed unlawful practices.

Informed law enforcement agencies of practices believed to be unlawful.

Testified or assisted in any proceeding.

Aided or encouraged a person to exercise or enjoy their rights.

If a tenant has engaged in any of the previously-referenced acts and the landlord or landlord's agent shortly thereafter engages in any of the following acts, there will be good evidence that the landlord or landlord's agent has retaliated against the tenant for engaging in protected activities:

Refusal to rent or negotiate for the rental of housing accommodations.

Any other denial or withholding of housing accommodations.

Provision of inferior conditions, privileges, facilities, or services in connection with those housing accommodations.

Cancellation or termination of a rental agreement.

See also the box "Retaliation Is Illegal" in "Chapter 6: Repairs and Services" and "What Can You Do?" at the end of this chapter.

Sexual Discrimination

See the section "What Can You Do?" at the end of this chapter for how to deal with sexual harassment which is also sexual discrimination. Also, see "Sexual Harassment" in "Chapter 8: Harassment."

Undocumented Immigrants

A landlord or agent of the landlord is prohibited from making any inquiry regarding the immigration or citizenship status of an occupant or prospective occupant of residential rental property, or disclosing the information to the Immigration and Customs Enforcement (ICE) or elsewhere for the purpose of harassment. (CA Civil Code § 1940.3, § 1942.5) In addition, it is illegal to threaten to disclose information related to the immigration or citizenship status of an occupant or another person known by the landlord to be related to the occupant for the purpose of influencing the tenant to vacate the dwelling. (CA Civil Code § 1940.2, § 1940.35) A landlord may not evict an occupant or person associated with the occupant because of the immigration or citizenship status unless complying with a federal law (such as rent limitations or assistance). (CA Code of Civil Procedure § 1161.4) The Fair Housing Amendments Act, FEHA, and the Unruh Civil Rights Act, also, prohibit discrimination on the basis of "national origin" but the courts have interpreted this phrase to *exclude* discrimination on the basis of immigration status.

Requests for citizenship status or Social Security numbers can be a form of tenant harassment. Often these requests come with new owners or in rental applications. You do not have to fill out this information if you already live in the building. If you are applying to a new building, its best to get in touch with the Human Rights Commission or Causa Justa when requested for this information and you think the request is discriminatory.

Article 33 of the San Francisco Police Code prohibits discrimination on the basis of "place of birth" and charges the Human Rights Commission with enforcement of this provision. It seems clear (although it has never been tested in court) that this "place of birth" classification would include immigration status, and the Human Rights Commission passed a resolution clarifying this point. The resolution clarifies that discrimination on the basis of "place of birth," includes discrimination on the basis of immigration status and *perceived* immigration status. The resolution also states that it is illegal to deny housing or refuse to make repairs or comply with other landlord obligations because of the tenant's immigration status. In addition, threatening a tenant with the ICE to circumvent eviction laws or to prevent the tenant from asserting their rights and requesting documentation from any tenant or prospective tenant is illegal. It explicitly lists several other illegal forms

of discrimination. The resolution asserts that the Commission will vigorously investigate complaints and prosecute any complaint with merit and/or refer the complaint to the City Attorney or the District Attorney.

What Can You Do?

1. Documentation in Writing

Discrimination can be difficult to prove. As with all legal disputes, it is very important that you document what is happening. Keep a log of each specific act that you think is discriminatory. **Put as much communication between you and your landlord in writing as possible**, keeping a copy and sending letters with a certificate of mailing or other proof of mailing. Write the landlord specifying what he has done and demanding that he stop. This letter is particularly important for people with disabilities because the landlord must know you have a disability (not necessarily what kind of disability) before you can gain the protections under the law. (See "Write Letters" in "Chapter 14: Taking Action" for more tips.)

2. Report the Discrimination

Report the behavior to the San Francisco Human Rights Commission so it can monitor the situation, help you with your case, and possibly help mediate with the landlord. (See "Appendix A: Resources" for the contact info.)

If you feel you have enough evidence to step up the legal action, you can go through the administrative process with the Department of Fair Employment and Housing (DFEH) for violations of the Fair Employment and Housing Act (FEHA) up to one year (extensions possible) after the alleged violations occurred. DFEH will attempt conciliation or recommend litigation. For anyone subject to the Unruh Act, a violation on "any...basis prohibited by [Unruh]" is a violation of the FEHA. (CA Government Code § 12955(d) To go through this process, file a complaint with the California Department of Fair Employment and Housing and/or the U.S. Department of Housing and Urban Development (HUD). More info can be found by looking in this book's index under "discrimination: resource, tenant" and in California Code of Regulations, Title 2, §§ 10035 through 10066.

3. File a Lawsuit

Alternatively, you could file a lawsuit. The statute of limitations (the time in which you can file in civil court) is two years for FEHA and one year for the Unruh Act. For a suit to be brought under the Fair Housing Act, consult with an attorney as soon as possible to determine the statute of limitations in your case. You can also sue for three times the actual damages or $1,000, whichever is greater, and other relief if bad faith on the part of the landlord can be proven under the Rent Ordinance. (SF Administrative Code § 37.10B) See "Sue Your Landlord" in "Chapter 14: Taking Action" for more info.

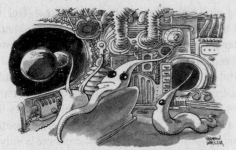

"When we're home, are we still aliens?"

Chapter 10: **Roommates**

Groups of unrelated or related individuals often set up shared households as high rents force people to pool their financial resources in order to remain in San Francisco. In order to help ensure that the friendly basis on which you established your household continues on the same good terms, it is important to know the rights and responsibilities that you have with one another and with your landlord, and to know some of the potential problem situations to avoid. Two things need to be figured out at the beginning:

(1) What will be the relationship between the owner and each individual roommate, including the critical question of how rent will be paid?

(2) What understandings will exist between the roommates regarding such things as cleaning duties, responsibility to pay bills, guest policies, etc.? A model roommate agreement is at the end of this chapter.

We will examine the rights and responsibilities between the tenant(s) and the landlord, and between household members.

Types of Tenant-Landlord Relationships

Different laws apply depending on the relationship between the landlord and the tenant(s).

The owner–household relationship is usually dictated by the owner when the tenants initially rent a home. Often, the owner will want all the roommates to be named on the rental agreement, if a written one is used. This way, the owner knows who is living in the dwelling and, therefore, who is responsible in case rent is unpaid or a problem arises.

A rental agreement does not have to be written, however. It may be oral or implied by conduct, such as acceptance of rent or other "consideration" (benefit) by the owner with a combination with other factors in exchange for the tenant's occupancy of the rental unit. Under the Rent Ordinance, the definition of a tenant is just "a person entitled by written or oral agreement, subtenancy approved by the owner, or by sufferance, to occupy a residential dwelling to the exclusion of others." (SF Administrative Code § 37.2(t)) The status of whether the tenant is a co-tenant or subtenant is bit not always clear, especially with oral agreements. (See the section later in this chapter "Proving That a Rental Agreement Directly with the Landlord Exists" for more information.)

It is very important to know what the legal relationship of each tenant is with the owner because this relationship determines whether and how much the owner can raise the rent which is discussed at the end of this chapter.

Roommates with Equal Rights

Co-tenants are tenants who are all considered equal in their relationship to the owner, usually with the same agreement and equal rights and responsibilities. Each co-tenant, usually, is considered to be "jointly and severally liable" for payment of the full rent and performance of the agreement. This means that if one co-tenant does not pay the rent or causes damage, the other tenants are liable for their own rent plus the unpaid rent and damage caused by the non-paying co-tenant(s). In written agreements, the named tenants are usually all co-tenants. Roommates added later and not named in the rental agreement are usually not co-tenants.

In a dispute between roommates, none of the co-tenants may evict another because they are all tenants renting from the owner. In a co-tenant situation, only the owner may bring an eviction action against the tenants. (See "Chapter 12: Evictions Defenses" for more info.)

Roommate(s) with a Master Tenant

An alternative situation is where one or more of the tenants is considered to be the master tenant and the other tenants are subtenants. A master tenant is defined under the Rent Ordinance (see "What Does the Rent Ordinance Cover?" in "Chapter 4: Renting Basics") as a landlord who is not the owner. (SF Rent Board Rules and Regulations § 6.15C) In addition, the landlord does not have to be the owner of the property; a landlord can be a "...lessor, or sublessor who receives or is entitled to receive rent..." (SF Administrative Code § 37.2(h)) Where a rental unit has a master tenant(s), the other tenants are usually considered to be subtenants of the master tenant and usually pay rent to the master tenant. In this situation, the master tenant(s) is ultimately responsible for the full payment of the rent. This means that the owner may look only to the master tenant(s) for the full rent payment and it is up to the master tenant(s) to make sure that the subtenants pay their parts. In written agreements, usually only the tenants named in the rental agreement are master tenants. If there are other tenants also living in the dwelling, they would then be subtenants.

Subletting

Subletting and assignment are two distinct legal concepts, although they may appear similar in practice. Subletting occurs when a tenant gives another person a partial or limited right to use of the tenant's place in exchange for rent or "reward." Vacation rentals and home exchanges are also considered subletting as long as there is a "reward" for the use of the property. (CA Civil Code § 1925) A common example is when a tenant will be out of town for a few months and rents her apartment to another person for this period. Another example is where there is only one name on the rental agreement and the named tenant rents space in the

unit to others. In both cases, a subletting has occurred, and a subtenancy has been created. Assignment of a rental agreement occurs when the tenant wants to give up all of his interests in the unit and completely transfer them to another person. See the section "Assignment of Rental Agreement to Another Tenant" later in this chapter. The subtenant ordinarily does not have a separate rental agreement with the owner; the only agreement is with the tenant from whom he is subletting.

When a tenant sublets all or part of the rental unit to another person, she becomes the master tenant—legally the landlord—in relation to the subtenant. She still continues to be responsible to the "real" landlord for payment of rent and for all other terms of the rental agreement. A subtenant's violation of the rental agreement that the master tenant has with the owner does not excuse the master tenant from responsibility.

A clear written agreement between the tenant and the subtenant which spells out the exact terms of the subtenancy will help prevent later problems. For example, there have been unfortunate instances in which a tenant has returned home from a vacation only to find that the subtenant was unwilling to move, and in fact even claimed that there was no agreement that he would do so, or when. Proper notice providing that the subtenant vacate by a certain date, or with adequate notice from the master tenant, usually will prevent such situations from occurring and protect everyone involved. However, if the rental unit is covered by the Rent Ordinance, then San Francisco Rent Board Rules and Regulations § 6.15C provides requirements that a master tenant must follow to terminate a tenancy.

Unless the rental agreement with the "real" landlord expressly prohibits subletting, the law presumes that tenants can transfer their rights. However, the right to sublet usually is restricted by the rental agreement, often including the condition that neither can be done without the landlord's consent. "Consent clauses" containing no express standard or condition for giving or withholding consent always have been judged by the law to include an implied standard that the landlord's consent may not be unreasonably withheld. (CA Civil Code § 1951.4) The Rent Board has adopted a specific set of requirements to deal with this situation in Rent Board Rules and Regulations § 6.15. (See the "Changing Roommates" and "Adding Non-Family Members," and "Adding Family Members" sections later in this chapter.)

Reasonable landlord objections to subletting might include the following: (1) the new occupant's inability to fulfill the terms of the agreement, (2) financial irresponsibility or instability, (3) unsuitability of the unit for the intended use and, (4) intended undesirable use of the premises. If factors such as these are not present, the courts probably would see the landlord's refusal to give consent as unreasonable and thus unenforceable. However, a landlord still can petition to remove the rent increase limitation under the Rent Ordinance if the master tenant is not a "tenant in occupancy." (See "Tenant Not in Occupancy" in "Chapter 7: Rent Increases.")

Even if the rental agreement prohibits subletting, under the Rent Ordinance partial sublets may be allowed. See the sections later in this chapter "Changing Roommates" and "Adding Non-Family Members," and "Adding Family Members" for more information.

If the rental unit is not covered by the Rent Ordinance, but is covered under California just cause eviction, the owner may evict the tenant for subletting in violation of the lease. (CA Civil Code § 1946.2(b)(1)(G)) If the rental unit is not covered by just cause eviction, the owner may also evict for breach of the rental agreement. (Code of Civil Procedure § 1161(3), (4))

The conversion of individual rental units to transient uses may be considered illegal use that is not curable. See "Airbnb, Home Exchanges, or Similar Uses" in "Chapter 11: Changes in Use" for more info.

Rights of Subtenants with Master Tenants Under the San Francisco Rent Ordinance

Roommate situations where there is a master tenant and subtenant relationship can get a bit sticky because, as we have explained, for most purposes the master tenant who collects rent is not just another roommate but is legally the subtenant's landlord. A master tenant has the same responsibilities towards her subtenants as any other landlord. Likewise, it is generally the master tenant—and not the owner of the property—who the subtenant must go up against if there are problems.

Rent Board Rules and Regulations § 6.15C gives both master tenants and their roommates rights and responsibilities if the rental unit. The truth is that some master tenants have proved to be just as nasty as some owners, and these rules were added precisely to prevent such master tenants from behaving like bad owners. That said, such master tenants are far more the exception than the rule, and many master tenants think of themselves simply as tenants and roommates rather than landlords. Nevertheless, they must follow the Rent Board rules.

Master tenants cannot evict subtenants who moved in on or after May 25, 1998, without one of the Rent Ordinance's " just causes" *unless* "prior to commencement of the tenancy, the master tenant informs the tenant in writing that the tenancy is not subject to the just cause provisions of the Rent Ordinance." This right to evict without just cause only applies to master tenants who reside in the same rental unit with his or her subtenant. (SF Rent Board Rules and Regulations § 6.15C(1)) In addition, for any tenancy which began on or after May 25, 1998, master tenants are required to "disclose in writing to a tenant prior to commencement of the tenancy the amount of

rent the master tenant is obligated to pay to the owner of the property." (SF Rent Board Rules and Regulations § 6.15C(2))

In *any* master tenant-subtenant situation where the parties are roommates, regardless of when the subtenant moved in, the master tenant "may charge the subtenant(s) no more than the subtenant(s)' proportional share of the total current rent paid to the landlord by the master tenant for the housing and housing services to which the subtenant is entitled under the sub-lease." (SF Rent Board Rules and Regulations § 6.15C(3)) The master tenant may not "rent gouge" the subtenants by charging them more than their "proportional share" for the housing and housing services to which they are entitled under their contract with the master tenant. If the master tenant is subleasing the entire unit—in other words, he doesn't live there himself—he may charge the subtenants no more than the rent the master tenant pays to the owner, on the initial occupancy of the subtenant. (SF Administrative Code § 37.3(c)) Charging subtenants more rent than what the master tenant pays may be illegal use, a just cause for eviction. If the master tenant provides services in addition to the services provided by the owner, the master tenant may be able to charge additional rent. However, the master tenant cannot charge for interacting with the landlord. It would be wise for subtenants to check that the rent paid to the master tenant is actually paid to the owner.

So, how is a "proportional share" of the rent determined? The law provides only limited guidance. Rules and Regulations 6.15C(3) (a) states that the allowable proportional share can be based on the "square footage shared with and/or occupied exclusively by the subtenant," or "an amount substantially proportional to the space occupied by and/or shared with the subtenant (for example, three people splitting the entire rent in thirds)" or "any other method" that means the subtenant's share of the rent is not an excessive share of the total rent for the unit.

For example, a subtenant might claim that requiring him to pay 60% of the rent is unfair because his room is smaller than the master tenant's. The master tenant could perhaps counter that she provides all appliances, electronics (such as the stereo and the computer), and kitchenware that the subtenant can use in the apartment, and also that she takes care of all the bills and dealings with the owner. Additional housing services provided by the master tenant (such as utilities), "special obligations" of the master tenant and "evidence of the relative amenities or value of rooms" (the subtenant has a large bay window and the master tenant does not, for instance) may be considered by the Rent Board in determining the proper split of the rent.

There is no simple rule for deciding what the "proportional share" of the rent is in every case. Under Rule 6.15C(3)(a) each situation will be decided on a case-by-case basis according to what the Rent Board judge thinks is equitable given the facts presented at a hearing. In general though, unless the rent seems outrageously out of proportion, the Rent Board will probably uphold it.

After the initial rent is set, the master tenant may only increase the rent as allowed by the Rent Ordinance. A master tenant whose landlord imposes a capital improvement passthrough may also impose a proportionate share of the passthrough on the subtenant. (SF Rent Board Rules and Regulations § 6.15C(3) (c)) If the total rent paid by the master tenant to the landlord increases due to a lawful rent increase or passthrough, the subtenant's share of the rent may be proportionately increased without regard to the subtenant's anniversary date. (Topic No. 359 on Rent Board website)

Either the subtenant or master tenant (but not the owner) may file a petition with the Rent Board for an adjustment of the subtenant's initial rent under Rule 6.15C(3)(b), however, the Rent Board cannot take cases where the master tenant does not fall under the jurisdiction of the Rent Board (for example, in a single residential unit that is exempt from rent control). Subtenants can also file a petition at the Rent Board ("Subtenant Petition") if they believe that their rent has been unlawfully raised by the master tenant, who must comply with the regular rent increase guidelines that apply to all landlords. However, a master tenant's violation of this is not a just cause for eviction. (SF Rent Board Rules and Regulations § 6.15C(3))

Tenants filing a petition with the Rent Board to dispute their share of the rent should remember that they will have to provide both the rent the master tenant pays the landlord, and also the rents of all the other subtenants to show that their own rent is too high. If the master tenant has refused to tell the subtenant the total rent, the tenant should send the master tenant a letter, copying the Rent Board, reminding her of Rule 6.15C(2), along with a copy of the regulation itself. The subtenant should also use any other evidence of the rent he can come up with in the Rent Board petition (conversations with the owner, or past tenants as witnesses, for example). For a decrease in housing services or failure to repair and maintain by the master tenant, the subtenant would attach the "Decrease in Housing Services" or "Failure to Repair and Maintain" petition to the "Subtenant Petition." (See "Chapter 6: Repairs and Services" for more info.)

Rights of Subtenants with Master Tenants Under the California Law Limiting Rent Increases

For rental units covered under the state law limiting rent increases (see "Protections for the Tenant Under the San Francisco Rent Ordinance and State Law" in "Chapter 4: Renting Basics"), the master tenant may not charge the subtenant(s) more than the total rent that is allowed by the law. (CA Civil Code § 1947.12(c))

Roommate(s) Living with Owner

The occupant becomes a lodger if he is the only person in the

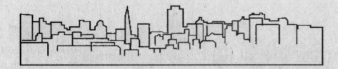

dwelling unit renting from the owner, and the owner has the right of access to all areas of the dwelling unit occupied by the lodger. The owner may evict the lodger after the appropriate notice without going to court and the owner is not required to have a just cause to evict. (CA Civil Code § 1946.5, SF Administrative Code § 37.9(b))

However, under the Rent Ordinance, if the sole person renting from the landlord is treated as having a separate unit, then the person is a tenant who is **not** exempt from just cause for eviction because of a shared unit. (*Chun v. Del Cid* (2019) B295140, Rent Board Case #T170945) For multiple tenants, the Rent Board has ruled in more than one case that the landlord has rented separate rental units by individually renting rooms with separate tenancies even though the rooms did not have locks. (Rent Board Case #T070119, #T130583)

If not covered under the Rent Ordinance, state law requiring just cause eviction may apply for tenants. (See "Protections for the Tenant Under the San Francisco Rent Ordinance and State Law" in "Chapter 4: Renting Basics.") The following exemptions are especially applicable:

1. Housing accommodations in which the tenant shares bathroom or kitchen facilities with the owner who maintains their principal residence at the property are exempt from just cause eviction.

2. Single-family owner-occupied residences, including where the owner-occupant rents no more than two units or bedrooms, including, but not limited to, an accessory dwelling unit are exempt from just cause eviction.

Adding Non-Family Members

This section only applies if the rental unit is covered under the Rent Ordinance. (See "What Does the Rent Ordinance Cover?" in "Chapter 4: Renting Basics" for more info.)

Although Rent Board Rules and Regulations 6.15A, B, and D have provided protections for tenants who want to replace roommates or add family members to their residence, most rental agreements have made it difficult or impossible for tenants to add new non-family occupants. The amended Rent Ordinance now prohibits evictions based on the addition of occupants if the landlord has unreasonably refused the tenant's written request, even if the lease prohibits subletting or limits the number of occupants. (SF Administrative Code § 37.9(a)(2)(C))

In addition, for breach-of-lease evictions based on unapproved subletting and/or occupants beyond the lease limit, the landlord must now provide a 10-day notice to cure or quit, and the tenant can cure the breach by requesting permission to add the unauthorized occupant. In situations where the tenant doesn't cure the breach, it is still unclear if landlords will also serve a 3 day notice to quit afterwards, or just simply start an unlawful detainer eviction proceeding through court. (See "Chapter 13: Eviction Process in Court" for more info.) Either way, it's best to try to comply within the 10 days notice period, if you have the option, in order to avoid an eviction case. See the box "What If There's Already a New Roommate?" for more information.

Further, the landlord may not increase the rent for the unit based on the addition of occupants, even when a pre-existing lease permits such an increase. (SF Administrative Code § 37.3(a)(11)) However, the landlord may petition the Rent Board to raise the rent for increased operating expenses. Tenants can protest such an increase. (See "Operating and Maintenance Expense Increase Passthrough" in "Chapter 7: Rent Increases" for more info.)

Rules and Procedures for Adding Non-Family Occupants

San Francisco Rent Board Rules and Regulations § 6.15E outlines specific rules and procedures for the addition of non-family occupants.

- In general, the number of occupants must not exceed *the lesser of*: (i) 2 persons in a studio unit, 3 persons in a one-bedroom unit, 4 persons in a two-bedroom unit, 6 persons in a three-bedroom unit, 8 persons in a 4-bedroom unit, etc.; or (ii) the maximum permitted under SF Housing Code § 503.

- The additional occupant(s) must not reside in the unit for fewer than 30 days.

- The tenant must request approval for a new occupant in writing. After receiving the tenant's request, the landlord has five days to request that the new occupant submit an application or information for a background check. The new occupant then has five days after receiving the landlord's request to respond (note that the five days begins on the day after actual receipt of the landlord's request).

- If the landlord fails to respond in writing, providing reasons for denying the request, the request shall be considered approved. Although the Ordinance states that the landlord must respond within 14 days of receiving the tenant's request, new clarifications of the timing mean that the landlord may have more than 14 days:

  - If the tenant's request is sent by mail, add five calendar days from the postmark date.

  - If the tenant's request is sent by email, add two calendar days.

  - If the tenant's request is personally delivered, no days are added.

  - If the last day is a weekend day or holiday, the time is extended to the end of the next business day. (CA Code of Civil Procedure § 12a)

The new legislation also clarifies that a landlord may deny a request for an additional occupant for any of the following reasons:

- The proposed occupant did not provide the requested application or information for a background check within the five-day time limit. The Rent Board recommends filling out the credit information, but the landlord may not use the lack of creditworthiness to deny the occupancy if the proposed occupant will not pay rent to the landlord because the other tenants are responsible for the entire rent.

- The new occupant has intentionally misrepresented significant facts on the application or provided significant misinformation that interferes with the landlord's ability to conduct a background check.

- The new occupant presents a direct threat to the health, safety or security of other residents, or to the physical structure of the property.

- The total number of occupants would exceed the allowable number of occupants, as specified in the previous paragraphs.

- The tenant resides in the same unit as the landlord. (See the previous section "Roommates(s) Living with Owner" for an argument that the tenant has a separate tenancy.)

- Adding an occupant would require the landlord to increase the electrical or hot water capacity in the building, or adapt other building systems or existing amenities, and such enhancements would present a financial hardship to the landlord.

- The proposed occupant will be paying some or all of the rent to the landlord, and the landlord can establish the new occupant's lack of creditworthiness. Note that if the new occupant will not be paying any of the rent to the landlord—i.e., if the other tenants will be responsible for the whole amount of the rent—the landlord may not reject the proposed occupant due to lack of creditworthiness.

If a request for a new occupant is refused, the tenant can petition the Rent Board for a significant rent reduction (decrease in services). This is safer than moving in a roommate.

Adding Family Members

If the rental agreement has no restrictions on the number of occupants allowed, or does not prohibit subletting, then tenants have the right to add family members. Also, rental agreements can be modified by either express or implied consent, so more occupants may be allowed than in the original rental agreement. The right for additional occupants if there is no restriction applies to both rental units covered and those not covered by the Rent Ordinance.

Rather than specifying how many occupants are allowed, San Francisco Housing Code § 503, which also applies to all residential units regardless of whether it is covered by the Rent Ordinance or not, is phrased in terms of how much space must be allowed for each person. The code specifies that "Every room which is used

for both … living and sleeping purposes shall have not less than 144 square feet of … floor area. Every room used for sleeping purposes shall have not less than 70 square feet of … floor area. When more than two persons occupy a room used for sleeping purposes the required…floor area shall be increased at the rate of 50 square feet for each occupant in excess of two….children under the age of six shall not be counted…" Only bedrooms are to be used for sleeping. (CA Civil Code § 1941.2) The Department of Building Inspection understands the shortage of housing in San Francisco, however, and will rarely cite residential units that are not legal for residential purposes, but for the occupancy limits, only counting rooms intended to be bedrooms is more likely to be in compliance with the laws.

For rental units covered under the Rent Ordinance (see "What Does the Rent Ordinance Cover?" in "Chapter 4: Renting Basics"), tenants have a clear right to add an immediate family member—spouse, domestic partner, grandparent, parent, sibling, child or grandchild or the spouses of such relatives—if the procedures of the Rent Ordinance are followed. This is true even if there is a restriction in the rental agreement limiting the number of occupants or prohibiting subletting. (SF Administrative Code § 37.9(a)(2)(B)) Tenants have the right to add such relatives up to a maximum number of occupants of two persons in a studio unit, three people in a one-bedroom unit, six in a three-bedroom unit and eight in a four-bedroom unit, etc. Families with children are further protected by San Francisco Police Code § 103, and other anti-discrimination laws. (See "Familial Status" in "Chapter 9: Discrimination.")

For units covered under the Rent Ordinance, the procedure for moving in relatives when the rental agreement would otherwise prohibit it is specified by Rent Board Rules and Regulations § 6.15D. Tenants must request in writing permission from the landlord that the relative be added to the household. If the landlord fails to respond in writing, providing reasons for denying the request, the request shall be considered approved. Although the Ordinance states that the landlord must respond within 14 days of receiving the tenant's request, new clarifications of the timing mean that the landlord may have more than 14 days:

- If the tenant's request is sent by mail, add five calendar days from the postmark date.

- If the tenant's request is sent by email, add two calendar days.

- If the tenant's request is personally delivered, no days are added.

- If the last day is a weekend day or holiday, the time is extended to the end of the next business day. (CA Code of Civil Procedure § 12a)

The landlord may require that the relative(s) complete the standard application form, and the landlord has five days to process the application. The addition could be denied, for example, if the relative has a history of damaging rental property or being evicted for nuisance, etc. The addition of the relative cannot be denied based on that person's credit history unless the additional roommate will be legally responsible for all or some of the rent. If the landlord denies the request to move in a relative, tenants can petition the Rent Board for a decrease in the rent.

San Francisco Administrative Code § 37.9(a)(2)(B) has yet to be tested in court. However, San Francisco Housing Code § 503, which includes a section promoting access to housing by families, has gone to court. § 503 prohibits landlords from denying dwelling units to families, where a family is defined as one or more persons related or unrelated, living together as a single integrated household. (SF Housing Code § 401) Although § 503 is still on the books, tenants should be aware that it may not be an effective eviction defense if more roommates than are permitted in the rental agreement (or by the conduct of the parties) are added over the landlord's objections. One appellate court, in the unpublished but influential decision described in the following paragraphs, has ruled that Housing Code § 503 is invalid because it is preempted by a state law, the California Fair Employment and Housing Act (FEHA). (CA Government Code §§ 12900 et. seq.)

In *Artal v. Sharp* ((2001) Cal. Superior Ct., App. Div. no. 5267), the tenant had a rental agreement naming her as the only tenant and prohibiting subletting. The tenant informed the landlord that she was engaged to be married and wanted her fiancé to move in. The landlord wrote back stating again the "one person only, no subletting" terms of her agreement. Nevertheless, the tenant's fiancé moved into the unit, the couple were married and the landlord filed an eviction for breach of the rental agreement.

The tenant won the first round—the trial court held the covenant in the rental agreement prohibiting the husband from moving in "unenforceable as a matter of public policy due to the marital relation existing between them." However, when the landlord appealed, the appellate court reversed the decision. It held that FEHA—ironically, the most important state law prohibiting discrimination—did not protect the newlyweds and that FEHA preempted Housing Code § 503, invalidating the part allowing tenants to add spouses! As a result, the court permitted eviction of the tenant for breaching the "one person only, no subletting" part of her rental agreement.

Instead of attempting an eviction, the landlord may try to raise the rent. Rent increases may not be allowed for households solely because of more adults than permitted in the rental agreement and even when a pre-existing lease permits such an increase. (SF Administrative Code § 37.3(a)(11)) Rent Board Rules and Regulations § 6.13 says, "No extra rent may be charged solely for an additional occupant to an existing tenancy, including a newborn child, regardless of the presence of a rental agreement which specifically allows for a rent increase for additional tenants." Even before § 6.13, a Rent Board hearing officer denied a landlord's request for a rent increase for an additional occupant even though the tenant did not contest the petition. (Rent Board Case #O001-02L) Also, San Francisco Police Code § 102(g) prohibits charging "additional rent, deposits, fees, or surcharges on the basis of actual or potential number or age of persons living in the housing accommodations."

What this means is that, even where a rental agreement specifies, for example, "no more than two adults," if the place is legally large enough and otherwise properly equipped to house the tenants in a safe and sanitary manner (according to the Housing Code), the landlord cannot raise the rent simply because of the additional number of occupants. The Police Code is not restricted to rent-controlled units nor specifically restricted to children. Rather, it seems to be an acknowledgment that San Francisco suffers from a severe shortage of affordable housing, and that, if a unit can properly accommodate additional tenants, public policy should permit this. However, this section of the Police Code has never been tested in court and it might be challenged because the surrounding paragraphs are about children, not adults, or because it may be preempted by state law. (See the box "Federal, State, and Local Anti-Discrimination Laws" in "Chapter 9: Discrimination" for more info.)

However, a right for additional keys is provided under the Rent Ordinance. A landlord cannot refuse keys in addition to those required for the adult occupants, within reason and at cost upon request. (SF Administrative Code § 37.13)

If there is already an unauthorized occupant in the unit, and the landlord attempts to evict the tenant(s) for breach of the lease for illegal subletting, the landlord must first provide a 10-day notice to cure or quit, and the tenant can request permission to add the unauthorized occupant. The law states that requesting permission is a cure of the breach, but because the timeline is complicated, it's probably safest for the unauthorized occupant to move out, while the other roommates wait to get permission, and deal with any background checks.

If you want to add family members, we caution:

(1) Be prepared to deal with an eviction attempt if the landlord refuses, despite negotiations, to accept additional tenants.

(2) If the unit is covered under the Rent Ordinance and the landlord can prove that the additional tenants have increased operating or maintenance expenses, he can petition for a rent increase. (See "Operating and Maintenance Expense Increase Passthroughs" in "Chapter 7: Rent Increases.")

(3) If the unit is not eviction-protected and tenants are merely on a month-to-month rental agreement, the landlord may simply evict the tenants. If that happens, the tenants' best defenses may be that the landlord was trying to discriminate against them as a family (see "Chapter 9: Discrimination") or that the landlord was retaliating against them for exercising their rights. (See the box "Retaliation Is Illegal" in "Chapter 6: Repairs and Services.")

Breaking Up

There are no easy ways to decide to split up a shared household unless all members of the household happen to be going their separate ways. In most situations, each person firmly believes that he has acted fairly and is behaving correctly in defending his rights. Except in the unusual situations where physical violence has been threatened or actually is happening, it is difficult and inappropriate to get the law involved. Here are some suggestions to help you deal with problems that may arise.

The first step, if you have been unable to resolve your differences in a way that would allow you to continue living together, is to look at each person's comparative needs to remain in the home. What is the financial situation of each roommate? Who has lived there the longest or otherwise has a stronger "claim" to the home? Who has a greater financial need to stay? Are children or pets involved which might make a move more difficult?

See the section "Assignment of Rental Agreement to Another Tenant" later in this chapter for information on assigning away a rental agreement. Also see the caution in the section "Rent Increase When Original Occupant Vacates" later in this chapter.

Be generous in allowing enough time for the roommate moving out to find a new home. The San Francisco housing shortage is so severe that 30 or even 60 days is an unreasonably short time in which to expect someone to find a decent place to live.

Be generous also with returning security deposits. Although departing tenants often expect to receive a refund of their security deposit from the owner, the owner is obligated to return the deposit only when the unit is completely vacated, and only to the tenant(s) with whom he had the original agreement. (See "Chapter 5: Security Deposits" for more info.) This can be a major issue when roommates leave, because a departing roommate will probably have to come up with a substantial sum of money to move into a new place. Perhaps the remaining tenants can chip in for moving expenses. A common solution is for the replacement roommate to pay her deposit to the vacating roommate. However, when the unit eventually is vacated by all the tenants, if the last tenant living in the rental unit is not an original tenant, she will likely not receive her deposit from the owner. She could try to recover the deposit from the original tenant who might receive it from the landlord. However, the original tenant may simply be long gone and impossible to locate. And if the original tenant is reachable, his right to the deposit from the owner comes with possible liability for rent or damages to the unit so he may refuse to request the refund of the deposit.

There is limited liability for rent for victims and household family members of domestic violence, sexual assault, stalking, elder or dependent adult abuse, or human trafficking. Such tenants may break a lease with 14-day notice and documentation. Domestic violence is defined for this purpose as "abuse" so does not require physical violence. Stalking includes a pattern of conduct intended to follow, alarm, place under surveillance, or harass the victim resulting in fear for her or an immediate family member's safety, or would cause a reasonable person to suffer substantial emotional distress. ("Immediate family" includes any person who regularly resides, or, within the six months preceding any portion of the pattern of conduct, regularly resided, in the victim's household.) The landlord is restricted from disclosing the information provided. (See CA Civil Code § 1946.7 in "Appendix D: California Law Excerpts" for more details.)

Before the household deteriorates to the point where it is impossible for the roommates involved to discuss the breakup, you may be able to agree on a neutral third person who would be willing to arbitrate your dispute and help the household reach a fair decision (or even find a way to stay together). Be sure that the third person you choose is not a close friend of any of the roommates, as that will likely lead to some hard feelings after the decision, no matter how carefully it's made. The Rent Board has a free Alternative Dispute Resolution program at which tenants can try to resolve their dispute with an Administrative Law Judge acting as a mediator. (There are other mediation services in this book's index under "mediation.")

If you are unable to reach a compromise, there may be little you can do other than to consider legal action. Who can initiate an eviction lawsuit depends on the legal status of the person who is being sued. If the tenant in question has been paying rent directly to the owner, *only* the owner can begin eviction proceedings. In this case, the owner would have to evict the tenants, as they are "jointly and severally liable." (See the section "Types of Tenant-Landlord Relationships" at the beginning of this chapter for more information.) If the tenant is subletting or paying rent directly to another tenant, the master tenant may be able to evict the subtenant. (See "Chapter 12: Eviction Defenses" for more info.) The San Francisco Tenants Union does not counsel anyone, including master tenants, on how to evict other tenants.

Things you should *never* do:

(1) **Never lock up or remove a person's possessions.** Even if someone is behind on rent payments, he has a right

to access his belongings. In addition, interfering with a person's belongings may subject you to a charge of theft, a criminal offense.

(2) **Lock a person out of his room or the common areas of the unit.** This is illegal and you could be sued for damages. (CA Civil Code § 789.3)

(3) **Harass, threaten, or intimidate a person out of his home.** This is also illegal. Only after completion of an eviction lawsuit can a person and his belongings be removed from the home and only the sheriff is allowed to do this after a court judgment.

See the following sections for information on replacing roommates and rent increases.

Changing Roommates

When a co-tenant wants to move out, he should give notice as described in the previous section "Breaking Up." In a unit covered under the Rent Ordinance (see "What Does the Rent Ordinance Cover?" in "Chapter 4: Renting Basics"), just because one co-tenant vacates does not mean that other co-tenants also have to move. Even if the landlord were to claim successfully that the co-tenant was only a subtenant, the landlord would need a just cause to evict under the Rent Ordinance. The court has ruled that "where a landlord agrees to an occupancy, characterization of the occupancy as a subtenancy does not prevent application of the Ordinance's requirements of cause for eviction." (*DeZerega v.*

Meggs (2000) 83 Cal. App. 4th 28) In other words, the remaining co-tenants may stay and probably will want to find a replacement to help meet the rent payments.

Most written rental agreements have a clause similar to the following: "a tenant may not sublet or assign any part of their rights to tenancy *without express consent by the owner.*" However, for rental units covered by the Rent Ordinance, the landlord cannot unreasonably refuse to permit tenants to replace one or more departing roommates with the same number of roommates. More precisely, (1) if the rental agreement itself specifies the number of tenants to reside in the unit, or (2) if the *open and established behavior of the landlord* and tenants has established that the tenancy includes more than one tenant, then the existing tenants cannot be evicted for breaching the rental agreement if the landlord *unreasonably* withholds consent to replace departing roommates with an equal number of roommates. (SF Administrative Code § 37.9(a)(2)(A), *Danekas v. San Francisco Residential Rent Stabilization & Arbitration Board* (2001) 95 Cal. App. 4th 638, 115 Cal. Rptr. 2d 694)

Withholding of consent by the landlord is *unreasonable* if the tenant has met the following requirements:

(1) The tenant has requested the landlord's permission *in writing* and *before* the proposed roommate moves in.

(2) If the landlord requests, the proposed roommate either completes the landlord's standard application or provides

---

What If There's Already a New Roommate?

If you already have a new roommate in a unit covered by the Rent Ordinance, but you haven't followed each requirement of San Francisco Rent Board Rules and Regulations § 6.15 to the letter, can the landlord evict you? No. Rule 6.15 says that if the tenant satisfies all the requirements of the Rule, the landlord is deemed to be unreasonable; it doesn't say that if you don't meet the requirements, then the landlord is being reasonable.

If you have no written rental agreement, or if your rental agreement doesn't explicitly state restrictions on subletting or assignment, then the law presumes that tenants can sublet or assign their rights. If yours does have restrictions on subletting or assignment, you want to look as reasonable as you can, so that the landlord looks unreasonable if she says the new roommate has to go. Try to show that you did most of the things listed in Rule 6.15 and that a reasonable landlord would have said yes. Write a letter giving the landlord all of the information specified in Rule 6.15. If you had already talked to her about the new roommate, refer to that in the letter. Let the landlord know that, of course, the new roommate is willing to sign on to the rental agreement just as you have. Point out that the new roommate has a good tenant history (or as good as the current tenants).

If you have always been allowed to get new roommates without prior consent, you could argue that the landlord shouldn't be allowed to say that you can't have a roommate now. Describe instances when the landlord has allowed you to have roommates without getting written approval and explain how you've come to rely on the informal method of getting roommates. (See the box "Waiver, Estoppel, and Change of Agreement: Unenforced Rental Agreement Provisions as Defenses to an Eviction" in *Chapter 12: Eviction Defenses* for more information.)

Finally, if the landlord does proceed with an eviction attempt, the landlord must first provide a 10-day notice to cure or quit, and the tenant can request permission to add the unauthorized occupant if the tenant has not already done so. (SF Administrative Code § 37.9(a)(2)(D)) The law states that requesting permission is a cure of the breach, but because the timeline is complicated, it's probably safest for the unauthorized occupant to move out until the time period for the landlord has expired as described in "Adding Non-Family Members" and "Changing Roommates." Also, a big defense can be that the landlord's main reason for evicting you is not that you got a new roommate without her consent, but rather that she could raise the rent (or get rid of a demanding tenant, etc.). For more information, see *Chapter 12: Evictions Defenses.*

sufficient information to allow the landlord to conduct a typical background check. A credit check can be required only if the new tenant will be paying rent directly to the landlord.

(3) The tenant has given the landlord five business days to process the new roommate's application.

(4) The proposed roommate meets the regular and reasonable application standards of the landlord.

(5) The proposed roommate agrees to sign and be bound by the already-existing rental agreement.

(6) The existing tenant has not requested the landlord's permission to replace roommates more than once per existing roommate in the previous 12 months without good cause (so-called "roommate churning").

(7) The tenant is requesting replacement of departing roommates with an equal number of new roommates.

(SF Rent Board Rules and Regulations § 6.15B)

If the landlord unreasonably withholds consent for the new roommates and the tenant has complied with Rule 6.15B, the tenant cannot be evicted on the ground that he breached the rental agreement. What is considered reasonable? As discussed in the earlier section "Subletting" and following section "Assignment of Rental Agreement to Another Tenant," the landlord needs to have a legitimate business-related reason for refusing a prospective tenant. Moreover, the standards are supposed to be "regular," so holding a new tenant to higher standards than the current tenants would be unreasonable. A new tenant does not have to have perfect credit; her credit only needs to be as good as the regular reasonable standards that the landlord has used for other tenants and her creditworthiness can only be required if the new tenant pays rent directly to the landlord.

If the rental agreement contains a clause *absolutely prohibiting* subletting or assignment with adequate disclosure, then the situation is similar to a consent required clause except that Rent Board Rules and Regulations § 6.15A applies instead of § 6.15B. Adequate disclosure is:

(1) The prohibition against subletting or assignment is enlarged or in boldface type in the rental agreement and initialed by the tenant; or

(2) The landlord has provided the tenant with a written explanation of the meaning of the absolute prohibition, as part of the rental agreement or in a separate declaration.

Not asking the landlord in writing *before the new roommate actually moves in* leaves you open to eviction for breach of the agreement. Your letter to the landlord should (1) explain that you intend to get a replacement roommate; (2) ask the landlord for

a standard application form for the new roommate, or else ask what reasonable background information, if any, the landlord wants; (3) include a copy of Rules and Regulations § 6.15 and Rent Ordinance § 37.2(g) (defining "housing services") with your letter, so that the landlord can read the law for herself and you can prove you gave her full disclosure before you made your move. Keep a copy of the letter and mail it with a certificate of mailing (different from certified) or, even better, send the letter with delivery confirmation. This shows good faith on your part, and should minimize any argument that the landlord could make at a later date. If you did not follow the proper procedure to sublet, see the box "What If There's Already a New Roommate?" for suggestions.

When a landlord unreasonably refuses consent for a suitable replacement roommate, the tenants already living in the unit can petition the Rent Board for a significant rent reduction on the grounds that the landlord has decreased their housing services. (See "Decrease in Housing Services Petitions" in "Chapter 6: Repairs and Services.") For example, if two roommates have been living in the unit and the landlord refuses to let the remaining tenant replace the departing roommate, the tenant may credibly petition the Rent Board for a rent reduction of 50%, since that remaining roommate's rent will double because of the landlord's unreasonable refusal to give consent. Refusal of consent may also be a back-door attempt to evict the remaining tenant(s) by an impossible rent increase. The Rent Board has been sympathetic to requests for rent reductions on this ground. The petition process is safer than fighting the landlord over what is reasonable or not since the landlord may decide to try to evict the tenant. The petition process also is easier than going through the time and expense of defending oneself in court and there is always a possibility of losing in court which would mean losing one's home.

If the landlord fails to respond in writing, providing reasons for denying the request, the request shall be considered approved. Although the Ordinance states that the landlord must respond within 14 days of receiving the tenant's request, new clarifications of the timing mean that the landlord may have more than 14 days:

- If the tenant's request is sent by mail, add five calendar days from the postmark date.
- If the tenant's request is sent by email, add two calendar days.
- If the tenant's request is personally delivered, no days are added.
- If the last day is a weekend day or holiday, the time is extended to the end of the next business day. (CA Code of Civil Procedure § 12a)

If there is already an unauthorized occupant in the unit, see the box "What If There's Already a New Roommate?"

The landlord has the right to consider only the remaining co-tenants as the "original" tenants, as discussed in the section "Rent Increase When Original Occupant Vacates" later in this chapter.

Assignment of Rental Agreement to Another Tenant

Assignment of a rental agreement occurs when the tenant wants to give up all of his interests in the unit and completely transfer them to another person. Assignment would occur, for instance, if the tenant is moving for a new job and wants a new tenant to take over his apartment permanently. It can also apply in a roommate situation when a co-tenant wants to leave and turn her room over to a new roommate. The assignee is directly liable to the landlord for everything the original tenant was liable for even if the assignee does not have a direct agreement with the landlord. (CA Civil Code § 822) However, an *assignment during the term of a lease does not terminate the responsibilities of the person moving out unless the landlord agrees*. If the agreement is month-to-month, you may be able to terminate your responsibilities.

A co-tenant or original tenant who wants to move out should give at least a thirty-day notice in writing to the other household members and to the owner. No court has ruled on if "one of the parties gives written notice to the other of his or her intention to terminate" means all original tenants, or a single original tenant

NOTICE OF TERMINATION OF TENANCY

NOTICE IS HEREBY GIVEN that thirty days from the date of this Notice, _____ does hereby terminate all possession, right, and interest in the premises located at _____, San Francisco, California.

This notice is not to be construed to affect the rights of _____ who will remain in possession of said premises and who will be responsible for payment of rent.

Dated: _____

_____ [Signature]

NOTICE OF REVOCATION OF PURPORTED "GUARANTEE"

NOTICE IS HEREBY GIVEN that, I, _____ do hereby elect, under Civil Code Section 2815, to revoke any and all guarantees, if any there be, with respect to performance of that rental agreement executed on or about _____, for rental of the premises at _____, San Francisco, California.

This notice shall not to be construed as any admission that any provision constitutes a guarantee of performance.

Dated: _____

_____ [Signature]

in California Civil Code § 1946. *Schmitt v. Felix* (1958) 157 Cal. App.2d 642 may allow release of liability from the landlord, however, *Schmitt v. Felix* may not apply if the rental unit requires just cause for eviction. *If possible, get the landlord's consent for terminating the rental agreement in writing.* If there is any hint of a "guarantor" (one who promises to answer for the default of another, CA Civil Code § 2787), give a notice revoking the guaranty (CA Civil Code § 2815).

Some landlords refuse to remove a departing co-tenant from the agreement until all the original co-tenants vacate the unit, leaving the departing co-tenant liable for default or damages by a replacement roommate. Though landlords are unlikely to chase down departed tenants, legally they may be able to do it. If the tenant wants to break a lease instead, see "Breaking a Lease" in "Chapter 4: Renting Basics."

Unless the rental agreement with the landlord expressly prohibits assignment, the law presumes that tenants can transfer their rights. However, the right to assign usually is restricted by the rental agreement, often including the condition that neither can be done without the landlord's consent. "Consent clauses" containing no express standard or condition for giving or withholding consent always have been judged by the law to include **an implied standard that the landlord's consent may not be unreasonably withheld**. The Rent Board has adopted a specific set of requirements to deal with this situation. (See the previous section "Changing Roommates.")

Reasonable landlord objections to assignment might include the following: (1) the new occupant's inability to fulfill the terms of the agreement, (2) financial irresponsibility or instability, (3) unsuitability of the unit for the intended use and, (4) intended undesirable use of the premises. If factors such as these are not present, the courts probably would see the landlord's refusal to give consent as unreasonable and thus unenforceable. However, a landlord still can petition to remove the rent increase limitation under the Rent Ordinance if the master tenant is not a "tenant in occupancy." (See "Tenant Not in Occupancy" in "Chapter 7: Rent Increases.")

Rent Increase When Original Occupant Vacates

There are two main laws and rules that allow owners to raise rent for roommates who moved in after the original occupancy began. One is a state law, the Costa-Hawkins Rental Housing Act (CA Civil Code §§ 1954.50-1954.53), and the other is San Francisco Rent Board Rules and Regulations § 6.14 (see "Protections for the Tenant Under the San Francisco Rent Ordinance and State Law" in "Chapter 4: Renting Basics," "Appendix C," and Appendix D.") Of these two, Costa-Hawkins is by far the most important and frequently used by the Rent Board; §6.14 usually comes into play only after analysis shows that an unlimited rent increase is not authorized under Costa-Hawkins. However, in some circumstances § 6.14 may separately allow an unlimited rent increase, *even if* Costa-Hawkins would *not* permit such an

increase. A survey of Rent Board decisions shows the Rent Board nearly always starts its analysis of rent increases for roommates by first applying Costa-Hawkins analysis, and usually will reach a § 6.14 analysis only if the question is not resolved under Costa-Hawkins. The notice of rent increase cannot be served until the last original occupant actually vacates. (CA Civil Code § 1954.53)

When landlords are not confident that they can increase the rent under the Costa-Hawkins Act, they sometimes try to claim in a lawsuit that the original tenant no longer lives in the unit and so any remaining roommates can have their rent increased. These lawsuits are called "declaratory relief" actions. Tenants can file a response ("demurrer") in court under the reasoning that landlords are trying to increase the rent by going to court to exhaust the resources of low-income tenants to defend against an illegal rent increase, and the matter is better resolved at the Rent Board.

Caution: If the original occupant moves out permanently and doesn't tell the owner, hoping to keep the current rent for the roommates, the original occupant should be aware that owner attorneys have sued the original occupant for the rent difference the owner claims she could have gotten under the Costa-Hawkins Rental Housing Act, had she known the original occupant had moved out. Seek advice from a tenant attorney in these cases. The original occupant should give notice of vacating (with proof of delivery) to the owner that he is vacating but the subtenants are remaining. Continuing to pay rent after vacating could also be considered fraud for which the owner can seek to recover for loss of increased rent.

Rent Increases Under the Costa-Hawkins Rental Housing Act

Any occupant authorized (by either implied or express consent or acquiescence) by the owner landlord at the inception of the tenancy, including children under the age of 18 who moved into the rental unit with their parent(s) with the landlord's consent at the beginning of the rental agreement, as well as any subtenants, qualify as original occupants for rent increase purposes under Costa-Hawkins. (*Mosser Companies v. San Francisco Residential Rent Stabilization and Arbitration Board* (2015) 233 Cal.App.4th 505; *T & A Drolapas v. San Francisco Residential Rent Stabilization and Arbitration Board* (2015) 238 Cal.App.4th 646)

For subsequent roommates, here are the two most pertinent sections of the Costa-Hawkins law which most frequently affect them:

(2) If the original occupant or occupants who took possession of the dwelling or unit pursuant to the rental agreement with the owner no longer permanently reside there, an owner may

increase the rent by any amount allowed by this section to a lawful sublessee or assignee <u>who did not reside at the dwelling or unit prior to January 1, 1996</u>....

(4) Acceptance of rent by the owner does not operate as a waiver or otherwise prevent enforcement of a covenant prohibiting sublease or assignment or as a waiver of an owner's rights to establish the initial rental rate, unless the owner has received written notice from the tenant that is party to the agreement and thereafter accepted rent.

CA Civil Code §§1954.53(d)(2) and (4)

So is a rent increase authorized under Costa-Hawkins in your case? Following are some guidelines to help you evaluate the situation. The two critical questions to ask are: (1) If the last original occupants who began the tenancy have permanently moved out of the unit, did the subsequent roommates move in before or after January 1, 1996? And (2) Did the subsequent roommates pay rent directly to the landlord?

(1) If the roommate(s) moved in before January 1, 1996, then even if they were subtenants paying rent to the original occupants (and not to the landlord), no Costa-Hawkins rent increase is authorized, because Costa-Hawkins only applies to "a lawful sublessee or assignee <u>who did not reside at the dwelling or unit prior to January 1, 1996.</u>"

(2) If the roommate(s) moved in <u>after</u> January 1, 1996, in order to avoid a Costa-Hawkins rent increase they would have to prove that they were not merely subtenants of the original occupants, but rather had a direct landlord-tenant relationship with the landlord. Remember, Costa-Hawkins applies only to "sublessees" and "assignees," that is, roommates whose rental agreements are only with another tenant and not with the landlord.

To put it another way, if a subsequent roommate who moved in after January 1, 1996 does have a rental agreement directly with the landlord, he is not a sublessee or assignee, and the rent cannot be raised under Costa-Hawkins even if the last original occupant moves out. Proving this relationship is the major challenge in contesting a Costa-Hawkins rent increase. (See the following section "Proving That a Rental Agreement Directly with the Landlord Exists.")

Even if a landlord can raise the rent, if the rent is increased substantially above market rate, a tenant may be able to successfully sue the landlord for wrongful eviction or harassment since the excessive rent increase could amount to an eviction without just cause. You can check for the current market rental rates by neighborhood on *https://www.padmapper.com*. (SF Administrative Code § 37.10A(i), (j); § 37.10B(a)(5))

An additional protection you may be able to claim under Costa-Hawkins would be to prove that there were serious code violations that had been cited by City inspectors that remained unabated at least 60 days prior to a tenant leaving. In this case the remaining

or replacement tenants may be able to claim protection from rent increases. (CA Civil Code § 1954.53(f)) See "Department of Building Inspection" in "Chapter 3: Researching Landlords, Buildings, and Laws" for more info on how to look up unabated code violations.

Proving That a Rental Agreement Directly with the Landlord Exists

So what, legally, does it take to prove the existence of a direct rental agreement between roommates and the landlord? As we discussed in "Chapter 4: Renting Basics," a rental agreement is a contract between the landlord and the tenant for the tenant's exclusive use and occupancy of the property during the contract's existence. As one court put it:

> "It is well established that a tenancy need not be created by a [written] lease but may be created by occupancy by consent…[I]n the ordinary course of business the occupancy of the premises by one person with the consent of the owner creates the relation of landlord and tenant." (*Parkmerced Co. v. San Francisco Rent Stabilization & Arbitration Board* (Abenheim) (1989) 215 Cal. App. 3d 490)

Or, as described in the language of numerous Rent Board decisions:

> "A tenancy is a contractual relationship, express or implied, between a landlord and a tenant. (*Ellingson v. Walsh, O'Connor & Barneson* (1940) 15 Cal. 2d 673) A tenancy may be created without a formal agreement by consent and acceptance of rent. (*Cobb v. City and County of San Francisco Rent Board* (2000) 98 Cal. App. 4th 345, 352; *Getz v. City of West Hollywood* (1991) 233 Cal. App. 3d 625, 629) Such conduct can create a landlord-tenant relationship despite the absence of a lease agreement, and such tenant may be entitled to invoke the protection of rent control laws. Whether consent and acceptance of rent creates a landlord-tenant relationship depends on the particular circumstances of each case."

So, the key for newer roommates to avoid an unlimited rent increase under Costa-Hawkins is to show that a rental agreement or tenancy has been established, explicitly and/or by conduct, directly between themselves and the landlord under California law. In addition to a written rental agreement with the newer tenant's name on it, the following elements can be useful to prove the existence of a direct rental agreement:

(1) By far the most important element is proof of payment of rent by the newer roommate(s) directly to, and acceptance of the rent from them by, the landlord.

(2) Direct, verifiable assertion of legal tenant rights and exercise of tenant remedies by the subsequent roommates(s)—for example, a communication with the landlord regarding "repair-and-deduct" to fix a problem in the unit.

(3) Verifiable evidence that, by his conduct, the landlord treated the subsequent roommates as tenants in their own right, as opposed to as subtenants of the original occupant. Examples of such evidence could include such things as: dealings directly with the landlord, such as repair requests and other communications, by the subsequent roommates; notices from the landlord, including rent increase notices, naming the subsequent roommates as "tenants"; payment of a security (or other) deposit in their names directly to the landlord by the subsequent roommates; and service of eviction (and/or other) notices naming the subsequent occupant(s) as a "tenant."

A separate way to show that an unlimited rent increase is not authorized under Costa-Hawkins is to prove that the landlord *waived* his right to such an increase. This can happen if the tenant(s) presents verifiable evidence that the owner has received *written* notice from the last of the original occupants (who started the tenancy) that they have vacated or intend to vacate, and thereafter has accepted rent directly from the subsequent roommate(s). **But note**: this notice from the former tenant(s) **must be written**; oral and/or constructive notice will *not* suffice under the specific language of Costa-Hawkins. (CA Civil Code § 1954.53(d)(4)) In addition, the landlord would probably not have waived his right if he had promptly given the tenant a rent increase notice.

Finally, for single residential units including condominiums, if the original occupancy began before January 1, 1996 and a newer tenant moved in after that date but paid rent directly to the landlord, this newer tenancy would be considered to be a continuing tenancy. Therefore when the original occupants vacate, an unlimited rent increase would not be permitted under Costa-Hawkins. (See "Single Residential Unit" in "Chapter 4: Renting Basics" for more info.)

Rules and Regulations § 6.14

Even if an unlimited rent increase is not authorized under Costa-Hawkins, the landlord might still be able to increase the rent under Rules and Regulations § 6.14 after the last original occupant who began the tenancy no longer "inhabits" the unit. This is because Rules and Regulations § 6.14 is under a different statute than Costa-Hawkins and has separate criteria for rent increases. If a landlord is going to increase the rent under § 6.14, she must have served the tenants with a notice of the statute, commonly known as a "6.14 Notice," as explained in the following sections.

However, § 6.14 is now far less important than Costa-Hawkins, and is not meant to enlarge or diminish rights under Costa-Hawkins (§ 6.14(f)), so is usually only used in two circumstances: first, for subsequent (those who moved in after the original

occupant(s) took possession) subtenants who moved in before January 1, 1996; and second, for co-tenants (in some cases also known as co-occupants) who moved in at any time. Also, note that § 6.14 is concerned only with rent increases; there is *nothing in § 6.14 that authorizes a landlord to terminate the tenancy*, even though many 6.14 Notices incorrectly assert that eviction is also one of the landlord's options under that statute.

Subtenants

For subsequent subtenants who moved in before January 1, 1996, the landlord can raise the rent when the last original occupant moves out only if the landlord served the subsequent roommates with a 6.14 Notice within a reasonable time of his actual knowledge of the new subtenants' occupancy. Failure to give the 6.14 Notice within 60 days establishes a rebuttable presumption that the notice was not given within a reasonable period of time, and the rent cannot be raised when the last original occupant vacates. (SF Rent Board Rules and Regulations § 6.14(b))

For subsequent subtenants who moved in on or after January 1, 1996, where the last original occupant moved out on or after April 25, 2000, the landlord can raise the rent under Costa-Hawkins, even if no 6.14 Notice was ever served.

Co-Tenants (in Some Cases Also Known as Co-Occupants)

Under specific circumstances, § 6.14(b) permits an unlimited rent increase *even for subsequent tenants who have a rental agreement directly with the landlord*, regardless of when they moved in:

"if the landlord served on the subsequent occupant(s), within a reasonable time of actual knowledge of occupancy, a written notice that when the last of the original occupant(s) vacates the premises, a new tenancy is created for purposes of determining the rent under the Rent Ordinance [a "6.14 Notice"]. *Failure to give such a notice within 60 days of the landlord's actual knowledge of the occupancy by the subsequent occupant(s) establishes a rebuttable presumption that notice was not given within a reasonable period of time.* If the landlord has not timely served such a notice on the subsequent occupant(s), a new tenancy is not created for purposes of determining the rent under the Rent Ordinance when the last of the original occupant(s) vacates the premises." (SF Rules and Regulations § 6.14(b)) [*Emphasis added.*]

In plain English, for roommate(s) who moved in after the original occupancy began and have a direct relationship with the landlord, a timely-served 6.14 Notice will permit an unlimited rent increase even if Costa-Hawkins would not. The landlord's failure to serve a timely 6.14 Notice on co-occupants should defeat an attempted rent increase under Rules and Regulations § 6.14.

Applying Costa-Hawkins and Rules and Regulations § 6.14 can be quite subtle and complicated. Tenants should speak with the Tenants Union, a tenant attorney and/or the Rent Board staff for assistance with Costa-Hawkins and 6.14 questions. The full text of both laws is found in *Appendices C and D: Law Excerpts and Regulations* in this book. An additional option for educating yourself on how the Rent Board has evaluated arguments and decided past cases is to go to the Rent Board's office and ask a counselor how to look up decisions on the computers by the front desk (the decisions are not online outside the Rent Board). There are numerous cases that have dealt with Costa-Hawkins and Rules and Regulations § 6.14, as well as all other issues that were decided in past cases. They can be read in full there, and printed out at cost.

Rules and Regulations § 1.21

Rent Board Rules and Regulations § 1.21 allows a landlord to petition the Rent Board for a rent increase if a tenant is not using the dwelling as her principal place of residence. (See "Tenant Not in Occupancy" in "Chapter 7: Rent Increases" for more info.) However, since approved subtenants (by either explicit or implied approval) qualify as tenants (SF Administrative Code § 37.2(t)), a rent increase under 1.21 would not be allowed if an approved subtenant uses the dwelling as his principal place of residence.

Guests

There is no law defining a "guest," but one rule of thumb has it that a guest does not pay rent or provide "reward" for temporary possession of the property (CA Civil Code § 1925), and stays no longer than fourteen days in a year.

If, for example, your lover is there five days out of every week and the landlord claims that he is therefore an "illegal subtenant," you will need to decide whether to ask your friend to leave or prepare for a possible eviction attempt. It will be important to be able to prove that money has not exchanged hands or other "reward" given, that the "guest" has a primary place of residence elsewhere, and that the "guest" is not in violation of the agreement's legal limitation on the number of occupants. (See the "Adding Non-Family Members, and "Adding Family Members" sections earlier in this chapter.) If the rental agreement includes a guest time limit and requires the landlord to give permission for a guest in excess of the time limit, the landlord cannot unreasonably refuse permission. Under the Rent Ordinance, a landlord cannot refuse keys in addition to those required for the adult occupants, within reason and at cost upon request. (SF Administrative Code § 37.13)

Hotel residents are the tenants most likely to be hassled for having visitors. The Uniform Hotel Visitor Policy gives single room occupancy hotel (SRO) residents rights for visitors. See "Uniform Hotel Visitor Policy" under "San Francisco Administrative Code" in "Appendix C: San Francisco Law and Regulations Excerpts."

Model Roommate Agreement

I. Amount and Method of Payment of Rent

Unless otherwise expressly agreed in writing, each roommate shall be responsible for an equal per capita proportion of rent lawfully owed to the landlord under the terms of the rental agreement, subject to any subsequent lawful rent adjustment. Each roommate shall be furnished an individual copy of the rental agreement; if the rental agreement is oral, each roommate shall promptly be informed of its complete contents.

(Check one alternative below:)

_____ Rent shall be tendered individually by each roommate when due to one designated roommate, who shall submit all rent owed in a timely fashion (as per the rental agreement with the landlord) to the landlord or to the landlord's designated agent.

_____ Rent shall be tendered individually by each roommate when due to the landlord or to the landlord's designated agent.

II. Termination of Tenancy by Roommate; 30-Day Written Notice to Other Roommate(s) Required

Any roommate intending to terminate his or her tenancy shall so inform the remaining roommates(s) in possession in writing a minimum of thirty (30) days before vacating the premises. Whenever possible, the vacating roommate shall reasonably assist the remaining roommate(s) in finding a suitable replacement roommate. The vacating roommate shall be responsible for any and all current and outstanding charges, costs or fees incurred by him or her during the course of his or her tenancy and/or caused as a result of the vacation of his or her tenancy.

III. Household Expenses, Charges and/or Costs

Each roommate shall be responsible for an equal per capita proportion of common household expenses, charges and/or costs, which amounts shall be paid promptly. Any additional charges, costs and/or fees incurred by an individual roommate shall be that individual roommate's sole responsibility. Such amounts shall be paid promptly by the roommate incurring them.

IV. Guests

Upon reasonable oral or written notice to the other roommate(s), a roommate may have an overnight guest stay in his/her room for a continuous period of up to seven (7) days. A minimum of twenty-four (24) hours shall be deemed to be reasonable notice in absence of evidence to the contrary. The "host" roommate shall be responsible for the actions and conduct of his or her guest. The "host" roommate's guest may remain beyond seven (7) days only with the express consent of the other roommate(s). If at any time the guest substantially interferes with the comfort, safety or enjoyment of the other roommate(s), any roommate may revoke said guest's license by expressly informing the "host" roommate and/or the guest that the guest's permission to stay in the rental unit has been revoked, along with the reason(s) for this revocation. After said guest and/or "host" roommate have been so informed, eight (8) hours shall be deemed a reasonable amount of time for the guest to vacate the rental unit, in the absence of substantial cause to the contrary (e.g., serious emergency, accident, etc.).

V. Involuntary Termination of Roommate Tenancy

Notwithstanding any other provision of law, no roommate shall be asked or required by another roommate to involuntarily terminate his/her tenancy unless:

1. The roommate has failed to pay:
   a. his or her agreed portion of the rent to which the landlord is lawfully entitled under the rental agreement,
   b. his or her agreed proportion of common household expenses, charges and/or costs, *or*
   c. any individually incurred expenses, charges and/or fees whose late payment or nonpayment will adversely affect the other roommate(s) (e.g., personal telephone bills); *or*

2. The roommate is committing or permitting to exist a substantial nuisance in, or is causing significant damage to, the rental unit, or is creating or permitting to exist a substantial interference with the comfort, safety or enjoyment of the landlord and/or the other roommates, and the nature of such nuisance, damage or interference is specifically stated in writing by the landlord or other tenant(s) and is not reasonably corrected or correctable; *or*

3. The roommate has violated a lawful obligation or covenant enumerated in the rental agreement between the landlord and roommate(s) without the express permission of the other roommate(s); *or*

4. The roommate substantially violates any additional express material agreement which may be created between him/her and the other roommate(s), on or subsequent to the roommate's occupancy, including, but not limited to, the terms of this present agreement.

_____   _____
Signature and Date   *Signature and Date*

_____   _____
Signature and Date   *Signature and Date*

Chapter 11: **Changes in Use**

Loss of Rental Units

As San Francisco's gentrification intensifies and property values soar, real estate speculators and investors are making huge profits through the conversion of thousands of rent-controlled apartments into other uses. Commonly, this process involves the conversion of a rental unit into an ownership unit, such as a condominium or tenancies in common (TICs). A landlord who focuses on rental income will receive large profits over time. A real estate speculator, in contrast, will make huge profits in a very short time by converting the rental units to owner-occupied units. The conversion of a four unit apartment building into four TICs, for example, typically yields an investor $750,000 – $1,000,000 profit.

Many other rental units are lost to demolitions, mergers (defined in the section "Demolition of a Rental Unit and Mergers" later in this chapter), tourist use and conversions into "corporate suites." Conversion of rental units has become a major threat to tenants over the years, and voters and elected officials have responded on a number of fronts. The 1979 Condominium Conversion Law limited the number of apartments that could be converted to condos to just 200 per year, and in 2013 an amendment to the law placed a moratorium on most condo conversions for at least 10 years. The 1986 Proposition M amended the Planning Code "General Plan Priorities." These amendments included the preservation of affordable housing as a top priority to be factored into all decisions related to development, land use and zoning.

These laws give tenants substantial power to fight conversions. For tenants to utilize these laws it is necessary to understand the nuances of the different types of conversions and the workings of the city's planning, zoning and permit processes as implemented by the Department of Public Works, the Department of Planning and Planning Commission, the Department of Building Inspection and the Board of Appeals.

Condominium Conversions

Most housing conversions in San Francisco are from rental units to condominiums. These conversions are former rent-controlled apartments in multiple-unit buildings in which *each unit* is now owned separately with the common areas jointly owned and managed by an owners' association. (See *Chapter 3: Researching Landlords, Building, and Laws* to find the status of your unit.)

The conversion of an apartment building into condos is legally a "subdivision"—similar to a suburban subdivision where a developer buys a large plot of land and subdivides it into individually owned lots. Condos are the same, except that each "lot" is an individual unit on shared land. Condo subdivisions are regulated by both state and city laws, which are described in the section "Condo Conversion Law" later in this chapter.

Owning a condo is much less risky than owning a tenancy in common, in which all the units are owned jointly, so a condominium is 20% more valuable than a TIC. However, in San Francisco, condominiums are usually created via the temporary creation of TICs. Because TICs are not subdivisions, they are exempt from the laws restricting condo conversions to protect tenants. So by creating TICs, real estate investors or landlords can avoid the tenant protections in the condo law and evict the tenants. Once the units are converted to TICs, the TIC owners can then apply to be selected as one of the 200 condo conversions allowed each year after the condo moratorium has passed. Because condo conversions usually happen via TICs, it's important to first understand what a TIC is.

Tenancies in Common (TICs)

A tenancy in common is a mutation of condominium ownership. In a condominium subdivision, the owner holds sole title to her unit, as a single residential unit. In a TIC, by contrast, the owners have a percentage share in the entire building and have a "side agreement" stipulating the unit belonging to each of them. For example, in a four unit TIC where all of the units are similar, each TIC owner would have a 25 percent ownership share of the building. Part of shared ownership is shared liability and, usually, a shared mortgage. If one owner defaults on his mortgage, usually all owners risk losing the building. Although there are a few fractionalized mortgages for TICs, lenders charge a higher interest rate for these mortgages because of their higher risk for liability. A shared mortgage and liability, as well as some TICs require agreement of all owners to sell, make the TIC a less desirable and less valuable form of ownership, so the ultimate goal is usually to subdivide the building into condos as soon as possible. Because TICs are not subject to the city's condo conversion law, TICs are commonly used to evict tenants and establish a "quasi-condo," in preparation for a subsequent legal condo subdivision.

TIC Regulation

There is no limit to the number of TIC conversions allowed per year nor protections for tenants as there are for condo conversions. However, because TIC owners usually want to ultimately convert into condominium subdivisions, the condo law does provide indirect regulation. Most notably, as of December 2013, only 2–4 unit buildings can be converted to condos, so TICs will generally be limited to 2-4 unit buildings. (SF Subdivision Code § 1396)

Amendments to the condo law adopted in 2013 also placed a moratorium through at least the year 2024 on condo conversions except for fully owner-occupied 2-unit buildings. This should provide an additional disincentive to TIC creation as owners

"Would you like any more apartments or just the check?"

will not be able to convert to condos for a considerable time. Sometimes, though, TICs can exist as TICs without having to become condominiums. This is usually done via "fractional loans" where the owner of each unit gets her own mortgage, thus overcoming the risk of a shared mortgage. Also, in wealthy San Francisco, buyers often pay all cash, so there is no mortgage (and thus no risk of a shared mortgage).

Fighting Conversion to TIC

TICs are usually created by real estate speculators who purchase rent-controlled buildings with 2–4 units (currently the only buildings which are allowed to convert to condominiums). The speculators will then empty the building of tenants and sell the units as TICs. However, creating a TIC is not a just cause for eviction under the Rent Ordinance, so landlords need to find a just cause in order to evict the tenants. The most common just cause used is the Ellis Act, under which the landlord may evict tenants in order to remove all the units from the rental market. Though there are many restrictions on re-renting the units, subsequently selling them as owner-occupied TIC or condo units is allowed under the Ellis Act. (See "Ellis Act" in "Chapter 12: Eviction Defenses" for more info.)

Once the building is owner-occupied, the TIC will get on the path to become one of the 200 housing units selected via an annual lottery to convert to condominiums. Because of the moratorium on condo conversions, though, there will be no conversions allowed each year until at least the year 2024 except for buildings already in the pipeline. (See the section "Limit on Annual Conversion" and the box "Condo Conversion Bypass for Existing TICs" later in this chapter for more info.)

Tenants may be able to stop a condo conversion by fighting the evictions done to create the TIC. The main leverage tenants have is that most evictions will trigger a permanent prohibition on condo conversion; in other words, the TIC would have to remain a TIC forever. As a result, TICs are most commonly created by buyouts. (See the section on condo conversion restrictions that follows, and the section "Buyouts, Almost Always a Bad Idea" in "Chapter 8: Harassment.") To coerce the tenant into accepting a buyout, the speculator creating the TIC will threaten an Ellis Act eviction (which is very difficult to defend against) and then offer the tenant money to move out. The combination of Ellis threat and buyout offer is like a poker game, and you have to

figure out whether the speculator is bluffing. Sometimes, when tenants refuse to take the buyouts, the speculator backs off and just becomes a landlord or sells the property to a landlord just interested in getting the rental income. Other times, the speculator will go ahead and carry out the threat and file an Ellis Act eviction, even though it means considerably less profit. Tenants in this situation should research at the San Francisco Rent Board to see if the speculator creating the TIC has ever done an Ellis eviction or other evictions.

In some cases, the speculator will not have emptied the building prior to selling the apartments as TICs but will instead put the burden of evictions on the TIC purchasers. In that situation, the most effective way to fight a TIC conversion is to start fighting the day a "for sale" sign is posted. Potential buyers often have not considered the fact that they may be evicting a family, a senior or disabled tenant. The potential buyers usually also have not considered the cost, in both time and money, to evict someone. The buyers often believe that you will move out the moment they buy the building. Educate prospective buyers! Let them know they will be evicting someone, and what this potentially devastating act will mean to the residents, as well as what it will mean to the landlord's pocketbook, schedule and psyche. You may be able to convince prospective buyers that they don't want to buy your building, because it looks like a lot of hassle. And you might slow down the process so much that the sale as TIC units becomes unprofitable. Many tenants have fought their TIC evictions this way.

In addition, there are increasing restrictions on condo conversion for TICs created through evictions. Potential buyers should be told that condo conversion of TICs created through specific types of evictions are prohibited or restricted. (See the section "Conversions Not Allowed If Certain Evictions, Buyouts, Rent Increases, or Discrimination Preceded Application" later in this chapter.) Further, even if they get past that, TICs where senior or disabled tenants have been evicted are given the lowest priority in the condo conversion lottery. Make sure potential buyers know that there is a moratorium on condo conversions which will last until at least the year 2024.

Also, TICs in buildings with five or more units are directly regulated by the California Bureau of Real Estate (BRE). The BRE has taken the position (because of state Attorney General opinions) that TICs are subdivisions and thus subject to state regulation which provides for regulation of the subdivision of five or more parcels. (CA Business and Profession Code § 11004.5)

The regulation is mainly aimed at protecting buyers of the TIC units, because TICs can be so risky. BRE requires that the subdivider of TICs with five or more units must first obtain a "public report" from BRE before the units can be offered, financed or sold. (CA Business and Profession Code § 11010) Getting this public report can be a long process (6–12 months) and costly (usually at least $20,000 in 2011). BRE looks particularly at the financing of the property and, because TIC owners all share the same mortgage, usually requires that substantial sums be placed in escrow in event of a mortgage default by one of the TIC owners. Thus, many TIC developers in buildings with five or more units just don't file this public report.

Tenants in five or more unit buildings being converted to TICs should file complaints of illegal subdivision with BRE if the units are being offered for sale without a public report (*www.dre.ca.gov/Consumers/FileComplaint.html*). BRE has limited enforcement ability but has stopped such activity in the past. Tenants filing such complaints should also notify the developer who is their landlord and the realtor involved that the complaint has been filed and demand that the complaint be disclosed to prospective buyers. (Under disclosure laws, failure to disclose a complaint of illegal subdivision could subject the realtor and landlord to significant damages.) Make sure potential buyers are informed that the sale of the units is potentially illegal and that an illegal subdivision complaint has been filed.

Failure to obtain a BRE report can be utilized as a defense to an eviction under the Ellis Act. (See "Chapter 12, Eviction Defenses.") In 2005, tenants won a significant case against a real estate speculator seeking to evict them and sell the units as TICs. The units were offered for sale without a BRE report and a San Francisco Superior Court judge ruled that to be a violation of the Subdivided Lands Act and threw out the Ellis evictions.

Fighting the Sale of Your Home

Estoppel Agreements/Tenant Questionnaires: Do not sign any "Estoppel Agreements" or anything else the landlord or realtor wants you to sign, unless your rental agreement requires you to do so. An important exception is if you are a senior, disabled, household with children or school worker, or have a familial relationship with a child or school worker, you must disclose this status upon request or you may lose important protection.

- **Access by landlord or landlord's agent is restricted:** Entry for photographing the unit for display to potential buyers may be ruled by some judges as legal, since it is for the purpose of exhibiting the unit to potential buyers. However, let your landlord know your objection to the possibly illegal entry. If she insists on entry, let her know that you will be documenting the entry through photographs, videotape and witnesses for potential violation of your right to privacy. (California Constitution Article 1, § 1, *Hill v. National Collegiate Athletic Association (1994) 7 Cal. 4th 1*) Cover your belongings with a sheet which might deter the photographing as it would be unattractive for advertising as well as hiding your belongings from public view.

The realtor may want to show your apartment at all hours of the day and on short notice to prospective buyers. Remember, the law says the landlord must give 24 hours

"There are two bedrooms in this unit."

notice before entering your apartment. The notice may be oral if written notice was given up to 120 days before the oral notice. (CA Civil Code § 1954)

This access must be during "normal business hours," and the right to enter cannot be abused. Don't feel forced into agreeing to frequent open houses or buyers walking in and out at all times with little or no notice. However, the courts have ruled that "normal business hours" includes entry on weekends because those hours are the customary hours realtors use for open houses. (*Dromy v. Lukovsky* (2013) 219 Cal.App.4th 278) The judgment allowed open houses twice a month from 1:00 pm–4:30 pm with a licensed real estate agent present. The tenant was allowed to propose alternative days for the open houses after receiving notice by email 10 days in advance of the proposed weekend open house dates. The tenant had 48 hours after receipt of the notice to propose alternative dates.

However, the court did not decide what would happen if the tenant proposed alternative dates and the realtor did not accept those dates. Therefore, tenants should make an effort to appear reasonable in such negotiations, since it is a just cause for eviction if a tenant has after written notice to cease, refused the landlord access to the rental unit as required by law. If you are willing to allow the landlord (or agent) to come in during some other time, for example, when you're present, make sure to suggest this in a letter to the landlord and keep a copy.

Finally, be creative in how you cooperate—delay cleaning for a few days so the place is a mess for the open house, or invite friends over for a noisy party!

- **Post Signs:** Signs in your window and on your door and inside your apartment which say things like "Buyers Beware: We Will Fight Any Eviction to the End!" or "Beware, If You Buy This Unit and Evict Us, You Will Be Evicting Children (Seniors/People with Disabilities, etc.)" or "Buyers: Ask Your Lawyer How Much It Will Cost to Evict Us" will let potential buyers know that they are in for a fight, and can get them thinking about the emotional and financial toll they cause if they evict the tenants. (Be 100% truthful which means saying, for example, "if you evict us" instead of "when you evict us.") Put up bright notes pointing out every defect!

- **Picket Open Houses:** If an open house is scheduled, get your friends and neighbors together and set up a picket line that buyers have to cross. Carry signs and give out the flyers. You will be surprised at how many potential buyers will leave. The Tenants Union may be able to organize people who would join such a picket, so call us if you need help with this.

- **Hand Out Flyers**: Handouts that you can give to prospective buyers are very powerful. Describe yourself and other tenants and tell why you want to remain living there. Humanize the eviction for them and many buyers will back off. Again, let them know that you plan to fight to the bitter end. Also, if you know for a fact that your rental unit has certain defects, such as a leaky roof, a bad heating system or electrical problems, let the prospective buyer know about them.

- **Monitor Disclosure:** Owners of properties with two or more residential units are required to disclose to any prospective purchaser the legal grounds for terminating the tenancy of each unit to be delivered vacant at the close of escrow and whether the unit was occupied by an elderly or disabled tenant at the time the tenancy was terminated. (SF Administrative Code § 37.10A(g)) Disclosure on a flier available at open houses and tours is sufficient. The landlord is also required to disclose in writing to the proposed buyer, prior to entering into a contract for the sale of any property of two or more residential units, the legal ground(s) for the termination of the tenancy of each residential unit to be delivered vacant at the close of escrow. Violation of this disclosure to the buyer is subject to prosecution. (SF Administrative Code § 37.10A(f), (j)

- **Inform Yourself of the Status:** Your landlord is unlikely to tell you what is happening with your home, so you will have to make an effort to find out the status of the building sale. Have a friend contact the realtor to see how the building is being marketed.

- **Permits Can Be Blocked**: Request an alert or Block Book Notice from the Department of Planning so that you will be notified of any permit requests before the permits are issued in case either the new landlord or the old one has any plans to do any work to the building that might affect you. You can object to their permits if they affect your living situation. (See the section "Permit Process" at the end of this chapter.)

THE APARTMENT COMPLEX

Condo Conversion Law

California law requires notification to tenants when a rental unit is converted to a condominium to allow the tenant to protest the conversion. (CA Government Code § 66427.1, § 66451.3) Landlords are also required to disclose to potential tenants that the rental unit has been approved for sale as a condo. (CA Government Code § 66459)

However, the strong protection is in San Francisco where condo conversions are regulated by Division 1, Article 9 of the San Francisco Subdivision Code (also called "the condo conversion law," which can be found at *https://www.amlegal.com*). This law restricts the type of buildings that may be converted into condos, how many apartments can be converted each year, and tenants' rights regarding condo conversions. Additional rights are described in "Single Residential Unit" in "Chapter 4: Renting Basics." Amendments made in 2013 to the condo conversion law have significantly reduced the number of buildings which are eligible for condo conversion and enacted a moratorium on condo conversions until at least the year 2024 with the exception of 2-unit buildings where both units are owner-occupied. (SF Subdivision Code § 1396.5)

What Building Types Can Be Converted into Condos

The current law allows only buildings containing two to four units which meet "owner occupancy" requirements to be converted from rental units to condominium units. (SF Subdivision Code § 1396) The owner-occupancy requirements are:

- 2-unit buildings in which both units have been owner-occupied for 1 year or more are eligible for conversion *and* are exempt from the annual conversion limit (see the following section "Limit on Annual Conversion"). Both units must have been occupied for 1 year by separate owners who each own at least a 25% interest.

- 2-unit buildings with at least 1 of the units continuously occupied by an owner for 3 years prior to the date of registration for the lottery. This requirement is also satisfied by having been a tenant in the unit for 3 years if the tenant becomes an owner by the time of the registration and application for the lottery.

- 3-unit buildings with at least 2 units which have been continuously occupied by an owner for 3 years prior to the date of registration for the lottery. This requirement is also satisfied by having been a tenant in the unit for 3 years if the tenant becomes an owner by the time of the registration and application for the lottery.

- 4-unit buildings with at least 3 units which have been continuously occupied by an owner for 3 years prior to the date of registration for the lottery. This requirement is also satisfied by having been a tenant in the unit for 3

Condo Conversions Prohibited			
	All Tenants	**Senior**	**Disabled**
SF Subdivision Code § 1396.2. Cannot convert in these cases if the T was evicted for SF Administrative Code § 37.9(a)(8) LMI, *37.9(a)(10)* demolition, *37.9(a)(11)* capital improvement, or *37.9(a)(13)* Ellis Act.	No condo conversion for 10 years if the building had 2 or more evictions of the listed types. 2-unit buildings exempt from the lottery after 10 years owner occupancy (instead of 1 year). *§ 1396.2(a), (f)*	No conversion ever if 1 eviction of the listed types where T was 60 years or older with 10 years or more tenancy.	No conversion ever if 1 eviction of the listed types where T was disabled under ADA, *42 USC § 12102(2)(A)* (really *12102(1)*, *substantially* limits a major life activity, *before* mitigating measures with the exception of ordinary eyeglasses or contact lenses).
SF Subdivision Code § 1396. No conversion if the T evicted for *SF Administrative Code § 37.9(a)(8)-(14)* (LMI, sale of after condo conversion, demolition, capital improvement, substantial rehabilitation, Ellis Act, or lead abatement), or for *SF Administrative Code § 37.9E* (buyout agreement).	No conversion unless applicant certifies that no unit was vacated by a T for 7 years prior to the lottery registration because of an eviction or eviction notice of the listed types except: (1) if for LMI, was the only LMI and the LL or relative lived in the unit for the 3 years preceding registration; (2) if for capital improvement or lead abatement, eviction was temporary; (3) if for demolition, no replacement unit built.	n/a	n/a
Buyout Agreement. *SF Subdivision Code § 1396(e)(4).* Restricts conversion after vacancy for *SF Administrative Code § 37.9E.*	No condo conversion for 10 years if the building had 2 or more Ts who were bought out.	No conversion ever where T was 60 years or older with 10 years or more tenancy at the time of the buyout agreement.	No conversion ever if T was disabled under ADA, *42 USC § 12102* (*substantially* limits a major life activity, *before* mitigating measures with the exception of ordinary eyeglasses or contact lenses) with 10 years or more tenancy at the time of the buyout agreement, except 5 years tenancy for catastrophically ill T.
Condo Conversion Bypass Prohibited. *SF Subdivision Code § 1396.4(b)(10).* No conversion if T was evicted for *SF Administrative Code § 37.9(a)(8)-(14)* (LMI, sale of after condo conversion, demolition, capital improvement, substantial rehabilitation, Ellis Act, or lead abatement).	No bypass unless applicant certifies that no unit was vacated by a T after 3/31/13 because of an eviction or eviction notice of the listed types except if the eviction(s) was for capital improvement or lead abatement, the eviction was temporary.	n/a	n/a

years if the tenant becomes an owner by the time of the registration and application for the lottery.

Limit on Annual Conversion

The subdivision code has a moratorium (SF Subdivision Code § 1396.5) until at least the year 2024 on the 200 annual condo conversions (SF Subdivision Code § 1396) which were previously allowed. This moratorium does not include 2-unit buildings where both of the units have been owner-occupied for a year or more, as these buildings can be converted without limit.

When the moratorium is lifted, landlords who want to convert their eligible, non-exempt buildings to condos must first register for the annual lottery, which chooses 200 units from the hundreds of units that satisfy the initial requirements of the condo conversion process. *Only after winning the lottery can the landlord begin the process of applying for a condo conversion.* If the landlord wins the lottery for condo conversion, the law requires that the landlord then meet certain tenants' rights criteria. 175 of the 200 annual condo conversions are reserved for buildings where there have been no evictions under San Francisco Administrative Code § 37.9(a)(8)–(14) of long-term senior or disabled tenants. (SF Subdivision Code § 1396.1(g))

Conversions Not Allowed If Certain Evictions, Buyouts, Rent Increases, or Discrimination Preceded Application

A building is permanently prohibited from being converted to condos if a senior (60 years or older) with 10 or more years tenancy, or a disabled tenant of any length tenancy, has been evicted for the Ellis Act, owner move-in, capital improvement, or demolition from any of the units on or after May 1, 2005. (SF Subdivision Code § 1396.2. See "Chapter 12: Eviction Defenses" for more info on these types of evictions.) Because the definition of disability for this law is very broad (a physical or mental impairment that substantially limits one or more of the major life activities of such individual without regard to mitigating measures other than ordinary eyeglasses or contact lenses) the overwhelming majority of buildings will have at least one disabled tenant in them. In addition, condo conversions are prohibited for 10 years in buildings which have had no senior or disabled tenants evicted, but which have had those types of evictions from two or more units.

For tenants who vacated under a buyout agreement (as defined in SF Administrative Code § 37.9E) after October 31, 2014, there are similar prohibitions on conversions to condos. No conversions to condos are allowed if the buyout was within 10 years prior to the condo conversion application and two or more tenants vacated. No conversion ever if a senior or disabled tenant vacated. A senior is a tenant who was 60 years or older with 10 years or more tenancy at the time of the buyout agreement. A tenant is considered disabled if the disability substantially limits a major life activity before mitigating measures with the exception of ordinary eyeglasses or contact lenses (42 USC § 12102) and has 10 years or more tenancy at the time of the buyout agreement, except the tenancy only needs to be 5 years for catastrophically ill tenants. (See "Buyouts, Almost Always a Bad Idea" in "Chapter 8: Harassment" for more info.)

In addition to these limitations and prohibitions, conversion is prohibited if any single eviction occurred under San Francisco Administrative Code § 37.9(a)(8)-(14) (capital improvement, demolition, Ellis Act, owner move-in, lead abatement, sale after a condo conversion, or substantial rehabilitation) within the seven years preceding the application for condo conversion unless the applicant can demonstrate:

- Capital Improvement Eviction: If the eviction was for capital improvement, that the evicted tenant was given the opportunity to return after the work was completed.

- Demolition Eviction: If the eviction was for demolition of the unit, that the demolition was ordered by the City and no replacement unit has been built on the property.

- Owner Move-In Eviction (OMI): If the eviction was for OMI, that only one OMI occurred during the seven year period, the landlord or relative who moved into the unit has lived in the unit as their principal place of residency for at least the three years preceding the lottery registration, and is one of the owners of the property at the time of application for condo conversion.

- Lead Abatement Eviction: If the eviction was for lead abatement, that the evicted tenant was given the opportunity to return after the work was completed.

- Ellis Act Eviction: Though rare, a single Ellis Act eviction in the seven years preceding the application for condo conversion would trigger a condo conversion ban.

(SF Subdivision Code § 1396(e)(3)(A))

See also the "Condo Conversions Prohibited" chart for more info.

In addition to these prohibitions on conversion following certain evictions, Subdivision Code § 1386 prevents the approval of tentative subdivision maps that fit its criteria, but § 1386 has been rarely enforced by the Department of Public Works (DPW). § 1386 says that the tentative subdivision map application shall be denied if, during the 5 years preceding the filing of the condominium subdivision application, there have been evictions, displacement of senior or disabled tenants, discrimination against senior or disabled tenants seeking to rent, or "vacancies… have been increased…for the purpose of preparing the building for conversion" or if rent increases in excess of the annual amount allowed by the Rent Board (except for increases reasonably related to construction of code-required capital improvements directly related to code enforcement, or to recover those costs) occur within eighteen months prior to the filing.

One problem with § 1386 is that the date of filing for the subdivision (which triggers the five-year eviction look-back) comes after the building has been selected in the lottery. Since it typically takes well over five years for a building to be selected in the lottery, any evictions which took place have usually happened too long ago to be covered by § 1386. At least, DPW has been matching condo conversion applications with Rent Board eviction records.

Expedited Conversion Bypass for Existing TICs

There has been a partial suspension of the Expedited Condo Conversion program due to a United States District Court challenge (*Pakdel v. City and County of San Francisco, et al.*). Only applications with the final and effective tentative parcel map or map approval on or before June 27, 2017 or buildings without non-owning tenants may proceed to conversion. For updates and more info, see *www.sfpublicworks.org/services/ subdivisions-and-mapping*.

The Expedited Condo Conversion program imposed a moratorium of at least 10 years on annual condo conversions and restricted condo conversions to 2-4 unit buildings. Existing tenancies in common (TICs) created prior to April 15, 2013 which have been seeking to convert to condos will be allowed to become condos by paying a fee to the city rather than going through the annual lottery. Tenants living in these buildings get certain rights, notably the right to a lifetime lease.

Eligible Buildings (SF Subdivision Code § 1396.4(b))

Owner occupancy requirements: At least 1 unit continuously occupied as required in the preceding list by the same owner in a 2-4 unit building. At least 50% of units continuously occupied by the same owners in 5 and 6 unit buildings. Buildings which did not participate in the 2012/2013 lottery may have a single change in ownership in 1 unit as long as owner occupancy is maintained..

- Participants in the 2012 or 2013 lottery.

  - If the building met owner occupancy requirements since at least 4/15/08, eligible to apply.

- If the building met owner occupancy requirements since 4/15/11, eligible to apply.

- Buildings with a TIC agreement and have met owner occupancy requirements as of 4/15/13 are eligible to apply.

Eviction under San Francisco Subdivision Code § 1396.2 exclusion: Under 1396.2, no building subject to the permanent ban on condo conversions following an eviction of a senior or disabled tenant is eligible for the bypass. Nor is any building subject to the 10-year ban on condo conversions for multiple evictions eligible if the ten years is still running, except that 5- and 6-unit buildings subject to the 10-year ban will be eligible when the 10-year ban ends for individual buildings.

Rights for Tenants

See also the "Condo Conversions Require Lease Options" chart.

Eviction Protections (SF Subdivision Code § 1396.4(b)(10)):

In addition to the existing bans on conversion following evictions, if a unit(s) is vacated by a tenant after 3/31/13, the applicant for the bypass must certify that the tenant left voluntarily. Or, if an eviction or eviction notice occurred, it was not pursuant to San Francisco Administrative Code § 37.9(a)(8)-(14) (no fault evictions) except if the evictions were temporary under § 37.9(a)(11) or § 37.9(a)(14).

Lifetime Lease (SF Subdivision Code § 1396.4(g) and www. sfpublicworks.org/services/subdivisions-and-mapping*)*:

All the tenants in the buildings must be offered, in writing, a

(Continued on next page)

Challenging a Condo Conversion

At least 20 days before the issuance of a "tentative map," DPW must publish the addresses of buildings being considered for approval on its Web site and any interested party may contest the eligibility and request a hearing. It may be possible to challenge eligibility sooner than the "tentative map" point.

Lawsuit for Treble Damages

The Subdivision Code provides current and former tenants with the right to sue for violations of the Subdivision Code and to receive injunctive relief and money damages of not less than three times actual damages. (SF Subdivision Code § 1304)

Legal Action by the City Attorney or District Attorney

Violations are both civil and criminal violations. (SF Subdivision Code § 1304)

Rights in Condo Conversions When Tenants Remain in Unit

When a condo conversion happens without the interim TIC creation (rare), or if the TIC is created and the TIC owners have elected to keep one or more of the units as rentals, the condo conversion law provides specific protections for tenants throughout the conversion process. These protections are described in the following sections. There are other rights for tenants living in previously created TICs which have been allowed to bypass the annual conversion limitation as part of the 2013 law limiting condo conversions; see the box "Expedited Conversion Bypass for Existing TICs."

Agreement of Tenants to Convert and Right to Purchase Unit

The condo law provides that forty percent of the building's "tenants" must agree to the conversion and tenants must be offered the right to buy their unit. (SF Subdivision Code §

(Continued from previous page)

lifetime lease. The lifetime lease must be in the form approved by the City of San Francisco. If the owner submits the required form, but then seeks to modify this language through an addendum, the owner may be in violation of Section 1396.4(g). The bypass application must include a signed and notarized copy of the lifetime lease that each tenant was offered, and is recorded on the deed. The tenant has two years to accept the offer, and if accepted, the lease is also recorded at the San Francisco Assessor-Recorder's Office. The lease provisions must include:

- Rent is what the rent was at the time of application for the bypass, and any increases are tied to the residential rent component of the San Francisco Bay Area Consumer Price Index or other rent increase laws.

- The lease shall state it does not alter the rights of the tenant in carrying out the terms of the pre-existing rental agreement including the landlord is obligated to maintain the same level of services.

- The tenant may terminate the lease with a 30-day notice.

The lifetime lease expires when the tenant voluntarily vacates the unit or upon the death of the tenant, except if there is a household member of the tenant who is a spouse, domestic partner or blood relative and is either senior (62 years old at the time of the death of the tenant), or disabled (no definitions), the lease expires upon the death of the household member.

If the bypass applicant seeks to sell before the conversion is complete, she must record on the deed the lease restrictions.

Remedies for Tenants in Bypass Buildings

Department of Public Works (DPW) Hearing to Challenge Building Eligibility (SF Subdivision Code § 1396.4(c))

At least 20 days before the issuance of a "tentative map" of the subdivision, DPW must publish the addresses of buildings being considered for approval on its website. Any "interested party" may submit info contesting the eligibility and request a hearing. Most commonly, tenants will challenge the owner occupancy or the eviction history. Presumably, tenants will be able to request notification by DPW and can track the progress of individual addresses via the website by searching for "tracking." Since "interested party" is not defined, it seems a challenge to a building's eligibility could be made sooner than when the addresses being considered are published at the "tentative map" point.

Planning Commission Review and Board of Supervisors Approval for 5- and 6-Unit Buildings

All condo conversions in 5- and 6-unit buildings must be reviewed by the Planning Commission and the subdivision map approved by the Board of Supervisors. Under state law, both bodies have limited abilities to stop the condo conversion at this point, but they can do so on the basis that applicants lied on their application (e.g., about owner occupancy or evictions and displacement of tenants).

Lawsuit for Treble Damages (SF Subdivision Code § 1304)

Right to sue for violations, receive injunctive relief and money damages of not less than three times actual damages.

Legal Action by the City Attorney or District Attorney (SF Subdivision Code § 1304)

Both civil and criminal violations of the Subdivision Code.

1388) However, "tenants" mean "occupants" of the building—meaning that owners are classified as tenants when calculating the percentage ownership requirements. (SF Subdivision Code § 1308) Requiring 40% of all tenants to agree is quite different from requiring 40% of all occupants to agree, especially since many condo conversions will involve buildings with more than one owner already residing there. For example, in a 3-unit building where two units are occupied by owners, 40% of occupants can be met by the two owners. This interpretation of the definition of "tenants" can be challenged during the conversion process, or even during the eviction process. Assuming it stands, it will still often mean that the landlord will need at least one tenant to agree to the conversion.

Tenant agreement is obtained via nonbinding "Intent to Purchase" agreements which the landlord will ask tenants to sign. This goes hand in hand with a second tenant right: the right of first refusal to purchase the unit. (SF Subdivision Code § 1387, CA Government Code § 66427.1) Given that these two rights work together, tenants need to carefully weigh their ability to actually purchase the unit before signing this agreement, and take into consideration that their signature will be used to verify that the landlord has the tenant's permission to convert. Although the landlord will stress that the intent is nonbinding and will lock in the offered price, keep in mind that once it is signed, the "Intent to Purchase" is irrevocable; the tenant can't sign it and then retract their permission for the conversion. This is an important time for tenants in the building to organize themselves to make sure that everyone understands the implications of tenant permission and right of first refusal.

Seniors or Permanently Disabled Have Right to Lifetime Lease for Condo Conversion

At the time of the filing of the "Final Map," which completes the condo conversion process, tenants aged 62 or older or who are permanently disabled (not defined) must be offered a lifetime lease at the same rent (with allowable annual rent increases established by the Rent Board or other law). This lifetime lease must provide for the right of the tenant to vacate at any time with 30-day notice. The lease expires upon the death of the last household member who is related to the tenant by blood or marriage and aged 62 or older at the tenant's death. (SF Subdivision Code § 1391)

Right to One-Year Lease and Relocation Payment for Tenants Not Senior or Permanently Disabled

On or after the filing of the "final map," tenants who are not age 62 or older or are not permanently disabled will receive a notice asking them either to agree to a one-year lease starting the date of approval of the Final Map or to vacate within 120 days and receive $1,000 in actual relocation expenses or a fixed amount allowed by the Central Relocation Services agency of the City and County of San Francisco. (SF Subdivision Code §§ 1391, 1392) Tenants who opt for the lease extension can be evicted at the end of that lease but only for one of the just causes in the Rent Ordinance, as explained next.

Evictions after Condo Conversion

Since rental units built after 1979 are automatically subdivided, only pre-1979 rental units need to go through a condo conversion process. *Tenants who have opted for a lease extension can be evicted after the lease ends only if the landlord has one of the just causes to evict in the Rent Ordinance.* Landlords will most often use the just cause which allows evictions in good faith for sale of a unit converted under the subdivision code. (SF Administrative Code § 37.9(a)(9)) Under this just cause, tenants do not receive relocation payments. If not evicted for this just cause, tenants will likely be evicted for owner move-in. (See "Chapter 12: Eviction Defenses" for more info.)

Tenants who are residing in a building undergoing condo conversion should not think their eviction is guaranteed. Evictions for condo conversion typically happen before the condo conversion process has begun (when the tenancy in common is created). Any units which are renter-occupied at the time of condo conversion are likely renter-occupied because the landlord wants the rental income for that unit and does not intend to sell it.

Other Tenant Protections in the Condo Law

- **Temporary relocation**: If the tenant needs to relocate because the landlord is renovating the unit as part of the condo conversion process, the landlord must find the tenant equivalent substitute housing and pay the tenant any *additional* cost for this housing while the renovations occur. However, the amount is limited to the amount required under California Civil Code § 1947.9 for relocation of less than 20 days ($275 per day which may be adjusted for inflation). The tenant has the right to return to the unit, at the same rent, after the renovations are complete. (SF Subdivision Code § 1389) The unit needs to be brought up to code before it is subdivided. (SF Subdivision Code § 1380.1)

- **Rent increases**: If the unit is not under rent control, rent increases are prohibited for two years from the time the landlord submits the application for condo subdivision, until the tenant moves or until the application is withdrawn or denied. For a one-year period after the initial two year period, the rent can be increased only by the annual rent increase determined by the Rent Board, unless other laws allow for additional rent increases. (SF Subdivision Code § 1390)

- **Award for triple damages**: The Subdivision Code provides current and former tenants with the right

Condo Conversions Require Lease Options

	All Tenants	Senior	Disabled
Lifetime Lease Offered for Seniors/Disabled, Other Ts Offered 1 Year Lease *SF Subdivision Code § 1391.* Qualifying Ts offered a lifetime lease with right to vacate with 30 days notice.	Must be offered either a 1 year lease extension or to vacate within 120 days with $1,000 relocation payment.	62 years or older. Expires upon the death of the T's last household member, if related by blood or marriage and aged 62 or older at T's death.	Permanently disabled (not defined).
Condo Conversion Bypass. Must Offer Lifetime Lease. *SF Subdivision Code § 1396.4(g).* Qualifying Ts offered a lifetime lease with right to vacate with 30 days notice.	Must be offered a lifetime lease in writing with documentation.	Expires on the death of the T's household member if spouse, domestic partner, or blood relative and aged 62 years or older at T's death.	Expires on the death of the T's household member if spouse, domestic partner, or blood relative of T, and disabled (not defined).

to sue for violations of the Subdivision Code and to receive injunctive relief and monetary damages of not less than three times actual damages. (SF Subdivision Code § 1304)

Vacation and Corporate Guest Suite Rentals by the Landlord

The conversion of individual rental units (including both units not covered under rent control and rent-controlled units) into transient use "hotelization" or "corporate suites" are regulated by Chapter 41A of the San Francisco Administrative Code, the Residential Unit Conversion Ordinance, also known as the hotel conversion law. Hotelization is a serious problem for tenants as short-term rentals such as Airbnb reduce vacant rental housing stock by as much as 43 percent making homes even less affordable. (*https://www.sfexaminer.com/news/airbnb-rentals-cut-deep-into-sf-housing-stock-report-says*)

In addition, "hotelization" is often disturbing to the permanent residents since the building is occupied by large numbers of transient guests who may not care about being good neighbors and are most interested in having a good time while on vacation. The landlords who seek to "hotelize" often renovate the buildings to provide more hotel-type amenities and try to pass the renovation costs on to the permanent tenants through capital improvement rent increases. (See "Capital Improvements" in "Chapter 7: Rent Increases" for more info.) Such renovation causes noisy disruption of homes.

In an attempt to reduce the negative impact on tenants, Chapter 41A restricts rentals on short-term/vacation rentals (short-term rentals are rentals for less than a 30-day period) to the owner's primary residence. The short-term rental is supposed to be registered with the San Francisco Planning Department which allows public review of the registry.

A tenant may pursue his own remedy by suing for wrongful eviction if a tenant were evicted from the rental unit to illegally convert the unit to a vacation rental. Most likely however, the owner will hide her track by having a friend register units which the owner controls in an attempt to disguise the illegal conversion by the owner. If you suspect that your landlord or a landlord within 100 feet of your rental unit is running an unsanctioned hotel report it to the city's Office of Short-Term Rentals (see the listing under Government Agencies: San Francisco in "Appendix A: Resources"). A permanent resident in an affected building (including neighbors in a different property within 100 feet) can also sue.

A landlord can go through a discretionary review to take units off the residential rental market in order to make them vacation rentals, but it is almost impossible to do. If successful, the landlord would have to register with the City and pay hotel tax. Each property is zoned differently, so the tenant must call the

Department of Planning to determine restrictions. Regardless of zoning, a landlord must get a conditional use permit or go through a discretionary review. See "Permit Process" at the end of this chapter for more details.

Another type of conversion is the conversion of individual apartments into hotel-type suites rented by corporations, or in some cases schools, for their employees and visiting executives. This problem is especially prevalent in larger apartment complexes. San Francisco Planning Code § 202.10 has limitation on intermediate length occupancies that are defined as more than 30 days but less than 1 year (SF Planning Code § 102).

The conversion of residential hotels into tourist hotels is generally prohibited by the law. In some circumstances, landlords can convert if they contribute sizable sums to the city's affordable housing fund for the creation of "replacement units." A number of hotels have been partially converted, and via court agreements, these buildings must maintain a number of units for residential usage. Most of the damage of hotel conversions occurred prior to the passage of Chapter 41A but some landlords occasionally will try to get away with it today. The Tenderloin Housing Clinic (see "Appendix A: Resources") has generally assumed much of the responsibility for enforcement of the hotel conversion law.

Airbnb, Home Exchanges, or Similar Uses by the Tenant

With rents in San Francisco at stratospheric heights, some tenants are using Airbnb or home exchange services to sublet part or all of their unit and get some rent relief. These tenants should be aware that they are putting themselves at risk for eviction based upon an alleged violation of Chapter 41A (the Residential Unit Conversion Ordinance) referenced in the previous section. Vacation rentals and home exchanges are considered subletting as long as there is a "reward" for the use of the property. (CA Civil Code § 1925)

Renting space in your apartment—whether you are on the premises or not—is an extremely risky venture without the permission of the landlord. Most leases prohibit subletting without the permission of the landlord and some landlords are looking for any excuse to evict so they can raise the rent. Tenant attorneys have reported a rash of eviction notices related to short-term rentals done without the landlord's permission, so **understand**

"It'll have to be your place tonight.
I Airbnb'd myself out of my apartment."

the risks. In addition to the landlords, annoyed neighbors and homeowners associations are reporting illegal vacation rentals to the Office of Short-Term Rentals. The hosting platform's Web site (such as Airbnb) is required to warn the tenant immediately prior to listing the rental to check their rental agreement for restrictions on short-term rentals, and require the tenant to acknowledge the warning. (CA Business and Professions Code §§ 22590, 22592, 22594) Short-term rentals have reduced housing stock by up to 43% and Ron Conway, an Airbnb investor, has been funding politicians and legislation against rent-control. The Tenants Union has successfully reduced Airbnb's illegal listings, but they remain a problem. The Office of Short-Term Rentals has the requirements for short-term rentals. (See "Appendix A: Resources.")

Removal of Parking, Storage, or Laundry Room

See the following section "Accessory Dwelling Units" or "Parking, Storage, or Laundry Room Severance" in *Chapter 6: Repairs and Services*" for info.

Accessory Dwelling Units

Accessory Dwelling Units (ADUs), often called in-law units, if included under San Francisco Administrative Code § 37.2(r)(4)(D) are still covered under the Rent Ordinance even though they are new and legal. (See also the following section "Unauthorized Units." which are also sometimes called in-law units.) These units are constructed with a waiver of code requirements. However, severance of parking, storage, and laundry still requires a just cause for eviction and a building permit is not a just cause. (See "Parking, Storage, or Laundry Room Severance" in "Chapter 6: Repairs and Services" for more info.)

The owner is required to file with the Rent Board a declaration signed under penalty of perjury that the project will comply with the requirements of SF Administrative Code § 37.2(r) and § 37.9 relating to severance or reduction of a housing service. The owner will cause a notice describing the proposed project to be delivered to each unit (including unauthorized units) at the property and posted in an accessible common area of the building for at least 15 days before submitting an application to construct an ADU. The property owner shall submit proof of these notices to the Planning Department as part of the application. These notices shall also include instructions on how a tenant may petition the Rent Board for a written determination on the declaration. (SF Planning Code Section 207(c)(4)(C) and (J))

The permit to construct an accessory dwelling unit will be denied for buildings with two to four dwelling units if in the 5 years prior to filing the permit application a tenant was evicted for owner move-in, or if 10 years prior to filing a tenant had been evicted for the just causes of Ellis Act, demolition that was not a development agreement with the City of San Francisco, capital

improvement or lead paint abatement without the right to return, sale of a condo conversion, or substantial rehabilitation. Some single residential units will also be denied permits in these circumstances. (Planning Code § 207(c)(4) in "Appendix C: San Francisco Law and Regulations Excerpts." See also "San Francisco Rent Ordinance Evictions" in "Chapter 12: Eviction Defenses" and SF Department of Building Inspection Info Sheet G-23, Attachment B for more info.)

Unauthorized Units

San Francisco has thousands of illegal or unauthorized apartments. Often called "in-law" units, they are frequently found in garages and basements underneath formerly single residential unit houses and two-to-four unit buildings. (See also the previous section "Accessory Dwelling Units, a different type of "in-law" unit.) Many have existed for decades and new ones are constructed every year. How do you determine if your unit is illegal? You can do a quick check online by going to *https://sfassessor.org*. Click on the "Parcel Info" button. If your property lists all the units, then your unit is legal. If your unit is not counted, it may be unauthorized or the record may be out-of-date. The most reliable method is to go to the Department of Building Inspection and ask to see the "Street Files" for your address and see if your unit is officially on file with the city. Some newer in-law units are legal and still covered under the Rent Ordinance even though they would normally be exempt due to their post-1979 certificate of occupancy. (See "What Does the Rent Ordinance Cover?" in "Chapter 4: Renting Basics" for more info.)

Unauthorized units are defined as one or more rooms within a building that:

- have been used, without the benefit of a building permit, as a separate living or sleeping space; and

- is independent from residential units on the same property, meaning that (i) the space has access that does not require entering another residential unit, and (ii) there is no open or visual connection to another residential unit.

(SF Planning Code § 317(b)(13))

A typical characteristic of an unauthorized unit is that it shares a PG&E meter with another residential unit. In such cases, landlord is required to have a mutually agreed upon written agreement with the tenant for the payment of gas or electricity. (CA Civil Code § 1940.9)

The "illegality" is technical: the San Francisco Planning Code restricts density in neighborhoods. Illegality does not exempt these units from the Rent Ordinance. However, if the unit is rented with the main house under one rental agreement, the Rent Board considers it a single unit and therefore, usually, partially exempt from the Rent Ordinance. (CA Civil Code § 1954.52, SF Rent Board Topic No. 019)

The real illegality is found in unauthorized units which do not meet the basic housing and building codes—for example, ceilings less than seven feet high, inadequate heating and ventilation, etc. The twist is that if a tenant in an unauthorized unit complains to the Department of Building Inspection (DBI) about code violations, DBI may order the landlord to shut the unit down since, technically, unauthorized units are illegal. However, as of February 2014, "...[f]or building permits to remove an unpermitted unit where there is a feasible path to legalize the unit, the Department [of Building Inspection] will recommend that the current housing affordability crises creates an "exceptional and extraordinary" circumstance such that the Commission should deny the permit and preserve the unit." (DBI response to Executive Directive 13-01, SF Planning Code § 317(g)(6)) If a demolition permit is issued, you can protest the permit. (See the next section "Demolition of a Rental Unit and Mergers" for more info.) The Department of Public Health (DPH) says that they are required to report housing code violations to DBI, but tenants may be able to prevent the code violations being reported to DBI by telling DPH that they cannot pass on the info. DBI cannot cite the unit unless they come in the unit because of a complaint or warrant.

For illegal residential use of warehouses, it may help to have a community event with art, education, history, etc. to show inspectors how your warehouse benefits the community, but be careful about requirements for gatherings. Inspectors have been impressed in the past with these community benefits.

Tenants who live in these more affordable units must use caution in dealing with their landlords. Still, if you pay rent, you are a tenant and are entitled to tenant rights. Don't let your landlord make you think that you are the one committing the illegal act! You may have a successful lawsuit on the grounds of fraud if you were not aware of the illegality of the unit when you entered into the rental agreement. (CA Civil Code § 1598, *Carter v. Cohen* (2010) 188 Cal.App.4th 1038) Damages awarded to the tenant have been in the six figures. See "Illegal Use," and "Demolition Evictions" in "Chapter 12: Eviction Defenses" for more info on evictions from unauthorized units.

Demolition of a Rental Unit and Mergers

Landlords may attempt to evict tenants from unauthorized units by demolition (removal of the housing unit from housing use) or through a merger with another housing unit. These changes

in use can be done legally by obtaining approval from the Department of Planning and Department of Building Inspection or done illegally. Either way, a tenant can, and should, fight. See "Demolition Evictions" in "Chapter 12: Eviction Defenses" for more info.

A Department of Building (DBI) Inspection Notice of Violation for an unauthorized unit would require the property owner to file a permit to legalize the unit unless the Planning Commission approves removal of the unit through conditional use authorization or DBI finds the unit is not able to be legalized. Reasons for not being able to legalize include the building is a serious and imminent hazard or is not affordable or financially accessible for housing. (SF Planning Code § 317(d))

State law requires that the landlord notify the tenant of the plan to demolish the unit prior to applying for the permit, as well as the earliest possible approximate date on which the demolition will occur and approximately when the landlord will evict the tenant. Failure to do so has statutory penalties of actual damages and $2,500 (CA Civil Code § 1940.6), as well as being a defense to the eviction. The landlord is supposed to post a sign and notice of the application should be hand delivered or mailed to the tenants in the building. Demolition work shall not begin until 15 days after issuance of the permit except for work under a conditional use authorization. DBI should revoke any permit where the applicant has not substantially complied with the signage. (SF Building Code § 106A.3.2.3, § 106A.4.6; SF Planning Code § 311)

Mergers often occur when a landlord combines units for her own personal use to create a larger dwelling. To effect a merger, landlords may try to evict tenants in two units for a owner move-in. If the landlord is already living in the building, she may try to evict tenants in another unit. To merge units covered under the Rent Ordinance (see "What Does the Rent Ordinance Cover?" in "Chapter 4: Renting Basics"), a landlord must first have a just cause to evict (see "Chapter 12: Eviction Defenses") and a conditional use authorization is required except where there is no path to legalization or is economically unfeasible (unsound). Usually, an owner move-in eviction will not be allowed for such a merger unless the landlord obtains permits to physically merge the two units, as opposed to claiming she simply wants to use two separate units. Generally if the cost to upgrade the unit(s) to safe and habitable standards costs more than 50% of the cost to replace the existing unit(s) at the same size, it would be considered unsound.

The Department of Planning holds public hearings of merger applications unless it is a listed exception. (SF Planning Code § 317) See the section "Permit Process" at the end of this chapter for more info.

Demolition of a Building

A landlord needs to obtain approval from the City of San Francisco to demolish a building. See the previous section "Demolition of a

"Quick Lassie! Our neighborhood is being gentrified! Get help!"

Rental Unit and Mergers," the following section "Permit Process, " and "Demolition Evictions" in "Chapter 12: Eviction Defenses" for more info including protesting the permits.

Permit Process

Generally, there are two types of permits, one or both of which apply to changes for a building: (1) building or construction permits, which relate to physical changes in the building; and (2) conditional use permits and occasionally variances, which relate to the zoning or allowed uses of the building. More info on the types of physical changes that require a permit can be found by doing a search on *https://sfdbi.org* for "G-20." For more info see the Department of Building Inspection and Department of Planning under "San Francisco" in "Governmental Agencies" in "Appendix A: Resources," and "Department of Building Inspection" in "Chapter 6: Repairs and Services."

Tenants contesting permits should obtain the application packets for the permits. The packets provide detail on what is required for the permit, what the process is, and the criteria for granting or denying the permit.

Building Permits

If an owner wants to merge, demolish (remove from housing use including just removing a stove range), alter a unit, or construct a wireless communications services facility, he usually must file an application for a building permit with the Central Permit Bureau of the Department of Building Inspection (DBI). (See also the previous sections "Demolition of a Rental Unit and Mergers" and "Demolition of a Building.") The City requires the owner to produce drawings and blueprints for work that is significant in scope, for example, knocking down or building walls, changing locations of plumbing facilities, building additions, etc. Depending on the district and type of application, the Department of Planning will cause mailing to the tenant (including in unauthorized residential units) and posting on the site of a notice of the application. (SF Planning Code § 311, § 317)

If the owner is only removing a stove, kitchen, or bathroom, the application must include an affidavit, signed under penalty of perjury, that the work is not removing a dwelling unit. Such affidavit shall be posted prominently for at least fifteen days in a conspicuous common area within the building and delivered by hand delivery or US mail to all tenants residing in the building. (SF Building Code § 106A.3.1)

Permits and complaints by address may be found at *https://dbiweb02. sfgov.org/dbipts*. If you think that your landlord is planning to apply for a permit, you can request free alerts for both the Department of Building Inspection and the Department of Planning at *https:// sfdbi.org/buildingeye* or you can request a Block Book Notification for a fee for your property from the Department of Planning in case you don't get the notice from the Department of Planning or your landlord. The owner of the property will be notified of the request for a Block Book Notification. (On *https://sfplanning.org*,

Proposition M (1986): Priority General Plan Policies

Underlying the whole permit process for changes in use is the 1986 San Francisco initiative, Proposition M. (SF Planning Code § 101.1) This initiative set forth eight priority policies and modifications to San Francisco Planning Code §§ 320 and 321 that projects such as permit applications must follow. Generally, the granting or denial of a permit must contain "Proposition M findings" to demonstrate adherence, or inapplicability, to these policies. The eight priority policies (with the key housing policies in italics) are as follows:

- Existing neighborhood-serving retail uses must be preserved and future opportunities for resident employment in and ownership of such businesses must be enhanced.

- *Existing housing and neighborhood character must be conserved and protected in order to preserve the cultural and economic diversity of our neighborhoods.*

- *The city's supply of affordable housing must be preserved and enhanced.*

- Commuter traffic must not impede Muni transit service or overburden our streets or neighborhood parking.

- A diverse economic base must be maintained by protecting our industrial and service sectors from displacement due to commercial office development, and future opportunities for resident employment and ownership in these sectors must be enhanced.

- The city must achieve the greatest possible preparedness to protect against injury and loss of life in an earthquake.

- Landmarks and historic buildings must be preserved.

- Our parks and open space and their access to sunlight and vistas must be protected from development.

search for "Block Book Notification.") Once you have done this, any permit requests for your property should be reported to you before the permits are issued. Because of the short time limit to appeal a permit, it is wise for tenants to monitor the status of the permit themselves.

If you go in person, the **Permit Services** has the records of permits issued for property in San Francisco. The **Help Desk,** on the second floor, assists the public and gives the status of a permit. To view plans, and other building records, you will have to complete a Record Request Form (*https://sfdbi.org/records*) from the **Records Management Division** and mail or fax it in. Wait for a confirmation, then bring your form and photo identification when picking up the files. After reviewing the file, you may ask the clerk to make copies, except for blueprints and building plans; you cannot get a copy unless you have written authorization from the building's owner. **These copies must be certified to be used as evidence in court.** If you discover that the landlord does not have the approved permits on file with the DBI, an affidavit can be prepared that states that the custodian of records conducted a search of the files and no permit for the site address could be located.

It is strongly advised that the tenant review the file of the proposed work at the DBI or Department of Planning for a better understanding of the application. Once you know that permits have been requested, you can request discretionary review by the Planning Commission before the permits are issued, on the basis that the neighborhood will be adversely impacted, or on public policy grounds such as violation of the 1986 Proposition M guidelines. (See the box "Proposition M (1986): Priority General Plan Policies.") The discretionary review has a fee of $682 (8/21). When the fee affects the requestor's ability to pay for the necessities of life, the requestor may apply for a fee waiver. Neighborhood organizations may also qualify. See "Department of Planning" under "Government Agencies" of "Appendix A: Resources" for more info.

The landlord is supposed to post a sign outside the building to put tenants and neighbors on notice that a permit has been granted. After the permit is issued, the appeal process then begins. (SF Planning Code § 308) Usually, appeals must be filed within 15 days from the date the permit is issued. (*https://sfgov.org/bdappeal/appeal-process*, SF Business and Tax Regulations Code § 8) Fees range from $100-$600. Contact the Board of Appeals for more info. Besides the personal impact the work may cause the tenant, larger policy issues should be raised in the appeal. Proposition M has become the standard policy raised against development projects.

Variances also require approval but the appeal usually must be filed within 10 days. The Planning Code has standards for buildings that govern such features as rear yards, front setbacks, usable open space, height, and parking. There may be special circumstances that make it difficult for a project to meet all of the Planning Code requirements. In those instances, an owner may request that the Zoning Administrator grant a Variance from the Code provisions. The owner is supposed to post a sign outside the building about the hearing for a more than 10% Variance.

The landlord is usually not allowed to proceed with any work until the appeal is heard. In addition, a tenant usually cannot be evicted for demolition or renovation until the appeal is heard. It is advisable to watch a few appeals before you perform your own case. Although a lawyer is not required to present the appeal, it may be helpful to consult with one beforehand.

A Conditional Use is a use that is not usually permitted in a particular Zoning District. Conditional Uses require a Planning Commission hearing in order to determine if the proposed use is necessary or desirable to the neighborhood, whether it may potentially have a negative impact on the surrounding neighborhood, and whether the use complies with the San Francisco General Plan. During this public hearing the Planning Commission will "condition" the use by applying operational conditions that may minimize neighborhood concerns as well as apply conditions that may be required by the Department and the Planning Code. The owner is supposed to post a sign outside the building about the conditional use authorization hearing. The Planning Commission decision is final unless appealed by the Board of Supervisors within 30 days.

The Board of Appeals has five commissioners who review the arguments and supporting evidence offered by the property owner and opponents. The appeal is difficult to win since at least four of the five commissioners need to vote in your favor, and they seem primarily interested in whether DBI thinks there were any procedural defects in the permit application. The Board of Appeals will let stand a City departmental decision unless at least four members vote for the appeal even if one member is absent. However, even if lost, the appeal has the benefit of delaying the eviction and usually causing the landlord to testify under oath which may be useful in a later lawsuit if the landlord misrepresents the case.

In preparing either for a Board of Appeals, Discretionary Review, or Conditional Use Authorization hearing, it is important to organize support from neighbors and community organizations who will write letters and testify at the public hearing. Neighborhood groups can assist. When you first find out what is going on, contact these groups and ask for their support.

Chapter 12: *Eviction Defenses*

What Is an Eviction? What Is Not an Eviction?

If you are a San Francisco tenant, the odds are that you will be faced with the possibility of eviction at some point. Although each tenant is in a unique situation, we can explain the basics of evictions and defenses. This chapter will look at the reasons a landlord can use to evict a tenant and the defenses the tenant can present before the court process of eviction. (See "Chapter 13: Eviction Process in Court" for info on the court process.)

What Is NOT an Eviction?

Eviction is a legal process, usually through the court, called an "unlawful detainer" lawsuit. It consists of the landlord taking a series of steps that will result, he hopes, in a court judgment ordering the tenant to vacate the premises.

With one exception, your landlord cannot evict you without filing a lawsuit and getting a court judgment ordering you to move. The only person who can then physically remove you from your home is the sheriff, after a court judgment. The exception is for a sole lodger—only one renter living with the owner who retains access to the renter's unit. (See "Bypassing the Courts: Lodgers and Hotels" in Chapter 13: Eviction Process in Court.) Unless you are a lodger, you must be given a chance to defend yourself against the eviction in court. **But beware! Eviction actions move much more quickly than any other kind of lawsuit.** They can be the legal equivalent of the bobsled: a dizzying plunge through the court system and onto the streets. The cold comfort is that the landlord must at least usually go through the court process to evict a tenant.

*You do **not** have to move out as a result of any of the following:*

- Your landlord cannot evict you by *verbally* telling you to move or by stating "you are evicted."

- Your landlord cannot evict you by changing the locks on your door, nailing your door shut, cutting off your utilities, or moving your stuff out of your home, unless you are a lodger. These "self-help" expulsion attempts by landlords, except for evicting a lodger, are *illegal* in California and most other states. (See "Chapter 8: Harassment" for more info on these illegal evictions.)

- Unless you are a lodger, your landlord cannot evict you by merely serving you with written notice of eviction. Such notice is only the first step in the eviction process. Unless you are a lodger, you do not have to leave until a court judgment is entered that orders you to vacate.

Landlords often give tenants notices including dire statements such as "you must vacate the premises within three days" or some other insanely short time period. **No matter what the notice says, you are legally entitled to remain in your home until a judge or jury says otherwise and the landlord pays the sheriff to remove you from the premises, unless you are a sole lodger.** With the exception for a lodger, if you did move out after one of these notices or if you moved out because the place was uninhabitable, the landlord is liable for a wrongful eviction.

What IS an Eviction?

To repeat, an eviction is a legal procedure almost always requiring a court judgment against the tenant. Evictions must always start with a written eviction notice, unless the lease terminated and the rental unit is not covered under the Rent Ordinance or state law requiring just cause eviction. See "Protections for the Tenant Under the San Francisco Rent Ordinance and State Law" in "Chapter 4: Renting Basics" for info about if a tenant must be evicted with just cause. If the tenant is not out at the end of the eviction notice period, the landlord still isn't allowed to lock the tenant out, except for a sole lodger. (See "Bypassing the Courts: Lodgers and Hotels" in "Chapter 13: Eviction Process in Court.") The landlord must sue for eviction in court. (See "Chapter 13: Eviction Process in Court.")

Under what circumstances can your landlord legally bring an effective eviction against you? There is an important **difference in the eviction protection provided for you under California state law and San Francisco's Rent Ordinance.** See the following chart "SF v. CA Just Cause for Eviction" for more information. The eviction *process* is governed by state law, so it is the same whether or not the rental unit is protected by the Rent Ordinance, but there is a difference in the allowable *reasons* for eviction.

Illegal Reasons for Evictions If the Unit Is Not Covered Under Just Cause

California state law and the San Francisco Rent Ordinance usually require a "just cause" to evict. Even for tenants not covered by just cause, evictions for no just cause look bad for the landlord, so organizing public opposition can be useful. (See "Chapter 14: Taking Action.") In addition, the following types of evictions are illegal for all California tenants:

Retaliation

The landlord cannot evict as retaliation for action of the tenant's. (CA Civil Code § 1942.5)

Discrimination

The landlord cannot evict because of discrimination. (See "Chapter 9: Discrimination.")

SF v. CA Just Cause for Eviction

	SF Administrative Code § 37.9	**California Civil Code § 1946.2**
Length of Tenancy Requirement	Rooms in hotels, motels, inns, tourist houses, rooming and boarding houses where the tenant has occupied the room fewer than 32 consecutive days are exempt from the Rent Ordinance. (SF Administrative Code § 37.2(r)(1))	Tenant must have continuously occupied the residential property for 12 months. If additional adult tenants are added to the lease then only applies if all the tenants have continuously occupied the residential property for 12 months or one of the tenants have continuously occupied the residential property for 24 months. California Civil Code § 1946.2(a)
Disclosure Required in Addition to Eviction Notice	None	As of 7/1/20 for new or renewed tenancies, 8/1/20 for continuing tenancies, disclose rent control and just cause eviction requirement. California Civil Code § 1946.2(f)
Nonpayment of Rent or Habitual Late Payment	SF Administrative Code § 37.9(a)(1)	California Civil Code § 1946.2(b)(1)(A) and (B)
Breach of Rental Agreement	SF Administrative Code § 37.9(a)(2)	California Civil Code § 1946.2(b)(1)(B)
Nuisance or Waste (Substantial Damage to the Unit)	SF Administrative Code § 37.9(a)(3)	California Civil Code § 1946.2(b)(1)(C) and (D)
Illegal Use	SF Administrative Code § 37.9(a)(4). If the unit is unauthorized for residential use, this just cause would not apply.	California Civil Code § 1946.2(b)(1)(F) and (I)
Refusal to Renew Rental Agreement	SF Administrative Code § 37.9(a)(5).	California Civil Code § 1946.2(b)(1)(E)
Refused Landlord Entry Required by Law	SF Administrative Code § 37.9(a)(6).	California Civil Code § 1946.2(b)(1)(H)
Unapproved Subtenant	SF Administrative Code § 37.9(a)(2) for breach of rental agreement, and § 37.9(a)(7) for only unapproved subtenant still remaining in the unit.	California Civil Code § 1946.2(b)(1)(G)
Employee/Agent/Licensee's Failure to Vacate After Termination	Not applicable (not a tenant).	California Civil Code § 1946.2(b)(1)(J)
Termination by Tenant Who Fails to Vacate	Not applicable (not a tenant).	California Civil Code § 1946.2(b)(1)(K)
Owner or Relative of Owner Move-In	SF Administrative Code § 37.9(a)(8)	California Civil Code § 1946.2(b)(2)(A)
Sale of Unit Converted to Condo	SF Administrative Code § 37.9(a)(9)	Not applicable.
Demolition Not for an Agreement with the City of SF	SF Administrative Code § 37.9(a)(10). Removal from housing use which is not a development agreement with the city.	California Civil Code § 1946.2(b)(2)(C) and (D)
Temporary Capital Improvement or Rehabilitation	SF Administrative Code § 37.9(a)(11)	Not applicable.
Substantial Rehabilitation/Remodel of Unit	SF Administrative Code § 37.9(a)(12). For a building that is essentially uninhabitable.	California Civil Code § 1946.2(b)(2)(C) and (D)
Ellis Act	SF Administrative Code § 37.9(a)(13)	California Civil Code § 1946.2(b)(2)(B)
Lead Paint Abatement	SF Administrative Code § 37.9(a)(14). *Temporary* removal from housing use.	California Civil Code § 1946.2(b)(2)(C) and (D)
Demolition for an Agreement with the City of SF	SF Administrative Code § 37.9(a)(15)	Not applicable.
Good Samaritan Occupancy Status Expires	SF Administrative Code § 37.9(a)(16).	Not applicable.
Relocation Payment	See the table "Relocation Payment for Evictions Under the SF Rent Ordinance."	Relocation payment or waiver of one month of rent for no-fault eviction within 15 calendar days of service of the termination notice. California Civil Code § 1946.2(d)

Chapter 12 – Eviction Defenses

Domestic Violence, Sexual Assault, Stalking, Abuse of an Elder or Dependent Adult or Human Trafficking

The landlord cannot usually evict if the tenant or a tenant's household member is a victim of domestic violence, sexual assault, stalking, abuse of an elder or dependent adult, or human trafficking if there is documentation of a protective order and the abuser is not sharing the dwelling unit with the victim. If the landlord believes the abuser is a threat to the legal rights of others, the landlord may evict after repeated warnings. (CA Code of Civil Procedure § 1161.3)

Servicemembers

Servicemembers have some protection under the Servicemembers Civil Relief Act, also known as the Soldiers' and Sailors' Relief Act of 1940. Except for a court order during military service, servicemembers or their dependents may not be evicted from premises that are intended as a residence and for which the monthly rent does not exceed $4,214.28 for 2022. (50 U.S.C. § 3951) The updated amount may be found by searching online for "secretary of defense (1)(A)(ii) housing price inflation [year]."

Natural Disaster

A landlord may not evict a tenant for a period of 30 days after a natural disaster declaration or extension and increase the rent over what the evicted tenant could have been charged. (CA Penal Code § 396)

Tax Credit Units for Low-Income Housing

For tenants who live in low-income housing units with tax credits, the landlord must give the tenant a "good cause" and explanation for ending the landlord-tenant arrangement. To find out if the unit is a tax credit unit, look for the property on the California Tax Credit Allocation Committee website, *www.treasurer.ca.gov/ctcac*.

The Eviction Process Before Going to Court

Notice to (Cure or) Quit

The eviction process almost always begins when the landlord or his agent gives the tenant a notice, commonly called a "Notice to Quit," which is usually a 3-day or 60-day notice. This notice does not come from the court. While the Notice to Quit can be handwritten or typed, formal or informal, *it must be in writing*, regardless of whether your rental agreement is oral or written. A mere oral demand by the landlord that you leave is not a legal eviction notice that a court will acknowledge. The notice must also adequately identify the premises. Usually this is done by providing the address, including the apartment number. See the following

---

10 Day Warning Notice

This legislation has been put on hold. Contact the Anti-Displacement Coalition for the latest status.

Eviction for nonpayment of rent excluding non-payment due between March 1, 2020 and March 31, 2022, breach of rental agreement, nuisance excluding imminent risk of physical harm to persons or property, illegal use, refusal to renew rental agreement, and refusal for legal entry by landlord (Sections 37.9(a)(1)-(6)) shall not apply unless the violation is not cured within ten days after the landlord has provided the tenant a written warning that describes the alleged violation and informs the tenant that a failure to correct such violation within ten days may result in eviction proceedings. (SF Administrative Code § 37.9(o))

---

sections for more notice requirements for specific types of notices.

Remember, the *landlord's Notice to Quit is not the same as an eviction unless you are a sole lodger*. Except for a lodger, the simple fact that you have received a notice of any type from the landlord does not mean that you must leave at the end of the notice period; it merely is the first step in the eviction process. (See "Chapter 13: Eviction Process in Court" for more info.)

If the tenant is covered by the Rent Ordinance (see "What Does the Rent Ordinance Cover?" in "Chapter 4: Renting Basics") **or state law for eviction with just cause, a Notice to Quit always needs to be served on the tenant in order to evict the tenant.** There are a few circumstances where the landlord is not required to give the tenant a Notice to Quit before filing an eviction lawsuit against the tenant if the tenant is not covered by the Rent Ordinance. However, even in those cases, the landlord still has to use the courts and go through the court process; that is, the landlord cannot simply remove the tenant.

In the following cases, the landlord does not have to serve a Notice to Quit prior to filing the Unlawful Detainer lawsuit.

- The tenant is not covered by the San Francisco Rent Ordinance or state law for eviction with just cause and has given the landlord a written 30-day notice to terminate the tenancy, and the tenant has not vacated the premises at the end of the 30-day period.

- The tenant is not covered by the Rent Ordinance or state law for eviction with just cause, and the landlord seeks to evict the tenant at the end of a fixed-term lease.

- The resident is not covered under state law for eviction with just cause and is a "servant, employee, licensee, or agent" of the landlord and her "employment, agency, or license" has been legally terminated. (See "Resident Managers and California Law Requiring Just Cause Eviction" in "Chapter 4: Renting Basics" for more info.)

Invalid Notices

Caution: Even if you are absolutely positive that the landlord's notice is invalid, this does not prevent the landlord from filing an eviction lawsuit — a lawsuit you will lose if you do not respond to it properly! Rather, an invalid notice gives you effective ammunition to fight the lawsuit once you correctly respond to it. In other words, an invalid notice does not magically stop the eviction process. You must still take effective action when the time comes. Also, some errors in the notice may be easily cured or are not considered defective. (See the "Unlawful Detainer Procedural Defenses" section in *Chapter 13: Eviction Process in Court* for ways to respond to an invalid notice.)

You may not want to let the landlord know that the notice is invalid as that will tip him off about correcting the notice, something he might otherwise have been unaware of. (Although the Rent Board may inform the landlord of required missing info.) It is not your responsibility to educate your landlord. However, it is important to act in good faith to present a good case. If you receive any type of eviction notice, you should immediately contact the San Francisco Tenants Union or see the box "Right to an Attorney for Eviction Notices."

Right to an Attorney for Eviction Notices

Free attorneys are available to tenants in an eviction, although not all tenants will receive full representation due to limited resources. (Former tenants who receive an unlawful detainer may also receive representation.) This service is not available when a landlord, including a master tenant, lives with the tenant. (Proposition F, 2018; SF Administrative Code § 58.4) However, if a subtenant is being evicted with the master tenant, the subtenant will receive an attorney. An attorney may be assigned where the tenant believes the unit is not shared with the landlord. Contact the Eviction Defense Collaborative for assistance. (See "Appendix A: Resources.")

In addition to complying with the requirements of state and local law, the landlord must also comply with the requirements of the rental agreement.

Sixty- and Thirty-Day Notices

Where the tenant has not done anything wrong, but the landlord still wants her out, the landlord must usually give a 60-day notice. If the tenant is covered under the Rent Ordinance or state law for eviction with just cause, the landlord must also have a just cause to evict. (See the chart earlier in this chapter "SF v. CA

Just Cause for Eviction" and "Right to an Attorney for Eviction Notices.") If a tenant has been in the rental unit for less than 1 year, however, the landlord can give only a 30-day notice instead. 30 days is also enough if the unit is not covered by just cause eviction and the landlord is selling a single residential unit (including a condominium where the "unit is alienable from the title to any other dwelling unit") to a natural person or people, not a corporation, the sale went into escrow no more than 120 days before the notice is given, the landlord has not previously given the tenant a 30 or 60-day notice, and the buyer intends to live in the unit for at least 1 year. A 30 or 60-day notice must include a statement that the former tenants can reclaim their property at their former address. (CA Civil Code § 1946, § 1946.1)

If you've received a notice that is longer than three days **you must still pay the rent during the notice period** or you may be evicted sooner, with a 3-day notice to pay or quit and have a mark against you on your credit record. A landlord may give a tenant both a 3-day notice to pay/cure or quit and a 30 or 60-day notice for termination of tenancy for another reason.

Other Notice Periods Besides Sixty/Thirty/Three

Evictions under the Ellis Act are required to give at least a 120-day notice which is extended for senior and disabled tenants to a 1-year notice if the tenant has given proper notice of their senior or disabled status. (See the section "Ellis Act" later in this chapter.)

Subletting breaches of the rental agreement for rental units covered under the San Francisco Rent Ordinance give the tenant the option to stop the breach within 10 days. (See the section later in this chapter "Breach of Rental Agreement" and also "Chapter 10: Roommates" for more info on subletting where the rental agreement restricts subletting.)

For a government contract that limits the rent the tenant must pay, such as Section 8, the landlord must give a 90-day termination notice. (CA Civil Code § 1954.535, *Wasatch Property Management v. Degrate* (2005) 35 Cal. 4th 1111) If the rental agreement requires 14-day notice for nonpayment of rent (as do leases with the San Francisco Housing Authority) or 10-day notice (as for many project-based Section 8 leases), then failure to give the appropriate notice would be a defense.

Three-Day Notices

State law allows a three-day notice when the landlord believes that the tenant has broken a specific part of the rental agreement. (CA Code of Civil Procedure § 1161) By far, the most common reason for a three-day notice is the tenant's failure to pay rent, in whole or in part. (See the section "Nonpayment of Rent" later in this chapter for more info.) With some exceptions, the three-day notice must give the tenant the option to cure the problem—that is, pay the rent or stop breaching other clauses in the rental agreement, or leave. These notices *must* be phrased in the alternative—as "Notice to Cure or Quit" or "Notice to Perform

Covenant or Quit." The tenant has three days *either* to correct the violation or to move out. If the offense requires an option to cure and does not include that option in the notice, the notice is defective, providing the tenant a strong defense to the eviction. Whether a problem can or cannot be corrected is not ultimately up to the landlord but must be decided by a court. Just because a tenant receives a three-day notice does not mean she has to leave

in three days. It merely is an allegation by the landlord which must be proved in court.

For details about specific types of evictions, see later in this chapter.

A landlord may give a tenant both a three-day notice to pay/cure

---

Credit Reports and Tenant Screening Agencies

As of January 1, 2017, access to court records for eviction lawsuits are restricted (masked) for the first sixty days. If a landlord wins within the sixty days, the records are available to anyone after the sixty days have passed, however, most judgments are not reached until after the sixty days. If the judgment is obtained after sixty days, the records are unmasked only with a court order. This law was not applied retroactively so anyone with an eviction record prior to 2017 so would not benefit from the masking protections.

The restriction allows access to the records for the first sixty days of the lawsuit (unless a court order prevents access) for:

(1) a party to the action

(2) a person who provides the names of a tenant and a landlord and address of the premises

(3) a resident of the premises who shows proof of residency and the name of either the tenant or landlord or case number

(4) by court order. If the judgment against the tenant is overruled after the sixty days has passed, the restrictions for sixty days begin again.

(Code of Civil Procedure § 1161.2)

Even if they are able to find the info (which is usually collected in bulk, not individualized as required by masked records), most of the big credit agencies like EquiFax, Trans Union, and Experian will not report lawsuits with no judgment, but negative judgments for money will affect the credit score. Also, if your landlord used a debt collector for nonpayment of rent, the collection account will show up on the credit report. Judgments that do not involve money also show up on the credit report if found, although it does not affect the credit score.

Much less commonly, tenant screening agencies obtain eviction info directly from landlords who sometimes report eviction info to these agencies. These agencies are supposed to give a complete, accurate picture of your record, so if the case was dismissed they should report that as well.

You should be aware of the possible mark on your credit record if you get an unlawful detainer notice. Here are some things you might do:

(1) If you get a three-day notice for nonpayment, consider paying the money within the three days. If you don't owe the landlord that money (because the apartment is not habitable, for example, or because you made necessary repairs and properly deducted the cost from your rent), you can then sue the landlord for the money instead of having the landlord sue you for unlawful detainer.

(2) In a settlement to an eviction lawsuit, make one of the conditions of the settlement that the landlord gives you a positive written referral. This doesn't cost the landlord anything, so she may be willing to do it, and it helps counter the fact that you have an unlawful detainer on your record. Of course, in any settlement you will want the landlord to vacate the judgment and to file a dismissal of the action with prejudice. (See the section in *Chapter 13: Eviction Process in Court*, "Negotiating Evictions: Settlements and Other Alternatives" for more info.)

(3) If you think some credit reporting agency is incorrectly or incompletely reporting your eviction history, call them up and ask them what they have on you. (To find tenant screening services, search online for "Credit Reporting Agencies.") If they are missing something, tell them in writing to correct it. They will probably want to verify what you tell them by checking to see that the case was indeed dismissed, for example, but they should correct it fairly promptly. Double check to make sure they do, and hound them or sue them if they continue to give incorrect info.

Both state and federal law require consumer credit reporting agencies to "follow reasonable procedures to assure maximum possible accuracy of the info concerning the individual about whom the report relates." (§ 1785.14(b) of the California Consumer Credit Reporting Agencies Act, CA Civil Code § 1785.1-1785.36; see also the almost identical provision in § 1681e(b) of the federal Fair Credit Reporting Act. A tenant can likely win a case against a tenant screening service for refusing to include additional clarifying info in their report. (*Schoendorf v. U.D. Registry, Inc.* (2002) 97 Cal. App. 4th 227, 238. Page 231 of this decision contains the full text of a letter that can be used as a model when writing a recalcitrant tenant screening service.)

or quit and a thirty or sixty-day notice for termination of tenancy for another reason.

Calculating the Notice Period

Weekends and holidays **are** counted in **noncurable** eviction notices unless it is the last day (CA Code of Civil Procedure § 12). Weekend days and judicial holidays are not counted for **curable** notices to quit (CA Code of Civil Procedure § 1161(2), (3)). If the last day falls on a weekend or holiday, then the next regular business day is considered the final day. (CA Code of Civil Procedure § 12a)

If the notice has been delivered directly to the tenant (personal service), the days start running on the day after the personal service. For example, if the tenant is personally served with a three day notice on Wednesday, then Thursday is Day One, Friday is Day Two, and because Day Three would fall on a weekend, the tenant has at least until the close of business on Monday to comply.

If the notice was served to a substitute person because personal service could not be made, the notice must also be mailed to the address of the property. If the notice is "nailed and mailed" because neither personal nor substitute service could be made, the notice may be attached to a conspicuous place of the property and also mailed. For these two types of service that require two notices each, the days start the day after both notices are served. (*Walters v. Meyers* (1990) 226 Cal. App. 3d Supp. 15) For a mailed notice, the first day is the day after the posting of the mail (dropped off at the post office or in the collection box). California Code of Civil Procedure § 1013 does not extend the notice period if mailed. (*Losornio v. Motta* (1998) 67 Cal.App.4th 110)

It is safer to comply with the notice by the close of business on the last day, especially if the landlord is a business. During this period, there is nothing the tenant can do to automatically stop the eviction process.

Service of the Eviction Notice

Whether the landlord's notice is for three, thirty, or sixty days, the landlord must deliver or "serve" it to the tenant in a manner authorized by law to increase the chances for the tenant to receive the notice. (For three day notices: CA Code of Civil Procedure § 1162, Civil Code § 789, *Borsuk v. Superior Court* (2015) 23 Cal. App.4th Supp.1. For thirty or sixty day notices: Civil Code § 1946, § 1946.1) If the rental agreement has special service requirements for the notice, then the landlord must follow those requirements as well. If the notice is not correctly served, the tenant has a defense which must be alleged in response to the eviction lawsuit. (See "Chapter 13: Eviction Process in Court.") The burden of proof is on the landlord that the landlord gave notice. Do not, however, count on an improperly served notice stopping the eviction, because judges may not see this as a fatal flaw.

The notice may be served on the tenant by the following methods:

(1) Personal service: The notice is delivered directly to the tenant.

(2) Substituted service: If personal delivery cannot be made, the landlord may deliver the notice to anyone who answers the door who is capable and of suitable age. If this method is used, the landlord also must send the tenant a copy of the notice by mail. (Regular mail is allowed.)

(3) Nail and mail: If the tenant cannot be served by either of the methods of numbers 1 or 2, the landlord may attach the notice to a conspicuous place on the property, such as the front door, and send a copy of the notice to the tenant by mail. (Regular mail is allowed.)

(4) 30-day, 60-day or 120-day notices to quit may be served by certified or registered mail; trying to serve the notice by personal delivery is not required.

If the rental agreement has special service requirements for the notice, then the landlord must follow those requirements or else the tenant has a basis to fight the eviction.

If the tenant is covered by the Rent Ordinance, the landlord must file a copy of the eviction notice with the Rent Board, within ten days of serving the tenant, in almost all cases. The exception is three-day notices for nonpayment of rent. (SF Administrative Code § 37.9(c)) Amendments must also be filed with the Rent Board.

Acceptance of Rent May Waive Notice

The tenant can try to void the eviction notice entirely by offering the landlord rent in the usual manner when it next comes due. For example, if the landlord claimed the tenant had been subletting in violation of the rental agreement, if the landlord accepts any portion of the rent for the period after the notice has expired, the landlord may have "waived" the notice and it may be effectively canceled. (CA Civil Code § 1945, *EDC Associates Ltd v. Gutierrez* (1984) 153 Cal. App. 3d 167) If the notice does not contain a forfeiture declaration, the tenant may pay the rent due after the expiration of the notice and retain possession. (*Briggs v. Electronic Memories & Magnetics Corp.* (1975) 53 Cal. App. 3d 900, 905) See the box "Waiver, Estoppel, and Change of Agreement: Unenforced Rental Agreement Provisions as Defenses to an Eviction" later in this chapter for more info.)

For example, if you get a valid 60-day notice to terminate your tenancy on March 1, the tenancy would expire on April 30. If

your landlord accepts rent for May, the March 1 notice may no longer be valid. In order to evict, the landlord may need to serve you with a new notice and wait another 60 days before taking further court action. If the landlord agrees to accept the rent, be sure to get the confirmation of the acceptance of rent in writing with the landlord's signature and the date to avoid unpleasant surprises later.

One good way to offer this rent is with a money order, because this provides you with a dated receipt which supports your assertion that rent was offered on that date. If the money order is returned by the landlord, you can cash it in and get the funds back. However, if you normally pay rent by personal check, you may want to use the same form of payment you usually use, in order not to arouse the landlord's suspicions. Just be certain to have proof the rent was offered to the landlord such as getting a receipt. (See "Paying Rent" in "Chapter 4: Renting Basics" for more info.)

San Francisco Rent Ordinance Evictions

The San Francisco Rent Ordinance requires (see "What Does the Rent Ordinance Cover?" in "Chapter 4: Renting Basics," also see following sections specific to certain types of evictions):

- At least one of the grounds for eviction in the notice is the **dominant and allowable motive**. Sixteen of the reasons, referred to as "just causes," are described in the following sections and summarized in the chart earlier in this chapter "SF v. CA Just Cause for Eviction." The seventeenth reason is the landlord may evict a tenant sharing the unit with the landlord. (See "Roommate(s) Living with Owner" in "Chapter 10: Roommates" for more info on the definition of sharing a unit.)

- Include a **Rent Board form** informing the tenant:

  · A timely response needed to avoid eviction.

  · Advice from the Rent Board is available.

  · Eligibility for affordable housing programs from the Mayor's Office of Housing and Community Development.

- For evictions under SF Administrative Code § 37.9(a) (8) owner move-in, (9) condo sale, (10) demolition not part of a development agreement with the City of San Francisco, (11) capital improvement, and (14) lead abatement, state the **rent at the time the notice was issued**.

- Notice be in the primary **language of the tenant** if it is Chinese, English, Russian, Spanish, Tagalog, or Vietnamese.

- All notices, except for nonpayment of rent, must be **filed with the Rent Board** within 10 days of service of the notice to vacate.

(SF Administrative Code § 37.9(c))

Just Causes for Eviction Under the SF Rent Ordinance

One way to divide up the just causes is to distinguish between "fault" and "no-fault" evictions. Those for "fault" are causes, such as nonpayment of rent, where the landlord claims that the tenant did something wrong or did not do something the tenant should have done. "No-fault" evictions are ones where the actions or inactions of the tenant play no part in the eviction, such as a owner move-in eviction. Historically, these no-fault evictions have been the ones most often abused by landlords trying to get more money for their units, since they typically are based on such subjective issues as the landlord's alleged intentions, rather than on facts. However, more and more landlords are using minor perceived (or invented) wrongs by the tenant as a pretext for eviction.

Seven of the sixteen just causes are for "fault" evictions, based on the tenant's failure to fulfill her obligations: paying the rent, paying the rent on time, following the rental agreement, refraining from causing a nuisance or damaging the property, signing an identical lease renewal offered by the landlord at the end of the lease, allowing the landlord to enter the unit as required by law, and refraining from using the rental unit for an illegal purpose.

The rest of the causes are the "no-fault" evictions, in which the tenant has not done anything to cause the eviction. These include eviction to allow the landlord to live in the unit or let a relative live in the building if the landlord is also going to live in the building (owner move-in/owner move-in), to sell the unit and evict the tenant towards the end of a pre-approved condo conversion, to demolish the unit, to get the tenant out temporarily so the landlord can do work on the building if the work is hazardous to the tenant (capital improvement or lead abatement eviction), to evict the tenant so the landlord can do major work on the building when the building is essentially uninhabitable (eviction for substantial rehabilitation), to stop renting all units in the building under the state "Ellis Act," or when a tenant's Good Samaritan occupancy status ends.

Under the Rent Ordinance, the mere fact that ownership of your building has been or may be transferred to new owners is not in itself a just cause for eviction. All previous rental agreements continue to apply, as well as rent and eviction controls. Even when the bank has foreclosed on the landlord, the bank still has to have one of the just causes to evict the tenant. (See "Foreclosure by a Bank" in "Chapter 4: Renting Basics" for more info.)

Rent Board Reports of Alleged Wrongful Eviction

Tenants in units covered by the Rent Ordinance (see "What Does the Rent Ordinance Cover?" in "Chapter 4: Renting Basics") may understandably think about filing a Report of Alleged Wrongful Eviction ("AWE") with the Rent Board, hoping that the Board will nip the eviction in the bud. Tenants need to know that there is a difference of opinion within the San Francisco Tenants Union as to the merits of this procedure. This section discusses the opposing viewpoints to give tenants a choice of tactics to defend their homes.

Be advised that an AWE may be of limited usefulness. Tenants should check with a SFTU counselor or an attorney before filing a Rent Board complaint. Why? Because the Rent Board has absolutely no legal power to stop any eviction, even a wrongful one. Only the courts can do this. Relying solely on the Rent Board might give you a false sense of security. Filing the Report may even assist the landlord by calling attention to errors and providing the opportunity to correct them before the eviction goes to court. (The landlord can look up the AWE at the Rent Board but it is not necessarily sent to the landlord.)

The only real powers the Rent Board has are: (1) to determine the correct amount of rent, and (2) to refer an alleged unlawful eviction to the District Attorney for criminal prosecution or to the City Attorney for civil prosecution (such prosecutions are rare). Since it can take months for the Rent Board to refer a case and they may never prosecute, you should always defend your eviction in court before you spend time fighting before the Rent Board.

So, why file an AWE? The reason for filing an AWE can best be summed up in three words: "**uncertainty breeds settlement**." AWEs can, and often do:

(1) Throw seeds of doubt into the landlord's mind about the strength of his claims. Suggest that a jury of San Francisco renters would be unsympathetic, and imply why (for example, the reasons stated in the notice may be merely a pretext; the eviction may be retaliation for calling the Building Inspector, etc.).

(2) Make the landlord understand that (a) a city agency is now involved, is investigating, and may hold a hearing; (b) the tenant's claims are now a matter of public record (including documenting a tenant in an illegal unit). The record may discourage future potential buyers or renters. Also, the San Francisco Planning Department and Department of Public Works will take into consideration AWEs for permit requests and property rights; and (c) a referral to the City Attorney or District Attorney is a possibility.

(3) Demonstrate that the tenant is aware of tenants rights and will exercise those rights, causing the landlord to hire a lawyer which makes the eviction expensive and time-consuming.

(4) Get free discovery from the landlord to find out what the landlord is claiming.

(5) Improve the ability to have a police escort for a lockout.

Often (around 40%) a landlord will rescind the eviction notice after an AWE is filed (for example, when the landlord understands there is no legal reason to evict). Other times, the landlord and tenant are able to come to a settlement in which either the tenant stays or the tenant gets time and money to move. Finally, even if the landlord goes on to file the eviction lawsuit, nothing has been lost, provided that the tenant does not teach the landlord how to do the eviction.

Filing an AWE is free. The Rent Board is a city agency that deals with everyone, so it will not advise how to write the petition, or give legal advice, or compose an eviction notice, but Rent Board counselors may point out relevant parts of the Rent Ordinance to landlords. They may also recommend that the landlord speak with an attorney. The Rent Board cannot recommend individual attorneys to either landlords or tenants, but if the Rent Board motivates your landlord to hire an attorney, that could work to your disadvantage. However, the notice of the AWE will be sent directly to all parties, including the landlord and tenant, not just their attorneys. This means that the Rent Board's actions are not filtered through the landlord's attorney. This direct communication may help tenants in negotiating with the landlord.

Procedure for Filing a Report of Alleged Wrongful Eviction

The Rent Board usually takes a week to ten days to process the AWE and send a notice to the landlord. **Do not wait until the last few days before the eviction notice is to expire** to file with the Rent Board since Rent Board backlogs can vary. However, even if the notice period expires tomorrow, there is still a reason to file the AWE. The landlord may not make his next move immediately, so it may still help. If you are filing late in the process, point this out to the Rent Board counselor. You may even want to write "URGENT—NOTICE EXPIRES IN TWO DAYS!" on the top of the AWE to call attention to it, but don't assume this will put you at the top of the list.

An eviction may be wrongful because the correct legal procedure is not being followed (for example, the eviction notice is defective for technical reasons) or the substance of the eviction is wrongful (for example, brought in bad faith, with dishonest motives, unlawful intent, in retaliation, or without a legal "just cause"). Tenants should state as clearly as possible why they believe the eviction is wrongful. Tenants should also provide *copies* of all relevant documents, such as the eviction notice (written notice is not required, oral notice can be sufficient), correspondence with the landlord, the rental agreement, Building Inspection reports, and anything else that can show what is wrongful about the eviction. However, take care not to disclose info that can help the landlord win the case should it go to court.

Relocation Payment for Evictions Under SF Law

Dollar amounts are correct as of March 1, 2022. Amounts increase each year in March. See *sfrb.org* for updates.

	All Tenants	Senior	Disability	Other
Owner Move-In, Demolition, Capital Improvements, and Substantial Rehabilitation Relocation Payments *SF Administrative Code § 37.9C* and *California Civil Code § 1947.9*. For evictions under *SF Administrative Code § 37.9(a)(8)* LMI, *37.9(a)(10)* demolition, *37.9(a)(11)* capital improvements, *37.9(a)(12)* substantial rehabilitation, and evictions for less than 20 days.	Each "authorized occupant" (includes children), with 1 year or more tenancy, receives $7,421. Maximum of $22,262/unit but this limit does not apply to the additional amount for seniors/disabled/children. *CA Civil Code § 1947.9* limits compensation where the tenant is displaced for less than 20 days to $402/day/household and moving expenses; comparable dwelling may be provided instead.	60 years or older, with 1 year or more tenancy. A senior receives $4,948 additional payment. If tenant is both senior and disabled, tenant only receives 1 additional payment.	Disabled under *CA Gov't Code § 12926* (any physical or mental condition that, if left untreated, would limit a major life activity, or history or perception of such condition), with 1 year or more tenancy. Each disabled person receives $4,948 additional payment.	Each "household" with at least one child under 18 years of age receives $4,948 additional payment.
Ellis Act Relocation Payments *SF Administrative Code § 37.9A(e)(3)*. For evictions under *SF Administrative Code § 37.9(a)(13)* Ellis Act.	Tenants (including children) have a right to the relocation payment of $7,426.54 for each tenant up to a maximum of $22,279.62 per household.	Seniors receive an additional $4,951.02.	Disabled tenants receive an additional $4,951.02.	Children are eligible tenants.
Conversion to Condo Relocation Payments *SF Subdivision Code § 1392* and *SF Subdivision Code § 1391*	n/a	n/a	n/a	Tenants who are not senior or permanently disabled have an option of a one year lease extension or to vacate within 120 days and receive $1,000 in actual relocation expenses.
Lead Abatement *SF Administrative Code § 37.9(a)(14)* and *California Civil Code § 1947.9*.	Payments increase the longer the lawful occupant is forced to vacate. (*SF Administrative Code § 72.3*) *CA Civil Code § 1947.9*, limits compensation where the tenant is displaced for < 20 days to $402/day/household and moving expenses; comparable dwelling may be provided instead.	n/a	n/a	n/a

In addition, parking, storage, laundry rooms, decks, patios, or gardens, or kitchen facilities or lobbies in single room occupancy hotels, supplied in connection with the use of a unit, may only be taken away from the tenant with just cause, except for required temporary seismic retrofit. Any reduction allowed by just cause should have a corresponding decrease in rent. (SF Administrative Code § 37.2(r)) See "Petitions for Lack of Services" in "Chapter 6: Repairs and Services" for more info.)

The Rent Ordinance provides penalties including treble damages for landlords who attempt to evict tenants without having one of the 16 just causes for eviction or sharing the unit with the tenant, or who fraudulently or without good faith claim a just cause for eviction when no such cause exists. (SF Administrative Code § 37.9(f)) A tenant has a complete defense to an eviction if it can be shown that the landlord did not base the eviction on a just cause, or the just cause listed is nonexistent. If the tenant can show that the landlord was acting in bad faith, she can win a lawsuit for wrongful eviction. The difficulty is in proving the bad faith on the landlord's part. (See "Sue Your Landlord" in "Chapter 14: Taking Action" for more info.) Moreover, although this may ultimately provide some compensation for loss of the tenant's home, the tenant usually can't move back in as a result of such a lawsuit.

Contesting the Just Cause for Eviction Under the SF Rent Ordinance

Just about any of the 16 just causes may be used as a pretext for an eviction, often when what the landlord really intends is to substantially raise the rent after she has forced the tenant out of the unit, or to sell the building at a substantial premium. The just causes provide tenants with a basis to fight an eviction by convincing the judge or jury that the reason the landlord is evicting is false. The landlord's dominant motive for bringing the eviction is an issue for almost any eviction under the Rent Ordinance. Some of the just causes (like owner move-in and demolition) add the more stringent requirement that the eviction be brought "in good faith, without ulterior reasons and with honest intent." But even without this requirement, any evidence that the landlord's main reason is, say, to raise the rent or to sell the building for more money, rather than what he says it is, can help save your home. If the landlord says something indicating a different motive, write an email to the landlord confirming that conversation, or have a witness watch you send a letter of confirmation, and keep a copy. See also the following sections for more defense strategies for specific types of evictions.

Fighting "Fault" Evictions

Nonpayment of Rent

All of this section except as noted applies to both rent-controlled (SF Administrative Code § 37.9(a)(1)](A), CA Civil Code § 1946.2(b)(1) (A)) and non-rent-controlled tenancies.

COVID-19 Recovery Period (For updates, contact the Anti-Displacement Coalition, sfadc.org)

October 2021-March 2022 (See Assembly Bill 2179 for updates.)
- A 3-day pay or quit notice must include language telling tenants about how to apply for rent relief and encouraging them to do so within 15 days. (CA Code of Civil Procedure § 1179.10(a))

- Through June 2022, a landlord cannot get a summons for unlawful detainer without certifying to the court that they applied for rent relief and the application was denied or that they applied for rent relief and that they were not notified that the tenant had applied for relief for the period demanded in the notice. (CA Code of Civil Procedure § 1179.11(a)))

When Is the Rent Due?

Most rental agreements, written or oral, specify a date by which the rent must be paid. If the rent due date falls on a Sunday or holiday, the due date for paying the rent on time is extended to the next business day. (CA Civil Code § 11, § 7; Government Code §6700-6730) It

may be hard to enforce a due date in an oral agreement, but unless you have an agreement to pay in advance, state law says that the rent is due at the end of the month or week or whatever the term is, up to a year. (CA Civil Code § 1947)

There is no automatic grace period for paying rent, as many tenants believe. If you don't pay your rent by the due date, it can be considered unpaid and an evictable offense. Many rental agreements state that there will not be a late fee until the rent is more than five days late. However, the rent would still be late if paid after the due date; there merely is no late fee. Rent paid late as few as three times in one year may be ruled habitual late payment, an incurable offense leading to eviction. Mail your rent payments early!

Notice to Pay or Quit

A landlord who wants to evict for nonpayment is required to give a written notice giving the tenant three days to pay the rent or vacate the unit without proceeding to eviction court, a "three-day notice to pay or quit." The landlord cannot have it both ways; she cannot serve the tenant with notice to pay rent and to quit the premises.

Saturdays, Sundays or judicial holidays are excluded in counting the days. The notice must state the name, telephone number, and address of the person to whom the rent payment shall be made, and, if payment may be made personally, the usual days and hours that person will be available to receive the payment. If payment may not be made personally, then payments made by mail are conclusively presumed received on the date of mailing if the tenant has proof of mailing. Instead of specifying a person to pay the rent to, the landlord can choose to give a bank account number, along with the name and street address of the bank, provided it's located within five miles of the rental property. (CA Code of Civil Procedure § 1161(2))

Nonpayment of rent notices must not overstate the amount of money that is due. (CA Code of Civil Procedure § 1161, *Baugh v. Consumers Associates, Ltd.* (1966) 241 Cal. App. 2d 672, 674) Where a notice to pay or quit seeks any sum which is in excess of the precise sum due, even if the amount is minimal, the notice is ineffective. (*Nourafchan v. Minor* (1985) 169 Cal. App. 3d 746, 215 Cal.Rptr. 450, *Del Monte Properties v. Dolan* (2018) Case No. CV170392)

SUMMONS
(CITACION JUDICIAL)
UNLAWFUL DETAINER—EVICTION
(RETENCIÓN ILÍCITA DE UN INMUEBLE—DESALOJO)

SUM-130

FOR COURT USE ONLY
(SOLO PARA USO DE LA CORTE)

NOTICE TO DEFENDANT:
(AVISO AL DEMANDADO):

YOU ARE BEING SUED BY PLAINTIFF:
(LO ESTÁ DEMANDANDO EL DEMANDANTE):

You have **5 CALENDAR DAYS** after this summons and legal papers are served on you to file a written response at this court and have a copy served on the plaintiff. (To calculate the five days, count Saturday and Sunday, but do not count other court holidays. If the last day falls on a Saturday, Sunday, or a court holiday then you have the next court day to file a written response.) A letter or phone call will not protect you. Your written response must be in proper legal form if you want the court to hear your case. There may be a court form that you can use for your response. You can find these court forms and more information at the California Courts Online Self-Help Center (www.courtinfo.ca.gov/selfhelp), your county law library, or the courthouse nearest you. If you cannot pay the filing fee, ask the court clerk for a fee waiver form. If you do not file your response on time, you may lose the case by default, and your wages, money, and property may be taken without further warning from the court.

There are other legal requirements. You may want to call an attorney right away. If you do not know an attorney, you may want to call an attorney referral service. If you cannot afford an attorney, you may be eligible for free legal services from a nonprofit legal services program. You can locate these nonprofit groups at the California Legal Services Web site (www.lawhelpcalifornia.org), the California Courts Online Self-Help Center (www.courtinfo.ca.gov/selfhelp), or by contacting your local court or county bar association.

Tiene **5 DÍAS DE CALENDARIO** después de que le entreguen esta citación y papeles legales para presentar una respuesta por escrito en esta corte y hacer que se entregue una copia al demandante. (Para calcular los cinco días, cuente los sábados y los domingos pero no los otros días feriados de la corte. Si el último día cae en sábado o domingo, o en un día en que la corte esté cerrada, tiene hasta el próximo día de corte para presentar una respuesta por escrito). Una carta o una llamada telefónica no lo protegen. Su respuesta por escrito tiene que estar en formato legal correcto si desea que procesen su caso en la corte. Es posible que haya un formulario que usted pueda usar para su respuesta. Puede encontrar estos formularios de la corte y más información en el Centro de Ayuda de las Cortes de California (www.courtinfo.ca.gov/selfhelp/espanol/), en la biblioteca de leyes de su condado o en la corte que le quede más cerca. Si no puede pagar la cuota de presentación, pida al secretario de la corte que le dé un formulario de exención de pago de cuotas. Si no presenta su respuesta a tiempo, puede perder el caso por incumplimiento y la corte le podrá quitar su sueldo, dinero y bienes sin más advertencia.

Hay otros requisitos legales. Es recomendable que llame a un abogado inmediatamente. Si no conoce a un abogado, puede llamar a un servicio de remisión a abogados. Si no puede pagar a un abogado, es posible que cumpla con los requisitos para obtener servicios legales gratuitos de un programa de servicios legales sin fines de lucro. Puede encontrar estos grupos sin fines de lucro en el sitio web de California Legal Services, (www.lawhelpcalifornia.org), en el Centro de Ayuda de las Cortes de California, (www.courtinfo.ca.gov/selfhelp/espanol) o poniéndose en contacto con la corte o el colegio de abogados locales.

1. The name and address of the court is:
   (El nombre y dirección de la corte es):

   CASE NUMBER:
   (Número del caso):

2. The name, address, and telephone number of plaintiff's attorney, or plaintiff without an attorney, is:
   (El nombre, la dirección y el número de teléfono del abogado del demandante, o del demandante que no tiene abogado, es):

3. *(Must be answered in all cases)* An unlawful detainer assistant (Bus. & Prof. Code, §§ 6400–6415) ☐ did not ☐ did for compensation give advice or assistance with this form. *(If plaintiff has received any help or advice for pay from an unlawful detainer assistant, complete item 6 on the next page.)*

Date:
(Fecha)

Clerk, by _____, Deputy
(Secretario) *(Adjunto)*

(For proof of service of this summons, use Proof of Service of Summons (form POS-010).)
(Para prueba de entrega de esta citatión use el formulario Proof of Service of Summons, (POS-010)).

[SEAL]

4. **NOTICE TO THE PERSON SERVED:** You are served
   a. ☐ as an individual defendant.
   b. ☐ as the person sued under the fictitious name of *(specify):*
   c. ☐ as an occupant
   d. ☐ on behalf of *(specify):*

   under: ☐ CCP 416.10 (corporation)   ☐ CCP 416.60 (minor)
   ☐ CCP 416.20 (defunct corporation)   ☐ CCP 416.70 (conservatee)
   ☐ CCP 416.40 (association or partnership) ☐ CCP 416.90 (authorized person)
   ☐ CCP 415.46 (occupant)   ☐ other *(specify):*

5. ☐ by personal delivery on *(date):*

Page 1 of 2

Form Adopted for Mandatory Use
Judicial Council of California
SUM-130 [Rev. January 1, 2004]

SUMMONS—UNLAWFUL DETAINER—EVICTION

Code of Civil Procedure §§ 412.20, 415.456, 1167

American LegalNet, Inc.
www.USCourtForms.com

Warning: If a tenant receives an eviction notice that looks like this, their landlord has begun the court part of the eviction. The tenant must file a response within five days or lose the case immediately—by "defaulting"—no matter how sound the case is. Go to the Eviction Defense Collaborative or get other legal help against unlawful detainers as early as possible during this five day period! A notice such as this should be taken care of promptly!

The rent can be too high simply because the landlord didn't calculate it correctly, or it can be wrong because the landlord imposed an illegal rent increase. Rent-controlled tenants who are facing a nonpayment of rent eviction should check their rent history for possible illegal rent increases. (See "Chapter 7: Rent Increases" for more info.) If the notice includes rent that is not yet overdue (because it was served on the date the rent is due, for

example), or an amount that is not rent, such as a late fee, then the notice is defective. The landlord cannot recover financial loss from before the unlawful detainer process began, except for the loss of rent. (CA Code of Civil Procedure § 1161, (*Chase v. Peters* (1918) 37 Cal. App. 358, 361 and *Vasey v. California Dance Company, Inc.* (1977) 70 Cal. App. 3d 742, 748))

Notices for nonpayment of rent are not allowed to include rent that became due more than one year prior to the service of the notice. (CA Code of Civil Procedure § 1161(2)) Commonly, however, landlords apply rent payments to the oldest amount due. Tenants get first choice as to what the payment should be applied to, provided they specify this at the time they make the payment. Generally, tenants who are a month behind in their rent should state that they are paying the next month's rent on time rather than the previous month's rent a month late by writing on the check the month and year the rent is for. This strategy can prevent the landlord from demanding rent due over a year ago, as well as preventing eviction for habitual late payment. (CA Civil Code § 1479) However, the landlord could sue for the unpaid rent in a separate case from the eviction case. The Eviction Defense Collaborative has a program where tenants may get one-time assistance with back rent if they show an ability to pay the ongoing rent in the future. (See "Appendix A: Resources.")

Additional Defenses

If you are disputing a nonpayment notice, collect all receipts, canceled checks, or other proof of payment to prove that the rent was actually paid, and include copies of these documents in a letter to the landlord disagreeing with the nonpayment. Do this immediately, as silence can be interpreted as agreement. (CA Evidence Code § 622) If a tenant mails rent at a landlord's direction and, through no fault of the tenant, the landlord does not receive it, the tenant is not in default in the payment of rent in an unlawful detainer action. (*Sleep EZ v. Mateo* (2017) 13 Cal. App. 5th Supp. 1)

If you can pay the amount demanded, it is safer to pay the full amount and then contest it. If you prevail, the landlord will have to refund the excess. It is a good idea to write "Paid Under Protest" on the back of the check where the landlord will need to sign and write "See attached note" in the memo line on the front of the check. Attach a general statement disputing the eviction notice without educating your landlord on how to fix the notice.

Just because a notice is defective, however, it doesn't mean you are out of the woods if you haven't paid your rent. The landlord can

simply start the eviction process over again with a correct notice.

See the sections "Three-Day Notices" earlier in this chapter for more info and the following subsections for specific types of defenses. If you are late with the rent more than once a year, read the following section "Habitual Late Payment of Rent."

Refused Rent After Notice to Pay or Quit

If the tenant offers the full amount demanded before the notice expires, the landlord is supposed to accept the money and not proceed with an eviction lawsuit for nonpayment. However, sometimes landlords refuse the money. See the discussion of "Refused Rent," in the following section for more info. If the tenant pays the overdue rent on the *fourth* day, the landlord could still proceed with the eviction process. However, the tenant still may be able to persuade the landlord to cancel the notice. This is a situation where it's worth looking as reasonable as possible.

Habitability

The most common defense to eviction based on nonpayment of rent is that the landlord failed to maintain the rental unit adequately. Tenants may have the right to withhold rent for lack of repairs or to make repairs and deduct the cost from the rent. (See "Chapter 6: Repairs and Services" for more info.) A tenant who can show that there are significant habitability issues that the landlord knew or should have known about but failed to repair can win an eviction for nonpayment of rent. (See "Affirmative Defenses" in "Chapter 13: Eviction Process in Court" for more info.) [In order to use physical evidence, (for example, documents, photographs, etc.) at the trial, your witnesses must be able to "authenticate" the item. That means that your client or the witness must be able to testify, from first-hand info, what the item is, where it came from and how it was obtained.

Generally, when a tenant wins on the basis of habitability, the court will set a reduced rent that the tenant then has to pay within five days. If the tenant doesn't pay within this period, the tenant's victory is converted into a defeat and the sheriff would be scheduled to do the eviction.

Unknown New Landlord

If your unit has been sold and you do not know who to send the rent to, the new owner may not seek to evict you for a nonpayment of rent during the period the new owner did not provide updated info on where to send the rent. (CA Civil Code § 1962)

Motive of Landlord Not Based on Overdue Rent

If the landlord refuses to let the tenant stay because the cure came one day late, that might be useful in showing that the landlord's dominant motive was not actually the alleged breach but rather something else entirely. In theory, the landlord's motive can be a defense to an eviction based on nonpayment of rent. In practice, however, judges

don't like to allow tenants to present such a defense. The retaliation statute doesn't apply to evictions based on nonpayment of rent, but there is still a common-law doctrine prohibiting retaliation that should apply. You would want to show that the landlord has a uniform business practice that was not applied in your case. For instance, if the landlord regularly waits until the rent is three months late before serving a three-day notice but gives a notice the day after the rent is due to a tenant who has been living in her unit for 23 years and has recently started demanding that the landlord fix the heat, it might be possible to convince a judge that this was retaliation.

Interest on Security Deposit Has Not Been Paid

If your landlord has not been paying the interest on your deposit, you have another possible defense to nonpayment of rent. (See "Interest on Deposits" in "Chapter 5: Security Deposits" for more info.) The argument is that, by failing to pay the interest, the landlord has chosen to take it off the rent. If you have paid late charge fees that are excessive, that is also a possible defense since the excessive payment should have been credited to your rent. (See "Late Charge" in "Chapter 4: Renting Basics" for more info.) The same argument applies if you share a gas or electric meter with an area outside of your rental unit and pay for the utility service without the required mutual agreement for payment. (CA Civil Code § 1940.9)

Debt Collectors

The Fair Debt Collection Practices Act requires debt collectors acting on behalf of the landlord to inform debtors within five days of the first time they write them that they have thirty days in which to dispute the debt. (15 U.S.C. Section 1692g(a)) "Debt collectors," are defined, in part, as one "who regularly collects or attempts to collect, directly or indirectly, debts owed or due or asserted to be owed or due another." So, a letter from an attorney about a debt the landlord claims you owe, including a three-day notice to pay rent or quit, also is supposed to tell you that you have thirty days in which to dispute the debt except it's possible that an occasional letter from an attorney to collect a landlord debt does not bring the attorney under the federal law if her debt collection practices are very limited.

If the tenant writes back saying they don't agree with any or all of the debt, the debt collector is supposed to stop all collection activity until they have verified the debt. This step is often easily satisfied by the debt collector calling the landlord to ask whether the figures are correct.

There is no case law saying the eviction process stops during the

thirty days a tenant is supposed to be able to dispute the debt, so it's still an open question. However, you can sue the attorney if she doesn't follow the rules. This can be one more piece of bargaining power for stopping the landlord from proceeding with the eviction.

Waiver of Notice

Accepting rent when that rent is for a period after the expiration of the notice may serve as a waiver of the notice, as discussed in the "Acceptance of Rent May Waive Notice" section earlier in this chapter.)

Refused Rent

However you offer payment, if the landlord refuses to accept it, document that you tried to pay the rent and when you submitted it. As recommended earlier, a money order is better proof of the date of a payment to the landlord than a check. A cashier's check is even better, but is harder to cancel than a money order. A cheaper method for evidence of delivery is to have a reliable friend accompany you when you pay the rent. A more expensive option, which may be viewed as clearer evidence of delivery, is to use a reliable courier service or process server. Sometimes the address provided for paying the rent or giving notice to the landlord does not allow for personal delivery. In this case, the date you post the rent (the date the mail is dropped in the mailbox on the street or at the post office) is considered the date it is received by the owner, if the tenant can show proof of mailing. (CA Code of Civil Procedure § 1161(2)) To show proof of mailing, mail rent with a certificate of mailing from the post office; this does not require a signature from the receiver. Even better, send the rent with delivery confirmation.

You can use the refused rent to open a new separate account at a bank and notify the landlord of the account (mail the notice with a certificate of mailing). You can open the account in your name as trustee for your landlord. You could even open an account in your landlord's name, but that would make the funds inaccessible by you, if later you want to recover the funds. Also, some banks refuse to open an account without the permission of the account holder. The advantage of this tactic is that the landlord would be bound to "constructive acceptance" of the rent. (CA Civil Code § 1500, *Guy F. Atkinson Co. of Calif. & Subsidiaries v. Commr. of Int. Rev. Serv.* (1987) 814 F2d 1388) If you do open a separate account, the landlord cannot later claim that the rent was not available, and you will be able to show that the rent was offered and is sitting untouched in the bank, safe and sound.

In addition, if you are covered under the Rent Ordinance (see "What Does the Rent Ordinance Cover?" in "Chapter 4: Renting

Basics"), the landlord may be penalized for failing to accept your rent. Statutory penalties include $1,000, or three times actual damages (including damages for mental or emotional distress), whichever is greater, if the landlord refuses to accept or acknowledge receipt of a tenant's lawful rent payment or refuses to cash a rent check for over thirty days, in bad faith. A landlord that violates this law is also potentially subject to a criminal penalty of imprisonment in the County Jail for up to 6 months if bad faith on the part of the landlord can be proven. (SF Administrative Code § 37.10B) The landlord must, at the time of the rent payment, specify any objection he may have to the rent or be prevented from objecting afterwards. (CA Code of Civil Procedure § 2076) If you need to document the attempt to pay but your bank account does not have enough money for a second payment, your written offer to pay is equivalent to paying if the offer is refused. (CA Code of Civil Procedure § 2074) Inform the landlord of these laws in addition to having proof of offering the rent.

Remember that nonpayment of rent is by far the most common reason for which tenants are actually evicted. And no matter how sound your defenses to an eviction may be, the cardinal rule is: **Don't spend your rent before you win your case!** See "Paying Rent" in "Chapter 4: Renting Basics" for tips on paying rent.

Bounced Check Rent Payments

If the tenant covered under the Rent Ordinance frequently pays rent with checks that bounce, the landlord can evict the tenant for this just cause for eviction. (SF Administrative Code § 37.9(a)(1)(C) A tenant not covered under the Rent Ordinance can also be evicted for this reason. Landlords usually use a sixty-day eviction notice in these cases for tenants who have been in occupancy for at least a year, and a thirty-day notice for tenants with an occupancy of less than a year. (CA Civil Code § 1946.1) A landlord may be able to use a three-day notice if it can be argued that the tenant violated the written rental agreement. See the following section "Breach of Rental Agreement" for defenses for a breach allegation.

Habitual Late Payment of Rent

If the tenant covered under the Rent Ordinance (see "What Does the Rent Ordinance Cover?" in "Chapter 4: Renting Basics") habitually does not pay his rent by the date it is due, the landlord can evict him for habitual late payment of rent. (SF Administrative Code § 37.9(a)(1)(B) Landlords usually use a sixty-day eviction notice in these cases for tenants who have been in occupancy for at least a year, and a thirty-day notice for tenants with an occupancy of less than a year. (CA Civil Code § 1946.1) A landlord may be able to use a three-day notice if it can be argued that the tenant violated (breached) the written rental agreement which could also be used under state law requiring just cause for eviction. See the following section "Breach of Rental Agreement" for defenses for a breach allegation. There is **NOT** an automatic grace period for when rent is due. Any grace period for late fees only means that the late fee is not charged until after the grace period; the rent is still late.

There is no set standard as to what constitutes "habitual," but paying rent late three times a year may be habitual. The landlord should have documentation (for example, three-day notices, warning letters, etc.).

What constitutes "late" can also be an issue here. If the agreement is oral, then it can be almost impossible for a landlord to evict for habitual late payment since it is hard to show when the rent is due. Unless you typically pay the rent in advance or have an agreement to pay in advance, state law says that the rent is due at the end of the month or week or whatever the term is, up to a year. (CA Civil Code § 1947)

Just as in a breach of a rental agreement eviction, what is written in the rental agreement is not always enforceable. (See the box on

"Waiver, Estoppel, and Change of Agreement: Unenforced Rental Agreement Provisions as Defenses to an Eviction" for more info.) If your landlord told you that you could pay on the fifth of the month because your SSI check always comes on the third of the month, document that fact in a letter to the landlord to create proof of the new agreed-upon date (keep a copy and mail with proof of mailing). Your landlord is also required to make reasonable accommodation for a disability, which could include changing when your rent is due. (See "Disability" in "Chapter 9: Discrimination.") Document your disagreement in a letter to the landlord (with proof of mailing) since silence can be interpreted as agreement. (CA Evidence Code § 622)

Breach (Violation) of Rental Agreement

Definition

This section will discuss breaches besides the breach for

Waiver, Estoppel, and Change of Agreement: Unenforced Rental Agreement Provisions as Defenses to an Eviction

If the landlord claims you have substantially breached (violated) the rental agreement and wants to evict you, first, take a careful look at your rental agreement. Close reading of the agreement can sometimes show that the landlord is trying to evict for something that is not prohibited by the agreement.

Look at the actual pattern and practice of the parties. Did the landlord know about this alleged breach earlier and then just ignore it? Did she say that this action, which was later alleged to be a breach, didn't really matter? Did she accept rent after she knew about the breach? Does evidence shows that the terms were changed? (CA Civil Code § 1698) If so, you may be able to argue that the landlord waived any right to enforce this term of the rental agreement. Or else you may be able to show that, since the landlord allowed the action, there was a change in the terms of the rental agreement. In order to enforce previously unenforced terms of a signed agreement, the landlord may need to give thirty days notice before the terms are enforceable.

Often rental agreements have a provision that a failure of a landlord to enforce a covenant of the agreement shall not be deemed a waiver of that provision, coupled with a provision that the written agreement is the entirety of the agreement and can't be changed except in writing. These provisions may limit your ability to use waiver or change of agreement defenses, but they still leave another related basis to defend a breach eviction: "estoppel." (CA Evidence Code § 623) If you can show that you did something to your detriment relying on what the landlord indicated to you, then you can argue that the landlord shouldn't be able to change his mind now. Let's say your rental agreement

specifies no pets, but the manager told you that it would be okay to get a pet, so long as it was no bigger than a breadbox. If you got a cat relying on that promise, then even if there's a clause in your rental agreement saying that the agreement can only be changed in writing, you can still argue that the landlord should be *estopped* from evicting you since you relied on the landlord's agent's statement. (The difference between waiver and estoppel is in a waiver, the landlord did something. In an estoppel argument, the landlord did something and you relied on it. Laches are where the landlord did not do something, in other words, sat on their rights. Estoppel and laches arguments rarely go to trial.) Your defense would be even stronger if you could show, for example, that you gave up another, cheaper apartment because you could keep your cat at this apartment but not the new one.

To establish that you have these defenses, it's useful to write a letter establishing the facts: "As you know, in March 2022, you told me that it would be okay for me to get a cat. Relying on that promise, I got Tiger that fall, and I gave up the chance to move into an even nicer, cheaper apartment because no pets were allowed in that building. You have seen Tiger on a number of occasions when you came over to fix things or to pick up the rent, and you commented on what a good pet Tiger was." Even if the facts in your case aren't quite as strong as these, think about your situation, and document anything that might show that the landlord somehow gave up any right to evict for breach of the agreement.

Finally, as in almost any eviction under the Rent Ordinance, you have the defense that the landlord's real motive is to raise the rent or sell the building. The landlord's dominant motive is required to be what she says it is. Also, retaliation and discrimination are defenses regardless of whether the Rent Ordinance applies.

nonpayment of rent which was discussed earlier. **Breach of the rental agreement (including leases)** applies to rental units covered under the San Francisco Rent Ordinance (SF Administrative Code § 37.9(a)(2)) and non-rent-controlled tenancies (CA Code of Civil Procedure § 1161(3), (4)). **Breach of a lease only** applies under state law requiring just cause for eviction for units not covered by the Rent Ordinance. (CA Civil Code § 1946.2(b)(1)(B))

Breach of a rental agreement is violation of a "material" and lawful clause in the agreement. A "material" clause is one that is significant to the contract, one that matters a lot. For example, you probably would not be evicted for violating a covenant that requires you to put your rent in a pink envelope. Further, the landlord can only evict for breach of an *express* provision of the agreement, not for a provision that is merely implied, so landlords generally cannot evict for breach of an oral rental agreement.

Notice Period

The eviction notice is usually three days except some subletting breaches under the Rent Ordinance require a ten day notice. (See "Adding Non-Family Members," "Adding Family Members," and "Changing Roommates" in "Chapter 10: Roommates.") Saturdays, Sundays or holidays are excluded in counting the days for curable three-day notices under state law. (CA Code of Civil Procedure § 1161(3))

Disagreement with Allegation

Landlords are increasingly using breach of a rental agreement to evict tenants with affordable rents for allegedly violating clauses. Attempted evictions on this basis can often be fought successfully, but the tenant significantly improves his chances if he makes his position look reasonable. (*Boston LLC v. Juarez* (2016) 245 Cal. App.4th 75, which takes precedence over the 2015 *Boston LLC v. Juarez* ruling. Because of the differences in law between this Los Angeles case and San Francisco law, the eviction would likely have failed even before the appeal in San Francisco.) The tenant should document disagreement with the allegation of a breach of the rental agreement in a letter to the landlord (with proof of mailing) since silence can be interpreted as agreement. (CA Evidence Code § 622) For more info on contracts, see "Leases and Rental Agreements" in "Chapter 4: Renting Basics."

Waiver of Breach

Clauses in agreements can be modified via passive consent and the parties' actions. (See the box "Waiver, Estoppel, and Change of Agreement: Unenforced Rental Agreement Provisions as Defenses to an Eviction.") For tenants covered by the Rent Ordinance, the landlord may not evict for violating a clause that was unilaterally imposed and not part of the original agreement or mutually agreed on, unless the change in the rental agreement is authorized by law and the change was accepted in writing after written notice that the tenant did not need to accept the change. (SF Rent Board Rules and Regulations § 12.20) If the landlord has made an illegal change to the rental agreement, the tenant should respond promptly in writing that she does not consent to the change and mail the letter with proof of mailing.

Some rental agreements contain a provision that any waiver of a breach of a covenant does not act to change the terms of the agreement or act as a waiver of any future breaches. (*Salton Community Service District v. Southard* (1967) 256 Cal.App.2d 526) If your rental agreement contains such a provision and, for instance, the landlord accepts your rent after the notice has expired (in other words, waives the breach), the landlord is not required to give you another notice in order to evict you for the same breach in the future.

Curing (Fixing) the Breach

The Rent Ordinance requires all notices based on breach of the rental agreement to allow the tenant the option to fix ("cure," also called "perform covenant") the breach or move out ("quit") without the case going to eviction court. State law for residential units covered by just cause for eviction (see "Protections for the Tenant Under the San Francisco Rent Ordinance and State Law" in "Chapter 4: Renting Basics") also requires giving a tenant a chance to cure a violation. (CA Civil Code § 1946.2(c)) In addition, under state law, including where a just cause is not required for evictions, a breach of a restriction to a designated person is curable. *Richard v. Degen & Brody, Inc.* (1960) 181 Cal. App.2d 289) If the breach is curable, the breach must be clearly stated in the eviction notice. (CA Code of Civil Procedure § 1161(3)) If there is an authorized subtenant, the subtenant must be named in the eviction notice so that he has an opportunity to cure the breach. (*Briggs v. Electronic Memories & Magnetics Corp.* (1975) 53 Cal. App. 3d 900, 905, *Kwok v. Bergren* (1982) 130 Cal. App. 3d 597) Only one co-tenant, however, needs to be served of all the co-tenants. (*University of Southern California v. Weiss* (1962) 208 Cal. App. 2d 759) Therefore, if the tenant receives such a notice, it is prudent to stop the activity immediately and provide the landlord with written confirmation within the notice period that there is no such activity occurring. (Do not confirm that the activity happened in the past, just state that the activity is not occurring.) If the breach is not curable, a notice stated in the alternative will not invalidate the notice. (*Richard v. Degen & Brody, Inc.*) However, allowing the breach to be curable is advisable for the notice since judges and juries are likely to be unsympathetic to continued eviction attempts if breaches have been cured.

If the tenant cures the breach within the notice period, the notice is void and no longer may be used by the landlord to evict the tenant. (CA Code of Civil Procedure § 1161.5) But if the tenant cures the breach after this period, the landlord could still proceed

with the eviction process. However, the tenant still may be able to persuade the landlord to cancel the notice. This is a situation where it's worth looking as reasonable as possible. If the landlord refuses to let the tenant stay because the cure came one day late, that might be useful in showing that the landlord's dominant motive was not the breach but something else.

Subletting or Assignment (Transfer of Rights to Another Occupant)

Subletting by adding or replacing roommates, or while out of town temporarily, is complex, and is discussed in detail in "Chapter 10: Roommates." Subletting can also be fought on the basis of discrimination. See "Disability" in "Chapter 9: Discrimination" for more info.

In a few cases, even though the rental unit was covered under the Rent Ordinance which requires the option to cure for a subletting breach, judges have not allowed a cure. All of the cases that have allowed eviction for sublease without an opportunity to cure involve long-term, full assignments such as renting out the apartment on Airbnb when the tenant doesn't live there. (*https://www.tobenerlaw.com/tenants-and-airbnb*) The conversion of individual rental units to transient uses ("hotelization," including Airbnb and home exchanges) may be considered illegal use, which is not curable. See "Airbnb, Home Exchanges, or Similar Uses" in "Chapter 11: Changes in Use" for more info.

Animals and Other Reasonable Accommodation

Assistance animals (including for mental health), and alterations in violation of a rental agreement can also be fought on the basis of discrimination. See "Disability" in "Chapter 9: Discrimination" for more info.

Nuisance

An eviction for "nuisance" generally alleges that the tenant is seriously interfering with the quiet enjoyment of the neighbors or creates a nuisance for the landlord. An eviction for nuisance applies to both the San Francisco Rent Ordinance (SF Administrative Code § 37.9(a)(2)) and California law (CA Code of Civil Procedure § 1161(4), CA Civil Code § 1946.2(b)(1)(C)). In fighting an eviction for interfering with the quiet enjoyment of the neighbors, one of the most helpful bargaining chips is neighbors' signatures saying that you are a good neighbor, not a nuisance.

For a nuisance eviction to be successful, there should be a paper trail of warnings, except for serious nuisances such as a tenant videotaped urinating in the common laundry room. In serious nuisance cases, the notice would only need to be a three-day notice which does not need to give an option to cure. If the last day of the three-day notice is on a weekend or holiday, the period for moving out ("quitting") before the case goes to eviction court is extended to the end of the next business day. (CA Code of Civil Procedure § 12a) The Rent Ordinance requires that the notice state the nature of the nuisance. (SF Administrative Code § 37.9(a)(3))

Sometimes a tenant may be a nuisance as a result of mental health impairment. Federal, state, and local fair housing law requires that a landlord provide reasonable accommodations in their rules, practices, policies and services to enable a disabled tenant to access and retain her housing. (See "Disability" in "Chapter 9: Discrimination" for more info.) Domestic violence, sexual assault, stalking, human trafficking, or abuse of an elder or a dependent adult against the tenant or a tenant's household member is also a defense for eviction for nuisance if the domestic violence, sexual assault stalking, human trafficking, or abuse of an elder or a dependent adult is the reason for the eviction. (CA Code of Civil Procedure § 1161.3, SF Administrative Code § 37.9(a)(3.1)) The tenant must have documentation by a qualified third party. The person who was accused cannot be a tenant of the same dwelling unit as the victim. A landlord may terminate a tenancy if she reasonably believes that the presence of the person who was accused still poses a threat to the quiet possession of other tenants or invitees on the property.

Document your disagreement on the eviction notice in a letter to the landlord (with proof of mailing) since silence can be interpreted as agreement. (CA Evidence Code § 622)

Waste (Destruction of Rental Unit)

An eviction notice to quit based on "waste" (destruction of the property) is allowed only if there is an explicit rental agreement provision that prohibits waste. This type of eviction is not a just cause for eviction under the Rent Ordinance, however, the landlord may use the just cause of nuisance instead. (See the previous section.)

There must be "permanent" or substantial reduction in the value of the premises for the damage to constitute waste. A tenant should not permanently or substantially diminish the property value by neglecting to do what an ordinarily prudent person would do in preserving his own property. Property damage such as punching holes in the walls, pulling out sinks and fixtures and knocking down doors could constitute waste. However, case history showed that $4,000 damage caused by a tenant's pet (due to having to replace the floor and repair the walls) was not enough to establish waste. These technical details can give a tenant a good defense to an eviction based on waste. An eviction for waste needs only a three-day notice, with no option to cure. (CA Code of Civil Procedure § 1161(4), CA Civil Code § 1946.2(b)(1)(D)) If the last day of the three-day notice is on a weekend or holiday, the period for quitting is extended to the end of the next business day. (CA Code of Civil Procedure § 12a)

Be careful about making improvements without proof of the landlord's consent since improvements could be considered waste, especially when landlords are looking for opportunities to evict long-term tenants. Even if the waste changes the property in a positive way, the tenant may still have committed waste because he did not maintain the rental unit according to the rental agreement.

Document your disagreement with allegations of waste in the eviction notice in a letter to the landlord (with proof of sending), since silence can be interpreted as agreement. (CA Evidence Code § 622) Additional documentation would be photos, witnesses, letters, etc. disputing claims of damage.

Illegal Use

An example of an eviction for illegal use is if the tenant is using the rental unit to sell illegal drugs or engaging in some other activity that is clearly illegal. An eviction notice for illegal use does not usually need to give an option to cure and applies to both the San Francisco Rent Ordinance (SF Administrative Code § 37.9(a)(4)) and California law (CA Code of Civil Procedure § 1161(4), CA Civil Code § 1946.2(b)(1)(F), (I)). However, first time violations of the short-term rental regulation cannot be used to evict the tenant if cured with thirty days of the written notice to the tenant, and the rental unit is covered under the Rent Ordinance. Otherwise, the notice is a three-day notice, but if the last day of the notice is on a weekend or holiday, the period for moving out ("quitting") before the case goes to court is extended to the end of the next business day. (CA Code of Civil Procedure § 12a) Document disagreement with allegations in the eviction notice in a letter to the landlord (with proof of sending) since silence can be interpreted as agreement. (CA Evidence Code § 622) Also, if the landlord knew of the illegal use, this can be used as a defense by asserting that any previous and current use has been with the landlord's knowledge.

Working at Home

Some landlords try to use this just cause to evict a tenant who works at home—for example, a tenant who has a graphic arts business at home—citing illegal use as a business in an all-residential neighborhood. However, illegal use probably would not apply unless the at-home business entailed the conversion of the rental unit to commercial use or a high-traffic business such as auto repair, and which clearly was a violation of the zoning restrictions for that location. (SF Planning Code § 204.1) Also an exception to the general rule of no business use is the "office of a professional person" residing in the residence. This exception recognizes that some occupations have traditionally been practiced in San Francisco homes before the introduction

of zoning regulations, and so should be allowed to continue. A "professional person" is defined as "a person legally qualified to practice dentistry, medicine, psychiatry, chiropractic, law, architecture or engineering." Additional professions have been added including massage therapy and acupuncture. (*https://sfplanning.org/resource/accessory-uses-dwellings-all-zoning-districts*) Additionally, a landlord may not evict a tenant for operating a licensed family day care if the tenant has provided the required notice and complies with the requirements for day care. (CA Health and Safety Code § 1597.40)

Subletting

Some types of subletting may be considered illegal use such as improper conversion of individual rental units to transient uses ("hotelization," including Airbnb and home exchanges). See "Airbnb, Home Exchanges, or Similar Uses" in "Chapter 11: Changes in Use." Also, charging subtenants more rent than the total rent owed by the master tenant to the landlord may be considered illegal use under the Rent Ordinance (SF Administrative Code § 37.3(c)) or California law (CA Civil Code § 1947.12(c)). However, charging subtenants a disproportionately high share of the rent cannot be the basis for eviction under the Rent Ordinance. (SF Rent Board Rules and Regulations § 6.15C(3))

Illegal Unit

The Rent Ordinance has been changed to clarify that the illegal use just cause is not to be used for evicting tenants from units that are unauthorized for residential use. Further, the landlord is not entitled to back rent. (*Gruzen v. Henry* ((1978) 84 Cal. App. 3d 515, 148 Cal. Rptr. 573) In addition, a tenant could not be evicted for nonpayment from an illegal unit. (*North 7th Street Associates v. Guillermo Constante* (2016) 7 Cal. App. 5th Supp. 1. See "Unauthorized Units" in "Chapter 11: Changes in Use" for more info.) Nor can charging subtenants a disproportionately high share of the rent be the basis for eviction under the Rent Ordinance. (SF Rent Board Rules and Regulations § 6.15C(3))

If the tenant has not impaired habitability by using the living room for a bedroom, the tenant would probably not be evicted for this technically illegal use.

Marijuana and Secondhand Smoke

Although still illegal under federal law, state law allows adults 21 years or older to smoke or ingest marijuana, give away up to 28.5 grams to other adults, and cultivate up to six plants. (CA Health and Safety Code § 11362.1) Medical use allows for cultivation of additional plants. (See "Reasonable Accommodations and Modifications" in "Chapter 9: Discrimination" for more info.) However, secondhand smoke and other odors may be considered a nuisance and an interference with a neighbor's right to quiet enjoyment of his home. See "Air Quality (Besides Lead, Mold, Filth) and Fire Hazards" in "Chapter 6: Repairs and Services" for more info.

Renewal of Rental Agreement Refused by Tenant

If, at the termination of the rental agreement, the tenant refuses to sign a new agreement that is materially the same as the previous one, the landlord may evict, even if the tenant is covered under the Rent Ordinance (SF Administrative Code § 37.9(a)(5)) or state law requiring just cause eviction (CA Civil Code § 1946.2(b)(1)(E)). If the tenancy is covered under just cause for eviction, the landlord would give a sixty-day notice of eviction if the tenant has lived in the unit at least a year, a thirty-day notice of eviction for a tenancy of less than a year. (CA Civil Code § 1946.1) This type of eviction notice would demand that the tenant vacate without the opportunity to cure by signing the rental agreement. If the tenant is not covered under just cause, and the landlord wants to evict at the end of the lease, no notice is required (nor does the landlord need a reason). There is no extension of the time to renew a rental agreement due to a weekend or holiday since the time to comply relies only on the contract not a statute. (*Gans v. Smull* (2003) 111 Cal.App.4th 985)

A tenant cannot be evicted for refusing to enter into a new agreement which differs from the current one in any material way—for instance, if the previous agreement allowed a pet and the new agreement prohibits pets. If the landlord wants the tenant to sign a written agreement that is materially the same as the oral agreement, it would be safer for the tenant to comply. If the tenant were on a month-to-month, and the landlord wants the tenant to agree to a lease with the same terms except for the time period, it would also be safer to comply. Rent increases allowed under the Rent Ordinance or California rent control would not be considered materially different.

Access for Landlord Denied

If the tenant fails to allow the landlord access to the dwelling as required by California Civil Code § 1954, then the landlord may use this just cause for eviction for both the San Francisco Rent Ordinance (SF Administrative Code § 37.9(a)(6)) and California law (CA Civil Code § 1946.2(b)(1)(H)). See "Privacy and Landlord Entry" in "Chapter 8: Harassment" for more info.

So, what is reasonable access? If the tenant has allowed the landlord to hold open houses and show the dwelling without restriction and then one time refuses because his child is sick that day, the landlord would be unreasonable for trying to evict. On the other hand, if the tenant continually and without fail refused to let the landlord in to show the dwelling, even after a written demand to cease refusing entry, a court might

hold that the tenant was unreasonable.

If the tenant refuses to allow access after the notice of entry, the landlord must then give another notice demanding that the tenant cease denying access. Up to that point, the tenant can be uncompromising (although appearing reasonable is certainly useful). Once a tenant receives the second notice, however, she should consider letting the landlord in even if she thinks the landlord is being unreasonable. The tenant then should write a letter to the landlord (with proof of mailing) stating that she has let the landlord in but also stating why she thinks the landlord is being unreasonable.

If the tenant continues to refuse to let the landlord in, then the landlord may attempt to evict on this basis. The eviction notice would be a sixty-day notice for tenants who have been in occupancy for at least a year, and a thirty-day notice for tenants with an occupancy of less than a year, unless this is a breach of a clause in the rental agreement in which case the rules for breach would apply; see the earlier "Breach of Rental Agreement" section. (CA Civil Code § 1946.1, Code of Civil Procedure § 1161(3) This just cause does not give the landlord the right to a key to the dwelling; the tenant may just provide legally required access. However, the landlord may rekey the locks (giving the tenant a copy of the new key) to obtain legal access.

Subtenant Holding Over Is Unapproved

This section applies to the San Francisco Rent Ordinance (SF Administrative Code § 37.9(a)(7)) although landlords can evict for unapproved subtenants in rental units not covered under the Rent Ordinance as well. (See the earlier "Breach of Rental Agreement" section.) Eviction for an unapproved subtenant remaining after the approved tenant has vacated (holding over) differs from an eviction for violating a subletting clause of a rental agreement, and applies when the only subtenants remaining are those whom the landlord never approved, either actively or passively. The landlord could evict with a three-day notice to cure or quit, if the unapproved subtenant remaining after the approved tenant vacates is considered a breach of a written agreement.

An eviction for an unapproved subtenant remaining after the approved tenant has vacated can be contested on the basis that the subtenant was approved by the landlord either directly or through the landlord's actions, such as accepting rent and responding to requests for repairs from the subtenant. The tenant or subtenant should document the disagreement with the eviction notice in a letter to the landlord (with proof of sending) since silence can be interpreted as agreement. Note that a subtenant who receives a 6.14 notice declaring her not to be an "original tenant" is in fact an approved subtenant and cannot be evicted under this just cause. She could, however, have her rent raised to market rate once the last original tenant moves out. (See "Chapter 10: Roommates" for more info.)

Chapter 12– Eviction Defenses

Fighting "No-Fault" Evictions

Owner Move-In Under California Law Requiring Just Cause Eviction

If a rental unit is not covered under the San Francisco Rent Ordinance but is covered by the California law requiring just cause for eviction (see "Protections for the Tenant Under the San Francisco Rent Ordinance and State Law" in "Chapter 4: Renting Basics"), the owner may evict if the intent is to occupy the rental unit by the owner or their spouse, domestic partner, children, grandchildren, parents, or grandparents. For leases entered into on or after July 1, 2020, the owner can evict for this just cause only if the tenant agrees, in writing, to the termination, or the lease allows this just cause. (CA Civil Code § 1946.2(b)(2)(A)) The eviction notice is a sixty-day eviction notice for tenancies of at least a year, a thirty-day notice for tenancies of less than a year. (CA Civil Code § 1946.1)

Relocation Assistance or Rent Waiver

The owner shall notify the tenant of the tenant's right to relocation assistance or rent waiver. For the rent waiver, the notice shall state the amount of rent waived and that no rent is due for the final month of the tenancy. The amount of relocation assistance or rent waiver shall be equal to one month of the rent when the owner issued the notice to terminate the tenancy. Any relocation assistance shall be provided within 15 calendar days of service of the notice. (CA Civil Code § 1946.2(d))

Owner Move-In/Landlord Move-In Under the San Francisco Rent Ordinance

Along with Ellis Act evictions (discussed in the next section), the most common no-fault evictions in San Francisco, where the tenant hasn't done anything wrong, have been for owner or relative move-in (OMI, SF Administrative Code § 37.9(a)(8)). Over the years, landlords learned how to exploit this loophole in the Rent Ordinance to evict tenants with affordable rents or to bypass the city's condo conversion law and evict tenants for tenancies in common.

The OMI loophole was closed considerably via legislation at the Board of Supervisors and a tenant-initiated ballot measure. The 1998 amendments limit when a landlord can evict for OMI, expand the tenant's defenses, and provide relocation payments if a tenant is eventually evicted. In addition, some buildings where an OMI has occurred are not allowed to convert to condos. Since conversion to condos is usually the ultimate goal when tenants

are evicted for no fault, stopping the conversion can be a powerful defense. (See "Condo Conversion Law" in "Chapter 11: Changes in Use" for more info.) The current requirements and restrictions on owner move-in evictions are summarized in the chart "Ellis Act v. Owner Move-In Eviction Under SF Rent Ordinance" later in this chapter.

Also, if the owner wanted to add an accessory dwelling unit to the building, the permit will be denied for buildings with two to four dwelling units if in the 5 years prior to filing the permit application a tenant was evicted for owner move-in. Some single residential units will also be denied permits in these circumstances. (See "Accessory Dwelling Units" in "Chapter 11: Changes in Use" for more info.)

Tenants threatened with an owner move-in eviction should let the landlord know that they are aware of all the restrictions including for condo conversions, will be monitoring the building for compliance for years, and will sue with the assistance of tenant advocates such as the San Francisco Tenants Union (which has settled for hundreds of thousands of dollars in some cases) if the requirements are not met.

The OMI eviction is supposed to be limited to situations where a landlord honestly wants to move either himself or closely related family members (if the landlord already lives in the building or is moving in simultaneously) into a building he owns. Since evicting only one unit for OMI is much easier than evicting for two or more units, which would require the landlord's close relatives to move in, it's important for all the tenants to stick together as a building to have as much power as possible to fight the eviction. The intent of the landlord (and relatives) to live in the unit must be in good faith. If new owners want to evict for OMI, they cannot start the process until the sale is 100% complete and is recorded. Tenants may be able to have representation by the Tenderloin Housing Clinic for bad faith OMIs. The Justice & Diversity Center may be able to provide representation for low-income tenants. (See "*Appendix A: Resources.*")

Some landlords will try to buy out tenants to avoid the restrictions on re-renting the property or to more easily sell the property for a higher price. (See "Buyouts, Almost Always a Bad Idea" in "Chapter 8: Harassment.") If the eviction notice for owner move-in has already been served, it may not be rescinded if the tenant agrees to move out.

"Protected" Tenants for OMI Under SF Rent Ordinance

Senior, Disabled, and Dying Tenants

OMI evictions are prohibited, **with a few exceptions** described after the prohibitions, if the tenants are **one of the following** (SF Administrative Code § 37.9(i)(1)):

- Senior tenants at least 60 years of age who have ten or more years of tenancy.

• Disabled tenants: generally those receiving Supplemental Security Income (SSI) or meet the standard for disability under SSI who have ten or more years of tenancy. (SF Rent Board Rules and Regulations § 12.14) A tenant who is engaged in work that involves significant and productive physical or mental duties and is usually done for pay or profit will not qualify for SSI. The impairment must have lasted or is expected to last for 12 continuous month or will result in death.

• Catastrophically ill tenants who have a diagnosis of a life threatening illness and who receive SSI or are eligible for SSI, and have five or more years of tenancy.

The exceptions are: (SF Administrative Code § 37.9(i)(2))

• The tenant is residing in a dwelling unit that is separate from title to any other dwelling unit (for example, a single-family house without an in-law unit), or is a subdivided interest in a subdivision (for example, a condominium) and the landlord owns no other dwelling units in the subdivision.

• Every unit in the building besides the unit occupied by the landlord is occupied by people who are either long-term seniors, disabled and/or catastrophically ill *and* the landlord is evicting for a relative who is age 60 or older.

The prohibition on owner move-in evictions of senior, disabled, and catastrophically ill tenants provides that a landlord who wants to move himself and/or his close relative(s) into a rental unit may request info from the tenants on whether or not they are in one of the protected categories. If the tenant who is in a protected category fails to respond with supporting evidence to the landlord's request within 30 days, then the tenant will not be covered by the owner move-in eviction prohibition for such tenants. (SF Administrative Code § 37.9(i)(4)) If the tenant falls into a protected category and is asked for this info (for example, on an estoppel agreement when the building is for sale), it is critical to provide the info within 30 days or the tenant will lose protection! Mail the info with a certificate of mailing or other confirmation of sending the info. If the tenant was not a member of the protected class at the time the info is requested but then becomes a member of the protected class after the 30 days has expired, the tenant may still be protected once the landlord is given notice of the protected status.

Children

OMI evictions are prohibited, **if all of the following** apply (SF Administrative Code § 37.9(j)(1)):

• The tenant has a custodial or family relationship with a child under age 18 who is residing in the unit. "Custodial relationship" means that the person is a legal guardian, or has a court-recognized caregiver authorization affidavit for the child, or that the person has provided full-time custodial care of the child by permission of the child's legal guardian or court-recognized caregiver and has been providing that care for at least one year or half of the child's lifetime, whichever is less. The term "family relationship" means that the person is the parent, grandparent, brother, sister, aunt or uncle of the child, or the spouse or domestic partner of such relations.

• The tenant has resided in the unit for 12 months or more.

• The effective date of the termination notice falls during the school year. "School year" means the first day of instruction for the Fall Semester through the last day of instruction for the Spring Semester, as posted on the San Francisco Unified School District Web site.

If the tenant falls in the protected category, and fails to respond to the landlord's request for this info with supporting evidence within 30 days, then the tenant will not be covered by the owner move-in eviction prohibition for such tenants.

School Workers

San Francisco school workers and their families are protected from owner move-in evictions during the school year where the tenant has resided in the unit for 12 months or more. "School" means any state-licensed child care center/family day care, or any public, private, or parochial institution that provides educational instruction for students in any of the grades from kindergarten through twelfth grade. If the tenant falls in the protected category, and fails to respond to the landlord's request for this info with supporting evidence within 30 days, then the tenant will not be covered by the owner move-in eviction prohibition for such tenants. (SF Administrative Code § 37.9(j))

Other Restrictions for OMI Under SF Rent Ordinance

One Eviction per Building Except for Close Relatives of Landlord

When there are multiple owners of a building, only one of the landlords is allowed to perform an OMI eviction. This provision limits the number of conversions of apartments into owner-occupied units. For example, four 25% owners of a 4-unit building cannot each evict tenants in the separate units. (SF Administrative Code § 37.9(a)(8)(vi)) However, a single landlord still can evict tenants from one unit to live in it himself and evict tenants from other units for close relatives to move in. (See the following section "Relatives of Landlord Living in Building Who

Chapter 12–Eviction Defenses

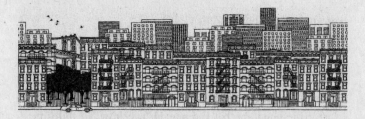

Qualify for Additional OMI.")

Relatives of Landlord Living in Building Who Qualify for Additional OMI

OMI evictions for relatives are allowed only in the same building where the landlord already lives or when the landlord is *simultaneously* evicting to live in the building himself. This is the only time more than one OMI eviction is allowed per building. In other words, if the landlord lives in Palo Alto, a tenant cannot be evicted for a son to move into the apartment in San Francisco.

A landlord can evict *all* the tenants in a building for the purpose of moving in relatives if the landlord lives in the building or is simultaneously evicting to move in. Relatives are defined under the OMI rules as grandparents, grandchildren, parents, children, brother or sister, or the spouse or registered domestic partner of the landlord or of one of these relatives. (SF Administrative Code § 37.9(a)(8)(ii))

Same Unit for Future OMIs

After a landlord has evicted a tenant for OMI for the landlord's personal occupancy, any subsequent OMI eviction for the landlord's personal occupancy in that building can happen only in the unit where the first eviction took place. For example, the tenants in Unit A are evicted under an OMI. Six years later the landlord sells the building to a buyer who wants to live in Unit B. That new landlord cannot use an OMI to evict the tenants of Unit B unless he could show "disability or similar hardship," such as being unable to climb stairs to an upper unit. (SF Administrative Code § 37.9(a)(8)(vi)) This limit went into effect December 18, 1998. You can look up records of previous OMIs at the Rent Board, on the deed at the Assessor's Office, and online by names of parties on the Superior Court's Web site if the eviction is not recorded elsewhere.

Procedural Requirements for OMI Under SF Rent Ordinance

Ownership

Be the owner of record with at least a 25% interest in the building if purchased on or after February 22, 1991; and be the owner of record of at least 10% if purchased before February 22, 1991. (SF Administrative Code § 37.9(a)(8)(iii) and Rent Board Rules and Regulations § 12.14) It is only the actual landlord who can evict for OMI and must move into the unit so if new owners want to evict for OMI, they cannot start the process until the sale is 100% complete and recorded.

The landlord must be a natural person or group of natural persons; a corporation or a trust would not qualify except for a family trust. (SF Rent Board Rules and Regulations § 12.14) Only the landlord or current 25% or more lifetime beneficiary of a family trust would be able to do the owner move-in eviction.

Eviction Notice for Tenant

Serve a sixty-day eviction notice for tenancies of at least a year, a thirty-day notice for tenancies of less than a year. (CA Civil Code § 1946.1) The notice must include or have attached:

- Rent amount that is legal in a statement at the time the notice was issued. (SF Administrative Code § 37.9(c))

- Declaration from the landlord under penalty of perjury that the landlord seeks to recover the unit in good faith for occupancy as the principal place of residence of the landlord or relative (identified by name and relation) for at least 36 continuous months as required. (SF Administrative Code § 37.9(a)(8)(v))

- Address change form prepared by the Rent Board that the tenant can use to inform the Rent Board of future addresses. (SF Administrative Code § 37.9(a)(8)(v))

Disclosure to Tenant

Disclose in writing to the tenant within ten days after service of the notice to vacate:

- The names, percentage of ownership, and the dates that ownership was recorded in the county records for each of the owners of the property where the landlord is evicting.

- The name of the landlord or relative who wants to move into the unit and a description of the current residence(s) and relationship to the landlord.

  For family trusts, the deed most likely will read "[Landlord Name], as trustee of the [Landlord Name] Revocable Living Trust." If it is a revocable living trust, which it would be 99% of the time, then the landlord is the owner and the other family members are future or "remainder" beneficiaries. If it is an irrevocable trust, different rules may apply. If the name of the trust does not say "irrevocable" then it is revocable.

- A description of all residential property owned by the landlord and any relative for whom the landlord is evicting.

- The current rent and the right to re-rent at the same rent with adjustment for rent increases allowed by the Rent Ordinance, for a period of five years following service of the notice to quit if the landlord re-rents within that time.

• The right to a relocation payment, the amount, and a copy of San Francisco Administrative Code § 37.9C.

• A copy of § 37.9B of San Francisco Administrative Code.

(SF Administrative Code § 37.9B)

• If the landlord served a notice to vacate for 37.9(a)(8) for a different unit.

• If the landlord has recovered possession of other rental units in San Francisco for any reason under San Francisco Administrative Code 37.9(a) other than nonpayment of rent in which the tenant who was displaced had resided for at least 36 consecutive months.

• Warn the tenant that the tenant must submit a statement to the landlord within 30 days of service of the notice to vacate, with supporting evidence, if the tenant claims to be a member of a protected class under San Francisco Administrative Code 37.9(i) or (j), and that failure to do is deemed an admission that the tenant is not protected.

• Other disclosures required for evictions under the Rent Ordinance. See the earlier section "San Francisco Rent Ordinance Evictions."

(SF Rent Board Rules and Regulations § 12.14)

• A statement of occupancy from the landlord is disclosed to the Rent Board which will send a copy to the displaced tenant or a notice that the landlord did not file the required statement of occupancy.

(SF Administrative Code § 37.9(a)(8)(vii))

Relocation Payment

For 3/22-2/23, pay relocation costs of $7,421 to each authorized occupant who has lived in the unit for 12 months or more, up to a total of $22,262 per household. Half of the relocation payment must be paid at the time of service of the eviction notice and half when the unit is vacated. Authorized occupants who are seniors (60 years of age or older), or disabled (the disability limits one or more major life activities *without regard to mitigating measures*), and households with at least one child receive an additional $4,948. If the authorized occupant is both senior and disabled, that person would receive only one additional payment. However, if the authorized occupant were a disabled child, there would be two additional payments.

Half of the additional payments must be paid within 15 calendar days of the landlord's receipt of the written notice with supporting evidence of the occupant's right to the payment, and the remaining half when the occupant vacates the unit even if evicted by the sheriff. (SF Administrative Code § 37.9C)

Check the Rent Board's Web site news section on *https://sfrb.org*, for updated amounts. Acceptance of payment for relocation shall not waive any rights a tenant may have under law. (SF Administrative Code § 37.9C(d))

Vacant Units Available

Withdraw the eviction notice if there are comparable vacant units owned by the landlord in the property or other property, or if such a comparable unit becomes vacant prior to the tenant moving out. (SF Administrative Code § 37.9(a)(8)(iv) This means the landlord must not evict the tenant if there is a comparable vacant unit, however, "comparable" has not been defined. If a non-comparable unit is available, the landlord must offer it to the tenant, but the courts have ruled that non-comparable units are offered as new tenancies, not continuations of existing tenancies, so landlords can charge whatever rent they want for non-comparable units. (*Bullard v. San Francisco Residential Rent Stabilization Board* (2003) 106 Cal. App. 4th 488)

Disclosure to Rent Board

• Request for info from tenant of tenant's "protected" status within 10 days of service on the tenant. (SF Administrative Code § 37.9 § 37.9 (i), (j))

• "Disclosures to Tenant" in the previous section must also be disclosed to the Rent Board within ten days after service of the notice to vacate together with the notice to vacate and proof of service. An OMI eviction is recorded on the deed after the filing at the Rent Board. (SF Administrative Code § 37.9B, § 37.9(c)) See the section "Assessor and Recorder" in "Chapter 3: Researching Landlords, Buildings, and Laws" for info.)

• Statement of occupancy under penalty of perjury within 90 days of the date of service of the eviction notice and an updated statement every 90 days afterwards if the landlord is still seeking recovery of possession of the unit. If the statement discloses the recovery of possession has occurred, the landlord must file updated statements once a year for five years. Each statement of occupancy after recovery of possession must disclose the date of recovery, whether the landlord or relative for whom the tenant was evicted is occupying the unit as that person's principal residence with two forms of supporting documentation, the date such occupancy began (or alternatively. the reasons why occupancy has not begun), the rent charged for the unit if any, and other info the Rent Board may require. The Rent Board shall make a reasonable effort

to send the displaced tenant a copy of each statement of occupancy within 30 days of the date of filing or a notice that the landlord did not file a statement of occupancy. In addition, the Rent Board shall impose an administrative penalty on any landlord who fails to comply. (SF Administrative Code § 37.9(a)(8)(vii))

- Re-rental offer within 15 days of the offer. (SF Administrative Code § 37.9B)

- Other disclosures as required by SF Rent Board Rules and Regulations § 12.14.

Occupancy by Landlord

Move into the unit within three months after the tenant vacates it and reside in the unit as his principal residence for three years, unless legitimate unforeseen circumstances, such as an unexpected job transfer to the East Coast, forces him to move. (SF Administrative Code § 37.9(a)(8)(v), Rent Board Rules and Regulations § 12.14)

Re-Rental Restrictions

Re-rental within five years after the eviction (for notices to vacate served on or after January 1, 2018, SF Administrative Code § 37.9B(a), (b)): Must allow the evicted tenant to return to the unit at the same rent she was paying when evicted, plus any increases that would have been allowed under the Rent Ordinance during that time by mailing an offer to the address the tenant has provided to the landlord or on file with the Rent Board if the landlord was not given the address. If the Rent Board also does not have an address, then the offer is mailed to the unit the tenant from which he was displaced and to any other physical or electronic address of which the landlord has knowledge. The tenant has 30 days from receipt of the offer to accept. If accepted, the tenant shall reoccupy the unit within 45 days of receipt of the offer. If the landlord rents the unit to someone else within the five years, the rent cannot be greater than the rent the evicted tenant was paying, plus any allowed annual rent increases. The Anti-Eviction Mapping Project maps these evictions. (See *Appendix A: Resources* for more info.) Also, the Rent Board will send notice of the maximum rent to the affected unit for five years. (SF Administrative Code §§ 37.9, 37.3(f), 37.10A, 37.9B(e))

Is the Landlord Evicting in Good Faith for OMI?

If the landlord appears to meet all the requirements of an OMI eviction, then the basic defense to an eviction applies: Is the landlord acting in good faith, without ulterior motives and with honest intent, as the law requires? This is the key issue for OMI evictions. This particular just cause eviction provision gets abused because it is easy for a landlord to claim an intention to live in your unit, but the question remains whether the landlord honestly intends to live there. Is the eviction based on retaliation because you asserted your rights, such as complaining to the building department? Is the landlord evicting because you have low rent or because the landlord does not like you or because a vacant unit sells for more than a rented unit? Assess the situation based on what you know about your landlord, such as how much money motivates his actions, and your past relationship with the landlord.

In any eviction lawsuit you have the right to a jury trial. Convincing a San Francisco jury that the landlord is acting in bad faith is easier than convincing a judge. There is usually not any one thing that convincingly shows bad faith; it's a few things combined. To fight, you will need to turn yourself into a part time private investigator. This is made considerably easier by the OMI disclosure requirements, but tenants should also double-check the info that is disclosed. Here are some places to start:

- Talk to your landlord informally if you have a relationship that allows for this. Have a friend along, as unobtrusively as possible, to act as a corroborating witness to what the landlord said. Write a letter to the landlord confirming what he said, especially any incriminating info, but try to do it in a way that doesn't make it too obvious. Once you know the landlord's cover story, you can try to find any info that doesn't fit.

- Research info about your landlord. See "Chapter 3: Researching Landlords, Buildings, and Laws."

- Check out the place where the landlord lives. What does it look like, how big is it, what's the neighborhood like, are there schools nearby for his children, is it near where he works? Your goal is to get a sense of how likely is it that the landlord is going to move to your rental unit.

- Check out any other properties owned by the landlord or by anyone connected to the landlord. Who lives there? Are there any vacancies? How much is the rent?

- If the landlord had done a previous OMI eviction within the last three years, the landlord is required to live in that previously evicted unit for three years (with rare exceptions).

During the court phase of the eviction process, you or your attorney also get a chance to "depose" your landlord and ask questions which the landlord must answer under oath. You will often get much of your info this way, but it's a good idea to do research ahead of time so you will know what to ask.

Ellis Act v. Owner Move-In Eviction Under SF Rent Ordinance

Dollar amounts are correct as of March 1, 2022. Amounts increase March 1 of each year.

	Ellis Act	Owner Move-In (OMI)
General Purpose	Owner may evict all tenants in building in order to remove the building from the rental market.	Owner may evict tenant in a particular unit in order to move herself or a close relative in.
Applicable Law	CA Government Code §§ 7060, et seq.; CA Government Code § 12926; SF Administrative Code §§ 37.9(a)(13), 37.9A, 47.2, 47.3	SF Administrative Code §§ 37.3(f), 37.9(a)(8), 37.9(c), 37.9(f), 37.9(i), 37.9(j), 37.9B, 37.9C, 37.10A, 37.11A, 47.2, 47.3; CA Civil Code § 1946.1
General Limitations	Cannot be used to withdraw only some units; must be entire building; cannot be used to evict single room occupancy (SRO) hotel tenants for pre-1990 SRO hotel.	Owner limited to 1 unit per building except for relatives, and once OMI has occurred, all future OMIs limited to that unit (even for future owners).
Preliminary Requirements Before Eviction	Owner must file Notice of Intent to Withdraw with the Rent Board.	Owner must own at least 25% interest in building if purchased on or after 2/22/91 or at least 10% if purchased before 2/22/91. Owner must file ownership and rental info with the Rent Board.
Eviction Notice Period	120 days except longer for Senior/Disabled Tenants; see below.	60 days, or 30 days if any tenant has resided less than 1 year.
Relocation Payment	$7,426.54 for each tenant up to a maximum of $22,279.62 per household. Additional $4,951.02 for senior/disabled.	$7,421 to each authorized occupant with 1 year or more tenancy, up to a total of $22,262 per household. Additional $4,948 for senior/disabled/household with minor children.
Senior Tenants	62 years or older: 1 year notice required rather than 120 days if senior has lived in unit for 1 year or more. Additional $4,421.58 relocation payment (not subject to household cap).	*60 years or older with 10 years or more tenancy*: Prohibition on OMI eviction except: (1) single family home/condo and owner owns no other condos in building; (2) all units in building other than owner's are occupied by "protected" tenants and owner moving in 60 years or older relative. *60 years or older and 1 year or more tenancy*: Additional $4,419 relocation payment (not subject to household cap).
Disabled Tenants	Broad Fair Employment and Housing Act definition of disabled: Any physical or mental condition that limits a major life activity, without regard to mitigating measures. 1 year notice required rather than 120 days if disabled tenant has lived in unit for 1 year or more. Additional $4,421.58 relocation payment (not subject to household cap).	Eligible for SSI and with 10 or more years tenancy: Prohibition on OMI eviction except for same exceptions as for Senior Tenants above. Broad definition of disabled and 1 year or more tenancy: Additional $4,419 relocation (not subject to household cap, but if both senior and disabled only 1 additional payment).
Catastrophically Ill Tenants	No additional protection. (See Disabled Tenants.)	Diagnosis of a terminal illness, eligible for SSI and 5 or more years tenancy: Prohibition on OMI eviction except for same exceptions as for Senior Tenants above. Same relocation payment as for disabled.
Households with or Familial Relationship with Children	No *additional* relocation payments, but each child is a "tenant" entitled to a relocation payment.	Possible prohibition on OMI during school year for tenancy of 1 year or more with minor(s) or familial or custodial relationship with minor. Additional $4,419 relocation payment per household, not subject to household cap. Each child counts as an "occupant."
Households with or Familial Relationship with School Worker	No additional restriction.	Possible prohibition on OMI during school year for tenancy of 1 year or more with school worker(s) or familial or custodial relationship with school worker.
Requirements After Eviction	If units are returned to the rental market within: 5 years, units must be re-rented at the old rent with allowable rent increases such as for inflation; 10 years: evicted tenant has first right to return. Tenants in rental units for which a Notice of Intent to Withdraw was filed with the Rent Board may be eligible for preference for Displaced Tenant Housing Preference Program.	Owner must move in within 3 months of tenant vacating and reside in the unit as their principal residence for 3 years, except for legitimate unforeseen circumstance. For re-rental within 5 years must re-rent at old rent with allowable rent increases such as for inflation with first right of refusal for evicted tenant. Evicted tenants 10 years or more tenancy may be eligible for Displaced Tenant Housing Preference Program.

Chapter 12– Eviction Defenses

Procedural Defenses for OMI Under SF Rent Ordinance

You can fight an OMI eviction based on common procedural errors that landlords make in the eviction notice, disclosures, and relocation payments. At a minimum, this will gain you extra time and bargaining power, and, if the landlord's motives are shaky, often can be enough to stop the eviction.

The tenant or Rent Board may sue for at least three times the actual damages, emotional distress, attorney fees and costs, and injunctive relief for wrongful eviction within five years of the first filing of the statement of occupancy or three months of recovering possession, whichever is earlier. An organization such as the San Francisco Tenants Union may also sue within three years after the tenant knew or should have known of the violation. The subsequent tenant may also sue for at least three times the excessive rent collected in the three years before the filing of the lawsuit and the period between the filing and the court date, as well as injunctive relief and attorney fees. (SF Administrative Code § 37.9(f), § 37.11A) Also, see the discussion on settlements and strategy near the end of "Chapter 13: Eviction Process in Court."

Housing Assistance After OMI Under SF Rent Ordinance

San Francisco tenants who received an eviction notice for OMI on or after January 1, 2010 may be eligible for a Displaced Tenant Housing Preference Certificate for housing funded by the City of San Francisco or inclusionary housing development. The tenant must have continuously occupied the residence for at least 10 years at the time the eviction notice was filed with the Rent Board and meet the rules for the housing unit including maximum and minimum income requirements. (SF Administrative Code §§ 47.2, 47.3) See "*Appendix A: Resources*" for info about the Displaced Tenant Housing Preference Program under "Government Agencies" > "Mayor's Office" > "Housing and Community Development."

Ellis Act

An Ellis Act eviction is for the purpose of withdrawing (removing) all of the rental units in a building from the rental market. (CA Government Code § 7060-7060.7) Using the Ellis Act, a landlord may evict tenants for multiple nonfamily owners to move in, unlike owner move-in evictions. The Ellis Act is included in the just causes under the Rent Ordinance (SF Administrative Code § 37.9(a)(13)) and California law (CA Civil Code § 1946.2(b)(2) (B)). Ellis Act evictions are being used to turn apartments into tenancies in common as a transition to condos.

The Ellis Act is often used to evict long-term tenants with

affordable rents. However, landlords are prohibited from using the Ellis Act to evict tenants in single-room occupancy (SRO) hotels that are in a city and county (such as San Francisco) or in a city with a population over 1 million and has a permit of occupancy before 1990. (CA Government Code § 7060)

Fighting an Ellis Eviction

Contact the Tenderloin Housing Clinic for a free attorney. (See "*Appendix A: Resources*.") Tenants who fight the Ellis eviction win surprisingly often. Tenants who don't win often drag out the eviction for well over a year and get into a position where they can settle on their terms.

Public Pressure for Fighting an Ellis Eviction

It can be useful to put public pressure on a landlord who is doing an Ellis Act eviction. These evictions are more blatantly morally wrong than most evictions, since the landlord isn't even claiming to be doing anything socially redeeming after the evictions are completed, so neighbors and the media can often be made to see the tenant's side clearly. See "Neighborhood or Citywide Action" at the end of "Chapter 14: Taking Action for more info."

California Law Requiring Just Cause for Ellis Eviction

The owner shall notify the tenant of the tenant's right to relocation assistance or rent waiver. For the rent waiver, the notice shall state the amount of rent waived and that no rent is due for the final month of the tenancy. The amount of relocation assistance or rent waiver shall be equal to one month of the rent when the owner issued the notice to terminate the tenancy. Any relocation assistance shall be provided within 15 calendar days of service of the notice. (CA Civil Code § 1946.2(d)) The other requirements for an Ellis Act eviction under California law requiring just cause are similar to the requirements under the San Francisco Rent Ordinance. For the details, see California Government Code § 7060-7060.7.

San Francisco Rent Ordinance Ellis Eviction

Ellis Eviction Threat

Many landlords will utilize Ellis threats, telling tenants that they will be doing an Ellis eviction in the future. They do this because actually evicting tenants via the Ellis Act is a serious step which goes on the title of the building and which will immediately lower the value of the building by thousands of dollars. If a landlord is able to get tenants out by threatening an Ellis and not leaving evidence of the threat, often in conjunction with buyout offers, the restrictions on re-rentals will not apply. (See "Buyouts, Almost Always a Bad Idea" in Chapter 8: Harassment for more info.) A landlord can then re-rent at higher rents or, if selling the units, can get a significantly higher price for vacant units.

Many landlords are thus using Ellis Act eviction as a bluff,

successfully using the Ellis eviction threat to get tenants to leave, even when the landlord has no intention of removing the units from the rental market. Other landlords will ultimately do the Ellis eviction, but will first try to get tenants out by just threatening the Ellis eviction. Tenants who receive Ellis threats should research the landlord at the Rent Board and see if that landlord has ever done an Ellis eviction or other evictions. If he hasn't and owns, or has owned, other property in San Francisco, then it may very well be a bluff. If the landlord seems likely to go ahead with an Ellis eviction, the next section has strategies for defending an actual Ellis eviction.

Organize the Building to Fight an Ellis Eviction

If one tenant can successfully claim any of the following defenses, then the eviction is stopped for the entire building since the landlord is then prevented from withdrawing all of the units. (However, one tenant claiming disability or senior status that requires notice of one year would not prevent eviction of the other tenants after 120 days.) Thus, it is especially important for tenants fighting an Ellis eviction to organize. If the landlord buys out enough units so that there are only two units that are tenant occupied, the landlord may be able to market the building as a owner move-in for one unit and a close relative move-in for the other unit with fewer restrictions, decreasing the tenants' fighting power. See "Building-Wide Collective Action" in "Chapter 14: Taking Action" for more info.

Inform Landlord of Restrictions on Ellised Property Under the SF Rent Ordinance

Evictions using the Ellis Act entail restrictions that are binding on current and future owners. If the landlord re-rents within two years of an Ellis Act eviction, the evicted tenant may sue the landlord for actual and exemplary damages. (See the later section "Return at Same Rent If Re-Rented After Ellis Eviction Under the SF Rent Ordinance.") If the units are returned to the rental market by the landlord or any subsequent landlord within five years of withdrawal under the Ellis Act, the maximum rent which can be charged to any tenant is the same rent that the evicted tenant was paying, plus any increases that would have been allowed under the Rent Ordinance. (See the later section "Re-Rent to New Tenant at Same Rent After Ellis Eviction Under the SF Rent Ordinance.") If the landlord re-rents within ten years of an Ellis Act eviction, the displaced tenant has the first right of refusal. If the building is demolished after an Ellis Act eviction and units in a newly-constructed building on that site are offered for rent within five years of the date of withdrawal, these units are covered by the Rent Ordinance, and the allowable initial rent would be determined by

the Rent Board. (SF Administrative Code § 37.9A(b))

Some buildings may not be allowed to convert to condos where an Ellis eviction has occurred. Since conversion to condos is usually the goal when tenants are evicted for no fault, stopping the conversion can be a powerful defense. See the chart "Condo Conversions Prohibited" and the section "Condo Conversion Law" in "Chapter 11: Changes in Use" for more info.

If the owner wanted to add an accessory dwelling unit to the building, the building permit will be denied for buildings with two to four dwelling units if in the 10 years prior to filing the application for the permit a tenant had been evicted for the Ellis Act. (See "Accessory Dwelling Units" in "Chapter 11: Changes in Use" for more info.)

Tenants in an Ellis Act eviction should be sure to let the landlord know that they are aware of all the restrictions and will be monitoring the building for compliance for years.

Procedural Defenses for an Ellis Eviction Under the SF Rent Ordinance

The Ellis Act says that landlords have the unconditional right to "go out of business." This means that, for an Ellis eviction, the landlord must remove all of the units in the building from the rental market; the landlord must evict all tenants and cannot single out one tenant or remove just one unit from the rental market. (See the section "Demolition Evictions" later in this chapter for a discussion of demolition or removal from housing use of a single unit.) Further, all the tenants in the entire building must be evicted simultaneously, though seniors or disabled tenants can get an extension of the eviction notice period.

The notices and paperwork required in filing an Ellis Act eviction are particularly complex, and courts are consistently ruling that the process must be adhered to exactly. For example, a number of Ellis evictions have been defeated by tenants because the eviction notices stated that relocation payment was due to the tenants but failed to state the dollar amount. These procedural issues are particularly fatal in an Ellis eviction because the extended notice periods (120 days and 1 year for senior or disabled tenants) means that when an eviction gets tossed out in court it can be more than a year after the landlord first filed the eviction notices. See the following section "Procedural Requirements for an Ellis Eviction Under the SF Rent Ordinance" for more info.

Procedural Requirements for an Ellis Eviction Under the SF Rent Ordinance

Ellis evictions require at least a 120-day notice, with at least a one-year notice for senior (age 62) or disabled (defined in CA Government Code § 12955.3 and § 12926) tenants who have lived in their unit for one year or more. Senior and disabled tenants must assert their right to receive the one-year notice within 60 days after the landlord delivers to the Rent Board the Notice of

Intent to Withdraw Residential Units. If the landlord disputes the tenant's claim of requirement for an extension to a one-year notice, the landlord must give written notice to the Rent Board and the affected tenant within 90 days of delivery to the Rent Board of the Notice of Intent to Withdraw of the dispute. (SF Administrative Code § 37.9A(f)(4))

Disability is defined significantly more broadly under the Ellis Act than for owner move-in evictions. Any physical or mental disability defined by the California Fair Employment and Housing Act constitutes a disability for purposes of the Ellis Act. Essentially, any physical or mental condition that limits a major life activity (physical or mental) constitutes a disability, and would require a one-year notice under the Ellis Act. The law also disregards assistive devices and medication which would remove the limitation, so a tenant who is very near-sighted when not wearing her glasses should qualify as disabled. (CA Government Code § 12926(j) and § 12926(m))

The process of an Ellis eviction is as follows:

1. The landlord serves all tenants eviction notices effective 120 days after filing of the Notice of Intent (SF Administrative Code § 37.9A(f)), unless the tenant qualifies as senior or disabled, in which case the notice would be effective one year after the filing. The landlord also pays the tenant half of the relocation payment at the time of the service of the notice. The other half is paid when the tenant vacates. The eviction notices must be served before the landlord can file the Notice of Intent. The landlord also informs the tenants of the tenants' re-occupancy and relocation rights. At some point, the Rent Board will also inform tenants of the filing and of relocation rights and re-occupancy rights, as well as provide a form for tenants to record their wish to re-occupy if the unit is re-rented.

2. The landlord files a Notice of Intent to Withdraw Residential Units from the Rental Market with the Rent Board.

3. Before the effective date of withdrawal, the landlord records with the County Recorder a memorandum summarizing the Notice of Intent.

4. 120 days or 1 year after the Notice of Intent is filed with the Rent Board, the building is legally withdrawn from the rental market.

5. Once the building is legally withdrawn from the rental market and the eviction notice to the tenants has expired, the landlord can initiate an Unlawful Detainer lawsuit against any tenants remaining in the building.

6. The Rent Board records the Ellis Act eviction at the County Recorder within 30 days of withdrawal. The Rent Board will seek to do this within five days of the date the building is withdrawn.

Ellis Act eviction notices cannot expire until on or after the day the building is considered withdrawn from the rental market. For example, suppose that on April 15 a landlord files the Notice of Intent, stating that the units will be withdrawn on August 13 (120 days after filing). If the landlord gives the tenants eviction notices stating that they must move by August 1, then the eviction notices will be defective. This means the tenants can protest and the landlord would have to start the 120-day or 1-year notice for seniors and disabled tenants again.

Relocation Payments for an Ellis Eviction Under the SF Rent Ordinance

Tenants evicted by the Ellis Act have a right to a relocation payment. Children are included as "eligible tenants." (SF Administrative Code § 37.9A(e)(3)) The amount from 3/22-2/23 is $7,426.54 for each tenant up to a household maximum of $22,279.62. In addition, tenants who are senior (age 62 or more) or disabled (broadly defined previously) receive an additional $4,951.02 each. Check *https://sfrb.org* news for updated amounts each year. If there are more than three tenants in the household, the payment per household would be divided among the tenants.

Half of the relocation payments must be paid at the time of the service of the eviction notice and the remainder at the time the tenant vacates, even if evicted by the sheriff. Half of the additional payment for senior or disabled tenants must be paid within fifteen days of the landlord receiving written notice from the tenants of their right to the additional payments, the other half when the tenant vacates. Such tenants should describe briefly their age or disability, when notifying their landlord of their right to the additional relocation payments. No supporting evidence is required at the time of informing the landlord, although evidence may be required later if the landlord disputes the tenant's claim.

Housing Assistance After Ellis Eviction Under the SF Rent Ordinance

San Francisco tenants in rental units for which a Notice of Intent to Withdraw was filed with the Rent Board on or after January 1, 2010 that the tenant's landlord plans to evict under the Ellis Act may be eligible for a Displaced Tenant Housing Preference Certificate for housing funded by the City of San Francisco or an inclusionary housing development. The Certificate holder must still meet the rules for the housing unit including maximum and minimum income requirements. (SF Administrative Code §§ 47.2, 47.3) See *Appendix A: Resources* for info about the Displaced Tenant

Housing Preference Program under "Government Agencies" > "Mayor's Office" > "Housing and Community Development."

Return at Same Rent If Re-Rented After Ellis Eviction Under the SF Rent Ordinance

For five years after the rental units are withdrawn from the rental market, if the units are put back on the rental market, including just one unit (CA Government Code § 7060.7(d)), evicted tenants have the right to return at the rent in effect at the time the Notice of Intent to Withdraw was filed, plus any adjustments which would have been allowed under the Rent Ordinance. However, tenants must notify the landlord and Rent Board of their wish to have this right of return. (SF Administrative Code § 37.9A(a), (c)) Within 30 days of vacating, such tenants are required to notify the landlord of their current address and their wish to re-occupy the unit at the same rent, if it is rented again. (Tenants should send the letter with proof of mailing, and keep a copy.) This letter does not obligate the tenant to move back in, but it does give the tenant stronger grounds for a lawsuit if the landlord doesn't notify the tenant. The landlord is supposed to contact the tenant for any re-rental within two years. The Rent Board also will provide tenants with a form to fill out and maintains a list of tenants who wish to return with their current addresses, phone numbers, etc. Tenants should keep the landlord and Rent Board informed of any address and phone number changes.

The tenant also has 30 days in which to request an offer to re-rent the unit after the owner notified the Rent Board of the intent to re-rent. The landlord is required to keep the Rent Board notified of the intent to re-rent for 10 years after withdrawal. If the landlord re-rents to someone other than the tenant within two years of an Ellis Act eviction, the tenant may sue the landlord for actual damages (including the difference between the old rent-controlled rent and market rent) plus exemplary damages. Such a suit must be brought within three years of the date the landlord withdrew the unit from the rental market. (SF Administrative Code § 37.9A(d)) From two years to ten years after withdrawal, if the landlord does not notify the Rent Board of any re-rental, the displaced tenant can sue for up to six months of the rent that was in the rental agreement. (SF Administrative Code § 37.9A(c))

Re-Rent to New Tenant at Same Rent After Ellis Eviction Under the SF Rent Ordinance

If units vacated by tenants after receiving an Ellis Act eviction notice are re-rented (including if only one unit) to anyone

within five years following the removal of the units from the rental market, then the initial rent must be the same rent that the evicted (or previous) tenant was paying, plus any adjustments which would have been allowed under the Rent Ordinance. This "vacancy control" provision lasts for all subsequent rentals during those five years, not just the first re-rental, and it applies even if the landlord changes his mind and does not withdraw all the units from rental. In the latter case, where the landlord changes his mind about the Ellis notices and keeps renting, the five years start from the date the original Notice of Intent to Withdraw the units was filed at the Rent Board. The Ellis Act eviction notices can be revoked only if no tenants moved as a result of the notice. (SF Administrative Code § 37.9A(a)) The Rent Board maintains a list of Ellis filings, with each unit's rent. Also, the Anti-Eviction Mapping Project maps these evictions. See *Appendix A: Resources* for more info.

Capital Improvement Temporary Evictions

Capital improvement evictions under the SF Rent Ordinance (SF Administrative Code § 37.9(a)(11)) should only be temporary evictions in good faith for tenants in units that will be uninhabitable during capital improvement work. (See "Capital Improvements" in "Chapter 7: Rent Increases" for more info on the definition of capital improvement.) Since the tenant is only temporarily vacating not giving up the tenancy, these evictions should not affect the length of residency which helps protect the tenant from landlord move-in evictions. Rent is not due if the displacement is for twenty or more days. For displacement under twenty days, rent may be due under California Civil Code § 1947.9. These evictions are not supposed to exceed three months unless the Rent Board approves an extension of time. (SF Rent Board Rules and Regulations § 12.15)

The eviction notice is a 60-day notice for tenancies of at least a year, a 30-day notice for tenancies of less than a year. (CA Civil Code § 1946.1) The notice must state the legal rent at the time the notice was issued. (SF Administrative Code § 37.9(c)) Copies of all necessary permits, a description of the work to be done and a reasonable approximate date when the tenant can re-occupy the unit should be given to the tenant on or before the date the notice to vacate is served. In addition, the landlord must provide a form from the Rent Board that advises the tenant that the tenant's failure to timely act in response to a notice to vacate may result in a lawsuit by the landlord to evict the tenant, advice regarding the notice to vacate is available from the Rent Board, the tenant may be eligible for affordable housing programs through the Mayor's Office of Housing and Community Development, his right to return, and a form that the tenant can use to inform the Rent Board of any change in address. The landlord must advise the tenant in writing on or before the date the notice to vacate is given that the rehabilitation or capital improvement plans are on file with the Central Permit Bureau of the Department of Building Inspection and that the tenant can arrange to review such plans.

The landlord is required to inform the tenant in writing,

promptly, when the work has been completed, allow the tenant to re-occupy the unit as soon as the work is completed, and not increase the rent more than allowed by the Rent Ordinance. The landlord must file a copy of the offer with the Rent Board within 15 days of the offer. The tenant has 30 days from receipt of the landlord's offer of re-occupancy to notify the landlord of acceptance and 45 days to re-occupy the unit after receipt of the offer. If the landlord does not notify the tenant promptly that the unit is ready for re-occupancy, the tenant may file a Decrease in Housing Services petition for the difference in rent between the original unit and the replacement unit he has been living in. (SF Rent Board Rules and Regulations § 12.16) If the landlord rents the unit to someone else within five years, the rent cannot be greater than the rent the evicted tenant was paying, plus any allowed annual rent increases. (SF Administrative Code § 37.3(f)) The Anti-Eviction Mapping Project maps these evictions. (See *Appendix A: Resources* for more info.) The Rent Board will also send a notice to the unit within one year of the offer to rerent informing the occupant that the rent may be restricted.

It is sometimes possible to prevent a capital improvement eviction by protesting the permits. (See "Permit Process" in "Chapter 11: Changes in Use" for more info.) If possible, it is best to stay in the unit while capital improvement work is being done so that this eviction cause is not abused. Landlords often fail to inform tenants when the work has been completed or delay doing the work or notifying the tenant of its completion.

Some buildings may not be allowed to convert to condos where a capital improvement eviction has occurred. Since conversion to condos is often the goal when tenants are evicted for no fault, stopping the conversion can be a powerful defense. See the chart "Condo Conversions Prohibited" and the section "Condo Conversion Law" in "Chapter 11: Changes in Use" for more info.

Also, if the owner wanted to add an accessory dwelling unit to the building, the permit will be denied for buildings with two to four dwelling units if in the 10 years prior to filing the permit application, a tenant had been evicted for capital improvement without the right to return. Some single residential units will also be denied permits in these circumstances. (See "Accessory Dwelling Units" in "Chapter 11: Changes in Use" for more information.)

Relocation Payment for Capital Improvement Eviction

Each authorized occupant who has lived in the unit at least one year is to be provided with relocation payment. If the displacement is for more than nineteen days, the payment is $7,421 for 3/22-2/23 per occupant, up to a total of $22,262 per household. Half of the relocation payment must be paid at the time of service of the eviction notice and half when the unit is vacated. Authorized occupants who are seniors (at least 60 years of age), or disabled (the disability limits one or more of a person's major life activities without regard to mitigating measures), and households with at least one child receive an additional $4,948. Half of the additional payments must be paid within 15 calendar days of the landlord's receipt of the written notice of the occupant's right to the additional payment with supporting evidence, and the remaining half when the occupant vacates. If the authorized occupant is both senior and disabled, that person would receive only one additional payment. However, if the authorized occupant were a disabled child, there would be two additional payments. (Check the *https://sfrb.org* news section for the updated relocation payment amounts.) A copy of San Francisco Administrative Code § 37.9C shall be provided to the tenant by the time of the service of the notice. (SF Administrative Code § 37.9C) When the tenant is displaced for less than twenty days the compensation for 3/22-2/23 is limited to $402 per day per household, adjusted for inflation by the Rent Board, and moving expenses. A comparable dwelling may be provided instead of the compensation. (CA Civil Code § 1947.9)

Households with Children or School Workers Protected During School Year from Capital Improvement Evictions

These evictions cannot occur during the school year for tenants that have a child or a San Francisco school worker in the household or have a familial relationship with a child or school worker. "School" means any state-licensed child care center/family day care, or any public, private, or parochial institution that provides educational instruction for students in any of the grades from kindergarten through twelfth grade. The tenant must have resided in the unit for 12 months or more. (SF Administrative Code § 37.9(j)) The landlord must warn the tenant to submit a statement to the landlord within 30 days of service of the notice to vacate, with supporting evidence, if the tenant claims to be a member of a protected class under Ordinance Sections 37.9(j), and that failure to do so shall be deemed an admission that the tenant is not protected by Sections 37.9(j). (SF Rent Board Rules and Regulations § 12.15)

Lead Abatement Evictions

Lead Abatement Eviction Under California Law Requiring Just Cause

Evictions for lead abatement are a just cause if the abatement cannot be reasonably accomplished in a safe manner with the tenant in place and requires the tenant to vacate the unit for at least 30 days. (CA Civil Code § 1946.2(b)(2)(C), (D)) The eviction notice is a sixty-day eviction notice for tenancies of at least a year, a thirty-day notice for tenancies of less than a year. (CA Civil Code § 1946.1)

Relocation Assistance or Rent Waiver

The owner shall notify the tenant of the tenant's right to relocation assistance or rent waiver. For the rent waiver, the notice shall state the amount of rent waived and that no rent is due for the final month of the tenancy. The amount of relocation assistance or rent waiver shall be equal to one month of the rent when the owner issued the notice to terminate the tenancy. Any relocation assistance shall be provided within 15 calendar days of service of the notice. The relocation assistance or rent waiver required by this subdivision shall be credited against any other relocation assistance required by any other law. (CA Civil Code § 1946.2(d))

Lead Abatement Eviction Under the SF Rent Ordinance

These types of evictions should be temporary and for the purpose in good faith of lead paint remediation when a child in the household has an elevated lead level and the landlord has been ordered to correct lead paint hazards. (SF Administrative Code § 37.9(a)(14)) Since the tenant is only temporarily vacating not giving up the tenancy, these evictions should not affect the length of residency which helps protect the tenant from owner move-in evictions. Rent is not due if the displacement is for twenty or more days. For displacement under twenty days, rent may be due under California Civil Code § 1947.9.

If possible, it is best to stay in the unit while lead abatement work is being done so that this eviction cause is not abused. Landlords often fail to inform tenants when the work has been completed, or delay doing the work and notifying the tenant of its completion.

The eviction notice is a 60-day notice for tenancies of at least a year, a 30-day notice for tenancies of less than a year. (CA Civil Code § 1946.1) The notice must state the legal rent at the time the notice was issued. (SF Administrative Code § 37.9(c)) If the landlord rents the unit to someone else within five years, the rent cannot be greater than the rent the evicted tenant was paying, plus any allowed annual rent increases. (SF Administrative Code § 37.3(f))

Relocation payments, which increase the longer the tenant is forced to vacate, must be paid to the tenant. (SF Administrative Code § 72.3) However, compensation is limited where the tenant is displaced for less than twenty days. (CA Code § 1947.9) No additional payments are given to seniors or disabled people. See "Lead Abatement" in the chart "Relocation Payments for Evictions Under SF Law" earlier in this chapter for more info.

The landlord is required to allow the tenant to re-occupy the unit as soon as the work is completed, and not increase the rent more than allowed by the Rent Ordinance. (SF Administrative Code § 72.5) These temporary evictions are very few. See "Lead Paint and Lead Hazards" in "Chapter 6: Repairs and Services" for more info.

Some buildings may not be allowed to convert to condos where a lead abatement eviction has occurred. Since conversion to condos is sometimes the goal when tenants are evicted, stopping the conversion can be a powerful defense to eviction. See the chart "Condo Conversions Prohibited" and the section "Condo Conversion Law" in "Chapter 11: Changes in Use" for more info.

Also, if the owner wanted to add an accessory dwelling unit to the building, the permit will be denied for buildings with two to four dwelling units if in the 10 years prior to filing the permit application, a tenant had been evicted for lead abatement without the right to return. Some single residential units will also be denied permits in these circumstances. (See "Accessory Dwelling Units" in "Chapter 11: Changes in Use" for more info.)

Demolition Evictions

Demolition Under California Law Requiring Just Cause

Evictions for demolition (removal from housing use) of a residential unit are a just cause. (CA Civil Code § 1946.2(b)(2) (C), (D) The eviction notice is a sixty-day eviction notice for tenancies of at least a year, a thirty-day notice for tenancies of less than a year. (CA Civil Code § 1946.1))

The owner shall notify the tenant of the tenant's right to relocation assistance or rent waiver. For the rent waiver, the notice shall state the amount of rent waived and that no rent is due for the final month of the tenancy. The amount of relocation assistance or rent waiver shall be equal to one month of the rent when the owner issued the notice to terminate the tenancy. Any relocation assistance shall be provided within 15 calendar days of service of the notice. (CA Civil Code § 1946.2(d))

Demolition Under the SF Rent Ordinance

There are two just causes for eviction for a demolition under the San Francisco Rent Ordinance. One is to remove the unit from housing use without a development agreement with the City of San Francisco, the other is with the development agreement.

Removing a Unit from Housing Use Without a City Development Agreement (SF Administrative Code § 37.9(a)(10))

The first demolition just cause is an eviction in good faith for the purpose of removing a unit from *all housing use* where there is *not an agreement between a developer and the City of San Francisco*. Tenants can fight this eviction by fighting the permits the landlord must obtain to demolish the unit. (See "Permit Process" in "Chapter 11: Changes in Use.")

The eviction notice is a 60-day notice for tenancies of at least a year, a 30-day notice for tenancies of less than a year. (CA Civil Code § 1946.1) The notice must state the legal rent at the time the notice was issued. (SF Administrative Code § 37.9(c)) If the landlord rents the unit to someone else within five years, the rent cannot be greater than the rent the evicted tenant was paying, plus any allowed annual rent increases. (SF Administrative Code § 37.3(f)) The Anti-Eviction Mapping Project maps these evictions. See *Appendix A: Resources* for more info.

Each authorized occupant who has lived in the unit for 12 months or more is to be provided with $7,421 for 3/22-2/23 in relocation payment, up to a total of $22,262 per household. Half of the relocation payment must be paid at the time of service of the eviction notice and half when the unit is vacated. Authorized occupants who are seniors (60 years of age or older), or disabled (the disability limits a major life activity without regard to mitigating measures), and households with at least one child receive an additional $4,948. If the authorized occupant is both senior and disabled, that person would receive only one additional payment. However, if the authorized occupant were a disabled child, there would be two additional payments. Half of the additional payments must be paid within 15 calendar days of the landlord's receipt of written notice of the occupant's right to the payment with supporting evidence, and the remaining half when the occupant vacates the unit. Check the *https://sfrb. org* news section for updated amounts. A copy of San Francisco Administrative Code § 37.9C shall be provided to the tenant by the time of the service of the notice. (SF Administrative Code § 37.9C)

Generally, the legitimate purpose for one of these evictions would be to demolish an unauthorized unit which the Department of Building Inspection had ordered removed from housing use. Note that "demolish" can mean simply removing a stove, toilet, etc. to make the unit unfit for housing use. The landlord must still obtain the appropriate permits and follow the just cause eviction process. See "Unauthorized Units" in "Chapter 11: Changes in Use" for more info.

Sometimes a landlord wants to demolish a tenant's unit and merge it into the landlord's unit. In such a case the eviction can be fought because, under the Rent Ordinance, the unit to be demolished must be removed from all housing use, which would not be the case if it were merged into the landlord's unit. Historically, however, judges have been pretty bad about supporting tenants raising this defense.

In addition, some buildings may not be allowed to convert to condos where this type of demolition eviction has occurred. Where conversion to condos are the goal, stopping the conversion can be a powerful defense. See the chart "Condo Conversions Prohibited" and the section "Condominium Conversions" in "Chapter 11: Changes in Use" for more info.

Also, if the owner wanted to add an accessory dwelling unit to the building, the permit will be denied for buildings with two to

four dwelling units if in the 10 years prior to filing the permit application, a tenant had been evicted for this type of demolition. (See "Accessory Dwelling Units" in "Chapter 11: Changes in Use" for more info.)

These evictions cannot occur during the school year for tenants that have a child or a San Francisco school worker in the household or have a familial relationship with a child or school worker. "School" means any state-licensed child care center/family day care, or any public, private, or parochial institution that provides educational instruction for students in any of the grades from kindergarten through twelfth grade. The tenant must have resided in the unit for 12 months or more. (SF Administrative Code § 37.9(j))

Development Agreement with the City of San Francisco (SF Administrative Code § 37.9(a)(15))

The second just cause for eviction for demolition was added as a result of a development agreement between the City of San Francisco and Trinity Properties. However, this just cause has also been used to evict many tenants in other developments such as Park Merced and Kirkham Heights, and other evictions are anticipated using this just cause. It is particularly important in these cases to organize as tenants. (See Chapter 14: Taking Action for more info.) The eviction notice is a 60-day notice for tenancies of at least a year, a 30-day notice for tenancies of less than a year. This just cause must be in good faith and applies only in these very specific cases.

Condo Conversion for Sale Evictions Under the SF Rent Ordinance

When rental units have been converted to condos, the owner may use this just cause under the Rent Ordinance for evicting a tenant to sell the unit after a condo conversion. (SF Administrative Code § 37.9(a)(9)) The eviction notice is a 60-day notice for tenancies of at least a year, a 30-day notice for tenancies of less than a year. (CA Civil Code § 1946.1) The notice must state the legal rent at the time the notice was issued. (SF Administrative Code § 37.9(c)) If the landlord rents the unit to someone else within five years, the rent cannot be greater than the rent the evicted tenant was paying, plus any allowed annual rent increases. (SF Administrative Code § 37.3(f))

See the chart "Relocation Payments for Evictions Under SF Law" earlier in this chapter for info on relocation payments to tenants. Because landlords usually use other types of evictions before converting to condos, this type of eviction is rare. To evict for this just cause, the landlord must first have approval to convert

to condos and go through most of the condo conversion process. See "Chapter 11: Changes In Use" for more info on condo conversions.

These evictions cannot occur during the school year for tenants that have a child or a San Francisco school worker in the household or have a familial relationship with a child or school worker. The tenant must have resided in the unit for 12 months or more.

Also, if the owner wanted to add an accessory dwelling unit to the building, the permit will be denied for buildings with two to four dwelling units if in the 10 years prior to filing the permit application, a tenant had been evicted for sale after a condo conversion. (See "Accessory Dwelling Units" in "Chapter 11: Changes in Use" for more info.)

Substantial Rehabilitation/Remodel Evictions

Substantial Remodel Eviction Under California Law Requiring Just Cause

Evictions for substantial remodel are a just cause. "Substantially remodel" means the replacement or substantial modification of any structural, electrical, plumbing, or mechanical system that requires a government permit, or the abatement of hazardous materials, including mold, in accordance with law, that cannot be reasonably accomplished in a safe manner with the tenant in place and that requires the tenant to vacate for at least 30 days. (CA Civil Code § 1946.2(b)(2)(C), (D)) The eviction notice is a sixty-day eviction notice for tenancies of at least a year, a thirty-day notice for tenancies of less than a year. (CA Civil Code § 1946.1)

Relocation Assistance or Rent Waiver

The owner shall notify the tenant of the tenant's right to relocation assistance or rent waiver. For the rent waiver, the notice shall state the amount of rent waived and that no rent is due for the final month of the tenancy. The amount of relocation assistance or rent waiver shall be equal to one month of the rent when the owner issued the notice to terminate the tenancy. Any relocation assistance shall be provided within 15 calendar days of service of the notice. (CA Civil Code § 1946.2(d))

Substantial Rehabilitation Eviction Under the SF Rent Ordinance

Substantial rehabilitation is renovation work on a building that is at least fifty years old and essentially uninhabitable. These just causes for eviction under the Rent Ordinance (SF Administrative Code § 37.9(a)(12)) are very few. Work not compensated by insurance must cost the landlord 75% or more of comparable construction and the landlord must have all the permits before the eviction notices in good faith can be issued. (SF Rent Board Rules and Regulations § 1.18) The eviction notice is a sixty-day notice for tenancies of at least a year, a thirty-day notice for

tenancies of less than a year. (CA Civil Code § 1946.1) The Rent Board certifies and maintains a list of these buildings, and the building is removed from Rent Ordinance coverage.

These evictions can be most successfully fought during the permit stage at the Department of Planning and Board of Permit Appeals. (See "Permit Process" in "Chapter 12: Changes in Use.") Also, since some buildings may not be allowed to convert to condos where this type of eviction has occurred, this may discourage the landlord from renovating. (See the chart "Condo Conversions Prohibited" and the section "Condo Conversion Law" in "Chapter 11: Changes in Use" for more info.)

Tenants are not able to return at the same rent. However, each authorized occupant is entitled to relocation payments with additional payments for seniors, disabled, and household with children after notice to the landlord. San Francisco Administrative Code § 37.9C shall be provided to the tenant by the time of the service of the notice. (SF Administrative Code § 37.9C)

These evictions cannot occur during the school year for tenants that have a child or a San Francisco school worker in the household or have a familial relationship with a child or school worker. The tenant must have resided in the unit for 12 months or more.

Also, if the owner wanted to add an accessory dwelling unit to the building, the permit will be denied for buildings with two to four dwelling units if in the 10 years prior to filing the permit application, a tenant had been evicted for substantial rehabilitation. (See "Accessory Dwelling Units" in "Chapter 11: Changes in Use" for more info.)

Good Samaritan Occupancy Status Termination Under the SF Rent Ordinance

Good Samaritan occupancy status is a temporary occupancy following an emergency such as a fire or earthquake that required the tenant to vacate his unit unexpectedly. The "Good Samaritan" landlord agrees to rent the tenant a replacement unit at a reduced rent for a specified period of up to twelve months. A landlord has just cause under the Rent Ordinance to evict a tenant from the replacement unit when the tenant's Good Samaritan status has expired (SF Administrative Code § 37.2(a)(D)), and the landlord serves a notice within sixty days after expiration of the Good Samaritan status period of termination of tenancy. (SF Administrative Code § 37.9(a)(16))

Chapter 13: Eviction Process in Court

With rare exception (a sole lodger sharing the unit with the owner), an eviction can be carried out only by the sheriff, not by the police or landlord, and the sheriff can do so only after a court order. An eviction is a complicated legal process. In the following sections, we will break the court process down into a series of steps and explain each as we go along. However, if the tenant receives a document called "Summons and Complaint for Unlawful Detainer," it is recommended that the tenant obtain assistance from the Eviction Defense Collaborative or other experienced agencies that provide free attorneys (see the box in "Chapter 12: Eviction Defenses" "Right to an Attorney for Eviction Notices") or private attorneys that can guide the tenant through the court process. The San Francisco Tenants Union usually is not able to assist with an Unlawful Detainer but can provide a list of attorneys who only represent tenants. This chapter applies to both rent-controlled and non-rent-controlled units.

Summary of the Eviction Process

- Notice to (cure or) quit is served on tenant (usually 3- or 60-day notices; sometimes 10-, 14-, 30-, 90-, or 120-day). This notice is not required at the end of a lease period.

- Lawsuit (a "complaint" called an "unlawful detainer") is filed in court and served on the tenant. This lawsuit is not required if the occupant is a lodger. (See the section "Bypassing the Courts: Lodgers and Hotels" later in this chapter.)

- Answer is filed by tenant to the complaint as a defense.

- Court date is set.

- Court conference and a trial if there is no settlement.

- Judgment taken to the sheriff by landlord if tenant loses.

- Sheriff serves tenant with a Notice to Vacate.

- Sheriff evicts five days after serving the Notice to Vacate.

(See also the flowchart "Unlawful Detainer Procedures & Time Diagram" later in this chapter.)

The eviction process usually begins when the landlord or their agent, such as the manager, gives the tenant a notice, commonly called a "Notice to Quit," which is usually a 3- or 60-day notice.

Right to a Free Attorney

See the box in Chapter 12 "Right to an Attorney for Eviction Notices" for more info about your right to a free attorney for evictions.

This notice does not come from the court. See "Notice to (Cure) or Quit" in "Chapter 12: Eviction Defenses" for more info.

Eviction Lawsuit Is Filed

After the tenant has been served with the eviction notice and the eviction notice period has expired, the landlord's next step is to go to court and file formal legal papers beginning a lawsuit against the tenant for possession of the premises. The legal term for the eviction lawsuit is "unlawful detainer." You will often see this term used instead of the word "eviction" once the formal legal papers are filed.

If the total back rent due is more than $25,000, the landlord may bring the case in the Unlimited Jurisdiction of the Superior Court. If the amount of back rent sought is less than $25,000, the lawsuit may be brought in Limited Jurisdiction. In actual practice, most eviction lawsuits are filed in Limited Jurisdiction, which has streamlined, "express-line" procedures regulating eviction cases, which make it easy for the landlord to prosecute his eviction lawsuit.

Bypassing the Courts: Lodgers and Hotels

The only exceptions to the requirement that the landlord go through the court process to evict are for "lodgers," short-term residential hotel occupants, and occupants in true tourist hotels. A "lodger" is an occupant who lives in the same unit as the owner where the owner retains control of the entire unit, and does not rent to anyone else. The owner may evict a lodger without going to court. (CA Civil Code § 1946.5) A lodger can be evicted with a notice of the same period as the rental agreement. (For example, if the rental agreement is month-to-month, the eviction notice would be a 30-day notice even if the lodger has lived in the rental unit for more than 1 year.) § 1946.5 would not apply to rooming houses or apartments with multiple tenants, residential hotels, or tenants in separate in-law units.

In addition, a landlord may evict an occupant in a hotel without going to court if the occupant has lived there for no more than thirty days or who hasn't paid the full rent for the first thirty days. (CA Civil Code § 1940(b)(1) and Revenue and Taxation Code § 7280) This eviction without going to court only applies if the room is subject to the hotel tax. The landlord is not supposed to make a residential hotel occupant change rooms or check out temporarily in order to prevent the occupant from gaining rights as a tenant. (CA Civil Code § 1940.1) On day thirty-one, the landlord must go through the court process in order to do an eviction, although the Rent Ordinance doesn't kick in until day thirty-three. SF Administrative Code § 37.2(r)(1)) Due to the lack of rights in the first thirty days, it is in the best interest of the occupant to be on their best behavior as much as possible. Tourist hotel occupants may also be evicted without the court eviction process if the hotel owner retains control of the room and offers safe storage of personal belongings, central phone service, maid,

UNLAWFUL DETAINER PROCEDURES & TIME DIAGRAM

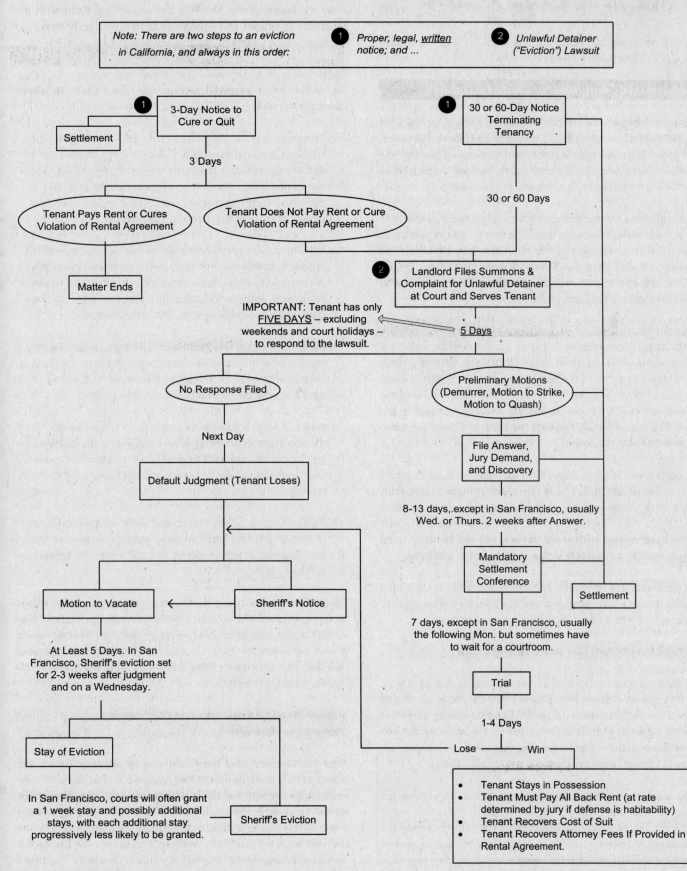

Note: There are two steps to an eviction in California, and always in this order:

1 Proper, legal, _written_ notice; and ...

2 Unlawful Detainer ("Eviction") Lawsuit

1 3-Day Notice to Cure or Quit

Settlement

3 Days

Tenant Pays Rent or Cures Violation of Rental Agreement

Tenant Does Not Pay Rent or Cure Violation of Rental Agreement

Matter Ends

1 30 or 60-Day Notice Terminating Tenancy

30 or 60 Days

2 Landlord Files Summons & Complaint for Unlawful Detainer at Court and Serves Tenant

IMPORTANT: Tenant has only <u>FIVE DAYS</u> – excluding weekends and court holidays – to respond to the lawsuit.

5 Days

No Response Filed

Next Day

Default Judgment (Tenant Loses)

Preliminary Motions (Demurrer, Motion to Strike, Motion to Quash)

File Answer, Jury Demand, and Discovery

8-13 days, except in San Francisco, usually Wed. or Thurs. 2 weeks after Answer.

Mandatory Settlement Conference

Settlement

Motion to Vacate

Sheriff's Notice

At Least 5 Days. In San Francisco, Sheriff's eviction set for 2-3 weeks after judgment and on a Wednesday.

7 days, except in San Francisco, usually the following Mon. but sometimes have to wait for a courtroom.

Trial

1-4 Days

Lose — Win

Stay of Eviction

In San Francisco, courts will often grant a 1 week stay and possibly additional stays, with each additional stay progressively less likely to be granted.

Sheriff's Eviction

- Tenant Stays in Possession
- Tenant Must Pay All Back Rent (at rate determined by jury if defense is habitability)
- Tenant Recovers Cost of Suit
- Tenant Recovers Attorney Fees If Provided in Rental Agreement.

mail, and room service, rental for less than one week, and food service. (CA Civil Code § 1940(b)(2))

Summons and Complaint for Unlawful Detainer

The landlord begins the eviction lawsuit by filing a formal legal document with the court called a Complaint for Unlawful Detainer. Upon this filing, the court issues a Summons to accompany the Complaint. These two legal documents are "wedded" to each other in that one is useless unless accompanied by the other.

The Complaint is the document that formally states the landlord's case: she has served you with notice, the notice has expired, and you are still in possession of the premises. (CA Code of Civil Procedure § 1166) If the San Francisco Rent Ordinance applies, the complaint also must state that the landlord has complied with the requirements of the Rent Ordinance.

The Summons is a separate piece of paper on top of the Complaint. (See the sample Summons in "Chapter 12: Eviction Defenses.") It is a formal notice to you from the court that you are being sued. It must state the name of the party suing you (the landlord), and the names of all persons being sued. It must also tell you how long you have to formally file papers with the court in response to the lawsuit. The tenant usually has only five days after being served to file a response with the court.

The courts provide a Summons form that landlords are required to use, and most landlords also use the court-provided Complaint forms as well. These forms contain blank spaces for the landlord to make his allegations against the particular tenant. **If your landlord serves you with these papers, you are being evicted and you need to act quickly if you want to keep your home!**

Some landlords and/or landlord attorneys prefer to use their own Complaint forms. They are permitted to do so. You will recognize it because it will be titled "Complaint" on the first page.

Notice of the Unlawful Detainer from the Court

The courts are supposed to send a notice to tenants who have been sued for unlawful detainer letting them know the phone number of the local Bar Association and Legal Aid and informing them that access to the court records are restricted for 60 days. (See the box "Credit Reports and Tenant Screening Agencies" in "Chapter 12: Eviction Defenses" for more info on court records access.)

If you receive a notice from the court but don't receive the Summons and Complaint from the landlord, it can be worth finding out what's going on, especially if you are concerned the landlord might have someone pretend to serve the Summons and Complaint without actually delivering it.

Serving the Summons and Complaint

After the landlord files the Summons and Complaint with the court, the Summons and Complaint must be properly served on the tenant. (CA Code of Civil Procedure §§ 415.10-415.95)

The tenant must be served in one of the following ways, however, the tenant must **respond within the time limit to allege improper service:**

1. Personal Service: Someone over 18 who is not the landlord or a relative (CA Code of Civil Procedure § 414.10) delivers the notice to the tenant in person. The server just has to say they're a process server and tell the defendant they're being served. Then they can leave the papers as close to the defendant as possible.

2. Substitute Service: Substituted service occurs only after repeated attempts to personally serve the papers have failed. A copy is left with a competent adult, other than the person being sued, at the residence or business of the person being sued, and a second copy is mailed to the residence.

3. Mail with Acknowledgement of Receipt of Summons: Service of a summons is complete on the date a written acknowledgement of receipt of summons is executed, if such acknowledgement is returned to the sender.

4. Nail and Mail: If repeated attempts to serve have failed *and* the court grants an order after a request by the landlord, service can be completed by posting a copy of the Summons and Complaint at the residence and mailing a copy to the tenant.

5. Publication: as a last resort, and only with permission of the court, the landlord may publish a copy of the complaint in a "newspaper of record" where the tenant's residence is located.

The landlord may not serve the tenant themselves. Someone who is "not a party to the action" must serve the tenant. The landlord may employ a professional process server or the sheriff's department to have the tenant served. The person serving the tenant also must complete, sign and date a form called a Proof of Service to verify that the tenant was served.

Responding to a Summons and Complaint: Beware the Time Limit!

After the landlord files the Complaint in Superior Court, the tenant usually *must* file a formal written response to the Summons and Complaint with the court **within five days after the day of service** to avoid being evicted by default! If the tenant does not properly respond in writing to the Summons and Complaint, the landlord wins automatically, without a trial. (See the discussion on default judgments in the "Eviction Timelines" section.)

Obtain assistance from the Eviction Defense Collaborative or other experienced agencies that provide free attorneys. (See the box in "Chapter 12: Eviction Defenses" "Right to an Attorney for Eviction Notices") You can also hire a private attorney. The San Francisco Tenants Union usually is not able to assist with an Unlawful Detainer but can provide a list of attorneys who only represent tenants.

As of September 1, 2019, you calculate the five day period starting the day after you are served with the Summons and Complaint excluding weekend days and court holidays. So, if you are served on a Sunday, Day One is Monday. Day Two is Tuesday, Day Three is Wednesday, Day Four is Thursday, and Day Five is Friday. Thus, your written response would have to be filed before the court clerk's office closes on Friday. If the fifth day falls on a day when the court is closed, either a weekend or court holiday, the response must be filed by the close of the next court business day. (CA Code of Civil Procedure § 1167)

The tenant may be able to gain additional time by filing a paper called "Ex Parte Request for Order Extending Time," in which the tenant explains, for example, that she is not an attorney and is in the process of seeking legal advice. Although extensions of time of up to 10 days are authorized by law (CA Code of Civil Procedure § 1167.5), the practice of the judges is to grant extensions of only 2-5 days.

Also, additional time is allowed if you are served by either "substitute service," "nail and mail," or "publication" (see the previous section "Serving the Summons and Complaint"). If the Summons and Complaint is not served personally, the tenant is supposed to get an additional ten days to respond. (Later on in the case, after the tenant has responded to the original complaint, service of a new complaint by mail only adds five days, not ten,) However, it is a good idea to respond within the five days, just in case the landlord claims that you were personally served.

Don't gamble with the service time! File within the five-day period or seek a court order to extend your filing time.

"Motions" and "Answers"

There are special rules for the requirements for legally acceptable court documents. The terms "Motion" and "Answer" are legal terms, which mean that they have a special meaning in law and must be presented in a manner acceptable to the court.

For the purposes of this discussion, "Motions" are legal documents a tenant may file challenging some portion of the landlord's Summons, Complaint, or service of the Summons and Complaint on procedural grounds. (See the "Motions" section that follows for more detail.)

The "Answer" refers to one specific legal document that lays out all the issues that the defendant wants to raise if the case should go to trial. The judge can prevent the tenant from raising a defense if it is not properly raised in the Answer. The Answer contains the tenant's response to the allegations in the landlord's "Complaint" as well as any other issues (called "affirmative defenses") that the tenant may wish to raise to show that she is entitled to remain in her home. It generally is filed after any applicable procedural motions are made. These legal documents are the front line of the tenant's defense to an eviction action. In defending an eviction action, the tenant is racing against the clock. By taking full advantage of legal rights, the tenant gains time, which is the most valuable commodity in an eviction.

If you find yourself faced with an eviction lawsuit (Unlawful Detainer), it is *strongly recommended* that you obtain qualified legal assistance immediately. The law at this level is technical and your defense must be organized and presented in the proper legal form.

Unlawful Detainer Procedural Defenses

This section outlines some of the legal procedures you can use in defending an Unlawful Detainer, but we recommend that you find good legal assistance before responding on your own.

"Motions" — Procedural Defenses

Because unlawful detainer is a "summary proceeding" (a priority case which moves much faster through the courts), a landlord has the added burden to comply strictly with all legal requirements. (CA Civil Code § 1442, *Briggs v. Electronic Memories & Magnetics Corp.* (1975) 53 Cal. App. 3d 900, 905) Thus, the Notice to Quit, whether 3-day or 60-day, and the Complaint must be properly written. In addition, the tenant must be properly "served" with the lawsuit. If the landlord makes a mistake, the court may throw out the case and the eviction returns to square one. The tenant, however, must bring the mistake to the attention of the court at the right time, or the case will proceed to trial.

There are three types of procedural responses available to a tenant being sued for eviction: the Motion to Quash, the Demurrer, and the Motion to Strike. We will discuss briefly what these are and when they may be used.

Motion to Quash

The law requires that a person being sued must be provided with correct notice of that fact, so that they may have a fair opportunity to respond. Otherwise, the case is not properly within the court's jurisdictional purview and cannot proceed through the court process.

The law therefore requires that the Summons and Complaint be served on the named respondents. As mentioned in the previous section "Serving the Summons and Complaint," there are three usual ways to serve a lawsuit: (1) personal service; (2)

substituted service; and (3) "nail and mail."

The most important reason for distinguishing what type of service was used is this: if a tenant is personally served she has only five days to file a response. If the other manners of service are used, the response period is 15 days.

A Motion to Quash is an option for the tenant who is not served legally by one of the methods allowed. For instance, the tenant returns home and discovers a copy of the Complaint lying on the floor inside the apartment and no copy is ever mailed to the tenant subsequently. Another example might be substituted service given to a minor, not an adult.

The tenant should file the appropriate papers **on or before the response due date**. A court hearing will be held within seven days, at which time the court may take testimony from the tenants and from the process server who allegedly served the papers. However, even if the tenant wins the Motion to Quash, it is more than likely that the tenant will be re-served immediately after the hearing, often right outside the courtroom. Still, this shows the landlord and the landlord's attorney that the tenant is serious about defending the eviction and will force them to follow the proper legal procedures. More importantly, the tenant has gained valuable time.

Demurrer

A Demurrer to a Complaint is a technical attack on the way that the landlord has couched the eviction lawsuit. (CA Code of Civil Procedure § 430.10) It has nothing to do with whether the landlord's allegations are true or false. A Demurrer only concerns the contents and quality of the Complaint itself and any documents attached to it, such as the Notice to Quit or rental agreement. The judge will not look at anything other than the papers filed with the court. A Demurrer can be brought for the following reasons:

(1) The Court in which the case was filed does not have jurisdiction to hear the case.

(2) The plaintiff (i.e., the landlord) does not have the legal right to sue, (e.g., he does not own the property or there is no claim that the plaintiff is an agent of the owner).

(3) The Complaint has not stated facts sufficient to qualify it as an unlawful detainer action (e.g., it does not allege a landlord-tenant relationship, or coverage by or exemption from local rent control law).

(4) The Complaint is uncertain or ambiguous, i.e., a reasonable person cannot clearly understand what the landlord is suing for. For example, the landlord neglects to check a necessary box on the Complaint form which

leaves a significant fact in doubt, such as the exact amount of rent alleged to be due.

(5) The landlord has failed to specify whether the rental agreement is oral or written.

If a tenant has a basis to file a Demurrer she must do so before filing an Answer. A hearing will be scheduled in 15 to 20 days after filing, depending on the tenant's method of service of the Demurrer on the landlord or the landlord's attorney. Sometimes, the landlord's Complaint may simply be written so poorly that the landlord will have to restart the entire process. More often, however, the court will allow the landlord to amend, or correct, the Complaint and then re-serve the amended copy on the tenant. Even if this should happen, however, it may be possible to demur again if the landlord makes another error.

Motion to Strike

Sometimes a Complaint may include allegations or request relief that goes beyond what the landlord is entitled to in an unlawful detainer action. In certain instances, a tenant may move to strike portions of the complaint, such as the landlord's request for attorney's fees when there is no provision for them in the rental agreement, or a request for punitive damages because the tenant is "maliciously holding over." (CA Code of Civil Procedure §§ 435 and 436) If the landlord is a suspended corporation, this may be used as a defense since suspended corporations may not bring a lawsuit against the tenant. Look up the entity that sued you on the California Secretary of State website. (See "Appendix A: Resources.") If their status is "Suspended" or "Forfeited" they cannot legally sue you.

If the tenant wants to file a Motion to Strike, it must be filed at the same time a Demurrer is filed. The timing of the hearing for a Motion to Strike is the same as that for a Demurrer.

Once a tenant has exhausted all procedural defenses or if none can be brought, the tenant will have to file an Answer to the Complaint.

Discovery

"Discovery" is the process in which either party in a lawsuit may obtain info from the opposing party and its agents prior to trial. The Discovery process is very formal. It includes interrogatories, written questions requesting certain documents in the other party's possession, and depositions, a question-and-answer examination of the opponent under oath. Info gained by properly following these methods can be used as evidence in court.

The Answer

The Answer is a document which directly responds to the landlord's allegations in the Complaint. If your case goes to trial, or is submitted for judgment, the arguments raised in your

Answer will form the basis of your defense. The tenant's Answer is filed after any applicable motions are made, or, if no procedural challenges are available, it is filed as the tenant's initial response to the Complaint.

The courts provide pre-printed "fill in the blank" Answer forms for tenants to use, entitled "Answer: Unlawful Detainer." It consists of a series of statements which have been used repeatedly by tenants in eviction lawsuits. At the end of each section is a box labeled "other," which can be filled out by the tenant if the form responses are not appropriate or complete. If the tenant has an attorney, the attorney may substitute an Answer she has written for the standard form.

The Answer form for eviction actions sets out the basic requirements for an effective response to the landlord's Complaint. Remember, the Complaint consists of a series of allegedly factual claims made by the landlord. If the court accepts each of the landlord's statements as true, then the landlord will have proved his case and you will be out on the street.

Legally, there is no such thing as "no comment" to a claim made in the landlord's Complaint. Any allegation that you do not *expressly* deny will be deemed admitted as if it were the undisputed truth. Therefore, the first function of the Answer is to deny *anything and everything* stated in the Complaint that you do not personally know to be the truth. This can be done in one of two ways. You may deny "generally" or "specifically." A general denial means that you deny *everything* the landlord claims in the Complaint. It may be used when the amount of rent demanded by the landlord does not exceed $1,000. If this applies to your situation, it is the safest way to respond to the Complaint. If the amount of rent due exceeds $1,000 you may not use the general denial paragraph on the form. Instead you must go through the landlord's Complaint paragraph by paragraph and state *specifically* whether you admit or deny each allegation. If you do *not* deny something in your landlord's Complaint, it legally amounts to agreeing with it. Make no assumptions, even logical ones. If you don't know from your own personal knowledge whether the landlord's statement is true, you may "deny on the basis of lack of information."

Affirmative Defenses

The second function of the Answer is to assert any additional defenses a tenant may have to the eviction beyond what the landlord said. The most commonly raised defenses also are listed on the standard Answer form. These are called "affirmative defenses" because the tenant cannot assert them by merely denying the landlord's statements. In addition, the tenant must present facts which show entitlement to retain possession of the premises because of the existence of these facts. A brief discussion

of some affirmative defenses that are commonly raised follows.

Breach of the Implied Warranty of Habitability

This defense may be raised only for eviction for nonpayment of rent. It is available where there are *substantial* (not merely cosmetic) defects in the premises which the landlord has been or should have been aware, and has failed to repair. (CA Code of Civil Procedure § 1174.2, Civil Code § 1942.3) See "Rent Strikes" in "Chapter 6: Repairs and Services" for a detailed discussion of the Implied Warranty of Habitability. In order to use physical evidence, (documents, photographs, etc.) at the trial, your witnesses must be able to "authenticate" the item. That means that the tenant or the witness must be able to testify, from first-hand info what the item is, where it came from and how it was obtained. A tenant may defend against an eviction against a current landlord for rent currently claimed owed despite the uninhabitable conditions first existing under a former landlord. (*Knight v. Hallsthammer* (1981) 29 Cal. 3d 46)

Retaliation

Your landlord is not legally permitted to bring an eviction action against you to retaliate for your exercise or assertion of any right available to you as a tenant, except retaliation cannot be raised as a defense to an Ellis Act eviction. (See "Fighting an Ellis Eviction" in "Chapter 12: Eviction Defenses.") Your landlord may not take *any* retaliatory action, including eviction, against you for 180 days after you assert any tenant right. (CA Civil Code § 1942.5) This does not mean that your landlord is free to retaliate against you on the 181st day. It just makes retaliation, which is usually very hard to prove, easier to prove within the 180 day period.

The defense of retaliation also exists as common law. Cases have held that a landlord may not evict a tenant as punishment for lawful action taken by a tenant. (*Barela v. Superior Court*, 30 Cal.3d 244 (1981), *Custom Parking, Inc. v. Superior Court (MacAnnan)* (1982) 138 Cal. App. 3d 90) For example, where a landlord brought an eviction action against a tenant who complained about the landlord's criminal activity, that tenant successfully raised the defense of retaliation. For rental units covered under the Rent Ordinance (SF Administrative Code § 37.9(a)(6)), the Rent Ordinance also prohibits retaliation. (SF Administrative Code § 37.9(d))

Discrimination

Your landlord is not allowed to bring an eviction action against you to discriminate against you because of your color, disability, ethnicity, national origin, gender identity, marital status, race, religion, or sexual orientation, except discrimination can only be raised as a defense to an Ellis Act eviction if the tenant challenges the landlord's "good faith" intention to take the units off the rental market and can prove there is bad faith. (See "Fighting an Ellis Eviction" in "Chapter 12: Eviction

Chapter 13– Eviction Process in Court

Defenses.") In addition, California law forbids discrimination based on any "arbitrary classification," such as lifestyle. (For more info, see "Chapter 9: Discrimination.")

Although your landlord may very well have discriminatory motives in attempting to evict you, these are usually very hard to prove. If you think you are being evicted for these reasons, you should start gathering evidence to support your position. An eviction which results from the landlord finding out something that she does not like about you, (such as that you suffer from AIDS or are a member of a different political party), is illegal if it is based on discriminatory motives. You may fight an eviction by asserting this defense if the eviction is not based on nonpayment of rent. Even where you have not paid your rent, if you believe that *one* reason, if not the major reason, for your eviction is discrimination you may raise this defense in addition to whatever defense you have for nonpayment of rent.

Waiver or Cancellation of Landlord's Notice

If your landlord serves you with a notice to leave, and later waives, changes or cancels that notice, then that waiver, change or cancellation operates as a defense to an eviction action based on that notice. (CA Code of Civil Procedure § 1161.5) The landlord must start over and serve the tenant with a new notice. Be sure to get written proof of the waiver.

Also, your landlord may not be able to evict you if he accepts rent from you after service of the notice for any period after the expiration date of the notice terminating the tenancy. In this situation, your landlord will probably need to serve you with a new eviction notice and begin again.

Landlord's Failure to Perform Obligations under the Rental Agreement

Usually, the landlord's failure to repair dilapidated premises (see the previous section "Breach of the Implied Warranty of Habitability") constitutes the gist of this defense. However, if the landlord fails to meet other obligations promised in the rental agreement (for example, a specific promise that the landlord will provide a garage space as part of the tenancy) the tenant may be justified in claiming the rent should be lower until the landlord fulfills his obligation as a defense to the eviction. (See the "Petitions for Lack of Services" section in "Chapter 6: Repairs and Services.")

Landlord's Refusal to Accept Rent

This is a defense only to an eviction based on alleged nonpayment of rent. If the tenant offers *all* rent due before a three-day notice to pay rent or quit is served, *or* within three days after service of such a notice, the landlord must accept the rent. However, the landlord need *not* accept less than the full amount of rent due.

Landlord's Failure to Credit Tenant for Costs of Necessary Repairs Properly Deducted from Rent

This defense is available only when the eviction is based on nonpayment of rent. If the tenant *properly* exercises the right to make necessary repairs and then deducts the cost of repairs from the rent pursuant to California Civil Code § 1942 (see "Chapter 6: Repairs and Services"), but the landlord refuses to credit the tenant for the repairs and attempts to evict the tenant for paying less than the full amount of rent due, then the tenant may use § 1942 rights as a defense to that eviction.

Landlord Is Evicting the Tenant Without "Just Cause" as Required under Law

If the rental unit is covered under the San Francisco Rent Ordinance or state law requiring just cause eviction, the landlord can only evict for one of the just causes. See "Protections for the Tenant Under the San Francisco Rent Ordinance and State Law" in "Chapter 4: Renting Basics" and "Chapter 12: Eviction Defenses."

Filing Fees

It will cost money to file both the Answer and any necessary motions with the Court. Since the costs vary, it's best to call the Court Clerk for the current fee schedule. Fee info can also be found at *https://sfsuperiorcourt.org/forms-filing/fees*.

If you are poor, the court may allow you to proceed without paying these filing fees. The clerk can give you a form for this. Prop F (2018) also provides some funding for depositions, etc. but if the tenant wins the award, the tenant will need to reimburse the fees.

Eviction Timelines

The most commonly asked question about an eviction is "how long does it take?" How long depends on many factors. For instance, is the landlord using an experienced attorney familiar with the eviction process or trying to do it on her own? Will the Complaint or Notice to Vacate be full of errors which can be objected to for procedural mistakes or must the tenant file an immediate Answer within five days of service? If the landlord obtains a judgment for possession how long will it be before the Sheriff performs the actual eviction? Does the tenant want to stay in the unit for the foreseeable future or is the tenant only looking for a little time to save rent and move on?

If a tenant does nothing in response to a Summons and Complaint for Unlawful Detainer, a Default Judgment may be entered as early as the sixth day following personal service on the tenant. The Sheriff, upon receiving the court writ of execution, may then post a notice on the tenant's door giving the tenant five days to

move. Thus, the worst case timeline for a tenant who fails to respond to the Summons and Complaint is that they would have to move ten days after service of the Summons and Complaint. (See the "Unlawful Detainer Procedures & Time Diagram" near the beginning of this chapter.)

If a tenant wages a minimal defense (i.e., filing an Answer but losing at trial) the minimum total time will jump to approximately 30 to 35 days. This is because trials must be set 20 days after the Answer is filed. If a tenant aggressively defends the eviction lawsuit, the tenant can expect the process to take 60 days or longer, sometimes months. An aggressive unlawful detainer defense may include various procedural motions, such as a Demurrer or Motion to Strike, as well as the Answer. An aggressive defense may also utilize a Discovery Process before the trial. Before deciding to put on such a defense, be aware that if the tenant prevails or if the case is dismissed (after a settlement, for example) within 60 days of the original filing, the court record is closed so that no new landlord or credit agency can see that the eviction was filed (although tenant screening agencies may still show the eviction was filed). For tenants concerned about finding a new place, this may be of some concern, but other tenants may decide that the additional time is worth the risk of having a UD suit publicly available. You can get an attorney for free. (See the box "Right to an Attorney for Eviction Notices" in "Chapter 12: Eviction Defenses.") A tenant may also want to review the rental agreement regarding attorney fees.

Remember that during the eviction fight, a settlement agreement between landlord and tenant may be reached at any time. A common example of a settlement is a formally agreed-upon move-out date, a waiver by the landlord of back rent due and sometimes some amount of cash paid to the tenant. An aggressive defense in which the tenant has asserted legitimate affirmative defenses will sometimes result in a landlord willing to pay cash out of pocket. Essentially, the landlord is faced with weighing the costs of prosecuting an eviction against the costs of paying the tenant to move out in a timely manner.

If you don't file a written Answer, the legal effect is identical to agreeing with every one of your landlord's allegations, including the request that you be thrown out of your home! In other words, the landlord simply wins, without even trying, by your default. As soon as your time to answer the landlord's complaint expires, (on the 6th day after you are served with the Summons and Complaint,) your landlord may simply go to the court and ask for the default Judgment. A court Judgment will then be entered against you which is called a clerk's Judgment. The landlord may ask the court for an additional hearing to discuss back rent and the court may find that you owe the landlord money, but the eviction will proceed immediately. The landlord is permitted to take the clerk's Judgment (also called Default Judgment) directly

to the Sheriff — who will arrive at your door within a few days to remove you. In San Francisco, the Sheriff currently evicts only on Wednesday in most cases, and if the landlord brings a Judgment to the Sheriff, the Sheriff will usually come one week from Wednesday of the following week. (See the "Landlord Wins" section near the end of this chapter.)

Obviously, if the landlord gets a Default Judgment against you, the time before you have to move is shortened considerably — in most cases by two or more weeks. Time is your most valuable asset when you are being evicted, because even if you eventually plan to move, you need time to find a new place, pack, move, etc. By filing an Answer or other appropriate motion in response to an eviction, you gain time — at least a couple of weeks and possibly more. Moreover, if you don't respond to the Summons and Complaint, you don't get to raise any defenses you might have to the eviction. Once you lose your home, you lose it forever.

In very rare circumstances, it is possible to get a Default Judgment set aside (rescinded) by the court. This is *not* common, so don't count on it. If you think a Default Judgment has been entered against you erroneously or unfairly, you should immediately seek legal assistance. Think very carefully before you decide to allow a Default Judgment to be entered against you.

Trial

Defending yourself against eviction in Court can be complicated. The courts require that you make your defense in writing (in legal form) as well as in person. You and/or your attorney can file any number of pre-trial "Motions." You might succeed in having the whole case thrown out of court before trial, or at the very least, gain some time to prepare your defense.

Once you finish with all the Motions and have filed the Answer, a date for the trial will be requested by the landlord and set by the court. You have a right to a trial by jury, but you must request one **at least 10 days** before the trial date, and it's usually better to request the jury at the same time the Answer is filed. (Code of Civil Procedure § 1171) You will have to pay for each day of the trial unless you are poor and the court grants your petition allowing you to proceed without paying jury fees. You probably have a better chance with a jury because it's likely that most of the jurors are tenants. Most of the judges are not! In addition, a jury trial is automatically preceded by a settlement conference in which the judge will talk with the parties and urge settlement of the case.

The trial itself is a formal proceeding. There are many rules regarding the presentation of evidence and the questioning of witnesses that you or your lawyer will have to follow. After you, your landlord, and your lawyers have presented all of your evidence and witnesses, the judge or jury will decide the outcome. Either you or your landlord may appeal the decision, but if you lose, you will probably not be allowed to stay in your home while the appeal process goes on. Any stay of eviction pending appeal is at the discretion of a judge and is usually not granted.

The decision reached by the judge or jury is called the Judgment. The Judgment will state whether or not you have to move, who owes money to whom, and how much is owed. The Judgment may also include back rent, filing fees, court costs, and sometimes attorneys' fees (awarded if provided for in the written rental agreement). If you have a very low income, your landlord may not be able to force you to pay any of the money the Judgment says you owe. If the Judgment says that you have to move and you don't move voluntarily, your landlord **must go to the Sheriff's Department** to have them evict you. The landlord cannot remove you or your possessions without the Sheriff.

Why Fight?

Fighting an eviction is obviously a time and energy consuming process. It requires a willingness to learn your rights under the law, to be diligent in keeping on top of the process, to file papers on time, etc. It may require some financial outlay and the ability to maintain determination through a trying time. There are plenty of good reasons for doing it, though, even if you plan to move in the near future anyway. To name a few:

(1) You might win—depending on your particular situation and the reasons for eviction. You'll get to stay and may be able to sue the landlord for damages at some point.

(2) Even if you decide to move out at before the trial, you are increasing the bargaining stakes. A settlement right before the trial might include a few months' free back rent plus moving costs, whereas if you move as soon as you get the eviction notice, you get nothing.

(3) If you simply default and the landlord obtains a judgment, this will appear on your credit record.

(4) Every time a tenant decides to fight for her home, it is another blow against a corrupt system which allows tenants to be victimized by landlords' lust for profits.

Whatever your reasons might be, the San Francisco Tenants Union encourages you to fight for your home. We will be glad to give you more info regarding your specific situation or to give you referrals to other organizations or services which can help you. (See "Appendix A: Resources.")

Negotiate or Fight to the End?—Decide What You Want to Do

You do not have to decide this right away, but at some point think about what you want. Some tenants find it impossible to move, knowing that they will face a severe rent increase or must sever ties to their home and neighborhood, which are so strong that they absolutely feel they cannot move. Others may not want to

move right away but can afford new rent, or are not particularly tied to their home or neighborhood, and simply would like adequate time to move and maybe some help with relocation costs. What you know about your landlord's honest intent can help you decide.

Whatever you decide, your best negotiating strength is to make the landlord think that you will fight to the bitter end, and fight until you get what you want. Your main negotiating strength lies in your ability to force the landlord into a lengthy and costly eviction process. When the landlord realizes that he will have to pay thousands of dollars to evict you and may not get you out for some months, your offers to move by a certain date if you get relocation help will begin to make sense to the landlord.

Time Is On Your Side

"Delay, delay, delay" can be a good strategy to increase your negotiating power and make your landlord think twice about evicting you, especially if the landlord is not acting in good faith and with honest intent. For example, you could initially let the landlord think that you are looking hard for a new place. Toward the end of the 60-day notice period, you could send a letter explaining that the rental market is very tight and that you simply cannot find a place by the end of the month. Ask for more time and try to keep the landlord from filing the unlawful detainer for as long as possible.

Once the eviction lawsuit is filed, a tenant may use the procedural defenses discussed previously to get more time. If the landlord is not acting in good faith, make the eviction as frustrating as possible for the landlord! Also, judgments reached after sixty days are only obtainable with a court order, so are unlikely to appear on credit reports.

Negotiating Evictions: Settlements and Other Alternatives

Now that you have an idea of what the eviction process is, you have your first negotiating tool for working things out with your landlord. As you can see, the eviction process is long and tedious and can cost both landlord and tenant a great deal of money. Most evictions settle before they get to court. **Do not sign any papers until you have had a tenants rights counselor or attorney review them!**

The best time to start dealing with an eviction is when the eviction notice first arrives. If you receive a three-day notice for nonpayment of rent, it is advisable to sit down with your landlord and work out some way to pay the rent. If you do work something out, get the agreement *in writing* and *signed by the landlord*.

If you receive a 60-day notice, you will first want to find out why

you are being evicted. If you cannot work out an agreement so that you can stay, you may still be able to work out an extension of time until you must move and/or money to help with moving expenses along with a waiver of any rent due.

Remember a few basic guidelines and factors in your negotiation:

- Before you negotiate seriously, get a good sense of what the rental market is like. Look at listings and the dwellings, etc. Do not accept time and/or money based on the last time you went looking for a home. Even if that was just a few years ago, you will find that the rental market has drastically changed. The San Francisco housing market continues to get more expensive and finding decent housing becomes more difficult every year.

- If you agree to move as of a certain date, consider whether you can really do it. Your signature will be binding.

- Realistically assess the amount of money being awarded to you. Maybe $5,000 sounds like a lot, but these days that usually won't even pay first and last month's rent plus deposit on a new place. How badly do you want to stay?

- Do not waive your rights to sue later unless the landlord substantially increase the offer of time and/or money to you and you are confident the waiver is worth the additional time and/or money. In a owner move-in, there is a good chance that she is not really moving in if your landlord is insistent on this right being waived.

- Prepare as well as possible and consider how strong your evidence is. The more the landlord thinks you might actually win the case, the more likely it is that a good settlement will be offered. The cost of going to trial (and paying a lawyer for all of the time in trial) can be sufficient motivation to get the landlord to want to settle. Are you willing and committed enough to put up a full-fledged fight? Do you have the evidence to make a strong case if you do fight?

- Consider putting public, social pressure on the landlord. Especially in cases where the landlord looks unreasonable while the tenant's situation would make others sympathetic, the landlord has a history of speculation or the type of eviction is one that is commonly abused, public pressure can be very powerful in changing the terms of the negotiation. (See "More Tactics" in "Chapter 14: Taking Action.")

- How large a property owner is your landlord? Is she a person you can negotiate with or is your landlord a heartless corporation with deep pockets?

- What is the stated reason for the eviction? Do you think it's the real reason?

- Can the conflicts the kind be resolved by negotiations?

- Is your landlord financially able to take you to court and go all the way through with trial? What is your financial status? Are you "judgment-proof" (i.e., would it be impossible for a landlord to collect any judgment against you because you're poor)?

Some landlords are impossible to negotiate with and your only alternatives may be to go to court or move. If this is the case, reread the chapters relevant to your case and get prepared. Also, seek advice to be sure you understand what is happening.

After the Trial?

Tenant Wins

If the eviction was for nonpayment of rent, a judgment for the tenant in an eviction lawsuit will usually be conditioned on the tenant paying an amount of back rent determined by the judge or jury.

Example: The tenant withholds rent for two months because the landlord has failed to provide habitable premises. The landlord brings an eviction suit for nonpayment of rent against the tenant, who claims as the defense breach of the Implied Warranty of Habitability. In court, the judge or jury finds that the tenant has proven that the landlord breached the Implied Warranty of Habitability. Upon that finding, the judge (or jury) will determine what the reduced rental value of the premises is — if the rent is $2,000 per month, the judge/jury may find that because of its condition the unit was only worth $1,500 per month. Thus, the Judgment issued by the court would state that the tenant is entitled to maintain possession of the premises *conditioned upon payment* of the reduced amount of back rent, in this case $1,500 for each month not paid. This example shows the importance of setting aside unpaid rent in an eviction action. In this type of eviction action you can win the case and still lose your home if you cannot pay the back rent ordered by the court. Even if you live in a place that is so badly dilapidated the landlord should be paying *you* to live there, don't count on the judge (or jury) seeing it your way. **Set aside the full amount of your rent each month.**

When the eviction action is based on another reason besides nonpayment of rent, judgment for the tenant means that the tenant is entitled to retain possession of his home. Payment of rent accrued while waiting for the court date may be ordered as well, so the warning to set aside your rent during an eviction lawsuit still applies.

Chapter 13–Eviction Process in Court

Landlord Wins

Relief from Forfeiture

For evictions based on nonpayment of rent or breach of the agreement, the tenant can ask the court for permission to stay in the rental unit on the condition that the tenant pays all of the back rent and stops any breach of the agreement. (CA Code of Civil Procedure §§ 1174 and 1179) This is called "Relief from Forfeiture" since the tenant is asking the judge to continue to have rights under the rental agreement rather than forfeiting the agreement. A tenant without a lawyer can make this motion orally in court so long as the landlord attorney is present or after giving at least 25 hours notice. This can be a useful fallback position for a tenant who has the back rent and is willing to pay it in order to stay. Although the statute does not mention it, sometimes judges will require the tenant to pay at least some of the landlord's attorney fees, even if the landlord can't get these fees in the underlying case. The statute doesn't even explicitly require that a Judgment be entered before the tenant requests Relief from Forfeiture (although that's how it is typically used), so you could try asking for Relief from Forfeiture even before the trial. That can be a good way to get the judge to see that you really want to stay and are able to pay, and make the landlord look less reasonable.

Sheriff Evicts

The landlord will get a paper called a Writ of Possession from the court after winning the trial. She must then take the Writ to the Sheriff. The Sheriff will then come to your home and post a Notice to Vacate. This Notice will say that you have five days to move. In reality, you probably have a few more days. At present, the San Francisco Sheriff evicts only one day a week (Wednesday). So you will have at least five days or, in San Francisco, typically twelve to nineteen days from the date of Judgment to move. You may try to dismiss the judgment by filing a Motion to Vacate with assistance from the Access Center (see the entry under "Government Agencies" in "Appendix A: Resources"). If you absolutely cannot move on the scheduled date, you can usually get one extra week, a Stay of Eviction, if you can pay a week's worth of rent to the court, but don't count on this. You need to go to court *first thing* Tuesday morning, the morning before the eviction is scheduled, *with the papers* to ask for the extra week. You also must call the landlord's attorney 25 hours before the hearing to inform the attorney that you will be asking for the extra week. If you want to ask for this one week stay, go to the Eviction Defense Collaborative the week *before* the eviction is scheduled so they may assist you.

On the last day of the eviction, the Sheriff's deputies will come to your home with the landlord. On *rare* occasions, the Sheriff will delay the eviction by one week, typically if there is a senior or disabled tenant in the unit and the landlord didn't tell the Sheriff about that. Also, if there is a tenant not named in the eviction lawsuit *and* if the landlord didn't properly serve a "Prejudgment Claim of Right to Possession" form at the beginning of the case (usually these are served with the Summons, CA Code of Civil Procedure § 415.46), then that person may be able to get a chance to fight the case in their own name, thus stopping the sheriff's eviction. (Minors need not be named.) Otherwise, the Sheriff will then evict you and your landlord will take possession of the premises and any personal belongings you haven't removed.

Your landlord must put all these personal belongings into storage for a period of 15 days and notify you of their whereabouts. You have the right to reclaim your things as long as you pay the landlord the "reasonable costs of storage" within this time period. The landlord can't hold your possessions back pending payment of the Judgment. After the 15 days, he can sell your possessions and deduct the amount he gets for them from the Judgment. If the value of your property is over $700, the property must be sold at a public sale; if the property is valued under $700, the property may be "kept, sold or destroyed without further notice." (CA Civil Code § 1984) For more info about getting your possessions back, see California Code of Civil Procedure § 1174 and Civil Code §§ 1980-1991.

Watch for Evidence of Wrongful Eviction

Watch or have your former neighbors and friends watch your old home! Did the landlord do what was stated in the notice? Did the landlord or relative move in within three months if required? Was the unit actually demolished if required? Did the landlord stop renting all apartments after an Ellis eviction? If the apartment gets re-rented, talk to an attorney right away. Don't wait! The time to sue lasts only one year. After the first year following the eviction, did the landlord or relative live there for three years for a owner move-in eviction?

A landlord who wrongfully evicts is liable for criminal and civil penalties. You can sue for wrongful eviction and win substantial awards. (A case from southern California may limit wrongful eviction suits. Talk with an attorney or an experienced Tenants Union counselor to find out more.) City agencies will not police the landlords, though, so it will be up to you to monitor your landlord's compliance with the requirements.

Most landlords are likely to go through the motions of pretending to live there if required for the eviction. They will gamble that the evicted tenant will eventually stop watching the place and then re-rent it. Other times, the landlord will commence major remodeling of the apartment or building, which may go on for many months.

An attorney may take a solid wrongful eviction case on contingency, which means that the fee is deducted from the amount you collect. You do not have to pay up front and the attorney can help you find additional evidence to show that the landlord did not evict with honest intent.

Chapter 14: *Taking Action*

I t is good to know the law, but it's also important to remember that regardless of whether or not the law is on your side, there's always something you can do to defend your home. Attorneys, the courts, and city agencies often have other interests besides looking out for tenants, so don't rely solely on what experts say.

This chapter is about taking action for yourself and other tenants. Also, see "Chapter 3: Researching Landlords, Buildings and Laws" for more info on taking action.

Individual Action

Taking individual action is about you dealing directly with the landlord, possibly through the Rent Board or an attorney.

Read This Book

For more than 50 years, many tenant activists have poured countless hours of time and care into successive editions of this handbook. What you have in your hands is not just a description of state and local law as it applies to tenants, but also a distillation of decades of experience and struggles for the right to decent housing. Please read it and share your knowledge with other tenants!

Write Letters

When you have a problem, a phone call to your landlord may seem like a quick and easy way to deal with it. But even if you feel everything has been sorted out by the time you hang up the phone, you should always follow up a conversation with a letter restating the key points of your complaint and any agreements reached between you and your landlord. If talking with your landlord is impossible, a letter may be the only way to communicate.

A letter serves a number of purposes: to clarify with your landlord what was agreed upon; to ensure that in the future, recollections of the facts do not change; and to provide evidence of any events or agreements that a judge or jury might think is important later on. Documenting all of the facts that support your position is more important than citing the law in your letter.

Generally, it is not necessary to mail your letter "certified." (An exception would be if you were to give a termination of tenancy notice to your landlord since the law requires those notices to be certified or registered.) However, it is a good idea to document that a letter was sent to the landlord on a certain date. A cheaper option than certified mail is by "certificate of mailing," where the postal clerk gives you a postmarked receipt that says on x date you mailed something to your landlord's address. You can also send the letter with delivery confirmation, which also does not require a signature. Since neither certificate of mailing or delivery confirmation requires a signature, your landlord cannot claim he did not receive the letter since he never picked it up from the post office, unlike certified mail. It is then reasonable to assume that your landlord did receive the letter. If your landlord does sign for mail, then a letter with a return receipt request would be solid proof the landlord received the letter.

In your letter, *always*:

- Type your letter, if possible. If you have to write in longhand, be neat.

- Establish your good faith, reasonableness, and willingness to work things out.

- Make your point. Don't ramble or get off on tangents. Keep it simple and stick to the facts.

- Avoid "legalese." Use your own words.

- Show that you are willing to cooperate with the landlord.

- Date and sign your letters.

- Make at least one copy of everything you send and file it in a safe place.

Never:

- Use threatening or hostile language in your letters.

- Say something that you may regret later or which could come back to haunt you in court or at the Rent Board. ("I admit that I was a little late with the rent.")

Throughout this book there are examples of letters that you can use as templates for your own letter, depending on your situation.

Email is, probably, considered a less reliable delivery of a letter. Plus, if there is a legal requirement that the notice be written, email may not qualify as writing. Still, email would be a better record of communication than a verbal exchange.

Alternative Dispute Resolution

For both rent-controlled and non-rent-controlled units, the Rent Board has a program, the Alternative Dispute Resolution (ADR), to help tenants, landlords, roommates and neighbors resolve disagreements that may not be relevant to a petition or a lawsuit. Very often, disputes that the parties can't work out between themselves can be successfully resolved with a Rent Board Administrative Law Judge who is an attorney trained in mediation, and acting both as a neutral third party and as a guide.

A tenant may file a Request for Alternative Dispute Resolution (ADR) Session form at the Rent Board. A Rent Board mediator will contact all parties to see if they are willing to attend a mediation session. **The Rent Board will NOT, under any circumstances, mediate move-out agreements**.

ADR sessions are not Rent Board hearings, and they are not taped or otherwise recorded. At the ADR the parties may decide to write a document that summarized their agreement, or they may decide a written agreement is not necessary. It's up to them. An ADR session will not be scheduled unless all involved parties agree to meet, but the Rent Board mediators are skilled in persuading adversaries to come together to solve their problems, so you only lose some time if the ADR session is not successful. ADR is especially effective for noise and nuisance. Also, there is no charge for an ADR session. As of 2020, it can take 8 weeks for a session.

Finally, even if the mediation does not succeed in resolving the issues, you will know that you have tried in good faith to solve the problem, and can point out your attempt to mediate if the dispute recurs. Even if you don't think the other person would be willing to mediate, they might be thinking the same about you.

Petition the Rent Board

A tenant covered under the Rent Ordinance (see the section "What Does the Rent Ordinance Cover?" in "Chapter 4: Renting Basics") may file a free petition for the following reasons: to defer a rent increase due to the landlord's failure to repair and maintain; to request a rent decrease due to a substantial decrease in services; to contest a past or current rent increase that a tenant believes is unlawful; to request a rent decrease due to rent gouging by a master tenant; or to report an alleged wrongful eviction. A tenant may also protest landlord petitions such as capital improvement or operating and maintenance passthroughs. An attorney may be provided under Proposition F (2018) for large rent increases such as for subsequent occupants, Rent Board Rules and Regulations § 1.21, or loss of another unit creating a single residential unit.

There are a number of strategies for dealing with bad physical conditions, however, the Rent Board is often a good place to start but be aware that although a hearing is supposed to be scheduled for the tenant to present her case within 45 days of the date of filing the petition (SF Rent Board Rules and Regulations § 11.10), it may take months. (As of 4/19, it took 6-8 weeks for a hearing on large Costa-Hawkins rent increases and 6-8 more weeks for a decision, but mediation was within 1-2 months for a decrease in housing services. It took a year for a landlord operating and maintenance rent increase hearing.)

Petition forms are available at the Rent Board as well as online, and there is no fee for filing a petition, so it is usually much cheaper and easier than going to court. A petition can be filed with the Rent Board even though the tenant no longer resides in the rental unit. The favorable ruling can be then be used as

---

Bureaucracies

Whether it's the Department of Building Inspection, PG&E, the Rent Board, the police department, or any other large agency, we've all been through the routine: the endless waits on hold, rude and/or ignorant workers whose only answer seems to be "no."

Believe it or not, bureaucrats are also people, many of whom are willing and may even want to help you, if you give them a reasonable chance to do so. Here are some tips for dealing with bureaucracies and actually getting results.

- **Think in advance and write down the questions you want to ask** and what you want the employee to help you accomplish. Don't just ask vague questions like "What do I do now?" Get to the point quickly and stick to the subject of your inquiry. After all, you don't want the worker to beat around the bush, so why should you?

- **Be friendly and personable,** as opposed to impatient and rude. You'll be much more successful if you are able to get the person on your side so that she wants to work with you. Be patient, pleasant, and treat the worker with respect.

- **Take notes.** These should include the names and telephone numbers of the people you're speaking with, the date and time, and what the person says. This info can be very useful to you later.

- Always **give your name** and ask the person if you can get back to her directly if you have further questions later. You should explain that she is already familiar with your issues and you don't want to reinvent the wheel by starting all over again with another person.

- **Act confident**, and convey by your manner that you *know* the person will help you solve your problem. Don't take "no" for an answer. If the person you're speaking to either won't or can't help, ask them for suggestions to other agencies or organizations who can, and if there is a particular individual to ask for.

- If the person you're dealing with is genuinely rude, ignorant or truly out of her depth, **get the name of her supervisor, and contact the supervisor.** If the person actually hangs up on you or refuses to provide this info, call the main telephone number back again; hopefully you'll get a different person who *will* help you, or at least will point you in the right direction.

evidence in Small Claims Court where the judges are probably not as familiar with the Rent Ordinance. Sometimes, however, the tenant is awarded a substantially larger amount in court and a negative or insufficient ruling at the Rent Board will negatively affect the court ruling. Although retaliation against a tenant who seeks a rent reduction or asserts other rights is against the law, you might need to remind your landlord of this fact. (See the box "Retaliation Is Illegal" in "Chapter 6: Repairs and Services.") Also, the Rent Board will inform your landlord about any allowable banked rent increases that have not been given to you.

When filing a petition for a reduction of rent (Decrease in Housing Services Petition or Failure to Repair and Maintain Petition), remember that the Rent Board is only looking at whether or not the rent should be reduced. Tenants asking for money have the burden of proving that they are actually owed this money. It is essential that the tenant show three things:

(1) That the problem(s) exist.

(2) That the landlord is aware of the problem(s).

(3) That the problem(s) are substantial and significant, i.e., worth a decrease in rent.

It's generally better to not include additional supporting evidence in a petition to the Rent Board as an attachment that is referred to in the petition as "see attached," since that info will be given to the landlord before the hearing, and may allow the landlord to construct a defense. If there is no reference to "see attached" that info will not be given to the landlord but still allows the Rent Board staff to understand the case. All documents submitted for the petition will become part of the public record, however. Limited masking of info due to medical reasons may be permitted, but the opposing party may still need access. Supplements to the petition may be added up to around 10 days after filing. Amendments to the petition can also be added later, even after the hearing if the record has not been closed, by filing a Notice from Petitioner of Amended Petition and providing copies of the evidence for the landlord with proof of service as well as for the judge. You do need to amend the petition at least 10 days before the hearing if it affects the knowledge of the opposing party. Videos may be shown at the Rent Board if the judge allows it and if you provide the display device such as a laptop, but evidence must be submitted on paper. Other languages need to be translated into English. If multiple units are having the same problem, mail the petitions together to be heard together.

Previous rulings on similar cases may be looked up in the Rent Board's office and will give the tenant an idea of how the case will be ruled. See the section "Rent Board" in "Chapter 3: Researching Landlords, Buildings and Laws" for info on how to look up cases.

The filled out petitions may be mailed or faxed to the Rent Board, but it is recommended that you seek counseling from the Rent Board and/or the SF Tenants Union about filling the petitions out properly. The Rent Board gives advice on the logistics of filling out the petition. For strategy, it is better to seek counseling from the Tenants Union. If you give the Rent Board your phone number, they will try to call you if you are late up to 20 minutes to the mediation or arbitration session.

For more info on petitions for requesting a rent decrease or deferring a rent increase due to lack of services, see the "Petitions for Lack of Services" section in "Chapter 6: Repairs and Services." The sections "Summary Petition for Unlawful Rent Increases" and "Unlawful Rent Increase Petition" in "Chapter 7: Rent Increases" have more info on contesting rent increases. The Rent Increases chapter also has suggestions on contesting capital improvement and operating and maintenance passthroughs in the "Capital Improvements" and "Operating and Maintenance Expense Increase Passthroughs" sections. See the listing for the Rent Board under "Government Agencies: San Francisco" for more info for the Rent Board in "Appendix A: Resources." See "Chapter 6: Repairs and Services" and the "Sue Your Landlord" section later in this chapter for other types of strategies.

Mediation Before Arbitration at the Rent Board

Only Decrease in Housing Services and Failure to Repair and Maintain petitions may be mediated by the Rent Board before going to arbitration. (This is different from the Alternative Dispute Resolution which can be used for any type of disagreements between the tenant and landlord.) Landlord petitions for Capital Improvement or Operating and Maintenance passthroughs and tenant petitions for illegal rent increases cannot be mediated, and the Rent Board will *not* mediate "move-out agreements" or waiver of rent. The Rent Board can, however, mediate the value of a service.

The Rent Board will first schedule a mediation session in which the parties attempt to resolve their disputes with a mediator's assistance. The tenant or landlord may cancel the mediation. The role of the mediator, who is an Administrative Law Judge trained in mediation techniques, is to get all of the parties' disputes on the table, not necessarily just those in the tenants' petition—for example, eviction issues may be discussed and resolved even in Decrease in Housing Services mediations. The mediator then attempts to guide discussion of the issues in an open and productive fashion, and to help the parties resolve their differences and arrive at mutually beneficial understandings and solutions. In the course of the mediation session, the mediator often holds meetings with each party privately to discuss and clarify the issues. The mediation is not recorded to reduce the ability to hold what was discussed against the tenant in a possible future hearing. (The tenant can object as hearsay if the landlord claims to quote from what the tenant said during the mediation.)

The parties' final agreement is put in writing and signed by the mediator as well as all the parties. The mediation agreement itself should be designed to be self-enforcing. (For example, "if the windows are not repaired within 30 days, then the rent is reduced by $25 per month until they are repaired.") Since the mediation agreements are actually contracts, they cannot be appealed to the Rent Board, the Rent Board Commissioners or a court, but are enforceable in court. Unlike arbitrations, which can only result in a rent reduction for lack of housing services, mediations can lead to services being restored and repairs getting made. Also, unlike arbitrations, the mediation process is confidential—no taped record of the mediation session is made, and the parties can even agree that the final mediation agreement itself is to be confidential.

Mediation often offers a more productive alternative to the more traditional solution of disputes being ruled upon by an uninvolved third party, like an arbitrator or a judge. There is also no waiting for a decision as there is with an arbitration (typically several months); the parties can have an agreement when they leave the Rent Board, and they often have begun speaking to each other again, too. When successful, mediation offers many benefits, including facilitating communication between the parties, reaching a compromise they can live with, reducing the time of the overall process, and eliminating or limiting legal costs. A well-crafted mediation agreement, reached by the parties themselves, may send both landlord and tenant home satisfied and less likely to hold a grudge against one another. The majority of those opting for Rent Board mediation have apparently been satisfied with the process, and some ALJs have reported that tenants, in fact, often come out much better (including financially) with mediation than they would have had they chosen arbitration.

A well-designed mediation agreement may produce a settlement in which the landlord agrees both to a rent rebate for decreased services and to make repairs or restore the service, on pain of future rent reductions if she doesn't hold up their end of the bargain. Remember that mediation agreements represent the final resolution of the issues, are legally binding on both parties and, as contracts. Therefore, tenants should (1) come to the mediation prepared to clearly articulate their issues; (2) know what resolutions they want and how enforcement of these solutions should be expressed in the mediation contract itself; (3) be ready for and flexible in the give-and-take of negotiation, but have a firm "bottom line"; and (4) be fully prepared to arbitrate if the other party doesn't show up, or refuses to mediate.

The parties are given at least a 10-day advance notice of the mediation, usually more, and since Rent Board mediation is strictly voluntary, either party may choose to arbitrate instead if they wish. If, after mediation, the parties fail to reach an agreement, the Rent Board will then reschedule the case for an arbitration.

If the landlord, without "good cause," does not appear, an arbitration will be held immediately, so it is important for tenants to be prepared for this possibility; but if the tenant-petitioner fails to appear without "good cause," the tenant's petition will be dismissed "with prejudice," meaning it will be extremely difficult to get a new hearing on these issues. (SF Rent Board Rules and Regulations § 11.14) Examples of "good cause" include the illness of a party or representative, verified travel outside San Francisco scheduled before receipt of notice of the mediation session, or any other "unforeseen circumstances or verified prearranged plans which cannot be changed" that would make it impractical to appear on the scheduled date. "Mere inconvenience or difficulty in appearing shall not constitute 'good cause'..." Requests for postponement of a hearing must be made in writing at the earliest date possible, with supporting documentation attached. The person requesting a postponement should notify the other parties of the request and provide them with any supporting documentation. (SF Rent Board Rules and Regulations § 11.13) The Rent Board will quickly rule on the postponement request, notify all parties as to its decision and, if granted, reschedule the mediation or arbitration session.

If the landlord has a long track record of broken promises, or has been indifferent or unreachable when the tenant has made requests in the past, tenants should be wary of the landlord's broken record playing the same tune at a mediation. One suggestion is to try mediation anyway, but with the following strategy: (1) inform the mediator of the landlord's past history, either during the session while the landlord is present or during the private meeting between only the mediator and the tenant; (2) insist that the mediation agreement be extremely detailed and specific in its self-enforcement provisions (for example, "the repairs must meet the standards of the S.F. Housing Code, as verified by a Building Inspector," instead of "the landlord will fix the windows"); and (3) if the landlord will not agree to a strong mediation agreement, make it clear to the landlord and the mediator that under these circumstances you're ready, willing and fully prepared to arbitrate instead of signing off on vague, unenforceable promises with a landlord who has broken his word in the past. The mediator "shall not allow any tenant to waive his/her rights regarding the lawful base rent" (SF Rent Board Rules and Regulations § 11.15)

The Hearing Process

After a petition is filed, copies are sent to the other parties by the Rent Board by mail. If the tenant did not receive the notice of the petition, the tenant can appeal. Call the Rent Board 7-10 days after filing the appeal and give the address or case number. The case number is better since the address may have multiple cases.

As of April 2017, it typically takes 6-8 weeks to schedule the hearing and then 10-30 days after the scheduling for the actual hearing except non-urgent tenant petitions can take 3-4 months to schedule. Landlord petitions for Capital Improvement Passthroughs can take 6 months to schedule a hearing, and Operating and Maintenance Passthrough Petitions take a year. The decision is issued 6-8 weeks after the hearing. The Rent Board

staff member who screens the case can tell you an estimate of the timeframe. (See also the section later in this chapter "Expedited Hearing Process" for a faster process.) All parties will be given at least a ten-day notice of the date and time of the hearing and an estimate of the length of the hearing (usually 2-4 hours). Hearings are held at the Rent Board's office during business hours.

At any time before the hearing, a settlement may be reached. If this happens, it's advisable to put the terms of the settlement in writing and to notify the Rent Board. You must file a Withdrawal of Petition form with the Rent Board if you wish to withdraw your petition. If you simply don't show up for the hearing without notifying the Rent Board, your petition will be dismissed and you may not be able to re-file. You may have to appeal the dismissal and show good cause as to why you did not appear (not bothering to notify the Rent Board is *not* good cause). If you or a representative cannot attend the scheduled hearing due to unforeseen circumstances or prearranged plans which cannot be changed, you may request a postponement (continuance). Requests must be made in writing at the earliest possible date, with appropriate documentation verifying your inability to appear. Fill out a "Request for Postponement of Hearing" form at the Rent Board or mail or fax a letter with your documentation. If an emergency arises which precludes a written request, call the hearing coordinator at the Rent Board as soon as possible and the ALJ may grant a postponement "*...only for good cause and in the interest of justice...Mere inconvenience or difficulty in appearing shall not constitute 'good cause.'*" (SF Rent Board Rules and Regulations § 11.13) Before the hearing time, you should be notified of the determination on the postponement request (yes or no) either by telephone or by mail.

You may participate by phone or give a representative the "right to settlement" in writing according to Rules and Regulations § 11.22. However, Form 523 for Tenant Petition Based on Decreased Housing Services for Multiple Units in the Same Building states that the petition may be denied if the tenant does not personally appear for the arbitration even if the tenant has an authorized representative. So, ask the Rent Board about the process for participation by phone if you are unable to appear in person. You are required to provide your own interpreter, unless you are unable to afford an interpreter. The Rent Board will hire an interpreter upon proof of financial hardship. Hardship applications for interpreter services can be obtained at the Rent Board's office and must be filed at least 72 hours before the hearing or mediation.

An Administrative Law Judge, "ALJ," presides over the hearing and issues the decision on the petition. At the hearing, both tenant and landlord may present oral testimony and written documentation (including bills, canceled checks, photographs, and sworn statements or affidavits) to support their positions. Videos may be shown at the Rent Board if you provide the display device. The parties may cross-examine each other and any witnesses. Telephone testimony at hearings may also be permitted if arranged in advance with the Rent Board. The parties may be represented by an attorney or other (non-attorney) representative that was designated in writing (SF Rent Board Rules and Regulations § 11.22), if they wish, **but there is no necessity or requirement for an attorney.** Each rental unit is a separate petition except if the decrease in housing services involve multiple tenants in the building, see the section "'Preparation for "Decrease in Housing Services' and 'Failure to Repair and Maintain'" in "Chapter 6: Repairs and Services" for more info. (The Tenants Union does not represent tenants before the Rent Board, but does have info on attorneys who will provide such representation.)

The ALJ (who is an attorney) may try to bring the two sides to a compromise agreement called "mediation" before entering into a formal arbitration process. (See the previous "Mediation Before Arbitration at the Rent Board" section.) If an agreement cannot be reached at this point, a hearing—*not a trial*—will be scheduled either that day or at a later date. Some ALJs may be more relaxed, allowing people to talk it all out; others may be rather formal, directing the hearing in a straight-line approach. If one party believes it needs additional time to review the other person's documents or to gather other evidence to support its arguments, the ALJ will usually "keep the record open" if explicitly requested to do so. All arbitrations are tape-recorded.

Upon the completion of the hearing or close of the record, the ALJ prepares a written decision. The decision is reviewed by a senior ALJ for consistency. This decision will be mailed to all parties. If the landlord is granted a rent increase and if proper notice was given at least 30 days before (or 90 days if the increase is over 10 percent), the tenant is obligated to pay the increase within 15 days. If either party files an appeal, the decision issued by the ALJ remains in effect during the appeal process, except for that portion of the decision which permits payment, refund, offsetting, or adding of rent. (SF Administrative Code § 37.8(f)(8)) For example, if the ALJ finds that a tenant has overpaid rent and is due a refund, the landlord doesn't have to pay you until the appeal is decided. However, if your base rent has been reduced, this is effective immediately. Violation of the decision of the ALJ is a misdemeanor. (SF Administrative Code § 37.10A)

See the following section "Preparing for a Hearing" for more info.

Expedited Hearing Process

In certain circumstances, the Rent Board can speed up the hearing process. For dramatic rent increases or habitability problems, the Rent Board may choose to expedite the case. Write "Please Expedite" on the petition to flag these cases but it will usually still take 6-8 weeks for the hearing as of April 2019. Formal "expedited hearings" are available only when both the tenant and landlord agree to an expedited hearing and they are available only for some of the petitions which can be filed.

The benefit of this process is that the hearing will be held within 21 days of the filing of the petition (instead of 45 days for a regular hearing). Also, the ALJ will make a decision in 10 days (as opposed to 30). The drawback is that there is no appeal allowed of the ALJ's decision to either the full Rent Board or to the courts. But if either the landlord or tenant does not like the ALJ's decision, then they have 15 days after the decision is issued to file a written objection. This objection will cause the expedited hearing decision to be dissolved and the party objecting could file a new petition to hear the case via the regular hearing process. (SF Rent Board Rules and Regulations § 11.25)

Thus, these expedited hearings are probably best for cases where the issues and facts are clear. Only certain cases are eligible for the expedited hearing process. These cases are:

- **Capital Improvement Petitions for No More Than 10% of the Rent or $30 Per Month** — Landlord petitions for capital improvements where the tenant's base rent would increase by no more than either 10% or $30 per month.

- **Decrease in Service Petitions for $1,000 or less** — Tenant petitions for a rent reduction due to the loss of housing services of $1,000 or less.

- **Failure to Repair and Maintain Petitions** — Tenant petitions to postpone a rent increase, except for capital improvement, utility or bond measure passthroughs, until the requested repairs are made.

- **Unlawful Rent Increase Petitions of $1,000 or less** — Tenant petitions for rent overpayments of $1,000 or less as of the filing date of the petition.

- **Petitions Where Rent Board Jurisdiction Is the Only Issue** — This is typically a case where the landlord claims the building is exempt from rent control and the tenant claims otherwise (for example., a dispute over the date of issuance of the certificate of occupancy).

The length of the regular hearing process can be frustrating, and in some cases tenants may want to get it over with. But in any type of complicated case where it may take you time and effort to collect all your facts and testimony, having a shorter hearing process may work against you. There is also some danger since these decisions are not appealable. While you have 15 days after the decision to object and start all over, if some reason you do not file this objection within 15 days, your case is over and you have lost your ability to pursue it further.

If you file a petition and you have documented facts in hand (e.g., a letter which clearly indicates a wrongful rent increase), then you may want to take advantage of this process. But if you think the facts are disputable or are not clearly documented, you may not want to use this process. You should be especially cautious with any complicated petition (and may want to say "no" to any capital improvement petition). You and the landlord both must agree to this process; do not use it unless you know it will be to your advantage.

Preparing for a Hearing

In effect, every hearing before the Rent Board is an unlawful rent increase hearing. The tenant's rent history is examined at every hearing in which the base rent (rent charged a tenant upon initial occupancy plus allowable annual rent increases that was added) is at issue. Since every hearing involves some potential adjustment to the tenant's base rent, the tenant must be prepared to prove their rent history back to April 1982 (May of 1994 for Proposition I units), or the date they first occupied the unit. This means you should bring the following to every hearing and make two copies (one for the judge and one for the opposing side):

- Notices of rent increase.

- Rent checks or receipts for at least the month before and after each rent increase went into effect.

- Any correspondence with the landlord about your rent.

You don't need to calculate how much you think your rent should be or how much the landlord owes you. The formulas used by the Rent Board to determine rent overpayments are complicated. If you provide all the info to the judge, she will apply the formulas and make the decision.

If you are bringing a petition for an unlawful rent increase that happened years ago, be prepared to explain why you waited to file your petition, for example, you were afraid the landlord would retaliate, you didn't know about rent control, you didn't know the increase was illegal, etc. While the rent will be rolled back to its correct amount no matter how long ago the illegal increase happened, be aware that the Rent Board judge may order refunds of rent overpayments for no more than three years preceding the filing of the petition, plus the period between the month of filing and the date of the Rent Board judge's decision. (SF Administrative Code § 37.8 (e)(7))

Summary of steps for hearing preparation:

- Prepare a **written chronology** of your rent history with all supporting documents. This applies to all hearings.

- Prepare a **written summary** of key points to present.

- Prepare a **list of all documentation** you will present at the hearing. Label each document. Make at least two copies of each document (besides your own), one for the Administrative Law Judge (ALJ) and one for the landlord.

- *Don't* wait until the hearing to **organize your documents**. You waste a lot of time, hurt your credibility and risk not presenting your case effectively. You also don't earn brownie points from the ALJ.

- Make a **list of questions** you may want to ask the landlord at the hearing. (This list is not submitted to the ALJ.)

- Make a list for yourself of possible defenses the landlord will raise to what you say and be prepared with responses. This lessens your chances of being surprised at the hearing and will boost your confidence when you have a response.

- If you are requesting reports from government agencies, call them in advance to remind them to act on your (prior) written request. Ask for materials well before the hearing date.

- If the hearing will involve several tenants, call a meeting to make sure all tenants have their cases prepared. Jointly **plan each tenant's testimony** (short and to the point on key issues). You might want to **do a mock hearing** so that everyone feels comfortable with what they will be saying.

- Have your witnesses attend the hearing in person if possible. The Rent Board gives very little weight to letters or documents from witnesses who are not present at the hearing. Any letter from a witness should be sworn under penalty of perjury. If your witnesses are unable to attend, ask them if they are willing to testify by telephone and, if they are, inform the Rent Board as soon as possible before the hearing so they can make appropriate arrangements.

- Call your witnesses together a few days before the hearing to go over their testimony with them.

- If you want a recording of the hearing, you may get a copy of the official Rent Board tape within a couple of years of the hearing. (SF Rent Board Rules and Regulations § 11.20) The cost is $1 per CD.

- **Get advice** from the Rent Board or a counseling agency such as the Tenants Union (or attorney) before the hearing to make sure you are prepared. Practice your presentation. This will help you find any gaps in your evidence and help your confidence.

Presenting Your Case at the Hearing

- Arrive early to review your file and go over details with other tenants and witnesses. Confirm your hearing room, introduce yourself and your group to the Administrative Law Judge (ALJ), follow any special instructions, fill out appearance forms, etc. Phone and video instead of in person appearance is allowed but weak.

- Present your written material for each point. **Keep your verbal testimony short and to the point of each issue.** Respond clearly to any questions from the ALJ. Videos may be shown at the Rent Board if you provide the display device.

- **Don't alienate the ALJ!**

- **Don't yell at the landlord.** Ask the landlord questions to clarify points or get info. (Your written documentation, supported by clear presentation, should provide all the info needed to bring out weaknesses and inconsistencies in the landlord's case.)

- If the landlord provides new documentation at the hearing that you haven't had time to review, or if your documentation is incomplete, ask the ALJ to keep the case open. They will usually do so for at least five days, or longer if you can show a good reason. Keeping the case open must be requested.

- If the landlord presents hearsay evidence (in which someone testifies about facts they don't personally know but found out from others), you can object. If you object, the ALJ has to determine whether "based on all the circumstances, it is sufficiently reliable and trustworthy," before admitting it into evidence but if you don't object the ALJ may simply permit the hearsay to be admitted as evidence. (SF Rent Board Rules and Regulations § 11.17(c))

- Remember that a Rent Board hearing is not like a formal court trial. You don't need to act like a lawyer, nor should you be intimidated if the landlord has a lawyer. The Rent Board process should operate so that tenants with a little key knowledge of the law, and a lot of preparation, can be their own most effective advocates.

Conduct of Arbitration Hearings

The landlord and tenant both have the right to:

- Call and examine witnesses.

- Introduce exhibits.

- Cross-examine opposing witnesses on any relevant matter.

- To "impeach" any witness (e.g., show their contradictions).

- Rebut evidence.

In general the hearing "…need not be conducted according to the technical rules relating to evidence or witnesses…Any relevant evidence shall be admitted if it is the sort of evidence on which responsible persons are accustomed to rely in the conduct of serious affairs…in the absence of a timely and proper objection, relevant hearsay evidence is admissible for all purposes. Proffered hearsay evidence to which timely and proper objection is made is admissible for all purposes, including as the sole support for a finding, if (a) it would otherwise be admissible under the rules of evidence applicable in a civil action or (b) the Administrative Law Judge determines, in her discretion, that, based on all the circumstances, it is sufficiently reliable and trustworthy…." (Rent Board Rules and Regulations § 11.17)

For absent parties at hearings, see SF Rent Board Rules and Regulations § 11.14.

Appealing Decisions to the Rent Board Commission

If one or both parties object to the decision, a written appeal must be filed **within 15 calendar days** of the date the decision was **mailed, not when it was received**. (This period includes Saturdays, Sundays, and holidays.) However, the Rent Board may extend the time limit for "good cause," and proof of "good cause" for late filing must be included when filing the appeal. This includes situations where you didn't actually receive the decision, in which case you can file a "Declaration of Non-Receipt."

File an "Appeal to the Board" form together with documentation and enough copies for all the parties plus 10 copies for the Rent Board Commissioners. The appeal must state specific grounds as to why a new hearing is necessary. All errors or abuses of discretion by the Administrative Law Judge (ALJ) that you claim must be clearly spelled out in the appeal. A claim of bias on the part of the ALJ will be disfavored; you should be detailed with specific relevant facts. **The Commissioners will not accept any oral testimony at the meeting at which they decide to accept/reject the appeal, so the written materials must tell the story.** Financial hardship may also be raised as grounds for an appeal. (See the following section "Hardship Appeal at Tenant's Request.") The Commissioners will have access to the complete file but don't assume that they will necessarily read it, or if they do, that they will absorb it all.

Within 30 days after the appeal is filed, the Rent Board Commissioners will review the appeal during one of their regular meetings and decide whether or not to accept it. If accepted, the case may be sent back to the same ALJ ("remand") for another

hearing on the entire case or particular points or to a different ALJ. In some cases, the Board Commissioners may hear it themselves. The Commissioners may decide to hear the case as an entirely new hearing ("de novo" meaning "for the first time"). The Commission may decide to hear the entire case or focus only on some points.

In the majority of cases, the Rent Board Commissioners will deny the appeal, which means the decision of the ALJ is final. Both parties will be notified as to when the Rent Board Commissioners will decide it, and all parties may come and listen to the Commissioners briefly discuss the acceptance or rejection of the appeal, but *no testimony* will be taken at this meeting. If the Board decides to accept the appeal, either a totally new hearing or a limited review will be set within 45 days of the decision on the appeal. The previous decision issued by the ALJ after the first hearing remains in effect during the appeal process, except for that portion of the decision which permits payment, refund, offsetting, or adding of rent.

Appeal decisions are effective on the date mailed to the parties, except that portion of the decision affecting rent payments which becomes effective 30 days after it is mailed unless a stay is granted by a court. (SF Administrative Code § 37.8(f); *McHugh v. Santa Monica Rent Control Board* (1989) 49 Cal. 3d 348)

If a tenant is "aggrieved" by any decision of the Rent Board, the tenant may seek judicial review in Superior Court. This must be done after the appeals process in the Rent Board is exhausted, and will probably require hiring an attorney. This must be done **within 90 calendar days** of the date of mailing of an ALJ's or Rent Board Commission's decision. (SF Administrative Code 37.8(f) (9)) Superior Court may grant an appeal staying the rent payment part of the decision until the Court makes its own decision. Landlords also have a right to appeal decisions and get a stay. It is a rare Rent Board case that is appealed to the courts, however.

Hardship Appeal at Tenant's Request

The Tenant Financial Hardship Application (available from the Rent Board in multiple languages) can be filed for petitions for capital improvement passthroughs, general bond passthroughs, water revenue bond passthroughs, utility passthroughs, and operating and maintenance expense increases. (SF Administrative Code § 37.7(h) and (i), SF Rent Board Rules and Regulations § 10.15) The hardship does not become retroactive.

- *Capital Improvement Passthroughs*: a tenant may file a hardship appeal at any time after receipt of the notice of rent increase or the decision from the Rent Board is issued, whichever is earlier. The tenant need not pay the approved rent increase while the appeal is being processed and considered. The Rent Board will provide a notice of the application procedures for this hardship exemption with the landlord's petition for certification of capital improvement costs. (SF Administrative Code § 37.7(j))

- *General Obligation Bond Passthrough*: a tenant may file a hardship appeal after receiving the passthrough. (SF Administrative Code § 37.3(a)(6)(E))

- *Water Revenue Bond Passthroughs (SF Administrative Code § 37.3(a)(5)(B)) or Utility Passthroughs based on a utility passthrough calculation worksheet*: a tenant may file a hardship appeal within one year of the effective date of the passthrough.

- *Operating and Maintenance Expense Increase Passthrough* or *Utility Passthrough*, a tenant may file a hardship appeal within one year of the effective date of the passthrough.

Each tenant in the unit who is at least 18 years old, except for subtenants, must submit documentation under penalty of perjury that the approved rent increase will constitute a financial hardship for one of the following reasons:

(1) Tenant is a recipient of means-tested public assistance, such as Social Security Supplemental Security Income (SSI), General Assistance (GA), Temporary Assistance for Needy Families (TANF), CalFresh (SNAP/Food Stamps) or California Work Opportunity and Responsibility to Kids (CalWORKS). **Or**

(2) (a) Maximum monthly gross household income (this would include all roommates) as of August 20, 2021 is: for a single person $6,217, for 2 people $7,104, for 3 people $7,992, for 4 people $8,879, for 5 people $9,592, for 6 people $10,300, for 7 people $11,008, for 8 people $11,721. (See the Rent Board form for updated amounts.) Assistance from family, etc., counts as income if it is consistent. **And**

    (b) Rent is greater than 33% of gross household income. **And**

    (c) Assets, excluding retirement accounts and non-liquid assets (such as automobiles, furniture, etc.), do not exceed asset amounts permitted by the Mayor's Office of Housing when determining eligibility for below market rate home ownership, $60,000 for 2021. **Or**

(3) Exceptional circumstances exist, such as excessive medical bills. A hearing will be held for this type of claim which is not held for the other two types of claims.

Social Security numbers can be blocked out (redacted) entirely and the account numbers except for the last four digits since the info becomes public except access to info for the exceptional

circumstances can be restricted to only the landlord, tenant, and Rent Board. Everything in the application is sent to the landlord who has 15 days to request a hearing. A request for a hearing is usually granted in 4-6 weeks (4/19). A decision will be issued administratively by a Rent Board Judge unless the Judge determines a hearing is needed. Hardship appeals are routinely granted.

The passthrough can be imposed at a later date if the tenant's income changes (i.e., their rent falls below 33% of their income), but are not banked. In other words, the tenant does not pay later for the passthrough they were exempt from before due to low income. A landlord may request that the Rent Board review the exemption again, however. Tenants whose income changes should notify the Rent Board in writing within 60 days and send a copy to the landlord.

Decisions on hardship exemptions may be appealed to the Rent Board. The tenant will be sent a "Notice of Action on Appeal" on whether the Rent Board Commissioners will hear the appeal.

Hardship Appeal at Landlord's Request

If a landlord claims that a refund of rent overpayments to a tenant would be a financial hardship, she may file a Landlord Hardship Appeal. Documentation of the financial hardship is required for the hearing. If the landlord is granted a hardship, she will still have to pay but may be granted a longer time to do so.

Protest

Building Permits Can Be Blocked

Building permits may be necessary before some types of evictions (capital improvement, demolition, substantial rehabilitation, or lead abatement), or some types of rent increases (capital improvement passthrough), can be protested. See the section "Permit Process" in "Chapter 11: Changes in Use."

Direct Action

You might decide you need to bring attention to an ongoing injustice outside of the bureaucratic process. Direct action can involve varying levels of protest. One example of a protest is politely handing out flyers to prospective tenants or buyers at a property management company or open house. Putting up big signs in the windows of your building is another way to let the neighborhood know what's going on, and can also be a good conversation starter with your landlord! You could even take your ironing board, flyers and petitions to the landlord's place of business or set up in front of the church that the landlord attends. An assertive tactic is risking arrest by sitting in at the landlord's workplace until he agrees to meet with you. What do you want to accomplish by the action? Do you want to directly confront the landlord with your demands? Is the tone of the

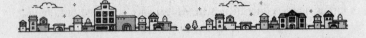

action intended to be educational, confrontational, angry, hurt, etc.?

Sue Your Landlord

Bringing a lawsuit against your landlord is serious business. We do not recommend that you take this step unless other alternatives do not work. Moreover, all lawsuits include an element of chance—even the most "airtight" cases have been known to sink in court for unfair reasons such as the judge relates better to landlords since the judge is a property owner. Weigh the pros and cons carefully before you throw down the gauntlet and file a lawsuit. You could incur not only financial loss, but you could possibly be sued yourself for bringing a "meritless" action if you knew your claims were false at the time you filed your lawsuit. Also, it can be difficult to enforce a judgment. (One way to collect is to use the landlord's checking account number which can often be found on the back of your rent check, but the checking account may have been closed.)

Petitioning the Rent Board, if your rental unit is covered under the Rent Ordinance, is often a better route to get compensation for the loss of housing services. If you win, the Rent Board will rule that you can pay a reduced amount of rent, so you are guaranteed a way to get compensation for your loss of housing services. Even if you no longer live in the home where the landlord caused the loss, a ruling in your favor will greatly strengthen your case in court, which is generally less knowledgeable about tenant rights under the Rent Ordinance. There are other ways to pressure the landlord, as well, such as reporting the poor housing conditions to city agencies. (See "Chapter 6: Repairs and Services" and "Chapter 7: Rent Increases" and the section "Petition the Rent Board" earlier in this chapter for more info.)

Some types of cases, however, even if eligible for a petition with the Rent Board, have a better chance at success in court. Researching outcomes for large amounts of money at the Rent Board and for lawsuits is recommended before choosing between the two. Although it is not essential to have an attorney to bring a lawsuit, it is highly recommended when suing in Superior Court. The laws and court procedures are very tricky —the rules of the game must be followed precisely or a case may be thrown out or gutted before it even gets to trial. Like any problem that requires technical know-how to solve (e.g., dentistry, plumbing, or car repair) hiring a professional may save you time and money.

Besides serving as your legal guide, a lawyer will be able to objectively assess the value of your case. It is almost impossible for a person involved in a dispute to step back and critically evaluate the merits of her own case. From your perspective, your case is the biggest injustice ever. But will it fly in court?

We suggest that you get at least three opinions from lawyers versed in tenant law before you make a decision to sue your landlord. Many tenant attorneys will consult with you initially for a small fee. The Tenants Union provides an attorney list which notes the attorneys' consultation policies.

More than likely, each attorney you talk to will have a unique opinion and consulting with several attorneys may provide you with some good ideas to strengthen your case. Also, talking with different attorneys will give you a broader range of choices when and if you decide to hire an attorney. Attorneys vary widely in their approaches. Consider that "shopping" for an attorney is similar to test riding assorted bicycle models (although admittedly not as much fun). Some attorneys put style before substance, others are safer, still others will zoom up the first hill but wear you out in the long haul.

How do you decide which, if any, is right for you? Ask yourself: What do I want from this lawsuit? Money? Time? Continued possession of my home? Correction of an existing problem? Compensation for injuries suffered in the past? Justice? Peace of mind? Or some combination of all of these?

If you have some idea of what you want from a lawsuit, you are in a better position to find an attorney whose skills match your goals. Even if you decide not to hire an attorney, consideration of your ultimate goal in bringing the lawsuit will help you frame your case.

Do You Have a Case?

Before assuming you can bring your landlord in to court, you should consult with the Tenants Union and tenant attorneys to make sure you have a strong legal case. Because you have been treated unjustly does not necessarily mean you have been treated illegally.

The person suing is the plaintiff; the person being sued is the defendant. The plaintiff has the burden of proving that the defendant's actions (or inaction) caused an injury to the plaintiff. The plaintiff must also show that he suffered damages as a result of this injury. It is critical that the tenant gather evidence to convince a judge or jury of the damages such as statements of witnesses, documents, pictures, or other physical proof.

For example, a tenant moved out based on the landlord's verbal notice that she was going to move in. Before moving out, the tenant should get the landlord's notice in writing. If this cannot be obtained, the tenant should write a letter confirming that the tenant was moving out based on the landlord's verbal statement of x date. If no such documentation exists, and the tenant sues the landlord for wrongful eviction, proof that the eviction was wrongful comes down to the tenant's word against the landlord's.

In addition to proving that the defendant (in this example, the landlord) caused harm to the plaintiff (tenant), the plaintiff needs to prove the amount of damages. These can be very difficult to assess. The "million dollar lawsuit" is extremely rare for tenant-landlord cases. Generally, your damages will bear some relation to the actual harm. The basic types of damages are:

- **Actual "out-of-pocket" or "benefit of the bargain" damages** are costs incurred by the plaintiff because of the defendant's conduct, such as money spent on repairs ignored by the defendant, temporary relocation costs if the plaintiff had to move out during renovation work, the difference in rent between the old rent and the new rent (*Chacon v. Litke* (2010) 181 Cal. App. 4th 1234 awarded the tenant twenty years of the projected difference in rent) and moving costs for wrongful eviction, and medical expenses for injury due to the defendant's negligence and other professional services.

- **Emotional distress damages** are less tangible. The methods of determining the worth of a person's psyche vary from case to case. What is critical, however, is to provide clear proof that the plaintiff experienced symptoms of discomfort, pain, humiliation, depression, or some other emotional disability as a result of the defendant's conduct. Usually a psychologist or psychiatrist would be needed to document these symptoms. "Severe" emotional distress is required, not just your normal day-to-day stress.

- **Punitive damages** are the other major form of damages that can be awarded in an affirmative lawsuit (claiming something is true as opposed to denying a claim). These are awarded when a defendant's behavior is found to be malicious, i.e., so outrageous to a reasonable person that society should punish the defendant by making them pay a large amount of money to teach them a lesson. The theory is, as the name indicates, *punishment* of a civil wrongdoer. The defendant must have acted intentionally or must have been grossly reckless in his conduct, e.g., after years of ignoring code violations, the building burns up due to faulty electrical wiring.

- **Statutory damages** are additional damages provided for by statute:

  - Debt collection violations. (CA Civil Code § 1788.30)

  - Demolition application was not disclosed. (CA Civil Code § 1940.6)

  - Evictions that were illegal (SF Administrative Code § 37.9(f), 37.10B(a)(14)) including for re-renting illegally under the Ellis Act (SF Administrative Code 37.9A(c)).

- Harassment. (SF Administrative Code § 37.10B(c)(5), CA Civil Code § 1940.2, CA Civil Code § 1942.5)

- Lead paint hazard violations. (42 U.S.C. § 4852d)

- Lockouts that were illegal. (CA Civil Code § 789.3)

- Maintenance required by law was not provided. (CA Civil Code § 1942.4) Bad faith can be proven on the part of the landlord and the unit is covered under the Rent Ordinance. (SF Administrative Code § 37.10B) Some courts have taken issue with the "bad faith" language in the ordinance.

- Rent is excessive after owner move-in eviction. (SF Administrative Code § 37.11A)

- Retaliation. (CA Civil Code § 1942.5)

- Security deposit not refunded in bad faith. (CA Civil Code § 1950.5(l))

- Subdivision Code violations. (SF Subdivision Code § 1304)

- Utility shutoff. (CA Civil Code § 789.3)

- **Attorneys' fees and costs** may be awarded if provided for by written contract (usually the rental agreement) or law:

  - Buyout agreement that did not provide the required disclosures to the tenant. (SF Administrative Code § 37.9E(k))

  - Debt collection harassment. (CA Civil Code § 1788.30)

  - Demolition application was not disclosed. (CA Civil Code § 1940.6)

  - Discrimination. (CA Government Code § 12980)

  - Evictions without just cause. (SF Administrative Code § 37.9(f), 37.10B(c)(6))

  - Rent increases that are illegal. (SF Administrative Code § 37.11A)

  - Repairs required by law were not provided. (CA Civil Code § 1942.4, CA Health and Safety Code § 17980.7)

  - Retaliation. (CA Civil Code § 1942.5, SF Administrative Code § 37.11A)

  - Rights under the San Francisco Rent Ordinance

interfered with by the landlord. (SF Administrative Code § 37.11A)

· Short-term rentals that are illegal in the building or within 100 feet of a permanent residence. (SF Administrative Code § 41A.5)

· Temporary restraining orders. (CA Code of Civil Procedure § 527.6(r)

· Utility shutoffs by the landlord. (CA Civil Code § 789.3, CA Public Utilities Code § 777.1)

The tenant may also sue for injunctive relief, a court-ordered act or prohibited act, including a restraining order. (See the section "Restraining Orders and Injunctions" in "Chapter 8: Harassment" for more info.)

Because lawsuits cost money, take time, and usually result in irreversible damage to the tenant-landlord relationship, you should always first consider this question: what do you want from the lawsuit? Your chances for recovery of damages will depend on both of the following:

• The type of damages you suffered.

• The extent to which you can prove these damages.

What if you're still in the home? Is an affirmative lawsuit a viable remedy for uninhabitable premises (in the court's opinion) that you still inhabit, rent overcharges, violations of the rental agreement, or other landlord abuses? The short answer is "Yes."

For example, one remedy for the landlord's breach of the Implied Warranty of Habitability (see the "Rent Strikes" section of "Chapter 6: Repairs and Services") is to sue your landlord for a "retroactive rent abatement," seeking a court judgment reducing your rent in an amount proportional to the habitability defects in your home. You may also sue your landlord if she seeks to wrongfully evict you by changing your locks, shutting off your utilities, etc.

When Can You Sue Your Landlord?

Your lawsuit also needs to be filed within the statute of limitations. If you are suing because an oral agreement was broken, you have two years to file after the agreement was broken. (CA Code of Civil Procedure § 339) For a written agreement, you have four years to file after the agreement was broken. (CA Code of Civil Procedure § 337) For a claim of wrongful eviction under the Rent Ordinance you have one year to file, except for owner move-in evictions the tenant has five years to file. (CA Code of Civil Procedure § 340) If your property was damaged, you have three

years to file after your property was damaged. If you are suing because you got hurt, you can file a claim for up to two years after you were hurt. (CA Code of Civil Procedure § 335.1) If you are suing because of fraud, you have three years to file after you find out about the fraud. (CA Code of Civil Procedure § 338) Fraud is when you lose money because someone lied to you or tricked you on purpose. Consult an attorney for more info.

What Court Should You Use?

Which court your case is filed in will depend on the monetary value of the damages sought and the length of time you are prepared to wait for judgment.

Small Claims Court is the quickest and cheapest way to bring your lawsuit. However, you can only sue for a maximum of $10,000. This is the "People's Court" where regular folks go and present their own cases. Small Claims Court proceedings are less formal and less concerned with the strict procedural rules that bind the larger courts and neither side may be represented by an attorney. However, plaintiffs have no right to appeal. Small Claims suits are commonly used where a landlord wrongfully refuses to return all or part of a security deposit. Injunctive relief (a court-ordered act or prohibition against an act) may also be awarded in Small Claims Court.

Before beginning the lawsuit, the plaintiff must, where possible, make a demand for payment. (CA Code of Civil Procedure § 116.320) Usually, parties in a small claims case must represent themselves. The most common exceptions (CA Code of Civil Procedure § 116.540):

•Property agent — A property agent may represent the owner of rental property if the property agent was hired principally to manage the rental of that property.

•Non-resident real property owner — A non-resident owner of real property located in California may defend a small claims case related to the property by submitting a declaration or sending a representative. However, the representative can't be compensated.

You may request an appearance by Zoom, but it is probably less effective than appearing in person. The form is on *https://sfsuperiorcourt.org/forms-filing/forms* under Civil/Small Claims. If a witness can't attend the hearing, you can ask the witness to write and sign a statement called a "declaration" for submission to the court. This statement should include everything that the witness would like to tell the judge about your claim or defense. At the end of the statement, the witness should write, "I declare under penalty of perjury under the laws of the State of California that the above is true and correct." The witness should then date and sign the statement, and write her city and telephone number at the time of signing. If the witness isn't living in California, the statement should be signed before a notary public. The witness should also include a telephone number (and perhaps an e-mail address) in case the judge needs to contact the witness. The judge isn't always required to accept a

written statement, so it's best to have an important witness come to the hearing. Since the judge may, also, want to ask the witness questions, a witness should attend if possible.

You may want to consult with the small claims clerk about whether the court will allow your witness to testify by telephone. Some, but not all, small claims judges will allow a witness, especially one who lives a long distance from court, or who will not be available for the hearing, to testify by telephone. It's a good idea to present a letter to the court from the witness explaining why the witness can't appear in person at the hearing. Even if the court generally permits telephone testimony from witnesses, you should ask for permission from the court in advance of the hearing.

If you are the plaintiff, and the defendant counter-sued you by filing a Defendant's Claim in response to your Plaintiff's Claim and you lose, you can appeal. A small claims appeal is a brand-new trial and is in Superior Court, so representation by attorneys is allowed.

Superior Court Limited Jurisdiction and Unlimited Jurisdiction have jurisdictional limits of $25,000 or less and $25,000 or more, respectively. The procedural requirements in these courts are more complicated, and the cost of breaking these rules more dear. Also, due to the backlog in court cases pending in these courts, it will almost certainly take longer for your case to be heard—in many cases over a year. A lawyer is not strictly necessary to bring a lawsuit in these courts, but it is highly recommended to have one when proceeding in Superior Court.

Federal district court is available if you are suing under a federal law (for example, federal anti-discrimination statutes) or in certain other circumstances.

Withhold Rent

See the "Repair and Deduct," and "Rent Strikes" sections of "Chapter 6: Repairs and Services" for info on rent withholding.

Prosecute Your Landlord

The San Francisco Rent Ordinance (SF Administrative Code § 37.10B, § 37.10A), state and federal laws specify criminal penalties for violations of the law. See this book's index under "crime: penalizing the landlord" for the relevant chapters with details of which section of the law to use for prosecution.

Group Tactics

You can use all of the same tactics that you use as an individual (writing letters, petitioning the Rent Board, protesting permits, suing the landlord, etc.) plus many other tactics, with a group.

Usually, using one tactic is not enough. It's best to start with less confrontational tactics and if they aren't successful, try others. All of these tactics should be used in conjunction with the long-term goals of your group. For example, if your long-term goal is getting heat in your building, you might combine letter writing with calling the building inspector and petitioning the Rent Board. On the other hand, if you are facing an Ellis Act eviction, you might put up big signs in the windows and do direct actions targeted at the people who can influence the landlord.

- Joint letters to the landlord. We've mentioned letter writing already—but how about a whole campaign? Rather than you, alone, writing to the landlord, you could have your neighbors, friends and workmates write letters in your support. Almost all of us have had our own troubles with an unreasonable or greedy landlord—allies in your struggle are all around you, waiting to be asked to lend a hand.

- Petitioning the Rent Board as a group if covered under the Rent Ordinance. You will need to file separate petitions, but you can request that the petitions be heard together. (See the "Petition the Rent Board" section of this chapter. For parallel decrease in housing services, see the section "Preparation for 'Decrease in Housing Services' and Failure to Repair and Maintain' Hearings" in *Chapter 7: Repairs and Services*.)

- Suing the landlord as a group. (See the "Sue Your Landlord" section of this chapter.)

- Finding out if the landlord owns other buildings where tenants might have similar problems to identify other allies. (See *Chapter 3: Researching Landlords, Buildings, and Laws*.)

- To identify the most effective ways to pressure the landlord to meet your demands, research the landlord's social, religious, business, and political relationships and affiliations. Consider who might have influence over the landlord even though they may not have decision-making power. This could include: coworkers, neighbors, customers, other parishioners, investors or funders, Board or Directors, or executives .

- When deciding what kind of action to take, consider the following:

  - Is the action intended primarily to draw the attention of the media?

  - Do you want to collect signatures for a big petition drive?

  - How many people do you need to have it be a successful action?

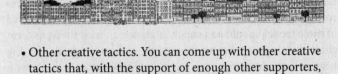

• Other creative tactics. You can come up with other creative tactics that, with the support of enough other supporters, could give you the power to win.

Building-Wide Collective Action

Organizing is the best way for tenants to gain negotiating power in a conflict with the landlord. Two tenants acting together are more than twice as powerful as one tenant acting alone, and tenants working together can share the work that must be done in waging a successful campaign. Another benefit of organizing is that your credibility increases. For example, if one tenant says something is wrong in the building, a judge or landlord may look skeptically at the complaint, but if several tenants in the building say the same thing, it's much harder to ignore. Organizing also guards against any one tenant being singled out. If only one tenant takes action, it's easy for the landlord to retaliate against that tenant, but if many tenants act together, it is very hard for the landlord to retaliate against everybody.

Additionally, a tenant acting individually against a landlord in the present exploitative housing market is already at a disadvantage because landlords are businesspeople maximizing their profits. Unfortunately they are doing it at your expense! They can generally be counted on to make decisions based on their own economic self-interest. Keeping this in mind, an individual tenant threatening to withhold rent may be an annoyance to the landlord, but a dozen tenants threatening to withhold rent can make a landlord listen and start negotiating. By working together as a group, we have a better chance of defending ourselves, and getting what we need!

To start with, you've got to get the word out to your neighbors, because a bad landlord is a problem for everybody sooner or later.

Starting a Tenants Union

Tenants unions can be powerful forces: the most effective way to work for positive changes in your building is with an active, well-organized tenants union. Most tenants unions are formed when a group of tenants have a common problem, such as long-delayed repairs, big rent increases, or unjust evictions. It is relatively rare in a multi-unit building for just one tenant to have repair or security problems, for example. Generally, the problems will be common throughout the building and unions emerge out of a struggle with the landlord over these issues.

(1) First, you need to ask—and answer—a few questions. What potential does your building have for forming an effective tenants union? Do the other tenants share the same housing problems that you have? Would they be interested in working together for better living conditions? Will they commit themselves to coming to the first and subsequent meetings? Are there other tenants who would

help you organize the first meeting?

(2) If you think your building has any organizing potential, begin planning the first meeting and remember, even two people acting together are better than one acting alone! Start keeping records of your communications with your landlord. Make a complete list of all problems and complaints related to the building. Make a list of the other tenants and begin talking to them. Start with the neighbors you know and knock on doors to identify other tenants who may have problems with the landlord. Request email addresses and phone numbers and get permission to share the email addresses with the other neighbors. You have a right to post or deliver flyers. (See the section "Posting and Distributing of Information by Tenant" in "Chapter 4: Renting Basics.") Ask any neighbors that express an interest to help you organize the first meeting. You can also set up an ironing board in front of your building and talk to your neighbors. Pass out flyers about the problems you are having. Or you can circulate a letter or ask people to sign a petition as a way to start talking to people. One of the great things about organizing is that it gives you an excuse to get to know your neighbors.

(3) If your building has five or more rental units that is organizing for the purpose of addressing housing conditions, community life, landlord-tenant relations, and/or similar issues of common interest or concern among tenants in the building, you have a right to form a Tenant Association under Chapter 49A of the SF Administrative Code. Provide your landlord a petition signed by tenants of 50% or more of the occupied units that you desire to form a Tenant Association, and identifying the Association. A landlord must on written request of a Tenant Association attend at least one Tenant Association meeting per calendar quarter. This requirement does not apply to some nonprofit landlords. Failure to comply with Chapter 49A is a decrease in housing services (see "Petitions for Lack of Services" in "Chapter 6: Repairs and Services.")

(4) Once you have done this work, look over the info and decide on a time to meet and on an agenda. Everyone may not be able to meet each time, but organizing is an ongoing process and those who do attend should let the others know what happened at the meeting. Meetings need a chairperson or facilitator and everything that happens at the meeting—especially any decisions that are made—should be written down. Communication between union members is vital to the health of the growing movement. Discuss problems by email if it is too hard to get everybody together.

(5) If you would like some outside help, contact the SF Tenants Union. We can sometimes even send out an organizer to attend your meeting and discuss what options

and opportunities might be available to you. Please try to give us at least a few days notice.

(6) At any meeting, be respectful and sensitive to personal and social dynamics. Meetings should be democratic and everybody should be encouraged to participate. Interpersonal friction should be noted and dealt with constructively and respectfully before things get out of hand. If you are interested in setting up democratic meetings that run well, read C.T. Butler's short book, *On Conflict and Consensus.*

Once you have taken the first steps, what can you expect to gain from your efforts? Many groups have had success in fighting unreasonable rent increases, getting repairs made, and stopping evictions. In fact, our experience indicates that almost all tenant unions will have at least some initial success. At the same time, there are no guarantees. The hardest part is to stay united until you have succeeded completely. Some groups, after an initial conflict with their landlord, fall apart either when tenants move, lose interest, or have conflict with each other. Still, over the years we have learned some of the critical factors and objectives that all groups should aim for.

- **Goals** — To start with, it is a good idea to concentrate on getting the landlord to resolve specific everyday problems faced by the tenants. Remember, small victories encourage people to keep trying for more complicated goals, while initial defeats have the opposite effect. Keep at it!

- **Structure** — Structure is a crucial element to establish within any group. Setting up a few ground rules and some routines, such as regular meetings, taking minutes or "passing the hat," allows for individuals to come and go while providing structure for the continuation of the group.

- **Money** — Small, individual contributions can be used to pay for the group's expenses as they arise. People are often willing to donate money to a cause they believe in, but they often won't unless they are asked.

Things to Think About

To get to the point of working together, it is necessary to meet to talk about what's going on, find out what common problems and goals are and make a plan:

Be careful in choosing the time and place of the first meeting. For instance, don't schedule it during a major holiday or event that might affect the ability of the people in your building to come to a meeting. Make flyers to announce each meeting and be sure to put one under every tenant's door as well as in common areas, if possible. Be aware that landlords and building management often have many eyes and ears. It is possible that the landlord may find out what was said before or at a meeting.

Try to include a little socializing. This could be coffee and cookies or anything else that will give people a little more incentive to come—and keep coming—to meetings. Use a committee structure for leadership. This will prevent many different kinds of problems that come up when a single person is "the leader" and get people to feel more involved.

Neighborhood or Citywide Action

If you or your tenants group *still* haven't gotten an adequate response from the landlord, you might want to take your struggle for justice to another level. Many of the laws that we have that support tenants rights were won by citywide tenant organizing. Though landlords, as a group, have a lot of money and power, tenants working together can and do continue to work to make the laws more fair to tenants. Contact the Tenants Union for info on getting support from community groups

Influence at the Neighborhood Level. Most neighborhoods in San Francisco have organized groups of residents who influence City Hall. Unfortunately, these groups frequently lack strong pro-tenant representation in leadership positions, in spite of the fact that more than half of us are renters! Consider having a member of your group attend the neighborhood association's meeting, so you can be sure that the tenants' point of view is in the mix. If that is not good enough, put together a "tenant slate" and run for office the next time the association holds an election.

Building Citywide Tenant Power. It's just not true that "you can't fight City Hall." Grassroots groups with little money, but plenty of people power, have fought and won—and will continue to fight and win—against big-money, politically-connected agendas at City Hall. Join the San Francisco Tenants Union or other large tenants associations if you haven't already. Keep informed of campaigns that the tenants union or other housing rights groups are working on and join them. If you see an injustice being done to tenants across the city, bring it to the San Francisco Tenants Union Steering Committee or other tenant groups to see if others want to start a campaign around it.

Get involved with grassroots groups, go to the SF Board of Supervisors hearings, Planning Commission meetings, and Rent Board Commission hearings where they are discussing changes to policy. And don't just sit there listening—stand up and say something, because if you don't challenge pro-landlord assumptions in the halls of government, landlords, real estate developers and others that profit off of providing shelter, landlords will continue to get their way! Instead, as an organized force, tenants can win victories that make the city a more just and humane place to live.

Appendix A: *Resources*

211

211 (telephone number)
Web Site: https://www.211bayarea.org

- Confidential information and referral on tenant services includes eviction prevention.
- Languages: multilingual.
- Hours: 24 hours a day, 7 days a week.

AIDS HOUSING ALLIANCE/SF

See Q Foundation.

AIDS LEGAL REFERRAL PANEL

(415) 701-1100
(415) 701-1200 (office)
Web Site: https://www.alrp.org

- Direct representation and referrals to a panel of volunteer attorneys for landlord/tenant disputes (including cases involving discrimination).
- Services limited to individuals with HIV/ AIDS living in the SF Bay Area.
- Call for assistance and leave a message. You will receive a return call within 48 business hours.

ALLIANCE OF CALIFORNIANS FOR COMMUNITY EMPOWERMENT

See *ACCE*

ANTI-EVICTION MAPPING PROJECT

Web Site: https://www.antievictionmap.com

- A data visualization, critical cartography, and digital storytelling collective documenting dispossession and resistance upon gentrifying landscapes.
- Eviction map.

ASIAN AMERICANS ADVANCING JUSTICE-ASIAN LAW CAUCUS

55 Columbus Avenue
San Francisco, CA 94111
(415) 295-2024 (legal assistance phone appointment, leave your name, phone number, and briefly describe the issue)
(415) 896-1701
(415) 896-1702 (fax)
Web Site: https://www.advancingjustice-alc.org

- Advocates including legal assistance for low-income residents in housing primarily in gateway communities for new immigrants, such as Chinatown.
- Free housing rights legal clinic including eviction

notices, unlawful detainer cases, rent increases, assistance for seniors, and discrimination on the first, third, and last Tuesday of each month, at 10am–12pm.

- Languages: Cantonese, Hindi, Mandarin and English. For other languages, please explain your specific language need when making an appointment.

ASIAN PACIFIC ISLANDER LEGAL OUTREACH (API LEGAL OUTREACH)

1121 Mission Street
San Francisco, CA 94103
(415) 567-6255
(415) 567-6248 (fax)
Web Site: https://www.apilegaloutreach.org

- Legal representation including against eviction and advocacy for Asian Pacific Islanders especially women, senior, recent immigrants, youth, and disabled.
- Free housing clinics.
- Languages: multilingual

(THE) BAR ASSOCIATION OF SAN FRANCISCO

See specific program.

BAY AREA LEGAL AID

(800) 551-5554 (legal assistance line)
711 (California Relay Service)
Web Site: https://baylegal.org

- Must meet income and location eligibility criteria.
- Provides free legal assistance with issues such as subsidized housing, eviction defense, housing conditions, rent control, discrimination, lockouts, utility shut-offs, residential hotels, and domestic violence.

BAY AREA MEDIATION SERVICES OF THE BAR ASSOCIATION OF SAN FRANCISCO

(415) 782-8905
Email: mking@sfbar.org
Web Site: https://www.sfbar.org/adr-services/bay-area-mediation-services

- Mediation services are confidential and voluntary. $295 per party for 2 hours of mediation and 1 hour of mediation preparation. 97% success rate.

BAYVIEW HUNTERS POINT COMMUNITY LEGAL

See Open Door Legal.

BILL SORRO HOUSING PROGRAM (BISHOP)

1110 Howard Street
San Francisco, CA 94103
415-513-5177
Email: info@bishopsf.org

Web Site: https://bishopsf.org

- Free education and advocacy on threats of eviction, landlord vs tenant disputes, rental assistance, decrease in housing services and other issues for San Francisco residents. Assistance in applying for the Displaced Tenant Housing Preference Program.

- Languages: Arabic, French, Spanish, Tagalog, and English

CALIFORNIA LAWYERS FOR THE ARTS
(888) 775-8995
Web Site: https://www.calawyersforthearts.org

- Provides lawyer referral services for art-related cases for landlord/tenant problems. Referrals usually take 3–5 business days. Free 30 minute initial consultation. May qualify for free program if near federal poverty guideline, otherwise $35 for nonmembers, $20 for members.

- Arts Arbitration and Mediation Services. Low sliding scale fees. (510) 990-6030

- Languages: multilingual

CAUSA JUSTA :: JUST CAUSE
Mailing Address: P. O. Box 7737, Oakland, CA 94601
(415) 487-9203 (leave name, phone number and brief description of problem)
Email: info@cjjc.org (no housing assistance by email)
Web Site: https://cjjc.org

- Free tenant counseling for mostly low-income Latino and black residents of San Francisco.

- Direct actions and coalition work for tenants.

- Languages: Spanish and English.

Mission District
2301 Mission Street, Suite 201

Bayview District
2145 Keith Street

CENTRAL CITY SRO COLLABORATIVE
472 Ellis St
San Francisco, CA 94102
(415) 775-7110
Web site: www.ccsroc.net

- Organizes tenants in single-room occupancy residential hotels (SROs).

- Languages: Spanish and English.

CHINATOWN COMMUNITY DEVELOPMENT CENTER
Housing Counseling
663 Clay Street
San Francisco, CA 94111
(415) 984-2728 (make appointment if cannot drop-in: leave your name, brief message, and phone number)

Web Site: https://www.chinatowncdc.org

- Educates, and organizes low-income residents on tenants' rights including: evictions, rent increases, repair and maintenance, translation and filing of forms and documents (e.g. Small Claims, Rent Board), and tenant/landlord mediations.

- Languages: Cantonese, Mandarin, and English.

CHINATOWN SRO COLLABORATIVE
A Program of the Chinatown Community Development Center
1525 Grant Avenue
San Francisco, CA 94133
(415) 984-2730

COMMUNITY BOARDS
601 Van Ness Avenue, Suite 2040
(415) 920-3820
Web Site: https://communityboards.org

- Mediation service for tenants/landlords, roommates, and neighbors. Mediation services are confidential and voluntary. $45–$100 to open a case, however this can be waived.

- Mediations can be scheduled for Monday–Sunday.

- Languages: Cantonese, Mandarin, Russian, Spanish, and English.

COMMUNITY UNITED AGAINST VIOLENCE
427 South Van Ness Avenue
San Francisco, CA 94103
(415) 333-HELP (4357, service request line)
(415) 777-5500 (business office)
Email: info@cuav.org
Web Site: https://www.cuav.org

- For the lesbian, gay, bisexual, and queer population.

- Support for people who have experienced domestic abuse to receive emotional support, safety planning, referrals, and limited case follow-up.

- Languages: Spanish and English.

CONFLICT INTERVENTION SERVICE (CIS)
(415) 782-8940
Email: cis@sfbar.org
Web Site: https://www.sfbar.org/adr-services/cis

- Resolve disputes/negotiate with landlord/roommate/neighbor.

- Confidential communication with CIS.

- Free to qualifying parties. Low cost services are available to anyone

- Languages: interpreter services.

COOPERATIVE RESTRAINING ORDER CLINIC
(415) 969-6711 (appointments)
(415) 864-1790 (administrative line)

ALICE IN HER STUDIO

Web Site: https://www.roclinic.org

- Assistance obtaining restraining orders for people facing domestic violence, sexual assault and stalking.

DEMOCRATIC SOCIALISTS OF AMERICA –SAN FRANCISCO

Web Site: https://dsasf.org

- Not a political party. Promotes and supports all tenants' efforts to stay in their homes. Capitalism is the cause of our housing issues. Mass organizing is the way forward.

DOLORES STREET COMMUNITY SERVICES

938 Valencia Street
San Francisco, CA 94110
(415) 282-6209
(415) 282-2826 (fax)

Web Site: https://www.dscs.org

- Advocates and organizes to minimize displacement and develop affordable housing in the Mission District.

- Languages: Spanish and English.

EVICTION DEFENSE COLLABORATIVE

1338 Mission Street, 4th Floor
(415) 659-9184 (for legal assistance)
(415) 470-5211 (financial assistance: RADCo)
(415) 947-0797 (recording)
(415) 947-0331 (fax, no assistance with individual cases)
Email: legal@evictiondefense.org (for legal assistance)
EDCRADCo@evictiondefense.org (financial assistance: RADCo)

Web Site: https://evictiondefense.org

- See the box "Right to an Attorney for Eviction Notices" in "Chapter 12: Eviction Defenses."

- The Rental Assistance Disbursement Component (RADCo) assists qualified tenants with back rent provided they can pay in the future.

- May be able to provide an attorney at Rent

Board hearings for rent increases due to:
- ·· Subsequent occupancy (original tenant moves out but another tenant remains).
- ·· Rent Board Rules and Regulations § 1.21 (not primary residence).
- ·· Single residential unit created by loss of another unit.
- ·· Reinstating original rent due to temporary rent reduction to benefit tenant.
- ·· Other special circumstances.
- Drop-In Hours: Monday, Wednesday, Friday, 10:00– 11:30 am and 1–2:30 pm except closed all court holidays.
- Languages: Chinese, Spanish, and English.

GENERAL ASSISTANCE ADVOCACY PROJECT

276 Golden Gate Avenue (at Hyde)
San Francisco, CA 94102
(415) 928-8191
(415) 928-1410 (fax)
Web Site: https://www.gaap.org

- Assists clients with landlord issues.

HOMELESS ADVOCACY PROJECT

A program of the Justice & Diversity Center of the Bar Association of San Francisco
125 Hyde Street
San Francisco, CA 94102
(415) 575-3130 or (800) 405-4HAP (4427)
(415) 575-3132 (fax)
Web Site: https://www.sfbar.org/jdc/jdc-legal-services-programs/hap

- Provides legal services (especially eviction defense) for people at risk of homelessness. Prioritizes mentally disabled and families.

- Referrals.

HOMELESS PRENATAL PROGRAM

2500 18th St.
San Francisco, CA 94110
(415) 546-6756
(415) 576-6778 (fax)
Email: info@homelessprenatal.org
Web Site: www.homelessprenatal.org

- Housing workshops that provide information on tenant rights and responsibilities.

- Counseling for housing issues and family violence.

HOUSING RIGHTS COMMITTEE OF SF

Web Site: hrcsf.org

- Counseling for free on tenant rights.

- Organizing.

- Public housing and Section 8 tenants call for an appointment for advocacy.

- Languages: Cantonese, Mandarin, Russian,

Spanish, and English.

Main Office
1663 Mission Street, Suite 504
San Francisco, CA 94103
(415) 703-8634

Richmond Branch
4301 Geary Boulevard/7th Avenue
San Francisco, CA 94118

(415) 947-9085

INDEPENDENT LIVING RESOURCE CENTER OF SAN FRANCISCO
825 Howard Street
San Francisco, CA 94103
(628) 231-2287 (info on legal services or to make a flexible appointment with a staff attorney)
(415) 543-6222 (office)
(415) 543-6318 (fax)
(415) 543-6698 (TTY)
Email: brandie@ilrcsf.org (for info on legal services or to make an appointment with a staff attorney), info@ilrcsf.org (general inquiries)
Web Site: https://www.ilrcsf.org

- Provides information, advocacy. or free representation on fair housing.
- Counseling and advocacy for housing focusing on tenant rights.
- Publications relative to housing and disabilities.
- Housing workshops.

JUSTICE & DIVERSITY CENTER
A program of The Bar Association of San Francisco
Web Site: https://www.sfbar.org/jdc
See also specific program.

LA CASA DE LAS MADRES
1269 Howard Street
San Francisco, CA 94103
(877) 503-1850 (adult crisis line, 24 hours, 365 days/year)
(877) 923-0700 (teen crisis line, 24 hours, 365 days/year)
(415) 503-0500 (counseling and supportive services)
(415) 200-3575 (text line)
Email: info@lacasa.org
Web Site: https://www.lacasa.org

- Provides women and children survivors of domestic violence free and confidential services of counseling, crisis intervention, support groups, referrals, and trainings.

LA RAZA CENTRO LEGAL
474 Valencia Street, Suite 295
(415) 575-3500 (legal services)
(415) 255-7593 (fax)
Web Site: https://lrcl.org

- The Senior Law Program assists seniors with consumer

debt. For appointment call (415) 553-3429 or email maribel@lrcl.org.

- Disabled adults also eligible for legal services for debt.
- Languages: Spanish and English.

LA RAZA COMMUNITY RESOURCE CENTER
474 Valencia Street, Suite 100
San Francisco, CA 94103
(415) 863-0764
Email: info@larazacrc.org
Web Site: https://www.larazacrc.org

- Provides information and referrals on topics including legal advice and housing for low-income, mostly Spanish-speaking individuals and families.
- Advocates for parents with service providers.
- Leadership development for parents.
- Languages: Spanish and English.

LA VOZ LATINA
456 Ellis Street
San Francisco, CA 94102
(415) 983-3970
Web Site: https://www.lavozlatinasf.org

- For low-income, monolingual Spanish-speaking immigrants.
- Aids with housing problems.
- Provides workshops on civil law.
- Languages: Spanish and English.

LAWYER REFERRAL & INFORMATION SERVICE
A program of the Justice & Diversity Center of the Bar Association of San Francisco
(415) 989-1616
TTY: (800) 735-2929
Web Site: https://www.sfbar.org/lris/need-a-lawyer

- Provides referrals within 2 business days to experienced attorneys in Landlord/Tenant law. In person 30-minute attorney consultations cost $35; no charge for consultations on injury matters. Reduced-fee legal services program is available for those who qualify.

LEGAL ADVICE AND REFERRAL CLINIC (LARC)
A program of the Justice & Diversity Center of the Bar Association of San Francisco
(415) 989-1616
Web Site: https://www.sfbar.org/jdc/jdc-legal-services-programs/legal-advice-and-referral-clinic

- Provides free legal advice and referrals.
- Assistance with filling out forms and writing letters.
- Languages: Chinese or Spanish may be available, and English.

LEGAL ASSISTANCE TO THE ELDERLY

1663 Mission Street, Suite 225
San Francisco, CA 94103
(415) 538-3333
Email: info@laesf.org (no legal advice by email)
Web Site: https://www.laesf.org

- Free full-scope representation for San Francisco residents, aged 60 or older, or adults with disabilities.
  - · Evictions
  - · Illegal Rent Increases
  - · Habitability
  - · Elder Abuse
  - · Significant Creditor Problems
  - · Reasonable Accommodation
  - · Does not assist for any problem for which representation by the private bar is available on a contingent fee basis. As a general rule, will not provide representation to:
    Respondents in restraining order cases.
    Master tenants seeking to evict subtenants.
- Will go to the client's place of residence, if necessary.
- Languages: Cantonese, Mandarin, Russian, Spanish, and English.

MENTAL HEALTH ASSOCIATION OF SAN FRANCISCO

870 Market Street, Suite 928
(855) 845-7415 (peer-run support and information)
(415) 421-2926 (office)
Email: info@mentalhealthsf.org
Web Site: https://www.mentalhealthsf.org

- Hoarders and clutterers support groups.
- Counseling, information and referrals.

MISSION SRO COLLABORATIVE

(415) 282-6209 ext. 150

- The Mission SRO Collaborative is a group of organizations that work together to organize SRO (single room occupancy) tenants in the Mission.
- Languages: Spanish and English.

OPEN DOOR LEGAL

(415) 735-4124
711 (TTY/TDD in English)
(800) 855-7200.(TTY/TDD in Spanish)
Email: info@opendoorlegal.org
Web Site: https://opendoorlegal.org

- Provides free legal services for housing needs for residents of specific zip codes (fill out the form on the website, call or go to the office to find out if you qualify). The appointment with a lawyer will be scheduled a minimum of two weeks after the application.
- Languages: Chinese, Spanish, and English.

Bayview Office
4634 3rd Street
San Francisco, CA 94124

Excelsior Office
60 Ocean Avenue
San Francisco, CA 94112
San Francisco, CA 94124

Western Addition Office
1113 Fillmore Street
San Francisco, CA 94115

OUR MISSION NO EVICTION

(415) 206-0577
Web Site: https://www.facebook.com/Our-Mission-NO-Eviction-533750263364322

- Opposes gentrification.

Q FOUNDATION

(415) 552-3242
Email: info@theqfoundation.org
Web Site: https://theqfoundation.org

- Formerly AIDS Housing Alliance.
- Promotes public policy to expand housing opportunities.

PEOPLE ORGANIZED TO DEMAND ENVIRONMENTAL AND ECONOMIC RIGHTS (PODER)

474 Valencia Street, Suite 125
San Francisco, CA 94103
(415) 431-4210
Email: info@podersf.org
Web Site: https://www.podersf.org

- PODER organizes the Mission and southeast San Francisco for solutions to environmental and economic inequities for low income communities of color.
- Languages: Spanish and English.

PLAZA 16 COALITION

Email: andy@plaza16.org
Web Site: https://www.facebook.com/Plaza16Coalition

- We are neighborhood residents, businesses, and community organizations from the Mission District. We believe in equitable development to ensure that low-income communities and communities of color participate in and benefit from the decisions that shape our neighborhoods.
- Languages: Spanish and English.

RILEY CENTER

A program of St. Vincent de Paul Society
1175 Howard Street
(415) 255-0165 (24 hour support line)
(415) 757-6490 (Spanish)
Web Site: https://svdp-sf.org/what-we-do/riley-center

- Offers confidential services for survivors of domestic violence, along with their children.

- Languages: Spanish and other possible translation.

SAN FRANCISCO ANTI-DISPLACEMENT COALITION

Email: sfantidisplacement@gmail.com
Web Site: sfadc.org

- A group of tenant organizations and allies to organize against evictions and rent increases which has resulted in the displacement through meetings, workshops and reports.

SAN FRANCISCO COMMUNITY LAND TRUST

Web Site: https://sfclt.org

- .Advocates conversions of rental buildings to limited equity cooperatives rather than condos.

SAN FRANCISCO LEGAL AID

See *Bay Area Legal Aid*

SAN FRANCISCO RISING

Email: information@sanfranciscorising.org
Web Site: https://www.sanfranciscorising.org

- A grassroots political fund that seeks to make lasting change for low income and working class communities of color.

SAN FRANCISCO SAFE (SAFETY AWARENESS FOR EVERYONE)

(415) 416-6435
Email: info@sfsafe.org
Web Site: https://sfsafe.org

- SAFE's Security Specialists will walk through your home with you and discuss ways that you can make it safer and more secure. Free.

SAN FRANCISCO TENANTS UNION

558 Capp Street (between 20th and 21st Street)
San Francisco, CA 94110
(415) 282-6622 (recording only)
Email: info@sftu.org (no counseling questions)

Web Site: https://www.sftu.org

- Campaigns, legislation, organizing, and counseling for tenant rights.

- No counseling of landlords or tenants who want to evict other tenants. If the shift is busy, tenants may be turned away.

- Membership or donation of $25 requested except the donation request is reduced for low-income clients.

- One-year membership includes:

  · *Tenants Rights Handbook.*
  · Drop-in counseling for one year. (No appointments.)

· Telephone counseling call-back for one year.
· Join online or by mailing a check with your name and address (and optional email address for emailing you about updates on legislation and actions affecting San Francisco tenants, and optional telephone number) for $50 regular income, $35 low income, and $65 for a household of more than one person. (Membership is $5 less if you do not want the handbook that would be mailed to you.)
- Languages: Spanish and English.

SELF-HELP FOR THE ELDERLY

731 Sansome Street, Suite 100
San Francisco, CA 94111
(415) 677-7600
711 (TDD/TYY)
Web Site: https://www.selfhelpelderly.org

- Assists seniors.

- Tenant rights information.

- Mediation assistance with landlord.

- Elder abuse prevention and intervention.

SENIOR AND DISABILITY ACTION

Mailing Address: P. O. Box 423388
San Francisco, CA 94142-3388
(415) 546-1333
Web Site: https://sdaction.org

- Mobilizes and educates seniors and people with disabilities to fight for individual rights and social justice.

- SRO Workgroup organizes seniors and the disabled in SRO hotels.

SOMCAN (SOUTH OF MARKET COMMUNITY ACTION NETWORK)

Web Site: https://www.somcan.org
Mailing Address: 1110 Howard Street
San Francisco, CA 94103
(415) 255-7693 (English)
(415) 552-5637 (Tagalog)

- Educates and organizes immigrant, people of color, and low-income residents for improvements to their quality of life.

- Info and referral on tenant rights by appointment only.

- Languages: Tagalog, and English.

SRO FAMILIES UNITED COLLABORATIVE

Program of the Chinatown Community Development Center, Chinese Progressive Association, Coalition on Homelessness, Dolores Street Community Services, South of Market Community Action Network
663 Clay Street

San Francisco, CA 94111
(415) 329-3809
Email: info@srofamilies.org
Web Site: https://www.srofamilies.org

- A collaborative of San Francisco organizations that educate and advocate for families living in Single Room Occupancy units.

TENANTS TOGETHER
(888) 495-8020 (tenants' rights hotline)
(415) 495-8100 (general inquiries)
Email: info@tenantstogether.org
Web Site: https://www.tenantstogether.org

- California's only statewide organization for renters' rights. Educates, organizes, and advocates for policy and legislative change at the state and local level.

TENANTS UNION
See *San Francisco Tenants Union*

TENDERLOIN HOUSING CLINIC (THC)
Web Site: https://www.thclinic.org
Legal Programs
(415) 771-9850 (intake phone interview)

- Represents San Francisco low-income tenants primarily seniors, the disabled, and minority and immigrant families as defendants in unlawful detainer actions, in affirmative lawsuits for wrongful eviction, and to address substandard housing.
- Representation for all tenants faced with evictions under the Ellis Act and some owner move-in evictions.
- Free, limited, legal counseling to tenants.

WOMAN, INC.
26 Boardman Place
San Francisco, CA 94103

(877) 384-3578 (24 hours)
(415) 864-4777 (office)
Web Site: www.womaninc.org

- Peer counseling, therapy, and support, and referrals for survivors of domestic violence and family or friends.
- Latinx Program provides case management to Spanish-speaking survivors of domestic violence.
- Languages: Spanish and English.

Governmental Agencies

United States

DEPARTMENT OF HOUSING AND URBAN DEVELOPMENT

Office of Fair Housing and Equal Opportunity
San Francisco Regional Office of FHEO
(415) 489-6524
(800) 347-3739
TTY (415) 436-6594
Civil Rights Complaints: ComplaintsOffice09@hud.gov
Web Site: https://www.hud.gov/program_offices/fair_housing_equal_opp

- Investigates housing discrimination and assists in filing an official discrimination complaint.

California

ACCESS CENTER
400 McAllister Street, Room 509
San Francisco, CA 94102
(415) 551-0605 (Your phone will need to be able to accept blocked calls in order to receive a return call from ACCESS staff.)
Web Site: https://sfsuperiorcourt.org/self-help

- Assists in representing oneself including filling out legal forms (including restraining orders), following court procedures, and finding resources or an attorney.
- Languages: multilingual.

BAY AREA AIR QUALITY MANAGEMENT DISTRICT
Web Site: https://www.baaqmd.gov/online-services/air-pollution-complaints

- For all complaints: The Air District will keep the complainant's personal information confidential, such as name, address, and telephone number, to the fullest extent permitted by law. It is also possible to file your complaint anonymously. Every complaint is investigated.

General Air Pollution
(800) 334-ODOR (6367, 24-hour) or complaint form online

- Report a complaint about odors, smoke, dust, or other air pollutants from gas stations, asbestos, idling trucks, locomotives and buses, open burning, and other commercial, manufacturing, and industrial facilities and operations.

Wood-Burning Devices (Including Fireplaces and Stoves) Complaints
(877) 4NO-BURN (466-2876, 24-hour complaint line) or complaint form online

BUREAU OF REAL ESTATE
See Under Department of Consumer Affairs

CALIFORNIA ENVIRONMENTAL PROTECTION AGENCY
Email: complaints@calepa.ca.gov
Web Site: https://calepacomplaints.secure.force.com/complaints

- Report an environmental problem that affects the quality of our air or water, the handling of hazardous or solid waste, or the use of pesticides.

DEPARTMENT OF CONSUMER AFFAIRS
(800) 952-5210
Web Site: https://www.dca.ca.gov
- Check a contractor's license.

Bureau of Real Estate
(877) DRE-4542 (373-4542)
Web Site: https://www.dre.ca.gov

- File a complaint against subdividers of property with at least 5 units that do not have a "public report" as required by law.

- Verify a real estate license.

- Free guide *California Tenants – A Guide to Residential Tenants' and Landlords' Rights and Responsibilities*

DEPARTMENT OF FAIR EMPLOYMENT AND HOUSING
(800) 884-1684
(800) 700-2320 (TTY)
Email: contact.center@dfeh.ca.gov
Web Site: https://www.dfeh.ca.gov

- Investigates discrimination.

SECRETARY OF STATE
Web Site: https://businesssearch.sos.ca.gov

- Information on corporation/partnership that are owners of your housing.

SMALL CLAIMS COURT
400 McAllister Street
San Francisco, CA 94102
(415) 551-0605 (Your phone will need to be able to accept blocked calls in order to receive a return call from ACCESS staff.)
Web Site: https://www.courts.ca.gov/selfhelp-smallclaims.htm

- Sue in amounts up to $10,000.
- No lawyers can represent either side.
- Filing fee (fee waivers for low income): $30 for claim of $0-$1,500, $50 for claim of $1,500.01-$5,000, $75 for claim of $5,000.01-$10,000
- 20-70 days until hearing date after filing. (*https://www.courts.ca.gov/1256.htm* > Going to Small Claims Court)
- Case information is available by party name or by case number online: *https://www.sfsuperiorcourt.org/online-services*
- For assistance, see Access Center.
- Languages: Court interpreters are not provided free of charge unless you are eligible for a fee waiver. (https://www.courts.ca.gov/1013.htm)

SUPERIOR COURT
400 McAllister Street
San Francisco, CA 94102
(415) 551-3802 (records)
(415) 551-4000 (recording)
(415) 551-4001 (TTY/TDD)
Web Site: https://www.sfsuperiorcourt.org

- Case information is available by party name or by case number
- File and defend lawsuits including unlawful detainers, and restraining orders.

San Francisco

311
311 (24 hours, 365 days/year)
(415) 701-2323 (TTY)
Web Site: https://sf311.org

- Request city services (including anonymously)

ADULT PROTECTIVE SERVICES
(800) 814-0009 (24 hours)
Web Site: https://www.sfhsa.org/services/protection-safety/adult-abuse

- Anyone can make a confidential report if they know or suspect that an elderly or disabled person who lives in San Francisco is being abused or neglected. If necessary, an Emergency Response Worker will make a home visit to investigate and to determine what services are needed.

ASSESSOR/RECORDER
1 Dr. Carlton B. Goodlett Place, Room 190
San Francisco, CA 94102
(415) 554-5596
Email: assessor@sfgov.org
Web Site: https://sfassessor.org

- Research property information, details in *Chapter 3: Researching Landlords, Buildings, and Laws*.

ANIMAL CARE & CONTROL
1419 Bryant Street
San Francisco, CA 94103
(415) 554-6364

(628) 652-8870 (TDD)
Web Site: https://www.sfanimalcare.org/services/service-support-animals

- Tags for service dogs and information about support animals.

BOARD OF APPEALS (PERMIT APPEALS)

(628) 652-1150/311
(415) 575-6885 (fax)
Email: boardofappeals@sfgov.org
Web Site: https://sfgov.org/bdappeal

- Appeal landlord demolition, construction, and conversion permits.
- Archived meetings may be viewed on request. Decisions online.

BOARD OF SUPERVISORS

1 Dr. Carlton B. Goodlett Place, Room 244
San Francisco, CA 94102-4689
(415) 554-5184
(415) 554-5163 (fax)
(415) 554-5227 (TTY)
Email: board.of.supervisors@sfgov.org
Web Site: https://sfbos.org

- Write, call, and/or attend hearings when tenant issues come before the Board.

CITY ATTORNEY

(415) 554-4700
Email: cityattorney@sfcityatty.org
Web Site: https://www.sfcityattorney.org

- The San Francisco City Attorney's Office regularly investigates violations of state and local housing and safety codes, and pursues civil actions to protect tenants from abusive landlords and predatory real estate practices. The City Attorney has won cases over the years to protect rent control, halt unlawful evictions and compel improvements to habitability. Successful efforts include suing CitiApartments to stop abusive anti-tenant practices, and invoking a state law to protect tenants from utility shutoffs during foreclosures.

DEPARTMENT OF BUILDING INSPECTION (DBI)

For more info on using DBI for repairs and services, see "Department of Building Inspection" in "Chapter 6: Repairs and Services." For more info on permits, see "Building Permits" in "Chapter 12: Changes in Use."
1660 Mission Street
San Francisco, CA 94103
(628) 652-3400 (Housing Inspection for housing code violations but not plumbing and electrical violations. See number below.)
(415) 558-6570 (Plumbing or Electrical Inspection Divisions for plumbing or electrical code violations)
(415) 558-6084 (code questions)
(415) 558-6088 (general information)

Email: dbicustomerservice@sfgov.org (call instead of email for a housing code violation inspection request)
Web Site: https://sfdbi.org (call instead of using the web form for a housing code violation inspection request)

- Contact when you have habitability problems except if you live in an illegal unit since DBI may evict you. Inspects buildings for compliance with building codes, building permits, and responds to complaints.
  - Housing Inspection enforces the Housing Code by inspecting buildings for residential maintenance. Also addresses complaints, and conducts inspections for interior/exterior lead-based paint disturbance.
- Research building permits, complaints, inspection reports, and citations online. Be notified about any permit applications for your block by a free alert at *https://sfdbi.org/buildingeye* or a "Block Book Notice."
- Has taken steps to protect tenants from utility shutoffs when property is being foreclosed.
- Code Enforcement Outreach Program (CEOP) answers questions about the Housing Code and habitability compliance, mediates with property owners and tenants especially for limited English speakers. Will not cite illegal unit. (628) 652-3700.

Single Room Occupancy (SRO) Task Force, Housing Inspection Services
Department of Building Inspection
49 South Van Ness Avenue, 4th Floor
San Francisco, CA 94103
(628) 652-3396
Email: jennifer.cheungjew@sfgov.org
Web Site: https://sfdbi.org/single-room-occupancy-sro-task-force

- Improves the quality of life for SRO residents by providing a discussion with city departments, SRO owners/managers, and nonprofit agencies. The Task Force's advises on policies, codes, and legislation.
- Meetings are accessible and open to the public, the third Thursday of every month from 9:00 am–10:30 am.
- Languages: To request an interpreter for a specific item during the meeting, contact Bernadette Perez at 628-652-3390 or Bernadette.Perez@sfgov.org at least 48 hours in advance.

DEPARTMENT OF PLANNING

49 South Van Ness Ave, Suite 140
San Francisco, CA 94103
(628) 652.7600
(415) 575-6863 (code enforcement complaint hotline)
Web Site: https://sfplanning.org

- Report potential code violations including anonymously online, *https://sfplanning.org/enforcement/filing-a-complaint*.
- Search for applications and permits, *https://aca-prod.accela.com/ccsf/Default.aspx*. Be notified about any permit applications for your block by a free alert at *https://sfdbi.org/buildingeye* or a Block Book Notice,

https://sfplanning.org/resource/block-book-notification.

Planning Information Center (PIC)
49 South Van Ness Ave, 2nd Floor
(628) 652-7300
Email: pic@sfgov.org

- Answers questions about zoning/land use, the Planning Code, a particular area plan, etc.

- Request Discretionary Review of a building permit application.

DEPARTMENT OF PUBLIC HEALTH (DPH)
Environmental Health
311 (Complaints. Their website states the complaints they handle. However reports are that they do not cite the landlord. Also, they are more likely to punish the tenant for mold or rodents. Usually mold and rodents come with building problems so it also falls under the Department of Building Inspection's jurisdiction which is usually more helpful.)
Web Site: https://www.sfdph.org/dph/EH

- Research complaints by address on *https://sanfrancisco.nextrequest.com.*

DEPARTMENT OF PUBLIC WORKS (DPW)
Telephone: 311
Web Site: https://sfpublicworks.org
Bureau of Street-Use and Mapping
(628) 271-2000
Email: subdivision.mapping@sfdpw.org
Website: https://sfpublicworks.org/services/subdivisions-and-mapping-office-city-and-county-surveyor

- Information on tenant rights during condominium conversions and addresses of buildings being considered for approval.

DISTRICT ATTORNEY
(628) 652-4000
Email: districtattorney@sfgov.org
Web Site: https://sfdistrictattorney.org

- Promotes the use of collaborative courts and restorative justice programs to hold individuals accountable and heal the harm caused to victims of crime.

- Victim Services Department: (628) 652-4100. Provides emotional and financial support, counseling, guidance in navigating the criminal justice system, temporary restraining order assistance, and referrals.

- Consumer Mediation Department: (628) 652-4311, consumer.mediation@sfgov.org

- Fraud Hotline: (628) 652-4311

- Languages: Translation/Interpretation will be provided to callers as needed via the Language Line.

FIRE DEPARTMENT
Web Site: https://sf-fire.org
- Records of inspection, permits, complaints

(*https://sanfrancisco.buildingeye.com/fire*) violations, incidents, and investigation reports. Can request records anonymously.

- A resource for fire code questions. May report fire hazards, but the Department of Building Inspection is a better department for making these complaints.

HEALTH DEPARTMENT
See *Department of Public Health*

HOUSING AUTHORITY
1815 Egbert Avenue
San Francisco, CA 94124
(415) 715-5200
Web Site: sfha.org

- Administrator of San Francisco housing for low income housing projects and Section 8 vouchers.

HUMAN RIGHTS COMMISSION
25 Van Ness Avenue, 8th Floor
San Francisco, CA 94102
(415) 252-2500
Email: hrc.info@sfgov.org
Web Site: https://sf-hrc.org

- Investigates and mediates complaints of discrimination based on: age, ancestry, creed, disability, familial status, gender identity, height, national origin, place of birth, race, religion, sex, sexual orientation, source of income, and weight.

LAW LIBRARY
1145 Market Street, 4th Floor
San Francisco, CA 94103
(415) 554-1772 (general information and circulation)
(415) 554-1797 (reference information)
Email: sflawlibrary@sfgov.org (general information)
Email: sfll.reference@sfgov.org (reference information)
Web Site: https://sflawlibrary.org

- While the staff cannot give legal advice, the librarians may assist in suggesting and locating resources. The staff may also be consulted for suggestions in research strategy. Other services include demonstrations of databases and assistance in using resources

- San Francisco, state and federal materials including digests.

- Extensive free legal databases including Westlaw, Lexis, and Court Forms.

OFFICE OF THE MAYOR
1 Dr. Carlton B. Goodlett Place, Room 200
San Francisco, CA 94102
(415) 554-6141
Web Site: https://sfmayor.org

- Write and call about tenant issues.

- Contact when having difficulty with city bureaucracies.

Appendix A– Resources

Mayor's Office of Housing and Community Development
1 South Van Ness, 5th Floor
San Francisco, CA 94103
(415) 701-5500
Email: sfhousinginfo@sfgov.org
Web Site: https://sfmohcd.org

- Displaced Tenant Housing Preference Program, *https://sfmohcd.org/displaced-tenant-housing-preference* for tenants evicted for Ellis Act, owner move-in, or fire. Email dthpcertificate@sfgov.org for more information.

OFFICE OF THE COUNTY CLERK
1 Dr. Carlton B. Goodlett Place, Room 168
San Francisco, CA 94102
(415) 701-2311
Web Site: https://sfgov.org/countyclerk

- Search for owners of registered businesses (fictitious business names), *https://countyclerk.sfgov.org/Fbn/FbnSearch.*
- Register domestic partners and obtain marriage licenses.
- SF City Identification Card Program.

OFFICE OF SHORT-TERM RENTALS
Email: shorttermrentals@sfgov.org
Web Site: https://sfplanning.org/office-short-term-rentals
(628) 652-7599

- If you suspect that a landlord is running an unsanctioned hotel report it (including anonymously).

POLICE DEPARTMENT
911 (emergency)
(415) 553-0123 (non-emergency situations)
Web Site: https://www.sanfranciscopolice.org

- Report crimes including anonymously.
- Obtain police reports.
- Languages: multilingual.

PUBLIC LIBRARY
Main Library
100 Larkin Street
San Francisco, CA 94102
(415) 557-4400
(415) 557-4433 (TTY)
Web Site: https://sfpl.org

- Collection of state codes, and copies of the San Francisco Tenants Union *Tenants Rights* Handbook (also at branches).

RENT BOARD (SAN FRANCISCO RESIDENTIAL RENT STABILIZATION AND ARBITRATION BOARD)
25 Van Ness Avenue, Suite 320
San Francisco, CA 94102
(415) 252-4600 (phone counseling)

(415) 252-4629 (hearing coordinator)
(415) 554-9845 (TTY)
Web Site: https://sfrb.org

- File free petitions to enforce the Rent Ordinance.
- The Rent Ordinance and Rules and Regulations online.
- Free Alternative Dispute Resolution (ADR) mediation service provided for residential San Francisco tenants for problems with their landlord, roommate and neighbors. Especially effective for noise and nuisance.
- Referrals for tenants.
- Drop-in and phone counseling generally limited to 10 minutes for the drop-in and 5 minutes for phone. Cannot give legal advice.
- Languages: Cantonese, Mandarin, Spanish, and English usually available. Telephone interpretation available in the office for 20 languages. The staff does not provide translation services at hearings or mediations. However, if you are unable to afford an interpreter, you can file a Hardship Application for interpreter services and the Rent Board will hire an interpreter for you. American Sign Language interpreters are also available upon 72 hours request.

Resources Outside of San Francisco

211
211 (telephone number)
Web Site: https://www.211bayarea.org

- Confidential information and referral on tenant services includes eviction prevention.
- Languages: multilingual.

ACCE (ALLIANCE OF CALIFORNIANS FOR COMMUNITY EMPOWERMENT)
213-863-4548
Email: info@calorganize.org
Web Site: https://www.acceaction.org

- A grassroots, member-led, statewide community organization to fight for the policies to improve our communities.

ALAMEDA RENTERS COALITION
(510) 473-2332
Email: alamedarenterscoalition@gmail.com
Web Site: https://www.thealamedarenterscoalition.org, https://www.facebook.com/AlamedaRentersCoalition

- A volunteer-run organization that advocates for renters.

AIDS LEGAL REFERRAL PANEL
See also AIDS Legal Referral Panel under *Non-Governmental Agencies in San Francisco* for more information.
1320 Webster Street
Oakland, CA 94610

ASIAN/PACIFIC ISLANDER LEGAL OUTREACH

See also Asian/Pacific Islander Legal Outreach under *Non-Governmental Agencies in San Francisco* for more information.
310 8th Street, Suite 305, Oakland, CA 94607
(510) 251-2846

BAY AREA LEGAL AID

See Bay Area Legal Aid under *Non-Governmental Agencies in San Francisco* for information.

BAY AREA MEDIATION SERVICES OF THE BAR ASSOCIATION OF SAN FRANCISCO

See Bay Area Mediation Services of the Bar Association of San Francisco under *Non-Governmental Agencies in San Francisco* for information.

BERKELEY TENANTS UNION

Email: info@berkeleytenants.org
Web Site: https://berkeleytenants.org

- Defends and advances the rights of Berkeley renters through grassroots organizing, outreach, and policy advocacy.

CALIFORNIA LAWYERS FOR THE ARTS

2140 Shattuck Avenue, Suite 310
Berkeley, CA 94704
(888) 775-8995
See also California Lawyers for the Arts under *Non-Governmental Agencies in San Francisco* for more information.

CAUSA JUSTA :: JUST CAUSE

See also Causa Justa :: Just Cause under *Non-Governmental Agencies in San Francisco* for more information.
1419 34th Ave., #203, Oakland, CA 94601
(510) 763-5877
(510) 763-5824 (fax)

Clinic
3340 International Blvd., Oakland, CA 94601
(510) 763-5877
(510) 763-5824 (fax)

CENTRO LEGAL DE LA RAZA

3400 E. 12th St., Oakland, CA 94601
Oakland, CA 94601
(510) 437-1554
Email: info@centrolegal.org
Web Site: https://centrolegal.org

- Only for tenants who meet Federal Housing and Urban Development Income Limits.

- Alameda County tenants (except Berkeley, Emeryville, and Albany) who want advice and a referral of needed, call the office.

- Drop-in clinic on tenant rights for Oakland tenants.

CITY OF BERKELEY RENT STABILIZATION BOARD

2125 Milvia Street
Berkeley, CA 94704
(510) 981-RENT (7368)
TTY: (510) 981-6903
Email: rent@cityofberkeley.info (Should include your name, address, a brief description of your issue, if you've received an eviction notice.)
Web Site: https://www.cityofberkeley.info/rent

- Provides information to Berkeley tenants about their rights and responsibilities by phone and email.

- Free mediation services between tenants and landlords.

- Hears petitions and issues decisions.

- Free workshops & seminars on rental law.

CITY OF OAKLAND RENT ADJUSTMENT PROGRAM

250 Frank H. Ogawa Plaza, Suite 5313
Oakland, CA 94612
(510) 238-3721
Email: rap@oaklandca.gov (Include your full name, telephone number, and address.)
Web Site: https://www.oaklandca.gov/topics/rent-adjustment-program

- Information about rent control laws including workshops.

- Free petitions and mediation for disputes.

DISABILITY RIGHTS ADVOCATES (DRA)

2001 Center Street, Fourth Floor
Berkeley, CA 94704
(510) 665-8644
(510) 665-8511 (fax)
Web Site: https://dralegal.org

- Seeks to remedy systemic problems through litigation, education, and advocacy.

EAST BAY COMMUNITY LAW CENTER

2921 Adeline Street
Berkeley, CA 94703
(510) 548-4040 extension 201 (Legal services: leave a brief message summarizing your housing issue (including any notices from your landlord or court), your city of residence, and your phone number)
Email: info@ebclc.org (No inquiries for legal services through email.)
Web Site: https://ebclc.org

- Provides tenant legal services for low income tenants of Alameda, Berkeley, Emeryville, and Oakland.

- Free legal assistance and referrals including eviction defense, housing subsidy termination, rent board hearings, tenant rights, assists tenants on representing themselves.

EVICTION DEFENSE CENTER

350 Frank Ogawa Plaza, Suite 703

Oakland, California 94612
(510) 452-4541
Web Site: https://www.evictiondefensecenteroakland.org

- For Berkeley and Richmond residents:
  legal services on housing matters.

- Alameda County residents:
  legal services if facing an eviction.

- Free or low cost.

HERA (HOUSING AND ECONOMIC RIGHTS ADVOCATES)

P. O. Box 29435
Oakland, CA 94604-0091
(510) 271-8443
(510) 868-4521 (fax)
800-735-2929 (TTY, English)
800-855-3000 (TTY, Spanish)
Email: inquiries@heraca.org
Web Site: heraca.org

- Provides legal advice on discrimination and
  wrongful credit reporting particularly to lower-
  income people, the elderly, immigrants, people
  of color and people with disabilities.

- Representation in court for some cases.

- Workshops for consumers and organizing.

- Languages: Arabic, Chinese, Russian,
  Spanish, Tagalog, and English.

HOUSING EQUALITY LAW PROJECT

180 South Spruce Avenue, Suite 250
South San Francisco, CA, 94080
(415) 434-9400
(650) 273-8143 (fax)
Web Site: housingequality.org

- Investigates housing discrimination. Educates
  and assists tenants, including mediation and
  representation at administrative hearings.

LAWYER REFERRAL & INFORMATION SERVICE

Also serves Marin counties. See Lawyer Referral & Information
Service under *Non-Governmental Agencies in San Francisco*.

LEGAL AID OF MARIN

1401 Los Gamos Drive Suite 101 (also other locations)
San Rafael, CA 94903
(628) 253-5755 (general information)
(415) 492-0230 extension 102 (Appointment request line: Leave
a message including your name, phone number and your town.)
(415) 492-0947 (fax)
Web Site: https://legalaidmarin.org

- Provides eviction defense and assistance with
  habitability, recovering security deposits.

- Organizes and educates tenants.

- Focuses on low-income residents of Marin County.

LEGAL AID SOCIETY OF SAN MATEO

Natalie Lanam Justice Center
Sobrato Center for Nonprofits
330 Twin Dolphin Drive, Suite 123
Redwood City, CA 94065
(800) 381-8898
(650) 558-0915
(650) 517-8973 (fax)
711 (for limited hearing or speaking)
(800) 854-7784 (Spanish)
Web Site: https://www.legalaidsmc.org

- For low-income tenants in San Mateo County.

- Legal assistance for problems with landlords.

- Help obtaining restraining orders.

- Languages: Spanish and English.

OAKLAND EVICTION DEFENSE CENTER

See *Eviction Defense Center*

OAKLAND TENANTS UNION

(510) 704-5276
Email: help@OaklandTenantsUnion.org
Web Site: www.oaklandtenantsunion.org

- Works with other organizations in pushing
  for more tenant-friendly laws.

- Tenant advice hours for Oakland tenants from
  3–5 pm on the 2nd and 4th Sunday of each month
  via Zoom or audio only. Register at: *http://bit.ly/
  otuadvice* by 12 pm on the Sunday of the session you
  want to attend or call and say you are registering for
  Virtual Tenant Advice Hours, and leave your full
  name, phone number and date you wish to attend.

- Available for questions at the Oakland Public
  Library Main Branch on the 1st Sunday of each
  month from 3:00-5:00 pm at the Veteran's Center
  in the main lobby. To schedule a consultation for
  3:15 PM, 3:45 PM, or 4:15 PM, call or email us.

TENANT AND NEIGHBORHOOD COUNCILS (TANC)

(510) 671-5747
Email: organizing@baytanc.com
Web Site: https://baytanc.com

- A member-run housing organization built out of
  the East Bay Democratic Socialists of America. We
  encourage all tenants to join us in organizing councils.

TENANTS TOGETHER

See Tenants Together under *Non-Governmental Agencies in San
Francisco* for information.

Morality, like art, means drawing a line someplace.
Oscar Wilde

Appendix B: List of Changes

Significant Changes to Chapters 3-14 of the 21ˢᵗ Edition of the Tenants Rights Handbook

Researching Landlords, Buildings, and Laws

1. Department of Planning > The Public Portal allows searches of applications and permits, https://aca-prod.accela.com/ccsf/Default.aspx.

2. Assessor and Recorder > If your Internet is too slow for the Assessor database, you may access the Recorder data at https://recorder.sfgov.org.

3. Rent Board > If a case was appealed to the Rent Board Commissioners, info might be found by searching for key words (including names) on the Rent Board's website, https://sfrb.org.

4. Laws on the Web > San Francisco's municipal codes (Administrative, Building, Electrical, Environment, Fire, Health, Housing, Mechanical, Planning, Plumbing, Police, and Subdivision Codes) can be found on https://www.amlegal.com and elaws.us.

Renting Basics, Chapter 4

1. Protections for the Tenant Under the San Francisco Rent Ordinance and State Law (and "Requirements and Protections in Rental Agreements") > Starting April 1, 2020, every online listing for a rental unit covered under the Rent Ordinance, excluding listings by landlords or master tenants who will reside in the same rental unit as their tenants or subtenants, must contain a disclosure in at least 12-point font that includes the following: "This unit is a rental unit subject to the San Francisco Rent Ordinance, which limits evictions without just cause, and which states that any waiver by a tenant of their rights under the Rent Ordinance is void as contrary to public policy." This text should also be included in print advertisements, if practicable. (SF Administrative Code § 37.9F)

2. SF v. CA Exemptions to Rent Control/Just Cause Eviction Table > > California Civil Code § 1946.2 and § 1947.12 > Disclosure > Required ~~for exemption from rent control/just cause~~ if covered, or if exempt as a single-family home.

   Mobilehomes added.

   Sharing Property with Landlord > A ~~duplex~~2 dwelling units structure where the owner occupied 1 of the units as his/her principal place of residence at the beginning of the tenancy and neither unit is an accessory dwelling unit, if the owner continues in occupancy.

   Single Residential Unit > Dwelling units separate from title to any other dwelling unit are ~~covered by~~exempt from rent control/just cause eviction unless...

3. Certificate of Occupancy Date > Effective January 2020, rental units with a certificate of occupancy after June 13, 1979 or which the Rent Board has certified has undergone a substantial rehabilitation are no longer exempt from the Rent Ordinance....

   - Replacement units under San Francisco Administrative Code § 37.9A(b). Search the "Recorded Documents for this property" on the San Francisco Assessor and Recorder's Office website for the restriction.

   - Accessory Dwelling Units with rent limitations under San Francisco Administrative Code § 37.2(r){4}{D}. Look for "ADU" under "Project Profile" for the planning applications....

- Development agreement with the City under San Francisco Administrative Code Chapter 56. <u>Within 10 days after the execution of the development agreement, the agreement shall be recorded with the County Recorder.</u>

4. *Government-Assisted Housing* > Units in project-based government-assisted or government-regulated housing are exempt from the Rent Ordinance <u>except Midtown Park Apartments receive benefits of the Rent Ordinance.</u> (SF Administrative Code § 37.2(r)(4)<u>, § 37B</u>)

5. Substantially Rehabilitated Housing (also the "SF v. CA Exemptions to Rent Control/Just Cause Eviction" chart) > Units that have undergone "substantial rehabilitation" as certified by the Rent Board are <u>no longer</u> exempt from the Rent Ordinance. ~~(SF Administrative Code § 37.2(r)(6), Rent Board Rules and Regulations § 1.18)~~ <u>However, these units are allowed to set the initial and subsequent rent with the same exceptions as the post-1979 certificate of occupancy units. (See the previous section "Certificate of Occupancy Date.")</u>

6. Just Cause Eviction Requirement for Single Residential Units > ~~It is critical to remember, however, that these protections usually apply only to units that received an initial certificate of occupancy before June 13, 1979.~~

7. California Law Disclosure and Ownership Requirement for Single Residential Unit Exception > For a tenancy in a single residential unit that began or renewed on or after July 1, 2020 <u>or if the lease is for a mobilehome July 1, 2022</u>...

8. Rights That CAN Be Signed Away > • The landlord informed the tenant, in writing, that the tenant did not need to accept a proposed change in the rental agreement and the tenant still accepted the change, in writing. <u>Even without this disclosure, the tenant should not agree to the change so the proposed change was unilateral and not allowed.</u>

9. Late Charge > ~~Although~~<u>Except for late rent payments due to COVID-19</u> with a declaration by the tenant <u>(CA Civil Code § 1942.9, check for amendment),</u> charges for late ~~payment of~~ rent may be valid...

10. Posting and Distributing of Information by Tenant (also Chapter 14)> <u>For buildings with 5 or more units, an occupant or guest may hang or place literature on the door of tenant units, or where that is not practical on the floor in front of the units which plainly include the name and telephone number and address of a distributor that the affected tenant may contact to opt out of future literature. (SF Administrative Code §49A.3)</u>

11. Notices and Other Communications Between Landlord and Tenant > In the case of the tenant's death <u>or incapacity to contract</u>, the estate of the deceased is not liable for the rent due to lack of notice to the landlord. (<u>CA Civil Code § 1934,</u> Miller & Desatnik Management Co. v. Bullock (1990) 221 Cal.App.3d Supp. 13)

12. Breaking a Lease > Also, for victims and household <u>or immediate</u> family members of domestic violence, sexual assault, stalking, elder or dependent adult abuse, ~~or~~ human trafficking, <u>or a crime that caused bodily injury or death or included the exhibition of a deadly weapon or threat of or use of force,</u> a tenant may break a lease with fourteen-day notice and documentation.... <u>If the tenant is terminating the tenancy because an immediate family member is a victim and the tenant did not live in the same household as the immediate family member at the time of the act, and no part of the act occurred within the dwelling unit or within 1,000 feet of the dwelling unit of the tenant, the tenant shall attach a statement including that the tenant intends to relocate as a result of the immediate family member being a victim of an eligible act....</u> ~~("Immediate family" includes any person who regularly resides, or, within the six months preceding any portion of the pattern of conduct, regularly resided, in the victim's household.)~~

Repairs and Services, Chapter 6

1. Obligations of the Landlord > <u>• The temperature of the hot water of not less than 110 degrees (CA Code of Regulations, Title 25, Division 1, Chapter 1, Subchapter 1, Article 5, § 32)</u>

2. Compensation for Retrofit > The required compensation <u>for units covered under the SF Rent Ordinance</u> does not exceed 15% of the monthly base rent, pro-rated, and a comparable service may be provided instead.

3. Disclosure Requirements for Smoke, Carbon Monoxide and Fire Safe<u>ty > (3)</u> ~~The location of all smoke alarms and carbon monoxide detectors in the dwelling unit, h~~How to confirm the <u>smoke alarms and</u> carbon monoxide detectors are in working condition, and when they ~~carbon monoxide detectors~~ were last replaced....

   ~~(7) The owner shall maintain a record of the disclosures by requesting each dwelling unit provide a Resident's Statement that the resident has received the disclosures to the owner upon occupancy and each subsequent year. A tenant's failure to provide a Resident's Statement is not a just cause for eviction.~~

4. Fire Extinguishers > Generally, the owner must provide a fire extinguisher on each floor which has common hallways. (*https://sf-fire.org/fire-safety-requirements-building-owners*)

5. <u>Ventilation for Urban Infill Sensitive Developments > Enhanced ventilation is required for urban infill sensitive use development within the Air Pollutant Exposure Zone. The map is available by searching on *sfdph.org* and the details in SF Health Code Article 38.</u>

6. Security > <u>Metal gates also have security requirements. (SF Building Code § 1003A.5)</u>

7. <u>Circuit Breaker Access > The legal occupant of the dwelling shall have access to all circuit breakers of their dwelling. (California Electrical Code § 240.24(B))</u>

8. Petitions for Lack of Services > <u>Under SF Administrative Code § 49A.5: right to organize and meet with the landlord.</u>

9. Parking, Storage, or Laundry Room Severance > <u>The tenant may also sue for an injunction which has been successful in the past, making it clear the tenant had a right to the parking without needing to go to trial.</u>

10. Retaliation Is Illegal > <u>There are limits to how often the retaliation may be asserted under California Civil Code § 1942.5.</u>

11. Heating Requirements > The requirement for hotels is 68 <u>degrees between the hours of 5:00 a.m. and 11:00 a.m. and 3:00 p.m. and 10:00 p.m.</u>

12. Compensation for Mold Problems > <u>If the tenant must move out temporarily under the SF Rent Ordinance, the requirements of a temporary capital improvement eviction applies. (See the section Capital Improvement Temporary Evictions" in *Chapter 12: Eviction Defenses*.")</u>

Rent Increases, Chapter 7

1. Rent Increases Under California Law > <u>(The California Apartment Association recommends using the March number for the prior calendar year if the April number is not available, *https://caanet.org/where-are-the-new-cpi-figures-for-rent-increases-under-ab-1482*.)</u>...rent increases over 10% of costs following a ~~natural disaster~~<u>state of emergency</u> declaration (CA Penal Code § 396, *https://caloes.ca.gov/cal-oes-divisions/legal-affairs/price-gouging*) are prohibited. <u>Tenants with rent debt due to COVID-19 and who have submitted a declaration may not have fees increased or charged for services previously provided without charge. (CA Civil Code § 1942.9, check for amendment)... You may request the SF Rent Board contact your landlord (use the request form called Report of Excessive Rent Increase Under the Tenant Protection Act) if you believe your landlord has increased your rent in noncompliance with California rent control. The Rent Board will not enforce the law, but having a government agency contacting your landlord may encourage compliance.</u>

Appendix B – List of Changes

2. Annual Rent Increases > <u>Starting July 1, 2022, a landlord is required to report information about their rental unit to the Rent Board to obtain a license to impose the rent increase.</u>

3. Gas, Electricity or Steam Heat Passthroughs > If payment of a utility passthrough causes a financial hardship for the tenant, the tenant may seek relief ~~from the passthrough. Where the landlord has filed a petition, the tenant can file an appeal based on financial hardship within fifteen days after the decision approving the passthrough is mailed to the tenant. Where the landlord has filed a Utility Passthrough Calculation Worksheet instead of a petition, the tenant can file~~ <u>by filing</u> a Hardship Application form with the Board within one year of the effective date of the passthrough. <u>Payment of the passthrough is suspended from the date of filing until a decision is made on the Tenant Financial Hardship Application. For a passthrough based on a petition from the landlord, the hardship application cannot be filed until the tenant receives the notice of rent increase or decision of the Administrative Law Judge, whichever is earlier.</u>

4. Required Seismic and Code Work Capital Improvement Passthroughs > <u>If the total monthly proposed capital improvement passthrough exceeds the greater of $30.00 or 10% of the tenant's base rent at the time the petition is filed, the landlord must limit the initial passthrough to $30.00 or 10% of the tenant's petition base rent, whichever is greater. The landlord may accumulate or "bank" the remaining portion of the passthrough and impose it in subsequent years at the rate of $30.00 or 10% of the tenant's petition base rent per year, until the full passthrough amount is completely imposed. (SF Rent Board Form 528)</u>

5. Filed after November 14, 2002 > For passthroughs filed after November 14, 2002, a tenant's rent cannot be increased more than 5% annually for properties with five or fewer units or 10% annually for properties with six or more units except see <u>previous sections for exceptions for work required by law and energy conservation, and</u> the following sections for variables related to 50% passthroughs and lifetime 15% cap.

Harassment, Chapter 8

1. Noise and Nuisance from a Neighbor > <u>(7) File a petition for Decrease in Housing Services with the Rent Board if you are covered under the Rent Ordinance. The Rent Board has awarded rent reductions for noise (SF Rent Board Case #AL 190090) or for the landlord's failure to provide quiet enjoyment (see definition of quiet enjoyment and case #AL180101) as long as the breach is not caused by the landlord.</u>

2. Stopping These Types of Harassment > • ~~File a petition with the Rent Board, if your unit is covered under the Rent Ordinance, for a decrease in housing services due to the landlord's failure to provide quiet enjoyment (see definition of quiet enjoyment and case #AL180101) or illegal entry.~~<u>For failure to exercise reasonable care in completing maintenance or to follow appropriate protocols to minimize exposure to noise, dust, mold, or building materials with potentially harmful health effects, in bad faith, file a petition for Decrease in Housing Services with the Rent Board if you are covered under the Rent Ordinance's rent control. (SF Administrative Code § 37.10B(a)(3))</u>

Discrimination, Chapter 9

1. Reasonable Accommodations and Modifications > <u>A landlord will be required to cease eviction proceedings at whatever stage they are in, even if made aware of the tenant's disability and need for an accommodation only after notice of the eviction was provided to the tenant, or after the eviction complaint was filed. (Radecki v. Joura, 114 F.3d 115 (8th Cir. 1997))</u>...~~Restoration of the property to the original condition is not required when modifications have been made to public or common use areas. (https://www.fairhousingfirst.org/documents/AccommodationsAndModifications.pdf)~~

2. Disability and Animal Support > The Fair Housing Amendments Act of 1988 applies to service animals in housing, not the Americans with Disabilities Act, which ~~does not address the topic~~only applies to housing made available by a public entity, and private entities that own, lease (to and from), and operate places of public accommodation.

Changes in Use, Chapter 11

1. Vacation and Corporate Guest Suite Rentals by the Landlord > San Francisco Planning Code § 202.10 has limitation on intermediate length occupancies that are defined as more than 30 days but less than 1 year (SF Planning Code § 102).

2. Accessory Dwelling Units > The owner is required to file with the Rent Board a declaration signed under penalty of perjury that the project will comply with the requirements of SF Administrative Code§ 37.2(r) and 37.9 relating to severance or reduction of a housing service. The owner will cause a notice describing the proposed project to be delivered to each unit (including unauthorized units) at the property and posted in an accessible common area of the building for at least 15 days before submitting an application to construct an ADU. The property owner shall submit proof of these notices to the Planning Department as part of the application. These notices shall also include instructions on how a tenant may petition the Rent Board for a written determination on the declaration. (SF Planning Code Section 207(c)(4)(C) and (J))

3. Demolition of a Rental Unit and Mergers > To merge units covered under the Rent Ordinance (see "What Does the Rent Ordinance Cover?" in "Chapter 4: Renting Basics"), a landlord must first have a just cause to evict (see "Chapter 12: Eviction Defenses") and a conditional use authorization is required except where there is no path to legalization or is economically unfeasible (unsound). Generally if the cost to upgrade the unit(s) to safe and habitable standards costs more than 50% of the cost to replace the existing unit(s) at the same size, it would be considered unsound. The Department of Planning ~~has been holding mandatory discretionary review or conditional use~~holds public hearings ~~of most merger applications~~unless it is a listed exception. ~~Housing that is not affordable or not sound does not require a public hearing. Generally if the cost to upgrade the unit(s) to safe and habitable standards costs more than 50% of the cost to replace the existing unit(s) at the same size, it would be considered unsound. Merger proposals also are supposed to provide notification by posting on the property.~~

Eviction Defenses, Chapter 12

1. 10 Day Warning Notice > This legislation has been put on hold, case # CPF-22-517718, SF Apartment Assoc. and Small Property Owners of San Francisco v. City and County of San Francisco.

2. Nonpayment of Rent > COVID-19 Recovery Period October 2021-March 2022

   • Tenants who cannot pay 100% of their rent each month from October 2021-March 2022 may be able to stop or delay an eviction with rental assistance .

   • A 3-day pay or quit notice must include language telling tenants about how to apply for rent relief and encouraging them to do so within 15 days. (CA Code of Civil Procedure § 1179.10(a))

   • The landlord cannot get a summons for unlawful detainer without certifying to the court that they applied for rent relief and the application was denied or that they applied for rent relief and that they were not notified that the tenant had applied for relief for the period demanded in the notice. (CA Code of Civil Procedure § 1179.11(a))

   • Tenants should not borrow money or not pay for other essentials to pay this rent if they are qualified for rent relief and have a pending application.

Appendix B – List of Changes

April 2022 and After If Covered Under the San Francisco Rent Ordinance > A tenant may not be evicted for nonpayment of rent if the tenant shows the inability to pay rent was due to COVID-19. (SF Administrative Code § 37.9(a)(1)(E))

3. Waiver, Estoppel, and Change of Agreement: Unenforced Rental Agreement Provisions as Defenses to an Eviction > (The difference between waiver and estoppel is in a waiver, the landlord did something. In an estoppel argument, the landlord did something and you relied on it. Laches are where the landlord did not do something, in other words, sat on their rights. Estoppel and laches arguments rarely go to trial.)

4. Senior, Disabled, and Dying Tenants > •   Catastrophically ill tenants who have a diagnosis of a ~~terminal illness~~life threatening illness and who receive SSI or are eligible for SSI, and have five or more years of tenancy.

5. Capital Improvement Temporary Evictions > In addition, the landlord must provide a form from the Rent Board that advises the tenant that the tenant's failure to timely act in response to a notice to vacate may result in a lawsuit by the landlord to evict the tenant, advice regarding the notice to vacate is available from the Rent Board, the tenant may be eligible for affordable housing programs through the Mayor's Office of Housing and Community Development....

6. Households with Children or School Workers Protected During School Year from Capital Improvement Evictions > The landlord must warn the tenant to submit a statement to the landlord within 30 days of service of the notice to vacate, with supporting evidence, if the tenant claims to be a member of a protected class under Ordinance Sections 37.9(j), and that failure to do so shall be deemed an admission that the tenant is not protected by Sections 37.9(j).

7. Re-Rent to New Tenant at Same Rent After Ellis Eviction Under the SF Rent Ordinance (also "Procedural Requirements for OMI Under SF Rent Ordinance" > "Re-Rental Restrictions," "Capital Improvement Temporary Evictions," "Removing a Unit from Housing Use Without a City Development Agreement (SF Administrative Code § 37.9(a)(10)" > Also, the Anti-Eviction Mapping Project maps these evictions. See Appendix A: Resources for more info.

Eviction Process, Chapter 13

1. Bypassing the Courts: Lodgers and Hotels > In addition, a landlord may evict an occupant in a ~~residential~~ hotel without going to court if the occupant has lived there for no more than thirty days, or who hasn't paid the full rent for the first thirty days.

Taking Action, Chapter 14

1. Hardship Appeal at Tenant's Request > • *Operating and Maintenance Expense Increase Passthrough* or *Utility Passthrough ~~based on a Utility Passthrough Petition~~*, a tenant may file a hardship appeal within one year of the effective date of the passthrough.

2. Starting a Tenants Union > If your building has five or more rental units that is organizing for the purpose of addressing housing conditions, community life, landlord-tenant relations, and/or similar issues of common interest or concern among tenants in the building, you have a right to form a Tenant Association under Chapter 49A of the SF Administrative Code. Provide your landlord a petition signed by tenants of 50% or more of the occupied units that you desire to form a Tenant Association, and identifying the Association. A landlord must on written request of a Tenant Association attend at least one Tenant Association meeting per calendar quarter. This requirement does not apply to some nonprofit landlords. Failure to comply with Chapter 49A is a decrease in housing services (see "Petitions for Lack of Services" in "Chapter 6: Repairs and Services.")

Appendix C: San Francisco Law and Regulations Excerpts

Uniform Hotel Visitor Policy

1. No operator, employee or agent of a Residential Hotel, as defined in San Francisco Administrative Code Section 41.4(p), may impose or collect a charge for any person to visit a guest or occupant of the hotel. Additionally, no owner or operator of a single room occupancy hotel (SRO) shall deny a guest or occupant of the hotel the right as to:

A. Day Time Visitors

1. To receive visitors between 9:00 a.m. and 9:00 p.m. daily. A maximum of two (2) day time visitors at a time per room may be imposed by management. There is no limit on the total number of visitors a tenant may have per day, week or month.

2. Children 13 years old and under shall not be counted towards the visitor limitation rule. However, a maximum of two (2) children per room at a time can be imposed by management.

3. Census workers shall be allowed access to Residential Hotels during the hours of 9 a.m. until 8 p.m. for the purpose of census activities. For the purposes of this subsection, the term "census activities" means any activity that has as its primary purpose encouraging SRO occupants to participate in the census, including but not limited to conducting surveys and distributing handbills, door hangers and flyers related to the census.

For the purposes of this subsection, the term "census worker" means an official employee of the U.S. Census Bureau or of an organization contracted by the City and County of San Francisco to perform Census outreach and education. Census employees shall present valid identification issued by the Bureau to a front desk clerk or property management staff. Employees of City-funded census outreach organizations shall present documentation from the Office of Citizen Engagement and Immigrant Affairs confirming that they are contracted with the City for Census outreach.

B. Overnight Guests

1. To have eight (8) overnight guests per month, limited to one visitor per tenant per night. Only tenants who have resided in their unit for thirty-two (32) continuous days or more shall be entitled to have overnight guests. Court-ordered custodial rights, which end at age seventeen (17), shall be honored for purposes of consecutive overnight stays but any such visits shall be counted toward the limitation on the number of overnight visitors.

2. For tenancies of two (2) persons per room, each tenant is permitted to have eight (8) overnight visitors per calendar month, but those tenants will have to reach agreement as to who will have the one (1) visitor per night if there is a dispute.

3. Tenants are entitled to have a visitor stay eight (8) days consecutively in a calendar month. Any visitor staying consecutive nights, as agreed upon, shall not be required to check in and out during the course of a consecutive stay. Otherwise, the visitor must check out by 11:00 a.m. or make arrangements with the desk to become a day time visitor.

4. Requests for overnight guests shall be made no later than 9:00 p.m. on the same day. If a request is made but no visitor stays past 9:00 that evening, the request shall not be counted against the tenant's allowed eight (8) overnight guests per month, as long as the tenant has informed management in writing by 6:00 p.m. the following day that no overnight visit took place. The visitor does not have to be present at the time the request is made and the visitor's name need not be provided until the visitor arrives at the hotel, after which time the visitor shall have the same in and out privileges as the resident.

C. Caregivers of disabled tenants shall be exempt from visitor limitations. The owner or operator of the hotel may request medical verification or a caregiver I.D. card.

2. Owners and operators of SROs shall have the right to adopt reasonable rules and regulations to ensure that the visitor rights set forth above do not infringe on the health and safety of the building and/or otherwise interfere with the tenants' right of quiet enjoyment.

A. Owners or operators are entitled to request that visitors produce identification as follows:

1. Only ONE valid California or out-of-state current government agency issued picture I.D. need be provided, including but not limited to: a valid and current passport, a California Department of Motor Vehicles (DMV) issued

I.D., a Mexican Consular Registration Card or Resident Alien Card, merchant seaman I.D., a Day Labor Program I.D., Veteran's Administration I.D or San Francisco City I.D. card.

2. Owners/managers cannot require that an I.D. be left with management during the visitor's stay. If an I.D. is not left with management, tenants must escort their visitors out of the building and make sure that they sign out. If a tenant's visitor does not sign out upon leaving, the tenant may lose their visitor privileges for thirty days, which must be put in writing within seven days.

3. A log must be maintained by management and the visitor must sign in and sign out. The log shall indicate when an I.D. is surrendered and when it is returned.

4. If an I.D. is lost or misplaced and not returned within 12 hours of the visitor's request to have it returned, the owner/manager shall pay the visitor $75.00 in cash immediately upon demand by the visitor as compensation for the loss and inconvenience of replacing the lost I.D.

B. Owners and operators shall have the specific right to restrict visitors on two (2) of the three (3) actual check days of each month. Providers are required to post those blackout dates at least five (5) days prior to the first blackout date on a minimum size of 8-1/2" x 11", to be posted prominently by the entrance or in the lobby. Blackout dates shall not apply to children thirteen (13) years of age and under, custodial children or consecutive visitors.

C. Owners and operators may deny visitor rights for 30 days to tenants who are repeat violators of hotel visiting rules. No penalty may be imposed until the second violation, and violations shall expire after 18 months. All notices of violation of the policy, including the first notice, must be in writing with a copy provided to the tenant. These limitations on the right to revoke visitor rights do not apply in the case of failing to ensure that a guest signs out upon leaving the building, as specified in Section 2A(2) above.

D. Tenants who disagree with the imposition of a penalty may either:

1. appeal to the operator or tenant representative (if one is present); or, in the alternative,

2. the tenant may go directly to the Rent Board for adjudication of their complaint.

E. Owners and operators shall also have the right to limit the number of nights any single visitor can make to the property to eight (8) per calendar month.

F. Tenants shall not be required to escort their visitors to the bathroom or other common areas of the building, except as specified in Section 2A(2) above. However, the tenant is responsible for the conduct of their unaccompanied visitor.

3. Nothing in this section shall interfere with the rights of owners and operators of SROs to exclude specific visitors who willfully or wantonly:

A. disturb the peaceful enjoyment of the premises by other tenants and neighbors;

B. destroy, deface, damage, impair, or remove any part of the structure or dwelling unit, or the facilities or equipment used in common; or,

C. have committed repeated violations of the visitor policy which can be construed as creating a nuisance on the property; or constituting substantial interference with the comfort, safety or enjoyment of the landlord or tenants, which can be a just cause for eviction under the Rent Ordinance, as determined by the courts.

D. Any time a tenant's visitor is excluded from the hotel, written notice must be delivered to the tenant after the fact with the visitor's name and the reason for the exclusion.

4. SRO owners or operators shall make available to their tenants a copy of any written Supplemental Visitor Policy that complies with this policy. SRO owners or operators are required to prominently post the Uniform Visitor Policy and any Supplemental Visitor Policy on a minimum size of 11" x 17" by the entrance or in the lobby.

5. Other than as a settlement of an unlawful detainer action, a tenant cannot waive the rights as outlined in this legislation. Any agreement between the SRO owner or operator and the tenant that reduces or limits the rights set forth in this legislation shall be deemed void and unenforceable.

6. Tenants are accorded certain and specific rights as a result of this legislation. If the SRO owner or operator violates this provision, a tenant will have legal recourse and will be encouraged to visit the San Francisco Rent Stabilization Board or the Police, as appropriate. Pursuant to Police Code Section 919.1(b), in addition to any available civil penalties, any operator, employee or agent of a Residential Hotel who violates any of the provisions of this Uniform Hotel Visitor Policy shall be guilty of an infraction, the penalty for which shall be a fine of not less than $50 nor more than $500, consistent with the California Government Code.

7. SRO owners or operators seeking a modification of the rights set forth above may file a petition with the San Francisco Rent Stabilization Board and receive a hearing on said petition. Notice of the time and date of said hearing shall be prominently posted by the SRO owner or operator above the front desk of

the hotel, in the lobby and at least five (5) copies shall be posted on each floor of the building.

8. The Rent Board shall translate the Uniform Visitor Policy into the predominant languages of the community and make them available as needed. (As amended March 30, 2010.)

§ 49.1 Security Deposit Defined

As provided in Section 1950.5 of the California Civil Code, a security deposit is any payment, fee, deposit or charge including, but not limited to, any of the following:

(1) The compensation of a landlord for a tenant's default in the payment of rent;

(2) the repair of damages to the premises caused by the tenant;

(3) the cleaning of the premises upon termination of the tenancy. **Leg. H.**1983.

§ 49.2 Interest on Security Deposits

(a) A landlord who is subject to the provisions of Section 1950.5 of the California Civil Code shall pay simple interest on all security deposits held for at least one year for his/her tenants; provided, however, that this requirement shall not apply where the rent is assisted or subsidized by any government unit, agency or authority.

(b) Interest shall begin accruing on September 1, 1983, or on whatever date the security deposit is received by the landlord after September 1, 1983, and shall accrue until the tenancy terminates. Beginning on September 1, 1984, or on any date thereafter upon which the security deposit has been held by the landlord for one year, and annually thereafter on the same month and day, a tenant shall be given the unpaid accrued interest in the form of ether a direct payment or a credit against the tenant's rent. The landlord shall choose between these two methods of payment.

(c) Upon termination of tenancy, a tenant whose security deposit has been held for one year or more shall be entitled to a direct pro-rata payment of any unpaid accrued interest no later than two weeks after the tenant has vacated the premises; provided, however, that a landlord may retain any portion of the unpaid accrued interest, subject to the limitations and requirements set forth in Section 1950.5(e) of the California Civil Code, where the security deposit alone is insufficient to remedy tenant default in the payment of rent, to repair damages to the premises caused by the tenant, exclusive of ordinary wear and tear, or to clean such premises, if necessary, upon termination of the tenancy.

(d) Nothing in this Chapter shall preclude a landlord from exercising his or her discretion in investing security deposits.

(e) Notwithstanding the provisions of (a) through (c) above, where a landlord seeks reimbursement for the annual Residential Rent Stabilization and Arbitration fee as provided in Section 37A.6 of this Code, the landlord may deduct said fee from the next interest payment owed to the tenant pursuant to this Chapter.

(f) The interest rate for interest payments required by this Chapter 49 shall be determined by the Residential Rent Stabilization and Arbitration Board (Rent Board), to be effective on March 1 of each year.

(1) For March 1, 2003 and prior years, the Rent Board shall calculate the rate as of the immediately preceding December 31st according to the historical Federal Reserve Discount Window Borrowing Rate, using an average of the twelve most recent monthly rates (rounded to the nearest tenth) as posted by the Federal Reserve on the Federal Reserve Statistical Release internet site.

(2) For March 1, 2004 through March 1, 2014, the Rent Board shall calculate the rate as of the immediately preceding December 31st according to the Federal Reserve 6-Month Certificate of Deposit rate, using an average of the twelve most recent monthly rates (rounded to the nearest tenth) as posted by the Federal Reserve on the Federal Reserve Statistical Release internet site.

(3) For March 1, 2015 and each year thereafter, the Rent Board shall calculate the rate according to the annual average of the 90-Day AA Financial Commercial Paper Interest Rate (rounded to the nearest tenth) for the immediately preceding calendar year as published by the Federal Reserve.

(g) The amount of interest due and payable by the landlord shall be the amount of the security deposit held by the landlord on the date the interest payment is due multiplied by either:

(1) The interest rate in effect on the date the annual payment is due, if the payment is due under Section 49.2(b); or

(2) The interest rate in effect on the date the tenant vacates the unit, if the tenant is entitled to a pro-rata interest payment under Section 49.2(c). **Leg. H.** 1983, 1989, 1990, 2002, 2003, 2004, 2014.

§ 49.3 Remedies

The rights, obligations and remedies of tenants and landlords under this Chapter shall be as provided in Subsections (f), (g), (h) and (j) of Section 1950.5 of the California Civil Code. **Leg. H.** 1983.

§ 49.4 Waiver

Any waiver by a tenant of rights under this Chapter shall be void as contrary to public policy. **Leg. H.** 1983.

§ 65A.1 Seismic Work Required for Building Code Chapter 34B Provides Tenant Compensation: Applicability

This Chapter shall apply to residential rental units subject to Administrative Code Chapter 37 "Residential Rent Stabilization and Arbitration Ordinance" when, in accordance with Administrative Code Section 37.2(r), one or more specified housing services will be temporarily severed from such a rental unit during the performance of seismic work required by Building Code Chapter 34B "Mandatory Earthquake Retrofit of Wood-Frame Buildings" ("mandatory seismic work"). Consistent with Section 37.2(r), the specified housing services covered by this Chapter 65A are: garage facilities, parking facilities, driveways, storage spaces, laundry rooms, decks, patios, or gardens on the same lot, or kitchen facilities or lobbies in single room occupancy (SRO) hotels, supplied in connection with the use or occupancy of a unit ("services"). Tenants in an affected unit shall be entitled to either compensation or a substitute housing service, as provided in this Chapter 65A. **Leg. H.** 2014.

§ 65A.2 Notice of Severance of Housing Services

The landlord shall provide 30-days written notice to temporarily sever the specified housing service(s), to the tenants in each affected unit. This notice shall include the length of time the specified housing service(s) will be temporarily severed. The landlord must obtain all necessary permits on or before the date the notice to temporarily sever is given. **Leg. H.** 2014.

§ 65A.3 Compensation for Required Seismic Work

Calculation and distribution of landlord compensation payments to tenants of affected units shall be as follows:

(a) If the rental unit lease or other written agreement states a rate for the housing service to be severed, that rate shall be used to calculate the amount due on a daily basis.

(b) If there is no rate stated in the lease or other written agreement for the housing service to be severed, the rate shall be equal to the current replacement value of the service to be severed; that rate shall be used to calculate the amount due on a daily basis.

(1) The amount due pursuant to this Subsection 65A.3(b) for each such temporarily severed housing service shall not exceed 15% of the monthly base rent for the rental unit, pro-rated on a daily basis.

(2) The replacement value of the severed housing service will depend on the facts of each case. The following factors may be considered in the determination of replacement value:

(A) The rates for parking or storage or other severed housing service in the same neighborhood at the time the tenant first rented the parking or storage space or other service, adjusted by the amount of the intervening annual allowable rent increases; the current replacement value of the parking or storage space or other service in the same neighborhood as the tenant's unit; and/or the amount the landlord charges other tenants in the same property for the same service.

(B) If the parking or storage space or other housing service was provided to the tenant after the inception of the tenancy and the tenant does not pay any additional rent for the service, no compensation will be due upon temporary severance of the service.

(3) One-half of the compensation payment shall be due upon service of the notice of temporary severance of housing service; the remaining one-half shall be due on the date that the temporary severance actually commences. **Leg. H.** 2014.

§ 65A.4 Substitute Housing Service as an Alternative

As an alternative to paying compensation as provided in Section 65A.3, the landlord may choose to provide a comparable housing service that is reasonably near the affected unit ("substitute housing service"). **Leg. H.** 2014

§ 65A.5 Rent Board Petitions for Required Seismic Work

Either a landlord or a tenant may file a petition with the Rent Board to determine the amount of compensation or sufficiency of the substitute housing service under this Chapter 65A. **Leg. H.** 2014.

§ 65A.6 Non-Tenants and Required Seismic Work

If an individual rents a parking or storage space or other service on a property but that service is not rented in connection with the use or occupancy of a housing unit owned or operated by the landlord, such a rental of the service alone is a commercial transaction that is not covered by this Chapter 65A or Administrative Code Chapter 37 (Residential Rent Stabilization and Arbitration Ordinance). **Leg. H.** 2014

San Francisco Housing Code

§ 204 SF Housing Code Enforcement Provisions

(a) Criminal Penalty for Violation; Citations.

(1) Any person or entity who violates, disobeys, omits, fails, neglects or refuses to comply with, or who resists or opposes the execution of any of the provisions of this Code, or any notice or order of the Director of the Department of Building Inspection made pursuant to this Code, relating to fire safety, the provision of heat or hot water, or the existence of conditions that endanger the life, limb, health or safety of any person or

the public may be charged with a misdemeanor pursuant to Section 204(b). The penalty upon conviction thereof shall be a fine of not less than $500 or more than $1,000, or imprisonment, no part of which may be suspended. A person convicted of violating this Code shall be deemed guilty of a separate offense for every day such violation, disobedience, omission, failure, neglect or refusal shall continue. Any person who shall do any work in violation of any of the provisions of this Code, or any order of the Director of the Department of Building Inspection made pursuant to this Code, and any person having charge of such work who shall permit it to be done, shall be liable for the penalty provided.

(2) Any person or entity who violates, disobeys, omits, fails, neglects or refuses to comply with any provision of this Code, or any notice or order of the Director of the Department of Building Inspection made pursuant to this Code which is not chargeable under Section 204(a)(1) may be charged with an infraction, and a citation may be issued pursuant to Section 204(b). Pursuant to California Government Code Section 36900 and 36901, the fine for infractions shall be as follows:

(i) A fine not exceeding $100 for the initial violation;

(ii) A fine not exceeding $200 for the second violation of the same section of the Code within one year of the first violation;

(iii) A fine not exceeding $500 for each additional violation of the same section of the Code within one year of the first violation.

(b) Department Members as Public Officers. In the performance of their duties of monitoring and enforcing compliance with the provisions of this Code, all persons authorized by the Housing Inspection Division of the Department of Building Inspection to conduct on-site inspections shall have the power, authority and immunity of a public officer and employee as set forth in California Penal Code Section 836.5, to make arrests without a warrant whenever such employees have reasonable cause to believe that a violation of this Code has taken place in their presence; provided, however, that no such arrest shall be made until the time period for compliance provided in the initial notice of violation has expired. In any case in which a person is arrested pursuant to this authority and the person arrested does not demand to be taken before a magistrate, the public officer or employee making the arrest shall prepare a written notice to appear and shall release the person on their promise to appear as prescribed by Chapter 5C (commencing with Section 853.6) of the California Penal Code.

The Director of the Department of Building Inspection, in coordination with the Chief of Police, shall establish and cause to be administered an enforcement training program designed to instruct each employee so authorized by this Section to exercise arrest and citation authority. Such training shall include guidance and instruction regarding the evidentiary

prerequisites to proper prosecution of violations thereof; the appropriate procedures for making arrests or otherwise prudently exercising such arrest and citation authority; and the legal and practical ramifications and limitations relevant to exercising enforcement authority.

(c) Presumption of Noncompliance with Order; Civil Penalty for Violation of Code.

(1) Notwithstanding any other provision of this Code, any person or entity served, in any manner permitted for service of process under the provisions of the Code of Civil Procedure, with a notice or order by the Director of the Department of Building Inspection setting forth the nature of the violation of this Code, demanding correction of such violation, and specifying the time within which such violation must be corrected, shall be presumed, in civil proceedings, to have failed to comply with said notice or order at and after the time given in said notice or order for correction of such violation has expired without correction of said violation.

(2) Any person or entity violating this Code shall be liable for a civil penalty of up to $1,000 for each day such violation is committed or permitted to continue, which penalty shall be assessed and recovered in a civil action brought in the name of the people of the City and County of San Francisco by the City Attorney in any court of competent jurisdiction. There shall be no more than one violation per building per day. In assessing the amount of the civil penalty, the court shall consider any one or more of the relevant circumstances presented by any of the parties to the case, but not limited to, the following: the nature and seriousness of the misconduct, the number of violations, the persistence of the misconduct, the length of time over which the misconduct occurred, the willfulness of the defendant's misconduct, and the defendant's asset's, liabilities and net worth. Any penalty assessed and recovered in an action brought pursuant to this paragraph shall be paid to the City Treasurer and credited to the Department of Building Inspection's Special Fund.

(3) The remedies in this Section are in addition to any other remedies provided by law. No provision in this Section shall preclude prosecution of actions for civil criminal penalties concurrently, sequentially or individually.

(d) Civil Remedies for Violation of Section 503(d). In addition to the penalties specified in Subsection (a) of this Section, Section 503(d) of this Code may also be enforced by a civil action authorized under this subsection.

(1) Any aggrieved person may enforce Section 503(d) of this Code by means of a civil action.

(2) Any person who violates Section 503(d) of this Code or who aids in the violation of Section 503(d) of this Code shall be liable for three times the amount of special and general

damages, or three times the amount of one month's rent that the landlord charges for the unit in question. The court may award in addition thereto, not less than $200 but not more than $400, together with punitive damages. The interested party instituting a civil proceeding, or the City suing to enforce Section 503(d), if prevailing parties, shall be entitled to the costs of enforcing Section 503(d), including reasonable attorney's fees, pursuant to a court order.

(3) Any person who commits, or proposes to commit, an action in violation of Section 503(d) may be enjoined therefrom by any court of competent jurisdiction.

(4) Any action under this subsection may be brought by any aggrieved person, by the District Attorney, by the City Attorney, or be any interested party on behalf of the aggrieved person.

(5) Any action brought under this subsection shall be filed within one year of the alleged violation.

(e) Special Assessment Lien to Recover Fees or Costs. Any person, the owner or their authorized agent, who violates, disobeys, omits, neglects, or refuses to comply with, or who resists or opposes the execution of any order of the provisions of this Code or any order of the Director of the Department of Building Inspection made pursuant to this Code, will be subject to the placement of a special assessment lien in the amount of the fee owed or delinquent, plus accrued interest, against the real property regulated under this chapter, for failure to pay items, including but not limited to: (1) required annual apartment/hotel license fees per Section 302 of this Code; (2) reinspection fees; and, (3) assessment of costs, pursuant to Sections 102A, 108A and 110A of the San Francisco Building Code.

(f) Continuing or Recurring Conditions Creating a Fire Hazard in Multi-Unit Residential Buildings. The Director of the Department of Building Inspection is expressly authorized, under this subsection (f) and Sections 102A.16.1, 102A.16.1.1, and 102A.16.1.2 of the Building Code, to order the owner of a residential building with three or more dwelling units to do one or more of the following to abate or mitigate a fire hazard in the building that continues or recurs notwithstanding the Department of Building Inspection's prior issuance of Notices of Violation and Administrative Orders:

(1) install a new fire sprinkler system;

(2) improve an existing fire sprinkler system or upgrade it to current code requirements;

(3) install a new fire alarm and/or detection system; or

(4) improve an existing fire alarm and/or detection system or upgrade it to current code requirements.

For purposes of this subsection (f), a "fire hazard" is as defined in Section 102A.1 of the Building Code.

The Director may exercise this authority in cases where:

(1) notwithstanding the Department's issuance of two or more NOVs and Administrative Orders under Sections 102A.4 and 102A.7 of the Building Code for violation of the fire safety requirements enforced by the Department of Building Inspection, a fire hazard (as defined in Section 102A.1) continues to exist or recurs after abatement in a residential building with three or more dwelling units; and

(2) while the cited code violations have not risen to the level of an imminent hazard that requires issuance of an emergency order under Section 102A.16 of the Building Code, the violations, are so extensive and of such a nature (including but not limited to a nonworking fire alarm or sprinkler system, a nonworking or chronically blocked fire escape, or locked or chronically blocked exits or egress system) that the health and safety of the residents and/or the general public is substantially endangered; and

(3) the property owner either has failed to abate or mitigate the violations in a timely way in accordance with an order issued pursuant to Section 102A.7 of the Building Code, or the violations recur after abatement.

Each NOV or Administrative Order issued pursuant to Sections 102A.4 and 102A.7 of the Building Code that includes a fire safety violation shall provide information about Building Code Section 102A.16.1 et seq. and the consequences for not abating fire safety violations within the specified compliance period. In addition, prior to issuance of a Fire Life Safety Notice and Order, the Building Official will send the warning letter required by Building Code Section 102A.16.1.1.3.

(g) Annual Report to Board of Supervisors.

(1) Six months from the effective date of this ordinance, the Director of the Department of Building Inspection shall provide the Board of Supervisors with information on the implementation of this Section 204.

(2) Each annual report of the Department of Building Inspection transmitted to the Board of Supervisors shall contain a statistical report detailing the number of citations issued during the preceding year, correlated with a general description of the types of violations for which they were issued.

(h) Partial Appropriation of Fines Collected. Up to 25% of the monies collected pursuant to Section 204(a), other than monies mandated by State law to be appropriated for specific purposes, shall be deposited directly to the Department of Building Inspection's Special Fund to partially offset the costs incurred by the Department of Building Inspection in issuing citations pursuant to this Section 204. for specific purposes, shall be deposited directly to the Department of Building Inspection's Special Fund to partially offset the costs incurred by the Department of Building Inspection in issuing citations pursuant to this Section. **Leg. H.** 1989, 1992, 1993, 1995, 1996, 1997, 2007, 2018.

§ 401 *Family Defined*

Family. One or more persons related or unrelated, living together as a single integrated household in a dwelling unit. **Leg.H.** 1989, 1992, 1995, 2007, 2014.

§ 503 *Room Dimensions and Housing Access to Families*

(a) Ceiling Heights. Unless legally constructed as such, no habitable room shall have a ceiling height less than seven feet six inches. Any room, other than a habitable room, shall have a ceiling height of not less than seven feet.

(b) Superficial Floor Area. Every dwelling unit and congregate residence shall have at least one room which shall have not less than 120 square feet of superficial floor area. Every room which is used for both cooking and living or both living and sleeping purposes shall have not less than 144 square feet of superficial floor area. Every room used for sleeping purposes shall have not less than 70 square feet of superficial floor area. When more than two persons occupy a room used for sleeping purposes the required superficial floor area shall be increased at the rate of 50 square feet for each occupant in excess of two. Guest rooms with cooking shall contain the combined required superficial areas of a sleeping and a kitchen, but not less than 144 square feet. Other habitable rooms shall be not less than 70 square feet.

Notwithstanding any provision of this Section, children under the age of six shall not be counted for purposes of determining whether a family with minor children complies with the provisions of this Code.

(c) Width. No habitable room except a kitchen shall be less than seven feet in width. Rooms used as guest rooms with cooking shall have a 10-foot minimum width.

(d) Housing Access. To promote access to housing by families, it shall be unlawful for the owner, lessor, lessee, sublessee, real estate broker, assignee, or other person having the rights of ownership, the right of possession, or other right to rent or lease any dwelling unit or any agent or employee of such person to refuse to rent or lease, or otherwise deny, a dwelling unit to a family, as defined in Section 401 of this Code, on the basis of the actual or potential number of occupants if the total number of persons occupying a room for sleeping purposes does not violate the minimum superficial floor area standards prescribed in Subsection (b) of this Section.

(e) Remedies. A violation of Subsection (d) of this Section shall be subject to the civil remedies specified in Section 204(e) of this Code. **Leg. H.** 1989, 1992, 1993, 1995, 2007.

§ 701 *Heating and Ventilation*

(a) Minimum Heat Requirements in Residential Rental Units.

(1) Except as provided in Section 701(c), every dwelling unit, guest room, and congregate residence shall be provided with heating facilities capable of maintaining a minimum room temperature of 70 degrees Fahrenheit (21.1 degrees Centigrade) at a point three feet above the floor· in all habitable rooms.

(2) Heat shall be furnished, within the dwelling unit, guest room, or congregate residence by heating units located within the dwelling unit, guest room, or congregate residence or from ductwork openings in the walls, floor or ceiling of said dwelling unit, guest rooms, or congregate residences. No direct openings for the entrance of heat shall be permitted between the exit corridor and the dwelling unit, guest room, or congregate residences.

(3) The cost of maintaining heat as required by this subsection (a) shall be a matter of agreement between the landlord and tenant.

(4) Such heating facilities shall be installed and maintained in a safe condition and in accordance with the Building Code and all other applicable laws.

(b) Requirements for Heaters. All individual heaters installed in dwelling units, guest rooms and guest room suites must be permanently attached and properly wired. Wiring for heaters shall conform to the San Francisco Electrical Code.

(c) Minimum Heat Requirements for Hotels. Hotels shall comply with the requirements set forth in Section 701(a) and (b) except that heating facilities capable of maintaining a room temperature of 68 degrees Fahrenheit (20 degrees Centigrade) at a point midway between the heating unit and the furthest wall and which point is three feet above the floor, shall be made available to each occupied habitable room for a total of 13 hours between the hours of 5:00 a.m. and 11:00 a.m. and 3:00 p.m. and 10:00 p.m.

(d) Buildings in Which the Heating System Is Not Under the Control of the Tenant or Occupant. In every building in which the heating system is not under the control of the tenant or occupant, a locking or nontamperable temperature-sensing device with a ±1½-degree Fahrenheit (0.8 degree Centigrade) tolerance shall be centrally located within the building in a habitable room to which heat is provided, whether occupied or unoccupied. The nontamperable device shall not be installed in a manager's unit or an owner's unit (except in an owner-occupied residential condominium). This device shall cause the heating system to cease heat production when the habitable room temperature exceeds the temperature required by subsection (a) or (c), as applicable, and reactivate the system when the habitable room temperature drops below the temperature required by subsection (a) or (c).

(1) A timeclock set to provide the amount and hours of heat required in this Section 701 shall be installed at or near the heating source (boiler, furnace, etc.) to control the heating system. A thermostat bypass switch wired in parallel with the thermostat shall be provided to allow testing of the boiler operation. This switch shall be located at or near the heating source.

(2) Except as otherwise provided in this subsection (d), remotely located switches which override timeclock operation shall be prohibited.

(e) Electrical Equipment. All electrical fixtures, wiring and appurtenances thereto and their maintenance shall comply with the San Francisco Electrical Code and all other applicable sections of the laws of the State of California and the Municipal Code.

(f) Mechanical Ventilation. The provisions and requirements of the San Francisco Mechanical Code shall govern the installation and operation of mechanical ventilation systems and equipment. **Leg. H.** 1989, 1992, 1995, 2002, 2007, 2019.

San Francisco Planning Code

§ 207(c)(4) *Accessory Dwelling Units in Zoning Districts Other Than RH-1(D). [RH-1(D) is residential house district, one-family detached dwellings.]*

...(c) Exceptions to Dwelling Unit Density Limits. An exception to the calculations under this Section 207 shall be made in the following circumstances:...

(4) Local Accessory Dwelling Unit Program: Accessory Dwelling Units in Multifamily Buildings; Accessory Dwelling Units in Single-Family Homes That Do Not Strictly Meet the Requirements in subsection (c)(6).

(A) Definition. An "Accessory Dwelling Unit" (ADU) is defined in Section 102.

(B) Applicability. This subsection (c)(4) shall apply to the construction of Accessory Dwelling Units on all lots located within the City and County of San Francisco in areas that allow residential use, except that construction of an Accessory Dwelling Unit is regulated by subsection (c)(6), and not this subsection (c)(4), if all of the following circumstances exist:

(i) only one ADU will be constructed;

(ii) the ADU will be located on a lot that is zoned for single-family or multifamily use and contains an existing or proposed single-family dwelling;

(iii) the ADU is either attached to or will be constructed entirely within the "living area" (as defined in subsection (c)(6)(B)(iii)) or the buildable area of the proposed or existing primary dwelling, or constructed within the built envelope of an existing and authorized auxiliary structure on the same lot; provided, however, that (A) when a stand-alone garage, storage structure, or other auxiliary structure is being converted to an ADU, an expansion to the envelope is allowed to add dormers even if the stand-alone garage, storage structure, or other auxiliary structure is in the required rear yard and (B) on a corner lot, a legal stand-alone nonconforming garage, storage structure, or other auxiliary structure may be expanded within its existing footprint by up to one additional story in order to create a consistent street wall and improve the continuity of buildings on the block.

(iv) the ADU will strictly meet the requirements set forth in subsection (c)(6) without requiring a waiver of Code requirements pursuant to subsection (c)(4)(G); and

(v) the permit application does not include seismic upgrade work pursuant to subsection (c)(4)(F).

(C) Controls on Construction. An Accessory Dwelling Unit regulated by this subsection (c)(4) is permitted to be constructed in an existing or proposed building under the following conditions:

(i) For lots that have four existing Dwelling Units or fewer or where the zoning would permit the construction of four or fewer Dwelling Units, one ADU is permitted; for lots that have more than four existing Dwelling Units or are undergoing seismic retrofitting under subsection (c)(4)(F) below, or where the zoning would permit the construction of more than four Dwelling Units, there is no limit on the number of ADUs permitted.

(ii) The Department shall not approve an application for construction of an ADU where a tenant on the lot has been evicted pursuant to Administrative Code Sections 37.9(a)(9) through (a)(12) and 37.9(a)(14) under a notice of eviction served within 10 years prior to filing the application for a building permit to construct the ADU or where a tenant has been evicted pursuant to Administrative Code Section 37.9(a)(8) under a notice of eviction served within five years prior to filing the application for a building permit to construct the ADU. This subsection (c)(4)(C)(ii) shall not apply if the tenant was evicted under Section 37.9(a)(11) or 37.9(a)(14) and the applicant(s) either (A) have certified that the original tenant reoccupied the unit after the temporary eviction or (B) have submitted to the Department and to the Residential Rent Stabilization and Arbitration Board (Rent Board) a declaration from the property owner or the tenant certifying that the property owner notified the tenant of the tenant's right to reoccupy the unit and the tenant chose not to reoccupy it.

(iii) Prior to submitting an application to construct an ADU under this subsection (c)(4), the property owner shall file with the Rent Board a written declaration, signed under penalty of perjury, demonstrating that the project will comply with the requirements of Administrative Code Sections 37.2(r) and 37.9 relating to severance, substantial reduction, or removal of a housing service. The Rent Board shall determine the form and content of said declaration, which shall include the following information: (1) a description of any housing services supplied in connection with the use or occupancy of any units on the subject property that are located in the area of the property or building where the ADU would be constructed; (2) whether construction of the ADU would result in the severance, substantial reduction, or removal of any such housing services; and (3) whether any of the just causes for eviction under Administrative Code Section 37.9(a) would apply. The property owner shall also file a copy of the notice required under Section 207(c)(4)(J) with the declaration.

(iv) Tenants at the subject property may contest the information in the declaration required by subsection 207(c)(4)(C)(iii) by petitioning for a written determination from the Rent Board verifying the presence and defining characteristics of the housing service or services in question, and whether any such housing services would be severed, substantially reduced, or removed by the project as proposed. Petitions must be filed with the Rent Board within 30 calendar days after the notice required under subsection 207(c)(4)(J) has been provided. If no such petition is timely filed, the Rent Board shall promptly transmit the declaration to the Planning Department. If any such petition is timely filed, the Rent Board shall endeavor to transmit the declaration and its final written determination on the petition to the Planning Department within 90 calendar days of receipt of said petition. The Department shall not approve an application to construct an ADU under this subsection (c)(4) unless (1) the Rent Board has transmitted the declaration and final written determination required by subsections (c)(4)(C)(iii) and (c)(4)(C)(iv), and (2) the materials transmitted by the Rent Board indicate that construction of the ADU would not result in the severance, substantial reduction, or removal without just cause of any tenant housing service set forth in Administrative Code Section 37.2(r) that is supplied in the area of the property or building where the ADU would be constructed, unless the property owner demonstrates that the tenant supplied with that housing service has given their express written consent

for the severance, substantial reduction, or removal of the housing service.

(v) Except as provided in subsections (vi) and (vii) below, an Accessory Dwelling Unit shall be constructed entirely within the buildable area of an existing lot, provided that the ADU does not exceed the existing height of an existing building, or within the built envelope of an existing and authorized stand-alone garage, storage structure, or other auxiliary structure on the same lot, as the built envelope existed three years prior to the time the application was filed for a building permit to construct the ADU. For purposes of this subsection (c)(4)(C)(v), the "built envelope" shall include the open area under a cantilevered room or room built on columns; decks, except for decks that are supported by columns or walls other than the building wall to which they are attached and are multi-level or more than 10 feet above grade; and lightwell infills provided that the infill will be against a blank neighboring wall at the property line and not visible from any off-site location; as these spaces existed as of July 11, 2016. An ADU constructed entirely within the existing built envelope, as defined in this subsection, along with permitted obstructions allowed in Section 136(c)(32), of an existing building or authorized auxiliary structure on the same lot, or where an existing stand-alone garage or storage structure has been expanded to add dormers, is exempt from the notification requirements of Section 311 of this Code unless the existing building or authorized auxiliary structure on the same lot is in an Article 10 or Article 11 District, in which case the notification requirements will apply. If an ADU will be constructed under a cantilevered room or deck that encroaches into the required rear yard, a pre-application meeting between the applicant and adjacent neighbors for all the proposed work is required before the application may be submitted.

(vi) When a stand-alone garage, storage, or other auxiliary structure is being converted to an ADU, an expansion to the envelope is allowed to add dormers even if the stand-alone garage, storage structure, or other auxiliary structure is in the required rear yard.

(vii) On a corner lot, a legal stand-alone nonconforming garage, storage structure, or other auxiliary structure may be expanded within its existing footprint by up to one additional story in order to create a consistent street wall and improve the continuity of buildings on the block.

(viii) An Accessory Dwelling Unit shall not be constructed using space from an existing Dwelling Unit except that an ADU may expand into habitable space on the ground or basement floors provided that it does not exceed 25% of the gross square footage of such space. The Zoning Administrator may waive this 25% limitation if (1) the resulting space would not be usable or would be impractical to use for other reasonable uses included but not limited to storage or bicycle parking or (2) waiving the limitation would help relieve any negative layout issues for the proposed ADU.

(ix) An existing building undergoing seismic retrofitting may be eligible for a height increase pursuant to subsection (c)(4)(F) below.

(x) Notwithstanding any other provision of this Code, an Accessory Dwelling Unit authorized under this subsection (c)(4) may not be merged with an original unit(s).

(xi) An Accessory Dwelling Unit shall not be permitted in any building in a Neighborhood Commercial District or in the Chinatown Community Business or Visitor Retail Districts if it would eliminate or reduce a ground-story retail or commercial space, unless the Accessory Dwelling Unit is a Designated Child Care Unit, as defined in Section 102, and meets all applicable standards of Planning Code Section 414A.6(e).

(D) Prohibition of Short-Term Rentals. An Accessory Dwelling Unit shall not be used for Short-Term Residential Rentals under Chapter 41A of the Administrative Code, which restriction shall be recorded as a Notice of Special Restriction on the subject lot.

(E) Restrictions on Subdivisions. Notwithstanding the provisions of Article 9 of the Subdivision Code, a lot with an Accessory Dwelling Unit authorized under this Section 207(c)(4) shall not be subdivided in a manner that would allow for the ADU to be sold or separately financed pursuant to any condominium plan, housing cooperative, or similar form of separate ownership; provided, however, that this prohibition on separate sale or finance of the ADU shall not apply to a building that (i) within three years prior to July 11, 2016 was an existing condominium with no Rental Unit as defined in Section 37.2(r) of the Administrative Code, and (ii) has had no evictions pursuant to Sections 37.9(a) through 37.9(a)(12) and 37.9(a)(14) of the Administrative Code within 10 years prior to July 11, 2016.

(F) Buildings Undergoing Seismic Retrofitting. For Accessory Dwelling Units on lots with a building undergoing mandatory seismic retrofitting in compliance with Chapter 4D of the Existing Building Code or voluntary seismic retrofitting in compliance with the Department of Building Inspection's Administrative Bulletin 094, the following additional provision applies: If allowed by the Building Code, a building in which an Accessory Dwelling Unit is constructed may be raised up to three feet to create ground floor ceiling heights suitable for residential use. Such a raise in height

(i) Shall be exempt from the notification requirements of Section 311 of this Code; and

(ii) May expand a noncomplying structure, as defined in Section 180(a)(2) of this Code and further regulated in Sections 172, 180, and 188, without obtaining a variance for increasing the discrepancy between existing conditions on the lot and the required standards of this Code.

(iii) On lots where an ADU is added in coordination with a building undergoing mandatory seismic retrofitting in compliance with Chapter 4D of the Existing Building Code or voluntary seismic retrofitting in compliance with the Department of Building Inspection's Administrative Bulletin 094, the building and the new ADU shall maintain any eligibility to enter the condo-conversion lottery and may only be subdivided if the entire property is selected on the condo-conversion lottery.

(iv) Pursuant to subsection (4)(C)(i), there is no limit on the number of ADUs that are permitted to be added in connection with a seismic retrofit.

(G) Waiver of Code Requirements; Applicability of Rent Ordinance. Pursuant to the provisions of Section 307(l) of this Code, the Zoning Administrator may grant an Accessory Dwelling Unit a complete or partial waiver of the density limits and bicycle parking, rear yard, exposure, or open space standards of this Code. If the Zoning Administrator grants a complete or partial waiver of the requirements of this Code and the subject lot contains any Rental Units at the time an application for a building permit is filed for construction of the Accessory Dwelling Unit(s), the property owner(s) shall enter into a Regulatory Agreement with the City under subsection (c)(4)(H) subjecting the ADU(s) to the San Francisco Residential Rent Stabilization and Arbitration Ordinance (Chapter 37 of the Administrative Code) as a condition of approval of the ADU(s). For purposes of this requirement, Rental Units shall be as defined in Section 37.2(r) of the Administrative Code.

(H) Regulatory Agreements. A Regulatory Agreement required by subsection (c)(4)(G) as a condition of approval of an Accessory Dwelling Unit shall contain the following:

(i) a statement that the ADU(s) are not subject to the Costa Hawkins Rental Housing Act (California Civil Code Section 1954.50) because, under Section 1954.52(b), the owner has entered into this agreement with the City in consideration for a complete or partial waiver of the density limits, and/or bicycle parking, rear yard, exposure, or open space standards of this Code or other direct financial contribution or other form of assistance specified in California Government Code Sections 65915 et seq. ("Agreement"); and

(ii) a description of the complete or partial waiver of Code requirements granted by the Zoning Administrator or other direct financial contribution or form of assistance provided to the property owner; and

(iii) a description of the remedies for breach of the Agreement and other provisions to ensure implementation and compliance with the Agreement.

(iv) The property owner and the Planning Director (or the Director's designee), on behalf of the City, will execute the Agreement, which shall be reviewed and approved by the City Attorney's Office. The Agreement shall be executed prior to the City's issuance of the First Construction Document for the project, as defined in Section 107A.13.1 of the San Francisco Building Code.

(v) Following execution of the Regulatory Agreement by all parties and approval by the City Attorney, the Regulatory Agreement or a memorandum thereof shall be recorded against the property and shall be binding on all future owners and successors in interest.

Any Regulatory Agreement entered into under this Section 207(c)(4) shall not preclude a landlord from establishing the initial rental rate pursuant to Section 1954.53 of the Costa Hawkins Rental Housing Act.

(I) Monitoring Program.

(i) Monitoring and Enforcement of Unit Affordability. The Department shall establish a system to monitor the affordability of the Accessory Dwelling Units authorized to be constructed by this subsection 207(c)(4) and shall use such data to enforce the requirements of the Regulatory Agreements entered into pursuant to subsection (c)(4)(H). Property owners shall provide the Department with rent information as requested by the Department. The Board of Supervisors recognizes that property owners and tenants generally consider rental information sensitive and do not want it publicly disclosed. The intent of the Board is for the Department to obtain the information for purposes of monitoring and enforcement but that its public disclosure is not linked to specific individuals or units. The Department shall consult with the City Attorney's Office with respect to the legal requirements to determine how best to achieve the intent of the Board.

(ii) Monitoring of Prohibition on Use as Short Term Rentals. The Department shall collect data on the use of Accessory Dwelling Units authorized to be constructed by this subsection (c)(4) as Short-Term Residential Rentals, as that term is defined in Administrative Code Section 41A.4, and shall use such data to evaluate and enforce Notices of Special Restriction pursuant to subsection 207(c)(4)(D) and the requirements of Administrative Code Chapter 41A.

(iii) Department Report. The Department shall publish a report annually until April 1, 2019, that describes and evaluates the types of units being developed and their affordability rates, as well as their use as Short-Term

Residential Rentals. The report shall contain such additional information as the Director or the Board of Supervisors determines would inform decision makers and the public on the effectiveness and implementation of this subsection (c)(4) and include recommendations for any amendments to the requirements of this Section 207(c)(4). The Department shall transmit this report to the Board of Supervisors for its review and public input. In subsequent years, this information on Accessory Dwelling Units shall be reported annually in the Housing Inventory.

(J) Notification. Prior to submitting an application to construct an ADU under this subsection (c)(4), the property owner shall cause a notice describing the proposed project to be posted in an accessible common area of the building for at least 15 calendar days prior to submitting an application to construct an ADU, and shall cause said notice to be mailed or delivered to each unit (including unauthorized units) at the subject property, also at least 15 calendar days prior to submitting the application. The property owner shall submit proof of these notices to the Planning Department as part of the application to construct an ADU. These notices shall have a format and content determined by the Zoning Administrator, and shall generally describe the project, including the number and location of the proposed ADU(s), and shall include a copy of the written declaration required by subsection (c)(4)(C)(iii). These notices shall also include instructions on how a tenant may petition the Rent Board for a written determination on the declaration as set forth in subsection (c)(4)(C)(iii), including the deadline for filing such petition, which shall be 30 calendar days after the notice has been provided. These notices shall also describe how to obtain additional information regarding the project and shall provide contact information for the Planning Department that complies with the requirements of the Language Access Ordinance, Chapter 91 of the Administrative Code, to provide vital information about the Planning Department's services or programs in the languages spoken by a Substantial Number of Limited English Speaking Persons, as defined in Chapter 91..... **Leg.H.** 1984, 1990, 2015, 2016, 2017, 2018, 2019, 2021.

San Francisco Police Code

Article 1.2 *Discrimination Against Families*

§ 103 **Occupancy Standards.** No provision of this Article shall be construed to authorize occupancies in violation of the floor-area standards of Section 501.1 of Article 5 of the San Francisco Housing code except that children under the age of six (6) shall not be counted for purposes of determining whether a family complies with the standards of the San Francisco Housing Code. **Leg.H.** 1987.

San Francisco Rent Ordinance

§ 37.2 *Rent Ordinance Definitions*

(a) Base Rent.

(1) That rent which is charged a tenant upon initial occupancy plus any rent increase allowable and imposed under this chapter; provided, however, that,

(A) Base rent shall not include increases imposed pursuant to Section 37.7.

(B) Base rent shall not include utility passthroughs or water revenue bond passthroughs or general obligation bond passthroughs pursuant to Sections 37.2(q), 37.3(a)(5)(B), and 37.3(a)(6).

(C) Base rent for tenants of RAP rental units in areas designated on or after July 1, 1977 shall be that rent which was established pursuant to Section 32.73-1 of the San Francisco Administrative Code. Rent increases attributable to the Chief Administrative Officer's amortization of a RAP loan in an area designated on or after July 1, 1977 shall not be included in the base rent.

(D) Good Samaritan Status. As of February 8, 2011 and after, Good Samaritan occupancy status occurs when a landlord and new tenant agree in writing for the tenant to commence temporary occupancy following an emergency such as fire, earthquake, landslide, or similar emergency situation, that required unexpected vacation of the tenant's previous unit, and the agreement includes a reduced rent rate for the replacement unit for a specified period of time up to twelve (12) months ("Original Good Samaritan Status Period"). "Reduced rent rate" means the base rent the tenant was paying for the previous unit at the time of the emergency or an amount up to ten (10) percent above that amount, except that if the owner of the previous unit is the same as the owner of the replacement unit then "reduced rent rate" means the rent the tenant was paying for the previous unit at the time of the emergency. For Good Samaritan Status to exist, the written agreement as referenced in this Subsection must include a statement that the agreement is temporary in nature, must refer to this Subsection, and must state that the tenant has been displaced from his or her previous unit as certified in Subsection (iii), below.

(i) The landlord and tenant may agree, in writing, to extend the reduced rent rate for a period of time beyond the Original Good Samaritan Status Period, up to a total of twenty-four (24) months from the beginning to the end of all Good Samaritan Status ("Extended Good Samaritan Status Period").

(ii) By accepting occupancy in Good Samaritan Status, a tenant does not waive any right to compensation or any right to return to the tenant's previous unit that he or she otherwise may have under Chapter 37 or other source of law based on the emergency vacation of the tenant's previous unit.

(iii) Good Samaritan Status may only be utilized upon certification in writing by one of the following officials, or his or her designee, that as a result of fire, earthquake, landslide, or similar emergency situation, the tenant's previous unit is in such condition that, as a matter of public health and safety and as a matter of habitability, the tenant cannot or should not reside there until the unit has been appropriately repaired: Mayor; Fire Chief; Director of the Department of Building Inspection; Director of the Department of Public Health; or Other Official as authorized by law. The Rent Board shall make a form available, that the Official may use for this purpose.

(iv) The tenant's rent increase anniversary date for a Good Samaritan occupancy shall be the date the tenancy commenced; the first annual allowable increase shall take effect no less than one year from the anniversary date, but when imposed after one year, shall set a new anniversary date for the imposition of future rent increases. The base rent used for calculation of the annual allowable increase pursuant to Section 37.3(a)(1) during a Good Samaritan occupancy, shall be the reduced rent rate in effect on the date the Good Samaritan occupancy commences.

(v) The landlord may serve a notice of termination of tenancy under Section 37.9(a)(16) within 60 days after expiration of the Original and any Extended Good Samaritan Status Period. Alternatively, within sixty (60) days after expiration of the Original and any Extended Good Samaritan Status Period, if the Good Samaritan rental agreement states the dollar amount of the tenant's initial base rent that can be imposed after expiration of the Original and any Extended Good Samaritan Status Period, the landlord may give legal notice of the rent increase to the tenant and then increase the tenant's rent from the temporary reduced rent rate to the previously agreed upon initial base rent for the unit.

(vi) The Rent Board shall make a form available that explains the temporary nature of tenant occupancy in Good Samaritan Status, and describes the other provisions of Section 37.2(a)(1)(D)(v).

The Good Samaritan landlord shall provide the tenant with this disclosure form prior to commencement of the Good Samaritan tenancy. However, failure by the landlord to provide the tenant with such disclosure form:

• Will not prevent the landlord from serving a notice of termination of tenancy under Section 37.9(a)(16) within sixty (60) days after expiration of the Original and any Extended Good Samaritan Status Period.

• Will not prevent the landlord from serving a notice of rent increase within sixty (60) days after expiration of the Original and any Extended Good Samaritan Status Period, to increase to the previously agreed upon initial base rent for the unit, as provided in Section 37.2(a)(1)(D)(v).

• Will not otherwise impact any rights that the landlord may have regarding the tenancy.

(2) From and after August 30, 1998, the base rent for tenants occupying rental units which have received certain tenant-based or project-based rental assistance shall be as follows:

(A) With respect to tenant-based rental assistance:

(i) For any tenant receiving tenant-based rental assistance as of August 30, 1998 under a program that does not establish the tenant's share of base rent as a fixed percentage of a tenant's income, such as in the Housing Choice Voucher Program or the Over-FMR Tenancy program, and continuing to receive such tenant-based rental assistance thereafter, the initial base rent for each unit occupied by such tenant shall be the rent payable for that unit under the housing assistance payments contract, as amended, between the San Francisco Housing Authority or the Human Services Agency and the landlord (the "HAP Contract") with respect to that unit immediately prior to August 30, 1998 (the "HAP Contract Rent").

(ii) For any tenant receiving tenant-based rental assistance under a program that does not establish the tenant's share of base rent as a fixed percentage of a tenant's income, such as in the Housing Choice Voucher Program or the Over-FMR Tenancy program, and commencing occupancy of a rental unit after August 30, 1998, the initial base rent for each unit occupied by such a tenant shall be the HAP Contract Rent in effect as of the date the tenant commences occupancy of such unit.

(iii) For any tenant receiving rental assistance under the HOPWA rental subsidy program as of May 17, 2016, and continuing to receive such assistance under the HOPWA rental subsidy program thereafter, the initial base rent for each unit occupied by such tenant shall be the HAP Contract Rent in effect as of May 17, 2016.

(iv) For any tenant receiving rental assistance under the HOPWA rental subsidy program who commenced occupancy of a rental unit after May 17, 2016, the initial base rent for each unit occupied by such tenant shall be the HAP Contract Rent in effect as of the date the tenant commences occupancy of such unit.

(v) For any tenant whose tenant-based rental assistance terminates or expires, for whatever reason, after August 30, 1998, the base rent for each such unit following expiration or termination shall be the HAP Contract Rent in effect for

that unit immediately prior to the expiration or termination of the tenant-based rental assistance.

(B) For any tenant occupying a unit upon the expiration or termination, for whatever reason, of a project-based HAP Contract under Section 8 of the United States Housing Act of 1937 (42 USC §1437f, as amended), the base rent for each such unit following expiration or termination shall be the "contract rent" in effect for that unit immediately prior to the expiration or termination of the project-based HAP Contract.

(C) For any tenant occupying a unit upon the prepayment or expiration of any mortgage insured by the United States Department of Housing and Urban Development ("HUD"), including but not limited to mortgages provided under sections 221(d)(3), 221(d)(4) and 236 of the National Housing Act (12 USC §1715z-1), the base rent for each such unit shall be the "basic rental charge" (described in 12 USC 1715z-1(f), or successor legislation) in effect for that unit immediately prior to the prepayment of the mortgage, which charge excludes the "interest reduction payment" attributable to that unit prior to the mortgage prepayment or expiration.

(b) Board. The Residential Rent Stabilization and Arbitration Board.

(c) Capital Improvements. Those improvements which materially add to the value of the property, appreciably prolong its useful life, or adapt it to new uses, and which may be amortized over the useful life of the improvement of the building.

(d) CPI. Consumer Price Index for all Urban Consumers for the San Francisco-Oakland Metropolitan Area, U.S. Department of Labor.

(e) Energy Conservation Improvements. Work performed pursuant to the requirements of Chapter 12 of the San Francisco Housing Code.

(f) Administrative Law Judge. A person, designated by the board, who arbitrates and mediates rental increase disputes, and performs other duties as required pursuant to this Chapter 37.

(g) Housing Services. Services provided by the landlord connected with the use or occupancy of a rental unit including, but not limited to: quiet enjoyment of the premises, without harassment by the landlord as provided in Section 37.10B; repairs; replacement; maintenance; painting; light; heat; water; elevator service; laundry facilities and privileges; janitor service; refuse removal; furnishings; telephone; parking; rights permitted the tenant by agreement, including the right to have a specific number of occupants, whether express or implied, and whether or not the agreement prohibits subletting and/or assignment; and any other benefits, privileges or facilities.

(h) Landlord. An owner, lessor, sublessor, who receives or is entitled to receive rent for the use and occupancy of any residential rental unit or portion thereof in the City and County of San Francisco, and the agent, representative or successor of any of the foregoing.

(i) Member. A member of the Residential Rent Stabilization and Arbitration Board.

(j) Over FMR Tenancy Program. A regular certificate tenancy program whereby the base rent, together with a utility allowance in an amount determined by HUD, exceeds the fair market rent limitation for a particular unit size as determined by HUD.

(k) Payment standard. An amount determined by the San Francisco Housing Authority that is used to determine the amount of assistance paid by the San Francisco Housing Authority on behalf of a tenant under the Housing Choice Voucher Program (24 CFR Part 982). The term "payment standard" shall also refer to the rent standard used to determine the amount of assistance paid by the Human Services Agency under the HOPWA rental subsidy program (24 CFR Part 574).

(l) RAP. Residential Rehabilitation Loan Program (Chapter 32, San Francisco Administrative Code).

(m) RAP Rental Units. Residential dwelling units subject to RAP loans pursuant to Chapter 32, San Francisco Administrative Code.

(n) Real Estate Department. A city department in the City and County of San Francisco.

(o) Rehabilitation Work. Any rehabilitation or repair work done by the landlord with regard to a rental unit, or to the common areas of the structure containing the rental unit, which work was done in order to be in compliance with State or local law, or was done to repair damage resulting from fire, earthquake or other casualty or natural disaster.

(p) Rent. The consideration, including any bonus, benefits or gratuity, demanded or received by a landlord for or in connection with the use or occupancy of a rental unit, or the assignment of a lease for such a unit, including but not limited to monies demanded or paid for parking, furnishings, food service, housing services of any kind, or subletting.

(q) Rent Increases. Any additional monies demanded or paid for rent as defined in item (p) above, or any reduction in housing services without a corresponding reduction in the monies demanded or paid for rent; provided, however, that: (1) where the landlord has been paying the tenant's utilities and the cost of those utilities increases, the landlord's passing through to the tenant of such increased costs pursuant to this Chapter does not constitute a rent increase; (2) where there has been a change in the landlord's property tax attributable to a general obligation bond approved by the voters between November 1, 1996 and November 30, 1998, or after November 14, 2002, the landlord's passing through to the

tenant of such increased costs in accordance with this Chapter (see Section 37.3(a)(6)) does not constitute a rent increase; (3) where there has been a change in the landlord's property tax attributable to a San Francisco Unified School District or San Francisco Community College District general obligation bond approved by the voters after November 1, 2006, the landlord's passing through to the tenant of such increased costs in accordance with this Chapter (see Section 37.3(a)(6)) does not constitute a rent increase; and (4) where water bill charges are attributable to water rate increases resulting from issuance of water revenue bonds authorized at the November 5, 2002 election, the landlord's passing through to the tenant of such increased costs in accordance with this Chapter (see Section 37.3(a)(5)(B)) does not constitute a rent increase.

(r) Rental Units. All residential dwelling units in the City and County of San Francisco together with the land and appurtenant buildings thereto, and all housing services, privileges, furnishings and facilities supplied in connection with the use or occupancy thereof, including garage and parking facilities.

Garage facilities, parking facilities, driveways, storage spaces, laundry rooms, decks, patios, or gardens on the same lot, or kitchen facilities or lobbies in single room occupancy (SRO) hotels, supplied in connection with the use or occupancy of a unit, may not be severed from the tenancy by the landlord without just cause as required by Section 37.9(a). Any severance, substantial reduction or removal of a housing service, even if permitted under Section 37.2(r) Section 37.9(a), shall be offset by a corresponding reduction in rent. Either a landlord or a tenant may file a petition with the Rent Board to determine the amount of the rent reduction. In addition, a tenant may petition the Rent Board for a determination on whether an Accessory Dwelling Unit proposed to be constructed under Planning Code Section 207(c)(4) would sever, substantially reduce, or remove a housing service, pursuant to the procedures set forth in subsection 207(c){4}{C}{iii}. The issuance of a permit for construction of an Accessory Dwelling Unit does not, in and of itself, constitute a just cause for the purpose of severing a housing service.

Notwithstanding the preceding paragraph, a landlord may temporarily sever one or more housing services listed in that paragraph in order to perform seismic work required by Building Code Chapter 34B "Mandatory Earthquake Retrofit of Wood-Frame Buildings" ("mandatory seismic work") if: (1) the landlord has given the notice to temporarily sever as required by Administrative Code Section 65A.2; (2) the landlord has obtained all necessary permits on or before the date the notice to temporarily sever is given; (3) the housing service(s) will only be severed for the minimum time required to complete the mandatory seismic work and in no event for a longer period than provided by Building Code Section 106A.4.4, Table B; and (4) the temporarily severed housing service(s) will be fully restored immediately upon completion of the mandatory seismic work. For such temporary severance of one or more of the specified housing services due to mandatory seismic work required by Building Code Chapter 34B, tenants will not be entitled to a reduction in rent, but tenants shall be entitled to either compensation or a substitute housing service as provided in Administrative Code Chapter 65A.

The term "rental units" shall not include:

(1) housing accommodations in hotels, motels, inns, tourist houses, rooming and boarding houses, provided that at such time as an accommodation has been occupied by a tenant for thirty-two (32) continuous days or more, such accommodation shall become a rental unit subject to the provisions of this chapter; provided further, no landlord shall bring an action to recover possession of such unit in order to avoid having the unit come within the provisions of this chapter. An eviction for a purpose not permitted under Sec. 37.9(a) shall be deemed to be an action to recover possession in order to avoid having a unit come within the provisions of this Chapter;

(2) dwelling units in non-profit cooperatives owned, occupied and controlled by a majority of the residents or dwelling units solely owned by a non-profit public benefit corporation governed by a board of directors the majority of which are residents of the dwelling units and where it is required in the corporate by-laws that rent increases be approved by a majority of the residents;

(3) housing accommodations in any hospital, convent, monastery, extended care facility, asylum, residential care or adult day health care facility for the elderly which must be operated pursuant to a license issued by the California Department of Social Services, as required by California Health and Safety Chapters 3.2 and 3.3, or in dormitories owned and operated by an institution of higher education, a high school, or an elementary school;

(4) except as provided in Subsections (A),(B) and (C), dwelling units whose rents are controlled or regulated by any government unit, agency or authority, excepting those unsubsidized and/ or unassisted units which are insured by the United States Department of Housing and Urban Development; provided, however, that units in unreinforced masonry buildings which have undergone seismic strengthening in accordance with Building Code Chapters 16B and 16C shall remain subject to the Rent Ordinance to the extent that the Ordinance is not in conflict with the seismic strengthening bond program or with the program's loan agreements or with any regulations promulgated thereunder;

(A) For purposes of sections 37.2, 37.3(a)(10)(A), 37.4, 37.5, 37.6. 37.9, 37.9A, 37.10A, 37.11A and 37.13, and the arbitration provisions of sections 37.8 and 37.8A applicable only to the provisions of section 37.3(a)(10)(A), the term "rental units" shall include units occupied by recipients of tenant-based rental assistance where the tenant-based rental assistance program does not establish the tenant's share of base rent as a fixed percentage of a tenant's income, such as in the Housing Choice voucher program and the Over-FMR

Tenancy program, and shall also include units occupied by recipients of tenant-based rental assistance under the HOPWA rental subsidy program;

(B) For purposes of sections 37.2, 37.3(a)(10)(B), 37.4, 37.5, 37.6, 37.9, 37.9A, 37.10A, 37.11A and 37.13, the term "rental units" shall include units occupied by recipients of tenant-based rental assistance where the rent payable by the tenant under the tenant-based rental assistance program is a fixed percentage of the tenant's income, such as in the Section 8 certificate program;

(C) The term "rental units" shall include units in a building for which tax credits are reserved or obtained pursuant to the federal low income housing tax credit program (LIHTC, Section 42 of the Internal Revenue Code, 26 U.S.C. Section 42), that satisfy the following criteria:

(i) Where a tenant's occupancy of the unit began before the applicable LIHTC regulatory agreement was recorded; and

(ii) Where the rent is not controlled or regulated by any use restrictions imposed by the City and County of San Francisco, the San Francisco Redevelopment Agency, the State of California Office of Housing and Community Development, or the United States Department of Housing and Urban Development.

Nothing in this Section 37.2(r)(4)(C) precludes a landlord from seeking an exemption from rent regulation on the basis of substantial rehabilitation under Section 37.3(g).

This Section 37.2(r)(4)(C) definition of "rental unit" shall apply to any unit where the qualifying tenant (see Section 37.2(r)(4)(C)(i)) is in possession of the unit on or after the effective date of this ordinance (Ord. No. 281-06) including but not limited to any unit where the tenant has been served with a notice to quit but has not vacated the unit and there is no final judgment against the tenant for possession of the unit as of the effective date of this ordinance (Ord. No. 281-06).

(s) Substantial Rehabilitation. The renovation, alteration or remodeling of residential units of 50 or more years of age which have been condemned or which do not qualify for certificates of occupancy or which require substantial renovation in order to conform the building to contemporary standards for decent, safe and sanitary housing. Substantial rehabilitation may vary in degree from gutting and extensive reconstruction to extensive improvements that cure substantial deferred maintenance. Cosmetic improvements alone such as painting, decorating and minor repairs, or other work which can be performed safely without having the unit vacated do not qualify as substantial rehabilitation.

(t) Tenant. A person entitled by written or oral agreement, subtenancy approved by the landlord, or by sufferance, to occupy a residential dwelling unit to the exclusion of others.

(u) Tenant-based Rental Assistance. Rental assistance provided directly to a tenant or directly to a landlord on behalf of a particular tenant, which includes but shall not be limited to certificates and vouchers issued pursuant to Section 8 of the United States Housing Act of 1937, as amended (42 U.S.C. §1437f) and the HOPWA program.

(v) Utilities. The term "utilities" shall refer to gas and electricity exclusively.

(w) Victims of Domestic Violence, Sexual Assault, or Stalking.

(1) "Victim of domestic violence or sexual assault or stalking" means any person who has been, or is currently being, subjected to one or more of the following:

(A) "Domestic violence," as defined in Section 13700 of the Penal Code or Section 6211 of the Family Code;

(B) "Sexual assault," as defined in Sections 261, 261.5, 262, 286, 288a, or 289 of the Penal Code; or

(C) "Stalking," as defined in Section 646.9 of the Penal Code or Section 1708.7 of the Civil Code.

(2) "Protective order" means a temporary restraining order or emergency protective order issued pursuant to Part 3 (commencing with Section 6240) or Part 4 (commencing with Section 6300) or Part 5 (commencing with Section 6400) of the Family Code, Section 136.2 of the Penal Code, Section 527.6 of the Code of Civil Procedure, or Section 213.5 of the Welfare and Institutions Code, that protects the tenant or household member from further domestic violence, sexual assault, or stalking.

(3) "Qualified third party" means a peace officer or victim advocate employed by a state or local law enforcement agency, or Licensed Clinical Social Worker (LCSW) or Marriage and Family Therapist (MFT), acting in his or her official capacity;

(4) "Written documentation from a qualified third party" means a document signed and dated within the preceding 60 days by a qualified third party stating all of the following:

(A) That the tenant notified the qualified third party that he or she was a victim of domestic violence or sexual assault or stalking;

(B) The time, date, and location of the act or acts that constitute the domestic violence or sexual assault or stalking; and

(C) That the tenant informed the qualified third party of the name of the alleged perpetrator of the act or acts of domestic violence or sexual assault or stalking, if known to the victim.

Leg. H. Amended 1980, 1982, 1983, 1984, 1986, 1993, 1994, 1995, 1998, 1999, 2000, 2003, 2006, 2007, 2008, 2009, 2010, 2011, 2014, 2015, 2016, 2019, 2021.

§ 37.3 *Rent Increase Limits*

(a) Rent Increase Limitations for Tenants in Occupancy. Landlords may impose rent increases upon tenants in occupancy only as provided below and as provided by subsections 37.3(d) and 37.3(g):

(1) Annual Rent Increase. On March 1 of each year, the Board shall publish the increase in the CPI for the preceding 12 months, as made available by the U.S. Department of Labor. A landlord who has reported the required information about their rental unit to the Rent Board as set forth in Section 37.15 shall have a license to impose annually a rent increase which does not exceed a tenant's base rent by more than 60% of said published increase. In no event, however, shall the allowable annual increase be greater than 7%.

(2) Banking. A landlord who refrains from imposing an annual rent increase or any portion thereof may accumulate said increase and, subject to Section 37.15, impose that amount on the tenant's subsequent rent increase anniversary dates. A landlord who, between April 1, 1982 and February 29, 1984, has banked an annual 7% rent increase (or rent increases) or any portion thereof may impose the accumulated increase on the tenant's subsequent rent increase anniversary dates.

(3) Capital Improvements, Rehabilitation, Energy Conservation Improvements, and Renewable Energy Improvements. A landlord may impose rent increases based upon the cost of capital improvements, rehabilitation, energy conservation improvements, or renewable energy improvements, provided that such costs are certified pursuant to Sections 37.7 and 37.8B below; provided further that where a landlord has performed seismic strengthening in accordance with Building Code Chapters 16B and 16C, no increase for capital improvements (including but not limited to seismic strengthening) shall exceed, in any twelve (12) month period, 10% of the tenant's base rent, subject to rules adopted by the Board to prevent landlord hardship and to permit landlords to continue to maintain their buildings in a decent, safe and sanitary condition. A landlord may accumulate any certified increase which exceeds this amount and impose the increase in subsequent years, subject to the 10% limitation. Nothing in this subsection shall be construed to supersede any Board rules or regulations with respect to limitations on increases based upon capital improvements whether performed separately or in conjunction with seismic strengthening improvements pursuant to Building Code Chapters 16B and 16C.

(4) Utilities. A landlord may impose increases based upon the cost of utilities as provided in Section 37.2(q) above.

(5) Water: Charges Related to Excess Water Use, and 50% Passthrough of Water Bill Charges Attributable to Water Rate Increases Resulting From Issuance of Water System Improvement Revenue Bonds Authorized at the November 2002 Election.

(A) Charges Related to Excess Water Use. A landlord may impose increases not to exceed fifty percent of the excess use charges (penalties) levied by the San Francisco Water Department on a building for use of water in excess of Water Department allocations under the following conditions:

(i) The landlord provides tenants with written certification that the following have been installed in all units: (1) permanently-installed retrofit devices designed to reduce the amount of water used per flush or low-flow toilets (1.6 gallons per flush); (2) low-flow showerheads which allow a flow of no more than 2.5 gallons per minute; and (3) faucet aerators (where installation on current faucets is physically feasible); and

(ii) The landlord provides the tenants with written certification that no known plumbing leaks currently exist in the building and that any leaks reported by tenants in the future will be promptly repaired; and

(iii) The landlord provides the tenants with a copy of the water bill for the period in which the penalty was charged. Only penalties billed for a service period which begins after the effective date of the ordinance [April 20, 1991] may be passed through to tenants. Where penalties result from an allocation which does not reflect documented changes in occupancy which occurred after March 1, 1991, a landlord must, if requested in writing by a tenant, make a good faith effort to appeal the allotment. Increases based upon penalties shall be pro-rated on a per room basis provided that the tenancy existed during the time the penalty charges accrued. Such charges shall not become part of a tenant's base rent. Where a penalty in any given billing period reflects a 25% or more increase in consumption over the prior billing period, and where that increase does not appear to result from increased occupancy or any other known use, a landlord may not impose any increase based upon such penalty unless inspection by a licensed plumber or Water Department inspector fails to reveal a plumbing or other leak. If the inspection does reveal a leak, no increase based upon penalties may be imposed at any time for the period of the unrepaired leak.

(B) Fifty Percent (50%) Passthrough of Water Bill Charges Attributable to Water Rate Increases Resulting From Issuance of Water System Improvement Revenue Bonds Authorized at the November 2002 Election. A landlord may pass through fifty percent (50%) of the water bill charges attributable to water rate increases resulting from issuance of Water System Improvement Revenue Bonds authorized

at the November 5, 2002 election (Proposition A), to any unit that is in compliance with any applicable laws requiring water conservation devices. The landlord is not required to file a petition with the Board for approval of such a cost passthrough. Such cost passthroughs are subject to the following:

(i) Affected tenants shall be given notice of any such passthrough as provided by applicable notice of rent increase provisions of this Chapter 37, including but not limited to Section 37.3(b)(3).

(ii) A tenant may file a hardship application with the Board, and be granted relief from all or part of such a cost passthrough;

(iii) If a tenant's hardship application is granted, the tenant's landlord may utilize any available Public Utilities Commission low-income rate discount program or similar program for water bill reduction, based on that tenant's hardship status;

(iv) A landlord shall not impose a passthrough pursuant to Section 37.3(a)(5)(B) if the landlord has filed for or received Board approval for a rent increase under Section 37.8(e)(4) for increased operating and maintenance expenses in which the same increase in water bill charges attributable to water rate increases resulting from issuance of any water revenue bonds authorized at the November 5, 2002 election was included in the comparison year cost totals.

(v) Where a tenant alleges that a landlord has imposed a water revenue bond passthrough that is not in compliance with Section 37.3(a)(5)(B), the tenant may petition for a hearing under the procedures provided by Section 37.8. In such a hearing the landlord shall have the burden of proving the accuracy of the calculation that is the basis for the increase. Any tenant petition challenging such a passthrough must be filed within one year of the effective date of the passthrough.

(vi) A tenant who has received a notice of passthrough or a passthrough under this Section 37.3(a)(5)(B) shall be entitled to receive a copy of the applicable water bill from the landlord upon request.

(vii) The amount of permissible passthrough per unit under this Section 37.3(a)(5)(B) shall be determined as follows:

(1) The San Francisco Public Utilities Commission will determine the charge per unit of water, if any, that is attributable to water rate increases resulting from issuance of water system improvement revenue bonds authorized at the November 5, 2002 election.

(2) The charge identified in Section 37.3(a)(5)(B)(vii) (1) shall be multiplied by the total units of water used by

each customer, for each water bill. The result is the total dollar amount of the water bill that is attributable to water rate increases resulting from issuance of water system improvement revenue bonds authorized at the November 5, 2002 election. That charge shall be a separate line item on each customer's water bill.

(3) The dollar amount calculated under Section 37.3(a)(5)(B)(vii)(2) shall be divided by two (since a 50% passthrough is permitted), and then divided by the total number of units covered by the water bill, including commercial units. The resulting dollar figure shall be divided by the number of months covered by the water bill cycle (most are two-month bill cycles), to determine the amount of that water bill that may be passed through to each residential unit for each month covered by that bill.

(4) These passthroughs may be imposed on a monthly basis. These passthroughs shall not become part of a tenant's base rent. The amount of each passthrough may vary from month to month, depending on the amount calculated under Sections 37.3(a)(5)(B)(vii)(1) through (3).

(viii) The Board may amend its rules and regulations as necessary to implement this Section 37.3(a)(5)(B).

(6) Property Tax. A landlord may impose increases based upon a 100% passthrough of the change in the landlord's property tax resulting from the repayment of general obligation bonds of the City and County of San Francisco approved by the voters between November 1, 1996, and November 30, 1998 as provided in Section 37.2(q).

A landlord may impose increases based upon a 50% passthrough of the change in the landlord's property tax resulting from the repayment of general obligation bonds of the City and County of San Francisco approved by the voters after November 14, 2002, as provided in Section 37.2(q), and subject to the following requirement: Any rent increase for bonds approved after the effective date of this initiative Ordinance [November 2000 Proposition H, effective December 21, 2000] must be disclosed and approved by the voters.

A landlord may impose increases based upon a 50% passthrough of the change in the landlord's property tax resulting from the repayment of San Francisco Unified School District or San Francisco Community College District general obligation bonds approved by the voters after November 1, 2006, as provided in Section 37.2(q).

The amount of such increases shall be determined for each tax year as follows:

(A) The Controller and the Board of Supervisors will determine the percentage of the property tax rate, if any, in each tax year attributable to the general obligation bonds and repayable within such tax year.

(B) This percentage shall be multiplied by the total amount of the net taxable value as of November 1 of the applicable tax year. The result is the dollar amount of property taxes for that tax year for a particular property attributable to the repayment of the general obligation bonds.

(C) The dollar amount calculated under subsection (a)(6)(B) shall be divided by the total number of all units in each property, including commercial units. That figure shall also be discounted to reflect the percentage passthrough that the voters authorized, as applicable: specifically, in the case of the 50% passthroughs authorized for general obligation bonds of the City and County of San Francisco approved by the voters after November 14, 2002 and general obligation bonds of the San Francisco Unified School District or San Francisco Community College District approved by the voters after November 1, 2006, the figure shall be divided by two. The figure shall then be divided by the total number of months that the passthrough may apply pursuant to subsection (a)(6)(D)(i), to determine the monthly per unit costs for that tax year of the repayment of general obligation bonds.

(D) Landlords may pass through to each unit in a particular property the dollar amount calculated under subsections (a)(6)(A), (B), and (C), as provided in this subsection (a)(6)(D).

(i) If a passthrough is imposed on or before December 31, 2020, it shall apply only for the 12-month period after it is imposed. Starting January 1, 2021, all passthroughs shall apply for the same number of months covered by the property tax bills used in the passthrough calculation, and the calculation may not be based on tax bills issued more than three years prior to the year in which the passthrough was imposed.

(ii) The landlord shall give affected tenants notice of the passthrough as provided by applicable notice of rent increase provisions of this Chapter 37, including but not limited to Section 37.3(b)(3). The passthroughs may be imposed at any time in the calendar year, provided that the landlord serves notice of such passthrough to be effective on the anniversary date of each tenant's occupancy of the property. The passthroughs shall not become a part of a tenant's base rent. The amount of each passthrough imposed pursuant to subsection (a)(6) may vary from year-to-year, depending on the amount calculated under subsections (a)(6)(A), (B), and (C). A landlord may impose the passthrough described in this subsection (a)(6) for a particular tax year only with respect to those tenants who were residents of a particular property on November 1 of the applicable tax year. A landlord shall not impose a passthrough pursuant to this subsection (a)(6) if the landlord has filed for or received Board approval for a rent increase under Section 37.8(e)(4) for increased operating and maintenance expenses in which the same increase in property taxes due to the repayment of general obligation bonds was included in the comparison year cost totals.

(E) A tenant who has received a passthrough under this subsection (a)(6) may file a financial hardship application with the Board, and the Board may grant the tenant complete or partial relief from that part of the passthrough that is attributable to general obligation bonds approved by the voters on or after November 5, 2019. The standards and procedures for the financial hardship application shall be as set forth in Sections 37.7(h)-(i).

(F) The Board shall have available a form which explains how to calculate the passthrough. Landlords must provide to tenants, on or before the date that notice is served on the tenant of a passthrough permitted under this subsection (a)(6), a copy of the completed form. This completed form shall be provided in addition to the Notice of Rent Increase required under Section 37.3(b). Where a tenant alleges that a landlord has imposed a charge which exceeds the limitations set forth in this subsection (a)(6), the tenant may petition for a hearing under the procedures provided by Section 37.8. In such a hearing, the landlord shall have the burden of proving the accuracy of the calculation that is the basis for the increase. Any tenant petition challenging such a passthrough must be filed within one year of the effective date of the passthrough.

(G) The Board may amend its rules and regulations as necessary to implement this subsection (a)(6).

(7) RAP Loans. A landlord may impose rent increases attributable to the Chief Administrative Officer's amortization of the RAP loan in an area designated on or after July 1, 1977 pursuant to Chapter 32 of the San Francisco Administrative Code.

(8) Additional Increases. A landlord who seeks to impose any rent increase which exceeds those permitted above shall petition for a rental arbitration hearing pursuant to Section 37.8 of this chapter.

(9) A landlord may impose a rent increase to recover costs incurred for the remediation of lead hazards, as defined in San Francisco Health Code Article 11 or 26. Such increases may be based on changes in operating and maintenance expenses or for capital improvement expenditures as long as the costs which are the basis of the rent increase are a substantial portion of the work which abates or remediates a lead hazard, as defined in San Francisco Health Code Article 11 or 26, and provided further that such costs are approved for operating and maintenance expense increases pursuant to Section 37.8(e)(4)(A) and certified as capital improvements pursuant to Section 37.7 below.

When rent increases are authorized by this subsection 37.3(a)(9), the total rent increase for both operating and maintenance expenses and capital improvements shall not exceed 10% in any twelve (12) month period. If allowable rent increases due to the costs of lead remediation and abatement work exceed 10% in any 12 month period, an Administrative Law Judge shall apply a portion of such excess to approved operating and maintenance expenses for lead remediation work, and the balance, if any, to certified capital improvements, provided, however, that such increase shall not exceed 10%. A landlord may accumulate any approved or certified increase which exceeds this amount, subject to the 10% limit.

(10) With respect to units occupied by recipients of tenant-based rental assistance:

(A) If the tenant's share of the base rent is not calculated as a fixed percentage of the tenant's income, such as in the Housing Choice Voucher Program and the Over-FMR Tenancy Program, or if the tenant is receiving assistance under the HOPWA rental subsidy program, then:

(i) If the base rent is equal to or greater than the Payment Standard, the rent increase limitations in Sections 37.3(a)(1) and (2) shall apply to the entire base rent, and the arbitration procedures for those increases set forth in section 37.8 and 37.8A shall apply.

(ii) If the base rent is less than the Payment Standard, the rent increase limitations of this Chapter shall not apply; provided, however, that any rent increase which would result in the base rent being equal to or greater than the Payment Standard shall not result in a new base rent that exceeds the Payment Standard plus the increase allowable under Section 37.3(a)(1).

(B) If the tenant's share of the base rent is calculated as a fixed percentage of the tenant's income, such as in the Section 8 Certificate Program, the rent increase limitations in Section 37.3(a)(1) and (2) shall not apply. In such circumstances, adjustments in rent shall be made solely according to the requirements of the tenant-based rental assistance program.

(11) Additional occupants.

(A) Except as provided in Section 37.3(a)(11)(B), a landlord may not impose increases solely because a tenant has added an additional occupant to an existing tenancy, including, but not limited to, a newborn child or family member as defined in Section 401 of the Housing Code. The prohibition on increases mandated by this Subsection (A) shall apply notwithstanding a rental agreement or lease that specifically permits a rent increase for additional occupants.

(B) A landlord may petition the Board for a rent increase pursuant to Section 37.3(a)(8) for costs associated with the addition of occupants authorized under Section 37.9(a)(2)(C).

(C) Rent increases otherwise permitted by the Costa-Hawkins Rental Housing Act, California Civil Code Section 1950 et seq. (as it may be amended from time to time) are not prohibited or limited by this Section 37.3(a)(11).

(b) Notice of Rent Increase for Tenants in Occupancy. On or before the date upon which a landlord gives a tenant legal notice of a rent increase, the landlord shall inform the tenant, in writing, of the following:

(1) Which portion of the rent increase reflects the annual increase, and/or a banked amount, if any;

(2) Which portion of the rent increase reflects costs for increased operating and maintenance expenses, rents for comparable units, and/or capital improvements, rehabilitation, energy conservation improvements, or renewable energy improvements certified pursuant to Section 37.7. Any rent increase certified due to increases in operating and maintenance costs shall not exceed seven percent.

(3) Which portion of the rent increase reflects the passthrough of charges for: gas and electricity; or the passthrough of increased water bill charges attributable to water rate increases resulting from issuance of water revenue bonds authorized at the November 2002 election as provided by Section 37.3(a)(5)(B)), which charges and calculations of charges shall be explained in writing on a form provided by the Board; or the passthrough of general obligation bond measure costs as provided by Section 37.3(a)(6), which charges shall be explained in writing on a form provided by the Board as described in Section 37.3(a)(6)(E);

(4) Which portion of the rent increase reflects the amortization of the RAP loan, as described in Section 37.3(a)(7) above.

(5) Nonconforming Rent Increases. Any rent increase which does not conform with the provisions of this section shall be null and void.

(6) With respect to rental units occupied by recipients of tenant-based rental assistance, the notice requirements of this Subsection (b) shall be required in addition to any notice required as part of the tenant-based rental assistance program.

(c) Initial Rent Limitation for Subtenants. A tenant who subleases his or her rental unit may charge no more rent upon initial occupancy of the subtenant or subtenants than that rent which the tenant is currently paying to the landlord.

(d) Costa-Hawkins Rental Housing Act (Civil Code Sections 1954.50, et seq.). Consistent with the Costa-Hawkins Rental Housing Act (Civil Code Sections 1954.50, et seq.) and

regardless of whether otherwise provided under Chapter 37:

(1) Property Owner Rights to Establish Initial and All Subsequent Rental Rates for Separately Alienable Parcels.

(A) An owner of residential real property may establish the initial and all subsequent rental rates for a dwelling or a unit which is alienable separate from the title to any other dwelling unit or is a subdivided interest in a subdivision as specified in subdivision (b), (d), or (f) of Section 11004.5 of the California Business and Professions Code. The owner's right to establish subsequent rental rates under this paragraph shall not apply to a dwelling or unit where the preceding tenancy has been terminated by the owner by notice pursuant to California Civil Code Section 1946 or has been terminated upon a change in the terms of the tenancy noticed pursuant to California Civil Code Section 827: in such instances, the rent increase limitation provisions of Chapter 37 shall continue to apply for the duration of the new tenancy in that dwelling or unit.

(B) Where the initial or subsequent rental rates of a Subsection 37.3(d)(1)(A) dwelling or unit were controlled by the provisions of Chapter 37 on January 1, 1995, the following shall apply:

(i) A tenancy that was in effect on December 31, 1995 remains subject to the rent control provisions of this Chapter 37, and the owner may not otherwise establish the subsequent rental rates for that tenancy.

(ii) On or after January 1, 1999 an owner may establish the initial and all subsequent rental rates for any tenancy created on or after January 1, 1996.

(C) An owner's right to establish subsequent rental rates under Subsection 37.3(d)(1) shall not apply to a dwelling or unit which contains serious health, safety, fire or building code violations, excluding those caused by disasters, for which a citation has been issued by the appropriate governmental agency and which has remained unabated for six months or longer preceding the vacancy.

(2) Conditions for Establishing the Initial Rental Rate Upon Sublet or Assignment. Except as identified in this Subsection 37.3(d)(2), nothing in this Subsection or any other provision of law of the City and County of San Francisco shall be construed to preclude express establishment in a lease or rental agreement of the rental rates to be applicable in the event the rental unit subject thereto is sublet, and nothing in this Subsection shall be construed to impair the obligations of contracts entered into prior to January 1, 1996, subject to the following:

(A) Where the original occupant or occupants who took possession of the dwelling or unit pursuant to the rental agreement with the owner no longer permanently reside there, an owner may increase the rent by any amount allowed by this section to a lawful sublessee or assignee who did not reside at the dwelling or unit prior to January 1, 1996. However, such a rent increase shall not be permitted while:

(i) The dwelling or unit has been cited in an inspection report by the appropriate governmental agency as containing serious health, safety, fire, or building code violations, as defined by Section 17920.3 of the California Health and Safety Code, excluding any violation caused by a disaster; and,

(ii) The citation was issued at least 60 days prior to the date of the vacancy; and,

(iii) The cited violation had not been abated when the prior tenant vacated and had remained unabated for 60 days or for a longer period of time. However, the 60-day time period may be extended by the appropriate governmental agency that issued the citation.

(B) This Subsection shall not apply to partial changes in occupancy of a dwelling or unit where one or more of the occupants of the premises, pursuant to the agreement with the owner provided for above (37.3(d)(2)), remains an occupant in lawful possession of the dwelling or unit, or where a lawful sublessee or assignee who resided at the dwelling or unit prior to January 1, 1996, remains in possession of the dwelling or unit. Nothing contained in this Subsection 37.3(d)(2) shall be construed to enlarge or diminish an owner's right to withhold consent to a sublease or assignment.

(C) Acceptance of rent by the owner shall not operate as a waiver or otherwise prevent enforcement of a covenant prohibiting sublease or assignment or as a waiver of an owner's rights to establish the initial rental rate unless the owner has received written notice from the tenant that is

party to the agreement and thereafter accepted rent.

(3) Termination or Nonrenewal of a Contract or Recorded Agreement with a Government Agency Limiting Rent. An owner who terminates or fails to renew a contract or recorded agreement with a governmental agency that provides for a rent limitation to a qualified tenant, shall be subject to the following:

(A) The tenant(s) who were beneficiaries of the contract or recorded agreement shall be given at least 90 days' written notice of the effective date of the termination and shall not be obligated to pay more than the tenant's portion of the rent, as calculated under that contract or recorded agreement, for 90 days following receipt of the notice of termination or nonrenewal.

(B) The owner shall not be eligible to set an initial rent for three years following the date of the termination or nonrenewal of the contract or agreement.

(C) The rental rate for any new tenancy established during the three-year period in that vacated dwelling or unit shall be at the same rate as the rent under the terminated or nonrenewed contract or recorded agreement, plus any increases authorized under this Chapter 37 after the date of termination/non renewal.

(D) The provisions of Subsections 37.3(d)(3)(B) and (C) shall not apply to any new tenancy of 12 months or more duration established after January 1, 2000, pursuant to the owner's contract or recorded agreement with a governmental agency that provides for a rent limitation to a qualified tenant unless the prior vacancy in that dwelling or unit was pursuant to a nonrenewed or canceled contract or recorded agreement with a governmental agency that provides for a rent limitation to a qualified tenant.

(4) Subsection 37.3(d) does not affect the authority of the City and County of San Francisco to regulate or monitor the basis or grounds for eviction.

(5) This Subsection 37.3(d) is intended to be and shall be construed to be consistent with the Costa-Hawkins Rental Housing Act (Civil Code Sections 1954.50. et seq.)

(e) Effect of Deferred Maintenance on Passthroughs for Lead Remediation Techniques.

(1) When lead hazards are remediated or abated pursuant to San Francisco Health Code Article 11 or 26, or are violations of state or local housing and/or health and safety laws, there shall be a rebuttable presumption that the lead hazards are caused or created by deferred maintenance as defined herein of the current or previous landlord. If the landlord fails to rebut the presumption, the costs of such work shall not be

passed through to tenants as either a capital improvement or an operating and maintenance expense. If the landlord rebuts the presumption, he or she shall be entitled to a rent increase if otherwise justified by the standards set forth in this Chapter.

(2) For purposes of the evaluation of petitions for rent increases for lead remediation work, maintenance is deferred if a reasonable landlord under the circumstances would have performed, on a regular basis, the maintenance work required to keep the premises from being in violation of housing safety and habitability standards set forth in California Civil Code Section 1941 and the San Francisco Municipal Code. In order to prevail on a deferred maintenance defense, a tenant must show that the level of repair or remediation currently required would have been lessened had maintenance been performed in a more timely manner.

(f) Costa-Hawkins Vacancy Control. Where a landlord has terminated the previous tenancy as stated in either subsection (1), (2) or (3) below, for the next five years from the termination, the initial base rent for the subsequent tenancy shall be a rent not greater than the lawful rent in effect at the time the previous tenancy was terminated, plus any annual rent increases available under this Chapter 37. This Section 37.3(f) is intended to be consistent with California Civil Code Section 1954.53(a)(1)(A)-(B).

(1) Where the previous tenancy was terminated by a notice of termination of tenancy issued under California Civil Code Section 1946.1 stating the ground for recovery of possession under Sections 37.9(a)(8), (9), (10), (11), or (14) of this Code. For purposes of the termination of the tenancy under Section 37.9(a)(9), the initial rent for the unit may be set by a subsequent bona fide purchaser for value of the condominium.

(2) Where the previous tenancy was terminated upon a change in terms of tenancy noticed under California Civil Code Section 827, except a change in rent permitted by law. Within 10 days after serving the notice of termination based upon a change in terms of tenancy under Civil Code Section 827, the landlord shall notify the Board in writing of the monthly rent the tenant was paying when the landlord gave the notice to the tenant, and provide a copy of the notice to the Board to the tenant.

(3) Where the landlord terminated or did not renew a contract or recorded agreement with a governmental agency that provided for a rent limitation to a qualified tenant. When a landlord terminates a tenant-based rental assistance program, the landlord shall, within 10 days after giving the notice of termination of the program to the tenant, notify the Board in writing of the monthly rent the tenant was paying and the monthly rent paid by the program to the landlord on behalf of the tenant when the landlord gave notice to the tenant, and provide a copy of the notice to the Board to the tenant.

(g) New Construction and Substantial Rehabilitation.

(1) An owner of a residential dwelling or unit which is newly constructed and first received a certificate of occupancy after the effective date of Ordinance No. 276-79 (June 13, 1979), or which the Rent Board has certified has undergone a substantial rehabilitation, may establish the initial and all subsequent rental rates for that dwelling or unit, except:

(A) where rent restrictions apply to the dwelling or unit under Sections 37.3(d) or 37.3(f);

(B) where the dwelling or unit is a replacement unit under Section 37.9A(b);

(C) as provided for certain categories of Accessory Dwelling Units under Section 37.2(r)(4)(D); and

(D) as provided in a development agreement entered into by the City under Administrative Code Chapter 56. **Leg.H.** 1984, 1987, 1991, 1992, 1996, 1998, 1999, 2000, 2003, 2004, 2006, 2015, 2016, 2019, 2019, 2020, 2021.

§ 37.8 *Arbitration of Rental Increase Adjustments*

(a) Authority of Board and Administrative Law Judges. In accordance with such guidelines as the Board shall establish, the Board and designated Administrative Law Judges shall have the authority to arbitrate rental increase adjustments and to administer the rent increase protest procedures with respect to RAP rental units as set forth in Chapter 32 of the San Francisco Administrative Code.

(b) Request for Arbitration.

(1) Landlords. Landlords who seek to impose rent increases which exceed the limitations set forth in Section 37.3(a) above must request an arbitration hearing as set forth in this section. The burden of proof is on the landlord. This Section 37.8(b)(1) applies, but is not limited, to Operating and Maintenance Expense petitions to increase base rent.

(A) Where a landlord Operating and Maintenance Expense petition to increase base rent is granted, based upon a petition pending or filed on or after October 28, 2003 for a property with six or more residential units, the same landlord shall not impose more than a total seven percent (7%) base rent increase on any unit in any five (5) year period due to increases in operating and maintenance costs.

(2) Tenants.

(A) Notwithstanding Section 37.3, tenants of non-RAP rental units and tenants of RAP rental units in areas designated on or after July 1, 1977 may request arbitration hearings where a landlord has substantially decreased services without a corresponding reduction in rent and/or has failed to perform ordinary repair and maintenance under state or local law and/or has failed to provide the tenant with a clear explanation of the current charges for gas and electricity passed through to the tenant and/or imposed a nonconforming rent increase which is null and void. The burden of proof is on the tenant.

(B) Tenants of RAP rental units in areas designated prior to July 1, 1977 may petition for a hearing where the landlord has noticed an increase which exceeds the limitations set forth in Section 32.73 of the San Francisco Administrative Code. After a vacancy has occurred in a RAP rental unit in said areas, a new tenant of said unit may petition for a hearing where the landlord has demanded and/or received a rent for that unit which exceeds the rent increase limitation set forth in Section 32.73 of the San Francisco Administrative Code. The burden of proof is on the landlord.

(c) Procedure for Landlord Petitioners.

(1) Filing. The request for arbitration must be filed on a petition form prescribed by the Board and shall be accompanied by such supporting material as the Board shall prescribe, including but not limited to, justification for the proposed rental increase.

(2) Filing Date. The petition must be filed prior to the mailing or delivering to the tenant or tenants legal notice of the rental increase exceeding the limitations as defined in Section 37.3.

(3) Effect of Timely Filing of Petition. Provided a completed petition is timely filed, that portion of the requested rental increase which exceeds the limitations set forth in Section 37.3 and has not been certified as a justifiable increase in accordance with Section 37.7 is inoperative until such time as the Administrative Law Judge makes findings of fact at the conclusion of the arbitration hearing.

(4) Notice to Parties. The Board shall calendar the petition for hearing before a designated Administrative Law Judge and shall give written notice of the date to the parties at least ten (10) days prior to the hearing.

(d) Procedure for Tenant Petitioners.

(1) Filing; Limitation. The request for arbitration must be filed on a petition form prescribed by the Board and must be accompanied by such supporting material as the Board shall prescribe, including but not limited to, a copy of the landlord's notice of rent increase. If the tenant petitioner has received certification findings regarding his rental unit in accordance with 37.7, such findings must accompany the petition. If the tenant petitioner has received a notification from the Chief Administrative Officer with respect to base rent and amortization of a RAP loan, such notification must

accompany the petition. A tenant petition regarding a gas and electricity passthrough must be filed within one year of the effective date of the passthrough or within one year of the date the passthrough was required to be recalculated pursuant to rules and regulations promulgated by the Board. A tenant petition regarding a water revenue bond passthrough under Section 37.3(a)(5)(B) must be filed within one year of the effective date of the passthrough. A tenant petition regarding a general obligation bond cost passthrough under Section 37.3(a)(6) must be filed within one year of the effective date of the passthrough.

(2) Notice to Parties. The Board shall calendar the petition for hearing before a designated Administrative Law Judge and shall give written notice of the date to the parties at least ten (10) days prior to the hearing. Responses to a petition for hearing may be submitted in writing.

(e) Hearings.

(1) Time of Hearing. The hearing must be held within forty-five (45) days of the filing of the petition. The level of housing services provided to tenants' rental units shall not be decreased during the period between the filing of the petition and the conclusion of the hearing.

(2) Consolidation. To the greatest extent possible, hearings with respect to a given building shall be consolidated.

(3) Conduct of Hearing. The hearing shall be conducted by an Administrative Law Judge designated by the Board. Both parties may offer such documents, testimony, written declarations or other evidence as may be pertinent to the proceedings. A record of the proceedings must be maintained for purposes of appeal.

(4) Determination of the Administrative Law Judge: Rental Units. Based upon the evidence presented at the hearing and upon such relevant factors as the Board shall determine, the Administrative Law Judge shall make findings as to whether the landlord's proposed rental increase exceeding the limitations set forth in Section 37.3 is justified or whether the landlord has effected a rent increase through a reduction in services or has failed to perform ordinary repair and maintenance as required by state or local law; and provided further that, where a landlord has imposed a passthrough pursuant to this Chapter 37, the same costs shall not be included in the calculation of increased operating and maintenance expenses pursuant to this subsection (4). In making such findings, the Administrative Law Judge shall take into consideration the following factors:

(A) Increases or decreases in operating and maintenance expenses, including, but not limited to, water and sewer service charges; janitorial service; refuse removal; elevator service; security system; insurance for the property; debt service and real estate taxes as set forth in subsections (i) and (ii); reasonable and necessary management expenses as set forth in subsection (iii); and routine repairs and maintenance as set forth in subsection (iv).

(i) For petitions filed before December 11, 2017, the Rent Board may consider increased debt service and increased real estate taxes; provided, however, that if the property has been purchased within two (2) years of the date of the previous purchase, consideration shall not be given to that portion of increased debt service which has resulted from a selling price which exceeds the seller's purchase price by more than the percentage increase in the "Consumer Price Index for All Urban Consumers for the San Francisco-Oakland Metropolitan Area, U.S. Department of Labor" between the date of previous purchase and the date of the current sale, plus the cost of capital improvements or rehabilitation work made or performed by the seller.

(ii) For petitions filed on or after December 11, 2017, the Rent Board shall not consider any portion of increased debt service, or that portion of increased real estate taxes that has resulted from an increased assessment due to a change in ownership; provided, however, that the Rent Board may consider that portion of increased real estate taxes that has resulted from the completion of needed repairs or capital improvements with respect to any petition filed on or after December 11, 2017; and provided, further, that the Rent Board may consider increased debt service and increased real estate taxes in a petition filed on or after December 11, 2017 pursuant to Section 37.8(e)(4)(A)(i), if the landlord demonstrates that it had purchased the property on or before April 3, 2018 and that it had reasonably relied on its ability to pass through those costs at the time of the purchase.

(iii) For petitions filed on or after July 15, 2018, the Rent Board may consider management expenses only to the extent those expenses are reasonable and necessary, based on factors such as the need to provide day-to-day management of the building; the level of management services previously required for the building; the reasonable cost of the services in an arms-length transaction; whether any tenants have objected that the cost and quality of the services are not in keeping with the socioeconomic status of the building's existing tenants; and other extraordinary circumstances.

(iv) The term routine repairs and maintenance shall not include any costs for installation or upgrade of a fire sprinkler system or fire alarm and/or detection system attributable to the landlord's compliance with a Fire Life Safety Notice and Order issued by the Building Official under Sections 107A.16.1 et seq. of the Building Code or the fire code official under Sections 109.3 et seq. of the Fire Code.

(B) The past history of increases in the rent for the unit and the comparison of the rent for the unit with rents for comparable units in the same general area.

(C) Any findings which have been made pursuant to Section 37.7 with respect to the unit.

(D) Failure to perform ordinary repair, replacement and maintenance in compliance with applicable state and local law.

(E) Any other such relevant factors as the Board shall specify in rules and regulations.

(5) Determination of the Administrative Law Judge: RAP Rental Units.

(A) Rap Rental units in RAP areas designated prior to July 1, 1977. The Administrative Law Judge shall make findings as to whether or not the noticed or proposed rental increase exceeds the rent increase limitations set forth in Section 32.73 of the San Francisco Administrative Code. In making such findings, the Administrative Law Judge shall apply the rent increase limitations set forth in Chapter 32 of the San Francisco Administrative Code and all rules and regulations promulgated pursuant thereto. The Administrative Law Judge shall consider the evidence presented at the hearing. The burden of proof shall be on the landlord.

(B) Rap rental units in RAP areas designated on or after July 1, 1977. The Administrative Law Judge shall make findings with respect to rent increases exceeding the limitations as set forth in Section 37.3 of this chapter. In making such findings, the Administrative Law Judge shall take into consideration the factors set forth in subsection (4) above and shall consider evidence presented at the hearing. The burden of proof is on the landlord.

(6) Findings of Fact. The Administrative Law Judge shall make written findings of fact, copies of which shall be mailed to the parties within 30 days of the hearing.

(7) Payment or Refund of Rents to Implement Arbitration Decision. Upon finding that all or any portion of the rent increase is or is not justified, or that any nonconforming rent increase is null and void, the Administrative Law Judge may order payment or refund of all or a portion of that cumulative amount within fifteen (15) days of the mailing of the findings of fact or may order the amount added to or offset against future rents; provided, however, that any such order shall be stayed if an appeal is timely filed by the aggrieved party. The Administrative Law Judge may order refunds of rent overpayments resulting from rent increases which are null and void for no more than the three-year period preceding the month of the filing of a landlord or tenant petition, plus the period between the month of filing and the date of the Administrative Law Judge's decision. In any case, calculation

of rent overpayments and re-setting of the lawful base rent shall be based on a determination of the validity of all rent increases imposed since April 1,1982, in accordance with Sections 37.3(b)(5) and 37.3(a)(2) above.

(8) Finality of Administrative Law Judge's Decision. The decision of the Administrative Law Judge shall be final unless the Board vacates his decision on appeal.

(f) Appeals.

(1) Time and Manner. Any appeal to the Board from the determination of the Administrative Law Judge must be made within fifteen (15) calendar days of the mailing of the findings of fact unless such time limit is extended by the board upon a showing of good cause. If the fifteenth day falls on a Saturday, Sunday or legal holiday, the appeal may be filed with the Board on the next business day. The appeal shall be in writing and must state why appellant believes there was either error or abuse of discretion on the part of the Administrative Law Judge. The filing of an appeal will stay only that portion of any Administrative Law Judge's decision which permits payment, refund, offsetting or adding rent.

(2) Record on Appeal. Upon receipt of an appeal, the entire administrative record of the matter, including the appeal, shall be filed with the Board.

(3) Appeals. The Board shall, in its discretion, hear appeals. In deciding whether or not to hear a given appeal, the board shall consider, among other factors, fairness to the parties, hardship to either party, and promoting the policies and purposes of this chapter, in addition to any written comments submitted by the Administrative Law Judge whose decision is being challenged. The Board may also review other material from the administrative record of the matter as it deems necessary. A vote of three (3) members shall be required in order for an appeal to be heard.

(4) Remand to Administrative Law Judge Without Appeal Hearing. In those cases where the Board is able to determine on the basis of the documents before it that the Administrative Law Judge has erred, the board may remand the case for further hearing in accordance with its instructions without conducting an appeal hearing. Both parties shall be notified as to the time of the re-hearing, which shall be conducted within thirty (30) days of remanding by the board. In those cases where the board is able to determine on the basis of the documents before it that the Administrative Law Judge's findings contain numerical or clerical inaccuracies, or require clarification, the board may continue the hearing for purposes of re-referring the case to said Administrative Law Judge in order to correct the findings.

(5) Time of Appeal Hearing; Notice to Parties. Appeals accepted by the board shall be heard within forty-five (45) days of the filing of an appeal. Within thirty (30) days of the filing of an appeal, both parties shall be notified in writing as to whether or not the appeal has been accepted. If the appeal has been accepted, the notice shall state the time of the hearing and the nature of the hearing. Such notice must be mailed at least ten (10) days prior to the hearing.

(6) Appeal Hearing; Decision of the Board. At the appeal hearing, both appellant and respondent shall have an opportunity to present oral testimony and written documents in support of their positions. After such hearing and after any further investigation which the board may deem necessary the board may, upon hearing the appeal, affirm, reverse or modify the Administrative Law Judge's decision or may remand the case for further hearing in accordance with its findings. The board's decision must be rendered within forty-five (45) days of the hearing and the parties must be notified of such decision.

(7) Notification of the Parties. In accordance with item (6) above, parties shall receive written notice of the decision. The notice shall state that this decision is final.

(8) Effective Date of Appeal Decisions. Appeal decisions are effective on the date mailed to the parties; provided, however, that that portion of any decision which orders payment, refund, offsetting or adding rent shall become effective thirty (30) calendar days after it is mailed to the parties unless a stay of execution is granted by a court of competent jurisdiction.

(9) Limitation of Actions. A landlord or tenant aggrieved by any decision of the Board must seek judicial review within ninety (90) calendar days of the date of mailing of the decision. **Leg.H.** 1979, 1980, 1982, 1983, 1986, 1989, 1991, 1992, 1993, 1998, 1999, 2000, 2003, 2004, 2018

§ 37.9 *Evictions [Stay (Hold) and Pending Legislation.]*

Notwithstanding Section 37.3, this Section 37.9 shall apply as of August 24, 1980, to all landlords and tenants of rental units as defined in Section 37.2(r).

(a) A landlord shall not endeavor to recover possession of a rental unit unless:

(1) The tenant:

(A) Has failed to pay the rent to which the landlord is lawfully entitled under the oral or written agreement between the tenant and landlord:

(i) Except that a tenant's nonpayment of a charge prohibited by Section 919.1 of the Police Code shall not constitute a failure to pay rent; and

"By God, for a minute there it all made sense!"

(ii) Except that, commencing August 10, 2001, to and including February 10, 2003, a landlord shall not endeavor to recover or recover possession of rental unit for failure of a tenant to pay that portion of rent attributable to a capital improvement passthrough certified pursuant to a decision issued after April 10, 2000, where the capital improvement passthrough petition was filed prior to August 10, 2001, and a landlord shall not impose any late fee(s) upon the tenant for such non-payment of capital improvement costs; or

(B) Habitually pays the rent late; or

(C) Gives checks which are frequently returned because there are insufficient funds in the checking account;

(D) Provided, however, that subsection (a)(1) shall not apply with respect to rent payments that initially became due during the time period when paragraph 2 of the Governor's Executive Order No. N-28-20 (as said time period may be extended by the Governor from time to time) was in effect, and where the tenant's failure to pay (i) arose out of a substantial decrease in household income (including, but not limited to, a substantial decrease in household income caused by layoffs or a reduction in the number of compensable hours of work, or substantial out-of-pocket expenses; (ii) that was caused by the COVID-19 pandemic, or by any local, state, or federal government response to COVID-19; and (iii) is documented. The types of documentation that a tenant may use to show an inability to pay due to COVID-19 may include, without limitation, bank statements, pay stubs, employment termination notices, proof of unemployment insurance claim filings, sworn affidavits, and completed forms prepared by the Rent Board. A tenant shall have the option, but shall not be required, to use third-party documentation such as a letter from an employer to show an inability to pay. The provisions of this subsection (a)(1)(D), being necessary for the welfare of the City and County of San Francisco and its residents, shall be liberally construed to effectuate its purpose, which is to protect tenants from being evicted for missing rent payments due to the COVID-19 pandemic. Nothing in this subsection (a)(1)(D) shall relieve a tenant of the obligation to pay rent, nor restrict a landlord's ability to recover rent due;

(2) The tenant has violated a lawful obligation or covenant of tenancy other than the obligation to surrender possession upon proper notice or other than an obligation to pay a charge prohibited by Police Code Section 919.1, the violation was substantial, and the tenant fails to cure such violation after having received written notice thereof from the landlord.

(A) Provided that notwithstanding any lease provision to the contrary, a landlord shall not endeavor to recover possession of a rental unit as a result of subletting of the rental unit by the tenant if the landlord has unreasonably withheld the right to sublet following a written request by the tenant, so long as the tenant continues to reside in the rental unit and the sublet constitutes a one-for-one replacement of the departing tenant(s). If the landlord fails to respond to the tenant in writing with a description of the reasons for the denial of the request within 14 days of receipt of the tenant's written request, the tenant's request shall be deemed approved by the landlord.

(B) Provided further that where a rental agreement or lease provision limits the number of occupants or limits or prohibits subletting or assignment, a landlord shall not endeavor to recover possession of a rental unit as a result of the addition to the unit of a tenant's child, parent, grandchild, grandparent, brother or sister, or the spouse or domestic partner (as defined in Administrative Code Sections 62.1 through 62.8) of such relatives, or as a result of the addition of the spouse or domestic partner of a tenant, so long as the maximum number of occupants stated in Section 37.9(a)(2)(B)(i) and (ii) is not exceeded, if the landlord has unreasonably refused a written request by the tenant to add such occupant(s) to the unit. If the landlord fails to respond to the tenant in writing with a description of the reasons for the denial of the request within 14 days of receipt of the tenant's written request, the tenant's request shall be deemed approved by the landlord. A landlord's reasonable refusal of the tenant's written request may not be based on the proposed additional occupant's lack of creditworthiness, if that person will not be legally obligated to pay some or all of the rent to the landlord. A landlord's reasonable refusal of the tenant's written request may be based on, but is not limited to, the ground that the total number of occupants in a unit exceeds (or with the proposed additional occupant(s) would exceed) the lesser of (i) or (ii):

(i) Two persons in a studio unit, three persons in a one-bedroom unit, four persons in a two-bedroom unit, six persons in a three-bedroom unit, or eight persons in a four-bedroom unit; or,

(ii) The maximum number permitted in the unit under state law and/or other local codes such as the Building, Fire, Housing and Planning Codes.

(C) Provided further that where a rental agreement or lease provision limits the number of occupants or limits or prohibits subletting or assignment, a landlord shall not endeavor to recover possession of a rental unit as a result of the addition by the tenant of additional occupants to the rental unit, so long as the maximum number of occupants does not exceed the lesser of the amounts allowed by Subsection (i) or Subsection (ii) of this Section 37.9(a)(2)(C), if the landlord has unreasonably refused a written request by the tenant to add such occupant(s) to the unit. If the landlord fails to respond to the tenant in writing with a description of the reasons for the denial of the request within 14 days of receipt of the tenant's written request, the tenant's request shall be deemed approved by the landlord. A landlord's reasonable refusal of the tenant's written request may not be based on either of the following: (1) the proposed additional occupant's lack of creditworthiness, if that person will not be legally obligated to pay some or all of the rent to the landlord, or (2) the number of occupants allowed by the rental agreement or lease. With the exception of the restrictions stated in the preceding sentence, a landlord's reasonable refusal of the tenant's written request may be based on, but is not limited to, the ground that the landlord resides in the same unit as the tenant or the ground that the total number of occupants in a unit exceeds (or with the proposed additional occupant(s) would exceed) the lesser of (i) or (ii):

(i) Two persons in a studio unit, three persons in a one-bedroom unit, four persons in a two-bedroom unit, six persons in a three-bedroom unit, or eight persons in a four-bedroom unit; or

(ii) The maximum number permitted in the unit under state law and/or other local codes such as the Building, Fire, Housing, and Planning Codes.

(iii) This Subsection 37.9(a)(2)(C) is not intended by itself to establish a direct landlord-tenant relationship between the additional occupant and the landlord or to limit a landlord's rights under the Costa-Hawkins Rental Housing Act, California Civil Code Section 1954.50 et seq. (as it may be amended from time to time).

(iv) For the purposes of this Subsection 37.9(a)(2)(C), the term "additional occupant" shall not include persons who occupy the unit as a Tourist or Transient Use, as defined in Administrative Code Section 41A.5.

(D) Before endeavoring to recover possession based on the violation of a lawful obligation or covenant of tenancy regarding subletting or limits on the number of occupants in the rental unit, the landlord shall serve the tenant a written notice of the violation that provides the tenant with an opportunity to cure the violation in 10 or more days. The tenant may cure the violation by making a written request to add occupants referenced in Subsection (A), (B), or (C) of Section 37.9(a)(2) or by using other reasonable means to

cure the violation, including, without limitation, the removal of any additional or unapproved occupant. Nothing in this Section 37.9(a)(2)(D) is intended to limit any other rights or remedies that the law otherwise provides to landlords.

(E) Notwithstanding any lease provision to the contrary, a landlord may not impose late fees, penalties, interest, liquidated damages, or similar charges due to a tenant's nonpayment of rent, if the tenant can demonstrate that it missed the rent payment due to the COVID-19 pandemic as set forth in subsection (a)(1)(D) and/or (a)(1)(E). A landlord may not recover possession of the unit due to a tenant's failure to pay such late charges when subsection (a)(1)(D) and/or (a)(1)(E) apply. The foregoing sentence shall not enlarge or diminish a landlord's rights with respect to such charges when subsection (a)(1)(D) and/or (a)(1)(E) do not apply; or

(3) The tenant is committing or permitting to exist a nuisance in, or is causing substantial damage to, the rental unit, or is creating a substantial interference with the comfort, safety or enjoyment of the landlord or tenants in the building, the activities are severe, continuing or recurring in nature, and the nature of such nuisance, damage or interference is specifically stated by the landlord in the writing as required by Section 37.9(c).

(3.1) Eviction Protection for Victims of Domestic Violence or Sexual Assault or Stalking:

(A) It shall be a defense to an action for possession of a unit under Subsection 37.9(a)(3) if the court determines that:

(i) The tenant or the tenant's household member is a victim of an act or acts that constitute domestic violence or sexual assault or stalking; and

(ii) The notice to vacate is substantially based upon the act or acts constituting domestic violence or sexual assault or stalking against the tenant or a tenant's household member, including but not limited to an action for possession based on complaints of noise, disturbances, or repeated presence of police.

(B) Evidence Required. In making the determination under Section 37.9(a)(3.1)(A) the court shall consider evidence, which may include but is not limited to:

(i) A copy of a temporary restraining order or emergency protective order issued pursuant to Part 3 (commencing with Section 6240) or Part 4 (commencing with Section 6300) or Part 5 (commencing with Section 6400) of the Family Code, Section 136.2 of the Penal Code, Section 527.6 of the Code of Civil Procedure, or Section 213.5 of the Welfare and Institutions Code, that protects the tenant or tenant's household member from further domestic violence, sexual assault, or stalking. And/or,

(ii) A copy of a written report by a peace officer employed by a state or local law enforcement agency acting in his or her official capacity, stating that the tenant or tenant's household member has filed a report alleging that he or she is a victim of domestic violence, sexual assault, or stalking. And/or

(iii) Other written documentation from a qualified third party of the acts constituting domestic violence or sexual assault or stalking.

(C) Mutual Allegations of Abuse Between Parties. If two or more co-tenants are parties seeking relief under Subsection 37.9(a)(3.1)(A), and each alleges that he or she was a victim of domestic violence or sexual assault or stalking perpetrated by another co-tenant who is also a party, the court may determine whether a tenant acted as the dominant aggressor in the acts constituting a domestic violence or sexual assault or stalking offense. In making the determination, the court shall consider the factors listed in Section 13701(b)(1) of the Penal Code. A tenant who the court determines was the dominant aggressor in the acts constituting a domestic violence or sexual assault or stalking offense is not entitled to relief under Subsection 37.9(a)(3.1)(A).

(D) Limitations on Relief. Unless the tenant or the tenant's household member has obtained a protective order against the alleged abuser to vacate or stay from the unit as a result of acts constituting domestic violence or sexual assault or stalking against the tenant or tenant's household member, the tenant may not obtain relief under Subsection 37.9(a)(3.1) if:

(i) The tenant was granted relief under Subsection 37.9(a)(3.1) in an action for possession of the unit within the previous five years; and

(ii) A subsequent action for possession of the unit has now been filed; and

(iii) The notice to vacate in this subsequent action for possession is substantially based upon continuing acts constituting domestic violence or sexual assault or stalking by the same person alleged to be the abuser in the previous action for possession.

(E) Nothing in this Subsection 37.9(a)(3.1) shall be construed to affect the tenant's liability for delinquent rent or other sums owed to the landlord, or the landlord's remedies in recovering against the tenant for such sums.

(F) The provisions of Subsection 37.9(a)(3.1) are intended for use consistent with Civil Code Section 1946.7.

(3.2) Confidentiality of Information Received from Victims of Domestic Violence or Sexual Assault or Stalking. A landlord shall retain in strictest confidence all information that is received in confidence from a tenant or a tenant's household member who is a victim of domestic violence or sexual assault or stalking, regarding that domestic violence or sexual assault or stalking, except to the extent that such disclosure (A) is necessary to provide for a reasonable accommodation for the victim, or (B) is otherwise required pursuant to applicable federal, state or local law. The victim may authorize limited or general release of any information otherwise deemed confidential under this Subsection 37.9(a)(3.2).

Or,

(4) The tenant is using or permitting a rental unit to be used for any illegal purpose, provided however that a landlord shall not endeavor to recover possession of a rental unit solely:

(A) as a result of a first violation of Chapter 41A that has been cured within 30 days written notice to the tenant; or,

(B) because the illegal use is the residential occupancy of a unit not authorized for residential occupancy by the City. Nothing in this Section 37.9(a)(4)(B) prohibits a landlord from endeavoring to recover possession of the unit under Section 37.9(a)(8) or (10) of this Chapter.

((5) The tenant, who had an oral or written agreement with the landlord which has terminated, has refused after written request or demand by the landlord to execute a written extension or renewal thereof for a further term of like duration and under such terms which are materially the same as in the previous agreement; provided, that such terms do not conflict with any of the provisions of this Chapter 37; or

(6) The tenant has, after written notice to cease, refused the landlord access to the rental unit as required by state or local law; or

(7) The tenant holding at the end of the term of the oral or written agreement is a subtenant not approved by the landlord; or

(8) The landlord seeks to recover possession in good faith, without ulterior reasons and with honest intent;

(i) For the landlords use or occupancy as his or her principal residence for a period of at least 36 continuous months;

(ii) For the use or occupancy of the landlords grandparents, grandchildren, parents, children, brother or sister, or the landlords spouse or the spouses of such relations, as their principal place of residency for a period of at least 36 months, in the same building in which the landlord resides as his or her principal place of residency, or in a building in which the landlord is simultaneously seeking possession of a rental unit under 37.9(a)(8)(i). For purposes of this Section 37.9(a)(8)(ii), the term "spouse" shall include Domestic Partners as defined in Administrative Code Chapter 62.1 through 62.8.

(iii) For purposes of this Section 37.9(a)(8) only, as to landlords who become owners of record of the rental unit on or before February 21, 1991, the term landlord shall be defined as an owner of record of at least 10 percent interest in the property or, for Section 37.9(a)(8)(i) only, two individuals registered as Domestic Partners as defined in San Francisco Administrative Code Chapter 62.1-62.8 whose combined ownership of record is at least 10 percent. For purposes of this Section 37.9(a)(8) only, as to landlords who become owners of record of the rental unit after February 21, 1991, the term landlord shall be defined as an owner of record of at least 25 percent interest in the property or, for Section 37.9(a)(8)(i) only, two individuals registered as Domestic Partners as defined in San Francisco Administrative Code Chapter 62.1-62.8 whose combined ownership of record is at least 25 percent.

(iv) A landlord may not recover possession under this Section 37.9(a)(8) if a comparable unit owned by the landlord is already vacant and is available, or if such a unit becomes vacant and available before the recovery of possession of the unit. If a comparable unit does become vacant and available before the recovery of possession, the landlord shall rescind the notice to vacate and dismiss any action filed to recover possession of the premises. Provided further, if a non-comparable unit becomes available before the recovery of possession, the landlord shall offer that unit to the tenant. It shall be evidence of a lack of good faith if a landlord times the service of the notice, or the filing of an action to recover possession, so as to avoid moving into a comparable unit, or to avoid offering a tenant a replacement unit.

(v) Commencing January 1, 2018, the landlord shall attach to the notice to vacate a form prepared by the Rent Board that the tenant can use to keep the Rent Board apprised of any future change in address, and shall include in the notice a declaration executed by the landlord under penalty of perjury stating that the landlord seeks to recover possession of the unit in good faith, without ulterior reasons and with honest intent, for use or occupancy as the principal residence of the landlord or the landlord's relative (identified by name and relation to the landlord), for a period of at least 36 continuous months, as set forth in subsections 37.9(a)(8)(i) and (ii). Evidence that the landlord has not acted in good faith may include, but is not limited to, any of the following: (1) the landlord has failed to file the notice to vacate with the Rent Board as required by Section 37.9(c), (2) the landlord or relative for whom the tenant was evicted did not move into the rental unit within three months after the landlord recovered possession and then occupy said unit as that person's principal residence for a minimum of 36 consecutive months, (3) the landlord or relative for whom the tenant was

evicted lacks a legitimate, bona fide reason for not moving into the unit within three months after the recovery of possession and/or then occupying said unit as that person's principal residence for a minimum of 36 consecutive months, (4) the landlord did not file a statement of occupancy with the Rent Board as required by Section 37.9(a)(8)(vii), (5) the landlord violated Section 37.9B by renting the unit to a new tenant at a rent greater than that which would have been the rent had the tenant who had been required to vacate remained in continuous occupancy and the rental unit remained subject to this Chapter 37, and (6) such other factors as a court or the Rent Board may deem relevant. Nothing in this Section 37.9(a)(8)(v) is intended to alter or diminish any other right to relief that a tenant may have based on a landlord's failure to comply with this Chapter 37.

(vi) Once a landlord has successfully recovered possession of a rental unit pursuant to Section 37.9(a)(8)(i), then no other current or future landlords may recover possession of any other rental unit in the building under Section 37.9(a)(8)(i). It is the intention of this section that only one specific unit per building may be used for such occupancy under Section 37.9(a)(8)(i) and that once a unit is used for such occupancy, all future occupancies under Section 37.9(a)(8)(i) must be of that same unit, provided that a landlord may file a petition with the Rent Board, or at the landlords option, commence eviction proceedings, claiming that disability or other similar hardship prevents him or her from occupying a unit which was previously occupied by the landlord.

(vii) A landlord who has recovered possession of a unit pursuant to Section 37.9(a)(8) on or after January 1, 2018 must complete a statement of occupancy under penalty of perjury on a form to be prepared by the Rent Board that discloses whether the landlord has recovered possession of the unit. The landlord shall file the statement of occupancy with the Rent Board within 90 days after the date of service, and shall file an updated statement of occupancy every 90 days thereafter, unless the statement of occupancy discloses that the landlord is no longer endeavoring to recover possession of the unit, in which case no further statements of occupancy need be filed. If the statement of occupancy discloses that the landlord has already recovered possession of the unit, the landlord shall file updated statements of occupancy once a year for five years, no later than 12 months, 24 months, 36 months, 48 months and 60 months after the recovery of possession of the unit. Each statement of occupancy filed after the landlord has recovered possession of the unit shall disclose the date of recovery of possession, whether the landlord or relative for whom the tenant was evicted is occupying the unit as that person's principal residence with at least two forms of supporting documentation, the date such occupancy commenced (or alternatively, the reasons why occupancy has not yet commenced), the rent charged for the unit if any, and such other information and documentation as the Rent Board may require in order to effectuate the purposes of this

Section 37.9(a)(8). The Rent Board shall make all reasonable efforts to send the displaced tenant a copy of each statement of occupancy within 30 days of the date of filing, or a notice that the landlord did not file a statement of occupancy if no statement of occupancy was filed. In addition, the Rent Board shall impose an administrative penalty on any landlord who fails to comply with this subsection (a)(8)(vii), in the amount of $250 for the first violation, $500 for the second violation, and $1,000 for every subsequent violation. The procedure for the imposition, enforcement, collection, and administrative review of the administrative penalty shall be governed by Administrative Code Chapter 100, "Procedures Governing the Imposition of Administrative Fines," which is hereby incorporated in its entirety.

(viii) If any provision or clause of this Section 37.9(a)(8) or the application thereof to any person or circumstance is held to be unconstitutional or to be otherwise invalid by any court of competent jurisdiction, such invalidity shall not affect other chapter provisions, and clauses of this chapter are held to be severable; or

(9) The landlord seeks to recover possession in good faith in order to sell the unit in accordance with a condominium conversion approved under the San Francisco subdivision ordinance and does so without ulterior reasons and with honest intent; or

(10) The landlord seeks to recover possession in good faith in order to demolish or to otherwise permanently remove the rental unit from housing use and has obtained all the necessary permits on or before the date upon which notice to vacate is given, and does so without ulterior reasons and with honest intent; provided that a landlord who seeks to recover possession under this Section 37.9(a)(10) shall pay relocation expenses as provided in Section 37.9C except that a landlord who seeks to demolish an unreinforced masonry building pursuant to Building Code Chapters 16B and 16C must provide the tenant with the relocation assistance specified in Section 37.9A(e) below prior to the tenant's vacating the premises; or

(11) The landlord seeks in good faith to remove temporarily the unit from housing use in order to be able to carry out capital improvements or rehabilitation work that would make the unit hazardous, unhealthy, and/or uninhabitable while work is in progress, and has obtained all the necessary permits on or before the date upon which notice to vacate is given, and does so without ulterior reasons and with honest intent. Any tenant who vacates the unit under such circumstances shall have the right to reoccupy the unit at the prior rent adjusted in accordance with the provisions of this Chapter 37. The landlord may require the tenant to vacate the unit only for the minimum time required to do the work.

(A) On or before the date upon which notice to vacate is given, the landlord shall: (i) advise the tenant in writing that the rehabilitation or capital improvement plans are on file with the Central Permit Bureau of the Department of Building Inspection and that arrangements for reviewing such plans can be made with the Central Permit Bureau, and (ii) provide the tenant a disclosure form prepared by the Board that advises the tenant of the tenant's right to return, and (iii) provide the tenant a form prepared by the Board that the tenant can use to keep the Board apprised of any future change in address.

(B) No landlord shall endeavor to recover possession of any unit subject to a RAP loan as set forth in Section 37.2(m) of this Chapter except as provided in Section 32.69 of the Administrative Code.

(C) The tenant shall not be required to vacate pursuant to this Section 37.9(a)(11), for a period in excess of three months; provided, however, that such time period may be extended by the Board (including its Administrative Law Judges) upon application by the landlord.

(i) In reviewing an application for an extension of time, the Board shall first determine whether the landlord has demonstrated that all of the work is reasonable and necessary to meet state or local requirements concerning the safety or habitability of the building or the unit, rather than elective in nature. If so, the Board shall only consider whether the landlord has delayed in seeking the extension; and the reasonableness of the landlord's time estimate.

(ii) Alternatively, if the Board determines that not all of the work is reasonable and necessary to meet state or local requirements concerning the safety or habitability of the building or the unit, the Board shall consider the degree to which the work is elective in nature; whether any tenants have objected that the cost of securing alternative housing during the time extension would cause them a financial hardship, and/or that they are 60 years of age or older or disabled; and any other extraordinary circumstances. The Board shall also consider whether the landlord has offered reasonable mitigation, other than the relocation expenses required by Section 37.9C, to address the hardship imposed upon the tenant, such as temporary occupancy of another vacant unit should one be available.

(iii) The Board may grant or deny an application for an extension of time or may approve a shorter period of time, based upon the consideration of the facts of the case. The Board shall adopt rules and regulations to implement the application procedure. If the landlord does not timely allow the tenant to reoccupy the unit, and upon completion of the work the subsequent occupant is someone other than the original tenant, there shall be a rebuttable presumption that the original tenant did not reoccupy the unit due to the delay and therefore, for purposes of restricting the rent as set forth in Section 37.3(f)(1), that the original tenancy was terminated by the landlord.

(D) Any landlord who seeks to recover possession under this Section 37.9(a)(11) shall pay relocation expenses as provided in Section 37.9C. [However, effective January 1, 2013, the amount of relocation payments for temporary displacement of a tenant household under Section 37.9(a)(11) for less than 20 days is governed by California Civil Code Section 1947.9 and not by Section 37.9C.]

(E) Immediately upon completion of the capital improvements or rehabilitation work, the landlord shall advise the tenant, in writing, and allow the tenant to reoccupy the tenant's unit. The tenant shall have 30 days from receipt of the landlord's offer of reoccupany to notify the landlord of acceptance or rejection of the offer, and if accepted, the tenant shall reoccupy the unit within 45 days of receipt of the landlord's offer. The landlord shall file a copy of the offer with the Rent Board within 15 days of the offer. The Board shall make all reasonable efforts to send a notice to the unit within one year of the date of filing, to inform the occupant that the rent may be subject to the rent restrictions set forth in Section 37.3(f) (1).

(12) The landlord seeks to recover possession in good faith in order to carry out substantial rehabilitation, as defined in Section 37.2(s), and has obtained all the necessary permits on or before the date upon which notice to vacate is given, and does so without ulterior reasons and with honest intent. Notwithstanding the above, no landlord shall endeavor to recover possession of any unit subject to a RAP loan as set forth in Section 37.2(m) of this Chapter except as provided in Section 32.69 of the San Francisco Administrative Code. Any landlord who seeks to recover possession under this Section 37.9(a)(12) shall pay relocation expenses as provided by Section 37.9C; or

(13) The landlord wishes to withdraw from rent or lease all rental units within any detached physical structure and, in addition, in the case of any detached physical structure containing three or fewer rental units, any other rental units on the same lot, and complies in full with Section 37.9A with respect to each such unit; provided, however, that guestrooms or efficiency units within a residential hotel, as defined in Section 50519 of the Health and Safety Code, may not be withdrawn from rent or lease if the residential hotel has a permit of occupancy issued prior to January 1, 1990, and if the residential hotel did not send a notice of intent to withdraw the units from rent or lease (Administrative Code Section 37.9A(f), Government Code Section 7060.4(a)) that was delivered to the Rent Board prior to January 1, 2004; or

(14) The landlord seeks in good faith to temporarily recover possession of the unit solely for the purpose of effecting lead remediation or abatement work, as required by San Francisco Health Code Articles 11 or 26. The tenant will vacate the unit only for the minimum time required to do the work. The relocation rights and remedies, established by San Francisco Administrative Code Chapter 72, including but not limited to, the payment of financial relocation assistance, shall apply to evictions under this Section 37.9(a)(14). [However, effective January 1, 2013, the amount of relocation payments for temporary displacement of a tenant household under Section 37.9(a)(14) for less than 20 days is governed by California Civil Code Section 1947.9.]

(15) The landlord seeks to recover possession in good faith in order to demolish or to otherwise permanently remove the rental unit from housing use in accordance with the terms of a development agreement entered into by the City under Chapter 56 of the San Francisco Administrative Code.

(16) The tenant's Good Samaritan Status (Section 37.2(a) (1)(D)) has expired, and the landlord exercises the right to recover possession by serving a notice of termination of tenancy under this Section 37.9(a)(16) within 60 days after expiration of the Original and any Extended Good Samaritan Status Period.

(b) A landlord who resides in the same rental unit with his or her tenant may evict said tenant without just cause as required under Section 37.9(a) above.

(c) A landlord shall not endeavor to recover possession of a rental unit unless at least one of the grounds enumerated in Section 37.9(a) or (b) above is (1) the landlord's dominant motive for recovering possession and (2) unless the landlord informs the tenant in writing on or before the date upon which notice to vacate is given of the grounds under which possession is sought. For notices to vacate under Sections 37.9(a)(1), (2), (3), (4), (5), or (6), the landlord shall prior to serving the notice to vacate provide the tenant a written warning and an opportunity to cure as set forth in Section 37.9(o). For notices to vacate under Sections 37.9(a)(8), (9), (10), (11), or (14), the landord shall state in the notice to vacate the lawful rent for the unit at the time the notice is issued before endeavoring to recover possession. The Board shall prepare a written form that (1) states that a tenant's failure to timely act in response to a notice to vacate may result in a lawsuit by the landlord to evict the tenant, and that advice regarding the notice to vacate is available from the Board; and (2) includes information provided by the Mayor's Office of Housing and Community Development regarding eligibility for affordable housing programs. The Board shall prepare the form in English, Chinese, Spanish, Vietnamese, Tagalog, and Russian and make the form available to the public on its website and in its office. A landlord shall attach a copy of the form that is in the primary language of the tenant to a notice to vacate before serving the notice, except that if the tenant's primary language is not English, Chinese, Spanish, Vietnamese, Tagalog or Russian, the landlord shall attach a copy of the form that is in English to the notice. A copy of all notices to vacate except three-day notices to pay rent or quit and a copy of any additional written documents informing the tenant of the grounds under which possession is sought shall be filed with the Board within 10 days following service of the notice to vacate. In any action to recover possession of the rental unit under Section 37.9, the landlord must plead and prove that at least one of the grounds enumerated in Section 37.9(a) or (b) and also stated in the notice to vacate is the dominant motive for recovering possession. Tenants may rebut the allegation that any of the grounds stated in the notice to vacate is the dominant motive.

(d) No landlord may cause a tenant to quit involuntarily or threaten to bring any action to recover possession, or decrease any services, or increase the rent, or take any other action where the landlord's dominant motive is retaliation for the tenant's exercise of any rights under the law. Such retaliation shall be a defense to any action to recover possession. In an action to recover possession of a rental unit, proof of the exercise by the tenant of rights under the law within six months prior to the alleged act of retaliation shall create a rebuttable presumption that the landlord's act was retaliatory.

(e) It shall be unlawful for a landlord or any other person who willfully assists the landlord to endeavor to recover possession or to evict a tenant except as provided in Section 37.9(a) and (b). Any person endeavoring to recover possession of a rental unit from a tenant or evicting a tenant in a manner not provided for in Section 37.9(a) or (b) without having a substantial basis in fact for the eviction as provided for in Section 37.9(a) shall be guilty of a misdemeanor and shall be subject, upon conviction, to the fines and penalties set forth in Section 37.10A. Any waiver by a tenant of rights under this Chapter 37 shall be void as contrary to public policy.

(f) Whenever a landlord wrongfully endeavors to recover possession or recovers possession of a rental unit in violation of Sections 37.9 and/or 37.10A as enacted herein, or wrongfitlly endeavors to sever, substantially reduce, or remove, or actually severs, substantially reduces, or removes a housing service supplied in connection with the use or occupancy of a rental unit as set forth in Section 37.2(r), the tenant or Rent Board may institute a civil proceeding for injunctive relief, money damages of not less than three times actual damages (including damages for mental or emotional distress as specified below), and whatever other relief the court deems appropriate. If the landlord has recovered possession pursuant to Section 37.9(8), such action shall be brought no later than five years after (1) the date the landlord files the first statement of occupancy with the Rent Board under Section 37.9(a)(8)(vii) or (2) three months after the landlord recovers possession, whichever is earlier. In the case of an award of damages for mental or emotional distress, said award shall only be trebled if the trier of fact finds that the landlord acted in knowing violation of or in reckless disregard of Section 37.9 or 37.10A herein. The prevailing party shall be entitled to reasonable attorney's fees

and costs pursuant to order of the court. The remedy available under this Section 37.9(f) shall be in addition to any other existing remedies which may be available to the tenant or the Rent Board.

(g) The provisions of this Section 37.9 shall apply to any rental unit as defined in Sections 37.2(r)(4)(A) and 37.2(r)(4)(B), including where a notice to vacate/quit any such rental unit has been served as of the effective date of Ordinance No. 250-98, but where any such rental unit has not yet been vacated or an unlawful detainer judgment has not been issued as of the effective date of Ordinance No. 250-98.

(h) With respect to rental units occupied by recipients of tenant-based rental assistance, the notice requirements of this Section 37.9 shall be required in addition to any notice required as part of the tenant-based rental assistance program, including but not limited to the notice required under 24 CFR 982.311(e)(2)(ii).

(i) The following additional provisions shall apply to a landlord who seeks to recover a rental unit by utilizing the grounds enumerated in Section 37.9(a)(8):

(1) A landlord may not recover possession of a unit from a tenant under Section 37.9(a)(8) if the landlord has or receives notice, any time before recovery of possession, that any tenant in the rental unit:

(A) Is 60 years of age or older and has been residing in the unit for 10 years or more; or

(B) Is disabled within the meaning of Section 37.9(i)(1)(B)(i) and has been residing in the unit for 10 years or more, or is catastrophically ill within the meaning of Section 37.9(i)(1)(B)(ii) and has been residing in the unit for five years or more:

(i) A disabled tenant is defined for purposes of this Section 37.9(i)(1)(B) as a person who is disabled or blind within the meaning of the federal Supplemental Security Income/California State Supplemental Program (SSI/SSP), and who is determined by SSI/SSP to qualify for that program or who satisfies such requirements through any other method of determination as approved by the Rent Board;

(ii) A catastrophically ill tenant is defined for purposes of this Section 37.9(i)(1)(B) as a person who is disabled as defined by Section 37.9(i)(1)(B)(i), and who is suffering from a life threatening illness as certified by his or her primary care physician.

(2) The foregoing provisions of Sections 37.9(i)(1)(A) and (B) shall not apply where there is only one rental unit owned by the landlord in the building, or where each of the rental units owned by the landlord in the same building where

the landlord resides (except the unit actually occupied by the landlord) is occupied by a tenant otherwise protected from eviction by Sections 37.9(i)(1)(A) or (B) and where the landlord's qualified relative who will move into the unit pursuant to Section 37.9(a)(8) is 60 years of age or older.

(3) The provisions established by this Section 37.9(i) include but are not limited to, any rental unit where a notice to vacate/quit has been served as of the date this amendment takes effect but where the rental unit has not yet been vacated or an unlawful detainer judgment has not been issued.

(4) Within 30 days of personal service by the landlord of a written request, or, at the landlords option, a notice of termination of tenancy under 37.9(a)(8), the tenant must submit a statement, with supporting evidence, to the landlord if the tenant claims to be a member of one of the classes protected by Section 37.9(i). The written request or notice shall contain a warning that a tenant's failure to submit a statement within the 30 day period shall be deemed an admission that the tenant is not protected by Section 37.9(i). The landlord shall file a copy of the request or notice with the Rent Board within ten days of service on the tenant. A tenant's failure to submit a statement within the 30 day period shall be deemed an admission that the tenant is not protected by Section 37.9(i). A landlord may challenge a tenant's claim of protected status either by requesting a hearing with the Rent Board or, at the landlord's option, through commencement of eviction proceedings, including service of a notice of termination of tenancy. In the Rent Board hearing or the eviction action, the tenant shall have the burden of proof to show protected status. No civil or criminal liability under 37.9(e) or (f) shall be imposed upon a landlord for either requesting or challenging a tenant's claim of protected status.

(5) This Section 37.9(i) is severable from all other sections and shall be of no force or effect if any temporary moratorium on owner/relative evictions adopted by the Board of Supervisors after June 1, 1998 and before October 31, 1998 has been invalidated by the courts in a final decision.

(j) The following additional provision shall apply to a landlord who seeks to recover a rental unit by utilizing the grounds enumerated in Sections 37.9(a)(8), (a)(9), (a)(10), (a)(11), or (a)(12).

(1) It shall be a defense to an eviction under Sections 37.9(a)(8), (a)(9), (a)(10), (a)(11), or (a)(12) if a child under the age of 18 or any educator resides in the unit, the child or educator is a tenant in the unit or has a custodial or family relationship with a tenant in the unit, the tenant has resided in the unit for 12 months or more, and the effective date of the notice of termination of tenancy falls during the school year.

(2) Section 37.9(j)(1) shall not apply where the landlord is seeking to temporarily evict or temporarily sever housing services in order to perform seismic work required by Building Code Chapter 34B and has provided notice and compensation as required by Administrative Code Chapter 65A.

(3) Within 30 days of personal service by the landlord of a written request, or, at the landlord's option, a notice of termination of tenancy under Sections 37.9(a)(8), (a)(9), (a)(10), (a)(11), or (a)(12), the tenant must submit a statement with supporting evidence to the landlord, if the tenant claims to be a member of the class protected from eviction by Section 37.9(j). The landlord's written request or notice shall contain a warning that a tenant's failure to submit a statement within the 30 day period shall be deemed an admission that the tenant is not protected from eviction by Section 37.9(j). The landlord shall file a copy of the landlord's request or notice with the Rent Board within 10 days of service on the tenant. A tenant's failure to submit a statement within the 30 day period shall be deemed an admission that the tenant is not protected from eviction by Section 37.9(j). A landlord may challenge a tenant's claim of protected status either by requesting a hearing with the Rent Board or, at the landlord's option, through commencement of eviction proceedings, including service of a notice of termination of tenancy. In the Rent Board hearing or the eviction action, the tenant shall have the burden of proof to show protected status. No civil or criminal liability under Section 37.9(e) or (f) shall be imposed upon a landlord for either requesting or challenging a tenant's claim of protected status.

(4) For purposes of this Section 37.9(j), the following terms have the following meanings:

"Custodial relationship" means, with respect to a child and a tenant, that the tenant is a legal guardian of the child, or has a court-recognized caregiver authorization affidavit for the child, or has provided full-time custodial care of the child pursuant to an agreement with the child's legal guardian or court-recognized caregiver and has been providing that care for at least one year or half of the child's lifetime, whichever is less.

"Educator" means any person who works at a school in San Francisco as an employee or independent contractor of the school or of the governing body that has jurisdiction over the school, including, without limitation, all teachers, classroom aides, administrators, administrative staff, counselors, social workers, psychologists, school nurses, speech pathologists, custodians, security guards, cafeteria workers, community relations specialists, child welfare and attendance liaisons, and learning support consultants.

"Family relationship" means that the person is the parent, grandparent, brother, sister, aunt, or uncle of the child or educator, or the spouse or domestic partner of such relations.

"School" means any state-licensed child care center, state-licensed family day care, and/or any public, private, or parochial institution that provides educational instruction for students in any or all of the grades from kindergarten through twelfth grade.

"School year" means the first day of instruction for the Fall Semester through the last day of instruction for the Spring Semester, as posted on the San Francisco Unified School District website for each year.

(k) Disclosure of Rights to Tenants Before and After Sale of Rental Units Subject to Section 37.9.

(1) Disclosure to Tenants By Seller of the Property. Before property containing rental units subject to Section 37.9 may be sold, the owner/seller shall disclose to tenants of the property the rights of tenants during and after the sale of the property. This disclosure shall be in writing and shall include:

(A) A statement in bold type of at least 12 points that tenants cannot be evicted or asked to move solely because a property is being sold or solely because a new owner has purchased that property.

(B) A statement in bold type of at least 12 points that tenants cannot have their rent increased above that permitted by Chapter 37 solely because a property is being sold or solely

(C) A statement in bold type of at least 12 points that the rental agreements of tenants cannot be materially changed solely because a property is being sold or solely because a new owner has purchased that property.

(D) A statement that the owner's right to show units to prospective buyers is governed by California Civil Code section 1954, including a statement that tenants must receive notice as provided by Section 1954, and a statement that a showing must be conducted during normal business hours unless the tenant consents to an entry at another time.

(E) A statement that tenants are not required to complete or sign any estoppel certificates or estoppel agreements, except as required by law or by that tenant's rental agreement. The statement shall further inform tenants that tenant rights may be affected by an estoppel certificate or agreement and that the tenants should seek legal advice before completing or signing an estoppel certificate or agreement.

(F) A statement that information on these and other tenants' rights are available at the San Francisco Rent Board, 25 Van Ness Ave, San Francisco, California, and at the counseling telephone number of the Rent Board and at its web site.

(2) Disclosure to Tenants by Purchaser of the Property. Within 30 days of acquiring title to rental units subject to Section 37.9, the new purchaser/owner shall disclose to tenants of the property the rights of tenants following this sale of the property. This disclosure shall be in writing and shall include:

(A) A statement in bold type of at least 12 points that tenants cannot be evicted or asked to move solely because a new owner has purchased that property.

(B) A statement in bold type of at least 12 points that tenants cannot have their rent increased above that permitted by Chapter 37 solely because a new owner has purchased that property.

(C) A statement in bold type of at least 12 points that the rental agreements of tenants cannot be materially changed solely because a new owner has purchased that property.

(D) A statement in bold type of at least 12 points that any tenants, sub-tenants or roommates who were lawful occupants at the time of the sale remain lawful occupants.

(E) A statement in bold type of at least 12 points: that tenants' housing services as defined in Section 37.2(r) first paragraph cannot be changed or severed from the tenancy solely because a new owner has purchased that property; and that tenants' housing services as defined in Section 37.2(r) second paragraph that were supplied in connection with the use or occupancy of a unit at the time of sale (such as laundry rooms, decks, or storage space) cannot be severed from the tenancy by the new purchaser/owner without just cause as required by Section 37.9(a).

(l) Hearings on Alleged Wrongful Endeavor to Recover Possession Through Tenant Harassment.

(1) Upon receipt of a tenant report alleging wrongful endeavor to recover possession of the tenant's unit through harassment, the Board through its Executive Director shall send a notice acknowledging receipt of the report and summarizing the rights and responsibilities of landlords and tenants regarding possession of, and eviction from, residential rental units. Upon consideration of such report, the Executive Director may schedule an investigative hearing on the allegations before a Board Administrative Law Judge, where both the tenant and the landlord may appear and make oral and/or written presentations, including presentation of other witnesses. Following such hearing, the Administrative Law Judge shall provide the Board with a summary of evidence produced at the hearing.

(2) Upon review of the evidence, the Board shall consider whether to undertake any further proceedings such as, but not limited to, civil litigation pursuant to Section 37.9(f), or referral to the District Attorney (see Section 37.9(e)).

(3) For purposes of this Subsection 37.9(l), harassment

includes but is not limited to the types of harassment defined in Section 37.10B(a)(1) – (6) and (8) – (14).

(m) Implementation of California Civil Code Section 1947.9(a)(1)(A). Notwithstanding any other provision of Administrative Code Chapter 37, and consistent with California Civil Code Section 1947.9, the daily compensation payment specified in Civil Code Section 1947.9(a)(1)(A) for a tenant household temporarily displaced for less than 20 days, shall increase annually, rounded to the nearest dollar, at the rate of increase in the "rent of primary residence" expenditure category of the Consumer Price Index (CPI) for All Urban Consumers in the San Francisco-Oakland-San Jose Region for the preceding calendar year, as that data is made available by the United States Department of Labor and published by the Board. This increase shall be calculated as of March 1 each year, commencing March 1, 2014.

(o) [Check updates for stay: case # CPF-22-517718.] Notice and Opportunity to Cure. The grounds for recovering possession set forth in Sections 37.9(a)(1), (2), (3), (4), (5), and (6) shall not apply unless the violation is not cured within ten days after the landlord has provided the tenant a written warning that describes the alleged violation and informs the tenant that a failure to correct such violation within ten days may result in the initiation of eviction proceedings. The Rent Board shall prepare a form that landlords may use for this purpose. However, this Section 37.9(o) shall not apply if a longer notice and cure period applies (for example, under the terms of the lease agreement between the parties); or if the landlord is seeking to recover possession based on the tenant causing or creating an imminent risk of physical harm to persons or property; or if the landlord is seeking to recover possession based on the non-payment of rent or any other unpaid financial obligation of a tenant under the tenancy that came due between March 1, 2020 and March 31, 2022. **Leg. H.** 1979, 1980, 1982, 1983, 1984, 1986, 1987, 1991,1996, 1998, 1999, 2000, 2001, 2002, 2003, 2004, 2005, 2006, 2007, 2008, 2009, 2010, 2011, 2013, 2014, 2015, 2016, 2017, 2019, 2020, 2021, 2022.

§ 37.9A *Ellis Act Eviction Rights for Tenant*

This Section 37.9A applies to certain tenant displacements under Section 37.9(a)(13), as specified.

(a) Rent Allowed.

(1) Except as provided in Section 37.9A(a)(2) below, any rental unit which a tenant vacates after receiving a notice to quit relying on Section 37.9(a)(13) (withdrawal of rental units from rent or lease under the Ellis Act, California Government Code Sections 7060 et seq.), if again offered for rent or lease, must be offered and rented or leased at a rent not greater than the lawful rent in effect at the time the notice of intent to withdraw rental units is filed with the Board, plus annual rent increases available under this Chapter 37.

(A) The provisions of Section 37.9A(a)(1) apply to all tenancies commenced during either of the following time periods:

(i) The five-year period after a notice of intent to withdraw the rental units is filed with the Board, whether or not the notice of intent is rescinded or the withdrawal of the units is completed pursuant to that notice;

(ii) The five-year period after the rental units are withdrawn.

(B) This Section 37.9A(a)(1) shall prevail over any conflicting provision of law authorizing the landlord to establish the rental rate upon the initial hiring of the unit.

(C) If it is asserted that the rent could have been increased based on capital improvements, rehabilitation or substantial rehabilitation, the owner must petition the Rent Board pursuant to the procedures of Section 37.7 of this Chapter. No increase shall be allowed on account of any expense incurred in connection with withdrawing any unit from rent or lease.

(2) If a new tenancy was lawfully created in a unit before January 1, 2003, following a lawful withdrawal of the unit from rent or lease under Section 37.9(a)(13), any subsequent new tenancies for that rental unit are not subject to the rent limitations in Section 37.9A(a)(1).

(b) Treatment of Replacement Units. If one or more units covered by subsection (a) is demolished, and one or more new units qualifying as rental units under this chapter but for the date on which they first receive a certificate of final completion and occupancy are constructed on the same property, and offered for rent or lease within five years of the date the last of the original units became vacant, the newly constructed units shall be offered at rents not greater than those reasonably calculated to produce a fair and reasonable return on the newly constructed units, notwithstanding Section 37.3(g) or any other provision of this chapter. The provisions of this chapter shall thereafter apply. The Board shall adopt rules for determining the rents necessary to provide a fair and reasonable return.

(c) Rights to Re-Rent. Any owner who again offers for rent or lease any unit covered by Subsection (a) shall first offer the unit for rent or lease to the tenants or lessees displaced from the unit as follows:

(1) If any tenant or lessee has advised the owner in writing within 30 days of displacement of his or her desire to consider an offer to renew the tenancy and has furnished the owner with an address to which that offer is to be directed, the owner must make such an offer whenever the unit is again offered for rent or lease within two years of withdrawal. That tenant, lessee, or former tenant or lessee may advise the owner at any time of a change of address to which an offer is to be directed.

(2) Notwithstanding Subsection (c)(1), if the unit is offered for rent or lease within 10 years of withdrawal, the owner shall notify the Rent Board in writing of the intention to re-rent the unit and make an offer to the tenant or lessee whenever the tenant or lessee requests the offer in writing within 30 days after the owner has notified the City of an intention to re-rent the unit. If the unit is offered for rent or lease more than two years after the date the unit was withdrawn from rent or lease, the owner shall be liable to any tenant or lessee who was displaced for failure to comply with this Subsection (c)(2), for punitive damages in an amount which does not exceed the contract rent for six months.

(3) If any former tenant or lessee has requested an offer to renew the tenancy, either directly to the landlord or after notice from the Rent Board, then the owner shall offer to reinstitute a rental agreement or lease at rents permitted under Subsection (a). This offer shall be deposited in the United States mail, by registered or certified mail with postage prepaid, addressed to the displaced tenant or lessee at the address furnished to the owner as provided by the tenant and shall describe the terms of the offer. The displaced tenant or lessee shall have 30 days from the deposit of the offer in the mail to accept the offer by personal delivery of that acceptance or by deposit of the acceptance in the United States mail by registered or certified mail with postage prepaid.

(4) If more than one tenant or lessee attempts to accept the offer for a given unit, the landlord shall notify each tenant or lessee so accepting that other acceptances have been received, and shall further advise each such tenant or lessee of the names and addresses of the others. If all such tenants or lessees do not within 30 days thereafter agree and notify the landlord of which tenant(s) or lessee(s) will reoccupy the unit, the tenant(s) or lessee(s) who first occupied the unit previously shall be entitled to accept the landlord's offer. If more than one eligible tenant or lessee initially occupied the unit on the same date, then the first such tenant or lessee to have originally sent notice accepting the landlord's offer shall be entitled to occupy the unit.

(d) Re-Rental Within Two Years. If a unit covered by Subsection (a) is offered for rent or lease within two years of the date of withdrawal:

(1) The owner shall be liable to any tenant or lessee who was displaced from the property for actual and exemplary damages. Any action by a tenant or lessee pursuant to this paragraph shall be brought within three years of withdrawal of the unit from rent or lease. However, nothing in this paragraph precludes a tenant from pursuing any alternative remedy available under the law.

(2) The City may institute a civil proceeding against the owner who has again offered the unit for rent or lease, for exemplary damages for displacement of tenants or lessees. Any action by

the City pursuant to this paragraph shall be brought within three years of the withdrawal of the unit from rent or lease.

(e) Relocation Payments to Tenants.

(1) Before August 10, 2004, Low Income, Elderly or Disabled. Where a landlord seeks eviction based upon Section 37.9(a)(13), and the notice of intent to withdraw rental units was filed with the Board before August 10, 2004, the relocation payments described in this Subsection 37.9A (e)(1) shall be limited to tenants who are members of lower income households, who are elderly, or who are disabled, as defined below.

(A) Tenants who are members of lower income households, as defined by Section 50079.5 of the California Health and Safety Code, and who receive a notice to quit based upon Section 37.9(a)(13), in addition to all rights under any other provisions of law, shall be entitled to receive $4,500, $2,250 of which shall be paid within fifteen (15) calendar days of the landlord's receipt of written notice from the tenants of their entitlement to the relocation payment, and $2,250 of which shall be paid when the tenants vacate the unit.

(B) With respect to Subsection 37.9A(e)(1)(A), the Mayor's Office of Housing or its successor agency shall annually determine the income limits for lower income households, adjusted for household size.

(C) Notwithstanding Subsection 37.9A(e)(1)(A), and irrespective of the size of the unit, any tenant who receives a notice to quit under Section 37.9(a)(13) and who, at the time such notice is served, is 62 years of age or older, or who is disabled within the meaning of Section 12955.3 of the California Government Code, shall be entitled to receive $3,000, $1,500 of which shall be paid within fifteen (15) calendar days of the landlord's receipt of written notice from the tenant of entitlement to the relocation payment, and $1,500 of which shall be paid when the tenant vacates the unit.

(D) The payments due pursuant to this Subsection 37.9A(e)(1) for any unit which is occupied by more than one tenant shall be divided equally among all the occupying tenants, excluding those tenants who are separately entitled to payments under Subsection 37.9A(e)(1)(C) above.

(2) On August 10, 2004 and until February 19, 2005. Where a landlord seeks eviction based upon Section 37.9(a)(13) and either (i) the notice of intent to withdraw rental units is filed with the Board on or after August 10, 2004 through February 19, 2005, or (ii) the notice of intent to withdraw rental units was filed with the Board prior to August 10, 2004 but the tenant still resided in the unit as of August 10, 2004, relocation payments shall be paid to the tenants as follows:

(A) Tenants who are members of lower income households, as defined by Section 50079.5 of the California Health and Safety Code, shall be entitled to receive $4,500, $2,250 of which shall be paid within fifteen (15) calendar days of the landlord's receipt of written notice from the tenants of their entitlement to the relocation payment, and $2,250 of which shall be paid when the tenants vacate the unit.

(B) Subject to Subsections 37.9A(e)(2)(C) and (D) below, tenants who are not members of lower income households, as defined by Section 50079.5 of the California Health and Safety Code, shall be entitled to receive $4,500, which shall be paid when the tenant vacates the unit;

(C) In the event there are more than three tenants in a unit, the total relocation payment shall be $13,500.00, which shall be divided equally by the number of tenants in the unit;

(D) Notwithstanding Subsection 37.9A(e)(2)(A) and (B), any tenant who, at the time the notice of intent to withdraw rental units is filed with the Board, is 62 years of age or older, or who is disabled within the meaning of Section 12955.3 of the California Government Code, shall be entitled to receive an additional payment of $3,000.00, $1,500.00 of which shall be paid within fifteen (15) calendar days of the landlord's receipt of written notice from the tenant of entitlement to the relocation payment, and $1,500.00 of which shall be paid when the tenant vacates the unit.

(3) On or After February 20, 2005. Where a landlord seeks eviction based upon Section 37.9(a)(13), and the notice of intent to withdraw rental units is filed with the Board on or after February 20, 2005, relocation payments shall be paid to the tenants as follows:

(A) Subject to Subsections 37.9A(e)(3)(B), (C), and (D) below, the landlord shall be required to pay a relocation benefit on behalf of each authorized occupant of the rental unit regardless of the occupant's age ("Eligible Tenant"). The amount of the relocation benefit shall be $4,500 per Eligible Tenant, one-half of which shall be paid at the time of the service of the notice of termination of tenancy, and one-half of which shall be paid when the Eligible Tenant vacates the unit;

(B) In the event there are more than three Eligible Tenants in a unit, the total relocation payment shall be $13,500, which shall be allocated proportionally among the Eligible Tenants based on the total number of Eligible Tenants in the unit; and

(C) Notwithstanding Subsections 37.9A(e)(3)(A) and (B), any Eligible Tenant who, at the time the notice of intent to withdraw rental units is filed with the Board, is 62 years of age or older, or who is disabled within the meaning of Section 12955.3 of the California Government Code, shall be entitled to receive an additional payment of $3,000, $1,500 of

which shall be paid within 15 calendar days of the landlord's receipt of written notice from the tenant of entitlement to the relocation payment, and $1,500 of which shall be paid when the Eligible Tenant vacates the unit.

(D) Commencing March 1, 2005, the relocation payments specified in Subsections 37.9A(e)(3)(A) and (B) and (C) shall increase annually at the rate of increase in the "rent of primary residence" expenditure category of the Consumer Price Index (CPI) for All Urban Consumers in the San Francisco-Oakland-San Jose Region for the preceding calendar year, as that data is made available by the United States Department of Labor and published by the Board.

(4) Any notice to quit pursuant to Section 37.9(a)(13) shall notify the tenant or tenants concerned of the right to receive payment under Subsections 37.9A(e)(1) or (2) or (3).

(f) Notice to Rent Board; Recordation of Notice; Effective Date of Withdrawal.

(1) Any owner who intends to withdraw from rent or lease any rental unit shall notify the Rent Board in writing of said intention. Said notice shall contain statements, under penalty of perjury, providing information on the number of residential units, the address or location of those units, the name or names of the tenants or lessees of the units, and the rent applicable to each residential rental unit. Said notice shall be signed by all owners of record of the property under penalty of perjury and shall include a certification that actions have been initiated as required by law to terminate existing tenancies through service of a notice of termination of tenancy. The notice must be served by certified mail or any other manner authorized by law prior to delivery to the Rent Board of the notice of intent to withdraw the rental units. Information respecting the name or names of the tenants, the rent applicable to any unit, or the total number of units, is confidential and shall be treated as confidential information by the City for purposes of the Information Practices Act of 1977, as contained in Chapter 1 (commencing with Section 1798) of Title 1.8 of Part 4 of Division 3 of the Civil Code. The City shall, to the extent required by the preceding sentence, be considered an "agency," as defined by Subdivision (b) of Section 1798.3 of the Civil Code.

(2) Prior to the effective date of withdrawal of rental units under this Section, the owner shall cause to be recorded with the County Recorder a memorandum of the notice required by Subsection (f)(1) summarizing its provisions, other than the confidential provisions, in substantially the following form:

Memorandum of Notice Regarding Withdrawal of

Rental Unit From Rent or Lease

This memorandum evidences that the undersigned, as the owner(s) of the property described in Exhibit A attached, has filed a notice, whose contents are certified under penalty of perjury, stating the intent to withdraw from rent or lease all units at said property, pursuant to San Francisco Administrative Code Section 37.9A and the Ellis Act (California Government Code Sections 7060 et seq.).

(Signature)

(3) For a notice of intent to withdraw rental units filled with the Rent Board on or before December 31, 1999, the date on which the units are withdrawn from rent or lease for purposes of this Chapter and the Ellis Act is 60 days from the delivery in person or by first-class mail of the Subsection (f)(1) notice of intent to the Rent Board.

(4) For a notice of intent to withdraw rental units filed with the Rent Board on or after January 1, 2000, the date on which the units are withdrawn from rent or lease for purposes of this Chapter and the Ellis Act is 120 days from the delivery in person or by first-class mail of the Subsection (f)(1) notice of intent to the Rent Board. Except that, if the tenant or lessee is at least 62 years of age or disabled as defined in Government Code § 12955.3, and has lived in his or her unit for at least one year prior to the date of delivery to the Rent Board of the Subsection (f)(1) notice of intent to withdraw, then the date of withdrawal of the unit of that tenant or lessee shall be extended to one year after the date of delivery of that notice to the Rent Board, provided that the tenant or lessee gives written notice of his or her entitlement to an extension of the date of withdrawal to the owner within 60 days of the date of delivery to the Rent Board of the Subsection (f)(1) notice of intent to withdraw. In that situation, the following provisions shall apply:

(A) The tenancy shall be continued on the same terms and conditions as existed on the date of delivery to the Rent Board of the notice of intent to withdraw, subject to any adjustments otherwise available under Administrative Code Chapter 37.

(B) No party shall be relieved of the duty to perform any obligation under the lease or rental agreement.

(C) The owner may elect to extend the date of withdrawal on any other units up to one year after date of delivery to the Rent Board of the Subsection (f)(1) notice of intent to withdraw, subject to Subsections (f)(4)(A) and (B).

(D) Within 30 days of the notification by the tenant or lessee to the owner of his or her entitlement to an extension of the date of withdrawal, the owner shall give written notice to the Rent Board of the claim that the tenant or lessee is entitled to stay in their unit for one year after the date of delivery to the Rent Board of the Subsection (f)(1) notice of intent to withdraw.

(E) Within 90 days of the date of delivery to the Rent Board of the notice of intent to withdraw, the owner shall give written notice to the Rent Board and the affected tenant or lessee of the following:

(i) Whether or not the owner disputes the tenant's claim of extension;

(ii) The new date of withdrawal under Section 37.9A(f)(4)(C), if the owner does not dispute the tenant's claim of extension; and,

(iii) Whether or not the owner elects to extend the date of withdrawal to other units on the property.

(5) Within 15 days of delivery of a Subsection (f)(1) notice of intent to the Rent Board, the owner shall provide notice to any tenant or lessee to be displaced of the following:

(A) That the Rent Board has been notified pursuant to Subsection (f)(1);

(B) That the notice to the Rent Board specified the name and the amount of rent paid by the tenant or lessee as an occupant of the rental unit;

(C) The amount of rent the owner specified in the notice to the Rent Board;

(D) The tenant's or lessee's rights to reoccupancy under Section 37.9A(c) if the rental unit is again offered for rent or lease by a current or future owner and to relocation assistance under Section 37.9A(e); and

(E) The rights of qualified elderly or disabled tenants as described under Subsection (f)(4), to extend their tenancy to one year after the date of delivery to the Rent Board of the Subsection (f)(1) notice of intent to withdraw.

(6) Within 30 days after the effective date of withdrawal of rental units under this Section 37.9A, the Rent Board shall record a notice of constraints with the County Recorder which describes the property and the dates of applicable restrictions on the property under this Section.

(g) Successor Owners. The provisions of this Section 37.9A shall apply to the owner of a rental unit at the time displacement of a tenant or tenants is initiated and to any successor in interest of the owner, subject to the provisions of Chapter 12.75 of Division 7 of Title 1 of the California Government Code (Sections 7060 et seq.).

(h) Reports Required.

(1) Not later than the last day of the third and sixth calendar months following the month in which notice is given to the Board under Subsection (f)(1), and thereafter not later than December 31st of each calendar year for a period of five years, beginning with the year in which the six-month notice is given, the owner of any property which contains or formerly contained one or more rental units which a tenant or tenants vacated pursuant to Section 37.9(a)(13) shall notify the Board, in writing, under penalty of perjury, for each such unit:

(A) Whether the unit has been demolished;

(B) If the unit has not been demolished, whether it is in use;

(C) If it is in use, whether it is in residential use;

(D) If it is in residential use, the date the tenancy began, the name of the tenant(s), and the amount of rent charged.

If the unit has been demolished, and one or more new units constructed on the lot, the owner shall furnish the information required by items (B), (C) and (D) for each new unit. The Board shall maintain a record of the notices received under Subsection (f) and all notices received under this Section for each unit subject to this reporting requirement.

(2) The Board shall notify each person who is reported as having become a tenant in a vacated or new unit subject to the reporting requirements of Subsection (h)(1) that it maintains the records described in Subsection (h)(1), and that the rent of the unit may be restricted pursuant to Subsection (a).

(3) The Board shall maintain a register of all rental units withdrawn from rent or lease under the Ellis Act and the rent applicable to each unit at the time of withdrawal. The Board shall inform tenants displaced from units withdrawn from rent or lease at the address provided by the tenant, when the owner notifies the Board that the unit or replacement unit will again be offered for rent or lease within ten years of the date of withdrawal.

(4) The Board may investigate whether a rental unit that was withdrawn from rent or lease has been again offered for rent or lease, and whether the owner has complied with the provisions of this Section.

(i) This Section 37.9A is enacted principally to exercise specific authority provided for by Chapter 12.75 of Division 7 of Title 1 of the California Government Code, originally enacted by Stats. 1985, Ch. 1509, Section 1 (the Ellis Act, California Government Code Sections 7060 et seq.). In the case of any amendment to Chapter 12.75 or any other provision of State law which amendment is inconsistent with this Section, this Section shall be deemed to be amended to be consistent with State law, and to the extent it cannot be so amended shall be interpreted to be effective as previously adopted to the maximum extent possible. **Leg. H.** 1986; 1994; 2000; 2003; 2005; 2006; 2014; 2015, Eff. 7/17; 2019, 2020.

§ 37.9B *Landlord Move-In Evictions Rights for Tenant*

(a) Any rental unit which a tenant vacates after receiving a notice to quit based on Section 37.9(a)(8), and which is subsequently no longer occupied as a principal residence by the landlord or the landlord's grandparent, parent, child, grandchild, brother, sister, or the landlord's spouse, or the spouses of such relations must, if offered for rent during the five-year period following service of the notice to quit under Section 37.9(a)(8), be rented in good faith at a rent not greater than that which would have been the rent had the tenant who had been required to vacate remained in continuous occupancy and the rental unit remained subject to this Chapter 37. If it is asserted that a rent increase could have taken place during the occupancy of the rental unit by the landlord if the rental unit had been subjected to this Chapter, the landlord shall bear the burden of proving that the rent could have been legally increased during that period. If it is asserted that the increase is based in whole or in part upon any grounds other than that set forth in Section 37.3(a)(1), the landlord must petition the Rent Board pursuant to the procedures of this Chapter. Displaced tenants shall be entitled to participate in and present evidence at any hearing held on such a petition. Tenants displaced pursuant to Section 37.9(a)(8) shall make all reasonable efforts to keep the Rent Board apprised of their current address. The Rent Board shall provide notice of any proceedings before the Rent Board to the displaced tenant at the last address provided by the tenant. No increase shall be allowed on account of any expense incurred in connection with the displacement of the tenant.

(b) (1) For notices to vacate served before January 1, 2018, any landlord who, within three years of the date of service of the notice to quit, offers for rent or lease any unit in which the possession was recovered pursuant to Section 37.9(a)(8) shall first offer the unit for rent or lease to the tenants displaced in the same manner as provided for in Sections 37.9A(c) and (d).

(2) For notices to vacate served on or after January 1, 2018, any landlord who, within five years of the date of service of the notice to quit, offers for rent or lease any unit in which the possession was recovered pursuant to Section 37.9(a) (8) shall first offer the unit for rent or lease to the tenants displaced, by mailing a written offer to the address that the tenant has provided to the landlord. If the tenant has not provided the landlord a mailing address, the landlord shall mail the offer to the address on file with the Rent Board, and if the Rent Board does not have an address on file, then to the unit from which the tenant was displaced and to any other physical or electronic address of the tenant of which the landlord has actual knowledge. The landlord shall file a copy of the offer with the Rent Board within 15 days of the

offer. The tenant shall have 30 days from receipt of the offer to notify the landlord of acceptance or rejection of the offer and, if accepted, shall reoccupy the unit within 45 days of receipt of the offer.

(c) In addition to complying with the requirements of Section 37.9(a)(8), an owner who endeavors to recover possession under Section 37.9(a)(8) shall inform the tenant of the following information in writing and file a copy with the Rent Board within 10 days after service of the notice to vacate, together with a copy of the notice to vacate and proof of service upon the tenant;

(1) The identity and percentage of ownership of all persons holding a full or partial percentage ownership in the property;

(2) The dates the percentages of ownership were recorded;

(3) The name(s) of the landlord endeavoring to recover possession and, if applicable, the names(s) and relationship of the relative(s) for whom possession is being sought and a description of the current residence of the landlord or relative(s);

(4) A description of all residential properties owned, in whole or in part, by the landlord and, if applicable, a description of all residential properties owned, in whole or in part, by the landlord's grandparent, parent, child, grandchild, brother, or sister for whom possession is being sought;

(5) The current rent for the unit and a statement that the tenant has the right to re-rent the unit at the same rent, as adjusted by Section 37.9B(a) above;

(6) The contents of Section 37.9B, by providing a copy of same; and

(7) The right the tenant(s) may have to relocation costs and the amount of those relocation costs.

(d) The landlord shall pay relocation expenses as provided in Section 37.9C.

(e) Within 30 days after the effective date of a written notice to vacate that is filed with the Rent Board under Section 37.9B(c) the Rent Board shall record a notice of constraints with the County Recorder identifying each unit on the property that is the subject of the Section 37.9B(c) notice to vacate, stating the nature and dates of applicable restrictions under Section 37.9(a)(8) and 37.9B. For notices to vacate filed under Section 37.9B(c) on or after January 1, 2018, the Rent Board shall also send a notice to the unit that states the maximum rent for that unit under Sections 37.9(a)(8) and 37.9B, and shall send an updated notice to the unit 12 months, 24 months, 36 months, 48 months and 60 months thereafter, or within 30 days of such date. If a notice of constraints is recorded but the tenant does

not vacate the unit, the landlord may apply to the Rent Board for a rescission of the recorded notice of constraints. The Rent Board shall not be required to send any further notices to the unit pursuant to this subsection (e) if the constraints on the unit are rescinded. **Leg.H.** 1998, 2002, 2006, 2017.

§ 37.9C *Relocation Payments for Qualifying Evictions*

[Editor's note: CA Civil Code § 1947.9 applies instead for displacements of less than 20 days.]

(a) Definitions.

(1) Covered No-Fault Eviction Notice. For purposes of this section 37.9C, a Covered No-Fault Eviction Notice shall mean a notice to quit based upon Section 37.9(a)(8), (10), (11), or (12). [However, effective January 1, 2013, the amount of relocation payments for temporary displacement of a tenant household under Section 37.9(a)(11) for less than 20 days is governed by California Civil Code Section 1947.9 and not by this Section.]

(2) Eligible Tenant. For purposes of this section 37.9C, an Eligible Tenant shall mean any authorized occupant of a rental unit, regardless of age, who has resided in the unit for 12 or more months.

(b) Each Eligible Tenant who receives a Covered No-Fault Eviction Notice, in addition to all rights under any other provision of law, shall be entitled to receive relocation expenses from the landlord, in the amounts specified in section 37.9C(e).

(c) On or before the date of service of a Covered No-Fault Eviction Notice, the landlord shall notify all occupant(s) in the unit in writing of the right to receive payment under this section 37.9C and the amount of that relocation and shall provide a copy of section 37.9C. Such notification shall include a statement describing the additional relocation expenses available for Eligible Tenants who are senior or disabled and for households with children. The landlord shall file a copy of this notification with the Rent Board within 10 days after service of the notice, together with a copy of the notice to vacate and proof of service upon the tenant.

(d) A landlord who pays relocation expenses as required by this section in conjunction with a notice to quit need not pay relocation expenses with any further notices to quit based upon the same just cause under Section 37.9(a) for the same unit that are served within 180 days of the notice that included the required relocation payment. The relocation expenses contained herein are separate from any security or other refundable deposits as defined in California Code Section 1950.5. Further, payment or acceptance of relocation expenses shall not operate as a waiver of any rights a tenant may have under law.

(e) Relocation expenses shall be:

(1) Each Eligible Tenant receiving a Covered No-Fault Eviction Notice shall receive $4,500, $2,250 of which shall be paid at the time of the service of the notice to quit, and $2,250 of which shall be paid when the unit is vacated. In no case, however, shall the landlord be obligated under this section 37.9C(e)(1) to provide more than $13,500 in relocation expenses to all Eligible Tenants in the same unit.

(2) In addition, each Eligible Tenant who is 60 years of age or older or who is disabled within the meaning of Section 12955.3 of the California Government Code, and each household with at least one Eligible Tenant and at least one child under the age of 18 years, shall be entitled to receive an additional payment of $3,000.00, $1,500.00 of which shall be paid within fifteen (15) calendar days of the landlord's receipt of written notice from the Eligible Tenant of entitlement to the relocation payment along with supporting evidence, and $1,500 of which shall be paid when the Eligible Tenant vacates the unit. Within 30 days after notification to the landlord of a claim of entitlement to additional relocation expenses because of disability, age, or having children in the household, the landlord shall give written notice to the Rent Board of the claim for additional relocation assistance and whether or not the landlord disputes the claim.

(3) Commencing March 1, 2007, these relocation expenses, including the maximum relocation expenses per unit, shall increase annually, rounded to the nearest dollar, at the rate of increase in the "rent of primary residence" expenditure category of the Consumer Price Index (CPI) for All Urban Consumers in the San Francisco-Oakland-San Jose Region for the preceding calendar year, as that data is made available by the United States Department of Labor and published by the Board.

(f) The provisions of this Ordinance shall apply to all notices to quit served on or after August 10, 2006. **Leg.H.** 2006; annotated to reference CA Civil Code § 1947.9, eff. 1/1/13.

§ 37.10A *Misdemeanors by Landlord*

(a) It shall be unlawful for a landlord to increase rent or rents in violation of the decision of an Administrative Law Judge or the decision of the board on appeal pursuant to the hearing and appeal procedures set forth in Section 37.8 of this chapter. It shall further be unlawful for a landlord to charge any rent which exceeds the limitations of this chapter. Any person who increases rents in violation of such decisions or who charges excessive rents shall be guilty of a misdemeanor.

(b) It shall be unlawful for a landlord to refuse to rent or lease or otherwise deny to or withhold from any person any rental unit because the age of a prospective tenant would result in the tenant acquiring rights under this Chapter. Any person who refuses to rent in violation of this subsection shall, in addition to any other penalties provided by state or federal law, be guilty of a misdemeanor.

(c) It shall be unlawful for a landlord or for any person who willfully assists a landlord to recover possession of a rental unit unless, prior to recovery of possession of the unit the landlord satisfies all requirements for recovery of the unit under Section 37.9(a) or (b).

(d) In any criminal or civil proceeding based on a violation of Section 37.10A(c), the landlord's failure to use a recovered unit for the Section 37.9(a) or (b) ground stated verbally or in writing to the tenant from whom the unit was recovered shall give rise to a presumption that the landlord did not have a good faith intention to recover the unit for the stated ground.

(e) If possession of a rental unit is recovered as the result of any written or verbal statement to the tenant that the landlord intends to recover the unit under one of the grounds enumerated in Section 37.9(a) or (b), the unit shall be subject to all restrictions set forth under this Chapter on units recovered for such stated purpose regardless of any agreement made between the landlord or the landlord's agent and the tenant who vacated the recovered unit. Any unit vacated by a tenant within 120 days after receiving any written or verbal statement from the landlord stating that the landlord intends to recover the unit under Section 37.9(a) or (b), shall be rebuttably presumed to have been recovered by the landlord pursuant to the grounds identified in that written or verbal statement.

(f) It shall be unlawful for a landlord to knowingly fail to disclose in writing to the buyer, prior to entering into a contract for the sale of any property consisting of two or more residential units, the specific legal ground(s) for the termination of the tenancy of each residential unit to be delivered vacant at the close of escrow.

(g) It shall be unlawful for a landlord/owner, when offering a property for sale in the City and County of San Francisco that includes two or more residential units, to knowingly fail to disclose in writing to any prospective purchaser:

(1) The specific legal ground(s) for the termination of the tenancy of each residential unit to be delivered vacant at the close of escrow; and,

(2) Whether the unit was occupied by an elderly or disabled tenant at the time the tenancy was terminated. For purposes of this Section 37.10A(g), "elderly" means a tenant defined as elderly by Administrative Code Sections 37.9(i)(1)(A), 37.9A(e)(1)(C), 37.9A(e)(2)(D), or 37.9A(e)(3)(C), or a tenant defined as "senior" by Subdivision Code Section 1359(d). For purposes of this Section 37.10A(g), "disabled" means a tenant defined as disabled by Administrative Code Sections 37.9(i)(1)(B)(i), 37.9A(e)(1)(C), 37.9A(e)(2)(D), or

37.9A(e)(3)(C), or by Subdivision Code Section 1359(d).

Any disclosure required by this Subsection (g) that is made on a flier or other document describing the property which is made available to prospective purchasers at each open house and at any tour through the property will constitute compliance with the disclosure requirements of this Subsection (g).

(h) It shall be unlawful for any landlord, within five years after service of the notice to quit under Section 37.9(a)(8), to charge a rent for the unit that exceeds the maximum rent for the unit as provided in Section 37.9B(a), unless the notice of constraints on the unit has been rescinded. Each month or portion thereof that the landlord charges an excessive rent in violation of Section 37.9B(a) shall constitute a separate violation.

(i) It shall be unlawful for a landlord to endeavor to recover possession of a rental unit that is exempt from rent increase limitations under Section 37.3(d) or Section 37.3(g) by means of a rent increase that is imposed in bad faith with an intent to defraud, intimidate, or coerce the tenant into vacating the rental unit in circumvention of Section 37.9(a), 37.9A, 37.9B, or 37.9C. Evidence of bad faith may include but is not limited to the following: (1) the rent increase was substantially in excess of market rates for comparable units; (2) the rent increase was within six months after an attempt to recover possession of the unit; and (3) such other factors as a court or the Rent Board may deem relevant.

(j) Any person who violates Section 37.10A(a),(b),(c), (f), or (h) is guilty of a misdemeanor and shall be punished by a mandatory fine of $1,000.00, and in addition to such fine may be punished by imprisonment in the County Jail for a period of not more than six months. Each violation shall constitute a separate offense.**Leg.H.** 1984, 1998, 2000, 2002, 2004, 2006, 2017, 1/2019, 12/2019, 2020.

§ 37.10B *Harassment by Landlord*

(a) No landlord, and no agent, contractor, subcontractor or employee of the landlord shall do any of the following in bad faith:

(1) Interrupt, terminate or fail to provide housing services required by contract or by State, County or local housing, health or safety laws;

(2) Fail to perform repairs and maintenance required by contract or by State, County or local housing, health or safety laws;

(3) Fail to exercise due diligence in completing repairs and maintenance once undertaken or fail to follow appropriate industry repair, containment or remediation protocols designed to minimize exposure to noise, dust, lead, paint, mold, asbestos, or other building materials with potentially harmful health impacts;

(4) Abuse the landlord's right of access into a rental housing unit as that right is provided by law;

(5) Influence or attempt to influence a tenant to vacate a rental housing unit through fraud, intimidation or coercion; for example and without limitation, by endeavoring to recover possession of a rental unit that is exempt from rent increase limitations under Section 37.3(d) or Section 37.3(g) by means of a rent increase that is imposed with an intent to defraud, intimidate, or coerce the tenant into vacating the rental unit in circumvention of Section 37.9(a), 37.9A, 37.9B, or 37.9C, in which case evidence of bad faith may include but is not limited to the following: (1) the rent increase was substantially in excess of market rates for comparable units; (2) the rent increase was within six months after an attempt to recover possession of the unit; and (3) such other factors as a court or the Rent Board may deem relevant;

(6) Attempt to coerce the tenant to vacate with offer(s) of payments to vacate which are accompanied with threats or intimidation;

(7) Continue to offer payments to vacate after tenant has notified the landlord in writing that they no longer wish to receive further offers of payments to vacate;

(8) Threaten the tenant, by word or gesture, with physical harm;

(9) Violate any law which prohibits discrimination based on actual or perceived race, gender, sexual preference, sexual orientation, ethnic background, nationality, place of birth, immigration or citizenship status, religion, age, parenthood, marriage, pregnancy, disability, AIDS or occupancy by a minor child;

(10) Interfere with a tenant's right to quiet use and enjoyment of a rental housing unit as that right is defined by California law;

(11) Refuse to accept or acknowledge receipt of a tenant's lawful rent payment;

(12) Refuse to cash a rent check for over 30 days;

(13) Interfere with a tenant's right to privacy;

(14) Request information that violates a tenant's right to privacy, including but not limited to residence or citizenship status or social security number;

(15) Other repeated acts or omissions of such significance as to substantially interfere with or disturb the comfort, repose,

peace or quiet of any person lawfully entitled to occupancy of such dwelling unit and that cause, are likely to cause, or are intended to cause any person lawfully entitled to occupancy of a dwelling unit to vacate such dwelling unit or to surrender or waive any rights in relation to such occupancy.

(b) Nothing in this Section 37.10B shall be construed as to prevent the lawful eviction of a tenant by appropriate legal means.

(c) Enforcement and penalties.

(1) Rent Board. Violation of Sections 37.10B(a)(1) – (3) is a substantial and significant decrease in services as defined in Section 37.2(g) and tenants may file a petition with the Rent Board for a reduction in rent.

(2) Criminal Penalty. Any person who is convicted of violating this Section shall be guilty of a misdemeanor and upon conviction shall be punished by a fine of not greater than one thousand dollars or by imprisonment in the County Jail for not more than six months, or by both such fine and imprisonment.

(3) Civil Action. Any person, including the City, may enforce the provisions of this Section by means of a civil action. The burden of proof in such cases shall be preponderance of the evidence. A violation of this Chapter may be asserted as an affirmative defense in an unlawful detainer action.

(4) Injunction. Any person who commits an act, proposes to commit an act, or engages in any pattern and practice which violates this Section 37.10B may be enjoined therefrom by any court of competent jurisdiction. An action for injunction under this subsection may be brought by an aggrieved person, by the City Attorney, or by any person or entity who will fairly and adequately represent the interest of the protected class.

(5) Penalties and Other Monetary Awards. Any person who violates or aids or incites another person to violate the provisions of this Section is liable for each and every such offense for money damages of not less than three times actual damages suffered by an aggrieved party (including damages for mental or emotional distress), or for statutory damages in the sum of one thousand dollars, whichever is greater, and whatever other relief the court deems appropriate. In the case of an award of damages for mental or emotional distress, said award shall only be trebled if the trier of fact finds that the landlord acted in knowing violation of or in reckless disregard of Section 37.9, 37.10A, or 37.10B herein. In addition, a prevailing plaintiff shall be entitled to reasonable attorney's fees and costs pursuant to order of the court. The trier of fact may also award punitive damages to any plaintiff, including the City, in a proper case as defined by Civil Code Section 3294. The remedies available under this Section shall be in addition to any other existing remedies which may be available to the tenant or the City.

(6) Defending Eviction Lawsuits. In any action to recover possession of a rental unit subject to the Chapter, unless the sole basis of the notice to quit is Section 37.9(b), the court shall award the tenant reasonable attorney fees and costs incurred in defending the action upon a finding that the tenant is the prevailing party under Code of Civil Procedure Section 1032(a)(4).

(d) Severability. If any provision or clause of this Section 37.10B, or Section 37.2(g), or the application thereof to any person or circumstance is held to be unconstitutional or to be otherwise invalid by any court of competent jurisdiction, such invalidity shall not affect other provisions of this Section 37.10B or Section 37.2(g) and all clauses of these Sections are declared to be severable. **Leg.H.** 2008, 2011, 1/2019, 12/2019, 2020.

§ 37.11A *Civil Actions Against Landlord*

(a) Whenever a landlord charges a tenant a rent which exceeds the limitations set forth in this Chapter, retaliates against a tenant for the exercise of any rights under this Chapter, or attempts to prevent a tenant from acquiring any rights under this Chapter 37, the tenant may institute a civil proceeding for injunctive relief and/or money damages, and in cases where the landlord has charged an excessive rent in violation of Section 37.9B(a), injunctive relief and/or money damages of not less than three times the amount of excess rent collected; provided, however, that any monetary award for rent overpayments resulting from a rent increase which is null and void pursuant to section 37.3(b)(5) shall be limited to a refund of rent overpayments made during the three-year period preceding the month of filing of the action, plus the period between the month of filing and the date of the court's order. In any case, calculation of rent overpayments and re-setting of the lawful base rent shall be based on a determination of the validity of all rent increases imposed since April 1, 1982, in accordance with Sections 37.3(b)(5) and 37.3(a)(2) above.

(b) Any organization with tax exempt status under 26 United States Code Section 501(c)(3) or 501(c)(4) that has a primary mission of protecting the rights of tenants in San Francisco may bring a civil action for injunctive relief and/or damages against a landlord who has wrongfully endeavored to recover, or has recovered, possession of a rental unit in violation of Section 37.9(a)(8), or who has collected excess rent in violation of Section 37.9B(a). Such action shall be filed within three years after an affected tenant knew, or through the exercise of reasonable diligence should have known, of the facts constituting the violation. However, before bringing any action under this Section 37.11A(b), the organization shall first provide 30 days' written notice of its intent to initiate civil proceedings by serving a draft complaint on the City Attorney's Office and on any known address(es) of the affected tenant(s), and may bring the action under this Section 37.11A(b) only if neither the City Attorney's Office nor the tenant(s) have initiated civil proceedings by the end of the 30 day period. Any monetary award for rent overpayments shall be for two times any excess amounts of rent charged, as well as any other sums reasonably expended to investigate and prosecute the claim, and shall be limited to the three-year period preceding the month of filing of the action, plus the period between the month of filing and the date of the court's order.

(c) The prevailing party in any civil action brought under this section 37.11A shall be entitled to recover reasonable attorneys' fees and costs. The remedy available under this Section 37.11A shall be in addition to any other existing remedies which may be available. **Leg.H.** 1984, 1993, 1998, 2017.

San Francisco Rent Board Rules and Regulations

§ 1.13 Capital Improvements Defined

"Capital Improvements" means those improvements which materially add to the value of the property, appreciably prolong its useful life, or adapt it to new uses, and which may be amortized over the useful life of the improvement of the building. Capital Improvements do not include normal routine maintenance and repair. (For example, the patching of a roof is not a capital improvement while the partial or complete replacement of the old roof is; repair of a foundation is considered a capital improvement and not a repair.) Repairs which are incidental to a capital improvement project, or replacement of an item normally considered a capital improvement, are also defined as capital improvements. Capital Improvements otherwise eligible are not eligible if the landlord charges a use fee such as where the tenant must deposit coins to use a landlord-owned washer and dryer. (Amended 1989.)

§ 1.17 Rental Units Defined

"Rental Unit" means a residential dwelling unit, regardless of zoning or legal status, in the City and County of San Francisco and all housing services, privileges, furnishings (including parking facilities supplied in connection with the use or occupancy of such unit), which is made available by agreement for residential occupancy by a tenant in consideration of the payment of rent. The term does not include:

(a) Housing accommodations in hotels, motels, inns, tourist homes, rooming and boarding houses, provided that at such time as an accommodation has been occupied by a tenant for thirty-two (32) continuous days or more, such accommodation shall become a rental unit;

(b) dwelling units in a non-profit cooperative owned, occupied, and controlled by a majority of the residents;

(c) housing accommodations in any hospital, convent, monastery, extended care facility, asylum, residential care or adult day health care facility for the elderly which must be operated pursuant to a license issued by the California Department of Social Services, as required by California Health and Safety Chapters 3.2 and 3.3, or in dormitories owned and operated by an institution of higher education, a high school, or an elementary school;

(d) dwelling units whose rents are controlled or regulated by any government unit, agency, or authority excepting those unsubsidized and/or unassisted units which are insured by the United States Department of Housing and Urban Development;

(e) commercial space where there is incidental and infrequent residential use;

(f) a residential unit, wherein at the inception of the tenancy there was residential use, there is no longer residential use and there is a commercial or other non-residential use. The presumption shall be that the initial use was residential unless proved otherwise by the tenant. (Amended 1989, 1995, 1995, 1997, 1999, 2020.)

§ 1.21 Tenant in Occupancy Defined

A tenant in occupancy is an individual who otherwise meets the definition of tenant as set forth in Ordinance Section 37.2(t), and who actually resides in a rental unit or, with the knowledge and consent of the landlord, reasonably proximate rental units in the same building as his or her principal place of residence. Occupancy does not require that the individual be physically present in the unit or units at all times or continuously, but the unit or units must be the tenant's usual place of return. When considering whether a tenant occupies one or more rental units in the same building as his or her "principal place of residence," the Rent Board must consider the totality of the circumstances, including, but not limited to the following elements:

(1) the subject premises are listed as the individual's place of residence on any motor vehicle registration, driver's license, voter registration, or with any other public agency, including Federal, State and local taxing authorities;

(2) utilities are billed to and paid by the individual at the subject premises;

(3) all of the individual's personal possessions have been moved into the subject premises;

(4) a homeowner's tax exemption for the individual has not been filed for a different property;

(5) the subject premises are the place the individual normally returns to as his/her home, exclusive of military service, hospitalization, vacation, family emergency, travel

necessitated by employment or education, or other reasonable temporary periods of absence; and/or

(6) Credible testimony from individuals with personal knowledge or other credible evidence that the tenant actually occupies the rental unit or units as his or her principal place of residence.

A compilation of these elements lends greater credibility to the finding of "principal place of residence" whereas the presence of only one element may not support such a finding. (2001, 2002.)

§ 6.13 *Additional Occupants Rent increase Prohibited*

No extra rent may be charged solely for an additional occupant to an existing tenancy (including a newborn child), regardless of the presence of a rental agreement or lease which specifically allows for a rent increase for additional tenants. Such provisions in written or oral rental agreements or leases are deemed to be contrary to public policy. (1986, 1998.)

§ 6.14 *Rental Rates for Subsequent Occupants*

(a) Definitions. The following terms have the following meaning for purposes of this Section 6.14:

(1) "Original occupant(s)" means one or more individuals who took possession of a unit with the express consent of the landlord at the time that the base rent for the unit was first established with respect to the vacant unit.

(2) "Subsequent occupant" means an individual who became an occupant of a rental unit while the rental unit was occupied by at least one original occupant.

(3) "Co-occupant" for purposes of this Section 6.14 only, is a subsequent occupant who has a rental agreement directly with the owner.

(b) Subsequent Occupants who commenced occupancy before January 1, 1996; Co-occupants who commenced occupancy before, on or after January 1, 1996. When all original occupant(s) no longer permanently reside in the rental unit, the landlord may raise the rent of any subsequent occupant who resided in the unit prior to January 1, 1996, or of any subsequent occupant who is a co-occupant and who commenced occupancy before, on or after January 1, 1996, without regard to the limitations set forth in Section 37.3(a) of the Rent Ordinance if the landlord served on the subsequent occupant(s), within a reasonable time of actual knowledge of occupancy, a written notice that when the last of the original occupant(s) vacates the premises, a new tenancy is created for purposes of determining the rent under the Rent Ordinance. Failure to give such a notice within 60 days of the landlord's actual knowledge of the occupancy by the subsequent occupant(s) establishes a rebuttable presumption

that notice was not given within a reasonable period of time. If the landlord has not timely served such a notice on the subsequent occupant(s), a new tenancy is not created for purposes of determining the rent under the Rent Ordinance when the last of the original occupant(s) vacates the premises.

(c) Subsequent Occupants who are not Co-occupants and who commenced occupancy on or after January 1, 1996, where the last Original Occupant vacated on or after April 25, 2000.

When all original occupant(s) no longer permanently reside in a rental unit, and the last of the original occupants vacated on or after April 25, 2000, the landlord may establish a new base rent of any subsequent occupant(s) who is not a co-occupant and who commenced occupancy of the unit on or after January 1, 1996 without regard to the limitations set forth in Section 37.3(a) of the Rent Ordinance unless the subsequent occupant proves that the landlord waived his or her right to increase the rent by:

(1) Affirmatively representing to the subsequent occupant that he/she may remain in possession of the unit at the same rental rate charged to the original occupant(s); or

(2) Failing, within 90 days of receipt of written notice that the last original occupant is going to vacate the rental unit or actual knowledge that the last original occupant no longer permanently resides at the unit, whichever is later, to serve written notice of a rent increase or a reservation of the right to increase the rent at a later date; or

(3) Receiving written notice from an original occupant of the subsequent occupant's occupancy and thereafter accepting rent unless, within 90 days of said acceptance of rent, the landlord reserved the right to increase the rent at a later date.

Where the landlord has waived the right to increase the rent under subsection (c)(1) or (c)(3) above, the subsequent occupant to whom the representation was made or from whom the landlord accepted rent shall thereafter have the protection of an original occupant as to any future rent increases under this Section 6.14. Where the landlord has waived the right to increase the rent under subsection (c)(2) above, any subsequent occupant who permanently resides in the rental unit with the actual knowledge and consent of the landlord (if the landlord's consent is required and not unreasonably withheld) at the time of the waiver shall thereafter have the protection of an original occupant as to any future rent increases under this Section 6.14.

(d) Subsequent Occupants who are not Co-occupants and who commenced occupancy on or after January 1, 1996, where the last Original Occupant vacated prior to April 25, 2000. When all original occupants no longer permanently reside in a rental unit and the last of the original occupants vacated prior to April 25, 2000, the landlord may establish a new base rent for any subsequent occupants who are not co-occupants and who commenced occupancy of the unit on or after January 1, 1996 without regard to the limitations set forth in Section 37.3(a) of the Rent Ordinance if:

(1) The landlord served on the subsequent occupant(s), within a reasonable time of actual knowledge of occupancy, a written notice that when the last of the original occupants vacates the premises, the new tenancy is created for purposes of determining the rent under the Rent Ordinance. Failure to give such a notice within 60 days of the landlord's actual knowledge of the occupancy by the subsequent occupant(s) establishes a rebuttable presumption that notice was not given within a reasonable period of time; or

(2) The landlord is entitled to establish a new base rent under the Costa Hawkins Rental Housing Act, California Civil Code Section 1954.53(d), even if no notice was served on the subsequent occupant(s) pursuant to subsection (d)(1) above.

(e) Subsequent Occupants of Proposition I Affected Units. When all original occupant(s) no longer permanently reside in a Proposition I Affected Unit, the landlord may raise the rent of any subsequent occupant who resided in the unit prior to February 15, 1995 without regard to the limitations set forth in Section 37.3(a) of the Rent Ordinance if the landlord served on the subsequent occupant(s), on or before August 15, 1995, a written notice that when the last of the original occupant(s) vacates the premises, a new tenancy is created for purposes of determining the rent under the Rent Ordinance. If the landlord has not timely served such a notice on the pre-February 15, 1995 subsequent occupant(s) of the Proposition I Affected Unit, a new tenancy is not created for purposes of determining the rent under the Rent Ordinance when the last of the original occupant(s) vacates the premises. For subsequent occupants who commenced occupancy in a Proposition I Affected Unit on or after February 15, 1995, the provisions of subsections (a) through (d) above apply.

(f) This Section 6.14 is intended to comply with Civil Code Section 1954.50 et seq. and shall not be construed to enlarge or diminish rights thereunder. (1989, 1995, 1996, 2000.)

§ 6.15A Subletting and Assignment—Prohibited in Rental Agreement

This Section 6.15A applies only when a lease or rental agreement includes an absolute prohibition against subletting and assignment.

(a) For agreements entered into on or after May 25, 1998, breach of an absolute prohibition against subletting or assignment may constitute a ground for termination of tenancy pursuant to, and subject to the requirements of, Ordinance Section 37.9(a)(2)(A) and subsection (b) below, only if such prohibition was adequately disclosed to and agreed to by the tenant at the commencement of the tenancy. For purposes of this subsection, adequate disclosure

shall include satisfaction of one of the following requirements:

(1) the prohibition against sublet or assignment is set forth in enlarged or boldface type in the lease or rental agreement and is separately initialed by the tenant; or

(2) the landlord has provided the tenant with a written explanation of the meaning of the absolute prohibition, either as part of the written lease or rental agreement, or in a separate writing.

(b) If the lease or rental agreement specifies a number of tenants to reside in a unit, or where the open and established behavior of the landlord and tenants has established that the tenancy includes more than one tenant (exclusive of any additional occupant approved under Ordinance Sections 37.9(a)(2)(B) or 37.9(a)(2)(C)), then the replacement of one or more of the tenants by an equal number of tenants, subject to subsections (c) and (d) below, shall not constitute a breach of the lease or rental agreement for purposes of termination of tenancy under Section 37.9(a)(2) of the Ordinance.

(c) If the tenant makes a written request to the landlord for permission to sublease in accordance with Section 37.9(a)(2)(A), and the landlord fails to deny the request in writing with a description of the reasons for the denial of the request, including specific facts supporting the reasons for the denial, within fourteen (14) days of receipt of the tenant's written request, the subtenancy is deemed approved pursuant to Ordinance Section 37.9(a)(2)(A). If the tenant's request is sent to the landlord by mail, the request shall be deemed received on the fifth calendar day after the postmark date. If the tenant's request is sent to the landlord by email, the request shall be deemed received on the second calendar day after the date the email is sent. If the tenant's request is personally delivered to the landlord, the request is considered received on the date of delivery. For purposes of this subsection 6.15A(c), the 14-day period begins to run on the day after the tenant's written request is received by the landlord.

(d)(1) The tenant's inability to obtain the landlord's consent to subletting or assignment to a person specified in subsection 6.15A(b) above shall not constitute a breach of the lease or rental agreement for purposes of eviction under Ordinance Section 37.9(a)(2), where the subletting or assignment is deemed approved pursuant to subsection (c) above or where the landlord has unreasonably denied, pursuant to subsection (e) below, the tenant's request to replace a departing tenant and the following requirements have been met:

(i) The tenant has requested in writing the permission of the landlord to the sublease or assignment prior to the commencement of the proposed new tenant's or new subtenant's occupancy of the unit.

(ii) The landlord has five calendar days after receipt of the tenant's written request to request the tenant to submit a completed standard form application for the proposed new tenant or subtenant or provide sufficient information to allow the landlord to conduct a typical background check, including full name, date of birth and references if requested. The 5-day period begins to run on the day after receipt of the tenant's written request for permission to replace a departing tenant or subtenant. The landlord may request credit or income information only if the new tenant or new subtenant will be legally obligated to pay some or all of the rent to the landlord. Nothing in Section 6.15A shall be construed as allowing a landlord to require a replacement roommate to pay some or all of the rent to the landlord.

(iii) The tenant has five calendar days after receipt of the landlord's timely request pursuant to subsection 6.15A(d)(1) (ii) to provide the landlord with the proposed new tenant's or new subtenant's application or typical background check information. The 5-day period begins to run on the day after actual receipt of the landlord's request.

(iv) The proposed new tenant or new subtenant meets the regular reasonable application standards of the landlord, except that creditworthiness may not be the basis for denial of the tenant's request to replace a departing tenant if the new tenant or new subtenant will not be legally obligated to pay some or all of the rent to the landlord;

(v) The proposed new tenant or new subtenant, if requested by the landlord, has agreed in writing to be bound by the current rental agreement between the landlord and the tenant;

(vi) The tenant has not, without good cause, requested landlord consent to replacement of a departing tenant pursuant to this section 6.15A more than one time per existing tenant residing in the unit during the previous 12 months;

(vii) The tenant is requesting replacement of a departing tenant or tenants with an equal number of new tenants.

(2) This subsection (d) shall not apply to assignment of the entire tenancy or subletting of the entire unit.

(e) Denial by the landlord of the tenant's written request to replace a departing tenant shall not be considered unreasonable in some circumstances, including but not limited to the following:

(1) where the proposed new tenant or subtenant will be legally obligated to pay some or all of the rent to the landlord and the landlord can establish the proposed new tenant's or new subtenant's lack of creditworthiness;

(2) where the landlord has made a timely request for the proposed new tenant or subtenant to complete the landlord's standard form application or provide sufficient information to allow the landlord to conduct a typical background check

and the proposed new tenant or subtenant does not, comply within five calendar days of actual receipt by the tenant of the landlord's request;

(3) where the landlord can establish that the proposed new tenant or subtenant has intentionally misrepresented significant facts on the landlord's standard form application or provided significant misinformation to the landlord that interferes with the landlord's ability to conduct a typical background check;

(4) where the landlord can establish that the proposed new tenant or subtenant presents a direct threat to the health, safety or security of other residents of the property; and,

(5) where the landlord can establish that the proposed new tenant or subtenant presents a direct threat to the safety, security or physical structure of the property.

(f) Nothing in this Section shall prevent the landlord from providing a replacement new tenant or new subtenant with written notice as provided under Section 6.14 that the tenant is not an original occupant as defined in Section 6.14(a)(1) and that when the last original occupant vacates the premises, a new tenancy is created for purposes of determining the rent under the Rent Ordinance. Furthermore, nothing in this Section 6.15A shall serve to waive, alter or modify the landlord's rights under the Costa-Hawkins Rental Housing Act (California Civil Code §§1954.50 et seq.) to impose an unlimited rent increase once the last original occupant(s) no longer permanently resides in the unit.

(g) Where a lease or rental agreement specifies the number of tenants to reside in a unit, or where the open and established behavior of the landlord and tenants has established that the tenancy includes more than one tenant, a landlord's unreasonable denial of a tenant's written request to replace one or more of the tenants by an equal number of tenants, subject to subsections 6.15A(d)(1)(i)-(vii) above, may constitute a decrease in housing services pursuant to Section 10.10 of these Regulations. For purposes of subsection 6.15A(g), a landlord's non-response to a tenant's written request within 14 calendar days shall be deemed an approval pursuant to subsection 6.15A(c) and shall not be deemed an unreasonable denial of a tenant's request to replace a departing tenant.

(h) In the event the landlord denies a tenant's request to replace a departing tenant under Section 6.15A, either the landlord or the tenant may file a petition with the Board to determine if the landlord's denial of the request was reasonable.

(i) Any petition filed under subsection 6.15A(g) or (h) shall be expedited. (Amended 2005, 2015.)

§ 6.15B Subletting and Assignment—Requires Landlord Consent in Rental Agreement

This Section 6.15B applies only when a lease or rental agreement includes a clause requiring landlord consent to assignment or subletting.

(a) If the lease or rental agreement specifies a number of tenants to reside in a unit, or where the open and established behavior of the landlord and tenants has established that the tenancy includes more than one tenant (exclusive of any additional occupant approved under Ordinance Sections 37.9(a)(2)(B) or 37.9(a)(2)(C)), then the replacement of one or more of the tenants by an equal number of tenants, subject to subsections (b) and (c) below, shall not constitute a breach of the lease or rental agreement for purposes of termination of tenancy under Section 37.9(a)(2) of the Ordinance.

(b) If the tenant makes a written request to the landlord for permission to sublease in accordance with Section 37.9(a)(2)(A), and the landlord fails to deny the request in writing with a description of the reasons for the denial, including specific facts supporting the reasons for the denial, of the request within fourteen (14) days of receipt of the tenant's written request, the subtenancy is deemed approved pursuant to Ordinance Section 37.9(a)(2)(A). If the tenant's request is sent to the landlord by mail, the request shall be deemed received on the fifth calendar day after the postmark date. If the tenant's request is sent to the landlord by email, the request shall be deemed received on the second calendar day after the date the email is sent. If the tenant's request is personally delivered to the landlord, the request is considered received on the date of delivery. For purposes of this subsection 6.15B(b), the 14-day period begins to run on the day after the tenant's written request is received by the landlord.

(c)(1) The tenant's inability to obtain the landlord's consent to subletting or assignment to a person specified in subsection 6.15B(a) above shall not constitute a breach of the lease or rental agreement for purposes of eviction under Ordinance Section 37.9(a)(2), where the subletting or assignment is deemed approved pursuant to subsection (b) above or where the landlord has unreasonably denied, pursuant to subsection (d) below, the tenant's request to replace a departing tenant and the following requirements have been met:

(i) The tenant has requested in writing the permission of the landlord to the sublease or assignment prior to the commencement of the proposed new tenant's or new subtenant's occupancy of the unit;

(ii) The landlord has five calendar days after receipt of the tenant's written request to request the tenant to submit a completed standard form application for the proposed new tenant or subtenant or provide sufficient information to allow the landlord to conduct a typical background check,

including full name, date of birth and references if requested. The 5-day period begins to run on the day after receipt of the tenant's written request for permission to replace a departing tenant or subtenant. The landlord may request credit or income information only if the new tenant or new subtenant will be legally obligated to pay some or all of the rent to the landlord. Nothing in Section 6.15B shall be construed as allowing a landlord to require a replacement roommate to pay some or all of the rent to the landlord.

(iii) The tenant has five calendar days after receipt of the landlord's timely request pursuant to subsection 6.15B(c)(1)(ii) to provide the landlord with the proposed new tenant's or new subtenant's application or typical background check information. The 5-day period begins to run on the day after actual receipt of the landlord's request.

(iv) The proposed new tenant or new subtenant meets the regular reasonable application standards of the landlord, except that creditworthiness may not be the basis for denial of the tenant's request to replace a departing tenant if the new tenant or new subtenant will not be legally obligated to pay some or all of the rent to the landlord;

(v) The proposed new tenant or new subtenant, if requested by the landlord, has agreed in writing to be bound by the current rental agreement between the landlord and the tenant;

(vi) The tenant has not, without good cause, requested landlord consent to replacement of a departing tenant pursuant to this section 6.15B more than one time per existing tenant residing in the unit during the previous 12 months;

(vii) The tenant is requesting replacement of a departing tenant or tenants with an equal number of new tenants.

(2) This subsection (c) shall not apply to assignment of the entire tenancy or subletting of the entire unit.

(d) Denial by the landlord of the tenant's written request to replace a departing tenant shall not be considered unreasonable in some circumstances, including but not limited to the following:

(1) where the proposed new tenant or subtenant will be legally obligated to pay some or all of the rent to the landlord and the landlord can establish the proposed new tenant's or new subtenant's lack of creditworthiness;

(2) where the landlord has made a timely request for the proposed new tenant or subtenant to complete the landlord's standard form application or provide sufficient information to allow the landlord to conduct a typical background check and the proposed new tenant or subtenant does not comply within five calendar days of actual receipt by the tenant of the

landlord's request;

(3) where the landlord can establish that the proposed new tenant or subtenant has intentionally misrepresented significant facts on the landlord's standard form application or provided significant misinformation to the landlord that interferes with the landlord's ability to conduct a typical background check;

(4) where the landlord can establish that the proposed new tenant or subtenant presents a direct threat to the health, safety or security of other residents of the property; and,

(5) where the landlord can establish that the proposed new tenant or subtenant presents a direct threat to the safety, security or physical structure of the property.

(e) Nothing in this Section shall prevent the landlord from providing a replacement new tenant or new subtenant with written notice as provided under Section 6.14 that the tenant is not an original occupant as defined in Section 6.14(a)(1) and that when the last original occupant vacates the premises, a new tenancy is created for purposes of determining the rent under the Rent Ordinance. Furthermore, nothing in this Section 6.15B shall serve to waive, alter or modify the landlord's rights under the Costa-Hawkins Rental Housing Act (California Civil Code §§1954.50 et seq.) to impose an unlimited rent increase once the last original occupant(s) no longer permanently resides in the unit.

(f) Where a lease or rental agreement specifies the number of tenants to reside in a unit, or where the open and established behavior of the landlord and tenants has established that the tenancy includes more than one tenant, a landlord's unreasonable denial of a tenant's written request to replace one or more of the tenants by an equal number of tenants, subject to subsections 6.15B(c)(1)(i)-(vii) above, may constitute a decrease in housing services pursuant to Section 10.10 of these Regulations. For purposes of subsection 6.15B(f), a landlord's non-response to a tenant's written request within 14 calendar days shall be deemed an approval pursuant to subsection 6.15B(b) and shall not be deemed an unreasonable denial of a tenant's request to replace a departing tenant.

(g) In the event the landlord denies a tenant's request to replace a departing tenant under Section 6.15B, either the landlord or the tenant may file a petition with the Board to determine if the landlord's denial of the request was reasonable.

(h) Any petition filed under subsection 6.15B(f) or (g) shall be expedited. (Amended 2005, 2015.)

§ 6.15C *Master Tenants*

(1) For any tenancy commencing on or after May 25, 1998, a landlord who is not an owner of record of the property and who resides in the same rental unit with his or her tenant (a "Master Tenant") may evict said tenant without just cause as required under Section 37.9(a) only if, prior to commencement of the tenancy, the Master Tenant informs the tenant in writing that the tenancy is not subject to the just cause provisions of Section 37.9. A landlord who is an owner of record of the property and who resides in the same rental unit with his or her tenant is not subject to this additional disclosure requirement.

(2) In addition, for any tenancy commencing on or after May 25, 1998, a Master Tenant shall disclose in writing to a tenant prior to commencement of the tenancy the amount of rent the Master Tenant is obligated to pay to the owner of the property.

(3) Partial Sublets. In the event a Master Tenant does not sublease the entire rental unit, as anticipated in Section 37.3(c), then the Master Tenant may charge the subtenant(s) no more than the subtenant(s) proportional share of the total current rent paid to the landlord by the Master Tenant for the housing and housing services to which the subtenant is entitled under the sub-lease. A master tenant's violation of this section shall not constitute a basis for eviction under Section 37.9.

(a) The allowable proportional share of total rent may be calculated based upon the square footage shared with and/or occupied exclusively by the subtenant; or an amount substantially proportional to the space occupied by and/or shared with the subtenant (e.g. three persons splitting the entire rent in thirds) or any other method that allocates the rent such that the subtenant pays no more to the Master Tenant than the Master Tenant pays to the landlord for the housing and housing services to which the subtenant is entitled under the sublease. In establishing the proper initial base rent, additional housing services (such as utilities) provided by, or any special obligations of, the Master Tenant, or evidence of the relative amenities or value of rooms, may be considered by the parties or the Rent Board when deemed appropriate. Any methodology that shifts the rental burden such that the subtenant(s) pays substantially more than their square footage portion, or substantially more than the proportional share of the total rent paid to the landlord, shall be rebuttably presumed to be in excess of the lawful limitation.

(b) The Master Tenant or subtenant(s) may petition the Board for an adjustment of the initial rent of the subtenant.

(c) If a portion of a capital improvement passthrough or a utility increase is allocated to a subtenant, it must be separately identified and not included in the subtenant's base rent. Such amounts are subject to the rules herein and must be discontinued or recalculated pursuant to the applicable rules. Any amount that is improperly calculated or not properly discontinued shall be disallowed.

(d) In the event of any dispute regarding any allowable

increase, or allocation, or any rental amount paid that is not rent, the subtenant may file a claim of unlawful rent increase to have the matter resolved between the subtenant and Master Tenant, as if the Master Tenant were the owner of the building. Disallowed or improper increases shall be null and void.

(e) For any sublease entered into on or before August 22, 2001, where the sublease rent was not calculated as provided for herein, the Master Tenant shall have six months from the effective date of this regulation to notice an adjusted proper rent and refund any overpayments paid after the effective date of this section. No petitions alleging overpayments may be filed during this time.

(f) For any sublease entered into after August 22, 2001, where the sublease rent was not calculated as provided for herein, the portion of the subtenant's rent that is in excess of the amount allowed pursuant to this Section 6.15C(3) shall be null and void. (Subsections (3)(a) through (f) added 2001, 2002.)

§ 6.15D Adding Family Members —Rental Agreement Limits Occupants or Subletting or Assignment

(a) This Section 6.15D applies when a lease or rental agreement includes a clause limiting the number of occupants or limiting or prohibiting subletting or assignment, and a tenant who resides in the unit requests the addition of the tenant's child, parent, grandchild, grandparent, brother or sister, or the spouse or the domestic partner (as defined in Administrative Code Sections 62.1 through 62.8) of such relatives, or the spouse or domestic partner of the tenant. This Section 6.15D does not apply when a lease or rental agreement includes neither a limit on the number of occupants nor any restriction on subletting or assignment.

(b) If the tenant makes a written request to the landlord for permission to add a person specified in subsection 6.15D(a) above, and the landlord fails to deny the request in writing with a description of the reasons for the denial of the request, including specific facts supporting the reasons for the denial, within fourteen (14) days of receipt of the tenant's written request, the tenant's request for the additional person is deemed approved pursuant to Ordinance Section 37.9(a)(2)(B). If the tenant's request is sent to the landlord by mail, the request shall be deemed received on the fifth calendar day after the postmark date. If the tenant's request is sent to the landlord by email, the request shall be deemed received on the second calendar day after the date the email is sent. If the tenant's request is personally delivered to the landlord, the request is considered received on the date of delivery. For purposes of this subsection 6.15D(b), the 14-day period begins to run on the day after the tenant's written request is received by the landlord.

(c) The tenant's inability to obtain the landlord's consent to the addition of a family member specified in subsection

6.15D(a) above shall not constitute a breach of the lease or rental agreement for purposes of eviction under Ordinance Section 37.9(a)(2), where the additional family member is deemed approved pursuant to subsection (b) above, or where the additional family member is a minor child allowed under subsection 6.15D(a) above, or where the landlord has unreasonably denied, pursuant to subsection (d) below, the tenant's request to add an additional family member allowed under subsection 6.15D(a) above who is not a minor child and the following requirements have been met:

(1) The tenant has requested in writing the permission of the landlord to add an additional family member to the unit, and stated the relationship of the person to the tenant.

(2) The landlord has five calendar days after receipt of the tenant's written request to request the tenant to submit a completed standard form application for the proposed additional family member or provide sufficient information to allow the landlord to confirm the relationship of the person to the tenant and to conduct a typical background check, including full name, date of birth and references if requested. The 5-day period begins to run on the day after receipt of the tenant's written request for permission to add an additional family member to the unit. The landlord may request credit or income information only if the additional family member will be legally obligated to pay some or all of the rent to the landlord. Nothing in Section 6.15D shall be construed as allowing a landlord to require an additional family member to pay some or all of the rent to the landlord.

(3) The tenant has five calendar days after receipt of the landlord's timely request pursuant to subsection 6.15D(c)(2) to provided the landlord with the additional family member's application or typical background check information. The 5-day period begins to run on the day after actual receipt of the landlord's request.

(4) The additional family member meets the regular reasonable application standards of the landlord, except that creditworthiness may not be the basis for denial of the tenant's request for an additional family member if the additional family member will not be legally obligated to pay some or all of the rent to the landlord;

(5) The additional family member, if requested by the landlord, has agreed in writing to be bound by the current rental agreement between the landlord and the tenant.

(6) With the additional family member, the total number of occupants does not exceed the lesser of (a) two persons in a studio rental unit, three persons in a one-bedroom unit, four persons in a two-bedroom unit, six persons in a three-bedroom unit or eight persons in a four-bedroom unit, or (b) the number of occupants permitted under state law and/or other local codes (e.g., Planning, Housing, Fire and Building

Codes).

(d) Denial by the landlord of the tenant's written request to add an additional family member allowed under subsection 6.15D(a) above shall not be considered unreasonable in some circumstances, including but not limited to the following:

(1) where the total number of occupants in the unit exceeds (or with the proposed additional occupant(s) would exceed) the lesser of:

(i) two persons in a studio unit, three persons in a one-bedroom unit, four persons in a two-bedroom unit, six persons in a three-bedroom unit, or eight persons in a four-bedroom unit; or

(ii) the maximum number permitted in the unit under San Francisco Housing Code Section 503;

(2) where the proposed additional family member will be legally obligated to pay some or all of the rent to the landlord and the landlord can establish the proposed additional family member's lack of creditworthiness;

(3) where the landlord has made a timely request for the proposed additional family member to complete the landlord's standard form application or provide sufficient information to allow the landlord to conduct a typical background check and the proposed additional family member does not comply within five calendar days of actual receipt by the tenant of the landlord's request;

(4) where the landlord can establish that the proposed additional family member has intentionally misrepresented significant facts on the landlord's standard form application or provided significant misinformation to the landlord that interferes with the landlord's ability to conduct a typical background check;

(5) where the landlord can establish that the proposed additional family member presents a direct threat to the health, safety or security of other residents of the property; and,

(6) where the landlord can establish that the proposed additional family member presents a direct threat to the safety, security or physical structure of the property.

(e) Nothing in this Section shall prevent the landlord from providing an additional family member occupant with written notice as provided under Section 6.14 that the occupant is not an original occupant as defined in Section 6.14(a)(1) and that when the last original occupant vacates the premises, a new tenancy is created for purposes of determining the rent under the Rent Ordinance. Furthermore, nothing in this Section 6.15D shall serve to waive, alter or modify the landlord's rights

under the Costa-Hawkins Rental Housing Act (California Civil Code §§1954.50 et seq.) to impose an unlimited rent increase once the last original occupant(s) no longer permanently resides in the unit.

(f) A landlord's unreasonable denial of a tenant's written request for the addition to the unit of a tenant's child, parent, grandchild, grandparent, brother or sister, or the spouse or domestic partner (as defined in Administrative Code Sections 62.1 through 62.8) of such relatives, or the spouse or domestic partner of a tenant, subject to subsections 6.15D(c)(1)-(6) above, may constitute a decrease in housing services pursuant to Section 10.10 of these Regulations. For purposes of subsection 6.15D(f), a landlord's non-response to a tenant's written request within 14 calendar days shall be deemed an approval pursuant to subsection 6.15D(b) and shall not be deemed an unreasonable denial of a tenant's request for the addition to the unit of a family member specified in subsection 6.15D(a) above.

(g) In the event the landlord denies a tenant's request for an additional family member under Section 6.15D, either the landlord or the tenant may file a petition with the Board to determine if the landlord's denial of the request was reasonable.

(h) Any petition filed under subsection 6.15D or (g) shall be expedited. (Added 2005, 2015.)

§ 6.15E Adding Non-Familial Occupants—Rental Agreement Limits Occupants or Subletting or Assignment

(a) This Section 6.15E applies when a lease or rental agreement includes a clause limiting the number of occupants or limiting or prohibiting subletting or assignment, and a tenant who resides in the unit requests the landlord's permission to add an additional occupant to the rental unit that will exceed the number of people allowed by the lease or rental agreement or by the open and established behavior of the parties. This Section 6.15E does not apply when a lease or rental agreement includes neither a limit on the number of occupants nor any restriction on subletting or assignment. For purposes of this Section 6.15E, the term "additional occupant" shall not include persons who occupy the unit as a Tourist or Transient Use, as defined in Administrative Code Section 41A.5 or persons who are considered family members under Section 6.15D(a).

(b) If the tenant makes a written request to the landlord for permission to add an additional occupant to the rental unit, and the landlord fails to deny the request in writing with a description of the reasons for the denial of the request, including specific facts supporting the reasons for the denial, within fourteen (14) days of receipt of the tenant's written request, the tenant's request for the additional occupant is deemed approved pursuant to Ordinance Section 37.9(a)(2)(C). If the tenant's request is sent to the landlord by mail, the request shall be deemed received on the fifth calendar day after the postmark date. If the tenant's request is sent to the landlord by email, the request shall be deemed received on the second calendar day after the date the email is sent. If the tenant's request is personally delivered to the landlord, the request is considered received on the date of delivery. For purposes of this subsection 6.15E(b), the 14-day period begins to run on the day after the tenant's written request is received by the landlord.

(c) The tenant's inability to obtain the landlord's consent to the addition of a person specified in subsection 6.15E(a) above shall not constitute a breach of the lease or rental agreement for purposes of eviction under Ordinance Section 37.9(a)(2), where the additional person is deemed approved pursuant to subsection (b) above or where the landlord has unreasonably denied, pursuant to subsection (d) below, the tenant's request to add an additional person allowed under subsection 6.15E(a) above and the following requirements have been met:

(1) The tenant has requested in writing the permission of the landlord to add an additional occupant to the unit.

(2) The landlord has five calendar days after receipt of the tenant's written request to request the tenant to submit a completed standard form application for the proposed additional occupant or provide sufficient information to allow the landlord to conduct a typical background check, including full name, date of birth and references if requested. The 5-day period begins to run on the day after receipt of the tenant's written request for permission to add an additional occupant to the unit. The landlord may request credit or income information only if the additional occupant will be legally obligated to pay some or all of the rent to the landlord. Nothing in Section 6.15E shall be construed as allowing a landlord to require an additional occupant to pay some or all of the rent to the landlord.

(3) The tenant has five calendar days after receipt of the landlord's timely request pursuant to subsection 6.15E(c) (2) to provide the landlord with the additional occupant's application or typical background check information. The 5-day period begins to run on the day after actual receipt of the landlord's request.

(4) The additional occupant meets the regular reasonable application standards of the landlord, except that creditworthiness may not be the basis for denial of the tenant's request for an additional occupant if the additional occupant will not be legally obligated to pay some or all of the rent to the landlord.

(5) The additional occupant, if requested by the landlord, has agreed in writing to be bound by the current rental agreement between the landlord and the tenant.

(6) With the additional occupant, the total number of occupants does not exceed the lesser of (a) two persons in a studio unit, three persons in a one-bedroom unit, four persons in a two-bedroom unit, six persons in a three-bedroom unit, or eight persons in a four-bedroom unit, or (b) the number of occupants permitted under state law and/or other local codes.

(d) Denial by the landlord of the tenant's written request to add an additional person allowed under subsection 6.15E(a) above shall not be considered unreasonable in some circumstances, including but not limited to the following:

(1) where the landlord resides in the same rental unit as the tenant;

(2) where the total number of occupants in the unit exceeds (or with the proposed additional occupant(s) would exceed) the lesser of:

(i) two persons in a studio unit, three persons in a one-bedroom unit, four persons in a two-bedroom unit, six persons in a three-bedroom unit, or eight persons in a four-bedroom unit; or

(ii) the maximum number permitted in the unit under San Francisco Housing Code Section 503;

(3) where the proposed additional occupant will be legally obligated to pay some or all of the rent to the landlord and the landlord can establish the proposed additional occupant's lack of creditworthiness;

(4) where the landlord has made a timely request for the proposed additional occupant to complete the landlord's standard form application or provide sufficient information to allow the landlord to conduct a typical background check and the proposed additional occupant does not comply within five calendar days of actual receipt by the tenant of the landlord's request;

(5) where the landlord can establish that the proposed additional occupant has intentionally misrepresented significant facts on the landlord's standard form application or provided significant misinformation to the landlord that interferes with the landlord's ability to conduct a typical background check;

(6) where the landlord can establish that the proposed additional occupant presents a direct threat to the health, safety or security of other residents of the property;

(7) where the landlord can establish that the proposed additional occupant presents a direct threat to the safety, security or physical structure of the property; and,

(8) where an additional occupant would require the landlord to increase the electrical or hot water capacity in the building, or adapt other building systems or existing amenities, and payment for such enhancements presents a financial hardship

to the landlord, as determined by a Rent Board Administrative Law Judge.

(e) Nothing in this Section shall prevent the landlord from providing an additional occupant with written notice as provided under Section 6.14 that the occupant is not an original occupant as defined in Section 6.14(a)(1) and that when the last original occupant vacates the premises, a new tenancy is created for purposes of determining the rent under the Rent Ordinance. Furthermore, nothing in this Section 6.15E shall serve to waive, alter or modify the landlord's rights under the Costa-Hawkins Rental Housing Act (California Civil Code §§1954.50 et seq.) to impose an unlimited rent increase once the last original occupant(s) no longer permanently resides in the unit.

(f) A landlord's unreasonable denial of a tenant's written request for the addition to the unit of a person specified in subsection 6.15E(a) above, subject to subsections 6.15E(c)(1)-(6) above, may constitute a decrease in housing services pursuant to Section 10.10 of these Regulations. For purposes of subsection 6.15E(f), a landlord's non-response to a tenant's written request within 14 calendar days shall be deemed an approval pursuant to subsection 6.15E(b) and shall not be deemed an unreasonable denial of a tenant's request for the addition to the unit of a person specified in subsection 6.15E(a) above.

(g) In the event the landlord denies a tenant's request for an additional person under Sections 6.15E, either the landlord or the tenant may file a petition with the Board to determine if the landlord's denial of the request was reasonable.

(h) Any petition filed under subsection 6.15E(f) or (g) shall be expedited. (2015.)

§ 10.10 Decrease in Services

(a) A tenant may petition for a reduction of base rent where a landlord, without a corresponding reduction in rent, has (1) substantially decreased housing services, including any service added after commencement of the tenancy and for which additional consideration was paid when it was provided, or (2) failed to provide housing services reasonably expected under the circumstances, or (3) failed to provide a housing service verifiably promised by the landlord prior to commencement of the tenancy.

(b) A petition for arbitration based on decreased services shall be filed on a form supplied by the Board. The petition shall be accompanied by a statement setting forth the nature and value of the service for which the decrease is being sought, and the date the decrease began and ended, if applicable.

(c) No rent decrease as requested in the tenant's petition will be allowed prior to one year preceding the filing of the petition except where one or more of the following is found:

(1) extraordinary circumstances;

(2) where the tenant establishes by a preponderance of the evidence that there has been long term notice, oral or written, from the tenant or other reliable source, regarding such decrease occurring in the interior of the tenant's unit, or where such condition existed in the interior of the unit at the commencement of the tenancy and the landlord had constructive notice of same; or

(3) where the tenant establishes by a preponderance of the evidence that there has been actual long term notice, oral or written, from the tenant or other reliable source, and/or constructive notice regarding such decrease occurring in any common area.

(d) For the purposes of this section, notice is defined as follows:

(1) Actual Notice: Actual notice occurs when the tenant or any reliable person or entity informs the landlord, or the landlord's agents, orally or in writing, of a decrease in housing services as defined in the Rent Ordinance at Section 37.2(g).

(2) Constructive Notice: Constructive notice occurs when a decrease in housing services exists and the landlord should have known about the condition. (For example, constructive notice may be found when a reasonable inspection would have revealed the condition in the common area at any time or in the unit prior to the commencement of the tenancy.)

(e) With respect to Newly Covered Units, the earliest permissible effective date for any rent decrease allowed under this Section 10.10 shall be December 22, 1994; provided, however, that the initial base rent, as defined by Section 37.12(a) of the Rent Ordinance shall include all housing services provided or reasonably expected on May 1, 1994, or as of the commencement of the tenancy, whichever is later.

(f) Except where a failure to repair and maintain results in a substantial decrease in housing services, any relief granted by the Board under this section shall preclude relief under Section 10.11 below. This provision shall not limit any civil remedies that would otherwise be available to a tenant or landlord. (Amended 1989, 1995, 1996.)

§ 12.14 Evictions under Section 37.9(a)(8)

(a) Definition of Landlord. For purposes of an eviction under Section 37.9(a)(8) of the Ordinance, the term "landlord" shall mean a natural person, or group of natural persons, and for evictions under Ordinance Section 37.9(a)(8)(i) only, the term "landlord" shall also mean two individuals registered as Domestic Partners as defined in San Francisco Administrative Code Chapter 62.1-62.8, who in good faith hold a recorded fee interest in the property and meet one of the following requirements:

(1) held a recorded fee interest of at least 10%, or a recorded equitable interest under contract of sale of at least 10%, or in the case of Domestic Partners a combined ownership of record of at least 10%, which interest was recorded on or before February 21, 1991, and continues to hold at least such a 10% interest on the date of service of the notice to vacate; or

(2) holds a recorded fee interest of at least 25%, or a recorded equitable interest under contract of sale of at least 25%, or in the case of Domestic Partners a combined ownership of record of at least 25%, on the date of service of the notice to vacate.

(b) Information to Accompany Notice to Vacate. In addition to general eviction notice requirements, a landlord who endeavors to recover possession under Ordinance Section 37.9(a)(8) shall provide the tenant with the following documents and information in writing on or before service of the notice to vacate and file a copy of same with the Rent Board within 10 days after service of the notice to vacate on the tenant, together with a copy of the notice to vacate and proof of service upon the tenant:

(1) the identity and percentage of ownership of all persons holding a full or partial percentage ownership in the property;

(2) the name(s) of the landlord endeavoring to recover possession and, if applicable, the name(s) and relationship of the relative(s) for whom possession is being sought and a description of the current residence of the person(s) for whom possession is being sought;

(3) the dates the current percentages of ownership were recorded;

(4) a description of all residential properties owned, in whole or in part, by the landlord and, if applicable, a description of all residential properties owned, in whole or in part, by the landlord's relative for whom possession is being sought;

(5) the current rent for the unit and a statement that if the unit is offered for rent during the five-year period following service of the notice to vacate under Section 37.9(a)(8), the tenant has the right to re-rent the unit at the same rent, as adjusted by Ordinance Section 37.9B(a);

(6) the contents of Ordinance Section 37.9B, by providing a copy of same;

(7) the right the tenant(s) may have to relocation costs under Ordinance Section 37.9C, the amount of those relocation costs, and a copy of Section 37.9C;

(8) a declaration executed by the landlord under penalty of perjury stating:

(i) the reason why the landlord or relative is moving from his/her current residence to the unit for which possession is being sought; (ii) that the landlord seeks to recover possession of the unit in good faith, without ulterior reasons and with honest intent, for use or occupancy as the principal residence of the landlord or the landlord's relative (identified by name and relation to the landlord), for a period of at least 36 continuous months, as set forth in Ordinance Sections 37.9(a)(8)(i) and (ii); (iii) whether the landlord served a notice to vacate pursuant to Ordinance Section 37.9(a)(8) for a different unit; and, (iv) whether the landlord has recovered possession of other rental units in the City and County of San Francisco for any reason under Ordinance Section 37.9(a) other than nonpayment of rent in which the tenant displaced from such rental unit had resided for at least 36 consecutive months;

(9) a warning that the tenant must submit a statement to the landlord within 30 days of service of the notice to vacate, with supporting evidence, if the tenant claims to be a member of a protected class under Ordinance Sections 37.9(i) or (j), and that failure to do so shall be deemed an admission that the tenant is not protected by Sections 37.9(i) or (j);

(10) a form prepared by the Rent Board stating that a tenant's failure to timely act in response to a notice to vacate may result in a lawsuit by the landlord to evict the tenant, that advice regarding the notice to vacate is available from the Rent Board, and that the tenant may be eligible for affordable housing programs through the Mayor's Office of Housing and Community Development; and

(11) a blank change of address form prepared by the Rent Board that the tenant can use to keep the Rent Board apprised of any future change of address.

(c) Principal Place of Residence. For purposes of an eviction under Section 37.9(a)(8) of the Ordinance, a landlord or landlord's relative can have only ONE "principal place of residence" which is defined as the permanent or primary home of the party claiming that a unit has that status attached to it. It is a unit that the party occupies for more than temporary or transitory purposes. Evidence that a unit is or is intended to be the party's "principal place of residence" includes, but is not limited to, the following elements, a compilation of which lends greater credibility to the claim of "principal place of residence of a party" whereas the presence of only one element may not support such claim:

(1) the subject premises are listed as the party's place of residence on any motor vehicle registration, driver's license, automobile insurance policy, homeowner's or renter's insurance policy, and with the party's current employer or any public agency, including State and local taxing authorities;

(2) utilities are installed under the party's name at the subject

premises;

(3) the party's personal possessions have been moved into the subject premises;

(4) a homeowner's tax exemption has been issued in the party's name for the subject premises;

(5) the party's current voter registration is for the subject premises;

(6) a U.S. Postal Change of Address form has been filed requesting that mail be forwarded to the subject premises;

(7) the subject premises are the place the party normally returns to as his/her home, exclusive of military service, hospitalization, vacation, or travel necessitated by employment;

(8) notice to move at another dwelling unit was given in order to move into the subject premises; and

(9) the party sold or placed on the market for sale the home he/she occupied prior to the subject premises.

(d) Definition of Disability for Protected Status. A tenant is disabled under Ordinance Section 37.9(i)(1)(B)(i) if the tenant meets the standard for blindness or disability under the federal Supplemental Security Income/California State Supplemental Program (SSI/SSP). In determining whether a tenant is disabled, a finder of fact shall consider relevant evidence, including:

(1) findings by any government entity concerning a disability;

(2) testimony concerning the disability; and

(3) medical evidence concerning the disability.

(e) Evidence of a Lack of Good Faith. For purposes of an eviction under Section 37.9(a)(8) of the Ordinance, evidence that is relevant to determining whether a landlord acted or is acting in good faith may include, but is not limited to, any of the following:

(1) the landlord has failed to file the notice to vacate with the Rent Board as required by Ordinance Sections 37.9(c) and 37.9B(c);

(2) the landlord or relative for whom the tenant was evicted did not move into the rental unit within three months after the landlord recovered possession and then occupy said unit as that person's principal residence for a minimum of 36 consecutive months;

(3) the landlord or relative for whom the tenant was evicted

lacks a legitimate, bona fide reason for not moving into the unit within three months after the recovery of possession and/or then occupying said unit as that person's principal residence for a minimum of 36 consecutive months;

(4) the landlord did not file a Statement of Occupancy with the Rent Board as required by Ordinance Section 37.9(a)(8)(vii) and Section 12.14(f) of these Rules and Regulations;

(5) the landlord violated Ordinance Section 37.9B during the five-year period following service of the notice to vacate under Ordinance Section 37.9(a)(8) by renting the unit to a new tenant at a rent greater than that which would have been the rent had the tenant who had been required to vacate remained in continuous occupancy and the rental unit remained subject to the Ordinance;

(6) the landlord served a notice to vacate pursuant to Ordinance Section 37.9(a)(8) for a different unit and has not sought a rescission or withdrawal of that notice;

(7) the landlord has recovered possession of multiple rental units in the same building within 180 days of the service of the notice to vacate pursuant to Ordinance Section 37.9(a)(8); and/or

(8) the landlord completed buyout negotiations as defined in Ordinance Section 37.9E(c) with any other tenant(s) in the building.

(f) Statement of Occupancy. A landlord who seeks to recover possession of a unit pursuant to Ordinance Section 37.9(a)(8) on or after January 1, 2018 must complete a Statement of Occupancy under penalty of perjury on a form to be prepared by the Rent Board that discloses whether the landlord has recovered possession of the unit. The landlord shall file a Statement of Occupancy with the Rent Board within 90 days after the date of service of the notice to vacate pursuant to Ordinance Section 37.9(a)(8), and shall file an updated Statement of Occupancy every 90 days thereafter; provided, however, if the Statement of Occupancy discloses that the landlord has recovered possession of the unit, the landlord shall then be required to file updated Statements of Occupancy once a year for five years, no later than 12 months, 24 months, 36 months, 48 months and 60 months after the date the landlord recovered possession of the unit. Each Statement of Occupancy filed after the landlord has recovered possession of the unit shall disclose the date of recovery of possession. If the Statement of Occupancy discloses that the landlord is no longer endeavoring to recover possession of the unit under Ordinance Section 37.9(a)(8) and the Rent Board has granted the landlord's written request for rescission of the notice to vacate pursuant to Ordinance Section 37.9B(e), no further Statements of Occupancy need be filed.

(1) If the Statement of Occupancy discloses that the landlord

has not yet recovered possession of the unit, the landlord shall provide the following information:

(i) whether the landlord is still pursuing an eviction of the tenant and, if not, the landlord shall: include proof that the landlord has notified the tenant in writing that the notice to vacate has been rescinded and that the Rent Board has granted the landlord's written request for rescission of the notice to vacate pursuant to Ordinance Section 37.9B(e); state whether any tenant still occupies the unit and provide the name(s) and contact information for each tenant still in occupancy; and, if any tenant still occupies the unit after written rescission of the notice to vacate and/or rescission by the Rent Board of the notice of constraints, include proof of the most recent rental payment received from the tenant and proof that the landlord has deposited or cashed it;

(ii) whether the landlord has filed an unlawful detainer action against the tenant to recover possession of the unit;

(iii) the identity and percentage of ownership of all persons holding a full or partial percentage ownership in the property;

(iv) the dates the current percentages of ownership were recorded;

(v) the name(s) of the landlord endeavoring to recover possession and, if applicable, the name(s) and relationship of the relative(s) for whom possession is being sought, a description of the current residence of the landlord or relative(s) for whom possession is being sought and an explanation of why the owner or relative is moving from his/her current residence to the unit;

(vi) a description of all residential properties owned, in whole or in part, by the landlord and, if applicable, a description of all residential properties owned, in whole or in part, by the landlord's relative for whom possession is being sought;

(vii) the current rent for the unit;

(viii) whether and when the landlord served a notice to vacate pursuant to Ordinance Section 37.9(a)(8)(i) for a different unit, and the address of such unit; and

(ix) whether and when the landlord has recovered possession of any other rental unit in the same building subsequent to the service of the notice to vacate pursuant to Ordinance Section 37.9(a)(8).

(2) If the Statement of Occupancy discloses that the landlord has already recovered possession of the unit and the owner or relative for whom the tenant was evicted is currently occupying the unit as that person's principal residence, the landlord shall provide the following information:

(i) the name(s) and ownership interest of the current occupant(s) of the unit, and the date such occupancy commenced;

(ii) at least two forms of the supporting documentation specified in Section 12.14(f)(4) below;

(iii) whether the current occupant's personal possessions have been moved into the unit;

(iv) the rent charged for the unit if any;

(v) whether the subject unit is listed as the owner's or relative's place of residence on any motor vehicle registration, driver's license, automobile insurance policy, homeowner's or renter's insurance policy, is used by or for the person's current employer and any public agency, including state and local taxing authorities;

(vi) whether utilities are installed at the unit under the owner's or relative's name;

(vii) whether the owner occupant has claimed a homeowner's tax exemption for the subject unit;

(viii) whether the occupant filed a U.S. Postal Service Change of Address form;

(ix) whether the subject unit is the place the owner or relative normally returns to as his/her home, exclusive of military service, hospitalization, vacation, or travel necessitated by employment;

(x) whether notice to move at another dwelling unit was given in order to move into the subject unit; and

(xi) whether the owner occupant sold or placed on the market for sale the home he/she occupied prior to the subject unit.

(3) If the Statement of Occupancy discloses that the landlord has already recovered possession of the unit and the owner or relative for whom the tenant was evicted is not occupying the unit as that person's principal residence, the landlord shall provide the following information:

(i) whether the owner or relative for whom the tenant was evicted ever occupied the unit as that person's principal residence, the dates of such occupancy, and the reasons why the unit is no longer occupied by that person;

(ii) if the owner or relative for whom the tenant was evicted never occupied the unit as that person's principal residence, the reasons why occupancy has not yet commenced;

(iii) If the owner or relative for whom the tenant was evicted has moved out of the unit within five years after service of the notice to vacate under Ordinance Section 37.9(a)(8), a copy of the written offer to the displaced tenant to re-rent the unit at a rent no greater than what the tenant would have paid had the tenant remained in continuous occupancy and the unit remained subject to the Rent Ordinance; and

(iv) If the owner or relative for whom the tenant was evicted has moved out of the unit within five years after service of the notice to vacate under Ordinance Section 37.9(a)(8) and the unit was re-rented to someone other than the displaced tenant, the amount of rent paid by the current tenant.

(4) Where the Statement of Occupancy discloses that the owner or relative for whom the tenant was evicted is currently occupying the unit as that person's principal residence, the landlord shall attach to the Statement of Occupancy at least two of the following forms of supporting documentation. Confidential information may be redacted from the supporting documentation prior to filing it with the Rent Board.

(i) current motor vehicle registration, plus a copy of the current insurance policy for the vehicle that shows the name of the insured, the address of the unit and the period of coverage, with proof of payment;

(ii) current driver's license;

(iii) Social Security statement of benefits that shows the name of the recipient, the address of the unit and the current period of coverage;

(iv) current voter registration;

(v) current homeowner's or renter's insurance policy for the contents of the unit showing the name of the insured, the address of the unit and the period of coverage, with proof of payment; and/or

(vi) the most recent state or federal tax return that shows the name and address of the owner or relative occupying the unit and proof of filing.

(5) The Rent Board shall make all reasonable efforts to send the displaced tenant a copy of each Statement of Occupancy with supporting documentation within 30 days of the date of filing, or a notice that the landlord did not timely file a Statement of Occupancy if no Statement of Occupancy was timely filed.

(6) The Rent Board shall impose an administrative penalty on any landlord who fails to timely file a Statement of Occupancy with the supporting documentation required by Section 12.14(f)(4) of these Rules and Regulations, in violation of Ordinance Section 37.9(a)(8)(vii) and Section

12.14(f). Penalties shall be in the following amounts: $250 for the first violation, $500 for the second violation, and $1,000 for every subsequent violation. The procedure for the imposition, enforcement, collection, and administrative review of the administrative penalty shall be governed by Administrative Code Chapter 100, "Procedures Governing the Imposition of Administrative Fines," which is hereby incorporated in its entirety. (Amended 1991, 1995, 1998, 2008, Subsections (a)-(d) amended and Subsections (e)-(f) added November 21.2017, effective January 1, 2018)

§ 12.15 *Evictions for Capital Improvement or Rehabilitation*

a. For purposes of an eviction under Section 37.9(a)(11) of the Ordinance, the capital improvement and/or rehabilitation work to be done must involve work that would make the unit hazardous, unhealthy, and/or uninhabitable while work is in progress. If there is a dispute between the landlord and the tenant as to whether the work that is to be performed creates a hazardous or unhealthy environment, the tenant may file a report of alleged wrongful eviction with the Board.

b. (1) Copies of all necessary permits, a description of work to be done and a reasonable approximate date (month and year) when the tenant can reoccupy the unit shall be given to the tenant on or before the date of service of the notice to vacate. On or before the date of service of the notice to vacate, the landlord also must advise the tenant in writing that the permit application and the rehabilitation or capital improvement plans, if required by the Building Inspection Department, are on file with the Central Permit Bureau of the Building Inspection Dept., located at 1660 Mission Street, and arrangements may be made to review such applications or plans.

(2) The tenant will vacate the unit only for the minimum time required to do the work as stated in the notice, not to exceed three months, unless the time is extended by the Board upon petition by the landlord pursuant to subsection (e) below.

c. Displaced tenants should advise the Board and the landlord of their temporary addresses during the period of displacement in order that they may be notified regarding their relocation.

d. Moving Costs

Any landlord who seeks to recover possession of a unit pursuant to Section 37.9(a)(11) of the Ordinance shall pay each relocation expenses as provided in Section 37.9C of the Ordinance.

e. Landlord's Petition for Extension of Time

1. Before giving the notice to vacate, if the landlord knows or should know that the work will require the removal of the tenant(s) for more than the three months authorized under

Ordinance Section 37.9(a)(11), the landlord shall petition the Rent Board for approval of displacement for more than three months. The petition shall include one original and copies for each involved tenant of the following documents:

A. A completed petition form;

B. Copies of all necessary building permits, showing approval has been granted;

C. A written breakdown of the work to be performed, detailing where the work will be done and the cost of the work;

D. An estimate of the time needed to accomplish the work and approximate date (month and day) each involved tenant may reoccupy.

2. If, after the notice to vacate has been given or after the work has commenced, it is apparent that the work will take longer than the three months authorized under Section 37.9(a)(11) or longer than the time approved by the Board, the landlord immediately shall file a petition pursuant to subsection (e)(1) above, along with a statement of why the work will require more time.

3. A hearing on the landlord's petition shall be scheduled within 30 days of the date of filing the petition and conducted pursuant to Part 11 of these Rules and Regulations. The hearing officer shall render a written decision as to the reasonableness of the landlord's time estimate. The tenants or the landlord may appeal this determination by filing an appeal with the Commissioners pursuant to Ordinance Section 37.8(f).

f. Nothing in this section shall preclude a tenant from filing a report of alleged wrongful eviction with the Board. (Amended 1987; eff. 2/14/87, applicable to notices served on or after that date; amended 2007.)

§ 12.19 *Other Displacements*

a. If a tenant is forced to vacate her/his unit due to fire or other disaster, the landlord shall, within 30 days of completion of repairs to the unit, offer the same unit to that tenant under the same terms and conditions as existed prior to her/his displacement. The landlord's offer shall be sent to the address provided by the tenant. If the tenant has not provided an address, the offer shall be sent to the unit from which the tenant was displaced and to any other address of the tenant of which the landlord has actual knowledge, including electronic mail (e-mail) addresses.

b. The tenant shall have 30 days from receipt of the landlord's offer to notify the landlord of acceptance or rejection of the offer and, if accepted, shall reoccupy the unit within 45 days of receipt of the landlord's offer.

c. However, the cost of capital improvements which are necessary before rerenting a unit which was damaged or destroyed as set forth in subsection (a) above, which cost was not reimbursed by insurance proceeds or by any other means (such as a satisfied judgment) may be passed through to the tenant by utilization of the capital improvement petition process as set forth in Part 7 above. Any rent increase under this section would require that a notice be served upon the tenant(s) pursuant to Civil Code Section 827.

d. The landlord who attempts to rerent a unit, but refuses to allow a tenant to return to her/his home under this section shall have wrongfully endeavored to recover or wrongfully recovered said tenant's rental unit in violation of Section 37.9 of the Ordinance and shall be liable to the displaced tenants for actual and punitive damages as provided by Ordinance Section 37.9(f). This remedy shall be in addition to any other remedy available to the tenant under the Rent Ordinance. (1989, 2013.)

§ 12.20 *Evictions for Unilaterally Imposed Terms of Rental Agreement under Section 37.9(a)(2)*

(a) Unilaterally Imposed Obligations and Covenants

Notwithstanding any change in the terms of a tenancy pursuant to Civil Code Section 827, a tenant may not be evicted for violation of a covenant or obligation that was not included in the tenant's rental agreement at the inception of the tenancy unless: (1) the change in the terms of the tenancy is authorized by the Rent Ordinance or required by federal, state or local law; or (2) the change in the terms of the tenancy was accepted in writing by the tenant after receipt of written notice from the landlord that the tenant need not accept such new term as part of the rental agreement. The landlord's inability to evict a tenant under this Section for violation of a unilaterally imposed change in the terms of a tenancy shall not constitute a decrease in housing service under the Rent Ordinance as to any other tenant. (1997, 2007, 2011, 2012.)

San Francisco Subdivision Code

§ 1396.2 *Prohibition on Condo Conversions for Certain Buildings*

(a) Notwithstanding any provisions in this Code to the contrary, including Section 1359, the Department of Public Works shall not sell residential condominium conversion lottery tickets to; shall not accept a residential condominium conversion subdivision application from; and shall deny a tentative subdivision or tentative parcel map for residential condominium conversion submitted by the owner(s) of a building that meets all of the following conditions:

(1) the building had two or more evictions with each eviction associated with a separate unit(s);

(2) issuance of each eviction notice occurred on or after May 1,

2005; and,

(3) issuance of the eviction notice(s) occurred pursuant to San Francisco Administrative Code Sections 37.9(a)(8), 37.9(a)(10), 37.9(a)(11), or 37.9(a)(13).

(b) Subsection (a) also shall apply to the owner(s) of a building with one or more evictions if the person(s) evicted was a senior, disabled, or catastrophically ill tenant and the issuance of the eviction notice occurred in accordance with the conditions of Subsections (a)(2) and(3).

(1) For purposes of this Subsection, a "senior" shall be a person who is 60 years or older and has been residing in the unit for ten years or more at the time of issuance of the eviction notice; a "disabled" tenant is defined for purposes of this Section as a person who is disabled within the meaning of Title 42 U.S.C. Section 12102(2)(A); and a "catastrophically ill" tenant is defined for purposes of this Subsection as a person who is disabled as defined above, and who is suffering from a life threatening illness as certified by his or her primary care physician.

(c) Subsections (a) and(b) shall apply to all buildings subject to such provisions without regard to whether the current owner(s) initiated or otherwise participated in the eviction(s).

(d) If the Department determines that an applicant has knowingly provided false material information concerning subsections (a) or (b) above, the Department shall immediately deny the application for the lottery, or if the applicant has submitted an application for conversion, shall immediately deny the application for conversion. Moreover, the Department, the Director, or other authorized person or entity may also enforce the provisions of this Section under section 1304 or any other applicable provision of law as warranted.

(e) For purposes of subsections (a) and(b), "eviction" shall mean the issuance of a written notice terminating tenancy pursuant to Administrative Code Sections 37.9(a)(8), 37.9(a)(10), 37.9(a)(11), or 37.9(a)(13); provided, however, that if the property owner(s) issues then withdraws the eviction notice prior to its expiration and the tenant receiving the notice remains in tenancy for at least 120 days following the expiration of the notice, the property owner's action shall not be deemed an eviction pursuant to this subsection.

(f) Notwithstanding the limitations set forth in Subsection (a), a building that meets the conditions of Subsections (a)(1)--(3) but did not result in the issuance of an eviction notice, as defined, to a senior, disabled, or catastrophically ill tenant shall be eligible for conversion ten (10) years following the date of the last eviction from the building. Conversion of a 2-unit building pursuant to this Section shall be subject to Section 1359 except that both units in the building shall be owner-occupied by the same owners of record for ten (10) years prior to the date of application for Conversion. Conversion of a building of up to six (6) units pursuant to this

section shall be subject to the provisions of Article 9 except that the owner occupancy requirements of Sections 1396(a) and(b) shall be ten (10) years prior to the date of registration for the lottery as selected by the Director.

(g) Notwithstanding the limitations set forth in Subsection (a) or (b), a building where one or more eviction notices, as defined, were issued after May 1, 2005, shall be exempt from this Section 1396.2 if each unit in the building was occupied by a separate owner of record on April 4, 2006, the introduction date of this legislation. **Leg.H.** 2006.

§ 1396.4 *Condo Conversion Fee and Expedited Conversion*

(a) Findings. The findings of Planning Code Section 415.1 concerning the City's inclusionary affordable housing program are incorporated herein by reference and support the basis for charging the fee set forth herein as it relates to the conversion of dwelling units into condominiums.

(b) Any building may be exempted from the annual lottery provisions of Section 1396 if the building owners for said building comply with Section 1396.3 (g)(1) and all the requirements of this Section 1396.4 . Notwithstanding the foregoing, no property or applicant subject to any of the prohibition on conversions set forth in Section 1396.2 , in particular a property with the eviction(s) set forth in Section 1396.2 (b), is eligible for the Expedited Conversion program under this Section 1396.4 . Eligible buildings as set forth in this Section (b) may exercise their option to participate in this program according to the following requirements:

(1) Any building that participated in but was not selected for the 2012 or 2013 condominium conversion lottery consisting of (a) four units or less in which one unit has been occupied continuously by one of the applicant owners of record for no less than five years prior to April 15, 2013, or (b) buildings consisting of five or six units in which 50 percent or more of the units have been occupied continuously by the applicant owners of record for no less than five years as of April 15, 2013, is eligible for conversion under this Subsection. The applicant(s) for the subject building seeking to convert under this Subsection shall pay the fee specified in Subsection (e) no later than April 14, 2014 for the entire building along with additional information as the Department may require including certification of continued eligibility; however, the deadline for an applicant to pay the fee may be extended pursuant to (j)(3) of this Section.

(2) Any building that participated in but was not selected for the 2012 or 2013 condominium conversion lottery consisting of (a) four units or less in which one unit has been occupied continuously by one of the applicant owners of record for no less than three years prior to April 15, 2014, or (b) buildings consisting of five or six units in which 50 percent or more of the units have been occupied continuously by the applicant owners of record for no less than three years as of April 15,

2014, is eligible for conversion under this Subsection. The applicant(s) for the subject building may apply for conversion under this Subsection on or after April 15, 2014 and shall pay the fee specified in Subsection (e) no later than January 23, 2015 along with additional information as the Department may require including certification of continued eligibility; however, the deadline for an applicant to pay the fee may be extended pursuant to (j)(3) of this Section.

(3) For Additionally Qualified Buildings consisting of (a) four units or less in which one unit has been occupied continuously by one owner of record for no less than six years as of April 15, 2015 or (b) buildings consisting of five or six units in which 50 percent or more of the units have been occupied continuously by owners of record for no less than six years as of April 15, 2015, the applicant(s) for the subject building may apply for conversion under this Subsection on or after April 15, 2015 and shall pay the fee specified in Subsection (e) no later than January 22, 2016 along with additional information as the Department may require including certification of continued eligibility.

(4) For Additionally Qualified Buildings consisting of (a) four units or less in which one unit has been occupied continuously by one owner of record for no less than six years as of April 15, 2016, or (b) buildings consisting of five or six units in which 50 percent or more of the units have been occupied continuously by owners of record for no less than six years as of April 15, 2016, the applicant(s) for the subject building may apply for conversion under this Subsection on or after April 15, 2016 and shall pay the fee specified in Subsection (e) no later than January 20, 2017 along with additional information as the Department may require including certification of continued eligibility.

(5) For Additionally Qualified Buildings consisting of (a) four units or less in which one unit has been occupied continuously by one owner of record for no less than six years as of April 15, 2017, or (b) buildings consisting of five or six units in which 50 percent or more of the units have been occupied continuously by owners of record for no less than six years as of April 15, 2017, the applicant(s) for the subject building may apply for conversion under this Subsection on or after April 15, 2017 and shall pay the fee specified in Subsection (e) no later than January 19, 2018 along with additional information as the Department may require including certification of continued eligibility.

(6) For Additionally Qualified Buildings consisting of (a) four units or less in which one unit has been occupied continuously by one owner of record for no less than six years prior to April 15, 2018, or (b) buildings consisting of five or six units in which 50 percent or more of the units have been occupied continuously by owners of record for no less than six years as of April 15, 2018, the applicant(s) for the subject building may apply for conversion under this Subsection on or after April

15, 2018 and shall pay the fee specified in Subsection (e) no later than January 25, 2019 along with additional information as the Department may require including certification of continued eligibility.

(7) For Additionally Qualified Buildings consisting of (a) four units or less in which one unit has been occupied continuously by one owner of record for no less than six years prior to April 15, 2019, or (b) buildings consisting of five or six units in which 50 percent or more of the units have been occupied continuously by owners of record for no less than six years as of April 15, 2019, the applicant(s) for the subject building may apply for conversion under this Subsection on or after April 15, 2019 and shall pay the fee specified in Subsection (e) no later than January 24, 2020 along with additional information as the Department may require including certification of continued eligibility. An Additionally Qualified Building subject to Subsection 9(A) shall be eligible to convert pursuant to this Subsection as long as there is fully executed written agreement in which the owners each have an exclusive right of occupancy to individual units in the building to the exclusion of the owners of the other units and 50 percent or more of the units have been occupied continuously by owners of record for no less than six years as of January 24, 2020.

(8) For applications for conversion pursuant to Subsections (3)-(7) only, a unit that is "occupied continuously" shall be defined as a unit occupied continuously by an owner of record for the six year period without an interruption of occupancy and so long as the applicant owner(s) occupied the subject unit as his/her principal place of residence for no less than one year prior to the time of application.

(A) Notwithstanding the occupancy requirements set forth above, each building may have one unit where there is an interruption in occupancy for no more than a three month period that is incident to the sale or transfer to a subsequent owner of record who occupied the same unit. For any unit with an interruption of occupancy, the applicant shall provide evidence to establish to the satisfaction of the Department that the period did not exceed three months.

(B) Notwithstanding the occupancy requirements set forth above, each building may have one unit where there is an interruption in occupancy for no more than a one year period if the sale or transfer to a subsequent owner of record who occupied the same unit was delayed during the term of a bank foreclosure against the former owner's interest in the building related to the subject unit. For any unit with an interruption of occupancy as a result of a foreclosure as described in Subsection (B), the applicant shall provide evidence to establish to the satisfaction of the Department that the period did not exceed one (1) year.

(9) An "Additionally Qualified Building" within the meaning of this Section is defined as a building in which the initially

eligible applicant owners of record have a fully executed written agreement as of April 15, 2013 in which the owners each have an exclusive right of occupancy to individual units in the building to the exclusion of the owners of the other units; provided, however, that said agreement can be amended to include new applicant owner(s) of record as long as the new owner(s) satisfy the requirements of Subsection (8) above. In addition to the requirements listed in this Subsection (8), an Additionally Qualified Building also includes a five or six unit building that: (A) on April 15, 2013, had 50 percent or more of the units in escrow for sale as a tenancy-in-common where each buyer shall have an exclusive right of occupancy to an individual unit in the building to the exclusion of the owners of other units or (B) is subject to the requirements of Section 1396.2 (f) and 50 percent or more of the units have been occupied continuously by owners of record for no less than ten years prior to the date of application as set forth in Subsections (3)-(7).

(10) In addition to all other provisions of this Section, the applicant(s) must meet the following requirements applicable to Subdivision Code Article 9, Conversions: Sections 1381, 1382, 1383,1386, 1387, 1388, 1389, 1390, 1391(a) and (b), 1392, 1393, 1394, and 1395. Also, the applicant(s) must certify that to the extent any tenant vacates his or her unit after March 31, 2013 and before recordation of the final parcel or subdivision map, such tenant did so voluntarily or if an eviction or eviction notice occurred it was not pursuant to Administrative Code Sections 37.9(a)(8)-(14). If an eviction has taken placed under 37.9(a)(11) or 37.9(a)(14) then the applicant(s) shall certify that th e original tenant reoccupied the unit after the temporary eviction.

(11) If the Department finds that a violation of this Section occurred prior to recordation of the final map or final parcel map, the Department shall disapprove the application or subject map. If the Department finds that a violation of this Section occurred after recordation of the final map or parcel map, the Department shall take such actions as are available and within its authority to address the violation.

(c) Decisions and Hearing on the Application.

(1) The applicant shall obtain a final and effective tentative map or tentative parcel map approval for the condominium subdivision or parcel map within one (1) year of paying the fee specified in Subsection (e).

(2) No less than twenty (20) days prior to the Department's proposed decision on a tentative map or tentative parcel map, the Department shall publish the addresses of building being considered for approval and post such information on its website. During this time, any interested party may file a written objection to an application and submit information to the Department contesting the eligibility of a building. In addition, the Department may elect to hold a public hearing

on said tentative map or tentative parcel map to consider the information presented by the public, other City department, or an applicant. If the Department elects to hold such a hearing it shall post notice of such hearing and provide written notice to the applicant, all tenants of such building, any member of the public who submitted information to the Department, and any interested party who has requested such notice. In the event that an objection to the conversion application is filed in accordance with this Subsection, and based upon all the facts available to the Department, the Department shall approve, conditionally approve, or disapprove an application and state the reasons in support of that decision.

(3) Any map application subject to a Departmental public hearing on the subdivision or a subdivision appeal shall have the time limit set forth in this Subsection (c)(1) extended for another six (6) months.

(4) The Director of the Department of Public Works is authorized to waive the time limits set forth in this Subsection (c)(1) as it applies to a particular building due to extenuating or unique circumstances. Such waiver may be granted only after a public hearing and in no case shall the time limit extend beyond two (2) years after submission of the application.

(d) Should the subdivision application be denied or be rejected as untimely in accordance with the dates specified above, or the tentative subdivision map or tentative parcel map disapproved, the City shall refund the entirety of the applicant's fee specified in Subsection (e).

(e) The fee amount is $20,000.00 per unit for all buildings that seek to convert under Subsection (b)(1)-(7). Said fee shall be adjusted annually in accordance with the terms of Section 1315 (f). Said fee is reduced for each year the building has participated in the condominium conversion lottery up to and including the 2013 lottery in accordance with the following formula:

(1) 2 years of participation, 20% fee reduction per unit;

(2) 3 years of participation, 40% fee reduction per unit;

(3) 4 years of participation, 60% fee reduction per unit; and

(4) 5 or more years of participation, 80% fee reduction per unit.

(f) For purposes of Section (e), a building's owner(s) shall get credit only for those years that he or she participated in the lottery even though such building could have qualified for and participated in other condominium conversion lotteries.

(g) Life Time Lease for Non-purchasing Tenants.

(1) Any application for conversion under this Section shall include a certification under penalty of perjury by the

applicants that any non-purchasing tenant(s) in the building has been given a written offer to enter into a life time lease in the form and with the provisions published and prescribed by the Department in consultation with the Rent Board. Such written offer for a life time lease shall be executed by the owners of the building(s) and recorded prior to the time of Final Map or Parcel Map approval. Any life time leases made pursuant hereto shall expire only upon the death or demise of the last such life-tenant residing in the unit or the last surviving member of the life-tenant's household, provided such surviving member is related to the life- tenant by blood, marriage, or domestic partnership, and is either disabled, catastrophically ill, or aged 62 or older at the time of death or demise of any such life-tenant, or at such time as the life-tenant(s) in the unit voluntarily vacates the unit after giving due notice of such intent to vacate.

(2) (A) Each lease shall contain a provision allowing the tenant to terminate the lease and vacate the unit upon 30 days' notice and a provision that rent charged during the term of the lease shall not exceed the rent charged at the time of filing of the application for conversion, plus any increases proportionate to the increases in the residential rent component of the "Bay Area Cost of Living Index, U.S. Dept, of Labor," provided that the rental increase provisions of this Section shall be operative only in the absence of other applicable rent increase or arbitration laws.

(B) The lease also shall state that it shall not alter or abridge the rights or obligations of the parties in performance of their covenants, including but not limited to the provision of services, payment of rent or the obligations imposed by Sections 1941, 1941.1, 1941.2, 1941.3, and 1941.4 of the California Civil Code and that there shall be no decrease in dwelling unit maintenance or other services historically provided to such units and such life-tenants.

(C) The lease shall include the following language:

Tenant agrees that this Lease shall be subject and subordinate at all times to (i) all ground leases or underlying leases that may now exist or hereafter be executed affecting the Real Property or any portion thereof; (ii) the lien of any mortgage, deed of trust, assignment of rents and leases or other security instrument (and any advances thereunder) that may now exist or hereafter be executed in any amount for which the Real Property or any portion thereof, any ground leases or underlying leases or Landlord's interest or estate therein, is specified as security; and (iii) all modifications, renewals, supplements, consolidations and replacements thereof, provided in all cases the mortgagees or beneficiaries named in mortgages or deeds of trust hereafter executed or the assignee of any assignment of rents and leases hereafter executed to recognize the interest and not disturb the possession, use and enjoyment of Tenant under this Lease, and, in the event of foreclosure or default, the lease will continue in full force and

effect by operation of San Francisco Administrative Code Chapter 37 , Section 37.9D , and the conditions imposed on each parcel or subdivision map pursuant to Section 1396.4 (g), as long as Tenant is not in default under the terms and conditions of this Lease. Tenant agrees to execute and deliver, upon demand by Landlord and in the form requested by Landlord, any additional reasonable documents evidencing the priority or subordination of this Lease with respect to any such ground leases, underlying leases, mortgages, deeds of trust, assignment of rents and leases or other security instruments. Subject to the foregoing, Tenant agrees that Tenant shall be bound by, and required to comply with, the provisions of any assignment of rents and leases with respect to the Building.

(3) The Department shall impose the following tentative map conditions on each parcel and subdivision map subject to this Subsection 1396.4 (g) and require that the conditions be satisfied prior to Final Subdivision Map or Parcel Map approval: (A) the property owner(s) of the building provide a written offer for a life time lease pursuant to this Subsection to the tenant(s) in the building and record such offer against the building's title, (B) at the time the tenant(s) accepts the life time lease offer, and even if such acceptance occurs after map approval, a binding agreement between the tenant(s) and the property owner(s) shall be executed and recorded against the property's title, and (C) a binding agreement between the City and the property owner(s) concerning the requirements of this Subsection be recorded against the property's title. For purposes of this Subsection, the Board of Supervisors delegates authority to the DPW Director, in consultation with the Mayor's Office of Housing, to enter in said agreement on behalf of the City and County of San Francisco.

(4) If the owner(s) of a building subject to the life time lease provisions of this Section 1396.4 (g) enters into any contract or option to sell or transfer any unit that would be subject to the lifetime lease requirements or any interest in any unit in the building that would be subject to the lifetime lease requirements at any time between the initial application and recording of the final subdivision map or parcel map, said contract or option shall be subject to the following conditions: (a) the contract or option shall include written notice that the unit shall be subject to the life time lease requirements of Subdivision Code Section 1396.4 (g), (b) prior to final execution of any such contract or option, the owner(s) shall record a notice of restrictions against the property that specifically identifies the unit potentially subject to the life time lease requirements and specifies the requirements of the life time lease as set forth in Section 1396.4 (g)(1), and (c) the recorded notice of restrictions shall be included as a note on the final subdivision map or parcel map. Prior to approval of a final subdivision map or parcel map, the applicant(s) shall certify under penalty of perjury to the Department that he, she, or they have complied with the terms of this Subsection as it applies to a building. Failure

to provide this certification from every current owner of a building shall result in disapproval of the map. The content of the notices and certifications required by this Subsection shall comply with the instructions and procedures developed by the Department.

(h) In recognition of the rental requirements of Section (g), the fee for each unit in which a non-purchasing tenant resides at the time specified in Section (g) who is offered a life time lease and is unrelated by blood, marriage, or domestic partnership to any owner of the building shall be refunded to the subdivider under the following formula:

(1) One unit, 10% fee reduction for such unit;

(2) Two units, 20% fee reduction for each unit;

(3) Three units, 30% fee reduction for each unit.

(i) Upon confirmation of compliance with the rental requirement, DPW or the City department in possession of the fee revenue shall refund the amount specified in Section (h) to the subdivider and have all remaining fee revenues transferred to the Citywide Affordable Housing Fund, established in Administrative Code Section 10.100-49, in the following percentage allocations:

(1) 25% to the Mayor's Office of Housing and Community Development's program for small site acquisition to purchase market rate housing and convert it to affordable housing; and

(2) 75% for the purpose of expanding affordable housing opportunities for low or moderate income households in San Francisco, including, but not limited to, expanding public housing opportunities.

(j) Waiver or Reduction of Fee Based on Absence of Reasonable Relationship.

(1) A project applicant of any project subject to the requirements in this Section may appeal to the Board of Supervisors for a reduction, adjustment, or waiver of the requirements based upon the absence of any reasonable relationship or nexus between the impact of development and the amount of the fee charged.

(2) Any appeal of requests under this clause shall be made in writing and filed with the Clerk of the Board no later than 15 days after the date the sponsor is required to pay and has paid to the Treasurer the fee as required in this Section. The appeal shall set forth in detail the factual and legal basis for the claim of waiver, reduction, or adjustment. Upon receipt of the appeal, the Clerk of the Board of Supervisors shall review the appeal in consultation with the City Attorney. If the Clerk of the Board determines that the appeal on its face challenges, on a factual or legal basis, the relationship or nexus between the impact of development and the amount of the fee charged,

then the Clerk of the Board shall schedule a hearing under Subsection (3). If the Clerk of the Board in consultation with the City Attorney determines that the appeal on its face does not challenge, on a factual or legal basis, the relationship or nexus, then the Clerk of the Board shall notify the members of the Board of Supervisors within three business days of the Clerk's receipt of the appeal. If any one member of the Board of Supervisors requests within three business days of the Clerk's notification that the Clerk schedule a hearing on the appeal, then the Clerk shall schedule a hearing under Subsection (3). If no member of the Board requests that the Clerk schedule a hearing, then the Clerk shall inform the appellant and the Department of Public Works, within ten business days from the date of the filing, that the filing does not allege a proper basis for appeal, and shall reject the appeal on behalf of the Board of Supervisors.

(3) If the Clerk of the Board schedules a hearing under this Section, the Board of Supervisors shall consider the appeal at the hearing within 60 days after the filing of the appeal. The appellant shall bear the burden of presenting substantial evidence to support the appeal, including comparable technical information to support appellant's position. If a reduction, adjustment, or waiver is granted, any change of use or scope of the project shall invalidate the waiver, adjustment or reduction of the fee. If the Board grants a reduction, adjustment or waiver, the Clerk of the Board shall promptly transmit the nature and extent of the reduction, adjustment or waiver to the Treasurer and Department of Public Works.

(k) Deferred Payment Based Upon Limited Means. A project applicant may apply to the Department of Public Works for a deferral of payment of the fee applied to a specific unit as described in Subsection (e) for the period beginning when the Department receives a complete application until six (6) months after recordation of the final parcel or subdivision map, provided that for the twelve months prior to the date of application, the applicant resided in his or her unit in the subject property as his or her principal place of residence and the applicant's household income was less than 120% of median income of the City and County of San Francisco as determined by the Mayor's Office of Housing. Prior to the final approval of a parcel or subdivision map for any building where an applicant(s) has obtained a fee deferral, the Department shall cause the recordation of a notice of restrictions or other similar document against the title of all owners of the subject property that guarantees payment of the deferred fee at the time set forth in this Subsection.

(l) Buildings that convert pursuant to this Section shall have no effect on the terms and conditions of Section 1341A , 1385A , or 1396 of this Code. **Leg.H.** 2013, 2014, 2015.

San Francisco Police Department Training Bulletin: Landlord/Tenant Disputes 84-05

Members are frequently called to mediate disputes between

landlords and their tenants. Although many of the problems between landlords and tenants are civil in nature, certain acts by the parties may give rise to violation of a penal statute. The information contained herein is the procedure to be followed when called to a landlord/tenant dispute. This bulletin supersedes and cancels any and all previous bulletins dealing with landlord/tenant disputes.

I. General Provisions

A. When called to a landlord/tenant dispute, members shall:

1. Attempt to determine if a violation of criminal law is involved. If it appears that a crime has been committed, prepare an incident report containing the pertinent facts.

2. If you have probable cause to believe that an offense has occurred in your presence, a citation shall be issued or an arrest made according to the provisions of General Order I-3, Citation Release Policy.

a. Either party may exercise their rights under Penal Code Section 837, Arrests by Private Persons, when the offense(s) in question occurred out of your presence.

3. If you determine an arrest is not to be made, advise the parties of possible civil remedies.

a. The landlord can obtain a lawyer for an eviction lawsuit through the Lawyer Referral Service of the Bar Association of San Francisco, or contact an eviction assistance organization (to help the landlord bring his own eviction lawsuit), or file a lawsuit in Small Claims Court at City Hall.

b. The tenant can obtain a lawyer through the Lawyer Referral Service; or if he/she cannot afford to hire a lawyer, obtain legal assistance or referral through the San Francisco Neighborhood Legal Assistance Foundation.

4. The Sheriff's Department has no jurisdiction in landlord/tenant matters until a landlord obtains a judgment against the tenant in court, and a Writ of Execution has been issued empowering the Sheriff to commence eviction proceedings.

a. The Sheriff's Department loses jurisdiction as soon as the writ is enforced and the premises returned to the landlord's possession.

b. The Sheriff's Department should not be contacted if a court action hasn't been commenced and a writ issued, or the writ has already been served.

B. If a member has any questions regarding a violation of the Penal Code in a particular case, such member shall request the assistance of a supervisor before acting.

II. Facts Related To Landlords

A. Lockouts

1. When a person occupies a room in a residential hotel or an apartment house, and such person has occupied the room for more than 30 days, a lockout or summary removal of such person is a violation of Section 418 of the Penal Code.

a. A tenant may rent by the day or week. The guiding factor is whether the tenant has occupied the premise for an uninterrupted period of more than 30 days.

b. Members should check hotel or motel ledgers, rent receipts and neighbors in order to establish the length of tenancy.

2. If a tenancy for more than 30 days can be established, or if a tenancy of more than 30 days is claimed and your investigation cannot show otherwise, summary removal of the tenant is prohibited. Members shall, in these cases, advise the property owner or agent to obtain a judgment against the tenant, and a Writ of Execution from the court if they wish to evict.

a. The lockout or summary removal of a worker/tenant whose salary includes lodging within a residential hotel, or an apartment house and who has been in possession for more than 30 days, violates Section 418 of the Penal Code.

1) Inquire about the status of the person whom the landlord is attempting to remove if the landlord claims the person has not leased the premises. A worker/tenant may have a verbal agreement for lodging as part of their salary, but may not have a lease.

3. If the property owner or agent refuses to let the tenant enter the premise, he is to be cited for violation of Section 418 of the Penal Code. Once cited, member shall again request that the property owner or agent let the tenant enter the premise. If he refuses, member shall arrest the property owner or agent for a continuing offense.

a. If the landlord is willing to let the tenant into the residence, the tenant may nevertheless insist upon exercising his/her rights under Penal Code Section 837 to arrest the landlord for a violation of Penal Code Section 418.

1) If the tenant does not wish to make a citizen's arrest, decline to act further and allow the matter to proceed civilly.

2) When a citizen's arrest is made, the person shall be cited or booked in accordance with the provisions of General Order I-3, Citation Release Policy .

4. Certain acts by a landlord have been held to give rise to violation of Section 418 of the Penal Code:

a. lock changed,

b. door jammed shut, or;

c. tenant otherwise denied entry to the premises.

B. A landlord may enter the real property of his tenant without the tenant's consent only in the following situations:

1. In an emergency.

2. To make necessary repairs or agreed upon repairs, or to show the property to prospective tenants, purchasers, workmen, contractors, or mortgage holders. The entry may be made only during normal business hours after providing reasonable advance notice to the tenant.

3. When the tenant has moved prior to expiration of the rental term.

4. When a court order authorizing entry is in effect.

Absent one of the above situations, or consent by the tenant, a landlord may be liable for arrest for violation of Section 602 of the Penal Code.

C. The intentional destruction by a landlord of property rented to the tenant may subject the landlord to violation of Section 594 of the Penal Code, Malicious Mischief.

D. Interfering with the gas supply of any hotel, lodging house, apartment house, or any house or building used as a dwelling may subject the landlord to criminal prosecution (Section 959 MPC). Section 961 of the MPC states that the penalty for violation of Section 959 of the MPC is a misdemeanor.

III. Facts Related To Tenants

A. California Penal Code Section 602. Trespasses upon lands enumerated states that, "Every person who willfully commits a trespass by any of the following acts is guilty of a misdemeanor."

1. 602(l) Entering and occupying real property or structures of any kind without the consent of the owner, his agent, or the person in lawful possession thereof.

2. 602(n) Refusing or failing to leave land, real property, or structures belonging to or lawfully occupied by another and not open to the general public, upon being requested to leave by (1) a peace officer and the owner, his agent, or the person in lawful possession thereof, or (2) the owner, his agent, or the person in lawful possession thereof; provided, however, that clause (2) of this subdivision shall not be applicable to persons engaged in lawful labor union activities which are permitted to be carried out on the property by the California Agricultural Labor Relations Act, Part 3.5 (commencing with Section 1140) of Division 2 of the Labor Code, or by the National Labor Relations Act.

B. Whenever members are asked by a property owner or agent to arrest a person for trespassing (602(l) P.C.), members shall handle the situation in the following manner:

1. Ask the alleged trespasser to provide any proof of their right to possession of the premises such as rent receipts, utility bills, cancelled checks processed by the landlord's bank, mail at the subject address or other similar materials.

a. If any material showing a right to possession is produced, however arguable it may be, the burden shifts to the property owner or agent to prove the elements required for a trespass violation.

2. If the person cannot produce any of the materials, but the member has doubts as to the person's status as a trespasser (based upon his investigation), decline to act further, and tell the property owner or agent to proceed civilly.

a. Members should not presume a person to be a trespasser.

3. If you determine that the person is a trespasser, inform the owner or agent that they must make a citizen's arrest if all the elements of the crime have not been committed in your presence.

a. If the owner or agent will not make a citizen's arrest, decline to act further and allow the matter to proceed civilly.

b. When a citizen's arrest is made, the person shall be cited or booked in accordance with the provisions of General Order I-3, Citation Release Policy. The violations charged may be based upon 602(l) or 602.5 P.C.

1) Do not advise a person accused of trespassing that such person can avoid being cited or booked by vacating the premises.

c. If a citation is given and the trespasser still refuses to leave, the refusal creates a continuing offense; the trespasser shall then be booked.

C. A tenant who unlawfully returns to a residence from which he/she has been evicted, and attempts to take possession of such residence is in violation of Section 419 of the Penal Code.

D. The intentional destruction by a tenant of the residential structure or the property rented may subject the tenant to violation of Section 603 or Section 594 of the Penal Code.

IV. Hotels and Motels

A. Penal Code Section 537, Defrauding an Innkeeper, is the appropriate charging section in cases where an occupant defrauds a hotel or motel keeper. If the value of the credit, food or accommodations is $400 or less, a misdemeanor has occurred. If the value of credit, food or accommodations is greater than $400, a felony has occurred.

B. California Penal Code Section 602(r) covers situations in which a party fails to leave a hotel or motel, where such party has obtained accommodations, and has refused to pay for those accommodations upon the request of the proprietor or manager. This section implies that no tenancy has been created (whether 30 days has lapsed or not), and that refusal to pay for such accommodations may be punished criminally.

1. Section 602(r) may be used as the violation charged to cite or book a person who has occupied a hotel or motel room in the situations as described below per Section 1940 of the California Civil Code:

a. Transient occupancy in a hotel, motel, residence club, or other facility when such occupancy is or would be subject to tax under Section 7280 of the Revenue and Taxation Code.

b. When the innkeeper retains a right of access to and control of the dwelling unit, and the hotel or motel provides or offers all of the following services to all of the residents:

1. facilities for safeguarding personal property.

2. central telephone service.

3. central dining, maid, mail, room and recreational services.

4. occupancy for periods less than 7 days.

Remember that it does not matter whether tenant has occupied a room for more than 30 days in this instance. If one of the provisions of sub-section a. or b. is present, no tenancy has been created.

Appendix D: *California Law Excerpts*

See also Appendix C: San Francisco Law Excerpts and Regulations

California Civil Code

§ 7 Holidays

Holidays within the meaning of this code are every Sunday and such other days as are specified or provided for as holidays in the Government Code of the State of California. **Leg.H.** 1872, 1880, 1889, 1893, 1897, 1907, 1909, 1911, 1925, 1955.

§ 11 Extension of Time to Perform Act Required by Law or Contract

Whenever any act of a secular nature, other than a work of necessity or mercy, is appointed by law or contract to be performed upon a particular day, which day falls upon a holiday, it may be performed upon the next business day, with the same effect as if it had been performed upon the day appointed. **Leg.H.** 1872.

§ 789 Estate at Will (30 Day Notice)

A tenancy or other estate at will, however created, may be terminated by the landlord's giving notice in writing to the tenant, in the manner prescribed by Section 1162 of the Code of Civil Procedure, to remove from the premises within a period of not less than 30 days, to be specified in the notice. **Leg.H.** 1872, 1911, 2002.

§ 789.3 Utility Shutoffs and Lockouts

(a) A landlord shall not with intent to terminate the occupancy under any lease or other tenancy or estate at will, however created, of property used by a tenant as his residence willfully cause, directly or indirectly, the interruption or termination of any utility service furnished the tenant, including, but not limited to, water, heat, light, electricity, gas, telephone, elevator, or refrigeration, whether or not the utility service is under the control of the landlord.

(b) In addition, a landlord shall not, with intent to terminate the occupancy under any lease or other tenancy or estate at will, however created, of property used by a tenant as his or her residence, willfully:

(1) Prevent the tenant from gaining reasonable access to the property by changing the locks or using a bootlock or by any other similar method or device;

(2) Remove outside doors or windows; or

(3) Remove from the premises the tenant's personal property, the furnishings, or any other items without the prior written consent of the tenant, except when done pursuant to the procedure set forth in Chapter 5 (commencing with Section 1980) of Title 5 of Part 4 of Division 3.

Nothing in this subdivision shall be construed to prevent the lawful eviction of a tenant by appropriate legal authorities, nor shall anything in this subdivision apply to occupancies defined by subdivision (b) of Section 1940.

(c) Any landlord who violates this section shall be liable to the tenant in a civil action for all of the following:

(1) Actual damages of the tenant.

(2) An amount not to exceed one hundred dollars ($100) for each day or part thereof the landlord remains in violation of this section. In determining the amount of such award, the court shall consider proof of such matters as justice may require; however, in no event shall less than two hundred fifty dollars ($250) be awarded for each separate cause of action. Subsequent or repeated violations, which are not committed contemporaneously with the initial violation, shall be treated as separate causes of action and shall be subject to a separate award of damages.

(d) In any action under subdivision (c) the court shall award reasonable attorney's fees to the prevailing party. In any such action the tenant may seek appropriate injunctive relief to prevent continuing or further violation of the provisions of this section during the pendency of the action. The remedy provided by this section is not exclusive and shall not preclude the tenant from pursuing any other remedy which the tenant may have under any other provision of law. **Leg.H.** 1971, 1979.

§ 827 Change of Rental Agreement Terms in Writing

(a) Except as provided in subdivision (b), in all leases of lands or tenements, or of any interest therein, from week to week, month to month, or other period less than a month, the landlord may, upon giving notice in writing to the tenant, in the manner prescribed by Section 1162 of the Code of Civil Procedure, change the terms of the lease to take effect, as to tenancies for less than one month, upon the expiration of a period at least as long as the term of the hiring itself, and, as to tenancies from month to month, to take effect at the expiration of not less than 30 days, but if that change takes effect within a rental term, the rent accruing from the first day of the term to the date of that change shall be computed at the rental rate obtained immediately prior to that change; provided, however, that it shall be competent for the parties to provide by an agreement in writing that a notice changing the terms thereof may be given at any time not less than seven days before the expiration of a term, to be effective upon the expiration of the term.

The notice, when served upon the tenant, shall in and of itself operate and be effectual to create and establish, as a part of the lease, the terms, rents, and conditions specified in the notice, if the tenant shall continue to hold the premises after the notice takes effect.

(b) (1) In all leases of a residential dwelling, or of any interest therein, from week to week, month to month, or other period less than a month, the landlord may increase the rent provided in the lease or rental agreement, upon giving written notice to the tenant, as follows, by either of the following procedures:

(A) By delivering a copy to the tenant personally.

(B) By serving a copy by mail under the procedures prescribed in Section 1013 of the Code of Civil Procedure.

(2) If the proposed rent increase for that tenant is 10 percent or less of the rental amount charged to that tenant at any time during the 12 months before the effective date of the increase, either in and of itself or when combined with any other rent increases for the 12 months before the effective date of the increase, the notice shall be delivered at least 30 days before the effective date of the increase, and subject to Section 1013 of the Code of Civil Procedure if served by mail.

(3) (A) If the proposed rent increase for that tenant is greater than 10 percent of the rental amount charged to that tenant at any time during the 12 months before the effective date of the increase, either in and of itself or when combined with any other rent increases for the 12 months before the effective date of the increase, the notice shall be delivered at least 90 days before the effective date of the increase, and subject to Section 1013 of the Code of Civil Procedure if served by mail.

(B) If the proposed rent increase for that tenant is caused by a change in a tenant's income or family composition as determined by a recertification required by statute or regulation, the notice shall be delivered at least 30 days before the effective date of the increase as described in paragraph (2), and subparagraph (A) of this paragraph shall not apply.

(c) If a state or federal statute, state or federal regulation, recorded regulatory agreement, or contract provides for a longer period of notice regarding a rent increase than that provided in subdivision (a) or (b), the personal service or mailing of the notice shall be in accordance with the longer period. **Leg.H.** 1874, 1907, 1929, 1937, 1939, 1947, 2000, 2001, 2002, 2004, 2019.

§ 1499 *Right to Receipt*

A debtor has a right to require from his creditor a written receipt for any property delivered in performance of his obligation. **Leg.H.** 1872.

§ 1500 *Constructive Acceptance of Payment*

An obligation for the payment of money is extinguished by a due offer of payment, if the amount is immediately deposited in the name of the creditor, with some bank or savings and loan association within this state, of good repute, and notice thereof is given to the creditor. **Leg.H.** 1872, 1981..

§ 1697 *Modification of Oral Contract*

A contract not in writing may be modified in any respect by consent of the parties, in writing, without a new consideration, and is extinguished thereby to the extent of the modification. **Leg.H.** 1872, 1873-74, 1976.

§ 1698 *Modification of Written Contract*

(a) A contract in writing may be modified by a contract in writing.

(b) A contract in writing may be modified by an oral agreement to the extent that the oral agreement is executed by the parties.

(c) Unless the contract otherwise expressly provides, a contract in writing may be modified by an oral agreement supported by new consideration. The statute of frauds (Section 1624) is required to be satisfied if the contract as modified is within its provisions.

(d) Nothing in this section precludes in an appropriate case the application of rules of law concerning estoppel, oral novation and substitution of a new agreement, rescission of a written contract by an oral agreement, waiver of a provision of a written contract, or oral independent collateral contracts. **Leg.H.** 1976.

§ 1927 *Warranty of Quiet Possession*

An agreement to let upon hire binds the letter to secure to the hirer the quiet possession of the thing hired during the term of the hiring against all persons lawfully claiming the same. **Leg.H.** 1872.

§ 1929 *Hirer's Duty for Repair*

The hirer of a thing must repair all deteriorations or injuries thereto occasioned by his want of ordinary care. **Leg.H.** 1872, 1905.

§ 1940 *Establishing Tenancy*

(a) Except as provided in subdivision (b), this chapter shall apply to all persons who hire dwelling units located within this state including tenants, lessees, boarders, lodgers, and others, however denominated.

(b) The term "persons who hire" shall not include a person who maintains either of the following:

(1) Transient occupancy in a hotel, motel, residence club, or other facility when the transient occupancy is or would be subject to tax under Section 7280 of the Revenue and Taxation Code. The term "persons who hire" shall not include a person to whom this paragraph pertains if the person has not made valid payment for all room and other related charges owing as of the last day on which his or her occupancy is or would be subject to tax under Section 7280 of the Revenue and Taxation Code.

(2) Occupancy at a hotel or motel where the innkeeper retains a right of access to and control of the dwelling unit and the hotel or motel provides or offers all of the following services to all of the residents:

(A) Facilities for the safeguarding of personal property pursuant to Section 1860.

(B) Central telephone service subject to tariffs covering the same filed with the California Public Utilities Commission.

(C) Maid, mail, and room services.

(D) Occupancy for periods of less than seven days.

(E) Food service provided by a food establishment, as defined in Section 113780 of the Health and Safety Code, located on or adjacent to the premises of the hotel or motel and owned or operated by the innkeeper or owned or operated by a person or entity pursuant to a lease or similar relationship with the innkeeper or person or entity affiliated with the innkeeper.

(c) "Dwelling unit" means a structure or the part of a structure that is used as a home, residence, or sleeping place by one person who maintains a household or by two or more persons who maintain a common household.

(d) Nothing in this section shall be construed to limit the application of any provision of this chapter to tenancy in a dwelling unit unless the provision is so limited by its specific terms. **Leg.H.** 1976, 1994, 1996.

§ 1940.1 Evading Tenancy in Residential Hotels

(a) No person may require an occupant of a residential hotel, as defined in Section 50519 of the Health and Safety Code, to move, or to check out and reregister, before the expiration of 30 days occupancy if a purpose is to have that occupant maintain

transient occupancy status pursuant to paragraph (1) of subdivision (b) of Section 1940. Evidence that an occupant was required to check out and reregister shall create a rebuttable presumption, which shall affect solely the burden of producing evidence, of the purpose referred to in this subdivision.

(b) In addition to any remedies provided by local ordinance, any violation of subdivision (a) is punishable by a civil penalty of five hundred dollars ($500). In any action brought pursuant to this section, the prevailing party shall be entitled to reasonable attorney's fees.

(c) Nothing in this section shall prevent a local governing body from establishing inspection authority or reporting or recordkeeping requirements to ensure compliance with this section. **Leg.H.** 1990, 1991, 2004.

§ 1940.2 Unlawful Actions by Landlord to Influence Tenant to Vacate

(a) It is unlawful for a landlord to do any of the following for the purpose of influencing a tenant to vacate a dwelling:

(1) Engage in conduct that violates subdivision (a) of Section 484 of the Penal Code.

(2) Engage in conduct that violates Section 518 of the Penal Code.

(3) Use, or threaten to use, force, willful threats, or menacing conduct constituting a course of conduct that interferes with the tenant's quiet enjoyment of the premises in violation of Section 1927 that would create an apprehension of harm in a reasonable person. Nothing in this paragraph requires a tenant to be actually or constructively evicted in order to obtain relief.

(4) Commit a significant and intentional violation of Section 1954.

(b) A tenant who prevails in a civil action, including an action in small claims court, to enforce his or her rights under this section is entitled to a civil penalty in an amount not to exceed two thousand dollars ($2,000) for each violation.

(c) An oral or written warning notice, given in good faith, regarding conduct by a tenant, occupant, or guest that violates, may violate, or violated the applicable rental agreement, rules, regulations, lease, or laws, is not a violation of this section. An oral or written explanation of the rental agreement, rules, regulations, lease, or laws given in the normal course of business is not a violation of this section.

(d) Nothing in this section shall enlarge or diminish a landlord's right to terminate a tenancy pursuant to existing state or local law; nor shall this section enlarge or diminish any ability of local government to regulate or enforce a prohibition against a landlord's harassment of a tenant. **Leg.H.** 2003.

§ 1940.6 *Demolition Permit Application Notice*

(a) The owner of a residential dwelling unit or the owner's agent who applies to any public agency for a permit to demolish that residential dwelling unit shall give written notice of that fact to:

(1) A prospective tenant prior to the occurrence of any of the following actions by the owner or the owner's agent:

(A) Entering into a rental agreement with a prospective tenant.

(B) Requiring or accepting payment from the prospective tenant for an application screening fee, as provided in Section 1950.6.

(C) Requiring or accepting any other fees from a prospective tenant.

(D) Requiring or accepting any writings that would initiate a tenancy.

(2) A current tenant, including a tenant who has entered into a rental agreement but has not yet taken possession of the dwelling unit, prior to applying to the public agency for the permit to demolish that residential dwelling unit.

(b) The notice shall include the earliest possible approximate date on which the owner expects the demolition to occur and the approximate date on which the owner will terminate the tenancy. However, in no case may the demolition for which the owner or the owner's agent has applied occur prior to the earliest possible approximate date noticed.

(c) If a landlord fails to comply with subdivision (a) or (b), a tenant may bring an action in a court of competent jurisdiction. The remedies the court may order shall include, but are not limited to, the following:

(1) In the case of a prospective tenant who moved into a residential dwelling unit and was not informed as required by subdivision (a) or (b), the actual damages suffered, moving expenses, and a civil penalty not to exceed two thousand five hundred dollars ($2,500) to be paid by the landlord to the tenant.

(2) In the case of a current tenant who was not informed as required by subdivision (a) or (b), the actual damages suffered, and a civil penalty not to exceed two thousand five hundred dollars ($2,500) to be paid by the landlord to the tenant.

(3) In any action brought pursuant to this section, the prevailing party shall be entitled to reasonable attorney's fees.

(d) The remedies available under this section are cumulative to other remedies available under law.

(e) This section shall not be construed to preempt other laws regarding landlord obligations or disclosures, including, but not limited to, those arising pursuant to Chapter 12.75 (commencing with Section 7060) of Division 7 of Title 1 of the Government Code.

(f) For purposes of this section:

(1) "Residential dwelling unit" has the same meaning as that contained in Section 1940.

(2) "Public agency" has the same meaning as that contained in Section 21063 of the Public Resources Code. **Leg.H.** 2002.

§ 1940.9 *Failure to Provide Separate Gas and Electric Meters for Each Dwelling Unit — Disclosure to Tenant*

(a) If the landlord does not provide separate gas and electric meters for each tenant's dwelling unit so that each tenant's meter measures only the electric or gas service to that tenant's dwelling unit and the landlord or his or her agent has knowledge that gas or electric service provided through a tenant's meter serves an area outside the tenant's dwelling unit, the landlord, prior to the inception of the tenancy or upon discovery, shall explicitly disclose that condition to the tenant and shall do either of the following:

(1) Execute a mutual written agreement with the tenant for payment by the tenant of the cost of the gas or electric service provided through the tenant's meter to serve areas outside the tenant's dwelling unit.

(2) Make other arrangements, as are mutually agreed in writing, for payment for the gas or electric service provided through the tenant's meter to serve areas outside the tenant's dwelling unit. These arrangements may include, but are not limited to, the landlord becoming the customer of record for the tenant's meter, or the landlord separately metering and becoming the customer of record for the area outside the tenant's dwelling unit.

(b) If a landlord fails to comply with subdivision (a), the aggrieved tenant may bring an action in a court of competent jurisdiction. The remedies the court may order shall include, but are not limited to, the following:

(1) Requiring the landlord to be made the customer of record with the utility for the tenant's meter.

(2) Ordering the landlord to reimburse the tenant for payments made by the tenant to the utility for service to areas outside of the tenant's dwelling-unit. Payments to be reimbursed pursuant to this paragraph shall commence from the date the

obligation to disclose arose under subdivision (a).

(c) Nothing in this section limits any remedies available to a landlord or tenant under other provisions of this chapter, the rental agreement, or applicable statutory or common law. **Leg.H.** 1989.

§ 1941 *Landlord to Keep Building Fit for Occupancy*

The lessor of a building intended for the occupation of human beings must, in the absence of an agreement to the contrary, put it into a condition fit for such occupation, and repair all subsequent dilapidations thereof, which render it untenantable, except such as are mentioned in section nineteen hundred and twenty-nine. **Leg.H.** 1872, 1874.

§ 1941.1 *Habitation Standard Characteristics*

(a) A dwelling shall be deemed untenantable for purposes of Section 1941 if it substantially lacks any of the following affirmative standard characteristics or is a residential unit described in Section 17920.3 or 17920.10 of the Health and Safety Code:

(1) Effective waterproofing and weather protection of roof and exterior walls, including unbroken windows and doors.

(2) Plumbing or gas facilities that conformed to applicable law in effect at the time of installation, maintained in good working order.

(3) A water supply approved under applicable law that is under the control of the tenant, capable of producing hot and cold running water, or a system that is under the control of the landlord, that produces hot and cold running water, furnished to appropriate fixtures, and connected to a sewage disposal system approved under applicable law.

(4) Heating facilities that conformed with applicable law at the time of installation, maintained in good working order.

(5) Electrical lighting, with wiring and electrical equipment that conformed with applicable law at the time of installation, maintained in good working order.

(6) Building, grounds, and appurtenances at the time of the commencement of the lease or rental agreement, and all areas under control of the landlord, kept in every part clean, sanitary, and free from all accumulations of debris, filth, rubbish, garbage, rodents, and vermin.

(7) An adequate number of appropriate receptacles for garbage and rubbish, in clean condition and good repair at the time of the commencement of the lease or rental agreement, with the landlord providing appropriate serviceable receptacles thereafter and being responsible for the clean condition and good repair of the receptacles under his or her control.

(8) Floors, stairways, and railings maintained in good repair.

(9) A locking mail receptacle for each residential unit in a residential hotel, as required by Section 17958.3 of the Health and Safety Code. This subdivision shall become operative on July 1, 2008.

(b) Nothing in this section shall be interpreted to prohibit a tenant or owner of rental properties from qualifying for a utility energy savings assistance program, or any other program assistance, for heating or hot water system repairs or replacement, or a combination of heating and hot water system repairs or replacements, that would achieve energy savings. **Leg.H.** 1970, 1979, 2002, 2007, 2012.

§ 1941.2 *Tenant Violation of Rental Obligations*

(a) No duty on the part of the landlord to repair a dilapidation shall arise under Section 1941 or 1942 if the tenant is in substantial violation of any of the following affirmative obligations, provided the tenant's violation contributes substantially to the existence of the dilapidation or interferes substantially with the landlord's obligation under Section 1941 to effect the necessary repairs:

(1) To keep that part of the premises which he occupies and uses clean and sanitary as the condition of the premises permits.

(2) To dispose from his dwelling unit of all rubbish, garbage and other waste, in a clean and sanitary manner.

(3) To properly use and operate all electrical, gas and plumbing fixtures and keep them as clean and sanitary as their condition permits.

(4) Not to permit any person on the premises, with his permission, to willfully or wantonly destroy, deface, damage, impair or remove any part of the structure or dwelling unit or the facilities, equipment, or appurtenances thereto, nor himself do any such thing.

(5) To occupy the premises as his abode, utilizing portions thereof for living, sleeping, cooking or dining purposes only which were respectively designed or intended to be used for such occupancies.

(b) Paragraphs (1) and (2) of subdivision (a) shall not apply if the landlord has expressly agreed in writing to perform the act or acts mentioned therein. **Leg.H.** 1970, 1979.

§ 1941.4 *Telephone Wiring*

The lessor of a building intended for the residential occupation of human beings shall be responsible for installing at least one usable telephone jack and for placing and maintaining the inside telephone wiring in good working order, shall ensure that the inside telephone wiring meets the applicable standards of the most recent California Electrical Code, and shall make any required repairs. The lessor shall not restrict or interfere with access by the telephone utility to its telephone network facilities up to the demarcation point separating the inside wiring.

"Inside telephone" for purposes of this section, means that portion of the telephone wire that connects the telephone equipment at the customer's premises to the telephone network at a demarcation point determined by the telephone corporation in accordance with orders of the Public Utilities Commission. **Leg.H.** 1991, 2013.

§ 1941.5 *Lock Change for Protected Tenant Not in Same Unit as Tenant with Restraining Order*

(a) This section shall apply if a person who is restrained from contact with the protected tenant under a court order or is named in a police report is not a tenant of the same dwelling unit as the protected tenant.

(b) A landlord shall change the locks of a protected tenant's dwelling unit upon written request of the protected tenant not later than 24 hours after the protected tenant gives the landlord a copy of a court order or police report, and shall give the protected tenant a key to the new locks.

(c) (1) If a landlord fails to change the locks within 24 hours, the protected tenant may change the locks without the landlord's permission, notwithstanding any provision in the lease to the contrary.

(2) If the protected tenant changes the locks pursuant to this subdivision, the protected tenant shall do all of the following:

(A) Change the locks in a workmanlike manner with locks of similar or better quality than the original lock.

(B) Notify the landlord within 24 hours that the locks have been changed.

(C) Provide the landlord with a key by any reasonable method agreed upon by the landlord and protected tenant.

(3) This subdivision shall apply to leases executed on or after the date the act that added this section takes effect.

(d) For the purposes of this section, the following definitions shall apply:

(1) "Court order" means a court order lawfully issued within the last 180 days pursuant to Section 527.6 of the Code of Civil Procedure, Part 3 (commencing with Section 6240), Part 4 (commencing with Section 6300), or Part 5 (commencing

with Section 6400) of Division 10 of the Family Code, Section 136.2 of the Penal Code, or Section 213.5 of the Welfare and Institutions Code.

(2) "Locks" means any exterior lock that provides access to the dwelling.

(3) "Police report" means a written report, written within the last 180 days, by a peace officer employed by a state or local law enforcement agency acting in his or her official capacity, stating that the protected tenant or a household member has filed a report alleging that the protected tenant or the household member is a victim of domestic violence, sexual assault, or stalking.

(4) "Protected tenant" means a tenant who has obtained a court order or has a copy of a police report.

(5) "Tenant" means tenant, subtenant, lessee, or sublessee. **Leg.H.** 2010.

§ 1941.6 *Lock Change for Protected Tenant in Same Unit as Tenant with Restraining Order*

(a) This section shall apply if a person who is restrained from contact with a protected tenant under a court order is a tenant of the same dwelling unit as the protected tenant.

(b) A landlord shall change the locks of a protected tenant's dwelling unit upon written request of the protected tenant not later than 24 hours after the protected tenant gives the landlord a copy of a court order that excludes from the dwelling unit the restrained person referred to in subdivision (a). The landlord shall give the protected tenant a key to the new locks.

(c) (1) If a landlord fails to change the locks within 24 hours, the protected tenant may change the locks without the landlord's permission, notwithstanding any provision in the lease to the contrary.

(2) If the protected tenant changes the locks pursuant to this subdivision, the protected tenant shall do all of the following:

(A) Change the locks in a workmanlike manner with locks of similar or better quality than the original lock.

(B) Notify the landlord within 24 hours that the locks have been changed.

(C) Provide the landlord with a key by any reasonable method agreed upon by the landlord and protected tenant.

(3) This subdivision shall apply to leases executed on or after the date the act that added this section takes effect.

(d) Notwithstanding Section 789.3, if the locks are changed

pursuant to this section, the landlord is not liable to a person excluded from the dwelling unit pursuant to this section.

(e) A person who has been excluded from a dwelling unit under this section remains liable under the lease with all other tenants of the dwelling unit for rent as provided in the lease.

(f) For the purposes of this section, the following definitions shall apply:

(1) "Court order" means a court order lawfully issued within the last 180 days pursuant to Section 527.6 of the Code of Civil Procedure, Part 3 (commencing with Section 6240), Part 4 (commencing with Section 6300), or Part 5 (commencing with Section 6400) of Division 10 of the Family Code, Section 136.2 of the Penal Code, or Section 213.5 of the Welfare and Institutions Code.

(2) "Locks" means any exterior lock that provides access to the dwelling.

(3) "Protected tenant" means a tenant who has obtained a court order.

(4) "Tenant" means tenant, subtenant, lessee, or sublessee. **Leg.H.** 2010.

§ 1942 *Repair and Deduct or Vacate*

(a) If within a reasonable time after written or oral notice to the landlord or his agent, as defined in subdivision (a) of Section 1962, of dilapidations rendering the premises untenantable which the landlord ought to repair, the landlord neglects to do so, the tenant may repair the same himself where the cost of such repairs does not require an expenditure more than one month's rent of the premises and deduct the expenses of such repairs from the rent when due, or the tenant may vacate the premises, in which case the tenant shall be discharged from further payment of rent, or performance of other conditions as of the date of vacating the premises. This remedy shall not be available to the tenant more than twice in any 12-month period.

(b) For the purposes of this section, if a tenant acts to repair and deduct after the 30th day following notice, he is presumed to have acted after a reasonable time. The presumption established by this subdivision is a rebuttable presumption affecting the burden of producing evidence and shall not be construed to prevent a tenant from repairing and deducting after a shorter notice if all the circumstances require shorter notice.

(c) The tenant's remedy under subdivision (a) shall not be available if the condition was caused by the violation of Section 1929 or 1941.2.

(d) The remedy provided by this section is in addition to any other remedy provided by this chapter, the rental agreement, or other applicable statutory or common law. **Leg.H.** 1872, 1874, 1970, 1979.

§ 1942.1 *Waiver of Rights; Public Policy*

Any agreement by a lessee of a dwelling waiving or modifying his rights under Section 1941 or 1942 shall be void as contrary to public policy with respect to any condition which renders the premises untenantable, except that the lessor and the lessee may agree that the lessee shall undertake to improve, repair or maintain all or stipulated portions of the dwelling as part of the consideration for rental.

The lessor and lessee may, if an agreement is in writing, set forth the provisions of Sections 1941 to 1942.1, inclusive, and provide that any controversy relating to a condition of the premises claimed to make them untenantable may by application of either party be submitted to arbitration, pursuant to the provisions of Title 9 (commencing with Section 1280), Part 3 of the Code of Civil Procedure, and that the costs of such arbitration shall be apportioned by the arbitrator between the parties. **Leg.H.** 1970.

§ 1942.3 *Unlawful Detainer Actions — Presumption of Breach of Habitability Requirements; Conditions*

(a) In any unlawful detainer action by the landlord to recover possession from a tenant, a rebuttable presumption affecting the burden of producing evidence that the landlord has breached the habitability requirements in Section 1941 is created if all of the following conditions exist:

(1) The dwelling substantially lacks any of the affirmative standard characteristics listed in Section 1941.1, is deemed and declared substandard pursuant to Section 17920.3 of the Health and Safety Code, or contains lead hazards as defined in Section 17920.10 of the Health and Safety Code.

(2) A public officer or employee who is responsible for the enforcement of any housing law has notified the landlord, or an agent of the landlord, in a written notice issued after inspection of the premises which informs the landlord of his or her obligation to abate the nuisance or repair the substandard or unsafe conditions identified under the authority described in paragraph (1).

(3) The conditions have existed and have not been abated 60 days beyond the date of issuance of the notice specified in paragraph (2) and the delay is without good cause.

(4) The conditions were not caused by an act or omission of the tenant or lessee in violation of Section 1929 or 1941.2.

(b) The presumption specified in subdivision (a) does not arise unless all of the conditions set forth therein are proven, but failure to so establish the presumption shall not otherwise affect the right of the tenant to raise and pursue any defense based on the landlord's breach of the implied warranty of habitability.

(c) The presumption provided in this section shall apply only to rental agreements or leases entered into or renewed on or after January 1, 1986. **Leg.H.** 1985, 2005.

§ 1942.4 *Collection of Rent for Untenantable Dwelling — Penalties*

(a) A landlord of a dwelling may not demand rent, collect rent, issue a notice of a rent increase, or issue a three-day notice to pay rent or quit pursuant to subdivision (2) of Section 1161 of the Code of Civil Procedure, if all of the following conditions exist prior to the landlord's demand or notice:

(1) The dwelling substantially lacks any of the affirmative standard characteristics listed in Section 1941.1 or violates Section 17920.10 of the Health and Safety Code, or is deemed and declared substandard as set forth in Section 17920.3 of the Health and Safety Code because conditions listed in that section exist to an extent that endangers the life, limb, health, property, safety, or welfare of the public or the occupants of the dwelling.

(2) A public officer or employee who is responsible for the enforcement of any housing law, after inspecting the premises, has notified the landlord or the landlord's agent in writing of his or her obligations to abate the nuisance or repair the substandard conditions.

(3) The conditions have existed and have not been abated 35 days beyond the date of service of the notice specified in paragraph (2) and the delay is without good cause. For purposes of this subdivision, service shall be complete at the time of deposit in the United States mail.

(4) The conditions were not caused by an act or omission of the tenant or lessee in violation of Section 1929 or 1941.2.

(b)(1) A landlord who violates this section is liable to the tenant or lessee for the actual damages sustained by the tenant or lessee and special damages of not less than one hundred dollars ($100) and not more than five thousand dollars ($5,000).

(2) The prevailing party shall be entitled to recovery of reasonable attorney's fees and costs of the suit in an amount fixed by the court.

(c) Any court that awards damages under this section may also order the landlord to abate any nuisance at the rental dwelling and to repair any substandard conditions of the rental dwelling, as defined in Section 1941.1, which significantly or materially affect the health or safety of the occupants of the rental dwelling and are uncorrected. If the court orders repairs or corrections, or both, the court's jurisdiction continues over the matter for the purpose of ensuring compliance.

(d) The tenant or lessee shall be under no obligation to undertake any other remedy prior to exercising his or her rights under this section.

(e) Any action under this section may be maintained in small claims court if the claim does not exceed the jurisdictional limit of that court.

(f) The remedy provided by this section may be utilized in addition to any other remedy provided by this chapter, the rental agreement, lease, or other applicable statutory or common law. Nothing in this section shall require any landlord to comply with this section if he or she pursues his or her rights pursuant to Chapter 12.75 (commencing with Section 7060) of Division 7 of Title 1 of the Government Code. **Leg.H.** 1985, 1990, 1992, 1993, 2003.

§ 1942.5 *Retaliation for Exercise of Tenant Rights*

(a) If the lessor retaliates against the lessee because of the exercise by the lessee of the lessee's rights under this chapter or because of the lessee's complaint to an appropriate agency as to tenantability of a dwelling, and if the lessee of a dwelling is not in default as to the payment of rent, the lessor may not recover possession of a dwelling in any action or proceeding, cause the lessee to quit involuntarily, increase the rent, or decrease any services within 180 days of any of the following:

(1) After the date upon which the lessee, in good faith, has given notice pursuant to Section 1942, has provided notice of a suspected bed bug infestation, or has made an oral complaint to the lessor regarding tenantability.

(2) After the date upon which the lessee, in good faith, has filed a written complaint, or an oral complaint which is registered or otherwise recorded in writing, with an appropriate agency, of which the lessor has notice, for the purpose of obtaining correction of a condition relating to tenantability.

(3) After the date of an inspection or issuance of a citation, resulting from a complaint described in paragraph (2) of which the lessor did not have notice.

(4) After the filing of appropriate documents commencing a judicial or arbitration proceeding involving the issue of tenantability.

(5) After entry of judgment or the signing of an arbitration award, if any, when in the judicial proceeding or arbitration the issue of tenantability is determined adversely to the lessor.

In each instance, the 180-day period shall run from the latest applicable date referred to in paragraphs (1) to (5), inclusive.

(b) A lessee may not invoke subdivision (a) more than once in any 12-month period.

(c) To report, or to threaten to report, the lessee or individuals known to the landlord to be associated with the lessee to immigration authorities is a form of retaliatory conduct prohibited under subdivision (a). This subdivision shall in no way limit the definition of retaliatory conduct prohibited under this section.

(d) Notwithstanding subdivision (a), it is unlawful for a lessor to increase rent, decrease services, cause a lessee to quit involuntarily, bring an action to recover possession, or threaten to do any of those acts, for the purpose of retaliating against the lessee because the lessee has lawfully organized or participated in a lessees' association or an organization advocating lessees' rights or has lawfully and peaceably exercised any rights under the law. In an action brought by or against the lessee pursuant to this subdivision, the lessee shall bear the burden of producing evidence that the lessor's conduct was, in fact, retaliatory.

(e) To report, or to threaten to report, the lessee or individuals known to the landlord to be associated with the lessee to immigration authorities is a form of retaliatory conduct prohibited under subdivision (d). This subdivision shall in no way limit the definition of retaliatory conduct prohibited under this section.

(f) This section does not limit in any way the exercise by the lessor of the lessor's rights under any lease or agreement or any law pertaining to the hiring of property or the lessor's right to do any of the acts described in subdivision (a) or (d) for any lawful cause. Any waiver by a lessee of the lessee's rights under this section is void as contrary to public policy.

(g) Notwithstanding subdivisions (a) to (f), inclusive, a lessor may recover possession of a dwelling and do any of the other acts described in subdivision (a) within the period or periods prescribed therein, or within subdivision (d), if the notice of termination, rent increase, or other act, and any pleading or statement of issues in an arbitration, if any, states the ground upon which the lessor, in good faith, seeks to recover possession, increase rent, or do any of the other acts described in subdivision (a) or (d). If the statement is controverted, the lessor shall establish its truth at the trial or other hearing.

(h) Any lessor or agent of a lessor who violates this section shall be liable to the lessee in a civil action for all of the following:

(1) The actual damages sustained by the lessee.

(2) Punitive damages in an amount of not less than one hundred dollars ($100) nor more than two thousand dollars

($2,000) for each retaliatory act where the lessor or agent has been guilty of fraud, oppression, or malice with respect to that act.

(i) In any action brought for damages for retaliatory eviction, the court shall award reasonable attorney's fees to the prevailing party if either party requests attorney's fees upon the initiation of the action.

(j) The remedies provided by this section shall be in addition to any other remedies provided by statutory or decisional law.

(k) A lessor does not violate subdivision (c) or (e) by complying with any legal obligation under any federal government program that provides for rent limitations or rental assistance to a qualified tenant.

(l) This section shall become operative on October 1, 2021. **Leg.H.** 1979, 2003, 2016, 2017, 2021.

§ 1944 *Length of Rental Period*

A hiring of lodgings or a dwelling-house for an unspecified term is presumed to have been for such length of time as the parties adopt for the estimation of the rent. Thus a hiring at a monthly rate of rent is presumed to be for one month. In the absence of any agreement respecting the length of time or the rent, the hiring is presumed to be monthly. **Leg.H.** 1872.

§ 1945 *Implied Renewal of Rental Agreement*

If a lessee of real property remains in possession thereof after the expiration of the hiring, and the lessor accepts rent from him the parties are presumed to have renewed the hiring on the same terms and for the same time, not exceeding one month when the rent is payable monthly nor in any case one year. **Leg.H.** 1872.

§ 1945.5 *Automatic Extension of Lease*

Notwithstanding any other provision of law, any term of a lease executed after the effective date of this section for the hiring of residential real property which provides for the automatic renewal or extension of the lease for all or part of the full term of the lease if the lessee remains in possession after the expiration of the lease or fails to give notice of his intent not to renew or extend before the expiration of the lease shall be voidable by the party who did not prepare the lease unless such renewal or extension provision appears in at least eight-point boldface type, if the contract is printed, in the body of the lease agreement and a recital of the fact that such provision is contained in the body of the agreement appears in at least eight-point boldface type, if the contract is printed, immediately prior to the place where the lessee executes the agreement. In such case, the presumption in Section 1945 of this code shall apply.

Any waiver of the provisions of this section is void as against public policy. **Leg.H.** 1965 c. 1664 operative 1/30/66, 1976.

§ 1946 *Notice Required to Terminate Tenancy*

A hiring of real property, for a term not specified by the parties, is deemed to be renewed as stated in Section 1945, at the end of the term implied by law unless one of the parties gives written notice to the other of that party's intention to terminate the same, at least as long before the expiration thereof as the term of the hiring itself, not exceeding 30 days; provided, however, that as to tenancies from month to month either of the parties may terminate the same by giving at least 30 days' written notice thereof at any time and the rent shall be due and payable to and including the date of termination. It shall be competent for the parties to provide by an agreement at the time the tenancy is created that a notice of the intention to terminate the same may be given at any time not less than seven days before the expiration of the term thereof. The notice herein required shall be given in the manner prescribed in Section 1162 of the Code of Civil Procedure or by sending a copy by certified or registered mail addressed to the other party. In addition, the lessee may give the notice by sending a copy by certified or registered mail addressed to the agent of the lessor to whom the lessee has paid the rent for the month prior to the date of the notice or by delivering a copy to the agent personally. The notice given by the lessor shall also contain, in substantially the same form, the following:

"State law permits former tenants to reclaim abandoned personal property left at the former address of the tenant, subject to certain conditions. You may or may not be able to reclaim property without incurring additional costs, depending on the cost of storing the property and the length of time before it is reclaimed. In general, these costs will be lower the sooner you contact your former landlord after being notified that property belonging to you was left behind after you moved out." **Leg.H.** 1872, 1931, 1937, 1941, 1947, 1969, 1973, 2012, 2018.

§ 1946.1 *Length of Notice Required to Terminate Tenancy*

(a) Notwithstanding Section 1946, a hiring of residential real property for a term not specified by the parties, is deemed to be renewed as stated in Section 1945, at the end of the term implied by law unless one of the parties gives written notice to the other of his or her intention to terminate the tenancy, as provided in this section.

(b) An owner of a residential dwelling giving notice pursuant to this section shall give notice at least 60 days prior to the proposed date of termination. A tenant giving notice pursuant to this section shall give notice for a period at least as long as the term of the periodic tenancy prior to the proposed date of termination.

(c) Notwithstanding subdivision (b), an owner of a residential dwelling giving notice pursuant to this section shall give notice at least 30 days prior to the proposed date of termination if any tenant or resident has resided in the dwelling for less than one year.

(d) Notwithstanding subdivision (b), an owner of a residential dwelling giving notice pursuant to this section shall give notice at least 30 days prior to the proposed date of termination if all of the following apply:

(1) The dwelling or unit is alienable separate from the title to any other dwelling unit.

(2) The owner has contracted to sell the dwelling or unit to a bona fide purchaser for value, and has established an escrow with a title insurer or an underwritten title company, as defined in Sections 12340.4 and 12340.5 of the Insurance Code, respectively, a licensed escrow agent, as defined in Sections 17004 and 17200 of the Financial Code, or a licensed real estate broker, as defined in Section 10131 of the Business and Professions Code.

(3) The purchaser is a natural person or persons.

(4) The notice is given no more than 120 days after the escrow has been established.

(5) Notice was not previously given to the tenant pursuant to this section.

(6) The purchaser in good faith intends to reside in the property for at least one full year after the termination of the tenancy.

(e) After an owner has given notice of his or her intention to terminate the tenancy pursuant to this section, a tenant may also give notice of his or her intention to terminate the tenancy pursuant to this section, provided that the tenant's notice is for a period at least as long as the term of the periodic tenancy and the proposed date of termination occurs before the owner's proposed date of termination.

(f) The notices required by this section shall be given in the manner prescribed in Section 1162 of the Code of Civil Procedure or by sending a copy by certified or registered mail.

(g) This section may not be construed to affect the authority of a public entity that otherwise exists to regulate or monitor the basis for eviction.

(h) Any notice given by an owner pursuant to this section shall contain, in substantially the same form, the following:

"State law permits former tenants to reclaim abandoned personal property left at the former address of the tenant, subject to certain conditions. You may or may not be able to reclaim property without incurring additional costs, depending on the cost of storing the property and the length of time before it is reclaimed. In general, these costs will be lower the sooner you contact your former landlord after being notified that property belonging to you was left behind after you moved out." **Leg.H.** 2006, 2009, 2012.

§ 1946.2 *Just Cause Eviction*

(a) Notwithstanding any other law, after a tenant has continuously and lawfully occupied a residential real property for 12 months, the owner of the residential real property shall not terminate the tenancy without just cause, which shall be stated in the written notice to terminate tenancy. If any additional adult tenants are added to the lease before an existing tenant has continuously and lawfully occupied the residential real property for 24 months, then this subdivision shall only apply if either of the following are satisfied:

(1) All of the tenants have continuously and lawfully occupied the residential real property for 12 months or more.

(2) One or more tenants have continuously and lawfully occupied the residential real property for 24 months or more.

(b) For purposes of this section, "just cause" includes either of the following:

(1) At-fault just cause, which is any of the following:

(A) Default in the payment of rent.

(B) A breach of a material term of the lease, as described in paragraph (3) of Section 1161 of the Code of Civil Procedure, including, but not limited to, violation of a provision of the lease after being issued a written notice to correct the violation.

(C) Maintaining, committing, or permitting the maintenance or commission of a nuisance as described in paragraph (4) of Section 1161 of the Code of Civil Procedure.

(D) Committing waste as described in paragraph (4) of Section 1161 of the Code of Civil Procedure.

(E) The tenant had a written lease that terminated on or after January 1, 2020, or January 1, 2022, if the lease is for a tenancy in a mobilehome, and after a written request or demand from the owner, the tenant has refused to execute a written extension or renewal of the lease for an additional term of similar duration with similar provisions, provided that those terms do not violate this section or any other provision of law.

(F) Criminal activity by the tenant on the residential real property, including any common areas, or any criminal activity or criminal threat, as defined in subdivision (a) of Section 422 of the Penal Code, on or off the residential real property, that is directed at any owner or agent of the owner of the residential real property.

(G) Assigning or subletting the premises in violation of the tenant's lease, as described in paragraph (4) of Section 1161 of the Code of Civil Procedure.

(H) The tenant's refusal to allow the owner to enter the residential real property as authorized by Sections 1101.5 and 1954 of this code, and Sections 13113.7 and 17926.1 of the Health and Safety Code.

(I) Using the premises for an unlawful purpose as described in paragraph (4) of Section 1161 of the Code of Civil Procedure.

(J) The employee, agent, or licensee's failure to vacate after their termination as an employee, agent, or a licensee as described in paragraph (1) of Section 1161 of the Code of Civil Procedure.

(K) When the tenant fails to deliver possession of the residential real property after providing the owner written notice as provided in Section 1946 of the tenant's intention to terminate the hiring of the real property, or makes a written offer to surrender that is accepted in writing by the landlord, but fails to deliver possession at the time specified in that written notice as described in paragraph (5) of Section 1161 of the Code of Civil Procedure.

(2) No-fault just cause, which includes any of the following:

(A) (i) Intent to occupy the residential real property by the owner or their spouse, domestic partner, children, grandchildren, parents, or grandparents.

(ii) For leases entered into on or after July 1, 2020, or July 1, 2022, if the lease is for a tenancy in a mobilehome, clause (i) shall apply only if the tenant agrees, in writing, to the termination, or if a provision of the lease allows the owner to terminate the lease if the owner, or their spouse, domestic partner, children, grandchildren, parents, or grandparents, unilaterally decides to occupy the residential real property. Addition of a provision allowing the owner to terminate the lease as described in this clause to a new or renewed rental agreement or fixed-term lease constitutes a similar provision for the purposes of subparagraph (E) of paragraph (1).

(B) Withdrawal of the residential real property from the rental market.

(C) (i) The owner complying with any of the following:

(I) An order issued by a government agency or court relating to habitability that necessitates vacating the residential real property.

(II) An order issued by a government agency or court to vacate the residential real property.

(III) A local ordinance that necessitates vacating the residential real property.

(ii) If it is determined by any government agency or court that the tenant is at fault for the condition or conditions triggering the order or need to vacate under clause (i), the tenant shall not be entitled to relocation assistance as outlined in paragraph (3) of subdivision (d).

(D) (i) Intent to demolish or to substantially remodel the residential real property.

(ii) For purposes of this subparagraph, "substantially remodel" means the replacement or substantial modification of any structural, electrical, plumbing, or mechanical system that requires a permit from a governmental agency, or the abatement of hazardous materials, including lead-based paint, mold, or asbestos, in accordance with applicable federal, state, and local laws, that cannot be reasonably accomplished in a safe manner with the tenant in place and that requires the tenant to vacate the residential real property for at least 30 days. Cosmetic improvements alone, including painting, decorating, and minor repairs, or other work that can be performed safely without having the residential real property vacated, do not qualify as substantial rehabilitation.

(c) Before an owner of residential real property issues a notice to terminate a tenancy for just cause that is a curable lease violation, the owner shall first give notice of the violation to the tenant with an opportunity to cure the violation pursuant to paragraph (3) of Section 1161 of the Code of Civil Procedure. If the violation is not cured within the time period set forth in the notice, a three-day notice to quit without an opportunity to cure may thereafter be served to terminate the tenancy.

(d) (1) For a tenancy for which just cause is required to terminate the tenancy under subdivision (a), if an owner of residential real property issues a termination notice based on a no-fault just cause described in paragraph (2) of subdivision (b), the owner shall, regardless of the tenant's income, at the owner's option, do one of the following:

(A) Assist the tenant to relocate by providing a direct payment to the tenant as described in paragraph (3).

(B) Waive in writing the payment of rent for the final month of the tenancy, prior to the rent becoming due.

(2) If an owner issues a notice to terminate a tenancy for no-fault just cause, the owner shall notify the tenant of the tenant's right to relocation assistance or rent waiver pursuant to this section. If the owner elects to waive the rent for the final month of the tenancy as provided in subparagraph (B) of paragraph (1), the notice shall state the amount of rent waived and that no rent is due for the final month of the tenancy.

(3) (A) The amount of relocation assistance or rent waiver shall be equal to one month of the tenant's rent that was in effect when the owner issued the notice to terminate the tenancy. Any relocation assistance shall be provided within 15 calendar days of service of the notice.

(B) If a tenant fails to vacate after the expiration of the notice to terminate the tenancy, the actual amount of any relocation assistance or rent waiver provided pursuant to this subdivision shall be recoverable as damages in an action to recover possession.

(C) The relocation assistance or rent waiver required by this subdivision shall be credited against any other relocation assistance required by any other law.

(4) An owner's failure to strictly comply with this subdivision shall render the notice of termination void.

(e) This section shall not apply to the following types of residential real properties or residential circumstances:

(1) Transient and tourist hotel occupancy as defined in subdivision (b) of Section 1940.

(2) Housing accommodations in a nonprofit hospital, religious facility, extended care facility, licensed residential care facility for the elderly, as defined in Section 1569.2 of the Health and Safety Code, or an adult residential facility, as defined in Chapter 6 of Division 6 of Title 22 of the Manual of Policies and Procedures published by the State Department of Social Services.

(3) Dormitories owned and operated by an institution of higher education or a kindergarten and grades 1 to 12, inclusive, school.

(4) Housing accommodations in which the tenant shares bathroom or kitchen facilities with the owner who maintains their principal residence at the residential real property.

(5) Single-family owner-occupied residences, including both of the following:

(A) A residence in which the owner-occupant rents or leases no more than two units or bedrooms, including, but not limited to, an accessory dwelling unit or a junior accessory dwelling unit.

(B) A mobilehome.

(6) A property containing two separate dwelling units within a

single structure in which the owner occupied one of the units as the owner's principal place of residence at the beginning of the tenancy, so long as the owner continues in occupancy, and neither unit is an accessory dwelling unit or a junior accessory dwelling unit.

(7) Housing that has been issued a certificate of occupancy within the previous 15 years, unless the housing is a mobilehome.

(8) Residential real property, including a mobilehome, that is alienable separate from the title to any other dwelling unit, provided that both of the following apply:

(A) The owner is not any of the following:

(i) A real estate investment trust, as defined in Section 856 of the Internal Revenue Code.

(ii) A corporation.

(iii) A limited liability company in which at least one member is a corporation.

(iv) Management of a mobilehome park, as defined in Section 798.2.

(B) (i) The tenants have been provided written notice that the residential property is exempt from this section using the following statement:

"This property is not subject to the rent limits imposed by Section 1947.12 of the Civil Code and is not subject to the just cause requirements of Section 1946.2 of the Civil Code. This property meets the requirements of Sections 1947.12 (d)(5) and 1946.2 (e)(8) of the Civil Code and the owner is not any of the following: (1) a real estate investment trust, as defined by Section 856 of the Internal Revenue Code; (2) a corporation; or (3) a limited liability company in which at least one member is a corporation."

(ii) (I) Except as provided in subclause (II), for a tenancy existing before July 1, 2020, the notice required under clause (i) may, but is not required to, be provided in the rental agreement.

(II) For a tenancy in a mobilehome existing before July 1, 2022, the notice required under clause (i) may, but is not required to, be provided in the rental agreement.

(iii) (I) Except as provided in subclause (II), for any tenancy commenced or renewed on or after July 1, 2020, the notice required under clause (i) must be provided in the rental agreement.

(II) For any tenancy in a mobilehome commenced or

renewed on or after July 1, 2022, the notice required under clause (i) shall be provided in the rental agreement.

(iv) Addition of a provision containing the notice required under clause (i) to any new or renewed rental agreement or fixed-term lease constitutes a similar provision for the purposes of subparagraph (E) of paragraph (1) of subdivision (b).

(9) Housing restricted by deed, regulatory restriction contained in an agreement with a government agency, or other recorded document as affordable housing for persons and families of very low, low, or moderate income, as defined in Section 50093 of the Health and Safety Code, or subject to an agreement that provides housing subsidies for affordable housing for persons and families of very low, low, or moderate income, as defined in Section 50093 of the Health and Safety Code or comparable federal statutes.

(f) An owner of residential real property subject to this section shall provide notice to the tenant as follows:

(1) (A) Except as provided in subparagraph (B), for any tenancy commenced or renewed on or after July 1, 2020, as an addendum to the lease or rental agreement, or as a written notice signed by the tenant, with a copy provided to the tenant.

(B) For a tenancy in a mobilehome commenced or renewed on or after July 1, 2022, as an addendum to the lease or rental agreement, or as a written notice signed by the tenant, with a copy provided to the tenant.

(2) (A) Except as provided in subparagraph (B), for a tenancy existing prior to July 1, 2020, by written notice to the tenant no later than August 1, 2020, or as an addendum to the lease or rental agreement.

(B) For a tenancy in a mobilehome existing prior to July 1, 2022, by written notice to the tenant no later than August 1, 2022, or as an addendum to the lease or rental agreement.

(3) The notification or lease provision shall be in no less than 12-point type, and shall include the following:

"California law limits the amount your rent can be increased. See Section 1947.12 of the Civil Code for more information. California law also provides that after all of the tenants have continuously and lawfully occupied the property for 12 months or more or at least one of the tenants has continuously and lawfully occupied the property for 24 months or more, a landlord must provide a statement of cause in any notice to terminate a tenancy. See Section 1946.2 of the Civil Code for more information."

The provision of the notice shall be subject to Section 1632.

(g) (1) This section does not apply to the following residential real property:

(A) Residential real property subject to a local ordinance requiring just cause for termination of a residential tenancy adopted on or before September 1, 2019, in which case the local ordinance shall apply.

(B) Residential real property subject to a local ordinance requiring just cause for termination of a residential tenancy adopted or amended after September 1, 2019, that is more protective than this section, in which case the local ordinance shall apply. For purposes of this subparagraph, an ordinance is "more protective" if it meets all of the following criteria:

(i) The just cause for termination of a residential tenancy under the local ordinance is consistent with this section.

(ii) The ordinance further limits the reasons for termination of a residential tenancy, provides for higher relocation assistance amounts, or provides additional tenant protections that are not prohibited by any other provision of law.

(iii) The local government has made a binding finding within their local ordinance that the ordinance is more protective than the provisions of this section.

(2) A residential real property shall not be subject to both a local ordinance requiring just cause for termination of a residential tenancy and this section.

(3) A local ordinance adopted after September 1, 2019, that is less protective than this section shall not be enforced unless this section is repealed.

(h) Any waiver of the rights under this section shall be void as contrary to public policy.

(i) For the purposes of this section, the following definitions shall apply:

(1) "Owner" includes any person, acting as principal or through an agent, having the right to offer residential real property for rent, and includes a predecessor in interest to the owner.

(2) "Residential real property" means any dwelling or unit that is intended for human habitation, including any dwelling or unit in a mobilehome park.

(3) "Tenancy" means the lawful occupation of residential real property and includes a lease or sublease.

(j) This section shall not apply to a homeowner of a mobilehome, as defined in Section 798.9.

(k) This section shall remain in effect only until January 1, 2030, and as of that date is repealed. **Leg.H.** 2019, 2020, 2021.

§ 1946.5 *Hiring of Room by Lodger; Termination; Notice*

(a) The hiring of a room by a lodger on a periodic basis within a dwelling unit occupied by the owner may be terminated by either party giving written notice to the other of his or her intention to terminate the hiring, at least as long before the expiration of the term of the hiring as specified in Section 1946. The notice shall be given in a manner prescribed in Section 1162 of the Code of Civil Procedure or by certified or registered mail, restricted delivery, to the other party, with a return receipt requested.

(b) Upon expiration of the notice period provided in the notice of termination given pursuant to subdivision (a), any right of the lodger to remain in the dwelling unit or any part thereof is terminated by operation of law. The lodger's removal from the premises may thereafter be effected pursuant to the provisions of Section 602.3 of the Penal Code or other applicable provisions of law.

(c) As used in this section, "lodger" means a person contracting with the owner of a dwelling unit for a room or room and board within the dwelling unit personally occupied by the owner, where the owner retains a right of access to all areas of the dwelling unit occupied by the lodger and has overall control of the dwelling unit.

(d) This section applies only to owner-occupied dwellings where a single lodger resides. Nothing in this section shall be construed to determine or affect in any way the rights of persons residing as lodgers in an owner-occupied dwelling where more than one lodger resides. **Leg.H.** 1986.

§ 1946.7 *Tenant May Terminate Tenancy for Domestic Violence, Sexual Assault, Stalking, Elder/Dependent Adult Abuse, Human Trafficking or a Crime of Bodily Injury/ Death or Included a Deadly Weapon or Threat/Use of Force*

(a) A tenant may notify the landlord that the tenant intends to terminate the tenancy if the tenant, a household member, or an immediate family member was the victim of an act that constitutes any of the following:

(1) Domestic violence as defined in Section 6211 of the Family Code.

(2) Sexual assault as defined in Section 261, 261.5, 286, 287, or 289 of the Penal Code.

(3) Stalking as defined in Section 1708.7.

(4) Human trafficking as defined in Section 236.1 of the Penal Code.

(5) Abuse of an elder or a dependent adult as defined in Section 15610.07 of the Welfare and Institutions Code.

(6) A crime that caused bodily injury or death.

(7) A crime that included the exhibition, drawing, brandishing, or use of a firearm or other deadly weapon or instrument.

(8) A crime that included the use of force against the victim or a threat of force against the victim.

(b) A notice to terminate a tenancy under this section shall be in writing, with one of the following attached to the notice:

(1) A copy of a temporary restraining order, emergency protective order, or protective order lawfully issued pursuant to Part 3 (commencing with Section 6240) or Part 4 (commencing with Section 6300) of Division 10 of the Family Code, Section 136.2 of the Penal Code, Section 527.6 of the Code of Civil Procedure, or Section 213.5 or 15657.03 of the Welfare and Institutions Code that protects the tenant, household member, or immediate family member from further domestic violence, sexual assault, stalking, human trafficking, abuse of an elder or a dependent adult, or any act or crime listed in subdivision (a).

(2) A copy of a written report by a peace officer employed by a state or local law enforcement agency acting in the peace officer's official capacity stating that the tenant, household member, or immediate family member has filed a report alleging that the tenant, the household member, or the immediate family member is a victim of an act or crime listed in subdivision (a).

(3) (A) Documentation from a qualified third party based on information received by that third party while acting in the third party's professional capacity to indicate that the tenant, household member, or immediate family member is seeking assistance for physical or mental injuries or abuse resulting from an act or crime listed in subdivision (a).

(B) The documentation shall contain, in substantially the same form, the following:

Tenant Statement and Qualified Third Party Statement

under Civil Code Section 1946.7

Part I.Statement By Tenant

I, [insert name of tenant], state as follows:

I, or a member of my household or immediate family, have been a victim of:

[insert one or more of the following: domestic violence, sexual assault, stalking, human trafficking, elder abuse, dependent adult abuse, or a crime that caused bodily injury or death, a crime that included the exhibition, drawing, brandishing, or use of a firearm or other deadly weapon or instrument, or a crime that included the use of force against the victim or a threat of force against the victim.]

The most recent incident(s) happened on or about:

[insert date or dates.]

The incident(s) was/were committed by the following person(s), with these physical description(s), if known and safe to provide:

[if known and safe to provide, insert name(s) and physical description(s).]

(signature of tenant)(date)

Part II.Qualified Third Party Statement

I, [insert name of qualified third party], state as follows:

My business address and phone number are:

[insert business address and phone number.]

Check and complete one of the following:

____I meet the requirements for a sexual assault counselor provided in Section 1035.2 of the Evidence Code and I am either engaged in an office, hospital, institution, or center commonly known as a rape crisis center described in that section or employed by an organization providing the programs specified in Section 13835.2 of the Penal Code.

____I meet the requirements for a domestic violence counselor provided in Section 1037.1 of the Evidence Code and I am employed, whether financially compensated or not, by a domestic violence victim service organization, as defined in that section.

____I meet the requirements for a human trafficking caseworker provided in Section 1038.2 of the Evidence Code and I am employed, whether financially compensated or not, by an organization that provides programs specified in Section 18294 of the Welfare and Institutions Code or in Section 13835.2 of the Penal Code.

____I meet the definition of "victim of violent crime advocate" provided in Section 1947.6 of the Civil Code and I am employed, whether financially compensated or not, by a reputable agency or organization that has a documented record of providing services to victims of violent crime or provides those services under the auspices or supervision of a court or a law enforcement or prosecution agency.

_____I am licensed by the State of California as a:

[insert one of the following: physician and surgeon, osteopathic physician and surgeon, registered nurse, psychiatrist, psychologist, licensed clinical social worker, licensed marriage and family therapist, or licensed professional clinical counselor.] and I am licensed by, and my license number is:

[insert name of state licensing entity and license number.]

The person who signed the Statement By Tenant above stated to me that the person, or a member of the person's household or immediate family, is a victim of:

[insert one or more of the following: domestic violence, sexual assault, stalking, human trafficking, elder abuse, dependent adult abuse, or a crime that caused physical injury, emotional injury and the threat of physical injury, or death.]

The person further stated to me the incident(s) occurred on or about the date(s) stated above.

I understand that the person who made the Statement By Tenant may use this document as a basis for terminating a lease with the person's landlord.

(signature of qualified third party)(date)

(C) The documentation may be signed by a person who meets the requirements for a sexual assault counselor, domestic violence counselor, a human trafficking caseworker, or a victim of violent crime advocate only if the documentation displays the letterhead of the office, hospital, institution, center, or organization, as appropriate, that engages or employs, whether financially compensated or not, this counselor, caseworker, or advocate.

(4) Any other form of documentation that reasonably verifies that the crime or act listed in subdivision (a) occurred.

(c) If the tenant is terminating tenancy pursuant to subdivision (a) because an immediate family member is a victim of an eligible act or crime listed in subdivision (a) and that tenant did not live in the same household as the immediate family member at the time of the act or crime, and no part of the act or crime occurred within the dwelling unit or within 1,000 feet of the dwelling unit of the tenant, the tenant shall attach to the notice and other documentation required by subdivision (b) a written statement stating all of the following:

(1) The tenant's immediate family member was a victim of an act or crime listed in subdivision (a).

(2) The tenant intends to relocate as a result of the tenant's immediate family member being a victim of an act or crime listed in subdivision (a).

(3) The tenant is relocating to increase the safety, physical well-being, emotional well-being, psychological well-being, or financial security of the tenant or of the tenant's immediate family member as a result of the act or crime.

(d) The notice to terminate the tenancy shall be given within 180 days of the date that any order described in paragraph (1) of subdivision (b) was issued, within 180 days of the date that any written report described in paragraph (2) of subdivision (b) was made, within 180 days of the date that a crime described in paragraph (6), (7), or (8) of subdivision (a) occurred, or within the time period described in Section 1946.

(e) If notice to terminate the tenancy is provided to the landlord under this section, the tenant shall be responsible for payment of rent for no more than 14 calendar days following the giving of the notice, or for any shorter appropriate period as described in Section 1946 or the lease or rental agreement. The tenant shall be released from any rent payment obligation under the lease or rental agreement without penalty. If the premises are relet to another party prior to the end of the obligation to pay rent, the rent owed under this subdivision shall be prorated.

(f) Notwithstanding any law, a landlord shall not require a tenant who terminates a lease or rental agreement pursuant to this section to forfeit any security deposit money or advance rent paid due to that termination. A tenant who terminates a rental agreement pursuant to this section shall not be considered for any purpose, by reason of the termination, to have breached the lease or rental agreement. Existing law governing the security deposit shall apply.

(g) This section does not relieve a tenant, other than the tenant who is, or who has a household member or immediate family member who is, a victim of an act or crime listed in subdivision (a) and members of that tenant's household, from their obligations under the lease or rental agreement.

(h) For purposes of this section, the following definitions apply:

(1) "Household member" means a member of the tenant's family who lives in the same household as the tenant.

(2) "Health practitioner" means a physician and surgeon, osteopathic physician and surgeon, psychiatrist, psychologist, registered nurse, licensed clinical social worker, licensed marriage and family therapist, or licensed professional clinical counselor.

(3) "Immediate family member" means the parent, stepparent, spouse, child, child-in-law, stepchild, or sibling of the tenant, or any person living in the tenant's household at the time

the crime or act listed in subdivision (a) occurred who has a relationship with the tenant that is substantially similar to that of a family member.

(4) "Qualified third party" means a health practitioner, domestic violence counselor, as defined in Section 1037.1 of the Evidence Code, a sexual assault counselor, as defined in Section 1035.2 of the Evidence Code, or a human trafficking caseworker, as defined in Section 1038.2 of the Evidence Code.

(5) "Victim of violent crime advocate" means a person who is employed, whether financially compensated or not, for the purpose of rendering advice or assistance to victims of violent crimes for a reputable agency or organization that has a documented record of providing services to victims of violent crime or provides those services under the auspices or supervision of a court or a law enforcement or prosecution agency.

(i) (1) A landlord shall not disclose any information provided by a tenant under this section to a third party unless the disclosure satisfies any one of the following:

(A) The tenant consents in writing to the disclosure.

(B) The disclosure is required by law or order of the court.

(2) A landlord's communication to a qualified third party who provides documentation under paragraph (3) of subdivision (b) to verify the contents of that documentation is not disclosure for purposes of this subdivision.

(j) An owner or an owner's agent shall not refuse to rent a dwelling unit to an otherwise qualified prospective tenant or refuse to continue to rent to an existing tenant solely on the basis that the tenant has previously exercised the tenant's rights under this section or has previously terminated a tenancy because of the circumstances described in subdivision (a). **Leg.H.** 2016, 2018, 2019, 2020, 2021.

§ 1947.9 Relocation Payment Limits for Tenant Displaced Less Than 20 Days

(a) (1) Notwithstanding any local law to the contrary, for those units governed by the local rent stabilization ordinance in the City and County of San Francisco, levels of compensation for the temporary displacement of a tenant household for less than 20 days shall be limited to both of the following:

(A) Temporary housing and living expenses, of two hundred seventy-five dollars ($275) per day per tenant household. This limit may be adjusted annually by the city and county in an amount equal to the Consumer Price Index, beginning on January 1, 2014.

(B) Actual moving expenses if it is necessary to move the possessions of the tenant household.

(2) The landlord shall have the option to provide a comparable dwelling unit and pay any actual moving expenses, in lieu of the compensation specified in subparagraph (A) of paragraph (1). The rental housing shall be comparable to the tenant household's existing housing in location, size, number of bedrooms, accessibility, type, and quality of construction, and proximity to services and institutions upon which the displaced tenant household depends.

(b) This section shall not be construed to do any of the following:

(1) To terminate, interrupt, or amend, in any way, a tenancy subject to the lease provisions, or the rights and obligations of either party, including, but not limited to, the payment of rent.

(2) To create or affect any grounds for displacement or requirements of a landlord seeking temporary displacement, except the payment of relocation fees pursuant to subdivision (a) for displacement not exceeding 20 days.

(3) To affect the authority of a public entity that may regulate or monitor the basis for eviction.

(c) If a federal or state law regarding relocation compensation is also applicable to the temporary displacement, the tenant may elect to be compensated under those other provisions, and subdivision (a) shall be inapplicable.

(d) This section shall affect only levels of compensation for a temporary displacement of less than 20 days, and does not affect any other local procedures governing temporary relocation. **Leg. H.** 2012.

§ 1947.12 Rent Increase Limitation

(a) (1) Subject to subdivision (b), an owner of residential real property shall not, over the course of any 12-month period, increase the gross rental rate for a dwelling or a unit more than 5 percent plus the percentage change in the cost of living, or 10 percent, whichever is lower, of the lowest gross rental rate charged for that dwelling or unit at any time during the 12 months prior to the effective date of the increase. In determining the lowest gross rental amount pursuant to this section, any rent discounts, incentives, concessions, or credits offered by the owner of such unit of residential real property and accepted by the tenant shall be excluded. The gross per-month rental rate and any owner-offered discounts, incentives, concessions, or credits shall be separately listed and identified in the lease or rental agreement or any amendments to an existing lease or rental agreement.

(2) If the same tenant remains in occupancy of a unit of residential real property over any 12-month period, the gross rental rate for the unit of residential real property shall not be increased in more than two increments over that 12-month period, subject to the other restrictions of this subdivision governing gross rental rate increase.

(b) For a new tenancy in which no tenant from the prior tenancy remains in lawful possession of the residential real property, the owner may establish the initial rental rate not subject to subdivision (a). Subdivision (a) is only applicable to subsequent increases after that initial rental rate has been established.

(c) A tenant of residential real property subject to this section shall not enter into a sublease that results in a total rent for the premises that exceeds the allowable rental rate authorized by subdivision (a). Nothing in this subdivision authorizes a tenant to sublet or assign the tenant's interest where otherwise prohibited.

(d) This section shall not apply to the following residential real properties:

(1) Housing restricted by deed, regulatory restriction contained in an agreement with a government agency, or other recorded document as affordable housing for persons and families of very low, low, or moderate income, as defined in Section 50093 of the Health and Safety Code, or subject to an agreement that provides housing subsidies for affordable housing for persons and families of very low, low, or moderate income, as defined in Section 50093 of the Health and Safety Code or comparable federal statutes.

(2) Dormitories owned and operated by an institution of higher education or a kindergarten and grades 1 to 12, inclusive, school.

(3) Housing subject to rent or price control through a public entity's valid exercise of its police power consistent with Chapter 2.7 (commencing with Section 1954.50) that restricts annual increases in the rental rate to an amount less than that provided in subdivision (a).

(4) Housing that has been issued a certificate of occupancy within the previous 15 years, unless the housing is a mobilehome.

(5) Residential real property that is alienable separate from the title to any other dwelling unit, including a mobilehome, provided that both of the following apply:

(A) The owner is not any of the following:

(i) A real estate investment trust, as defined in Section 856 of the Internal Revenue Code.

(ii) A corporation.

(iii) A limited liability company in which at least one member is a corporation.

(iv) Management of a mobilehome park, as defined in Section 798.2.

(B) (i) The tenants have been provided written notice that the residential real property is exempt from this section using the following statement:

"This property is not subject to the rent limits imposed by Section 1947.12 of the Civil Code and is not subject to the just cause requirements of Section 1946.2 of the Civil Code. This property meets the requirements of Sections 1947.12 (d)(5) and 1946.2 (e)(8) of the Civil Code and the owner is not any of the following: (1) a real estate investment trust, as defined by Section 856 of the Internal Revenue Code; (2) a corporation; or (3) a limited liability company in which at least one member is a corporation."

(ii) For a tenancy existing before July 1, 2020, or July 1, 2022, if the lease is for a tenancy in a mobilehome, the notice required under clause (i) may, but is not required to, be provided in the rental agreement.

(iii) For a tenancy commenced or renewed on or after July 1, 2020, or July 1, 2022, if the lease is for a tenancy in a mobilehome, the notice required under clause (i) must be provided in the rental agreement.

(iv) Addition of a provision containing the notice required under clause (i) to any new or renewed rental agreement or fixed-term lease constitutes a similar provision for the purposes of subparagraph (E) of paragraph (1) of subdivision (b) of Section 1946.2.

(6) A property containing two separate dwelling units within a single structure in which the owner occupied one of the units as the owner's principal place of residence at the beginning of the tenancy, so long as the owner continues in occupancy, and neither unit is an accessory dwelling unit or a junior accessory dwelling unit.

(e) An owner shall provide notice of any increase in the rental rate, pursuant to subdivision (a), to each tenant in accordance with Section 827.

(f) (1) On or before January 1, 2030, the Legislative Analyst's Office shall report to the Legislature regarding the effectiveness of this section and Section 1947.13. The report shall include, but not be limited to, the impact of the rental rate cap pursuant to subdivision (a) on the housing market within the state.

(2) The report required by paragraph (1) shall be submitted in compliance with Section 9795 of the Government Code.

(g) For the purposes of this section, the following definitions shall apply:

(1) "Consumer Price Index for All Urban Consumers for All Items" means the following:

(A) The Consumer Price Index for All Urban Consumers for All Items (CPI-U) for the metropolitan area in which the property is located, as published by the United States Bureau of Labor Statistics, which are as follows:

(i) The CPI-U for the Los Angeles-Long Beach-Anaheim metropolitan area covering the Counties of Los Angeles and Orange.

(ii) The CPI-U for the Riverside-San Bernardo-Ontario metropolitan area covering the Counties of Riverside and San Bernardino.

(iii) The CPI-U for the San Diego-Carlsbad metropolitan area covering the County of San Diego.

(iv) The CPI-U for the San Francisco-Oakland-Hayward metropolitan area covering the Counties of Alameda, Contra Costa, Marin, San Francisco, and San Mateo.

(v) Any successor metropolitan area index to any of the indexes listed in clauses (i) to (iv), inclusive.

(B) If the United States Bureau of Labor Statistics does not publish a CPI-U for the metropolitan area in which the property is located, the California Consumer Price Index for All Urban Consumers for All Items as published by the Department of Industrial Relations.

(C) On or after January 1, 2021, if the United States Bureau of Labor Statistics publishes a CPI-U index for one or more metropolitan areas not listed in subparagraph (A), that CPI-U index shall apply in those areas with respect to rent increases that take effect on or after August 1 of the calendar year in which the 12-month change in that CPI-U, as described in subparagraph (B) of paragraph (3), is first published.

(2) "Owner" includes any person, acting as principal or through an agent, having the right to offer residential real property for rent, and includes a predecessor in interest to the owner.

(3) (A) "Percentage change in the cost of living" means the percentage change, computed pursuant to subparagraph (B), in the applicable, as determined pursuant to paragraph (1), Consumer Price Index for All Urban Consumers for All Items.

(B) (i) For rent increases that take effect before August 1 of any calendar year, the following shall apply:

(I) The percentage change shall be the percentage change in the amount published for April of the immediately preceding calendar year and April of the year before that.

(II) If there is not an amount published in April for the applicable geographic area, the percentage change shall be the percentage change in the amount published for March of the immediately preceding calendar year and March of the year before that.

(ii) For rent increases that take effect on or after August 1 of any calendar year, the following shall apply:

(I) The percentage change shall be the percentage change in the amount published for April of that calendar year and April of the immediately preceding calendar year.

(II) If there is not an amount published in April for the applicable geographic area, the percentage change shall be the percentage change in the amount published for March of that calendar year and March of the immediately preceding calendar year.

(iii) The percentage change shall be rounded to the nearest one-tenth of 1 percent.

(4) "Residential real property" means any dwelling or unit that is intended for human habitation, including any dwelling or unit in a mobilehome park.

(5) "Tenancy" means the lawful occupation of residential real property and includes a lease or sublease.

(h) (1) This section shall apply to all rent increases subject to subdivision (a) occurring on or after March 15, 2019, except as provided in subdivision (i).

(2) In the event that an owner has increased the rent by more than the amount permissible under subdivision (a) between March 15, 2019, and January 1, 2020, both of the following shall apply:

(A) The applicable rent on January 1, 2020, shall be the rent as of March 15, 2019, plus the maximum permissible increase under subdivision (a).

(B) An owner shall not be liable to the tenant for any

corresponding rent overpayment.

(3) An owner of residential real property subject to subdivision (a) who increased the rental rate on that residential real property on or after March 15, 2019, but prior to January 1, 2020, by an amount less than the rental rate increase permitted by subdivision (a) shall be allowed to increase the rental rate twice, as provided in paragraph (2) of subdivision (a), within 12 months of March 15, 2019, but in no event shall that rental rate increase exceed the maximum rental rate increase permitted by subdivision (a).

(i) (1) Notwithstanding subdivision (h), this section shall apply only to rent increases for a tenancy in a mobilehome subject to subdivision (a) occurring on or after February 18, 2021.

(2) In the event that an owner has increased the rent for a tenancy in a mobilehome by more than the amount permissible under subdivision (a) between February 18, 2021, and January 1, 2022, both of the following shall apply:

(A) The applicable rent on January 1, 2022, shall be the rent as of February 18, 2021, plus the maximum permissible increase under subdivision (a).

(B) An owner shall not be liable to the tenant for any corresponding rent overpayment.

(3) An owner of residential real property subject to subdivision (a) who increased the rental rate on that residential real property on or after February 18, 2021, but prior to January 1, 2022, by an amount less than the rental rate increase permitted by subdivision (a) shall be allowed to increase the rental rate twice, as provided in paragraph (2) of subdivision (a), within 12 months of February 18, 2021, but in no event shall that rental rate increase exceed the maximum rental rate increase permitted by subdivision (a).

(j) This section shall not apply to a homeowner of a mobilehome, as defined in Section 798.9.

(k) Any waiver of the rights under this section shall be void as contrary to public policy.

(l) This section shall remain in effect until January 1, 2030, and as of that date is repealed.

(m) (1) The Legislature finds and declares that the unique circumstances of the current housing crisis require a statewide response to address rent gouging by establishing statewide limitations on gross rental rate increases.

(2) It is the intent of the Legislature that this section should apply only for the limited time needed to address the current statewide housing crisis, as described in paragraph (1). This section is not intended to expand or limit the authority of local governments to establish local policies regulating rents consistent with Chapter 2.7 (commencing with Section 1954.50), nor is it a statement regarding the appropriate, allowable rental rate increase when a local government adopts a policy regulating rent that is otherwise consistent with Chapter 2.7 (commencing with Section 1954.50).

(3) Nothing in this section authorizes a local government to establish limitations on any rental rate increases not otherwise permissible under Chapter 2.7 (commencing with Section 1954.50), or affects the existing authority of a local government to adopt or maintain rent controls or price controls consistent with that chapter. **Leg.H.** 2019, 2020, 2021.

§ 1950 *Penalty for Double Letting of Room*

One who hires part of a room for a dwelling is entitled to the whole of the room, notwithstanding any agreement to the contrary; and if a landlord lets a room as a dwelling for more than one family, the person to whom he first lets any part of it is entitled to the possession of the whole room for the term agreed upon and every tenant in the building, under the same landlord, is relieved from all obligation to pay rent to him while such double letting of any room continues. **Leg.H.** 1872.

§ 1950.5 *Security Deposit*

(a) This section applies to security for a rental agreement for residential property that is used as the dwelling of the tenant.

(b) As used in this section, "security" means any payment, fee, deposit, or charge, including, but not limited to, any payment, fee, deposit, or charge, except as provided in Section 1950.6, that is imposed at the beginning of the tenancy to be used to reimburse the landlord for costs associated with processing a new tenant or that is imposed as an advance payment of rent, used or to be used for any purpose, including, but not limited to, any of the following:

(1) The compensation of a landlord for a tenant's default in the payment of rent.

(2) The repair of damages to the premises, exclusive of ordinary wear and tear, caused by the tenant or by a guest or licensee of the tenant.

(3) The cleaning of the premises upon termination of the tenancy necessary to return the unit to the same level of cleanliness it was in at the inception of the tenancy. The amendments to this paragraph enacted by the act adding this sentence shall apply only to tenancies for which the tenant's right to occupy begins after January 1, 2003.

(4) To remedy future defaults by the tenant in any obligation under the rental agreement to restore, replace, or return

personal property or appurtenances, exclusive of ordinary wear and tear, if the security deposit is authorized to be applied thereto by the rental agreement.

(c) (1) Except as provided in paragraph (2), (3), or (4), a landlord may not demand or receive security, however denominated, in an amount or value in excess of an amount equal to two months' rent, in the case of unfurnished residential property, and an amount equal to three months' rent, in the case of furnished residential property, in addition to any rent for the first month paid on or before initial occupancy.

(2) Notwithstanding paragraph (1), and except as provided in subparagraphs (A) and (B), a landlord shall not demand or receive security, however denominated, from a service member who rents residential property in which the service member will reside in an amount or value in excess of an amount equal to one months' rent, in the case of unfurnished residential property, or in excess of an amount equal to two months' rent, in the case of furnished residential property, in addition to any rent for the first month paid on or before initial occupancy. A landlord shall not refuse to enter into a rental agreement for residential property with a prospective tenant who is a service member because this paragraph prohibits the landlord from demanding or receiving a greater amount of security than that which is established in paragraph (1). For purposes of this paragraph, "service member" has the same meaning as in Section 400 of the Military and Veterans Code.

(A) A landlord may demand or receive security from a service member who rents residential property in which the service member will reside as provided in paragraph (1), if the tenant has a history of poor credit or of causing damage to the rental property or its furnishings.

(B) This paragraph does not apply to a situation in which the property is rented to a group of individuals, one or more of whom is not the service member's spouse, parent, domestic partner, or dependent.

(C) For purposes of this paragraph "resides" means that the service member will be listed as a tenant on the residential property lease agreement.

(3) This subdivision does not prohibit an advance payment of not less than six months' rent if the term of the lease is six months or longer.

(4) This subdivision does not preclude a landlord and a tenant from entering into a mutual agreement for the landlord, at the request of the tenant and for a specified fee or charge, to make structural, decorative, furnishing, or other similar alterations, if the alterations are other than cleaning or repairing for which the landlord may charge the previous tenant as provided by subdivision (e).

(d) Any security shall be held by the landlord for the tenant who is party to the lease or agreement. The claim of a tenant to the security shall be prior to the claim of any creditor of the landlord.

(e) The landlord may claim of the security only those amounts as are reasonably necessary for the purposes specified in subdivision (b). The landlord may not assert a claim against the tenant or the security for damages to the premises or any defective conditions that preexisted the tenancy, for ordinary wear and tear or the effects thereof, whether the wear and tear preexisted the tenancy or occurred during the tenancy, or for the cumulative effects of ordinary wear and tear occurring during any one or more tenancies.

(f) (1) Within a reasonable time after notification of either party's intention to terminate the tenancy, or before the end of the lease term, the landlord shall notify the tenant in writing of the tenant's option to request an initial inspection and of the tenant's right to be present at the inspection. The requirements of this subdivision do not apply when the tenancy is terminated pursuant to subdivision (2), (3), or (4) of Section 1161 of the Code of Civil Procedure. At a reasonable time, but no earlier than two weeks before the termination or the end of lease date, the landlord, or an agent of the landlord, shall, upon the request of the tenant, make an initial inspection of the premises prior to any final inspection the landlord makes after the tenant has vacated the premises. The purpose of the initial inspection shall be to allow the tenant an opportunity to remedy identified deficiencies, in a manner consistent with the rights and obligations of the parties under the rental agreement, in order to avoid deductions from the security. If a tenant chooses not to request an initial inspection, the duties of the landlord under this subdivision are discharged. If an inspection is requested, the parties shall attempt to schedule the inspection at a mutually acceptable date and time. The landlord shall give at least 48 hours' prior written notice of the date and time of the inspection if either a mutual time is agreed upon, or if a mutually agreed time cannot be scheduled but the tenant still wishes an inspection. The tenant and landlord may agree to forgo the 48-hour prior written notice by both signing a written waiver. The landlord shall proceed with the inspection whether the tenant is present or not, unless the tenant previously withdrew their request for the inspection. Written notice by the landlord shall contain, in substantially the same form, the following:

"State law permits former tenants to reclaim abandoned personal property left at the former address of the tenant, subject to certain conditions. You may or may not be able to reclaim property without incurring additional costs, depending on the cost of storing the property and the length of time before it is reclaimed. In general, these costs will be lower the sooner you contact your former landlord after being notified that property belonging to you was left behind after you moved out."

(2) Based on the inspection, the landlord shall give the tenant an itemized statement specifying repairs or cleanings that are proposed to be the basis of any deductions from the

security the landlord intends to make pursuant to paragraphs (1) to (4), inclusive, of subdivision (b). This statement shall also include the texts of paragraphs (1) to (4), inclusive, of subdivision (b). The statement shall be given to the tenant, if the tenant is present for the inspection, or shall be left inside the premises.

(3) The tenant shall have the opportunity during the period following the initial inspection until termination of the tenancy to remedy identified deficiencies, in a manner consistent with the rights and obligations of the parties under the rental agreement, in order to avoid deductions from the security.

(4) Nothing in this subdivision shall prevent a landlord from using the security for deductions itemized in the statement provided for in paragraph (2) that were not cured by the tenant so long as the deductions are for damages authorized by this section.

(5) Nothing in this subdivision shall prevent a landlord from using the security for any purpose specified in paragraphs (1) to (4), inclusive, of subdivision (b) that occurs between completion of the initial inspection and termination of the tenancy or was not identified during the initial inspection due to the presence of a tenant's possessions.

(g) (1) No later than 21 calendar days after the tenant has vacated the premises, but not earlier than the time that either the landlord or the tenant provides a notice to terminate the tenancy under Section 1946 or 1946.1, Section 1161 of the Code of Civil Procedure, or not earlier than 60 calendar days prior to the expiration of a fixed-term lease, the landlord shall furnish the tenant, by personal delivery or by first-class mail, postage prepaid, a copy of an itemized statement indicating the basis for, and the amount of, any security received and the disposition of the security, and shall return any remaining portion of the security to the tenant. After either the landlord or the tenant provides notice to terminate the tenancy, the landlord and tenant may mutually agree to have the landlord deposit any remaining portion of the security deposit electronically to a bank account or other financial institution designated by the tenant. After either the landlord or the tenant provides notice to terminate the tenancy, the landlord and the tenant may also agree to have the landlord provide a copy of the itemized statement along with the copies required by paragraph (2) to an email account provided by the tenant.

(2) Along with the itemized statement, the landlord shall also include copies of documents showing charges incurred and deducted by the landlord to repair or clean the premises, as follows:

(A) If the landlord or landlord's employee did the work, the itemized statement shall reasonably describe the work performed. The itemized statement shall include the time

spent and the reasonable hourly rate charged.

(B) If the landlord or landlord's employee did not do the work, the landlord shall provide the tenant a copy of the bill, invoice, or receipt supplied by the person or entity performing the work. The itemized statement shall provide the tenant with the name, address, and telephone number of the person or entity, if the bill, invoice, or receipt does not include that information.

(C) If a deduction is made for materials or supplies, the landlord shall provide a copy of the bill, invoice, or receipt. If a particular material or supply item is purchased by the landlord on an ongoing basis, the landlord may document the cost of the item by providing a copy of a bill, invoice, receipt, vendor price list, or other vendor document that reasonably documents the cost of the item used in the repair or cleaning of the unit.

(3) If a repair to be done by the landlord or the landlord's employee cannot reasonably be completed within 21 calendar days after the tenant has vacated the premises, or if the documents from a person or entity providing services, materials, or supplies are not in the landlord's possession within 21 calendar days after the tenant has vacated the premises, the landlord may deduct the amount of a good faith estimate of the charges that will be incurred and provide that estimate with the itemized statement. If the reason for the estimate is because the documents from a person or entity providing services, materials, or supplies are not in the landlord's possession, the itemized statement shall include the name, address, and telephone number of the person or entity. Within 14 calendar days of completing the repair or receiving the documentation, the landlord shall complete the requirements in paragraphs (1) and (2) in the manner specified.

(4) The landlord need not comply with paragraph (2) or (3) if either of the following applies:

(A) The deductions for repairs and cleaning together do not exceed one hundred twenty-five dollars ($125).

(B) The tenant waived the rights specified in paragraphs (2) and (3). The waiver shall only be effective if it is signed by the tenant at the same time or after a notice to terminate a tenancy under Section 1946 or 1946.1 has been given, a notice under Section 1161 of the Code of Civil Procedure has been given, or no earlier than 60 calendar days prior to the expiration of a fixed-term lease. The waiver shall substantially include the text of paragraph (2).

(5) Notwithstanding paragraph (4), the landlord shall comply with paragraphs (2) and (3) when a tenant makes a request for documentation within 14 calendar days after receiving the itemized statement specified in paragraph (1). The landlord

shall comply within 14 calendar days after receiving the request from the tenant.

(6) Any mailings to the tenant pursuant to this subdivision shall be sent to the address provided by the tenant. If the tenant does not provide an address, mailings pursuant to this subdivision shall be sent to the unit that has been vacated.

(h) Upon termination of the landlord's interest in the premises, whether by sale, assignment, death, appointment of receiver, or otherwise, the landlord or the landlord's agent shall, within a reasonable time, do one of the following acts, either of which shall relieve the landlord of further liability with respect to the security held:

(1) Transfer the portion of the security remaining after any lawful deductions made under subdivision (e) to the landlord's successor in interest. The landlord shall thereafter notify the tenant by personal delivery or by first-class mail, postage prepaid, of the transfer, of any claims made against the security, of the amount of the security deposited, and of the names of the successors in interest, their addresses, and their telephone numbers. If the notice to the tenant is made by personal delivery, the tenant shall acknowledge receipt of the notice and sign their name on the landlord's copy of the notice.

(2) Return the portion of the security remaining after any lawful deductions made under subdivision (e) to the tenant, together with an accounting as provided in subdivision (g).

(i) Prior to the voluntary transfer of a landlord's interest in the premises, the landlord shall deliver to the landlord's successor in interest a written statement indicating the following:

(1) The security remaining after any lawful deductions are made.

(2) An itemization of any lawful deductions from any security received.

(3) Their election under paragraph (1) or (2) of subdivision (h).

This subdivision does not affect the validity of title to the real property transferred in violation of this subdivision.

(j) (1) In the event of noncompliance with subdivision (h), the landlord's successors in interest shall be jointly and severally liable with the landlord for repayment of the security, or that portion thereof to which the tenant is entitled, when and as provided in subdivisions (e) and (g). A successor in interest of a landlord may not require the tenant to post any security to replace that amount not transferred to the tenant or successors in interest as provided in subdivision (h), unless and until the successor in interest first makes restitution of the initial security as provided in paragraph

(2) of subdivision (h) or provides the tenant with an accounting as provided in subdivision (g).

(2) This subdivision does not preclude a successor in interest from recovering from the tenant compensatory damages that are in excess of the security received from the landlord previously paid by the tenant to the landlord.

(3) Notwithstanding this subdivision, if, upon inquiry and reasonable investigation, a landlord's successor in interest has a good faith belief that the lawfully remaining security deposit is transferred to the successor in interest or returned to the tenant pursuant to subdivision (h), the successor in interest is not liable for damages as provided in subdivision (l), or any security not transferred pursuant to subdivision (h).

(k) Upon receipt of any portion of the security under paragraph (1) of subdivision (h), the landlord's successors in interest shall have all of the rights and obligations of a landlord holding the security with respect to the security.

(l) The bad faith claim or retention by a landlord or the landlord's successors in interest of the security or any portion thereof in violation of this section, or the bad faith demand of replacement security in violation of subdivision (j), may subject the landlord or the landlord's successors in interest to statutory damages of up to twice the amount of the security, in addition to actual damages. The court may award damages for bad faith whenever the facts warrant that award, regardless of whether the injured party has specifically requested relief. In an action under this section, the landlord or the landlord's successors in interest shall have the burden of proof as to the reasonableness of the amounts claimed or the authority pursuant to this section to demand additional security deposits.

(m) No lease or rental agreement may contain a provision characterizing any security as "nonrefundable."

(n) An action under this section may be maintained in small claims court if the damages claimed, whether actual, statutory, or both, are within the jurisdictional amount allowed by Section 116.220 or 116.221 of the Code of Civil Procedure.

(o) Proof of the existence of and the amount of a security deposit may be established by any credible evidence, including, but not limited to, a canceled check, a receipt, a lease indicating the requirement of a deposit as well as the amount, prior consistent statements or actions of the landlord or tenant, or a statement under penalty of perjury that satisfies the credibility requirements set forth in Section 780 of the Evidence Code. (p) The amendments to this section made during the 1985 portion of the 1985-86 Regular Session of the Legislature that are set forth in subdivision (e) are declaratory of existing law.

(q) The amendments to this section made during the 2003 portion of the 2003-04 Regular Session of the Legislature that are set forth in paragraph (1) of subdivision (f) are declaratory of existing law. **Leg.H.** 1977, 1985, 1985, 1986, 1993, 1994, 2002, 2003, 2006, 2012, 2013, 2019.

§ 1951.2 *Termination of Lease: What Lessor May Recover*

(a) Except as otherwise provided in Section 1951.4, if a lessee of real property breaches the lease and abandons the property before the end of the term or if his right to possession is terminated by the lessor because of a breach of the lease, the lease terminates. Upon such termination, the lessor may recover from the lessee:

(1) The worth at the time of award of the unpaid rent which had been earned at the time of termination;

(2) The worth at the time of award of the amount by which the unpaid rent which would have been earned after termination until the time of award exceeds the amount of such rental loss that the lessee proves could have been reasonably avoided;

(3) Subject to subdivision (c), the worth at the time of award of the amount by which the unpaid rent for the balance of the term after the time of award exceeds the amount of such rental loss that the lessee proves could be reasonably avoided; and

(4) Any other amount necessary to compensate the lessor for all the detriment proximately caused by the lessee's failure to perform his obligations under the lease or which in the ordinary course of things would be likely to result therefrom.

(b) The "worth at the time of award" of the amounts referred to in paragraphs (1) and (2) of subdivision (a) is computed by allowing interest at such lawful rate as may be specified in the lease or, if no such rate is specified in the lease, at the legal rate. The worth at the time of award of the amount referred to in paragraph (3) of subdivision (a) is computed by discounting such amount at the discount rate of the Federal Reserve Bank of San Francisco at the time of award plus 1 percent.

(c) The lessor may recover damages under paragraph (3) of subdivision (a) only if:

(1) The lease provides that the damages he may recover include the worth at the time of award of the amount by which the unpaid rent for the balance of the term after the time of award, or for any shorter period of time specified in the lease, exceeds the amount of such rental loss for the same period that the lessee proves could be reasonably avoided; or

(2) The lessor relet the property prior to the time of award and proves that in reletting the property he acted reasonably and in a good faith effort to mitigate the damages, but the recovery of damages under this paragraph is subject to any limitations specified in the lease.

(d) Efforts by the lessor to mitigate the damages caused by the lessee's breach of the lease do not waive the lessor's right to recover damages under this section.

(e) Nothing in this section affects the right of the lessor under a lease of real property to indemnification for liability arising prior to the termination of the lease for personal injuries or property damage where the lease provides for such indemnification. **Leg.H.** 1970 c. 89 operative 7/1/71.

§ 1953 *Certain Rental Agreement Provisions Void*

(a) Any provision of a lease or rental agreement of a dwelling by which the lessee agrees to modify or waive any of the following rights shall be void as contrary to public policy:

(1) His rights or remedies under Section 1950.5 or 1954.

(2) His right to assert a cause of action against the lessor which may arise in the future.

(3) His right to a notice or hearing required by law.

(4) His procedural rights in litigation in any action involving his rights and obligations as a tenant.

(5) His right to have the landlord exercise a duty of care to prevent personal injury or personal property damage where that duty is imposed by law.

(b) Any provision of a lease or rental agreement of a dwelling by which the lessee agrees to modify or waive a statutory right, where the modification or waiver is not void under subdivision (a) or under Section 1942.1, 1942.5, or 1954, shall be void as contrary to public policy unless the lease or rental agreement is presented to the lessee before he takes actual possession of the premises. This subdivision does not apply to any provisions modifying or waiving a statutory right in agreements renewing leases or rental agreements where the same provision was also contained in the lease or rental agreement which is being renewed.

(c) This section shall apply only to leases and rental agreements executed on or after January 1, 1976. **Leg.H.** 1975.

§ 1954 *Entry by Landlord*

(a) A landlord may enter the dwelling unit only in the following cases:

(1) In case of emergency.

(2) To make necessary or agreed repairs, decorations, alterations or improvements, supply necessary or agreed services, or exhibit the dwelling unit to prospective or actual purchasers, mortgagees, tenants, workers, or contractors or

to make an inspection pursuant to subdivision (f) of Section 1950.5.

(3) When the tenant has abandoned or surrendered the premises.

(4) Pursuant to court order.

(5) For the purposes set forth in Chapter 2.5 [water service] (commencing with Section 1954.201).

(6) To comply with the provisions of Article 2.2 (commencing with Section 17973) of Chapter 5 of Part 1.5 of Division 13 of the Health and Safety Code.

(b) Except in cases of emergency or when the tenant has abandoned or surrendered the premises, entry may not be made during other than normal business hours unless the tenant consents to an entry during other than normal business hours at the time of entry.

(c) The landlord may not abuse the right of access or use it to harass the tenant.

(d) (1) Except as provided in subdivision (e), or as provided in paragraph (2) or (3), the landlord shall give the tenant reasonable notice in writing of his or her intent to enter and enter only during normal business hours. The notice shall include the date, approximate time, and purpose of the entry. The notice may be personally delivered to the tenant, left with someone of a suitable age and discretion at the premises, or, left on, near, or under the usual entry door of the premises in a manner in which a reasonable person would discover the notice. Twenty-four hours shall be presumed to be reasonable notice in absence of evidence to the contrary. The notice may be mailed to the tenant. Mailing of the notice at least six days prior to an intended entry is presumed reasonable notice in the absence of evidence to the contrary.

(2) If the purpose of the entry is to exhibit the dwelling unit to prospective or actual purchasers, the notice may be given orally, in person or by telephone, if the landlord or his or her agent has notified the tenant in writing within 120 days of the oral notice that the property is for sale and that the landlord or agent may contact the tenant orally for the purpose described above. Twenty-four hours is presumed reasonable notice in the absence of evidence to the contrary. The notice shall include the date, approximate time, and purpose of the entry. At the time of entry, the landlord or agent shall leave written evidence of the entry inside the unit.

(3) The tenant and the landlord may agree orally to an entry to make agreed repairs or supply agreed services. The agreement shall include the date and approximate time of the entry, which shall be within one week of the agreement. In this case, the landlord is not required to provide the tenant a written notice.

(e) No notice of entry is required under this section:

(1) To respond to an emergency.

(2) If the tenant is present and consents to the entry at the time of entry.

(3) After the tenant has abandoned or surrendered the unit. **Leg.H.** 1975, 2002, 2003, 2016, 2018.

§ 1954.50 *Costa-Hawkins Rental Housing Act*

This chapter shall be known and may be cited as the Costa-Hawkins Rental Housing Act. **Leg.H.** 1995.

§ 1954.51 *Costa-Hawkins Definitions*

As used in this chapter, the following terms have the following meanings:

(a) "Comparable units" means rental units that have approximately the same living space, have the same number of bedrooms, are located in the same or similar neighborhoods, and feature the same, similar, or equal amenities and housing services.

(b) "Owner" includes any person, acting as principal or through an agent, having the right to offer residential real property for rent, and includes a predecessor in interest to the owner, except that this term does not include the owner or operator of a mobile home park, or the owner of a mobile home or his or her agent.

(c) "Prevailing market rent" means the rental rate that would be authorized pursuant to 42 U.S.C.A. 1437 (f), as calculated by the United States Department of Housing and Urban Development pursuant to Part 888 of Title 24 of the Code of Federal Regulations.

(d) "Public entity" has the same meaning as set forth in Section 811.2 of the Government Code.

(e) "Residential real property" includes any dwelling or unit that is intended for human habitation.

(f) "Tenancy" includes the lawful occupation of property and includes a lease or sublease. **Leg.H.** 1995.

§ 1954.52 *Costa-Hawkins Rent Decontrol*

(a) Notwithstanding any other provision of law, an owner of residential real property may establish the initial and all subsequent rental rates for a dwelling or a unit about which any of the following is true:

(1) It has a certificate of occupancy issued after February 1, 1995.

(2) It has already been exempt from the residential rent control ordinance of a public entity on or before February 1, 1995, pursuant to a local exemption for newly constructed units.

(3) (A) It is alienable separate from the title to any other dwelling unit or is a subdivided interest in a subdivision, as specified in subdivision (b), (d), or (f) of Section 11004.5 of the Business and Professions Code.

(B) This paragraph does not apply to either of the following:

(i) A dwelling or unit where the preceding tenancy has been terminated by the owner by notice pursuant to Section 1946.1 or has been terminated upon a change in the terms of the tenancy noticed pursuant to Section 827.

(ii) A condominium dwelling or unit that has not been sold separately by the subdivider to a bona fide purchaser for value. The initial rent amount of the unit for purposes of this chapter shall be the lawful rent in effect on May 7, 2001, unless the rent amount is governed by a different provision of this chapter. However, if a condominium dwelling or unit meets the criteria of paragraph (1) or (2) of subdivision (a), or if all the dwellings or units except one have been sold separately by the subdivider to bona fide purchasers for value, and the subdivider has occupied that remaining unsold condominium dwelling or unit as his or her principal residence for at least one year after the subdivision occurred, then subparagraph (A) of paragraph (3) shall apply to that unsold condominium dwelling or unit.

(C) Where a dwelling or unit in which the initial or subsequent rental rates are controlled by an ordinance or charter provision in effect on January 1, 1995, the following shall apply:

(i) An owner of real property as described in this paragraph may establish the initial and all subsequent rental rates for all existing and new tenancies in effect on or after January 1, 1999, if the tenancy in effect on or after January 1, 1999, was created between January 1, 1996, and December 31, 1998.

(ii) Commencing on January 1, 1999, an owner of real property as described in this paragraph may establish the initial and all subsequent rental rates for all new tenancies if the previous tenancy was in effect on December 31, 1995.

(iii) The initial rental rate for a dwelling or unit as described in this paragraph in which the initial rental rate is controlled by an ordinance or charter provision in effect on January 1, 1995, may not, until January 1, 1999, exceed the amount calculated pursuant to subdivision (c) of Section 1954.53. An owner of residential real property as described in this paragraph may, until January 1, 1999, establish the initial rental rate for a dwelling or unit only where the tenant has voluntarily vacated, abandoned, or been evicted pursuant to paragraph (2) of Section 1161 of the Code of Civil Procedure.

(b) Subdivision (a) does not apply where the owner has otherwise agreed by contract with a public entity in consideration for a direct financial contribution or any other forms of assistance specified in Chapter 4.3 (commencing with Section 65915) of Division 1 of Title 7 of the Government Code.

(c) Nothing in this section shall be construed to affect the authority of a public entity that may otherwise exist to regulate or monitor the basis for eviction.

(d) This section does not apply to any dwelling or unit that contains serious health, safety, fire, or building code violations, excluding those caused by disasters for which a citation has been issued by the appropriate governmental agency and which has remained unabated for six months or longer preceding the vacancy. **Leg.H.** 1995, 2001, 2004.

§ 1954.53 *Vacancy Decontrol*

(a) Notwithstanding any other provision of law, an owner of residential real property may establish the initial rental rate for a dwelling or unit, except where any of the following applies:

(1) The previous tenancy has been terminated by the owner by notice pursuant to Section 1946.1 or has been terminated upon a change in the terms of the tenancy noticed pursuant to Section 827, except a change permitted by law in the amount of rent or fees. For the purpose of this paragraph, the owner's termination or nonrenewal of a contract or recorded agreement with a governmental agency that provides for a rent limitation to a qualified tenant, shall be construed as a change in the terms of the tenancy pursuant to Section 827.

(A) In a jurisdiction that controls by ordinance or charter provision the rental rate for a dwelling or unit, an owner who terminates or fails to renew a contract or recorded agreement with a governmental agency that provides for a rent limitation to a qualified tenant may not set an initial rent for three years following the date of the termination or nonrenewal of the contract or agreement. For any new tenancy established during the three-year period, the rental rate for a new tenancy established in that vacated dwelling or unit shall be at the same rate as the rent under the terminated or nonrenewed contract or recorded agreement with a governmental agency that provided for a rent limitation to a qualified tenant, plus any increases authorized after the termination or cancellation of the contract or recorded agreement.

(B) Subparagraph (A) does not apply to any new tenancy of 12 months or more duration established after January 1, 2000, pursuant to the owner's contract or recorded agreement with a governmental agency that provides for a rent limitation to a qualified tenant, unless the prior vacancy in that dwelling or unit was pursuant to a nonrenewed or canceled contract or recorded agreement with a governmental agency that provides for a rent limitation to a qualified tenant as set forth in that subparagraph.

(2) The owner has otherwise agreed by contract with a public entity in consideration for a direct financial contribution or any other forms of assistance specified in Chapter 4.3 (commencing with Section 65915) of Division 1 of Title 7 of the Government Code.

(3) The initial rental rate for a dwelling or unit whose initial rental rate is controlled by an ordinance or charter provision in effect on January 1, 1995, may not until January 1, 1999, exceed the amount calculated pursuant to subdivision (c).

(b) Subdivision (a) applies to, and includes, renewal of the initial hiring by the same tenant, lessee, authorized subtenant, or authorized sublessee for the entire period of his or her occupancy at the rental rate established for the initial hiring.

(c) The rental rate of a dwelling or unit whose initial rental rate is controlled by ordinance or charter provision in effect on January 1, 1995, shall, until January 1, 1999, be established in accordance with this subdivision. Where the previous tenant has voluntarily vacated, abandoned, or been evicted pursuant to paragraph (2) of Section 1161 of Code of Civil Procedure, an owner of residential real property may, no more than twice, establish the initial rental rate for a dwelling or unit in an amount that is no greater than 15 percent more than the rental rate in effect for the immediately preceding tenancy or in an amount that is 70 percent of the prevailing market rent for comparable units, whichever amount is greater.

The initial rental rate established pursuant to this subdivision may not substitute for or replace increases in rental rates otherwise authorized pursuant to law.

(d) (1) Nothing in this section or any other provision of law shall be construed to preclude express establishment in a lease or rental agreement of the rental rates to be applicable in the event the rental unit subject thereto is sublet. Nothing in this section shall be construed to impair the obligations of contracts entered into prior to January 1, 1996.

(2) If the original occupant or occupants who took possession of the dwelling or unit pursuant to the rental agreement with the owner no longer permanently reside there, an owner may increase the rent by any amount allowed by this section to a lawful sublessee or assignee who did not reside at the dwelling or unit prior to January 1, 1996.

(3) This subdivision does not apply to partial changes in occupancy of a dwelling or unit where one or more of the occupants of the premises, pursuant to the agreement with the owner provided for above, remains an occupant in lawful possession of the dwelling or unit, or where a lawful sublessee or assignee who resided at the dwelling or unit prior to January 1, 1996, remains in possession of the dwelling or unit. Nothing contained in this section shall be construed to enlarge or diminish an owner's right to withhold consent to a sublease or assignment.

(4) Acceptance of rent by the owner does not operate as a waiver or otherwise prevent enforcement of a covenant prohibiting sublease or assignment or as a waiver of an owner's rights to establish the initial rental rate, unless the owner has received written notice from the tenant that is party to the agreement and thereafter accepted rent.

(e) Nothing in this section shall be construed to affect any authority of a public entity that may otherwise exist to regulate or monitor the grounds for eviction.

(f) This section does not apply to any dwelling or unit if all the following conditions are met:

(1) The dwelling or unit has been cited in an inspection report by the appropriate governmental agency as containing serious health, safety, fire, or building code violations, as defined by Section 17920.3 of the Health and Safety Code, excluding any violation caused by a disaster.

(2) The citation was issued at least 60 days prior to the date of the vacancy.

(3) The cited violation had not been abated when the prior tenant vacated and had remained unabated for 60 days or for a longer period of time. However, the 60-day time period may be extended by the appropriate governmental agency that issued the citation. **Leg.H.** 1995, 1996, 1999, 2004.

§ 1961 *Disclosure to Tenant by Owner*

This chapter shall apply to every dwelling structure containing one or more units offered to the public for rent or for lease for residential purposes. **Leg.H.** 1972 c. 941 operative 7/1/73, 1987.

§ 1962 *Disclosure to Tenant by Owner*

(a) Any owner of a dwelling structure specified in Section 1961 or a party signing a rental agreement or lease on behalf of the owner shall do all of the following:

(1) Disclose therein the name, telephone number, and usual street address at which personal service may be effected of each person who is:

(A) Authorized to manage the premises.

(B) An owner of the premises or a person who is authorized to act for and on behalf of the owner for the purpose of service of process and for the purpose of receiving and receipting for all notices and demands.

(2) Disclose therein the name, telephone number, and address of the person or entity to whom rent payments shall be made.

(A) If rent payments may be made personally, the usual days and hours that the person will be available to receive the payments shall also be disclosed.

(B) At the owner's option, the rental agreement or lease shall instead disclose the number of either:

(i) The account in a financial institution into which rent payments may be made, and the name and street address of the institution; provided that the institution is located within five miles of the rental property.

(ii) The information necessary to establish an electronic funds transfer procedure for paying the rent.

(3) Disclose therein the form or forms in which rent payments are to be made.

(4) Provide a copy of the rental agreement or lease to the tenant within 15 days of its execution by the tenant. Once each calendar year thereafter, upon request by the tenant, the owner or owner's agent shall provide an additional copy to the tenant within 15 days. If the owner or owner's agent does not possess the rental agreement or lease or a copy of it, the owner or owner's agent shall instead furnish the tenant with a written statement stating that fact and containing the information required by paragraphs (1), (2), and (3).

(b) In the case of an oral rental agreement, the owner, or a person acting on behalf of the owner for the receipt of rent or otherwise, shall furnish the tenant, within 15 days of the agreement, with a written statement containing the information required by paragraphs (1), (2), and (3) of subdivision (a). Once each calendar year thereafter, upon request by the tenant, the owner or owner's agent shall provide an additional copy of the statement to the tenant within 15 days.

(c) The information required by this section shall be kept current and this section shall extend to and be enforceable against any successor owner or manager, who shall comply with this section within 15 days of succeeding the previous owner or manager. A successor owner or manager shall not serve a notice pursuant to paragraph (2) of Section 1161 of the Code of Civil Procedure or otherwise evict a tenant for nonpayment of rent that accrued during the period of noncompliance by a successor owner or manager with this subdivision. Nothing in this subdivision shall relieve the tenant of any liability for unpaid rent.

(d) A party who enters into a rental agreement on behalf of the owner who fails to comply with this section is deemed an agent of each person who is an owner:

(1) For the purpose of service of process and receiving and receipting for notices and demands.

(2) For the purpose of performing the obligations of the owner under law and under the rental agreement.

(3) For the purpose of receiving rental payments, which may be made in cash, by check, by money order, or in any form previously accepted by the owner or owner's agent, unless the form of payment has been specified in the oral or written agreement, or the tenant has been notified by the owner in writing that a particular form of payment is unacceptable.

(e) Nothing in this section limits or excludes the liability of any undisclosed owner.

(f) If the address provided by the owner does not allow for personal delivery, then it shall be conclusively presumed that upon the mailing of any rent or notice to the owner by the tenant to the name and address provided, the notice or rent is deemed receivable by the owner on the date posted, if the tenant can show proof of mailing to the name and address provided by the owner. **Leg.H.** 1972 c. 941 operative 7/1/73, 1987, 2001, 2012.

§ 1962.5 *Posting Disclosure to Tenant by Landlord*

(a) Notwithstanding subdivisions (a) and (b) of Section 1962, the information required by paragraph (1) of subdivision (a) of Section 1962 to be disclosed to a tenant may, instead of being disclosed in the manner described in subdivisions (a) and (b) of Section 1962, be disclosed by the following method:

(1) In each dwelling structure containing an elevator a printed or typewritten notice containing the information required by paragraph (1) of subdivision (a) of Section 1962 shall be placed in every elevator and in one other conspicuous place.

(2) In each structure not containing an elevator, a printed or typewritten notice containing the information required by paragraph (1) of subdivision (a) of Section 1962 shall be placed in at least two conspicuous places.

(3) In the case of a single unit dwelling structure, the information to be disclosed under this section may be disclosed by complying with either paragraph (1) or (2).

(b) Except as provided in subdivision (a), all the provisions of Section 1962 shall be applicable. **Leg.H.** 1972 c. 941 operative 1/1/73, 1987, 2001.

Appendix D–California Law Excerpts

In the event an owner, successor owner, manager, or agent specified in Section 1961 fails to comply with the requirements of this chapter, service of process by a tenant with respect to a dispute arising out of the tenancy may be made by registered or certified mail sent to the address at which rent is paid, in which case the provisions of Section 1013 of the Code of Civil Procedure shall apply. **Leg.H.** 1987, 2001.

California Code of Civil Procedure

§ 12 Counting Days for Required Act

The time in which any act provided by law is to be done is computed by excluding the first day, and including the last, unless the last day is a holiday, and then it is also excluded. **Leg.H.** 1872.

§ 12a Extension of Due Date

(a) If the last day for the performance of any act provided or required by law to be performed within a specified period of time is a holiday, then that period is hereby extended to and including the next day that is not a holiday. For purposes of this section, "holiday" means all day on Saturdays, all holidays specified in Section 135 and, to the extent provided in Section 12b, all days that by terms of Section 12b are required to be considered as holidays.

(b) This section applies to Sections 659, 659a, and 921, and to all other provisions of law providing or requiring an act to be performed on a particular day or within a specified period of time, whether expressed in this or any other code or statute, ordinance, rule, or regulation. **Leg.H.** 1933, 1951, 1955, 1961, 1982, 1994;, 2001, 2007.

§ 1013 Notice Requirements If Mailed or Faxed

(a) In case of service by mail, the notice or other paper shall be deposited in a post office, mailbox, subpost office, substation, or mail chute, or other like facility regularly maintained by the United States Postal Service, in a sealed envelope, with postage paid, addressed to the person on whom it is to be served, at the office address as last given by that person on any document filed in the cause and served on the party making service by mail; otherwise at that party's place of residence. The service is complete at the time of the deposit, but any period of notice and any right or duty to do any act or make any response within any period or on a date certain after the service of the document, which time period or date is prescribed by statute or rule of court, shall be extended five calendar days, upon service by mail, if the place of address and the place of mailing is within the State of California, 10 calendar days if either the place of mailing or the place of address is outside the State of California but within the United States, and 20 calendar days if either the place of mailing or the place of address is outside the

United States, but the extension shall not apply to extend the time for filing notice of intention to move for new trial, notice of intention to move to vacate judgment pursuant to Section 663a, or notice of appeal. This extension applies in the absence of a specific exception provided for by this section or other statute or rule of court.

(b) The copy of the notice or other paper served by mail pursuant to this chapter shall bear a notation of the date and place of mailing or be accompanied by an unsigned copy of the affidavit or certificate of mailing.

(c) In case of service by Express Mail, the notice or other paper must be deposited in a post office, mailbox, subpost office, substation, or mail chute, or other like facility regularly maintained by the United States Postal Service for receipt of Express Mail, in a sealed envelope, with Express Mail postage paid, addressed to the person on whom it is to be served, at the office address as last given by that person on any document filed in the cause and served on the party making service by Express Mail; otherwise at that party's place of residence. In case of service by another method of delivery providing for overnight delivery, the notice or other paper must be deposited in a box or other facility regularly maintained by the express service carrier, or delivered to an authorized courier or driver authorized by the express service carrier to receive documents, in an envelope or package designated by the express service carrier with delivery fees paid or provided for, addressed to the person on whom it is to be served, at the office address as last given by that person on any document filed in the cause and served on the party making service; otherwise at that party's place of residence. The service is complete at the time of the deposit, but any period of notice and any right or duty to do any act or make any response within any period or on a date certain after the service of the document served by Express Mail or other method of delivery providing for overnight delivery shall be extended by two court days, but the extension shall not apply to extend the time for filing notice of intention to move for new trial, notice of intention to move to vacate judgment pursuant to Section 663a, or notice of appeal. This extension applies in the absence of a specific exception provided for by this section or other statute or rule of court.

(d) The copy of the notice or other paper served by Express Mail or another means of delivery providing for overnight delivery pursuant to this chapter shall bear a notation of the date and place of deposit or be accompanied by an unsigned copy of the affidavit or certificate of deposit.

(e) Service by facsimile transmission shall be permitted only where the parties agree and a written confirmation of that agreement is made. The Judicial Council may adopt rules implementing the service of documents by facsimile transmission and may provide a form for the confirmation of the agreement required by this subdivision. In case of service by facsimile transmission, the notice or other paper must be transmitted to a facsimile machine maintained by the person on whom it is served at the facsimile machine telephone number as last given by that person on any document which he or she has filed in the cause and served on the party making the service. The service is complete at the time of transmission, but any period of notice and any right or duty to do any act or make any response within any period or on a date certain after the service of the document, which time period or date is prescribed by statute or rule of court, shall be extended, after service by facsimile transmission, by two court days, but the extension shall not apply to extend the time for filing notice of intention to move for new trial, notice of intention to move to vacate judgment pursuant to Section 663a, or notice of appeal. This extension applies in the absence of a specific exception provided for by this section or other statute or rule of court.

(f) The copy of the notice or other paper served by facsimile transmission pursuant to this chapter shall bear a notation of the date and place of transmission and the facsimile telephone number to which transmitted or be accompanied by an unsigned copy of the affidavit or certificate of transmission which shall contain the facsimile telephone number to which the notice or other paper was transmitted.

(g) Electronic service shall be permitted pursuant to Section 1010.6 and the rules on electronic service in the California Rules of Court.

(h) Subdivisions (b), (d), and (f) are directory. **Leg.H.** 1872, 1874, 1907, 1929, 1931, 1949, 1967, 1968, 1974, 1980, 1992, 1995, 2001, 2010.

§ 1161 *Unlawful Detainer Defined*

A tenant of real property, for a term less than life, or the executor or administrator of the tenant's estate heretofore qualified and now acting or hereafter to be qualified and act, is guilty of unlawful detainer:

1. When the tenant continues in possession, in person or by subtenant, of the property, or any part thereof, after the expiration of the term for which it is let to the tenant; provided the expiration is of a nondefault nature however brought about without the permission of the landlord, or the successor in estate of the landlord, if applicable; including the case where the person to be removed became the occupant of the premises as a servant, employee, agent, or licensee and the relation of master and servant, or employer and employee, or principal and agent, or licensor and licensee, has been lawfully terminated or the time fixed for occupancy by the agreement between the parties has expired; but nothing in this subdivision shall be construed as preventing the removal of the occupant in any other lawful manner; but in case of a tenancy at will, it shall first be terminated by notice, as prescribed in the Civil Code.

2. When the tenant continues in possession, in person or by subtenant, without the permission of the landlord, or the

successor in estate of the landlord, if applicable, after default in the payment of rent, pursuant to the lease or agreement under which the property is held, and three days' notice, excluding Saturdays and Sundays and other judicial holidays, in writing, requiring its payment, stating the amount that is due, the name, telephone number, and address of the person to whom the rent payment shall be made, and, if payment may be made personally, the usual days and hours that person will be available to receive the payment (provided that, if the address does not allow for personal delivery, then it shall be conclusively presumed that upon the mailing of any rent or notice to the owner by the tenant to the name and address provided, the notice or rent is deemed received by the owner on the date posted, if the tenant can show proof of mailing to the name and address provided by the owner), or the number of an account in a financial institution into which the rental payment may be made, and the name and street address of the institution (provided that the institution is located within five miles of the rental property), or if an electronic funds transfer procedure has been previously established, that payment may be made pursuant to that procedure, or possession of the property, shall have been served upon the tenant and if there is a subtenant in actual occupation of the premises, also upon the subtenant.

The notice may be served at any time within one year after the rent becomes due. In all cases of tenancy upon agricultural lands, if the tenant has held over and retained possession for more than 60 days after the expiration of the term without any demand of possession or notice to quit by the landlord or the successor in estate of the landlord, if applicable, the tenant shall be deemed to be holding by permission of the landlord or successor in estate of the landlord, if applicable, and shall be entitled to hold under the terms of the lease for another full year, and shall not be guilty of an unlawful detainer during that year, and the holding over for that period shall be taken and construed as a consent on the part of a tenant to hold for another year.

An unlawful detainer action under this paragraph shall be subject to the COVID-19 Tenant Relief Act of 2020 (Chapter 5 (commencing with Section 1179.01)) if the default in the payment of rent is based upon the COVID-19 rental debt.

3. When the tenant continues in possession, in person or by subtenant, after a neglect or failure to perform other conditions or covenants of the lease or agreement under which the property is held, including any covenant not to assign or sublet, than the one for the payment of rent, and three days' notice, excluding Saturdays and Sundays and other judicial holidays, in writing, requiring the performance of those conditions or covenants, or the possession of the property, shall have been served upon the tenant, and if there is a subtenant in actual occupation of the premises, also, upon the subtenant. Within three days, excluding Saturdays and Sundays and other judicial holidays, after the service of the notice, the tenant, or any subtenant in actual occupation of the premises, or any mortgagee of the term, or other person interested in its continuance, may perform the conditions or covenants of the lease or pay the stipulated rent, as the case

may be, and thereby save the lease from forfeiture; provided, if the conditions and covenants of the lease, violated by the lessee, cannot afterward be performed, then no notice, as last prescribed herein, need be given to the lessee or the subtenant, demanding the performance of the violated conditions or covenants of the lease.

A tenant may take proceedings, similar to those prescribed in this chapter, to obtain possession of the premises let to a subtenant or held by a servant, employee, agent, or licensee, in case of that person's unlawful detention of the premises underlet to or held by that person.

An unlawful detainer action under this paragraph shall be subject to the COVID-19 Tenant Relief Act of 2020 (Chapter 5 (commencing with Section 1179.01)) if the neglect or failure to perform other conditions or covenants of the lease or agreement is based upon the COVID-19 rental debt.

4. Any tenant, subtenant, or executor or administrator of that person's estate heretofore qualified and now acting, or hereafter to be qualified and act, assigning or subletting or committing waste upon the demised premises, contrary to the conditions or covenants of the lease, or maintaining, committing, or permitting the maintenance or commission of a nuisance upon the demised premises or using the premises for an unlawful purpose, thereby terminates the lease, and the landlord, or the landlord's successor in estate, shall upon service of three days' notice to quit upon the person or persons in possession, be entitled to restitution of possession of the demised premises under this chapter. For purposes of this subdivision, a person who commits or maintains a public nuisance as described in Section 3482.8 of the Civil Code, or who commits an offense described in subdivision (c) of Section 3485 of the Civil Code, or subdivision (c) of Section 3486 of the Civil Code, or uses the premises to further the purpose of that offense shall be deemed to have committed a nuisance upon the premises.

5. When the tenant gives written notice as provided in Section 1946 of the Civil Code of the tenant's intention to terminate the hiring of the real property, or makes a written offer to surrender which is accepted in writing by the landlord, but fails to deliver possession at the time specified in that written notice, without the permission of the landlord, or the successor in estate of the landlord, if applicable.

6. As used in this section:

"COVID-19 rental debt" has the same meaning as defined in Section 1179.02.

"Tenant" includes any person who hires real property except those persons whose occupancy is described in subdivision (b) of Section 1940 of the Civil Code.

7. This section shall remain in effect until February 1, 2025, and

as of that date is repealed. **Leg.H.** 2008, 2009, 2011, 2018, 2020.

§ 1161.3 *Victim of Domestic Violence, Sexual Assault, Stalking, or Abused Elder or Dependent Adult May Not Be Evicted*

(a) Except as provided in subdivision (b), a landlord shall not terminate a tenancy or fail to renew a tenancy based upon an act or acts against a tenant or a tenant's household member that constitute domestic violence as defined in Section 6211 of the Family Code, sexual assault as defined in Section 1219, stalking as defined in Section 1708.7 of the Civil Code or Section 646.9 of the Penal Code, human trafficking as defined in Section 236.1 of the Penal Code, or abuse of an elder or a dependent adult as defined in Section 15610.07 of the Welfare and Institutions Code, if both of the following apply:

(1) The act or acts of domestic violence, sexual assault, stalking, human trafficking, or abuse of an elder or a dependent adult have been documented by one of the following:

(A) A temporary restraining order, emergency protective order, or protective order lawfully issued within the last 180 days pursuant to Section 527.6, Part 3 (commencing with Section 6240), Part 4 (commencing with Section 6300), or Part 5 (commencing with Section 6400) of Division 10 of the Family Code, Section 136.2 of the Penal Code, or Section 213.5 or 15657.03 of the Welfare and Institutions Code that protects the tenant or household member from domestic violence, sexual assault, stalking, human trafficking, or abuse of an elder or a dependent adult.

(B) A copy of a written report, written within the last 180 days, by a peace officer employed by a state or local law enforcement agency acting in his or her official capacity, stating that the tenant or household member has filed a report alleging that he or she or the household member is a victim of domestic violence, sexual assault, stalking, human trafficking, or abuse of an elder or a dependent adult.

(C) Documentation from a qualified third party based on information received by that third party while acting in his or her professional capacity to indicate that the tenant or household member is seeking assistance for physical or mental injuries or abuse resulting from an act of domestic violence, sexual assault, stalking, human trafficking, elder abuse, or dependent adult abuse.

(D) The documentation shall contain, in substantially the same form, the following:

Tenant Statement and Qualified Third Party Statement

under Code of Civil Procedure Section 1161.3

Part I.Statement By Tenant

I, [insert name of tenant], state as follows:

I, or a member of my household, have been a victim of:

[insert one or more of the following: domestic violence, sexual assault, stalking, human trafficking, elder abuse, or dependent adult abuse.]

The most recent incident(s) happened on or about:

[insert date or dates.]

The incident(s) was/were committed by the following person(s), with these physical description(s), if known and safe to provide:

[if known and safe to provide, insert name(s) and physical description(s).]

(signature of tenant)(date)

Part II.Qualified Third Party Statement

I, [insert name of qualified third party], state as follows:

My business address and phone number are:

[insert business address and phone number.]

Check and complete one of the following:

_____I meet the requirements for a sexual assault counselor provided in Section 1035.2 of the Evidence Code and I am either engaged in an office, hospital, institution, or center commonly known as a rape crisis center described in that section or employed by an organization providing the programs specified in Section 13835.2 of the Penal Code.

_____I meet the requirements for a domestic violence counselor provided in Section 1037.1 of the Evidence Code and I am employed, whether financially compensated or not, by a domestic violence victim service organization, as defined in that section.

_____I meet the requirements for a human trafficking caseworker provided in Section 1038.2 of the Evidence Code and I am employed, whether financially compensated or not, by an organization that provides programs specified in Section 18294 of the Welfare and Institutions Code or in Section 13835.2 of the Penal Code.

_____I am licensed by the State of California as a:

[insert one of the following: physician and surgeon, osteopathic physician and surgeon, registered nurse, psychiatrist, psychologist, licensed clinical social worker,

licensed marriage and family therapist, or licensed professional clinical counselor.] and I am licensed by, and my license number is:

[insert name of state licensing entity and license number.]

The person who signed the Statement By Tenant above stated to me that he or she, or a member of his or her household, is a victim of:

[insert one or more of the following: domestic violence, sexual assault, stalking, human trafficking, elder abuse, or dependent adult abuse.]

The person further stated to me the incident(s) occurred on or about the date(s) stated above.

(signature of qualified third party)(date)

(E) The documentation may be signed by a person who meets the requirements for a sexual assault counselor, domestic violence counselor, or a human trafficking caseworker only if the documentation displays the letterhead of the office, hospital, institution, center, or organization, as appropriate, that engages or employs, whether financially compensated or not, this counselor or caseworker.

(2) The person against whom the protection order has been issued or who was named in the police report or Tenant Statement and Qualified Third Party Statement regarding the act or acts of domestic violence, sexual assault, stalking, human trafficking, or abuse of an elder or dependent adult is not a tenant of the same dwelling unit as the tenant or household member.

(b) A landlord may terminate or decline to renew a tenancy after the tenant has availed himself or herself of the protections afforded by subdivision (a) if both of the following apply:

(1) Either of the following:

(A) The tenant allows the person against whom the protection order has been issued or who was named in the police report or Tenant Statement and Qualified Third Party Statement regarding the act or acts of domestic violence, sexual assault, stalking, human trafficking, or abuse of an elder or a dependent adult to visit the property.

(B) The landlord reasonably believes that the presence of the person against whom the protection order has been issued or who was named in the police report or Tenant Statement and Qualified Third Party Statement regarding the act or acts of domestic violence, sexual assault, stalking, human trafficking, or abuse of an elder or dependent adult poses a physical threat to other tenants, guests, invitees, or licensees, or to a tenant's right to quiet possession pursuant to Section

1927 of the Civil Code.

(2) The landlord previously gave at least three days' notice to the tenant to correct a violation of paragraph (1).

(c) Notwithstanding any provision in the lease to the contrary, the landlord shall not be liable to any other tenants for any action that arises due to the landlord's compliance with this section.

(d) (1) A landlord shall not disclose any information provided by a tenant under this section to a third party unless either of the following are true:

(A) The tenant has consented in writing to the disclosure.

(B) The disclosure is required by law or court order.

(2) A landlord's communication with the qualified third party who provides documentation in order to verify the contents of that documentation is not a disclosure for purposes of this subdivision.

(e) For the purposes of this section:

(1) "Tenant" means tenant, subtenant, lessee, or sublessee.

(2) "Health practitioner" means a physician and surgeon, osteopathic physician and surgeon, psychiatrist, psychologist, registered nurse, licensed clinical social worker, licensed marriage and family therapist, or licensed professional clinical counselor.

(3) "Qualified third party" means a health practitioner, domestic violence counselor, as defined in Section 1037.1 of the Evidence Code, a sexual assault counselor, as defined in Section 1035.2 of the Evidence Code, or a human trafficking caseworker, as defined in Section 1038.2 of the Evidence Code.

(f) The Judicial Council shall, on or before September 1, 2019, develop a new form or revise an existing form that may be used by a party to assert in the responsive pleading the grounds set forth in this section as an affirmative defense to an unlawful detainer action. **Leg.H.** 2010, 2013, 2018.

§ 1162 *Service of Notice Terminating Tenancy*

(a) Except as provided in subdivision (b), the notices required by Sections 1161 and 1161a may be served by any of the following methods:

(1) By delivering a copy to the tenant personally.

(2) If he or she is absent from his or her place of residence, and from his or her usual place of business, by leaving a copy with

some person of suitable age and discretion at either place, and sending a copy through the mail addressed to the tenant at his or her place of residence.

(3) If such place of residence and business cannot be ascertained, or a person of suitable age or discretion there can not be found, then by affixing a copy in a conspicuous place on the property, and also delivering a copy to a person there residing, if such person can be found; and also sending a copy through the mail addressed to the tenant at the place where the property is situated. Service upon a subtenant may be made in the same manner.

(b) The notices required by Section 1161 may be served upon a commercial tenant by any of the following methods:

(1) By delivering a copy to the tenant personally.

(2) If he or she is absent from the commercial rental property, by leaving a copy with some person of suitable age and discretion at the property, and sending a copy through the mail addressed to the tenant at the address where the property is situated.

(3) If, at the time of attempted service, a person of suitable age or discretion is not found at the rental property through the exercise of reasonable diligence, then by affixing a copy in a conspicuous place on the property, and also sending a copy through the mail addressed to the tenant at the address where the property is situated. Service upon a subtenant may be made in the same manner.

(c) For purposes of subdivision (b), "commercial tenant" means a person or entity that hires any real property in this state that is not a dwelling unit, as defined in subdivision (c) of Section 1940 of the Civil Code, or a mobilehome, as defined in Section 798.3 of the Civil Code. **Leg. H.** 1872, 1874, 1935, 2002, 2010.

§ 2074 *Written Offer to Pay Equivalent to Payment*

An offer in writing to pay a particular sum of money, or to deliver a written instrument or specific personal property, is, if not accepted, equivalent to the actual production and tender of the money, instrument, or property. **Leg.H.** 1872.

§ 2075 *Right to Receipt for Payment or Delivery*

Whoever pays money, or delivers an instrument or property, is entitled to a receipt therefor from the person to whom the payment or delivery is made, and may demand a proper signature to such receipt as a condition of the payment or delivery. **Leg.H.** 1872.

§ 2076 *Objections to Tender Must Be Specified*

The person to whom a tender is made must, at the time, specify any objection he may have to the money, instrument, or property, or he must be deemed to have waived it; and if the objection be to the amount of money, the terms of the instrument, or the amount or kind of property, he must specify the amount, terms, or kind which he requires, or be precluded from objecting afterwards. **Leg.H.** 1872.

California Government Code

§ 7060 *Prohibition Against Compelling Owner to Lease Accommodations (Ellis Act)*

(a) No public entity, as defined in Section 811.2, shall, by statute, ordinance, or regulation, or by administrative action implementing any statute, ordinance or regulation, compel the owner of any residential real property to offer, or to continue to offer, accommodations in the property for rent or lease, except for guestrooms or efficiency units within a residential hotel, as defined in Section 50519 of the Health and Safety Code, if the residential hotel meets all of the following conditions:

(1) The residential hotel is located in a city and county, or in a city with a population of over 1,000,000.

(2) The residential hotel has a permit of occupancy issued prior to January 1, 1990.

(3) The residential hotel did not send a notice of intent to withdraw the accommodations from rent or lease pursuant to subdivision (a) of Section 7060.4 that was delivered to the public entity prior to January 1, 2004.

(b) For the purposes of this chapter, the following definitions apply:

(1) "Accommodations" means either of the following:

(A) The residential rental units in any detached physical structure containing four or more residential rental units.

(B) With respect to a detached physical structure containing three or fewer residential rental units, the residential rental units in that structure and in any other structure located on the same parcel of land, including any detached physical structure specified in subparagraph (A).

(2) "Disabled" means a person with a disability, as defined in Section 12955.3 of the Government Code. **Leg.H.** 1985, 1999, 2003.

§ 7060.1 *Persons and Entities to Which Chapter (Ellis Act) Does Not Apply*

Notwithstanding Section 7060, nothing in this chapter does any of the following:

(a) Prevents a public entity from enforcing any contract or agreement by which an owner of residential real property has agreed to offer the accommodations for rent or lease in consideration for a direct financial contribution or, with respect to written contracts or agreements entered into prior to July 1, 1986, for any consideration. Any contract or agreement specified in this subdivision is not enforceable against a person who acquires title to the accommodations as a bona fide purchaser for value (or successors in interest thereof), unless (1) the purchaser at the time of acquiring title to the accommodations has actual knowledge of the contract or agreement, or (2) a written memorandum of the contract or agreement which specifically describes the terms thereof and the affected real property, and which identifies the owner of the property, has been recorded with the county recorder prior to July 1, 1986, or not less than 30 days prior to transfer of title to the property to the purchaser. The county recorder shall index such a written memorandum in the grantor-grantee index.

As used in this subdivision, "direct financial contribution" includes contributions specified in Section 65916 and any form of interest rate subsidy or tax abatement provided to facilitate the acquisition or development of real property.

(b) Diminishes or enhances, except as specifically provided in Section 7060.2, any power which currently exists or which may hereafter exist in any public entity to grant or deny any entitlement to the use of real property, including, but not limited to, planning, zoning, and subdivision map approvals.

(c) Diminishes or enhances any power in any public entity to mitigate any adverse impact on persons displaced by reason of the withdrawal from rent or lease of any accommodations.

(d) Supersedes any provision of Chapter 16 (commencing with Section 7260) of this division, Part 2.8 (commencing with Section 12900) of Division 3 of Title 2 of this code, Chapter 5 (commencing with Section 17200) of Part 2 of Division 7 of the Business and Professions Code, Part 2 (commencing with Section 43) of Division 1 of the Civil Code, Title 5 (commencing with Section 1925) of Part 4 of Division 3 of the Civil Code, Chapter 4 (commencing with Section 1159) of Title 3 of Part 3 of the Code of Civil Procedure, or Division 24 (commencing with Section 33000) of the Health and Safety Code.

(e) Relieves any party to a lease or rental agreement of the duty to perform any obligation under that lease or rental agreement. **Leg.H.** 1985, 2003.

§ 7060.2 *Regulation of Property Subject to Rent Control on Re-Offer for Rent After Withdrawal*

If a public entity, by valid exercise of its police power, has in effect any control or system of control on the price at which accommodations may be offered for rent or lease, that entity may, notwithstanding any provision of this chapter, provide by statute or ordinance, or by regulation as specified in Section 7060.5, that any accommodations which have been offered for rent or lease and which were subject to that control or system of control at the time the accommodations were withdrawn from rent or lease, shall be subject to the following:

(a) (1) For all tenancies commenced during the time periods described in paragraph (2), the accommodations shall be offered and rented or leased at the lawful rent in effect at the time any notice of intent to withdraw the accommodations is filed with the public entity, plus annual adjustments available under the system of control.

(2) The provisions of paragraph (1) shall apply to all tenancies commenced during either of the following time periods:

(A) The five-year period after any notice of intent to withdraw the accommodations is filed with the public entity, whether or not the notice of intent is rescinded or the withdrawal of the accommodations is completed pursuant to the notice of intent.

(B) The five-year period after the accommodations are withdrawn.

(3) This subdivision shall prevail over any conflicting provision of law authorizing the landlord to establish the rental rate upon the initial hiring of the accommodations.

(b) If the accommodations are offered again for rent or lease for residential purposes within two years of the date the accommodations were withdrawn from rent or lease, the following provisions shall govern:

(1) The owner of the accommodations shall be liable to any tenant or lessee who was displaced from the property by that action for actual and exemplary damages. Any action by a tenant or lessee pursuant to this paragraph shall be brought within three years of the withdrawal of the accommodations from rent or lease. However, nothing in this paragraph precludes a tenant from pursuing any alternative remedy available under the law.

(2) A public entity which has acted pursuant to this section may institute a civil proceeding against any owner who has again offered accommodations for rent or lease subject to this subdivision, for exemplary damages for displacement of tenants or lessees. Any action by a public entity pursuant to this paragraph shall be brought within three years of the withdrawal of the accommodations from rent or lease.

(3) Any owner who offers accommodations again for rent or lease shall first offer the unit for rent or lease to the tenant or lessee displaced from that unit by the withdrawal pursuant to this chapter, if the tenant has advised the owner in writing within 30 days of the displacement of the tenant's desire to consider an offer to renew the tenancy and has furnished the owner with an address to which that offer is to be directed. That tenant, lessee, or former tenant or lessee may advise the owner at any time during the eligibility of a change of address to which an offer is to be directed.

If the owner again offers the accommodations for rent or lease pursuant to this subdivision, and the tenant or lessee has advised the owner pursuant to this subdivision of a desire to consider an offer to renew the tenancy, then the owner shall offer to reinstitute a rental agreement or lease on terms permitted by law to that displaced tenant or lessee.

This offer shall be deposited in the United States mail, by registered or certified mail with postage prepaid, addressed to the displaced tenant or lessee at the address furnished to the owner as provided in this subdivision, and shall describe the terms of the offer. The displaced tenant or lessee shall have 30 days from the deposit of the offer in the mail to accept the offer by personal delivery of that acceptance or by deposit of the acceptance in the United States mail by registered or certified mail with postage prepaid.

(c) A public entity which has acted pursuant to this section, may require by statute or ordinance, or by regulation as specified in Section 7060.5, that an owner who offers accommodations again for rent or lease within a period not exceeding 10 years from the date on which they are withdrawn, and which are subject to this subdivision, shall first offer the unit to the tenant or lessee displaced from that unit by the withdrawal, if that tenant or lessee requests the offer in writing within 30 days after the owner has notified the public entity of an intention to offer the accommodations again for residential rent or lease pursuant to a requirement adopted by the public entity under subdivision (c) of Section 7060.4. The owner of the accommodations shall be liable to any tenant or lessee who was displaced by that action for failure to comply with this paragraph, for punitive damages in an amount which does not exceed the contract rent for six months, and the payment of which shall not be construed to extinguish the owner's obligation to comply with this subdivision.

(d) If the accommodations are demolished, and new accommodations are constructed on the same property, and offered for rent or lease within five years of the date the accommodations were withdrawn from rent or lease, the newly constructed accommodations shall be subject to any system of controls on the price at which they would be offered on the basis of a fair and reasonable return on the newly constructed accommodations, notwithstanding any exemption from the system of controls for newly constructed accommodations.

(e) The amendments to this section enacted by the act adding this subdivision shall apply to all new tenancies created after

December 31, 2002. If a new tenancy was lawfully created prior to January 1, 2003, after a lawful withdrawal of the unit under this chapter, the amendments to this section enacted by the act adding this subdivision may not apply to new tenancies created after that date. **Leg.H**. 1985, 1999, 2002, 2019.

§ 7060.3 Application of Rent Control to Successor in Interest of Withdrawn Property; Recorded Notice

If a public entity determines to apply constraints pursuant to Section 7060.2 to a successor in interest of an owner who has withdrawn accommodations from rent or lease, the public entity shall record a notice with the county recorder which shall specifically describe the real property where the accommodations are located, the dates applicable to the constraints and the name of the owner of record of the real property. The notice shall be indexed in the grantor-grantee index.

A person who acquires title to the real property subsequent to the date upon which the accommodations thereon have been withdrawn from rent or lease, as a bona fide purchaser for value, shall not be a successor in interest for the purposes of this chapter if the notice prescribed by this section has not been recorded with the county recorder at least one day before the transfer of title. **Leg.H.** 1985, 1986.

§ 7060.4 Notice to be Given by Owner on Withdrawal

(a) Any public entity which, by a valid exercise of its police power, has in effect any control or system of control on the price at which accommodations are offered for rent or lease, may require by statute or ordinance, or by regulation as specified in Section 7060.5, that the owner notify the entity of an intention to withdraw those accommodations from rent or lease and may require that the notice contain statements, under penalty of perjury, providing information on the number of accommodations, the address or location of those accommodations, the name or names of the tenants or lessees of the accommodations, and the rent applicable to each residential rental unit. Information respecting the name or names of the tenants, the rent applicable to any residential rental unit, or the total number of accommodations, is confidential information and for purposes of this chapter shall be treated as confidential information by any public entity for purposes of the Information Practices Act of 1977 (Chapter 1 (commencing with Section 1798) of Title 1.8 of Part 4 of Division 3 of the Civil Code). A public entity shall, to the extent required by the preceding sentence, be considered an "agency," as defined by subdivision (d) of Section 1798.3 of the Civil Code.

(b) The statute, ordinance, or regulation of the public entity may require that the owner record with the county recorder a memorandum summarizing the provisions, other than the confidential provisions, of the notice in a form which shall be prescribed by the statute, ordinance, or regulation, and require a certification with that notice that actions have been

initiated as required by law to terminate any existing tenancies. In that situation, the date on which the accommodations are withdrawn from rent or lease for purposes of this chapter is 120 days from the delivery in person or by first-class mail of that notice to the public entity. However, if the tenant or lessee is at least 62 years of age or disabled, and has lived in their accommodations or unit within the accommodations for at least one year prior to the date of delivery to the public entity of the notice of intent to withdraw pursuant to subdivision (a), then the date of withdrawal of the accommodations of that tenant or lessee shall be extended to one year after the date of delivery of that notice to the public entity, provided that the tenant or lessee gives written notice of their entitlement to an extension to the owner within 60 days of the date of delivery to the public entity of the notice of intent to withdraw. In that situation, the following provisions shall apply:

(1) The tenancy shall be continued on the same terms and conditions as existed on the date of delivery to the public entity of the notice of intent to withdraw, subject to any adjustments otherwise available under the system of control.

(2) No party shall be relieved of the duty to perform any obligation under the lease or rental agreement.

(3) The owner may elect to extend the tenancy on any other unit within the accommodations up to one year after date of delivery to the public entity of the notice of intent to withdraw, subject to paragraphs (1) and (2).

(4) Within 30 days of the notification by the tenant or lessee to the owner of their entitlement to an extension, the owner shall give written notice to the public entity of the claim that the tenant or lessee is entitled to stay in their accommodations or unit within the accommodations for one year after date of delivery to the public entity of the notice of intent to withdraw.

(5) Within 90 days of date of delivery to the public entity of the notice of intent to withdraw, the owner shall give written notice of the owner's election to extend a tenancy under paragraph (3) and the revised date of withdrawal to the public entity and any tenant or lessee whose tenancy is extended.

(6) The date of withdrawal for the accommodations as a whole, for purposes of calculating the time periods described in Section 7060.2, shall be the latest termination date among all tenants within the accommodations, as stated in the notices required by paragraphs (4) and (5). An owner's further voluntary extension of a tenancy beyond the date stated in the notices required by paragraphs (4) and (5) shall not extend the date of withdrawal.

(c) The statute, ordinance, or regulation of the public entity adopted pursuant to subdivision (a) may also require the owner to notify any tenant or lessee displaced pursuant to this chapter of the following:

(1) That the public entity has been notified pursuant to subdivision (a).

(2) That the notice to the public entity specified the name and the amount of rent paid by the tenant or lessee as an occupant of the accommodations.

(3) The amount of rent the owner specified in the notice to the public entity.

(4) Notice to the tenant or lessee of their rights under paragraph (3) of subdivision (b) of Section 7060.2.

(5) Notice to the tenant or lessee of the following:

(A) If the tenant or lessee is at least 62 years of age or disabled, and has lived in their accommodations for at least one year prior to the date of delivery to the public entity of the notice of intent to withdraw, then tenancy shall be extended to one year after date of delivery to the public entity of the notice of intent to withdraw, provided that the tenant or lessee gives written notice of their entitlement to the owner within 60 days of date of delivery to the public entity of the notice of intent to withdraw.

(B) The extended tenancy shall be continued on the same terms and conditions as existed on date of delivery to the public entity of the notice of intent to withdraw, subject to any adjustments otherwise available under the system of control.

(C) No party shall be relieved of the duty to perform any obligation under the lease or rental agreement during the extended tenancy.

(d) The statute, ordinance, or regulation of the public entity adopted pursuant to subdivision (a) may also require the owner to notify the public entity in writing of an intention to again offer the accommodations for rent or lease. **Leg.H.** 1985, 1999, 2004, 2019.

§ 7060.7 *Supersession Exclusions*

It is the intent of the Legislature in enacting this chapter to supersede any holding or portion of any holding in Nash v. City of Santa Monica, 37 Cal.3d 97 to the extent that the holding, or portion of the holding, conflicts with this chapter, so as to permit landlords to go out of business. However, this act is not otherwise intended to do any of the following:

(a) Interfere with local governmental authority over land use, including regulation of the conversion of existing housing to condominiums or other subdivided interests or to other nonresidential use following its withdrawal from rent or lease under this chapter.

(b) Preempt local or municipal environmental or land use regulations, procedures, or controls that govern the demolition and redevelopment of residential property.

(c) Override procedural protections designed to prevent abuse of the right to evict tenants.

(d) Permit an owner to do any of the following:

(1) Withdraw from rent or lease less than all of the accommodations, as defined by paragraph (1) or (2) of subdivision (b) of Section 7060.

(2) Decline to make a written rerental offer to any tenant or lessee who occupied a unit at the time when the owner gave the public entity notice of its intent to withdraw the accommodations, in the manner and within the timeframe specified in paragraph (3) of subdivision (b), or in subdivision (c), of Section 7060.2. But the requirements of this paragraph shall not apply to:

(A) A unit that was the principal place of residence of any owner or owner's family member at the time of withdrawal, provided that it continues to be that person's or those persons' principal place of residence when accommodations are returned to the rental market as provided in this section.

(B) A unit that is the principal place of residence of an owner when the accommodations are returned to the rental market, if it is the owners' principal place of residence, at the time of return to the rental market, as provided in this section. If the owner vacates the unit within 10 years from the date of withdrawal, the owner shall, within 30 days, offer to rerent if required under this paragraph.

(e) Grant to any public entity any power which it does not possess independent of this chapter to control or establish a system of control on the price at which accommodations may be offered for rent or lease, or to diminish any such power which that public entity may possess, except as specifically provided in this chapter.

(f) Alter in any way either Section 65863.7 relating to the withdrawal of accommodations which comprise a mobilehome park from rent or lease or subdivision (f) of Section 798.56 of the Civil Code relating to a change of use of a mobilehome park. **Leg.H.** 1999, 2019.

§ 12926 *Additional Definitions of Discrimination*

As used in this part in connection with unlawful practices, unless a different meaning clearly appears from the context:

(a) "Affirmative relief" or "prospective relief" includes the authority to order reinstatement of an employee, awards of backpay, reimbursement of out-of-pocket expenses, hiring, transfers, reassignments, grants of tenure, promotions, cease and desist orders, posting of notices, training of personnel, testing, expunging of records, reporting of records, and any other similar relief that is intended to correct unlawful practices under this part.

(b) "Age" refers to the chronological age of any individual who has reached a 40th birthday.

(c) Except as provided by Section 12926.05, "employee" does not include any individual employed by that person's parent, spouse, or child or any individual employed under a special license in a nonprofit sheltered workshop or rehabilitation facility.

(d) "Employer" includes any person regularly employing five or more persons, or any person acting as an agent of an employer, directly or indirectly, the state or any political or civil subdivision of the state, and cities, except as follows:

"Employer" does not include a religious association or corporation not organized for private profit.

(e) "Employment agency" includes any person undertaking for compensation to procure employees or opportunities to work.

(f) "Essential functions" means the fundamental job duties of the employment position the individual with a disability holds or desires. "Essential functions" does not include the marginal functions of the position.

(1) A job function may be considered essential for any of several reasons, including, but not limited to, any one or more of the following:

(A) The function may be essential because the reason the position exists is to perform that function.

(B) The function may be essential because of the limited number of employees available among whom the performance of that job function can be distributed.

(C) The function may be highly specialized, so that the incumbent in the position is hired based on expertise or the ability to perform a particular function.

(2) Evidence of whether a particular function is essential includes, but is not limited to, the following:

(A) The employer's judgment as to which functions are essential.

(B) Written job descriptions prepared before advertising or interviewing applicants for the job.

(C) The amount of time spent on the job performing the

function.

(D) The consequences of not requiring the incumbent to perform the function.

(E) The terms of a collective bargaining agreement.

(F) The work experiences of past incumbents in the job.

(G) The current work experience of incumbents in similar jobs.

(g) (1) "Genetic information" means, with respect to any individual, information about any of the following:

(A) The individual's genetic tests.

(B) The genetic tests of family members of the individual.

(C) The manifestation of a disease or disorder in family members of the individual.

(2) "Genetic information" includes any request for, or receipt of, genetic services, or participation in clinical research that includes genetic services, by an individual or any family member of the individual.

(3) "Genetic information" does not include information about the sex or age of any individual.

(h) "Labor organization" includes any organization that exists and is constituted for the purpose, in whole or in part, of collective bargaining or of dealing with employers concerning grievances, terms or conditions of employment, or of other mutual aid or protection.

(i) "Medical condition" means either of the following:

(1) Any health impairment related to or associated with a diagnosis of cancer or a record or history of cancer.

(2) Genetic characteristics. For purposes of this section, "genetic characteristics" means either of the following:

(A) Any scientifically or medically identifiable gene or chromosome, or combination or alteration thereof, that is known to be a cause of a disease or disorder in a person or that person's offspring, or that is determined to be associated with a statistically increased risk of development of a disease or disorder, and that is presently not associated with any symptoms of any disease or disorder.

(B) Inherited characteristics that may derive from the individual or family member, that are known to be a cause of a disease or disorder in a person or that person's offspring, or that are determined to be associated with a statistically increased risk of development of a disease or disorder, and that are presently not associated with any symptoms of any disease or disorder.

(j) "Mental disability" includes, but is not limited to, all of the following:

(1) Having any mental or psychological disorder or condition, such as intellectual disability, organic brain syndrome, emotional or mental illness, or specific learning disabilities, that limits a major life activity. For purposes of this section:

(A) "Limits" shall be determined without regard to mitigating measures, such as medications, assistive devices, or reasonable accommodations, unless the mitigating measure itself limits a major life activity.

(B) A mental or psychological disorder or condition limits a major life activity if it makes the achievement of the major life activity difficult.

(C) "Major life activities" shall be broadly construed and shall include physical, mental, and social activities and working.

(2) Any other mental or psychological disorder or condition not described in paragraph (1) that requires special education or related services.

(3) Having a record or history of a mental or psychological disorder or condition described in paragraph (1) or (2), which is known to the employer or other entity covered by this part.

(4) Being regarded or treated by the employer or other entity covered by this part as having, or having had, any mental condition that makes achievement of a major life activity difficult.

(5) Being regarded or treated by the employer or other entity covered by this part as having, or having had, a mental or psychological disorder or condition that has no present disabling effect, but that may become a mental disability as described in paragraph (1) or (2).

"Mental disability" does not include sexual behavior disorders, compulsive gambling, kleptomania, pyromania, or psychoactive substance use disorders resulting from the current unlawful use of controlled substances or other drugs.

(k) "Veteran or military status" means a member or veteran of the United States Armed Forces, United States Armed Forces Reserve, the United States National Guard, and the California National Guard.

(l) "On the bases enumerated in this part" means or refers to discrimination on the basis of one or more of the following: race, religious creed, color, national origin, ancestry, physical disability, mental disability, medical condition, genetic information, marital status, sex, age, sexual orientation, or veteran or military status.

(m) "Physical disability" includes, but is not limited to, all of the following:

(1) Having any physiological disease, disorder, condition, cosmetic disfigurement, or anatomical loss that does both of the following:

(A) Affects one or more of the following body systems: neurological, immunological, musculoskeletal, special sense organs, respiratory, including speech organs, cardiovascular, reproductive, digestive, genitourinary, hemic and lymphatic, skin, and endocrine.

(B) Limits a major life activity. For purposes of this section:

(i) "Limits" shall be determined without regard to mitigating measures such as medications, assistive devices, prosthetics, or reasonable accommodations, unless the mitigating measure itself limits a major life activity.

(ii) A physiological disease, disorder, condition, cosmetic disfigurement, or anatomical loss limits a major life activity if it makes the achievement of the major life activity difficult.

(iii) "Major life activities" shall be broadly construed and includes physical, mental, and social activities and working.

(2) Any other health impairment not described in paragraph (1) that requires special education or related services.

(3) Having a record or history of a disease, disorder, condition, cosmetic disfigurement, anatomical loss, or health impairment described in paragraph (1) or (2), which is known to the employer or other entity covered by this part.

(4) Being regarded or treated by the employer or other entity covered by this part as having, or having had, any physical condition that makes achievement of a major life activity difficult.

(5) Being regarded or treated by the employer or other entity covered by this part as having, or having had, a disease, disorder, condition, cosmetic disfigurement, anatomical loss, or health impairment that has no present disabling effect but may become a physical disability as described in paragraph (1) or (2).

(6) "Physical disability" does not include sexual behavior disorders, compulsive gambling, kleptomania, pyromania, or psychoactive substance use disorders resulting from the current unlawful use of controlled substances or other drugs.

(n) Notwithstanding subdivisions (j) and (m), if the definition of "disability" used in the federal Americans with Disabilities Act of 1990 (Public Law 101-336) would result in broader protection of the civil rights of individuals with a mental disability or physical disability, as defined in subdivision (j) or (m), or would include any medical condition not included within those definitions, then that broader protection or coverage shall be deemed incorporated by reference into, and shall prevail over conflicting provisions of, the definitions in subdivisions (j) and (m).

(o) "Race, religious creed, color, national origin, ancestry, physical disability, mental disability, medical condition, genetic information, marital status, sex, age, sexual orientation, or veteran or military status" includes a perception that the person has any of those characteristics or that the person is associated with a person who has, or is perceived to have, any of those characteristics.

(p) "Reasonable accommodation" may include either of the following:

(1) Making existing facilities used by employees readily accessible to, and usable by, individuals with disabilities.

(2) Job restructuring, part-time or modified work schedules, reassignment to a vacant position, acquisition or modification of equipment or devices, adjustment or modifications of examinations, training materials or policies, the provision of qualified readers or interpreters, and other similar accommodations for individuals with disabilities.

(q) "Religious creed," "religion," "religious observance," "religious belief," and "creed" include all aspects of religious belief, observance, and practice, including religious dress and grooming practices. "Religious dress practice" shall be construed broadly to include the wearing or carrying of religious clothing, head or face coverings, jewelry, artifacts, and any other item that is part of an individual observing a religious creed. "Religious grooming practice" shall be construed broadly to include all forms of head, facial, and body hair that are part of an individual observing a religious creed.

(r) (1) "Sex" includes, but is not limited to, the following:

(A) Pregnancy or medical conditions related to pregnancy.

(B) Childbirth or medical conditions related to childbirth.

(C) Breastfeeding or medical conditions related to breastfeeding.

(2) "Sex" also includes, but is not limited to, a person's gender. "Gender" means sex, and includes a person's gender identity and gender expression. "Gender expression" means a person's gender-related appearance and behavior whether or not stereotypically associated with the person's assigned sex at birth.

(s) "Sexual orientation" means heterosexuality, homosexuality, and bisexuality.

(t) "Supervisor" means any individual having the authority, in the interest of the employer, to hire, transfer, suspend, lay off, recall, promote, discharge, assign, reward, or discipline other employees, or the responsibility to direct them, or to adjust their grievances, or effectively to recommend that action, if, in connection with the foregoing, the exercise of that authority is not of a merely routine or clerical nature, but requires the use of independent judgment.

(u) "Undue hardship" means an action requiring significant difficulty or expense, when considered in light of the following factors:

(1) The nature and cost of the accommodation needed.

(2) The overall financial resources of the facilities involved in the provision of the reasonable accommodations, the number of persons employed at the facility, and the effect on expenses and resources or the impact otherwise of these accommodations upon the operation of the facility.

(3) The overall financial resources of the covered entity, the overall size of the business of a covered entity with respect to the number of employees, and the number, type, and location of its facilities.

(4) The type of operations, including the composition, structure, and functions of the workforce of the entity.

(5) The geographic separateness or administrative or fiscal relationship of the facility or facilities.

(v) "National origin" discrimination includes, but is not limited to, discrimination on the basis of possessing a driver's license granted under Section 12801.9 of the Vehicle Code.

(w) "Race" is inclusive of traits historically associated with race, including, but not limited to, hair texture and protective hairstyles.

(x) "Protective hairstyles" includes, but is not limited to, such hairstyles as braids, locks, and twists. **Leg.H.** 2011, 2012, 2013, 2014, 2016, 2017, 2019, 2020.

§ 12955.3 *Defining Disability*

For purposes of this part, "disability" includes, but is not limited to, any physical or mental disability as defined in Section 12926. **Leg.H.** 1992, 2000.

California Health & Safety Code

§ 17920.3 Substandard Building Conditions

Any building or portion thereof including any dwelling unit, guestroom or suite of rooms, or the premises on which the same is located, in which there exists any of the following listed conditions to an extent that endangers the life, limb, health, property, safety, or welfare of the public or the occupants thereof shall be deemed and hereby is declared to be a substandard building:

(a) Inadequate sanitation shall include, but not be limited to, the following:

(1) Lack of, or improper water closet, lavatory, or bathtub or shower in a dwelling unit.

(2) Lack of, or improper water closets, lavatories, and bathtubs or showers per number of guests in a hotel.

(3) Lack of, or improper kitchen sink.

(4) Lack of hot and cold running water to plumbing fixtures in a hotel.

(5) Lack of hot and cold running water to plumbing fixtures in a dwelling unit.

(6) Lack of adequate heating.

(7) Lack of, or improper operation of required ventilating equipment.

(8) Lack of minimum amounts of natural light and ventilation required by this code.

(9) Room and space dimensions less than required by this code.

(10) Lack of required electrical lighting.

(11) Dampness of habitable rooms.

(12) Infestation of insects, vermin, or rodents as determined by a health officer or, if an agreement does not exist with an agency that has a health officer, the infestation can be determined by a code enforcement officer, as defined in Section 829.5 of the Penal Code, upon successful completion of a course of study in the appropriate subject matter as determined by the local jurisdiction.

(13) Visible mold growth, as determined by a health officer or a code enforcement officer, as defined in Section 829.5 of the Penal Code, excluding the presence of mold that is minor and found on surfaces that can accumulate moisture as part of their properly functioning and intended use.

(14) General dilapidation or improper maintenance.

(15) Lack of connection to required sewage disposal system.

(16) Lack of adequate garbage and rubbish storage and removal facilities, as determined by a health officer or, if an agreement does not exist with an agency that has a health officer, the lack of adequate garbage and rubbish removal facilities can be determined by a code enforcement officer as defined in Section 829.5 of the Penal Code.

(b) Structural hazards shall include, but not be limited to, the following:

(1) Deteriorated or inadequate foundations.

(2) Defective or deteriorated flooring or floor supports.

(3) Flooring or floor supports of insufficient size to carry imposed loads with safety.

(4) Members of walls, partitions, or other vertical supports that split, lean, list, or buckle due to defective material or deterioration.

(5) Members of walls, partitions, or other vertical supports that are of insufficient size to carry imposed loads with safety.

(6) Members of ceilings, roofs, ceiling and roof supports, or other horizontal members which sag, split, or buckle due to defective material or deterioration.

(7) Members of ceilings, roofs, ceiling and roof supports, or other horizontal members that are of insufficient size to carry imposed loads with safety.

(8) Fireplaces or chimneys which list, bulge, or settle due to defective material or deterioration.

(9) Fireplaces or chimneys which are of insufficient size or strength to carry imposed loads with safety.

(c) Any nuisance.

(d) All wiring, except that which conformed with all applicable laws in effect at the time of installation if it is currently in good and safe condition and working properly.

(e) All plumbing, except plumbing that conformed with all applicable laws in effect at the time of installation and has been maintained in good condition, or that may not have conformed with all applicable laws in effect at the time of installation but is currently in good and safe condition and working properly, and that is free of cross connections and siphonage between fixtures. **Leg.H.** 1979, 1982, 2000, 2013, 2015.

Appendix E: *Table of Statutes, Regulations, and Cases.* See also Appendices C and D: Law Excerpts

San Francisco Building Code

San Francisco Business and Tax Regulations Code

San Francisco Environment Code

San Francisco Subdivision Code

United States Code

Table of Cases

Throughout this book, court cases are cited in the text. Most of the cases can be found by just searching for them online for the names of the plaintiff v. the defendant. To learn how to use the citations below to find the case in a law library, see the explanation in the "Law Libraries" section of the *Researching Landlord, Buildings, and Laws* chapter.

Artal v. Sharp (2001) Cal. Superior Court, App. Div. No. 5267; court permitted eviction of the tenant for breaching the "one person only, no subletting" part of her rental agreement. 105

Auburn Woods I Homeowners Association v. Fair Employment and Housing Commission (2004) 121 Cal.App.4th 1578: reasonable accommodations required for companion animal. 96

Barela v. Superior Court (1981) 30 Cal.3d 244; a landlord may not evict tenant as punishment for lawful action taken by tenant. 165

Baugh v. Consumers Associates, Ltd. (1966) 241 Cal. App. 2d 672, 674; nonpayment of rent notices must specify the precise amount of money that is due. 137

Birkenfeld v. City of Berkeley (1976) 17 Cal. 3d 129; rent control and just cause evictions do not materially interfere with state law. 17

Birke v. Oakwood Worldwide (2009) 169 Cal. App. 4th 1540; smoking from neighbor was a nuisance and caused allergy when allowed in common area 45

Borsuk v. Superior Court (2015) 23 Cal.App.4th Supp.1; landlord must serve three day notice in manner authorized by law. 133

Boston LLC v. Juarez (2016) 245 Cal.App.4th 75; breach must be material for eviction. 142

Bragdon v. Abbot (1998) 524 U.S. 624, 631; Fair Housing Amendments Act uses the term "handicap" to have the same legal meaning as "disability. 94

Briggs v. Electronic Memories & Magnetics Corp. (1975) 53 Cal. App. 3d 900, 905; since an unlawful detainer is a priority case which moves much faster through the courts, a landlord must comply strictly with legal requirements. 133, 142, 163

Bullard v. San Francisco Residential Rent Stabilization Board (2003) 106 Cal. App. 4th 488; noncomparable units are offered as new tenancies, not continuations of existing tenancies for owner move-in evictions. 149

Burien, LLC v. Wiley (2014) 230 Cal. App. 4th 1039; California Civil Code Section 1954.52, subdivision (a)(1), refers to certificates of occupancy issued prior to residential use of the unit. 18

Carter v. Cohen (2010) 188 Cal.App.4th 1038; awarded entire rent for illegal unit. 125

Chacon v. Litke (2010) 181 Cal. App. 4th 1234; awarded wrongfully evicted tenant twenty years of the projected difference in rent. 181

Chan v. Antepenko (1988) 203 Cal. App. 3d Supp. 21; if resident manager signs a contract as a "licensee," and occupancy is merely incidental to employment, the resident manager is not a "tenant" under the Rent Ordinance. 33

Chase v. Peters (1918) 37 Cal. App. 358, 361; Code of Civil Procedure § 1161 does not allow the landlord to recover financial loss from before the unlawful detainer process began, except for the loss of rent. 138

Chun v. Del Cid (2019) B295140; rooming house use exempt from Costa-Hawkins single family home definition. 20, 103

Citizens for Uniform Laws v. County of Contra Costa (1991) 223 Cal. App. 3d 1468; law that prohibits discrimination against people with AIDS is valid because it promotes public health. 93

City and County of San Francisco v. Post (2018) 22 Cal. App.5th 121; Section 8 voucher holders may not be discriminated against. 97

City and County of San Francisco v. The Regents of the University of California et al. (2019) S242835; state entity not exempt from local regulation. 19

City and County of San Francisco v. USPS, No. 12-15473 (9th Cir. 2013); A federal appeals court upheld that the U. S. Postal Service may deliver mail to the front desk or a central collection box rather than individual mailboxes. 19

Cobb v. City and County of San Francisco Rent Board (2000) 98 Cal. App. 4th 345, 352; a tenancy may be created without a formal agreement by consent and acceptance of rent. 111

Cunningham v. Universal Well Services, Inc. (2002) 98 Cal. App. 4th 1141; constructive eviction defined. 60

Custom Parking, Inc. v. Superior Court (MacAnnan) (1982) 138 Cal. App. 3d 90); a landlord may not evict tenant as punishment for lawful action taken by tenant. 165

Danekas v. San Francisco Residential Rent Stabilization & Arbitration Board (2001) 95 Cal. App. 4th 638, 115 Cal. Rptr. 2d 694; landlord cannot evict for breach of rental agreement after unreasonable withholding consent for replacing tenants. 107

Da Vinci Group v. San Francisco Residential Rent Stabilization Board (1992) 5 Cal. App.4th 24; illegal units that were brought up to code after June 13, 1979 are still covered under the Rent Ordinance. 18

Del Monte Properties v. Dolan (2018) 26 Cal.App.5th Supp. 20; the only circumstance under which the payment of a fixed amount for damages may be enforced is when it would be impracticable to fix the actual damage. 25

Del Monte Properties v. Dolan (2018) Case No. CV170392; where a notice to pay or quit seeks any sum which is in excess of the precise sum due, even if the amount is minimal, the notice is ineffective. 137

DeZerega v. Meggs (2000) 83 Cal. App. 4th 28; where a landlord agrees to an occupancy, characterization of the occupancy as a subtenancy does not prevent application of the Ordinance's requirements of cause for eviction. 107

Directors Guild of America v. Harmony Pictures (1998) 32

F. Supp. 2d 1184; California Commercial Code § 3311 (since more recent statute) gives up right to remainder of money of cashed check if landlord sent money in good faith. 42

Dromy v. Lukovsky (2013) 219 Cal.App.4th 278; open house limitations. 116

EDC Associates Ltd. v. Gutierrez (1984) 153 Cal. App. 3d 167; if the landlord accepts any portion of the rent for the period after the notice has expired, she may have "waived" the notice and it may be effectively canceled. 133

Ellingson v. Walsh, O'Connor & Barneson (1940) 15 Cal. 2d 673; a tenancy is a contractual relationship, express or implied, between a landlord and a tenant. 111

Gans v. Smull (2003) 111 Cal.App.4th 985: weekend or holiday does not extend time to comply with contract. 145

Getz v. City of West Hollywood (1991) 233 Cal. App. 3d 625, 629; a tenancy may be created without a formal agreement by consent and acceptance of rent. 111

Golden Gateway Center v. Gateway Tenants' Association (2001) 26 Cal. 4th 1013; can post/deliver flyers unless forbidden from all solicitors in hallways, hallways secured by locked doors from visitors, and rental agreement states prohibition. 26

Golden Gateway Center v. San Francisco Residential Rent Stabilization & Arbitration Board (1999) 73 Cal. App. 4th 1204, 1212; "reasonably necessary" repair and maintenance which does not substantially interfere with tenant's housing not decrease. 53

Green v. Housing Authority of Clackamas County (1998) 994 F.Supp. 1253, 1256 (U.S. District Court); landlord may not require proof of special training or certification for support animal. 96

Green v. Superior Court (1974) 10 Cal. 3d 616; "implied warranty of habitability." 43, 57

Gross v. Superior Court (1985) 171 Cal. App. 3d 265; tenant living in a home that is covered by the Rent Ordinance cannot be evicted by the foreclosure owner unless the owner has "just cause" for eviction. 32

Gruzen v. Henry (1978) 84 Cal.App.3d 515; when the landlord was entitled to an order of eviction, the landlord was not entitled to an award of rent for renting an illegal unit. 144

Guntert v. City of Stockton (1976) 55 Cal. App. 3d 131; lawsuit for breach of privacy. 84

Guy F. Atkinson Co. of Calif. & Susidiaries v. Commr. of Int. Rev. Serv. (1987) 814 F2d 1388; constructive acceptance. 140

Harris v. Capital Growth Investors XIV (1991) 52 Cal.3d 1142; arbitrary discrimination not allowed except for a valid business reason that is applied to all of that trait. 94

Hill v. National Collegiate Athletic Association (1994) 7 Cal. 4th 1 (Cal. 4th); the California Constitutional right to privacy. 116

Hinson v. Delis (1972) 26 Cal. App. 3d 62; "implied warranty of habitability." 58

Jaramillo v. JH Real Estate (2003) 111 Cal. App. 4th 394; you cannot sign away your right to sue your landlord. 24

Jordan v. Talbot ((1961) 55 Cal. 2d 597; cannot waive right to entry requirements for landlord. 24, 86

Kirk Corporation v. First American Title Co. (1990) 220 Cal. App. 3d 785, 809; if the building is sold, all of the provisions of the original agreement remain. 30

Knight v. Hallsthammer (1981) 29 Cal. 3d 46; rights of tenant in rent withholding. 58, 165

Kraus v. Trinity Management Services, Inc. (2000) 23 Cal. 4th 116, 141; security deposit uses. 37

Kulawitz v. Pacific Paper Company (1944) 25 Cal.2d 664; constructive eviction allows tenant to terminate tenancy without notice and rental obligations are extinguished. 60

Kwaitkowski v. Superior Trading Co. (1981) 123 Cal. App. 3d 324; landlord liable for robbery and rape of tenant in a dimly-lit doorway when landlord was aware of prior assault on one tenant and numerous complaints that defective lock allowed strangers in. 47

Kwok v. Bergren (1982) 130 Cal. App. 3d 597; authorized subtenant must be named in eviction notice for curable breach. 142

Ladas v. California State Automobile Assn. (1993) 19 Cal. App.4th 761, 770; an offer must be sufficiently definite, or must call
for such definite terms in the acceptance that the performance promised is
reasonably certain. 22

Larson v. City and County of San Francisco (2011) 192 Cal. App. 4th 1263; tenant can give up rights under the Rent Ordinance for buyouts. 25

Losornio v. Motta (1998) 67 Cal.App.4th 110: Code of Civil Procedure § 1013 does not extend notice prior to unlawful detainer. 133

Madhani v. Cooper (2003) 106 Cal. App. 4th 412; neighbor in the building repeatedly yelled and pushed tenant. Management did nothing despite repeated complaints and police report. Tenant attacked and severely injured by neighbor. Landlord must pay costs. 47

McHugh v. Santa Monica Rent Control Board (1989) 49 Cal. 3d 348; appeal decisions effective on date mailed to the parties except that portion of the decision affecting rent payments is effective 30 days after mailing unless granted stay. 178

McNairy v. C.K. Realty (2007) 150 Cal. App. 4th 1500; actual damages include emotional distress. 57

Miller & Desatnik Management Co. v. Bullock (1990) 221 Cal.App.3d Supp. 13, 18-19; death of tenant terminates

Index

F

Index

Index